JEWISH TRAVEL GUIDE 1999

International Edition

Published in association with
the *Jewish Chronicle*, London

Editor

MICHAEL ZAIDNER

VALLENTINE MITCHELL
LONDON • PORTLAND, OR

First published in 1999 in Great Britain by
VALLENTINE MITCHELL & CO. LTD.
Newbury House, 900 Eastern Avenue
London IG2 7HH

and in the United States of America by
VALLENTINE MITCHELL
c/o ISBS, Inc.
5804 N.E. Hassalo Street
Portland, Oregon 97213-3644

ISBN 0 85303 357 9
ISSN 0075 3750

Printed in Great Britain by
Creative Print and Design (Wales), Ebbw Vale

Contents

The Publishers always welcome additions changes and corrections to any of the material in this Guide.

Such information may be sent to us by post at our address in London or by fax to +44 (01) 181 599 8866 ; in this case please note that hand written items are not always legible when sent by fax.

Additionally it may be sent by Email to jtg@vmbooks.com

Potential advertisers may also use any of the above means of communication if they require advertising rates or any other information.

Details of The Jewish Year Book and all other Vallentine Mitchell publications are also available on our Website: www.vmbooks.com

Abridged Jewish Calendar

1999 (5759–5760)

Fast of Esther	Monday	March 1st
Purim	Tuesday	March 2nd
First Day Pesach	Thursday	April 1st
Second Day Pesach	Friday	April 2nd
Seventh Day Pesach	Wednesday	April 7th
Eighth Day Pesach (Yizkor)	Thursday	April 8th
Holocaust Memorial Day	Tuesday	April 13th
Israel Independence Day	Wednesday	April 21st
Lag B'Omer	Tuesday	May 4th
First Day Shavout	Friday	May 21st
Second Day Shavout (Yizkor)	Saturday	May 22nd
Fast of Tammuz	Thursday	July 1st
Fast of Av	Thursday	July 22nd
First Day Rosh Hashanah	Saturday	September 11th
Second Day Rosh Hashanah	Sunday	September 12th
Fast of Gedaliah	Monday	September 13th
Yom Kippur (Yizkor)	Monday	September 20th
First Day Succot	Saturday	September 25th
Second Day Succot	Sunday	September 26th
Shemini Atseret (Yizkor)	Saturday	October 2nd
Simchat Torah	Sunday	October 3rd
First Day Chanucah	Saturday	December 4th

2000 (5760-5761)

Fast of Esther	Monday	March 20th
Purim	Tuesday	March 21st
First Day Pesach	Thursday	April 20th
Second Day Pesach	Friday	April 21st
Seventh Day Pesach	Wednesday	April 26th
Eighth Day Pesach (Yizkor)	Thursday	April 27th
Holocaust Memorial Day	Tuesday	May 2nd
Israel independence Day	Wednesday	May 10th
Lag B'Omer	Tuesday	May 23rd
First Day Shavout	Friday	June 9th
Second Day Shavout (Yizkor)	Saturday	June 10th
Fast of Tammuz	Thursday	July20th
Fast of Av	Thursday	August 10th
First Day Rosh Hashanah	Saturday	September 30th
Second Day Rosh Hashanah	Sunday	October 1st
Fast of Gedaliah	Monday	October 2nd
Yom Kippur (Yizkor)	Monday	October 9th
First Day Succot	Saturday	October 14th
Second Day Succot	Sunday	October 15th
Shemini Atseret (Yizkor)	Saturday	October 21st
Simchat Torah	Sunday	October 22st
First Day Chanucah	Friday	December 22nd

Publisher's Note

Our regular readers will recall that last year's *Jewish Travel Guide* was published in a completely different format than that of previous years.

This new format has been extremely well accepted.

Behind the new presentation is a large data base of all the information contained within the *Jewish Travel Guide*. This year we have for the first time sent notifications to all those establishments which have an entry within the guide asking them to check the details and notifying us of all and any changes. This has again resulted in a substantial update.

This year the details to all countries have been revised, total population and Jewish population figures have, where available, been included and details of emergency phone numbers have been added. We have also added information in respect of individual cities which we feel may be of interest to the Jewish traveller. We would always be grateful to receive additional information which may be of use in this connection.

All readers should be aware that telephone area and local codes are continually being revised throughout the world. We have endeavoured to keep up to date with all such changes.

The revision has again been a mammoth task and the publisher would like to thank especially Kim Knight for all her hard work, and Daphne Money for her contribution to this endeavour.

Again as in previous years we must remind readers that establishments change hands from time to time, in some instances even ceasing to be kosher. It is therefore in the interest of travellers to consider obtaining confirmation of kashrut claims prior to visiting an establishment.

Extensive research is undertaken for each annual revision of the *Jewish Travel Guide* and every effort is made to ensure accuracy. Nevertheless, no responsibility can be accepted for any errors or omissions, or for kashrut and other claims by establishments listed in the guide.

As in previous years update forms and new entry forms are included in the back of the book for convenience of those wishing to notify us. Additionally we are quite prepared to receive information by post, fax or email. Please note however that the fax transfer system cannot adequately deal with hand written notes; they are often illegible when received.

Albania

There have been some Jews living on the territory now known as Albania since Roman times and there are remains in Dardania (in the north of the country) of an ancient synagogue. The community was re-established by Jews from Iberia escaping the Spanish Inquisition in the fifteenth and early sixteenth centuries. The famous false messiah, Shabbetai Zvi, died in exile in Albania in 1676, and an annual fair is held at the place where, it is believed, he was buried.

The strict communist regime which followed the war led to the isolation of the Jewish community. In 1991, almost the entire community, about 300, was airlifted to Israel. The few Jews who remained in Albania live in the capital, Tirana. The Albanian-Israel Friendship Society will be happy to provide any further information.

GMT + 1 hour	Total Population 3,401,000
Country calling code (355)	Jewish Population Under 100

Tirana

Contact Information
Albanian-Israel Friendship Society
Rruga 'Barrikatave' 226   (42) 22611

Algeria

Jews first settled in Algeria soon after the start of the diaspora following the destruction of the Second Temple.

In the present century, Algerian Jews suffered anti-semitism from both the local Muslim population and the wartime Vichy government. Following the Allied landings in 1942, the anti-Jewish laws were slowly lifted. After the civil war, which led to independence from France in 1962, most of the community moved to France, although some went to Israel, leaving very few behind. The present day community, centred in Algiers, has a synagogue but no rabbi.

GMT + 1 hour	Total Population 28,784,000
Country calling code (213)	Jewish Population Under 100

Algiers

Representative Organisations
Association Consistoriale Israélite d'Alger
6 rue Hassena Ahmed   (2) 62-85-72

Federation des Communautes Israelites d'Algerie
6 rue Hassena Ahmed   (2) 62-85-72

Synagogues
6 rue Hassena Ahmed   (2) 62-85-72

Argentina

The first Jewish arrivals (Marranos, or 'secret Jews') came in the sixteenth and seventeenth centuries from Portugal and Spain. They assimilated quickly. A more significant Jewish immigration occurred in the middle of the nineteenth century from western Europe, and at the end of the nineteenth century, many Jews arrived from eastern Europe, taking advantage of the 'open-door' policy towards immigrants. The new arrivals set up some Jewish agricultural settlements, but on the whole mixed with the local population. The largest Jewish community is in Buenos Aires, with smaller communities in 11 provincial centres. There are also some Jewish families remaining in the Jewish agricultural colonies, with Moiseville, Rivera and General Roca being the three most important. There are Jewish newspapers, restaurants and other institutions. The Delegation of Argentine Jewish Associations (DAIA) represents all Jewish organisations on a political level.

GMT – 3 hours
Country calling code (54)

Total Population 35,219,000
Jewish Population 230,000

Emergency Telephone (Police – 101) (Fire – 100) (Ambulance – 107)

Bahia Blanca

Contact Information
Beit Jabad Bahia Blanca
C.C. 405 8000 (91) 36582

Buenos Aires

Bakeries
Confitería Aielet
Aranguren 2911, Flores (1) 637-5419
Confitería Ganz
Paso 752, Once (1) 961-6918
Confitería Helueni
Tucumán 2620, Once (1) 961-0541
Confitería Mari Jalabe
Bogota 3228, Flores (1) 612-6991
Panadería Malena
Av. Pueyrredón 880, Once (1) 962-6290

Booksellers
Agudat Dodim
Bogota 2973, Flores (1) 613-7900
E. Milberg, Lavalle 2223 (1) 951-1979
Ediciones del Seminaro Rabínico
Latinoamericano
José Hernandez 1750, Belgrano (1) 783-2009
Editorial Yehuda
Lavalle 2168, Oficina 37

Kehot Lubavitch Sudamericana
San Luis 3281 1186 (1) 865-0625
Fax: (1) 865-0625
Email: kehot@iname.com
Web site: www.kehot-lubavitch.com.ar
Librería Editorial Sigal
Av. Corrientes 2854 1193
(1) 861-9501; 865-7208; 962-1131
Fax: (1) 962-7931; 865-7208
Email: lib-sigal@cybergal.com
Web site: www. libreria-sigal.com
Otzar Hatora
Viamonte 2712 (1) 865-7208
Fax: (1) 962-7931

Contact Information
Asociacion Shuva Israel
Paso 557, Once (1) 962-6255
Beit Jabad Belgrano
O'Higgins 2358, Belgrano 1428 (1) 781-3848
Beit Jabad Villa Crespo
Serrano 69 (1) 855-9822
Chabad Lubavitch Argentina
Agüero 1164, Flores 1425 (1) 963-1221

Congregacion Israelita de la Republica Argentina
Libertad 785, Centro   (1) 476-2474/371-8929
The total number of synagogues in Buenos Aires where there is a minyan at least Friday night and Shabbat morning exceeds fifty. Call either of the above numbers to locate the synagogue nearest you.
Jabad Lubavitch La Plata
Calle 50 No. 463 1900   (21) 25-8304
Kehot Lubavitch
S. Luis 3281 1186   (1) 865-0629

Embassy
Embassy of Israel
Av. de Mayo 701   (1) 342-1465

Groceries
Almacén Behar
Campana 347, Flores   (1) 613-2033
Almacén Shalom
San Luis 2513, Once   (1) 962-3685
Autoservicio Ezra
Ecuador 619, Once   (1) 963-7062
Autoservicio Siman Tov
Helguera 474, Flores   (1) 611-4746
Azulay, Helguera 507, Flores
Battías, Paso 706, Once
Kahal Jaredim
Argerich 386, Flores   (1) 612-4590
Kaler, San Luis 2810, Once
Kol Bo Brandsen
Brandsen 1389, Barracas
Kol Bo I, Ecuador 855, Once (1) 961-3838
Kol Bo II, Viamonte 2537, Once (1) 961-2012
Kosher Delights
La Pampa 2547, Belgrano   (1) 788-3150
La Esquina Casher
Aranguren 2999, Flores   (1) 637-3706
La Quesería
Viamonte 2438, Once   (1) 961-3171
La Tzorja, Ecuador 673, Once (1) 961-1096
Yehuda Kosher Foods
Moldes 2452, Belgrano   (1) 637-1465

Kashrut Information
The Central Rabbinate of the Vaad Hakehillot
Ecuador 1110, Once   (1) 961-2944
The Orthodox Ashkenazi Chief Rabbi of Argentina is Rabbi Shlomo Benhamu Anidjar.

Libraries
Sociedad Hebraica Argentino
Sarmiento 2233   (1) 952-5570
Also has art gallery.

YIVO Library
Pasteur 633, Third floor   (1) 45-2474

Media

Newspapers
Comunidades
Die Presse
Kesher Kehilari
La Voz Judia
Mundo Israelita
Nueva Sion

Mikvaot
Moldes 2449, Belgrano   (1) 783-2831
Helguera 270, Once   (1) 612-0410

Museums
Museo Judio de Buenos Aires
Libertad 769   (1) 372-2474;0014
                           Fax: (1) 372-2474
                Email: adaszko@mail.retina.ar.
Hours: Tuesday and Thursday 4pm to 7pm.

Representative Organisations
AMIA (Central Ashkenazi community)
Pasteur 633   (1) 953-9777; 953-2862
Asociacion Israelita Sefaradi Argentina (AISA)
Paso 493   (1) 952-4707
DAIA (Political representative body of Argentine Jewry)
Pasteur 633, Fifth floor
                       (1) 953-5380; 953-5394
ECSA (Central Sephardi body)
Larrea 674, Fourth floor
                       (1) 953-9777; 953-2862
Vaad Hakehillot
Pasteur 633, Second floor
                       (1) 953-9777; 953-2862

Restaurants
Burguer Cash'r
Viamonte 2613, Once   (1) 961-2440
D'el Gorro Blanco
1 piso Salon de Fiestas, Pueyrredon 900
                       (1) 963-8030/964-0109
Supervision: Casher Supervisado.
Parilla al Carbon. Comidas para llevar. Envios a domicilio.
Delicias Kasher
Argerich 404, Flores   (1) 637-1465
Dell Gorro Blanco
Av. Pueyrredón 900, Once   (1) 963-8030
Parrilla al Galope
Tucumán 2637, Once   (1) 963-6888
Restaurant Kasher
Av. Nazca 544, Flores   (1) 611-9686

Sucath David
Tucumán 2349, Once (1) 952-8878
Summer only.

Pizzerias

Roberto Helueni
Pinzón 1235, Barracas (1) 302-4341
Soultani, San Luis 2528, Once (1) 961-3913

Synagogues

Ashkenazi Orthodox

Baron Hirsh
Billinghurst 664 (1) 862-2624
Bet Rajel, Ecuador 522 (1) 862-2701
Brit Abraham
Antezana 145 (1) 855-6567
Etz Jaim, Julian Alvarez 745 (1) 772-5324
Sinagoga Israelita Lituana
Jose Evaristo Uriburu 348 (1) 952-7968
Torah Vaaboda
Julian Alvarez 667 (1) 854-0462
Zijron le David
Azcuenaga 736 (1) 953-0200

Conservative

Beit Hilel, Araoz 2854, Palermo (1) 804-2286
Colegio Wolfson, Comunidad Or-El
Amenabar 2972 (1) 544-5461
Comunidad Bet El
Sucre 3338 (1) 552-2365
Dor Jadash, Murillo 649, Villa Crespo
(1) 854-4467
Nueva Comunidad Israelita
Arcos 2319 (1) 781-0281
Or Jadash, Varela 850, Flores (1) 612-1171
Templo la Paz (Chalom)
Olleros 2876 (1) 552-6730

German Orthodox

Ajdut Yisroel
Moldes 2449 (1) 783-2831

Progressive

Benei Tikva
Vidal 2049 (1) 795-0380

Reform

Templo Emanu-El
Tronador 1455 (1) 552-4343
All Conservative synagogues are affiliated to the World Council of Synagogues; all Reform and Liberal synagogues to the World Council for Progressive Judaism.

Sephardi Orthodox

Aderet Eliahu
Ruy Diaz de Guzman 647 (1) 302-9306
Agudat Dodim
Avellaneda 2874 (1) 611-0056
Bajurim Tiferet Israeil
Helguera 611 (1) 611-3376
Comunidad Israelita
Camargo 870 (1) 854-1952; 854-0287
Etz Jaim, Carlos Calvo 1164 (1) 302-6290
Jaike Grimberg
Campana 460 (1) 672-2347
Kehal Jaredim
Helguera 270, Once (1) 612-0410
Od Yosef Jai
Tucuman 3326 (1) 963-2349
Or Misraj
Ciudad de la Paz 2555 (1) 784-5945
Shaare Tefila
Paso 733 (1) 962-2865
Shaare Tzion
Helguera 453 (1) 612-9484
Shalom, Olleros 2876 (1) 552-2720
Shuba Israel
Ecuador 627 (1) 862-0562
Sinagoga Rabino Zeev Gringberg
Canalejas 3047 (1) 611-3366
Sucath David
Paso 724 (1) 962-1091
Fax: (1) 962-1264
Email: perspect@satlink.com
Web site: www.judaicasite.com
Yeshurun, Republica de la India 3035
(1) 802-9310
Yesod Hadat
Lavalle 2449 (1) 961-1615

Concordia

Contact Information
Beit Jabad Concordia
Entre Rios 212 3200 (45) 21-1934
Fax: (45) 21-7898

Cordoba

Contact Information
Jabad Lubavitch Cordoba
Sucre 1380, Barrio Cofico 5000 (51) 71-0223

Groceries

Almacén
Sucre 1378, Barrio Cofico 5000 (51) 71-0223

Rosario

Contact Information
Beit Jabad Rosario
S. Lorenzo 1882 P.A. 2000   (41) 25-2899

Groceries
La Granja Kasher
Montevideo 1833   (41) 49-6210

San Luis

Restaurants
Gueulah, 1056 Bs. As.
          (783) 962-5249; 951-2330

Tucuman

Contact Information
Beit Jabad Tucuman
Lamadrid 752 4000   (81) 31-1257

Groceries
Almacén
Lamadrid 752 4000   (81) 31-1257
Almacén y Carnicería
9 de Julio 625   (81) 31-0227

Australia

The first Jews in Australia arrived with the convict ships from the United Kingdom in 1788 and regular, organised worship started in the 1820s. The community grew in the nineteenth century, with the first synagogue being established in the mid-1840s. Events such as the Australian gold rush and progroms in eastern Europe were catalysts for more Jewish immigration.

The Jewish contribution to Australian life has been prominent, with the commander of the ANZAC forces in the First World War being a practising Jew, Sir John Monash. The twentieth century saw some 7,000 Jewish refugees from Nazi Europe settling in Australia, and the community contains the largest percentage of Holocaust survivors in the world. They are a major influence on the present community, which is expanding and comparatively religious.

The community is led by the Executive Council of Australian Jewry. Seventy-five per cent of primary and 55 per cent of secondary Jewish school children attend Jewish schools and there is a low level of inter-marriage. Melbourne has the largest community (45,000), with 35,000 in Sydney. There are Jewish newspapers, radio programmes of Jewish interest and museums on Jewish themes.

GMT + 7 to 10 hrs	Total Population 18,057,000
Country calling code (61)	Jewish Population 95,000
Emergency Telephone (Police, Fire and Ambulance – 000)	

Australian Capital

Canberra

Embassy
Embassy of Israel
6 Turrana Street, Yarralumla 2600
(6) 73-1309

Synagogues
The A.C.T. Jewish Community Synagogue
National Jewish Memorial Centre, cnr Canberra Ave & National Circuit, Forrest 2603
(6) 295-1052
Fax: (6) 295-8608
Postal address: POB 3105, Manuka 2603

New South Wales

Newcastle

Synagogues
122 Tyrrell Street 2300
(49) 26-2820
Contact: Dr L.E. Fredman, 123 Dawson St, Cooks Hill, 2300 N.S.W.

Sydney

Bakeries
Carmel Cake Shop
14 O'Brien Street, Bondi
Supervision: NSW Kashrut Authority.

Booksellers
Geniza Book Shop
O'Brien Street, Bondi 2026
(2) 365-5783
Gold's Book & Gift Company
16 O'Brien Street, Bondi 2026
(2) 9300-0495
Fax: (2) 9221-3998
Email: goldsyd@matra.com.au
Shalom Gift and Book Shop
323 Pacific Highway, Lindfield 2070
(2) 9416-7076
Fax: (2) 9416-7076

Butchers
Eilat, 173 Bondi Road, Bondi
(2) 9387-8881
Supervision: NSW Kashrut Authority.
Hadassa, 17 O'Brien Street, Bondi
(2) 9365-4904
Fax: (2) 9130-4760
Supervision: NSW Kashrut Authority.

Contact information
Jewish Chaplain to the Olympic Games
166 Castlereagh Street 2000   (2) 9267-2477
                                Fax: (2) 9264-8871
Email: greatsyn@magna.com.au
For Religious matters relating to the Sydney
Olympics in 2000

Embassy
Consulate General
31 York Street 2000

Hospitals
Wolper Jewish Hospital
8 Trelawney Street, Woollahra   (2) 9328-6077

Kashrut Information
NSW Kashrut Authority
PO Box 206, Bondi 2026   (2) 9369-4286
                                Fax: (2) 9369-4329
Email: rabbig@ka.org.au
Web site: www.ka.org.au

Media
Newspapers
Australian Jewish News
146 Darlinghurst Road, Darlinghurst 2010
                                (2) 9360-5100
                                Fax: (2) 9332-4207

Mikvaot
117 Glenayr Avenue, Bondi   (2) 9130-2509

Museums
Sydney Jewish Museum
148 Darlinghurst Road, Darlinghurst 2010
                                (2) 9360-7999
                                Fax: (2) 9331-4245
Email: sydjmus@tmx.mhs.oz.au
Kosher restaurant (Milcig) on site.

Religious Organisations
Beth Din
166 Castlereagh Street 2000   (2) 9267-2477
                                Fax: (2) 9264-8871
Email: info @greatsynagogue.org.au

Representative Organisations
**Executive Council of Australian Jewry
(National Roof Body)**
146 Darlinghurst Road, Second floor,
Darlinghurst 2010   (2) 9360-5415
                                Fax: (2) 9360-5416
Email: aipgtmx.mhs.oz.au

Sydney Jewish Museum

Location	148 Darlinghurst Road, Darlinghurst 1.5km from centre of Sydney
Hours of Opening	Sunday 11 am–5 pm Monday-Thursday 10 am–4 pm Friday 10 am–2 pm
Admission	Adults $6, Family $15, Child $3, Concession $4
Phone	(02) 9360 7999

Restaurants

Grandma Moses
511 Old South Head Road, Rose Bay
(2) 9371-0874
Supervision: NSW Kashrut Authority.

Meat

Avivim, 49 Hall Street, Bondi   (2) 9365-7609
Supervision: NSW Kashrut Authority.
Glatt kosher.
Lewis Continental Kitchen
2 Curlewis Street, Bondi   (2) 9365-5421
Fax: (2) 9300-0037
Supervision: NSW Kashrut Authority.
Glatt kosher.
Savion, 1/38 Wairoa Avenue, Bondi
(2) 9130-6357
Supervision: NSW Kashrut Authority.
Glatt kosher. Hours: Sunday to Thursday, 9 am
to 10 pm; Friday, 9 am to 2 pm
Tibby's Kosher Restaurant
2d Campbell Parade, Bondi Beach
(2) 9130-5051
Fax: (2) 9365-6608
Supervision: NSW Kashrut Authority.
Open Saturday to Thursday for dinner.
Continental, Chinese, Sephardi and Israeli
food. Glatt kosher.

Pizzerias

Toovya the Milkman
379 Old South Head Road, North Bondi 2026
(2) 9130-4016
Supervision: NSW Kashrut Authority.
Not Cholov Yisrael. Vegetarian and vegan
food. Eat in or take away. Delivery to eastern
suburbs, including to your hotel room.
Personalised catering. Hours: Sunday to
Thursday, 5 pm to 10 pm; Saturday, after
Shabbat to midnight. Nearest metro: 387 bus
from Bondi junction to the door. Plenty of
parking.

Synagogues

Adath Yisroel
243 Old South Head Road, Bondi
(2) 9300-9447
Central Synagogue
15 Bon-Accord Avenue, Bondi Junction
(2) 9389-5622
Coogee Synagogue
121 Brook Street, Coogee   (2) 9315-8291
Cremorne & District
12a Yeo Street, Neutral Bay   (2) 9908-1853
Fax: (2) 9908-1852

Great Synagogue
166 Castlereagh Street   (2) 9267-2477
Fax: (2) 9264-8871
Houses the Rabbi L.A. Falk Memorial Library
and the A.M. Rosenblum Jewish Museum.
Illawarra Synagogue
502 Railway Parade, Allawah   (2) 9587-5643
Email: georgefoster1@compuserve.com
Kehillat Masada
9-15 Link Road, St Kilda 2075   (2) 9988-4417
Maroubra Synagogue (K.M.H.C.)
635 Anzac Parade, Maroubra   (2) 9344-6095
Fax: (2) 9349-6727
Mizrachi, 339 Old South Head Road, Bondi
(2) 9130-7221
North Shore Synagogue
15 Treatts Road, Lindfield   (2) 9416-3710
Fax: (2) 9416-7659
Paramatta Synagogue
116 Victoria Road, Paramatta   (2) 9683-5381
Sephardi Synagogue
40-42 Fletcher Street, Bondi Junction
(2) 9389-3355
Fax: (2) 9369-2143
Shearit Yisrael
146 Darlinghurst Road, Darlinghurst 2010
(2) 9365-8770
South Head & District Synagogue
666 Old South Head Road, Rose Bay
(2) 9371-7300
Fax: (2) 9371-7416
Strathfield & District Synagogue
19 Florence Street, Strathfield 2135
(2) 9642-3550
Fax: (2) 9642-4803
Western Suburbs Synagogue
20 Georgina Street, Newtown   (412) 340-212
Yeshiva, 36 Flood Street, Bondi (2) 9387-3822
Fax: (2) 9389-7652

Liberal

North Shore Temple Emanuel
28 Chatswood Avenue, Chatswood 2067
(2) 9419-7011
Fax: (2) 9413-1474
Email: nste@tmx.mhs.oz.au
Temple Emanuel
7 Ocean Street, Woollahra 2025
(2) 9328-7833

Sefardim

Beth Yosef, Ground Floor, 243 Old South
Head Road, Bondi

Tour information
(2) 9328-7604

For information about tours of Jewish Sydney, contact the Great Synagogue at the number listed above or Karl Maehrischel at this number.

Queensland

Brisbane

Bakeries
Brumby's Bakery
408 Milton Road, Auchenflower 4066
(7) 3371-8744

Community Organisations
Jewish Communal Centre
2 Moxom Road, Burbank 4156
(7) 3349-9749

Mikvaot
Queensland Mikvah
46 Bunya Street, Greenslopes 4120
(7) 3848-5886

Religious Organisations
Brisbane Chevra Kadisha
242 Kingsford Smith Drive, Hamilton 4007
(7) 3262-6564
The number listed is Mr Philips' home number.
Chabad House of Queensland
43 Cedar Street, Greenslopes 4120
(7) 3397-9025
Fax: (7) 3397-9025

Synagogues
Brisbane Hebrew Congregation
98 Margaret Street 4000 (7) 3229-3412
Givat Zion
43 Bunya Street, Greenslopes 4000
(7) 3397-9025
Fax: (7) 3397-9025
South Brisbane Hebrew Congregation
46 Burya Street, Greenslopes 4120
(7) 3397-9025
Temple Shalom
13 Koolatah Street, Camp Hill 4152
(7) 3398-8843

Gold Coast

Bakeries
Goldstein's Bakery
509 Olsen Avenue, Ashmore City 4214
(75) 5539-3133
Fax: (75) 5597-1064
Supervision: Rabbi Gurevitch, Gold Coast Hebrew Congregation.
Under the umbrella of the NSW Kashrut Authority. Challah and kosher breads available at 14 stores along the Gold Coast, including Surfers Paradise shop (Tel) 5531-5808

Community Organisations
Association of Jewish Organisations
31 Ranock Avenue, Benown Waters 4217
(75) 5597-2222

Religious Organisations
Chevra Kadisha
(75) 5597-2239

Synagogues
Gold Coast Hebrew Congregation
34 Hamilton Avenue, Surfers Paradise 4215
(75) 5570-1851
Temple Shalom
25 Via Roma Drive, Isle of Capri 4217
(75) 5570-1716

South Australia

Adelaide

Bakeries
Bagel Boys
134 Goodwood Road 5034 (8) 8271-0818
Open 7 days.
Bakers Delight
Frewville Shopping Centre, Green Osmond Road

Groceries
Kosher Imports
c/o Hebrew Congregation, 13 Flemington Street, Glenside 5065 (8) 9532-9994
Judaica and Kosher products available.

Synagogues

Orthodox

Adelaide Hebrew Congregation
13 Flemington Street, Glenside 5065
(8) 8338-2922
Fax: (8) 8379-0142
Mikva on premises. Mailing address: PO Box 320, Glenside 5065.

Progressive

Beit Shalom
41 Hackney Road, Hackney 5069
(8) 8362-8281
Fax: (8) 8362-4406
Mailing address: P.O.Box 47, Stepney 5069

Tasmania

Hobart

Contact Information
Jewish Centre
Chabad House, 93 Lord Street, Sandy Bay 7005
(3) 6223-7116
Fax: (3) 6223-7116
Contact in advance for Shabbat meals and Mikveh.

Synagogues
Hobart Synagogue
PO Box 128B 7001   (3) 6228-4097
The synagogue is the oldest in Australia, having been consecrated in July 1845. Open Saturday 10 am and every second Friday in the month at 6:15 pm. Other days by arrangement.

Launceston

Contact Information
Chabad House
(3) 6334-0705

Synagogues
PO Box 66, St John Street 7250
(3) 6343-1143
The synagogue in St John Street is the second oldest in Australia, founded in 1846.

Victoria

Ballarat

Synagogues
211 Drumond Street North 3350   32-6330

Melbourne

Bakeries
Big K Kosher Bakery
316 Carlisle Street,, Balaclava 3183
(3) 9527-4582
Supervision: Rabbi A.Z. Beck, Adass Israel.

Glicks Cakes and Bagels
330a Carlisle Street, Balaclava 3183
(3) 9527-2198
Supervision: Melbourne Kashrut.
Pat Yisrael.

Greenfield Cakes
7 Willow Street, Elsternwick   (3) 9528-4261
Supervision: Rabbi A.Z. Beck, Adass Israel.
At same location is King David Kosher Meals on Wheels (Refuah), hospital meals, airline and TV dinners.

Haymishe Bakery
320 Carlisle Street, Shop 4, Balaclava 3183
(3) 9527-7116
Supervision: Rabbi A.Z. Beck, Adass Israel.

Kosher Delight Bakery
75 Glen Eira Road, Ripponlea   (3) 9532-9994
Supervision: Rabbi A.Z. Beck, Adass Israel.

Lowy's Cakes & Catering
59 Gordon Street, Elsternwick   (3) 9530-0246
Supervision: Rabbi A.Z. Beck, Adass Israel.

Meal-Mart
251 Inkerman Street, St Kilda 3182
(3) 9525-4230
Fax: (3) 9525-4230
Supervision: Rabbi A.Z. Beck, Adass Israel.
Pies, salads, pre-cooked and frozen foods.

Booksellers
Golds Book & Gift Company
36 William Street, Balaclava 3183
(3) 9527-8775
Fax: (3) 9527-6434
Email: goldsd@minerva.com.au

Mazeltov Bookshop
275 Carlisle Street, East St Kilda 3183
(3) 9527-3462

Butchers
Continental Kosher Butchers
155 Glenferrie Road, Malvern 3144
(3) 9509-9822
Fax: (3) 9509-9099
Supervision: Rabbi J.S. Cohen and Rabbi M. Gutnick, Melbourne Kashrut..
Kosher meats and small goods. Distributor to other Australian states.

Melbourne Kosher Butchers
251 Inkerman Street, East St Kilda 3182
(3) 9525-4230
Fax: (3) 9525-4230
Supervision: Rabbi A.Z. Beck, Adass Israel.
Sell kosher products as well. Hours: Monday, 10 am to 5:30 pm; Tuesday to Thursday, 7 am to 5:30 pm; Friday, 7 am to 3 pm.

Solomon Kosher Butchers
140-144 Glen Eira Road, Elsternwick 3185
(3) 9532-8855
Fax: (3) 9532-8896
Supervision: Rabbi Y.D. Groner, Agudas
Chabad Kashrut Committee.
Hours: Monday to Thursday, 7 am to 5:30 pm;
Friday, 7 am to 3 pm.

Yumi's Kosher Seafoods
29 Glen Eira Road, Ripponlea 3183
(3) 9523-6444
Fax: (3) 9532-8189
Supervision: Rabbi A.Z. Beck, Adass Israel.
Suppliers of fresh fish.

Caterers

Fogels, 59 Glen Eira Road, Ripponlea 3183
(3) 9532-8309
Fax: (3) 9525-9197
Supervision: Rabbi A.Z. Beck, Adass Israel.

Kosher Meals on Wheels
572 Inkeman Street, Caulfield 3162
(3) 9527-5525
Supervision: Rabbi A.Z. Beck, Adass Israel.

Chocolatiers

Alpha Kosher Chocolates
17 William Street, Balaclava   (3) 9527-2453
Australia's only kohser chocolate factory. Hand
made chocolates of export quality. Visitors
welcome. Open Sunday mornings.

Contact Information

Mizrachi Hospitality Committee
81 Balaclava Road, Caulfield 3161
(3) 9525-9833
Fax: (3) 9527-5665
Mailing address: P.O.Box 2247. Caulfield
Junction. VIC 3161

Delicatessens

E.S. Delicatessen
74 Kooyong Road, Caulfield 3161
(3) 9576-0804
Supervision: Melbourne Kashrut.
Catering also undertaken.

Eshel Take-Away Foods & Catering
59 Glen Eira Road, Ripponlea 3161
(3) 9532-8309
Fax: (3) 9525-9197
Supervision: Rabbi A.Z. Beck, Adass Israel.

Groceries

Benedikt Imports
40 Pakington Street, St Kilda 3182
(3) 9534-8192
Importers of kosher foods and wines.

Dainty Foods (Kravsz)
62 Glen Eira Road, Ripponlea 3183
(3) 9523-8463
Grocers/Importers

Gefen Liquor Store
144 Chapel Street, Balaclava 3183
(3) 9531-5032
Fax: (3) 9525-7388
Australia's largest selection of kosher wines
and spirits. Hours: Monday to Thursday, 9 am
to 5 pm; Friday, 9 am to 4 pm. Public
transport access: #3 tram to corner of Carlisle
and Chapel Streets or Sandringham line train
to Balaclava Station.

Milecki's Balaclava Health Food
277 Carlisle Street, Balaclava 3183
(3) 9527-3350
Open every day except Shabbat and all Jewish
holidays. Hours: 9 am to 9 pm. Close to rail
station and on tram line.

Rishon Foods Party Ltd.
23 Williams Street, Balaclava 3183
(3) 9527-5142

Singers
57 Kooyong Road, Caulfield 3162
(3) 9509-2387
Fax: (3) 9509-2387

Tempo Kosher Supermarket
391 Inkerman Street, St Kilda 3183
(3) 9527-5021
Manufacturers of a range of kosher foods,
including cheese, butter and juice drinks.

Hospitals

Masada Hospital
26 Balaclava Road, East St Kilda
Supervision: Rabbi A.Z. Beck, Adass Israel.
Kosher kitchen only.

Hotels

Kimberley Gardens
441 Inkerman Street, Balaclava 3183
(3) 9526-3888
Fax: (3) 9525-9691
Strictly Glatt kosher.

Judaica

The Antique Silver Co.
253 Carlisle Street, Balaclava 3183
(3) 9525-8480
Fax: (3) 9525-8479
Large selection of Judaica and ritual objects,
not necessarily all silver. New and old.

Libraries

Kadimah Jewish Cultural Centre & National Library
7 Selwyn Street, Elsternwick 3185
(3) 9523-9817
Makor Library
306 Hawthorn Road, South Cantfield 3162
(3) 9272-5611
Fax: (3) 9272-5540

Media

Newspapers

Jewish News
PO Box 1000, South Cantfield
Publish weekly newspaper.
Yidishe Gesheften
(3) 9532-7323
Fax: (3) 9523-0106
Jewish advertising monthly.

Mikvaot

Lubavitch Mikva
38 Empress Road, East St Kilda 3183
(3) 9527-7555

Orthodox

Caulfield Mikva
9 Furneaux Grove, East St Kilda 3183
(3) 9528-1116/9525-8585
Hours: From sunset till 1 hour after nightfall.

Museums

Jewish Holocaust Centre
13 Selwyn Street, Elsternwick 3185
(3) 9528-1985
Jewish Museum of Australia
26 Alma Road, St Kilda 3182   (3) 9543-0083
Fax: (3) 9543-0844

Religious Organisations

Adass Israel Chevra Kadisha
St Kilda
(3) 9510-3377
Fax: (3) 9532-4241
Melbourne Chevra Kadisha
Inkerman Street, St Kilda 3182   (3) 9534-0208

Orthodox

Association of Rabbis and Ministers of Australia and New Zealand
c/o 12 Charnwood Grove, St Kilda 3182
(3) 9537-1433
Fax: (3) 9525-3759
Council of Orthodox Synagogues of Victoria
c/o Jetset House, 5 Queens Road 3000
(3) 9828-8000

Melbourne Beth Din
Synagogue Chambers, 572 Inkerman Road,
North Caulfield 3161   (3) 9527-8337
Fax: (3) 9527-8072
Rabbinical Council of Victoria
c/o Honorary Secretary, Rabbi Mordechai
Gutnick, 7 Meadow St, East St Kilda 3183
(3) 9525-9542
Fax: (3) 9525-9546

Progressive

Victorian Union for Progressive Judaism
78 Alma Road, St Kilda 3182   (3) 9510-1488
Fax: (3) 9521-1229
Email: Eampbeth@starnet.com.au

Representative Organisations

Jewish Community Council of Victoria
306 Hawthorn Road, South Cantfield 3161
(3) 9272-5566
Fax: (3) 9272-5560
Email: jccv@netspace.net.au
Head body of Melbourne Jewish community.

Restaurants

Lamzinnis, 219 Carlisle Street, Balaclava
(3) 9527-1283
Supervision: Melbourne Kashrut.

Dairy

Sheli's Coffee Shop
306 Hawthorn Road, South Cantfield 3162
(3) 9272-5607
Supervision: Melbourne Kashrut.
Chalav Yisrael. Catering also undertaken.

Pizzerias

Rutti's Place
223 Carlisle Street,, Balaclava 3183
(3) 9525-9939
Supervision: Melbourne Kashrut.
Catering also undertaken.

Synagogues

Caulfield Chabad House
441 Inkerman Street, East St Kilda
Chabad House
Duver Heights   (3) 9387-3822
Kollel Bes Yosef
22 Glen Eira Avenue, Ripponlea 3183
(3) 9527-5081
Lakewood Kollel Beth Hatalmud
362a Carlisle Street, East St Kilda 3183
(3) 9527-6156

KIMBERLEY GARDENS
VISITING MELBOURNE
Multi-Award Winning Boutique Hotel and Suites
KOSHER LUXURY
- accommodation • indoor swimming pool/spa/gym
- close to Synagogues, Schools and CBD

RATED ★★★★½ WITH ★★★★★ SERVICE

**441 INKERMAN STREET, EAST ST KILDA 3183, MELBOURNE, AUSTRALIA
TEL: (03) 9526 3888. FAX: (03) 9525 9691**

Independent

Bet Hatikva Synagogue
233 Nepean Highway, Gardenvale 3185
(3) 9576-9755

Liberal

Bentleigh Progressive Synagogue
549 Centre Road 3204   (3) 9563-9208
Leo Baeck Centre
33 Harp Road, East Kew 3102   (3) 9819-7160
Temple Beth Israel
76 Alma Road, St Kilda 3182   (3) 9510-1488

Orthodox

Brighton Synagogue
134 Marriage Road, East Brighton 3186
(3) 9592-9179
Burwood Hebrew Congregation
38 Harrison Avenue 3125   (3) 9808-3120
Caulfield Hebrew Congregation
572 Inkerman Road, Caulfield 3161
(3) 9525-9492
Fax: (3) 9527-8463
Email: chcmelb@ozemail.com.au
Elwood Talmud Torah Congregation
39 Dickens Street, Elwood 3184
(3) 9531-1547
Kew Synagogue
53 Walpole Street, Kew 3101   (3) 9853-9243
Fax: (3) 9853-1354

Melbourne Hebrew Congregation
Cnr. Toorak & St Kilda Roads, S. Yarra 3141
(3) 9866-2255
Fax: (3) 9866-2022
Email: mhc@bigpond.com
Mizrachi
81 Balaclava Road, Caulfield 3161
(3) 9525-9833
Fax: (3) 9527-5665
Moorabbin & District Synagogue
960 Nepean Highway, Moorabbin 3189
(3) 9553-3845
North Eastern Malvern Chabad
Glenferrie Road, Malvern
**Sephardic Synagogue Congregation
Rambam**
90 Hotham Street, East St Kilda 3183
(3) 9527-3285
South Caulfield Synagogue
47 Leopold Street, South Cantfield 3162
(3) 9578-5922
St Kilda Synagogue
12 Charnwood Grove, St Kilda 3182
(3) 9537-1433
Yeshiva Shule
92 Hotham Street, East St Kilda 3183
(3) 9525-3759

Tourist Site

North Eastern Jewish War Memorial Centre Inc.
6 High Street, Doncaster 3108   (3) 9816-3516
Fax: (3) 9857-4430

Western Australia

Perth

Representative Organisations
Council of Western Australian Jewry
J.P. PO Box 763, Morley 6062

Synagogues
Jewish Centre
Woodrow Avenue, Mt Yokine 6060
(8) 9276-8572
Northern Suburbs Congregation
4 Vernon Street, Noranda 6062 (8) 9275-5932

Perth Hebrew Congregation
Freedman Road, Menora 6050   (8) 9271-0539

Liberal
Temple David
34 Clifton Crescent, Mt Lawley 6050
(8) 9271-1485

Lubavitch
Chabad House
396 Alexander Drive, Dianella 6062
(8) 9275-4912

Austria

The arrival of Jews in this area of Europe (probably with the Romans) happened more than a 1,000 years ago. The community was expelled from Austria between 1420 and 1421, but were allowed to return in 1451. The Jews were granted their own quarter of Vienna in 1624, but were expelled again in 1670. The economy declined after the expulsion, and so they were asked to return.

It was not until 1782 that the situation became more stable when Joseph II began lifting the anti-Jewish decrees that his mother, Maria Theresa, had imposed on her Jewish subjects. The Jews received equal rights in 1848 and, in 1867, legal and other prohibitions were lifted.

Anti-semitism did continue, however, and many influential anti-semitic publications were available in Vienna and were keenly read by many people, including the young Adolf Hitler. After the First World War, Austria lost its empire (which included Czech lands and Galicia, which had a very large Jewish community), and the Jewish population fell accordingly. At the time of the Nazi take-over in 1938, 200,000 Jews lived in the country. Some 70,000 were killed in the Holocaust, the rest having escaped or hidden. Today there are several synagogues in Vienna. The city has an active ultra-orthodox community and kosher food is available. There are prayer rooms in some provincial cities.

GMT + 1 hour
Country calling code (43)
Emergency Telephone (Police – 133) (Fire – 122) (Ambulance – 144)

Total Population 8,106,000
Jewish Population 10,000

Baden

Cemeteries

Jewish Cemetery
Halsriegelstrasse 30   (2252) 85405
Contains some 3,000 graves.

Synagogues
Grabengasse 14
              (2236) 26383 or 2252-45705
Services are held Shabbat mornings from May to September. Contact Dr. Grossinger any time except Shabbos/holidays. Kosher catering possible. Event room (for 50 persons). Baden is R. Naftali Carlebach's last kehillah in Europe and the site of his distinguished sons R. Shlomo's z'tzal and R. Eliyahu Chaim's z'1 Barmitzvah. The Jewish cemetery, containing some 2,000 graves, is at Halsriegelstr. 30. Keys to be obtained at Tourist Information Centre, tel. 2252-4453157. Baden, 25km to the South of Vienna and easily accessible with public transport, used to be the third largest Jewish Community in Austria.

Edlach

Monument

A memorial to Dr Theodor Herzl, erected by the Viennese Jewish community, can be seen in the garden of the local sanatorium, where the founder of the Zionist movement died in 1904.

Eisenstadt

Cemeteries

The old cemetery, closed around 1875, contains the grave of Rav Meir ben Isak (Mram Asch), who died in 1744. To this day it is the scene of pilgrimages, particularly on the anniversary of his death. Keys to the cemetery are with the porter of the local hospital, which adjoins the old cemetery.

Museums
Austrian Jewish Museum
Unterbergstrasse 6 (2682) 65145
Fax: (2682) 65145; 65144
Email: info@oejudmus.or.at
The museum now also comprises the restored private synagogue of Samson Wertheimer, Hapsburg court Jew and Chief Rabbi of Hungary (1658–1724). The museum is open daily except Monday from 10 am to 5 pm. The Eruv Arch, spanning Unterbergstrasse, is at the end near the Esterhazy Palace. The road chain was used in former times to prevent vehicular traffic on Shabbat and Yom Tov.

Graz
Community Organisations
Community Centre
Synagogenplatz 1 (316) 912-468

Innsbruck
Community Organisations
Community Centre
Zollerstrasse 1 (512) 586-892

Kobersdorf
Cemeteries
Jewish Cemetery
Waldgasse
The keys of the cemetery on the Lampelberg are with Mr Piniel, Waldgasse 25 (one of the two houses to the left of the cemetery) and Mr Grässing, Haydngasse 4. The synagogue is currently being rebuilt.

Linz
Community Organisations
Community Centre
Bethlehemstrasse 26 (70) 779-805

Salzburg
Community Organisations
Community Centre
Lasserstrasse 8 5020 (662) 875-665
Community synagogue and mikva are to be found at the same address.

Semmering
Hotels
Hotel Alpenhof
Spital (663) 808-439
Open July through August.

Vienna
Vienna is now where most of Austrian Jewry live, and was always an important centre for Central European Jews. From 180,000 Jews in the 1930s, there are now about 10,000 Jews today. Professor Freud's clinic is a popular attraction, and the Jewish Museum in Vienna gives information on the history of the Jews in this attractive town.

Bakeries
Engländer
Hollandstrasse 10 1020 (1) 214-5617
Supervision: Rabbi Abraham Yonah Schwartz.

Bed & Breakfasts
Pension Lichtenstein
Grosse Schifgasse 19 1020 (1) 216-8498
Fax: (1) 214-7690
The pension consists of 'suites' (sleeping area, living area, kitchenette and bathroom). The stove can be used as a hot plate for Shabbat. It is within walking distance of the old Jewish quarter of Vienna in one direction, and 5-20 minutes from some small synagogues, kosher bakery in the other direction. Should be coordinated in advance as there is no front desk reception; the key is kept in the owner's office around the block. Recommended for families and couples interested in self-catering.

Booksellers
Chabad-Simcha-Center
Hollandstrasse 10 1020 (1) 216-2924
Chai Vienna
Praterstrasse 40 1020 (1) 216-4621
Fax: (1) 216-4621
Jewish Museum
Dorotheergasse 11 A-1010 (1) 512-5361
Hours: Sunday to Friday, 10 am to 6 pm; Thursday, 10 am to 9 pm. Cafeteria and bookshop on site. The cafeteria is not under supervision.

Butchers
B. Ainhorn
Stadtgutgasse 7 1020 (1) 214-5621
Supervision: Rabbi Abraham Yonah Schwartz.
Rebenwurzel
Grose Mohrengasse 19 1010 (1) 216-6640
Supervision: Rabbi Abraham Yonah Schwartz.
Sephardi Butcher
Volkertmarkt 1020 (1) 214-9650

Caterers

Shalom Bernholtz

(1) 214-914

Call for private food arrangements.

Cemeteries

Floridsdorfer Cemetery

Ruthnergasse 28 1210

Those wishing to visit must first obtain a permit from the community centre.

Rossauer Cemetery

Seegasse 9 1090

This is the oldest Jewish cemetery in Vienna, dating from the sixteenth century. It has now been restored after being devastated by the Nazis and is open daily from 8 am to 3 pm. Access is via the front entrance of the municipal home for the aged at Seegasse 9-11, but a permit must first be obtained from the community centre.

Vienna Central Cemetery

Simmering district 1110   (1) 76-6252

There is a Jewish section at Gate 4 and an older Jewish part at Gate 1.

Währinger Cemetery

Semperstrasse 64a 1180

Those wishing to visit must first obtain a permit from the community centre.

Contact Information

Jewish Community Centre

Seitenstettengasse 4   (1) 53104

Fax: (1) 533-1577

Email: lkg_adion@csi.com

Jewish Welcome Service Vienna

Stephansplatz 10 1010   (1) 533-2730

Fax: (1) 533-4098

Rabbi Paul Chaim Eisenberg

Chief Rabbi of Vienna   (1) 53104-17

Documentation Centres

Documentation Centre of Austrian Resistance Movement

Old City Hall, Wipplingerstrasse 8 1010

(1) 534-36-332

Documentation Centre of Union of Jewish Victims of the Nazis

Salztorgasse 6 1010   (1) 533-9131

Fax: (1) 535-0397

Embassy

Embassy of Israel

Anton-Frankgasse 20 1180   (1) 470-4741

Groceries

Kosher Supermarket & Shutnes Laboratory

Hollandstrasse 7 1020   (1) 26-96-75

Supervision: Rabbi Abraham Yonah Schwartz.

Raffi's

Ferdinandstrasse 1020   (1) 214-3394

Food imported from Belgium.

Vinothek Gross

Liechtensteinstrasse 32 1090   (1) 317-5277

Fax: (1) 317-5277

Vinothek Gross

Taborstrasse 15 1020   (1) 212-6299

Hotels

Hotel Stefanie

12 Tabor Strasse 1020   (1) 211-500

Fax: (1) 211-50160

Email: stefanie@schick-hotels.com

Four star hotel with kosher breakfast on request.

Kashrut Information

Vaad Hakashrut

Karmelitergasse 13 1020   (1) 33-73-64

Media

Maps and Guides

Jewish Vienna: Heritage and Mission

(1) 513-8892

Fax: (1) 513-4015

Newspaper

Die Gemeinde

(1) 531-0428

Fax: (1) 533-4516

Monthly.

Mikvaot

Agudas Yisroel

Tempelgasse 3 1020   (1) 214-9262

Machsike Haddas

Fleischmarkt 22 1010   (1) 512-5262

Museums

Jewish Museum of the City of Vienna

Dorotheergasse 11 A-1010   (1) 535-0431

Fax: (1) 535-0424

Hours: Sunday to Friday, 10 am to 6 pm; Thursday, 10 am to 8 pm. Cafeteria and bookshop on site.

Sigmund Freud Museum

Berggasse 19 1090   (1) 319-1596

Fax: (1) 317-0279

Email: freud-museum@t0.or.at

Web site: freud.t0.or.at

Restaurants

Vegetarian

Wrenkh, 1 Bauermarket 1010   (1) 533-1526

Hours: 11:30 am to 2:30 pm and 6 pm to midnight.

Austria

Sites
Mauthausen Memorial Site
(1) 072-38/24-39
Those wishing to visit the site should contact the Jewish Welcome Service.

Seitenstettengasse Synagogue
Seitenstettengasse 4 1010
Built in 1824-26 and partly destroyed during the Nazi period, this beautiful synagogue was restored by the community in 1988. Guides to the synagogue are available from the Jewish Community Centre. For information about guided tours, contact the Community Centre offices.

Snack Bar
Bernat Ainhorn
Grobe Stadtgutgasse 7, Wien 1020
(1) 214-5621

Synagogues

Orthodox

Agudas Yeshurun
Riemergasse 9 1010
Agudas Yisroel
Grünangergasse 1 1010 (1) 512-8331

Agudas Yisroel
Tempelgasse 3 1020 (1) 249-262
Machsike Haddas
Desider Friedmann-Platz 1010 (1) 214-1347
Misrachi
Judenplatz 8 1010 (1) 535-4153
Ohel Moshe
Lilienbrunngasse 19 1020 (1) 216-8864
Sephardi Centre
Tempelgasse 7 1020
Shomre Haddas
Glasergasse 17 1090
Thora Etz Chayim
Grosse Schiffgasse 8 1020 (1) 214-5206

Tour Information
The Vienna Tourist Board
(1) 513-8892
Fax: (1) 513-4015
Tourist Information Centre
Kärntnerstrasse 38 (1) 313-8892
Open daily, 9 am to 7 pm.

Azerbaijan

Azerbaijan has a remarkable Jewish history, which can be better explored now that the country is independent from the Soviet Union. The Tats (mountain Jews) believe that their ancestors arrived in Azerbaijan at the time of Nebuchadnezzar. They lived in several mountain villages, and adopted the customs of their non-Jewish neighbours. They spoke a north Iranian language, known as Judeo-Tat, to which they had added some Hebrew words. The Soviets clamped down on their way of life after 1928, changing the alphabet of their language from Hebrew to Latin and then, in 1938, to Cyrillic. Some of their synagogues were also closed down. Zionist feeling is high, with almost 30,000 emigrating to Israel since 1989.

The other strand in Azerbaijan's Jewish population are the Ashkenazis who arrived in the nineteenth century from Poland and other countries to the west.

The community has some 10–15 organisations in Baku, the capital, including Zionist and youth groups. The largest synagogue in Baku is the Tat synagogue, but there are also Ashkenazi and Georgian synagogues. Synagogues are found in other towns.

GMT + 5 hours	Total Population 7,595,000
Country calling code (994)	Jewish Population 20,000

Baku

Embassy
Embassy of Israel
Stroiteley Prospect 1

Synagogues
Mountain Jews
Dmitrova Street 39 370014
(12) 892-232-8867

Ashkenazi
Pervomoskaya Street 271   (12) 892-294-1571

Kuba

Synagogues
46 Kolkhoznaya Street

Bahamas

Luis de Torres, the official interpreter for Columbus, was the first Jew in the Bahamas, as well as being one of the first Europeans there. He was a Converso or Marrano, a 'secret Jew' who officially had converted to Catholicism, but who practised Judaism in private.

Today there are between 100 and 200 Jewish residents in the Bahamas. However, it is estimated that about 350,000 Jews visit the island every year as tourists. There is a conservative synagogue in Nassau, and also a separate Jewish cemetery. Freeport also has a synagogue.

GMT – 5 hours
Country calling code (1242)
Emergency Telephone (Police, Fire and Ambulance – 919)

Total Population 284,000
Jewish Population 200

Freeport

Synagogues
Luis de Torres Synagogue
East Sunrise Highway, PO Box F41761,
Freeport, Grand Bahama Island
(809) 373-2008
Services are held fairly regularly. The president of the congregation, Jack Turner, can be reached at 373-1041.

Tours of Jewish Interest
Freeport Hebrew Congregation
Freeport   (242) 373-4025
                        Fax: (242) 373-2130
                Email: hurst100@yahoo.com
Geoff Hurst is happy to make arrangements for tourists, and is the Bahamian Marriage Officer.

Barbados

Jewish history in Barbados starts in 1628, a year after the British first settled there. Jewish settlers came from Brazil, Surinam, England and Germany, and were mainly Sephardi. The first synagogue was established in Bridgetown (the capital) in 1654. Early settlers were engaged in cultivating sugar and coffee.

The synagogue was restored in 1987, and stamps were produced which commemorated its restoration. The Jewish population remains small, but it was a group of Barbadian Jews who founded the Caribbean Jewish Congress. The Jewish cemetery, one of the oldest in the Americas, is now back in use.

GMT – 4 hours
Country calling code (1246)

Total Population 261,000
Jewish Population Under 100

Community Organisations
Barbados Jewish Community
PO Box 651, Bridgetown   (809) 427-0703
                        Fax: (809) 436-8807
Caribbean Jewish Congress
PO Box 1331, Bridgetown   (809) 436-8163
Synagogue Restoration Project
PO Box 256, Bridgetown   (809) 432-0840
Local inquiries to Henry Altman, 'Sea Shell', Gibbes Beach, St Peter. Tel: 422-2664.

Synagogues
Barbados Synagogue
Synagogue Lane
Services are held Friday evenings at 7 pm at 'True Blue', Rockley New Road, Christ Church, during the summer, and at the synagogue in winter.

Belarus

For the adventurous traveller, who has a keen interest in Jewish history, Belarus (also known as White Russia) makes an interesting and unusual destination. Situated in the western side of the former Soviet Union, this largely flat country borders Poland and Lithuania to the west, Ukraine to the south and Russia to the east. Belarus finally achieved independence in 1991, and within its present borders are many towns and villages of Jewish interest, such as Minsk, Pinsk and Grodno. One of the most famous villages in Belarus is Lubavitch, a hamlet in the far east of the country, near the Russian border, where the world-wide Lubavitch movement had its origins.

The majority of this region's Jews died in the Holocaust and although emigration to Israel is high, the community is slowly rebuilding itself after the decades of Soviet control. Americans and Israelis are contributing rabbis to help in this revival, and Jewish schools have been set up. Yiddish is used far more here than in other parts of the former USSR.

GMT + 2 hours   Total Population 10,350,000
Country calling code (375)   Jewish Population 45,000
Emergency Telephone (Police, Fire and Ambulance – 03)

Baranovichi
Synagogues
39 Svobodnaya St.

Bobruisk
Synagogues
Engels St.

Borisov
Synagogues
Trud St.

Brest
Synagogues
Narodnaya St.

Gomel
Synagogues
13 Sennaya St.

Minsk
Embassy
Embassy of Israel
Partizanski Prospekt 6A 220002

Synagogues
22 Kropotkin St.   (0172) 558-270
Kommunisticheskaya St.

Moghilev
Synagogues
1 2nd Krutoy La.

Orsha
Synagogues
Nogrin St.

Rechitsa
Synagogues
120 Lunacharsky St.

Belgium

Jewish settlement in the area now known as Belgium dates back to the thirteenth century, and suffered a similar fate to other medieval European Jewish communities – taking the blame for the Black Death and suffering expulsions. The Sephardim were the first to resettle in Belgium, mainly in Antwerp. After the French Revolution, conditions for the Jews improved and more Jews began to settle there. The diamond centre of Antwerp was developing rapidly at that time, attracting many Jews from eastern Europe.

By 1939, the Jewish population had grown to 100,000, a large proportion of them being refugees hoping to escape to America. Some succeeded, but many became trapped after the German invasion. Some 25,000 Belgian Jews were deported and killed in the Holocaust. A national monument stands in Anderlecht in Brussels to their memory, listing the names of the victims.

The present Jewish population includes a large Chassidic community in Antwerp, where there are some 30 synagogues. There are also more than ten synagogues in Brussels. There are Jewish schools in Antwerp and Brussels, and Jewish newspapers and kosher food are easy to obtain in these two cities.

GMT + 1 hour
Country calling code (32)
Emergency Telephone (Police – 101) (Fire and Ambulance – 101)

Total population 10,160,000
Jewish Population 40,000

Antwerp

Seen by some as 'the last shtetl in Europe', Antwerp is a well known Hassidic centre. Antwerp's Jewish population (15,000) has one of the highest numbers of Ultra-Orthodox in continental Europe. It is served by 30 synagogues (many of them small shtiebels).

Bakeries
Gottesfeld, Mercatorstrasse. 20 (3) 230-0003
Grosz, Pelikaanstrasse 130 (3) 233-9110
Kleinblatt, Provinciestraat 206 (3) 233-7513; 226-0018
Fax: (3) 232-0920
Steinmetz, Lange Kievitstrasse 64

(3) 234-0947

Booksellers
Epstein, Van den Nestlei 7 (3) 232-7562
I. Menczer, Simonstrasse 40 (3) 232-3026
N. Seletsky
Lange Kievitstrasse 70 (3) 232-6966
Fax: (3) 226-9446
Stauber, Van Leriusstrasse 3 (3) 231-8031

Butchers
Berkowitz, Isabellalei 9 (3) 218-5111
Farkas, Lange Kievitstrasse 66 (3) 232-1385
Fruchter, Simonstrasse 22
(3) 233-1811; 1557
Fax: (3) 231-3903
Kosher King
Isabellalei 7 (3) 239-4189
Kosher King
Lange Kievitstrasse 40 (3) 233-6749
Mandelovics
Isabellalei 96 (3) 218-4779
Moszkowitz, Lange Kievitstrasse 47
(3) 232-6349
Fax: (3) 226-0471
Deli and Catering
Weingarten, Lange Kievitstrasse 124
(3) 233-2828

Contact Information
Machsike Hadass (Israelitische Orthodoxe Gemeente)
Jacob Jacobsstrasse 22 (3) 233-5567
Machsike Hadass Rabbinate
Jacob Jacobsstrasse 22 (3) 232-0021
Rabbi Ch. Kreiswirth, Quinten Matsijslei 35, 234-3148; Dayan E. Sternbuch, 233-7194; Dayan T. Weiss, 230-2163.

Shomre Hadass (Israelitische Gemeente)
Terliststrasse 35 2018   (3) 232-0187
                                     Fax: (3) 226-3123
Dayan J. Kohen, 230-3581; Rabbi D.
Lieberman, 239-1883

Embassy
Consulate General
Postbus 126 B- 2018 14

Groceries
Col-Bo, Jacob Jacobsstrasse 40   (3) 234-1212
Grosz-Modern
Terliststrasse 28   (3) 232-4626
Herzl & Gold
Korte Kievitstrasse 38   (3) 232-2365
Stark, Mercatorstrasse 24   (3) 230-2520
Super Discount
Belgielei 104-108   (3) 239-0666

Media
Newspapers
Belgisch Israelitisch Weekblad
Pelikaanstrasse 106-108 2018   (3) 233-7094
                                     Fax: (3) 233-4810

Mikvaot
Machsike Hadass
Steenbokstrasse 22   (3) 239-7588
Shomre Hadass
Van Diepenbeeckstrasse 42   (3) 239-0965

Museums
Plantin-Moretus Museum
Vrijdagmarkt (nr Groenplaats)   (3) 233-0688
Open daily (except Monday). Contains
examples of early Jewish printing, such as the
famous Polyglot Bible.

Restaurants
Blue Lagoon
Lange Herentalsestrasse 70   (3) 226-0114
Supervision: Machsike Hadass.
Also sell chocolates, contact R Suchowolski on
230-2871 or fax: 281-1702. Five minutes from
Central station..
Dresdner, Simonsstrasse 10   (3) 232-5455
Garden of Eden
Plantin En Moretuslei 10 2018   (3) 281-4281
Open: 12pm-2pm and 6pm-11pm.
Jacob, Lange Kievitstrasse 49   (3) 233-1124
Sam (Diamantbeurs)
Pelikaanstrasse 28   (3) 233-9289
Snack Bar, Romi Goldmuntz Centre,
Nerviersstrasse 12   (3) 239-3911
Snack Bar Hoffy's
Lange Kievitstrasse 52   (3) 234-3535

Synagogues
Orthodox
Machsike Hadass
Jacob Jacobsstrasse 22
Machsike Hadass
Oostenstrasse 43   (3) 239-3038

Tour Information
Antwerp Tourist & Inquiries Office
Grote Markt 15 2000   (3) 232-0103
                                     Fax: (3) 231-1937
                    Email: moerisme@antwerpen.be
                           Web site: /www.dma.be

Arlon
Synagogues
Rue St Jean   (63) 217-985
Established 1863. The secretary, J.C. Jacob, can
be reached at 11 rue des Martyrs, 6700. A
monument has been erected in the new Jewish
cemetery to the memory of the Jews of Arlon
deported and massacred by the Nazis.

Brussels
The capital of Belgian is less well endowned
with kosher facilities compared to Antwerp,
but nevertheless, there are 15,000 Jews living
in the city. The headquarters of the European
Union of Jewish Students is based there. The
Anderlecht area has a monument to the
Belgian Holocaust victims.

Bakeries
Bornstein, 62 rue de Suéde, St Gilles
                                          (2) 537-1679

Booksellers
Colbo, 121 rue du Brabant   (2) 217-2620
Menorah
12 Ave. J. Voldens 1060   (2) 537-5073

Butchers
Lanxner
121 rue de Brabant 1030   (2) 217-2620
Supervision: Rabbinate of the Jewish Orthodox
Community of Brussels.
Grocery: Jewish specialities, also Delicatessen.
Hours: Sun, Mon, Fri 8.30am to 13.00pm.
Tues 8.30am to 18.00pm. Wed-Thurs 8.30am
to 19.30pm.
Lanxner, 37 Ave Jean Volders   (2) 537-0608

Community Organisations
Centre Communautaire Laic Juif
52 rue Hotel des Monnaies   (2) 537-8216

Belgium

Contact Information
Beth Chabad
87 Ave du Roi   (2) 537-1158

Embassy
Embassy of Israel
40 Avenue de l'Observatoire 1180
                                 (2) 373-5500

Media
Newspapers
Centrale, 91 Av. Henri Jaspar   (2) 538-8036
Monthly
Fax De Jerusalem
68 Ave Ducpétiaux   (2) 538-5673
                            Fax: (2) 534-0236
            Email: alyabelgique@skynet.be
Weekly
Kehilatenou
2 rue Joseph Dupont   (2) 512-4334
Monthly
Regards, 52 rue Hotel des Monnaies
                                 (2) 538-4908
                            Fax: (2) 537-5565
Fortnightly

Mikvaot
Machsike Hadass
67a rue de la Clinique   (2) 537-1439

Museums
Jewish Museum
74 Ave de Stalingrad 1000   (2) 512-1963
                            Fax: (2) 513-4859
            Email: info@mjb.jmb.org
Hours: Mon-Thurs 12.00 – 5.00 pm. Sunday
10.00 am to 1.00 pm. Closed Friday, Saturday
and Jewish holidays.

Religious Organisations
Communaute Israelite de Bruxelles
2 Rue Joseph Dupont 1000   (2) 512-4334
                            Fax: (2) 512-9237
Consistoire Central Israelite de Belgique
2 Rue Joseph Dupont 1000   (2) 512-2190
                            Fax: (2) 512-3578
**Machsike Hadass (Communauté Israélite
Orthodoxe de Bruxelles)**
67a rue de la Clinique
                        (2) 524-1486; 521-1289
Machsike Hadass Beth Din
67a rue de la Clinique   (2) 522-0717

Restaurants
Centre Ben Gurion
89 Chaussee de Vleurgat   (2) 648-1859
Hours: daily, noon to 2:30 pm and 6 pm to 9
pm except Friday evenings and Shabbat
afternoons.
Chez Gilles
Rue de la Clinique 21 1070
Supervision: (O).
Kosher restaurant open from 9am – 5 pm Also
sells confectionery.

Sites
**National Monument to the Jewish Martyrs
of Belgium** corner rue Emile Carpentier and
rue Goujons, Square of the Jewish Martyrs,
Anderlecht. This monument commemorates
the Jews of Belgium who were deported to
concentration camps and killed by the Nazis
during the Second World War. The names of
all 23,838 are engraved on the monument.

Synagogues
Liberal
**Member of World Union for Progressive
Judaism**
96 Ave Kersbeek   (2) 332-2528

Orthodox
Adath Israel
126 rue Rogier, Schaerbeek   (2) 241-1664
Ahavat Reim
73 rue de ThySt Gilles   (2) 648-3837
Beth Hamidrash
rue du Chapeau, Anderlecht   (2) 524-1486
Beth Itshak
115 Ave du Roi 1060
                        (2) 538-3374; 520-1359
Maale, 11 Ave de Messidor   (2) 344-6094
Machsike Hadass
67a rue de la Clinique   (2) 522-0717
Or Hahayim
77 rue P. Decoster 1190   (2) 344-2342

Sephardi
Communauté Sepharade de Bruxelles
47 rue du Pavaillon 1030   (2) 215-0525
                            Fax: (2) 215-0242

Charleroi
Community Organisations
Community Centre
56 rue Pige-au-Croly

Ghent

Contact Information
Jacques Bloch
Veldstrasse 60   (9) 225-7085
The treasurer of the community, he will be happy to meet Anglo-Jewish visitors. As the community is a very small one, there is no permanent synagogue. Services are held on the High Holy Days.

Knokke

Restaurants
Maison Steinmetz
Piers de Raveschootlaan 129 8300
    (50) 61-0265

Open July-August.

Synagogues
30 Van Bunnenlaan   (50) 611-0372

Liège

Community Organisations
Community Centre
12 Quai Marcellis 4020

Museums
Musee Serge Kruglanski
19 rue L. Fredericq 4020   (43) 438-043
    Fax: (43) 226-0234

Synagogues
19 rue L. Frédéricq 4020   (41) 436-106

Mons

Contact Information
SHAPE 7010   (65) 445-808; 444-809
Nearby, at Casteau, the International Chapel of NATO's Supreme Headquarters Allied Powers Europe, includes a small Jewish community, established 1951, that holds regular services. Call for further information.

Ostend

Hotels
Hotel Royal Astor
Hertsstraat 15   (59) 803-773
Open for Sukkot

Synagogues
Van Maastrichtplein 3
Services during July and August. Inquiries to Mrs. Liliane Wulfowicz, Parklaan 21, B-8400, 802-405.

Bermuda

Jews have lived in Bermuda since the seventeenth century, but the first formal congregation was not established until the twentieth century. In April 1943, at the time of the Warsaw Ghetto Revolt, President Roosevelt organised a conference on the island about how to rescue Europe's Jews from the Nazis. Nothing transpired from his efforts, however.

The resident Jewish population is very small, but the transient population (of tourists largely from the USA, Britain and Canada) is much greater. High holy-day services are normally held at the US Naval Air Station Chapel. Friday services are held, usually monthly, at the Unity Foundation, 75 Reid Street, Hamilton.

GMT – 4 hours	Total Population 64,000
Country calling code (1)	Jewish Population Under 100
Emergency Telephone (Police – 112) (Fire – 113) (Ambulance -115)	

Ferry Reach

Contact Information
Diana Lynn
17 Biological Lane GE01   (441) 297-2267
                                              Fax: (441) 297-8143
                                              Email: dlynn@bbsr.edu

Hamilton

Community Organisations
Jewish Community of Bermuda
PO Box HM 1793 HM HX   (441) 291-1785

Bolivia

The history of the Jews of Bolivia dates back to the Spanish colonial period. Conversos (converts to Christianity who practised Judaism in secret, also known as Marranos) came with the Spaniards in the seventeenth century.

The main influx of Jews occurred in 1905, with immigrants from eastern Europe, but the number entering Bolivia was much smaller than that to other South American countries. In 1933 there were only some 30 Jewish families. At the end of the decade, however, there was a small increase in Jewish immigration as German and Austrian Jews fled from Europe. Ironically, the Jewish community did not grow very much, even though the government granted every Jew an entry visa.

Many Jews started to leave Bolivia in the 1950s because of political instability and the lack of educational opportunities. The present-day community has a central organisation known as the Circulo Israelita de Bolivia. There are synagogues in the capital, La Paz, and one rabbi. Kosher food is available.

GMT – 4 hours

Country calling code (591)

Total Population 7,593,000

Jewish Population 500

Cochabamba

Representative Organisations
Asociacion Israelita de Cochabamba
PO Box 349, Calle Valdivieso

Synagogues
Calle Junin y Calle Colombia, Casilla 349

La Paz

Synagogues
Circulo Israelita de Bolivia
Casilla 1545, Calle Landaeta 346, PO Box 1545
(2) 32-5925
Fax: (2) 34-2738
Representative body of Bolivian Jewry. All La Paz organisations are affiliated to it. Service Shabbat morning only.

Comunidad Israelita Synagogue
Calle Canada Stronguest 1846, PO Box 2198
Affiliated to the Circulo. Friday evening services are held here. There is a Jewish school at this address.

Tour information
Centro Shalom
Calle Canada Stronguest 1846

Santa Cruz

Community Organisations
Centro Cruceño
PO Box 469

Representative Organisations
WIZO, Castilla 3409

Bosnia-Hercegovina

Sephardi Jews were the first to arrive in the area, in the late sixteenth century. They established a Jewish quarter in Sarajevo, and this was home for poorer Jews until the Austrians conquered the land in 1878. It was the Turks who emancipated the Jews in the nineteenth century when Bosnia-Hercegovina was under Ottoman rule.

When Bosnia-Hercegovina became part of the newly formed Yugoslavia, after the First Word War, the community maintained its Sephardi heritage and joined the all-Yugoslav Federation of Jewish Religious Communities. The Jewish population numbered 14,000 in 1941. This number dropped sharply after the Germans conquered Yugoslavia.

After the war the survivors were joined by many who had decided to return. The Sephardi and Ashkenazi communities became unified. La Benevolencija, founded 100 years ago, is a humanitarian organisation which supported the plight of the community and became well known in the early 1990s at the time of the civil war. After the Yugoslav civil war, many made aliyah to Israel, reducing the community still further.

GMT + 1 hour
Country calling code (387)
Emergency Telephone (Police – 664 211) (Fire – 93) (Ambulance – 94)

Total Population 3,628,000
Jewish Population 500

Sarajevo

Cemeteries
Kovacici
This historic Jewish cemetery is in town. Not far from the centre of town, on a hill called Vraca, there is a monument with the names of the 7,000 Jews from the area who fell victim to the Nazis.

Museums
Jewish Museum
Mulamustafe Baseskije Street
This historic museum, placed in the oldest synagogue in Sarajevo, with priceless relics dating back to the expulsion from Spain, is temporarily closed to the public.

Novi Hram
This gallery is also located in a former synagogue. The president of the community will gladly show you around.

Synagogues
Synagogue and Community Centre
Hamdije Kresevljakovica 59   (71) 663-472
Fax: (71) 663-473
Email: labelova@utic.net.ba

Brazil

The first Jewish settlers in Brazil came with the Portuguese in 1500. They were mainly Marranos, escaping persecution in Portugal, and worked on the sugar plantations. The huge area which is called Brazil today was in the process of being conquered by the Dutch and the Portuguese. The Portuguese gained the upper hand in 1654, and there was much anti-Jewish persecution. Many fled and some went on to found the first Jewish community in New York, then known as New Amsterdam.

With Brazilian independence in 1822, conditions became more favourable for Jews and many immigrated from north Africa and Europe. The majority of Jews in Brazil today, however, originate from the immigration of east European Jews in the early twentieth century. From about 6,000 Jews in 1914, the community grew to 30,000 in 1930. From 1937 Brazil refused to allow Jewish immigrants into the country, but some limited immigration managed to continue despite the restrictions.

A central organisation was established in 1951 (the CONIB), and this includes 200 various Jewish organisations. Brazilian Jews are fortunate to live in an atmosphere of tolerance and posperity, and assimilation is prominent. There are synagogues in all the major cities.

GMT – 3 to 4 hrs

Country calling code (55)

Emergency Telephone (Police – 147) (Fire – 193) (Ambulance – 192)

Total Population 161,087,000

Jewish Population 130,000

Amazonas

Manaus

Community Organisations
Grupo Kadima
Rua Ramos Ferreira 596

Bahia State

Salvador

Synagogues
Rua Alvaro Tiberio 60   (71) 3-4283
Community centre and Zionist organisation are at the same address.

Brasilia

Embassy
Embassy of Israel
Av. das Nacoes Sul, Lote 38
       (61) 244-7675; 7875; 5886; 4886

Synagogues
ACIB, Entrequadras Norte 305-306, Lote A
       (61) 23-2984
Community centre is at the same address.

Minas Gerais

Belo Horizonte

Contact Information
Lojinha do Beit Chabad
Av. Serzedelo Corrêa 276   (91) 241-2250

Mikvaot
Rua Rio Grande do Norte 477   (91) 221-0690

Representative Organisations
Associacão Israelita Brasileira
Rua Rio Grande do Norte 477   (91) 221-0690
Congregacao Israelita Mineira
Rua Rio Grande do Norte 477   (031) 224-6673
       Fax: (031) 224-6673
       Email: cim@honiz.com.br
Uniao Israelita de Belo Horizonte
Rua Pernambuco 326   (91) 224-6013

Synagogues
Av. Leonardo Malchez 630, Centro

Para

Belém

Community Organisations
Community Centre
Travessa Dr. Moraes 37

Contact Information
Lojinha do Beit Chabad
Av. Serzedelo Corrêa 276   (91) 241-2250

Synagogues
Eshel Avraham
Travessa Campos Sales 733
Shaar Hashamaim
Rua Alcipreste Manoel Theodoro 842

Parana

Curitiba

Community Organisations
Community Centre and S. Guelman School
Rua Nilo Pecanha 664   (41) 233-734

Synagogues

Orthodox

Francisco Frischman
Rua Cruz Machado 126

Pernambuco

Recife

Community Organisations
Community Centre
Rua da Gloria 215

Synagogues
Rua Martins Junior 29

Rio de Janeiro

Campos

Community Organisations
Community Centre
Rua 13 de Maio 52

Greater Rio de Janeiro

Embassy
Consulate General
Av. Copacabana 680   (21) 255-5432

Groceries
Kosher House
Rua Anita Garibaldi 37 lj. A, Copacabana
                              (21) 255-3891

Libraries
Biblioteca Bialik
Rua Fernando Osorio 16
Flamengo 22230   (21) 205-1946

Biblioteca Sholem Aleichem
Rua Sao Clemente 155
Botafogo 22260   (21) 226-7740

Mikvaot
Kehilat Yaakov
Rua Capelao Alvares da Silva 15
Copacabana 22041

Museums
Jewish Museum
Rua Mexico 90-1Andar

Religious Organisations
Chevre Kedishe
Rua Barao de Iguatemi 306   (21) 248-8716

Representative Organisations
Organição Israelita do Estado do Rio de Janeiro
Rua Mexico 90/5   (21) 532-0925
Rabinado do Rio de Janeiro
Rua Pompeu Loureiro 40
                              Fax: (21) 236-0249

Restaurants
Cafeteria no Rabinato
Rua Pompeu Loureiro 40 Copacabana
                              (21) 236-0249
Hours: 10am to 5pm Sunday to Thursday.

Synagogues
Grande Templo Israelita
Rua Tenente Possolo 8
Centro 20230   (21) 232-3656

Liberal

Associação Religiosa Israelita
Rua General Severiano 170
Botafogo 22290   (21) 226-9666; 237-9283

Orthodox

Agudat Israel
Rua Nascimento Silva 109
Ipanema 22421

Kehilat Yaakov
Rua Capelao Alvares da Silva
Copacabana 22041

Niteroi

Community Organisations
Centro Israelita
Rua Visconde do Uruguai 255 24030
Sociedade Hebraica
Rua Alvares de Azevedo 185, Icarai 24220

Petropolis

Religious Organisations
Machane Israel Yeshiva
Rua Duarte de Silveira 1246 25600
(242) 45-4952

Synagogues
Sinagoga Israelita Brasileira
Rua Aureliano Coutinho 48 25600

Rio Grande do Sul

Erechim

Synagogues
Av. Pedro Pinto de Souza 131

Passo Fundo

Synagogues
Rua General Osório 1049

Pelotas

Synagogues
Rua Santos Dumont 303

Porto Alegre

Butchers
Kosher Butcher
Rua Fernandes Vieira 518   (51) 250-441

Cultural Organisations
**Instituto Cultural Judaico Marc Chagall –
Projeto Memoria**
Rua Dom Pedro II, 1220/sala 216
(51) 343-5748

Mikvaot
Rua Francisco Ferrer 170

Museums
Museu Judaico
Rua João Telles 329   (51) 226-0379

Religious Organisations
City Rabbinate
Rua Henrique Dias 73   (51) 219-649

Synagogues
Liberal
SIBRA, Mariante 772   (51) 331-8133
Services on Shabbat only.

Orthodox
Beit Chabad
Rua Felipe Camarão 748   (51) 330-7078
Daily services.
Centro Israelita Porto Alegrense
Rua Henrique Dias 73   (51) 228-1935
Daily services.
Linath Ha-Tzedek
Rua Bento Figueredo 55   (51) 332-1065
Daily services.
Poilisher Farband
Rua João Telles 329   (51) 226-0379
Daily services.
União Israelita Porto Algrense
Rua Barros Cassal 750   (51) 224-6515
Daily services.

Sephardi
Centro Hebraico Riograndense
Rua Cel. Machado 1008
Services on Shabbat only.

São Paulo

Campinas

Synagogues
Beth Yacob, Rua Barreto Leme 1203
(19) 314-908
Fax: (19) 442-171

Guaruja

Synagogues
Beit Yaacov
Av. Leomil 628   (013) 387-2033
Neve Itzhak
Av. Leomil 950   (013) 386-3167

Mogi Das Cruzes

Community Organisations
Jewish Society
Rua Dep. Deodato Wertheimer 421
(11) 469-2505

S. Jose dos Campos

Synagogues

Beit Chabad
Rua Republica do Ira 91   (11) 3064-6322

Santo Andre

Synagogues

Beit Chabad
Rua 11 de Junho 172   (11) 449-1568

Santos

Community Organisations

Club, Rua Cons. Neblas 254   (132) 32-9016

Synagogues

Beit Sion, Rua Borges 264
Sinagoga Beit Jacob
Rua Campos Sales 137

São Caetano do Sul

Synagogues

Sociedade Religiosa S. Caetano do Sul
Rua Para 67   (11) 442-3514

São Paulo

Bakeries

Buffet Mazal Tov
Rua Peixoto Gomide 1724   (11) 883-7614
Fax: (11) 3064-5208
Matok Bakery
Al. Barros 921   (11) 66-7514
Supervision: Rabbi I. Dichi.
Matok Bakery
Rua P. João Manoel 709   (11) 3064-6668
Supervision: Rabbi I. Dichi.

Booksellers

Livraria Sêfer
Rua Conselheiro Brotero 986 01232-010
(11) 826-1366
Fax: (11) 826-4508
Email: seer@sefer.com.br
Web site: http:// www.sefer.com.br
Bookseller and Judaica
Oitzer Haseforim
Rua Augusta 2299/3   (11) 881-3255

Butchers

Casa de Carnes Casher
Rua Fortunato 241   (11) 221-2240
Under supervision of Rabbi Elyahu B. Valt.
Mehadrin, Rua S. Vicente de Paulo
(11) 67-9090
Under supervision of Rabbi M.A. Iliovitz.

Mehadrin, Rua Prates 689   (11) 228-1771
Under supervision of Rabbi M.A. Iliovitz.

Embassy

Consulate General
Rua Luis Coelho 308, 7th Floor
(11) 257-2111; 257-2814

Groceries

All Kosher, Rua Albuquerque Lins 1170
(11) 825-1131
Amazonas, Rua Amazonas 91   (11) 229-1336
Chazak, Rua Haddock Lobo 1002
(11) 3068-9093
Chazak, Rua Afonsa Pena 348a (11) 229-5607
Dom Bosco, Rua Guarani 114   (11) 228-6105
Mazal Tov, Rua Peixoto Gomide 1724
(11) 883-7614
Fax: (11) 3064-5208
Sta. Luzia, Al. Lorena 1471   (11) 883-5844
Look for kosher section.
Zilanna, Rua Itambé 506   (11) 257-8671

Media

Magazines

Morasha
Rua de Veiga, Filho-547, Higienopolis
01229-000   (11) 3662-2154
Email: morasha@uol.com.br

Newspapers

O Hebreu, Rua Cunha Gago 158
(11) 870-1616
Fax: (11) 816-1324
Monthly.
Resenha Judaica
Rua Antonio Carlos 582/5   (11) 255-8794
Weekly.
Tribuna Judaica
Rua Tanabi 299   (11) 871-3234
Fax: (11) 3675-0072
Email: tjudaica@uol.com.br
Weekly.

Mikvaot

Micre Taharat Menachem – Perdizes
Rua Dr. Manoel Maria Tourinho 261
(11) 3865-0615
By appointment only.

Orthodox

Congregacao Monte Sinai
Rua Piaui 624, Higienopolis 01241-000
(11) 3824-9229
Fax: (11) 3824-9229
Email: cmsinai@sanet.com.br

Religious Organisations

Centro Judaico Religioso de Sao Paulo
(11) 220-5642
Office hours: 9 am to 1 pm weekdays.
Comunidade Israelita Ortodoxa de Sao Paulo
Kehilat Hacharedim, Rua Haddock Lobo 1091
(11) 282-1562; 852-9710
This Community centre has two synagogues.

Restaurants

Hebraica Kosher Restaurant
Rua Hungria 1000
(11) 815-6788; 815-6980; 818-8831
Fax: (11) 815-6980
Supervision: Rabbi Elyahu B. Valt.
Buffet Mosaico inside the Hebraica São Paulo club. Closed Mondays, open Saturday night 1 1/2 hours after Shabbat.
Kosher Center
Rua Corrèa de Melo 68 01123-020
(11) 223-1175
Fax: (11) 223-3721
Supervision: Rabbi M.A. Iliovitch Shlita of Kehal Hachareidim.
Restaurant and Bakery. Hours: Sun 9.00am-4.00pm. Mon-Thurs 8.00am-6.00pm. Fri 7.30am-3.00pm
Kosher Deli
Rua Consolação 3679
(11) 852-6473; 853-1250
Kosher Pizza
Rua P. João Manoel 881   (11) 0800-114-666
Restaurant Beit Chinuch
Rua P. João Manoel 727   (11) 280-5111
Fax: (11) 280-4553
Email: lavne@uninet.com.br

Synagogues

Beit Chabad Perdizes
Rua Dr. Manoel Maria Tourinho 261
(11) 3865-0615
By appointment only.

Hasidic

Kehal Chassidim
Rua Mamore 597   (11) 224-0278

Hungarian

Adas Yereim
Rua Talmud Tora 86
(11) 282-1562; 852-9710

Liberal

Congregacao Israelita Paulista
Rua Antonio Carlos 653   (11) 256-7811
Fax: (11) 257-1446
Email: scrtgeral@dialdata.com.br
Web site: www.cip.sp.com.br

Orthodox

Beit Chabad Central
Rua Chabad 60   (11) 282-8711
Fax: (11) 280-2380
Beit Itzchak
Rua Haddock Lobo 1279   (11) 881-3804
Fax: (11) 881-3064, 0302
Kehal Machzikei Hadat
Rua Padre Joao Manuel 727   (11) 280-5111
Sinagoga Israelita Paulista – Beit Chabad
Rua Augusta 259 01305-000   (11) 258-7173

Sephardi

Templo Israelita Brasileiro Ohel Yaacov
Rua Abolicao 457   (11) 606-9982
Fax: (11) 227-6793

Travel Agencies

Carmel Tur, Rua Xavier de Toledo 121/10
(11) 257-2244
Sharontur, Rua de Graca 235   (11) 223-8388
Vertice, Rua Sao Bento 545/10
(11) 3115-1960
Fax: (11) 3068-0325

Sorocaba

Synagogues

Community Centre
Rua Dom Pedro II 56   (11) 31-3168

Bulgaria

Dating back to the Byzantine conquest, the community in Bulgaria was established by Greek Jews in Serdica (Sofia, the capital). The Jewish community grew when the Bulgarian state was founded in 681. Czar Ivan Alexander (1331–71) had a Jewish wife (who converted to Christianity).

The community included eminent rabbinic commentators, such as Rabbi Dosa Ajevani and Joseph Caro, the codifier of the Shulchan Aruch, who escaped to Bulgaria after the expulsion from Spain. The various Jewish groups joined to form a unified Sephardi community in the late seventeenth century.

Since the fall of communism, the community has been reconstituted and now has synagogues in Sofia and Plovdiv, but no rabbi. The community is ageing, although 100 children attend a Sunday school, run by the Shalom Organisation, the central Jewish organisation for Bulgaria.

GMT + 2 hours
Country calling code (359)
Emergency Telephone (Police – 166) (Fire – 160) (Ambulance – 150)

Total Population 8,468,000
Jewish Population 3,000

Pazardjik

Community Organisations
Community Centre
Asson Zlatarov St. 26   (34) 28-364

Plovdiv

Libraries
Library and House of Culture
Vladimir Zaimov St. 20   (32) 761-376

Synagogues
Tsar Kalojan St. 15
In the courtyard of a large apartment complex.

Russe

Synagogues
Community Centre
Ivan Vazov Sq. 4   (82) 270-540

Sofia

About half of Bulgarian Jewry lives in Sofia. The Great Synagogue of 1878 ranks amongst the largest of Sephardi synagogues. A musuem lies next to it, detailing the rescue of Bulgarian Jews in the Holocaust. The Central Jewish Religious Council is based in the city.

Cemeteries
Jewish Cemetery
Orlandovtzi suburb
Take a tram (Nos. 2, 10 or 14) to the last stop for this large Jewish cemetery.

Community Organisations
Social & Cultural Organisation of Bulgarian Jews
Shalom, Alexander Stambolisky St. 50   (2) 870-163
Publishes a periodical 'Evreiski Vesti' and a yearbook. It also maintains a museum devoted to 'The Rescue of Bulgarian Jews, 1941–1944'. At the same address are the offices of El Al, the Joint and the Jewish Agency.

Embassy
Embassy of Israel
Seventh floor, NDK Administrative Building, 1 Bulgaria Square

Religious Organisations
Synagogue & Central Jewish Religious Council
Ekzarh Josef St. 16
Above the synagogue is a museum dedicated to the history of Bulgarian Jewry.

Canada

The Jewish settlement of Canada began with the British expansion into Canada. In 1760, the Shearith Israel synagogue was founded in Montreal and in 1832 Jews received full civil rights. In the 1850s the community began to spread from Montreal to Toronto and Hamilton, with the first arrivals being those fleeing Lithuanian.

The community grew throughout the early twentieth century, from 16,000 in 1900 to 126,000 in 1921. After the war, Jewish immigration increased, and by 1961 the population was 260,000.

The headquarters of the Canadian Jewish Congress is in Montreal. This is the main national organisation for Canadian Jewry, and the community is provided with a full range of services, with Jewish schools, yeshivot, newspapers and the unique (in the Americas) Montreal Jewish Library. There are also several kosher restaurants.

GMT -3 to -8 hours   Total Population 29,680,000
Country calling code (1)   Jewish Population 360,000
Emergency Telephone (Police, Fire and Ambulance – 911) In remote areas, calls have to be made via the operator.

Alberta

Calgary

Delicatessens
Schaier's Meat & Kosher Deli
2515 90th Av. S.W.   (403) 251-2552
Wolf's Kosher World & Deli
42 180-94 Av. S.E   (403) 253-3354
Hours: Sunday to Thursday, 10 am to 8 pm; Friday, 10 am to 2 pm.

Media

Newspapers

Jewish Free Press
Box 72113, 16900 90th Av. S.W. T2V 5H9
       (403) 252-9423
       Fax: (403) 255-5640

Religious Organisations
Calgary Rabbinical Council
       (403) 253-8600
       Fax: (403) 253-7915

Representative Organisations
B'nai Brith Canada
Western Region, 10655 Southport Rd S.W., Suite 1400 T2W 4Y1   (403) 225-5256
       Fax: (403) 278-0176

Calgary Jewish Community Council
1607 90TH Av. S.W.   (403) 253-8600
       Fax: (403) 253-7915
       Web site: www.jewish-calgary.com
The Council issues a booklet 'Keeping Kosher in Calgary'.

Restaurants

Dairy and Meat

Karen's Cafe
Calgary Jewish Centre, 1607 90th Av. S.W.
       (403) 255-5311
Hours: Sunday to Thursday, 10 am to 7 pm; Friday, 10 am to 1 pm.

Synagogues

Conservative

Beth Tzedec
1325 Glenmore Trail S.W. T2Y 4Y8
       (403) 255-8688

Orthodox

House of Jacob
1613 92nd Av. S.W. T2V 5C9   (403) 259-3230

Reform

Temple B'nai Tikvah
Calgary Jewish Centre, 1607 90th Av. S.W.
T2V 4V7   (403) 252-1654

Edmonton

Butchers
Kosher Mart
14804 Stony Plain Rd T5N 3S5
(708) 453-3988

Delicatessens
Hello Deli, 10725-124 St   (708) 454-8527

Media

Newspapers

Edmonton Jewish Life
10342-47 St. T5J 2W2   (708) 488-7276
Fax: (708) 487-4342
Edmonton Jewish News
#330, 10036 Jasper Ave T5J 2W2
(708) 421-7966
Fax: (708) 424-3951

Representative Organisations
Edmonton Jewish Federation
7200 156th St. T5R 1X3   (708) 487-0585
Fax: (708) 481-1854
Email: edjfed@netcom.ca
Contact L. Jacobson, Exec. Director, for
additional information.

Restaurants
King David Pizza
1195 8770-170 St, West Edmonton Mall
(708) 486-9020
Kosher Restaurant at Jewish community
centre
7200-156 St T5R 1X3   (708) 444-4460

Synagogues
Beth Shalom
11916 Jasper Av. T5K 0N9   (708) 488-6333

Othodox

Beth Israel
10205 119th St. T5K 1Z3   (708) 482-2840

Reform

Temple Beth Ora
7200 156th St. T5R 1X3   (708) 487-4817
Fax: (708) 481-1854
Email: bethora@planet.eon.net

Lethbridge

Synagogues

Orthodox

Beth Israel
914 15th Street South T1J 3A5
(403) 327-8621

Medicine Hat

Synagogues
Sons of Abraham
540 5th Street South East T1A 1S6
(403) 526
Fax: (403) 3880

British Columbia

Kelowha

Synagogues

Traditional

Beth Shalom Sanctuary
OJCC, 102-1 North Glenmore Road V1V 2E2
(250) 862-2305
Fax: (250) 862-2365
Shabbat services last Saturday of the month,
9:30 am.

Richmond

Bakeries
Garden City Bakery
#360-9100 Blundell Road   (604) 244-7888
Supervision: Orthodox Rabbinical Council of
British Columbia.

Kashrut Information
Orthodox Rabbinical Council of British
Columbia
8080 Francis Road V6Y 1A4   (604) 275-0042
Fax: (604) 277-2225
Email: bckosher@direct.ca
Kashrut Director, Rabbi A. Feigelstock; Kashrut
Administrator, Rabbi Levy Teitlebaum.

Synagogues

Conservative

Beth Tikvah
9711 Geal Road V7E 1R4   (604) 271-6262
Friday, 8 pm; Shabbat, 9:30 am. Wheelchair
access.

Orthodox

Eitz Chaim
8080 Frances Road V6Y 1A4   (604) 275-0007
Fax: (604) 277-2225
Daily, 7 am and sunset; Shabbat, 9 am and
sunset; Sunday, 9 am. Wheelchair access.
Young Israel Congregation Schaare Tzion
8360 St Albans Road   (604) 272-2113
Monday and Thursday, 7 am; Sunday, 9 am;
Shabbat, 9:30 am. Wheelchair access.

Surrey – White Rock
Community Organisations
White Rock/South Surrey Jewish Community Centre
PO Box 75186 V4A   (604) 541-9995
Monthly Shabbat services. Wheelchair access.

Synagogues
Hasidic
The Centre for Judaism of the Lower Fraser Valley
2351 128th Street   (604) 541-4111
                Email: shfy@aol.com
Weekly Shabbat services. Wheelchair access.

Vancouver
Bakeries
Sabra
3844 Oak Street V6H 2M5   (604) 733-4912
                Fax: (604) 733-4911
Supervision: Orthodox Rabbinical Council of British Columbia.
Fresh kosher cookies, muffins, falafel, salads and more items. Take-out, eat-in and catering. Dairy, pareve (meat is take-out only). Hours: Monday to Thursday, 8:30 am to 8 pm; Friday, 8:30 am to 2 pm; Sunday, 10 am to 6:30 pm.

Cafeterias
Dairy
Cafe Sabra Too (Jewish Community Centre)
950 West 41st Avenue V5Z 2N7
                (604) 257-5111
Supervision: Orthodox Rabbinical Council of British Columbia.
Fresh kosher cookies, muffins, falafel, salads and more items. Take-out, eat-in and catering. Dairy, pareve (meat is take-out only). Hours: Monday to Thursday, 8:30 am to 8 pm; Friday, 8:30 am to 2 pm; Sunday, 10 am to 6:30 pm.

Community Organisations
Jewish Community Centre of Greater Vancouver
950 West 41st Avenue V5Z 2N7
                (604) 257-5111
Executive Director Gerry Zipursky

Contact Information
Jewish Federation of Greater Vancouver
950 West 41st Avenue, Suite 200 V5Z 2N7
                (604) 257-5100
                Fax: (604) 257-5110
                Email: dstaffenberg@jfgv.com
Executive Director Drew Staffenberg
Shalom Vancouver
950 West 41st Avenue V5Z 2N7
                (604) 257-5111
                Fax: (604) 257-5121
Jewish Information Referral & Welcome Service for newcomers and visitors. Publishes a 'Guide to Jewish life in British Columbia'. Co-ordinator Janet Kolof.

Media
Newspapers
Jewish Bulletin
#203-873 Beatty Street V6B 2M6
                (604) 689-1520
                Fax: (604) 689-1525

Restaurants
Dairy
Cohen's Gourmet
4054 Cambie Street   (604) 879-9044
Fresh kosher, vegetarian, dairy dishes and gourmet pizza. Dine in or take out. Hours: Monday to Thursday, 8 am to 8 pm; Friday, 8 am to 5 pm; Shabbat closed; Sunday, 11 am to 8 pm.

Meat
Aviv Kosher Meats
1011 West 49th Avenue   (604) 261-2727
Supervision: Orthodox Rabbinical Council of British Columbia.
Fresh meats, poultry, sandwiches, pastries, cakes and breads. Eat in, take out and catering. Hours: Monday to Thursday, 8 am to 8 pm; Friday, 7 am to 3 pm; Sunday, 8 am to 3 pm.
Omnitsky Kosher B.C.
5866 Cambie Street   (604) 321-1818
                Fax: (604) 321-1817
                Web site: www.escape.ca
Supervision: Orthodox Rabbinical Council of British Columbia.
Fresh meats, poultry. Manufacturers of all beef delicatessen products under B.C.K.

Synagogues

Conservative

Beth Israel
4350 Oak Street V6H 2N4   (604) 731-4161
Daily, 8 am (public holidays, 9 am) and 6 pm;
Friday, 8:15 pm; Shabbat, 9:15 am and 6 pm;
Sunday, 9 am and 6 pm. Wheelchair access.
Har El
North Shore
JCC, 1305 Taylor Way, West Vancouver V7T
2Y7   (604) 925-6488
Fax: (604) 922-8245
Friday, 7 pm; Shabbat, 10 am.

Hasidic

Chabad-Lubavitch
5750 Oak Street V6M 2V9   (604) 266-1313
Daily, 7 am and sunset; Shabbat, 10 am;
Sunday, 9 am. Wheelchair access.

Jewish Renewal

Or Shalom
710 East 10th Avenue V5T 2A7
(604) 872-1614
Or Shalom
710 East 10th Avenue V5T 2A7
(604) 872-1614
Wednesday, 7 am; family kabbalat Shabbat
and potluck dinner once a month, 6 pm;
Shabbat, 10 am. Wheelchair access.

Orthodox

Louis Brier Home
1055 West 41st Avenue V6M 1W9
(604) 261-9376
Daily mincha, 4:30 pm; Friday, 4:15 pm;
Shabbat, 9 am. Wheelchair access.
Schara Tzedeck
3476 Oak Street V6H 2L8   (604) 736-7607
Monday and Thursday, 7 am; Tuesday,
Wednesday and Friday, 7:15 am; weekdays,
sunset; Friday, 7:30 pm; Shabbat, 9 am and
half hour before sunset; Sunday, 8:30 am.

Reform

Temple Sholom
7190 Oak Street V6P 3Z9   (604) 266-7190
Fax: (604) 266-7126
Monday and Wednesday, 7:15 am; Friday, 8:15
pm; Shabbat, 10 am.

Sephardic Orthodox

Beth Hamidrash
3231 Heather Street V5Z 3K4
(604) 872-4222; 873-2371
Daily, 7 am; Shabbat, 9 am; Sunday and public
holidays, 8:30 am; Friday, 5 pm; Shabbat,
sunset.

Traditional

Burquest Jewish Community
(604) 526-7235
Oneg Shabbat services second Friday of each
month, 8 pm. Wheelchair access.
Shaarey Tefilah
785 West 16th Avenue   (604) 873-2700
Friday evening, call for time; Shabbat and
Sunday, 9 am. Wheelchair access.

Victoria

Synagogues

Conservative

Emanu-El
1461 Blanshard V8W 2J3   (250) 382-0615
Thursday, 7 am; Shabbat, 9 am. Wheelchair
access.

Manitoba

Winnipeg

Bakeries

City Bread
238 Dufferin Avenue R2W 2X6
(204) 586-8409
Goodies' Bake Shop
2 Donald Street R3L 0K5   (204) 489-5526
Gunn's
247 Selkirk Avenue R2W 2L5   (204) 582-2364
Miracle Bakery
1385 Main Street R2W 3T9   (204) 586-6140

Butchers

Omnitsky's
1428 Main Street R2W 3V4   (204) 586-8271
Tuxedo Quality Foods
1853 Grant Avenue R3N 1Z2   (204) 987-3830

Community Organisations

Winnipeg Jewish Community Council
200-370 Hargrave Street R3B 2K1
(204) 943-0406
Fax: (204) 956-0609

Cultural Organisations
Jewish Historical Society of Western Canada
404-365 Hargrave Street R3B 2K3
(204) 942-4822
Fax: (204) 942-9299

Groceries
Bathurst Street Market
1570 Main Street R2W 5J8   (204) 338-4911

Kashrut Information
Vaad Ha'lr
370 Hargrave Street R3B 2K1   (204) 949-9180
Fax: (204) 956-0609
The Vaad Ha'lr will be pleased to give
information about kashrut.

Libraries
Jewish Public Library
1725 Main Street R2V 1Z4   (204) 338-4048

Media
Newspapers

Jewish Post & News
117 Hutchings Street R2X 2V4
(204) 694-3332
Fax: (204) 694-3916
Jewish Radio Hour Weekly – Sundays, at 1:30
pm. Yiddish TV, Channel 11.

Mikvaot
Mikva Chabad-Lubavitch
455 Hartford Avenue R2V 0W9
(204) 339-4761

Restaurants
Dairy

Y.M.H.A. Jewish Community Centre
370 Hargrave Street R3B 2K1   (204) 946-5257
Kosher café.

Theatres
Winnipeg Jewish Theatre
504-365 Hargrave Street R3B 2K3
(204) 943-3222
Fax: (204) 949-1739

New Brunswick
Fredericton
Synagogues
Orthodox

Sgoolai Israel
Westmoreland Street E3B 3L7   (506) 454-9698
Mikva on premises.

Moncton
Synagogues
Tiferes Israel
56 Steadman Street E1C 4P4   (506) 858-0258
Mikva on premises.

Saint John
Museums
Jewish Historical Museum
29 Wellington Row E2L 3H4   (506) 633-1833
Fax: (506) 642-9926
Email: sjjhm@nbnet.nb.ca
May-September 10am to 4pm Monday to
Friday. Also, during July and August, Sunday
1pm to 4pm.

Synagogues
Conservative

Shaarei Zedek
76 Carleton Street E2L 2Z4   (506) 657-4790
Community centre on premises as well.

Newfoundland
St John's
Synagogues
**Hebrew Congregation of Newfoundland &
Labrador (Beth El)**
122-126 Elizabeth Avenue, PO Box 724 A1C
5L4   (709) 737-6548
Fax: (709) 737-6995

Nova Scotia
Glace Bay
Synagogues
Orthodox

1 Prince Street B1A 3C8   (902) 849-8605

Halifax
Community Organisations
Atlantic Jewish Council
1515 S. Park Street, Suite 304 B3J 2L2
(902) 422-7491
Also at this address: Canadian Jewish
Congress, Canadian Zionist Federation, United
Israel Appeal, ORT, Young Judea, B'nai B'rith,
Hadassah, Jewish National Fund, Atlantic
Provinces Jewish Student Federation and
Chabad Lubavitch.

Media

Newspapers

Shalom Magazine
1515 S. Park Street, Suite 305 B3J 2L2
(902) 422-7491
Fax: (902) 425-3722

Synagogues

Conservative

Shaar Shalom
1981 Oxford Street B3H 4A4   (902) 423-5848

Orthodox

Beth Israel
1480 Oxford Street B3H 3Y8   (902) 422-1301
Mikva on premises.

Sydney

Synagogues

Conservative

Temple Sons of Israel
P.O. Box 311, Whitney Avenue B1P 6H2
(902) 564-4650

Yarmouth

Contact Information
R & V Indiq
13 Parade Street B5A 3A5
Will be happy to provide details of the local
Jewish Community.

Ontario

Belleville

Synagogues

Conservative

Sons of Jacob
211 Victoria Avenue K8N 2C2 (613) 962-1433

Brantford

Synagogues

Orthodox

Beth David
50 Waterloo Street N3T 3R8   (519) 752-8950

Chatham

Synagogues

Conservative

Children of Jacob
29 Water Street N7M 3H4   (519) 352-3544

Cornwall

Synagogues
Beth-El
321 Amelia Street K6H 3P4   (613) 932-6373

Guelph

Synagogues

Traditional

Beth Isaiah
47 Surrey Street W. N1H 3R5   (519) 836-4338

Hamilton

Butchers
Hamilton Kosher Meats
889 King Street West L8S 1K5

Delicatessens
Westdale Deli
893 King Street West L8S 1K5 (905) 529-2605

Media

Newspapers

Hamilton Jewish News
P.O. Box 7528
Ancaster, Ancaster L9G 3N6   (905) 648-0605
Fax: (905) 648-8388

Representative Organisations
Hamilton Jewish Federation
1030 Lower Lions Club Road
P.O. Box 7258, Ancaster L9G 3N6
(905) 648-0605
Fax: (905) 648-8350

Synagogues

Conservative

Beth Jacob
375 Aberdeen Avenue L8P 2R7
(905) 522-1351

Orthodox

Adas Israel
125 Cline Avenue S. L8S 1X1   (905) 528-0039

Reform

Anshe Sholom
215 Cline Avenue N. L8S 4A1   (905) 528-0121

Kingston

Community Organisations
B'nai B'rith Hillel Foundation
26 Barrie Street   (613) 542-1120

Synagogues

Orthodox

Beth Israel
116 Centre Street K7L 4E6   (613) 542-5012

Reform

Temple Iyr Hamelech
331 Union Street West K7L 2R3
                                          (613) 789-7022

Kitchener

Synagogues
Temple Shalom
116 Queen Street North N2H 2H7
                                          (519) 743-0401

Traditional

Beth Jacob
161 Stirling Avenue South N2G 3N8
                                          (519) 743-8422

London

Community Organisations
Jewish Community Council
536 Huron Street N5Y 4J5   (519) 673-3310
                            Email: ljf@icis.on.ca
Communal inquiries to Executive Director at
the above number.
There are no kosher establishments, but kosher
frozen meat, prepared foods and select
groceries are available at local A&P and IGA
Loeb Stores.

Media

Newspapers

London Jewish Community News
536 Huron Street N5Y 4J5   (519) 673-3310
                            Fax: (519) 673-1161

Synagogues

Conservative

Congregation Or Shalom
534 Huron Street N5Y 4J5   (519) 438-3081
                            Fax: (519) 439-2994

Orthodox

Beth Tefilah
1210 Adelaide Street North N5Y 4T6
                                          (519) 433-7081
Mikva on premises.

Reform

Temple Israel
651 Windermere Road N5X 2P1
                                          (519) 858-4400
                            Fax: (519) 858-2070
                Email: jwitts@julian.uwo.ca

Mississauga

Synagogues
Solel Congregation
2399 Folkway Drive L5L 2M6   (905) 820-5915
                            Fax: (905) 820-1956

Niagara Falls

Synagogues

Conservative

B'nai Jacob
5328 Ferry Street L2G 1R7   (416) 354-3934

North Bay

Synagogues

Orthodox

Sons of Jacob
302 McIntyre Street West P1B 2Z1
                                          (705) 474-2170

Oakville

Synagogues

Reform

Shaarei-Beth El
186 Morrison Road L6L 4J4   (905) 845-0837

Oshawa

Synagogues

Orthodox

Beth Zion
144 King Street East L1H 1B6   (905) 723-2353

Ottawa

Bakeries
Rideau Bakery
384 Rideau St   (613) 234-1019
Kosher bread and other products are available in both branches.
Rideau Bakery
1666 Bank St   (613) 737-3355

Butchers
United Kosher Meat & Deli Ltd
378 Richmond Road   (613) 722-6556
Kosher meals and sandwiches available on weekdays.

Embassy
Embassy of Israel
Suite 1005, 50 O'Connor Street K1P 6L2

Religious Organisations
Vaad Ha'ir (Jewish Community Council)
151 Chapel Street K1N 7Y2   (613) 232-7306
                              Fax: (613) 563-4593
Vaad Hakashruth located here for all kashrut information.

Restaurants
JCC Drop in Diner
151 Chapel Street K1N 7Y2   (613) 789-1818
Tuesdays, 12 pm to 1:30 pm.

Dairy
Viva's, 1766 Carling Avenue   (613) 722-6645

Owen Sound

Synagogues
Conservative
Beth Ezekiel
3531 Bay Shore Road N4K 5N3
                              (519) 376-8774

Pembroke

Synagogues
Beth Israel
322 William Street K8A 1P3   (613) 732-7811

Peterborough

Synagogues
Conservative
Beth Israel
Waller Street   (705) 745-8398

Richmond Hill

Synagogues
Beth Rayim
9711 Bayview Avenue L4C 9X7
                              (905) 770-7639
The Country Shul
Carville Road and Bathurst Street
                              (905) 770-4191

St Catharine's

Community Organisations
Community Centre
Newman Memorial Building   (416) 685-6767

Synagogues
Reform
Temple Tikvah
83 Church Street, PO Box 484 L2R 3C7
                              (416) 682-4191

Traditional
B'nai Israel
190 Church Street L2R 4C4   (416) 685-6767
                              Fax: (416) 685-3100

Sudbury

Synagogues
Orthodox
Shaar Hashomayim
158 John Street P3E 1P4   (705) 673-0831

Thornhill

Booksellers
Israel's Judaica Centre
441 Clark Avenue West L4J 6W7
                              (905) 881-1010
Matana Judaica
248 Steeles Avenue West, #6 L4J 1A1
                              (905) 731-6543
                              Fax: (905) 882-6196
Also sells gifts.

Delicatessens
Marky's Delicatessen North
7330 Yonge Street L4J 1V8   (905) 731-4800
Wok'n'Deli
441 Clarke Avenue West L4J 6W7
                              (905) 882-0809

Restaurants

Dairy

Cafe Sheli
441 Clark Avenue West L4J 6W7
(905) 886-7450

King David Pizza
7000 Bathurst Street L4J 7L1   (905) 669-0660
My Zaidy's Cafe
7241 Bathurst Street L4J 6J8   (905) 731-3831
My Zaidy's Pizza
441 Clark Avenue West L4J 6W8
(905) 731-3029

Not Just Yoghurt
800 Steeles Avenue West L4J 7L2
(905) 738-1322

Thunder Bay

Synagogues

Orthodox

Shaarey Shomayim
627 Gray Street P7E 2E4   (905) 622-4867

Toronto

There has been one a half centuries of organised Jewish life in Toronto. The Jewish population increased significantly during the 1980s, and now Toronto is home for almost half of Canada's Jews. There is a good range of Jewish facilities in the city.

Bakeries

Bagels Galore
First Canadian Place M5X 1E1
(416/905) 363-4233

Booksellers

Israel's Judaica Centre
897 Eglinton Avenue West M6C 2C1
(416/905) 256-2858
Miriam's, 3007 Bathurst Street
(416/905) 781-8261
Negev Importing Co Ltd
3509 Bathurst Street M6A 2C5
(416/905) 781-9356
Pardes Hebrew Book Shop
4119 Bathurst Street   (416/905) 633-7113
Zucker's Books & Art
3453 Bathurst Street

Community Organisations

Bernard Betal Centre
1003 Steeles Avenue West M2R 3T6
(416/905) 225-2112
Has two separate minyanim: Beth Joseph and Tehilla Yerushalayim.
Jewish Federation of Greater Toronto
4600 Bathurst Street
North York M2R 3V2   (416) 635-2883
Fax: (416) 635-9565
Email: office@ujafed.org

Contact Information

Jewish Information Services
4588 Bathurst Street
Suite 345, Willowdale M2R 1W6
(416) 635-5600
Fax: (416) 636-5813
Email: jyerbin@ujafed.org
Publishes a Jewish Community of Services Directory for Greater Toronto.

Delicatessens

Marky's Delicatessen
280 Wilson Avenue, Downsview
(416/905) 638-1081

Mati's Fallafel House
3430 Bathurst Street M6A 1C2
(416/905) 783-9505
Sells dairy products only.

Embassy

Consulate General
180 Bloor Street West, Suite 700 M5S 2V6
(416) 961-1126
Israel Government Tourist Office: 964-3784

Media

Newspapers

Canadian Jewish News
10 Gateway Blvd
Suite 420, Don Mills M3C 3A1
(416/905) 422-2331
Fax: (416/905) 422-3790

Jewish Tribune
15 Hove Street
Downsview M3H 4Y8,   (416/905) 633-6227
Fax: (416/905) 630-2159

Memorials

Holocaust Education & Memorial Centre
4600 Bathurst Street
Willowdale M2R 3V2   (416/905) 635-2883

Religious Organisations
JEP/Ohr Somayach Centre
2939 Bathurst Street M6B 2B2
(416/905) 785-5899
Has a minyan.
Kashruth Council
4600 Bathurst Street, Ste 240 M2R 3V2
(416/905) 635 9550
Fax: (416/905) 635-8760
All enquiries about kashrut here.

Restaurants
Chicken Nest
3038 Bathurst Street M6B 4K2
(416/905) 787-6378
Hakerem
1045 Steeles Avenue West
Willowdale M2R 2S9   (416/905) 736-7227
Kosher Facilities
York University
4700 Keele Street, Downsview M3Y 1P3
(416/905) 736-5965
Kosher Hut
3428 Bathurst Street M6A 2C2
(416/905) 787-7999

Dairy
Brooklyn Pizza
3028 Bathurst Street M6B 3B6
(416/905) 256-1477
Dairy Treats Cafe
3522 Bathurst Street M6A 2C6
(416/905) 787-0309
King David Pizza
3020 Bathurst Street M6B 2B6
(416/905) 781-1326
Milk'n Honey
3457 Bathurst Street
Downsview M6A 2C5   (416/905) 789-7651
My Zaidy's Pizza
3456 Bathurst Street, Willowdale
(416/905) 789-0785
Tovli Pizza
5792 Bathurst Street
Willowdale M2R 1Z1   (416/905) 650-9800

Meat
King Solomon's Table
3705 Chesswood Drive
Downsview M3J 2P6   (416/905) 630-0666
Fax: (416/905) 630-4585
Open Monday to Thursday 12.00 noon to
10.00pm. Sunday 4.00pm to 10.00pm.
Closed Friday and Saturday. Open Saturday
night in the winter.

Windsor
Community Organisations
Jewish Community Council
1641 Ouellette Avenue N8X 1K9
(519) 973-1772

Media
Periodicals
Windsor Jewish Community Bulletin
Fax: (519) 973-1774

Synagogues
Orthodox
Shaar Hashomayim
115 Giles Blvd East N9A 4C1   (519) 256-3123
Shaarey Zedek
610 Giles Blvd East N9A 4E2   (519) 252-1594
Reform
Congregation Beth-El
2525 Mark Avenue N9E 2W2   (519) 969-2422

Quebec
Montreal
1760 saw the arrival of the first Jews in
Montreal, along with the British army. In the
1991 census, there were just over 100,000
Jews in the city, about a quarter of Canada's
Jews.

Bakeries
Biscuit Adar
5458 Westminister   (514) 484-1198
Supervision: Vaad Hair.
Kosher Cookies
Boulangerie-Adir
6795 Darligton   (514) 342-1991
Supervision: Vaad Hair.
Cite Cashere
4747 Van Horne   (514) 733-2838
Supervision: Vaad Hair.
Delice Cashere
4655 Van Horne   (514) 733-5010
Supervision: Vaad Hair.
Katzberg Home Bread and Cake Delivery
5355 Jeanne Mance   (514) 273-4042
Supervision: Vaad Hair.
Kleins Kosher Bakery
5540 Hutchison   (514) 274-4633
Supervision: Vaad Hair.

Kosher Quality Bakery
5855 Victoria   (514) 731-7883
                                Fax: (514) 731-0205
Supervision: Vaad Hair.
Hours: Sunday – Wednesday 6am to 9pm.
Thursday 6am to 10pm. Friday 6am winter
2pm or summer 4pm.
La Biscuit Adar
1204 Beaumont   (514) 343-0272
Supervision: Vaad Hair.
Montreal Kosher
7005 Victoria   (514) 739-3651
Supervision: Vaad Hair.
Montreal Kosher
2865 Van Horne, Wilderton Shopping Centre
                                (514) 739-3651
Supervision: Vaad Hair.
Montreal Kosher
2135 St. Louis, St. Laurent   (514) 747-5116
Supervision: Vaad Hair.
New Homemade Kosher Bakery
6685 Victoria   (514) 733-4141
Supervision: Vaad Hair.
New Homemade Kosher Bakery
6915 Querbes   (514) 270-5567
Supervision: Vaad Hair.
New Homemade Kosher Bakery
5638 Westminister   (514) 486-2024
Supervision: Vaad Hair.
New Homemade Kosher Bakery
1085 Bernard W.   (514) 276-2105
Supervision: Vaad Hair.
New Homemade Kosher Bakery
6795 Darlington   (514) 342-1991
Supervision: Vaad Hair.
Patisserie Chez Ma Souer
5095 Queen Mary   (514) 737-2272
Supervision: Vaad Hair.
Pita Royal, 5897 Van Horne   (514) 488-9414
Supervision: Vaad Hair.
Renfels Bakery
2800 Bates   (514) 733-5538
Supervision: Vaad Hair.

Booksellers
Rodal's Hebrew Book Store & Gift Shop
4689 Van Horne Avenue H3W 1H8
                                (514) 733-1876
                                Fax: (514) 733-2373
                        Email: rodals@ican.net
Kotel Book & Gift Store
6414 Victoria Avenue H3W 2S6
                                (514) 739-4142
                                Fax: (514) 739-7330

Victoria Gift Shop
5875 Victoria Avenue H3W 2R6
                                (514) 738-1414

Community Organisations
Federation CJA
5151 ch, de la Côte Ste-Catherine H3W 1M6
                                (514) 735-3541
Operates the Jewish Information and Referral
Service (JIRS), Tel: 737-2221.
Jewish Community Council
6333 Decarie, Suite 100 H3W 3E1
                                (514) 739-6363
                                Fax: (514) 739-7024
Visitors requiring additional information about
kosher establishments should contact the Vaad
Ha'ir at the above numbers. Also apply to them
for a list of kosher butchers, bakeries and
caterers.

Embassy
Consulate General
1155 Boulevard Rene Levesque Ouest, Suite
2620 H3B 4S5

Libraries
Jewish Public Library
5151 Côte Ste-Catherine Road H3W 1M6
                                (514) 345-2627
                                Fax: (514) 345-6477
                        Email: c-stern@hotmail.com

Media
Newspapers
Canadian Jewish News
6900 Decarie Blvd, #341 H3X 2T8
                                (514) 735-2612

Representative Organisations
**Canadian Jewish Congress National
Headquarters**
Samuel Bronfman House, 1590 Docteur
Penfield Avenue H3G 1C5   (514) 931-7531
                                Fax: (514) 931-0548
                        Email: mikec@cjc.ca
Publishes the National Synagogue Directory.
Contact to find out which of the many
synagogues in Montreal is nearest you.

Restaurants
**B'nai B'rith Hillel Foundation/Yossi's
Dizengoff Café**
3460 Stanley Street   (514) 845-9171
                                Fax: (514) 842-6405
                        Email: hillel@vir.com
Supervision: Vaad Hair.
Hours: Daily, 11 am to 6 pm.

David's Wok and Grill
6540 Darlington   (514) 734-8289
Supervision: Vaad Hair.
Exodus, 5395 Queen Mary   (514) 483-6610
Supervision: Vaad Hair.
Golden Age Cafeteria
5700 Westbury Avenue H3W 3E8
                         (514) 739-4731
Supervision: Vaad Hair.
Majestik, 5415 Royalmont   (514) 735-7911
Supervision: Vaad Hair.
Y.M.H.A. Cafeteria
5500 Westbury Avenue   (514) 737-8704
Supervision: Vaad Hair.

Dairy

Cholov Israel
5710 Victoria Avenue   (514) 731-7482
Supervision: Vaad Hair.
Pizza, pita and a variety of Milchig dishes.
Open 9.30am-11.30pm daily, Saturday night
until 2.30am.
Foxy's, 5987A Victoria Avenue
                         (514) 739-8777
Supervision: Vaad Hair.
La Casa Linga
5095 Queen Mary H3W 1X4   (514) 737-2272
Tatty's Pizza
6540 Darlington   (514) 734-8289
Supervision: Vaad Hair.

Meat

El Morocco II
3450 Drummond Street
          (514) 844-6888; 844-0203
Supervision: Vaad Hair.
Open for lunch and dinner until 10 pm.
Located downtown near hotels and boutiques.
Ernie's & Elie's Place
6900 Decarie Blvd H3X 2T8   (514) 842-6616
Supervision: Vaad Hair.
Kotel Restaurant
3429 Peel Street   (514) 987-9875
Supervision: Vaad Hair.

Quebec City

Cemetaries
Beth Israel Ohev Sholom
Boulevard Rene Levesque, Sainte-Foy
                         (418) 658-6677
This is an official monument and historic site
5 miles from the old center.

Synagogues

Orthodox

Beth Israel Ohev Sholom
20 Cremazie Street East G1R 1Y2
                         (418) 523-7346

Ste. Agathe-des-Monts

Synagogues
House of Israel Congregation
31 Albert Street J8C 1Z6   (819) 326-4320

Saskatchewan

Moose Jaw

Synagogues

Conservative

Moose Jaw Hebrew Congregation
937 Henry Street S6H 3H1   (306) 692-1644

Regina

Synagogues

Orthodox

Beth Jacob
4715 McTavish Street S4S 6H2
                         (306) 757-8643
                      Fax: (306) 352-3499

Reform

Temple Beth Tikvah
Box 33048, Cathedral Post Office S4T 7X2
                         (306) 761-2218

Saskatoon

Synagogues

Conservative

Agudas Israel
715 McKinnon Avenue S7H 6H2
                         (306) 343-7023
                      Fax: (306) 343-1244
Rabbi R. Pavey, 343-6960, will be pleased to
welcome visitors.

Cayman Islands

In addition to a very small permanent Jewish community there are a number of Jews who spent part of the year on the Islands.

GMT -5 hours
Country calling code (1345)

Total Population 32,000
Jewish Population Under 100

Grand Cayman

Contact Information
Harvey DeSouza
P.O. Box 72, Grand Cayman, Cayman Islands,
British West Indies   949-7739

Chile

Among the heroes of Chilean Independence were a number of the descendants of Conversos. The original Jewish settlers in Chile were Conversos (Marranos). Rodrigo de Orgonos, a Converso, was the first European to enter the country in 1535. The Inquisition curtailed the growth of the community because the Converso community was persecuted. The first legal Jewish immigration, albeit small, occurred only after Chile's independence in 1810. In 1914 the Jewish community numbered some 500, but this increased in the late 1930s with refugees from Nazism who were able to avoid the strict immigration laws. Anti-semitism, however, also grew, and the Comite Representativo was formed to respond to it.

There is an umbrella organisation and a large Zionist body in Chile. B'nai B'rith and WIZO also function. Most of the community is not religious, but some keep Kosher and there are several synagogues in Santiago (the capital) and a few kosher shops. There are two Jewish schools and several Jewish newspapers are published.

GMT -4 hours
Country calling code (56)
Emergency Telephone (Police – 133) (Fire – 132) (Ambulance – 131)

Total Population 14,421,000
Jewish Population 21,000

Arica

Community Organisations
Sociedad Israelita
Dr Herzl, Casilla 501

Iquique

Community Organisations
Comunidad Israelita
Playa Ligade 3263, Playa Brava

La Serena

Community Organisations
Community Centre
Cordovez 652

Rancagua

Community Organisations
Comunidad Israelita
Casilla 890

Santiago

The majority of Chilean Jews live in Santiago. The city has a couple of notable features in connection with its Jewish community – the Circulo Israelita Synagogue has an interesting stained glass design in its interior, and the 'Bomba Israel' is a fire service, manned by volunteers who include a few rabbis. Two of their fire engines carry the Chilean and Israeli flags.

Embassy
Embassy of Israel
San Sebastian 2812, Casilla 1224
(2) 246-1570

Representative Organisations
Communal Headquarters (Comite Representativo de las Entidades Judias de Chile)
Miguel Claro 196   (2) 235-8669

Restaurants
La Idishe Mama
M. montt 1273, Esquina Bilbao   (2) 209-8131
Kosher style.

Synagogues

Ashkenazi

Comunidad Israelita de Santiago
Serrano 214-218   (2) 639-387

German

Sociedad Cultural Israelita B'ne Jisroel
Portugal 810   (2) 221-993

Hungarian
Maze, Pedro Bannen 0166   (2) 274-2536

Orthodox
Bicur Joilim
Av. Matte 624
Jabad Lubavitch
Gloria 62, Las Condes   (2) 228-2240
Jafets Jayim
Miguel Claro 196

Sephardi
Maguen David
Av. R. Lyon 812

Temuco

Community Organisations
Comunidad Israelita
General Cruz 355

Valdivia

Community Organisations
Community Centre
Arauco 136 E.

Valparaiso

Community Organisations
Comunidad Israelita
Alvarez 490, Vina del Mar   (32) 680-373

China

Jews have been in China since the twelfth century. There was an established, thriving community in Kaifeng for some 700 years until it finally lost its identity. The town now has a small Jewish museum.

During the 1930s refugees from Germany fled to Shanghai and other cities. However, the community subsequently migrated and until the past year or so there was no Jewish life in the country. This has now changed.

Also included here is Hong Kong, previously listed as a separate entity, but, since July 1997, again a region of China.

GMT + 8 hours   Total Population 1,320,083,000
Country calling code (86)   Jewish Population Under 100

Hong Kong

Although there were some Jewish merchants trading out of Hong Kong over the centuries, the first permanent community consisted of Jews who came from Baghdad in the early nineteenth century. The first synagogue was not established until 1901, the early settlers preferring to organise communal events from the home. The majority of the community were Sephardi, but Nazi persecution led to more Ashkenazi settlers arriving in Hong Kong, via Shanghai. Since the Second World War many Chinese Jews have emigrated through Hong Kong to Australia and the USA, although some have remained in Hong Kong. Despite the reversion to Chinese control in mid-1997, the Jewish community is still thriving, and the mood is optimistic.

The Jews have contributed greatly to the building of the infrastructure of Hong Kong and, since the 1960s, many Western Jews, attracted by the success of this major financial centre, have made their homes there. The first communal hall was founded in 1905, but a new, multi-purpose complex (the Jewish Community Centre) has recently been opened, which is one of the most luxurious in the world. This centre includes everything, from a library and a strictly kosher restaurant to a swimming pool and sauna.

Community Organisations
Jewish Community Centre
1 Robinson Place, 70 Robinson Road,
Mid-Levels   2801-5440
                                   Fax: 2877-0917

A new facility with two kosher restaurants, kosher supermarket and banquet facilities under mashgiach supervision, swimming pool and leisure facilities and library/function facilities. Meals available on Shabbat. Take-away and kosher food delivery available.

Cultural Organisations
Hong Kong Jewish Historical Society
                                        2559-2890
                                   Fax: 2547-2550
Publishes monographs on subjects of Sino-Judaic interest and maintains an archive. Information from Dennis Leventhal.

Synagogues
Orthodox
Lubavitch in the Far East (Chabad)
18 Kennedy Road, #1A, Mid-Levels 2523-9770
                                   Fax: 2845-2772
Holds regular morning services in the Furama Hotel, Room 601. Daily Shacharit at 7:15 am and Mincha-Ma'ariv at 5:50 pm. Shabbat services are followed by Shabbat meals. Due to its popularity and limited space, meals have to be reserved and paid for in advance. Rooms at the Furama Hotel, as well as the Ritz Carlton, can be booked through Chabad at discounted rates. For meals and room reservation, fax requests to the above number. For room reservations, please include your credit card information for guarantee.

Ohel Leah Synagogue
70 Robinson Road, Mid-Levels   2589-2621
                                   Fax: 2548-4200
Friday night, Shabbat and weekday services are held.

Hong Kong Jewish Community Centre
community activities and supervised kosher restaurants

One Robinson Place, 70 RobinsonRoad,
Mid-Levels, Hong Kong.
Tel: (852) 2801 5440
Fax: (852) 2877 0917
JCC Web Home Page:
www.jcc.org.hk

Full programme of education, cultural and social activities and classes. Facilities are available to visitors on payment of a modest entry fee. Glatt Kosher Restaurants under full-time Mashgiach supervision. Take-away food and delivery service available. Kosher supermarket and banquet facilities. Library/Function facilities. Meals on the Sabbath. Swimming pool and leisure facilities.

Shuva Israel Beit Medrash and Community Centre
61 Connaught Road Central, 2/F, Fortune
House, Central   2851-6218; 2851-6300
Fax: 2851-7482
Sephardi service. Daily minyan during weekdays, Shacharit 7:15 am, Mincha-Maariv, 20 minutes before sunset; Shabbat times, Kabbalat Shabbat at sunset, Shacharit 8 am; Mincha and Seuda Shlishit 30 minutes before sunset.

Shuva Israel Synagogue
16-18 MacDonnel Road, 1-B,
Mid-Levels   2851-6218
Fax: 2851-7482
Sephardi service. Shabbat and holidays. A substantial discount can be arranged at a nearby hotel.

Zion Congregation
21 Chatham Road, 4th Floor, Kowloon
2366-6364
Fax: 2366-6364

Liberal/Reform

United Jewish Congregation of Hong Kong
Jewish Community Centre, Mid-Levels
2523-2985
Fax: 2523-3961
Email: jvujc@hk.super.net
The UJC is the only non-Orthodox community in Hong Kong. It encompasses Jews from Reform, Conservative and Liberal backgrounds. Friday evening services followed by communal Shabbat dinner; periodic Shabbat morning services; holidays.

Embassy

Israel Consulate-General
Admiralty Centre, Tower II, suite 701, 18
Harcourt Road   2529-6091
Fax: 2855-0220

Restaurants

Shalom Grill
61 Connaught Road Central, 2/F, Fortune
House, Central   2851-6218; 2851-6300
Fax: 2851-7482
Email: darvick@chevalier.net
Middle Eastern Glatt Kosher cuisine and grocery. Hours: Breakfast, 8 am to 9 am; Lunch, 12 pm to 2:30 pm; Dinner, 6:30 pm to 9:30 pm.

Cemeteries

The Jewish Cemetery
Located in Happy Valley   2589-2621
Fax: 2548-4200

Shanghai

Synagogues

A Bet Midrash
B'Nai Yisrael, 1277 Beijing Rd 19th floor
200040   (21) 6289-9903
Fax: (21) 6289-9957
Email: sjcchina@usa.net
A Jewish community has been established in Shangai – the first Jewish community here for 50 years.

Colombia

The first Jews in Colombia were Conversos, as was common in South America.

The present community is a mix of Ashkenazi and Sephardi elements, each having their own communual organisations. There are also youth and Zionist organisations. There is a central organisation for Colombian Jewry in Bogota (the capital). WIZO and B'nai B'rith are represented. There are also Jewish schools and synagogues (13 rabbis officiate in the country), and Jewish publications and radio programmes.

GMT – 5 hours

Country calling code (57)

Total Population 36,500,000

Jewish Population 6,000

Emergency Telephone (Police – 112) (Fire – 119) (Ambulance – 132)

Baranquilla

Community Organisations

Centro Israelita Filantropico
Carrera 43, No 85-95, Apartado Aereo 2537
(53) 342-310; 351-197

Comunidad Hebrea Sefaradita
Carrera 55, No 74-71, Apartado Aereo 51351
(53) 340-054; 340-050

Bogota

Media

Monthly
Menorah, Apartado Aereo 9081

Religious Organisations

Union Rabinica Colombiana
Tranversal 29, No 126-31
(1) 274-9069; 218-2500

Synagogues

Congregacion Adath Israel
Carrera 7a, No 94-20 (1) 257-1660; 257-1680
Mikva on premises.

Ashkenazi

Centro Israelita de Bogota
Transversal 29, No 126-31
(1) 274-9069
Kosher meals available by prior arrangement with Rabbi Goldschmidt, 218-2500.

German

Asociacion Israelita Montefiore
Carrera 20, No 37-54 (1) 245-5264

Orthodox

Comunidad Hebrea Sefaradi
Calle 79, No 9-66 (1) 256-2629; 249-0372
Mikva on premises.

Jabad House
Calle 92, No 10, Apt. 405
Rabbi's Tel: 257-4920

Cali

Representative Organisations

Union Federal Hebrea
Apartado Aereo 8918
(2) 443-1814
Fax: (2) 444-5544
An umbrella organisation co-ordinating all Jewish activities in Cali.

Synagogues

Ashkenazi

Sociedad Hebrea de Socoros
Av. 9a Norte # 10-15, Apartado Aereo 011652
(2) 668-8518
Fax: (2) 668-8521

German

Union Cultural Israelita
Apartado Aereo 5552
(2) 668-9830
Fax: (2) 661-6857

Sephardi

Centro Israelita de Beneficiencia
Calle 44a, Av. 5a Norte Esquina, Apartado
Aereo 77
(2) 664-1379
Fax: (2) 665-5419

Medellin

Community Organisations

Union Israelita de Beneficencia
Carrera 43B, No 15-150, Apartado Aereo 4702
(4) 668-560

Costa Rica

The first Jews arrived in Costa Rica in the nineteenth century, from nearby islands in the Caribbean, such as Jamaica. The next wave of immigrants came from eastern Europe in the 1920s. Thereafter Costa Rica did not welcome new Jewish immigrants, and passed laws against foreign merchants and foreign land ownership. However, the Jewish community in Costa Rica established a communal organisation in 1930, which includes WIZO, B'nai B'rith and other groups. There is a monthly newsletter, and a synagogue in San Jose. Most Jewish children attend the Haim Weizmann School, which has both primary and secondary classes.

It is interesting to note that the Costa Rican embassy in Israel is in Jerusalem, and not Tel Aviv, where most other embassies are situated.

GMT – 6 hours
Country calling code (506)
Emergency Telephone (Police, Fire and Ambulance 911)

Total Population 3,500,000
Jewish Population 2,500

San Jose

Contact Information
Centro Israelita Sionista de Costa Rica
Calle 22 y 22, Apdo 1473-1000   233-9222
Fax: 233-9321

Embassy
Embassy of Israel
Edificio Centro Colon, Piso 11,
P.O.Box 5147-1000   216-011; 216-444
Fax: 257-0867
Email: embofisr@sol.racsa.co.cr

Groceries
Little Israel Pita Rica
Frente a Shell, Pavas   290-2083
Fax: 296-4802
The only mini-market in Costa Rica.

Hotels
Barcelo San Jose Palacio
Apdo 458-1150   220-2034; 220-2035
Fax: 220-2036
Email: Palacio@sol.racsa.co.cr
Hotel has separated kosher kitchen and its key in the mashgiach's (Rabbi Levkovitz) hands. The hotel is about a half hour walk to the synagogue.

Camino Real
Autopista Prospero Fernandez y Blvd, Apdo 11856-1000   289-7000
Fax: 289-8930
Email: caminoreal@ticonet.co.cr
Hotel has new separated kosher kitchen, with the key in the mashgiach's (Rabbi Levkovitz) hands.

Melia Confort Corobici
PO Box 2443-1000   232-8122
Fax: 231-5834
Email: corobici@sol.racsa.co.cr
There is no separate kosher kitchen, but it is fairly close to the Orthodox synagogue.

Croatia

Jews were in the land now known as Croatia before the Croats themselves. The Croats arrived in the seventh century, the Jews some centuries before with the Romans: there is a third-century Jewish cemetery in Solin.

The Croatian Jews suffered greatly under the German occupation in the Second World War when the local Ustashe (Croatian Fascists) assisted the Germans. Despite their efforts, some Jews survived and even decided to rebuild their community when peace returned. Today, after the civil war, there are synagogues in towns across the country, but no rabbis. There are some Hebrew classes and newsletters are published. There are also many places of historical interest, such as Ulicia Zudioska (Jewish Street) in Dubrovnik.

GMT + 1 hour   Total Population 4,504,000
Country calling code (385)   Jewish Population 2,000
Emergency Telephone (Police – 92) (Fire – 93) (Ambulance – 94)

Dubrovnik

Synagogues
Zudioska Street 3
Zudioska means 'Street of the Jews'. This is the second oldest synagogue in Europe and is located in a very narrow street off the main street – the Stradun or Placa. The Jewish community office is in the same building. Zudiosla Street is the third turning on the right from the town clock tower. There are about 30 Jews in the city. Tourists help to make up a minyan in the synagogue on Friday night and High Holy Days.

Osijek

Community Organisations
Brace Radica Street 13   (31) 24-926
The community building contains objects from the synagogue that was destroyed during the Second World War. The community numbers about 150 members and has two cemeteries. No regular services are held. A former building of the second pre-war synagogue in Cvjetkova Street is a Pentecostal church today. There is a plaque at the site of the destroyed synagogue in Zupanijska Street.

Rijeka

Synagogues
Filipovieva ul. 9, PO Box 65 51000
                          (51) 425-156/336-032

The community numbers about 60. Services are held in the well maintained synagogue on Jewish holidays.

Split

Community Organisations
Zidovski Prolaz 1   (21) 45-672
The synagogue at Split is one of the few in Yugoslavia to have survived the wartime occupation. The Jewish community numbers about 200. There is a Jewish cemetery, established in 1578. More information from the community offices at the above number.

Zagreb

Community Organisations
Jewish Community of Zagreb
Palmoticeva Street 16, PO Box 986
                                (1) 434-619
                          Fax: (1) 434-638
              Email: jcz@public.stce.hr
Before the war Zagreb had 11,000 Jews. There are now only about 1,500, but they remain very active in Jewish communal life. Services are held in the community building on Friday evenings and holidays.

Media

Books
Voice of the Jewish Communities of Croatia
                    Email: jcz@oleh.srce.hr

Monuments
Central Synagogue
Praska Street 7
There is a plaque on the spot of this pre-war synagogue.

Mirogoj Cemetery

There is an impressive monument in this cemetery to the Jewish victims of the Second World War.

Cuba

There were Jewish converts among the first European settlers in 1492. Jews fleeing from Brazil during the seventeenth century also settled in Cuba.

Until 1898 there was, however, only a tiny Jewish population on the island. With the end of Spanish colonial rule in that year, Jews from nearby areas, such as Jamaica and Florida and Jewish veterans of the Spanish-American War, began to settle in Cuba. A congregation was established in 1904. The community was augmented by immigrants from eastern Europe who had decided to stay in Cuba, which being was used as a transit camp for those seeking to enter America. A central committee was established for all Jewish groups in the 1930s. Cuba clamped down on immigration at that time, and the story of the German ship *St Luis* (full of Jewish refugees), which was refused entry into Cuba, is well known.

About 12,000 Jews lived on the island in 1952. Havana had by far the largest community, and 75 per cent of the Cuban community was Ashkenazi. Although the Cuban revolution did not target Jews, many emigrated (as did many non-Jews) because their economic stability was ruined. The remaining community has synagogues, and a Sunday school. Kosher food is imported, mainly from Canada.

GMT – 5 hours
Country calling code (53)
Total Population 11,018,000
Jewish Population 800
Emergency Telephone (Police – 82 0116) (Fire – 81 1115) (Ambulance 404 551)

Havana

Synagogues

Conservative

Patronado de la Casa de la Comunidad Hebrea de Cuba
Calle 13 e I, Vedado   (7) 32-8953
Modern community centre as well.

Orthodox
Hadath Israel
Calle Picota 52, Habana Vieja   (7) 61-3495

Reform
The United Hebrew Congregation
Av. de los Presidentes 502
The Jewish cemetery is at Guanabacoa.

Cyprus

During the Roman Empire, Jewish merchants made their home on Cyprus. However, after a revolt which destroyed the town of Salamis, they were expelled. In medieval times, small Jewish communities were established in Nicosia, Limassol and other towns but the community was never large.

It is interesting to note that Cyprus was seen as a possible 'Jewish Homeland' by the early Zionists. Agricultural settlements were established at the end of the nineteenth century, but they were not successful. Herzl himself tried to persuade the British government to allow Jewish rule over Cyprus in 1902, but again met with failure.

Some German Jews managed to escape to Cyprus in the early 1930s. After the war, many Holocaust survivors who had tried to enter Palestine illegally were deported to special camps on the island. Some 50,000 European Jews were held there. Since the establishment of the state of Israel, the Jewish community on the island has become small, and the Israeli embassy has served as a centre for community activities.

GMT + 2 hours   Total Population 756,000
Country calling code (357)   Jewish Population Under 100
Emergency Telephone (Police, Fire and Ambulance – 112)

Nicosia
Community Organisations
Committee of the Jewish Community of Cyprus
PO Box 4784   (2) 427-982
Contact Mrs Z. Yeshurun for information.

Embassy
Embassy of Israel
4 Grypari Street

Czech Republic

Prague, the capital of this small central European country, is fast becoming a major tourist attraction. It is one of the few cities actively to promote its Jewish heritage, which dates from early medieval times. The oldest (still functioning) synagogue in Europe is there (the Altneuschul), as well as other interesting Jewish sites.

After the arrival of the first Jews in the country in the tenth century, the community suffered similar tragedies to those of other medieval Jewish communities – forced baptism by the Crusaders and expulsions, together with some tolerance. Full emancipation was reached in 1867 under the Hapsburgs. The celebrated Jewish writer, Franz Kafka, lived in Prague and did not neglect his Judaism, unlike many other Czech Jews who assimilated and intermarried.

The German occupation led to 85 per cent of the community (80,000 people) perishing in the Holocaust. Further difficulties were faced in the communist period after the war, but since the 1989 'Velvet Revolution', Judaism is being rediscovered. The community (mostly elderly) has several synagogues around the country, a kindergarten and a journal, and there are two kosher restaurants in the old Jewish quarter in Prague.

GMT + 1 hour
Country calling code (0161)
Emergency Telephone (Police – 158) (Fire – 150) (Ambulance – 155)

Total Population 10,251,000
Jewish Population 5,000

Boskovice

Sites
Medieval Ghetto

(501) 454601; 452077
Fax: (501) 452077
Email: museum@mas.cz
17th-century Jewish town, synagogue and cemetery.

Brno

Community Organisations
Community Centre
Kpt. Jarose 3   (5) 21-5710
The community president can be reached at 77 3233.

Synagogues
Skorepka 13

Holesov

Museums
Schach Synagogue

Dating from 1650, this synagogue is now a museum. Open in the mornings. At other times the curator will show visitors around, if contacted. The old cemetery is close by.

Karlovy Vary

Synagogues
Community Centre
Masaryka 39, Karlsbad
Services, Friday evening and Shabbat morning.

Liberec

Synagogues
Community Centre
Matousova 21
Reichenberg 46001   (48) 510-3340
Each weekday 9-11 a.m.

Mikulov

Sites
Nikolsburg, Nikolsburg
Only one synagogue, still being restored, remains of the many which flourished here when the town was the spiritual capital of Moravian Jewry and the seat of the Chief Rabbis of Moravia. The cemetery contains the graves of famous rabbis.

Olomouc

Synagogues
Community Centre
Komenskeho 7   (68) 522-3119

Ostrava

Synagogues
Community Centre
Ceskobratrska 17   (69) 611-2389

Plzen

Synagogues
Community Centre
Smetanovy Sady 5, Pilsen   (19) 723-5749
Services Friday evenings. The Great Synagogue is now closed.

Prague

The impact of the Jews in Prague has been great – the Golem has entered Prague folklore, and the Altneushul is the oldest functioning synagogue in Europe. The Jewish Quarter in the old town contains other historical sites.

Cemeteries
Old Jewish Cemetery
The oldest cemetery in Europe, containing the graves of such famour rabbis & scholars as Avigdor Karo (died 1439), Yehuda Low ben Bezalel (1609), David Gans (1613) & David Oppenheim (1736).

Contact Information
Jewish Town Hall
Maislova 18 1
Houses the Federation of Jewish Communities in the Czech Republic as well as the Shalom restaurant.

Embassy
Embassy of Israel
Badeniho Street 2 7

Groceries
Kosher Shop
Brehova 5 1   (2) 232-4729
Osem products are available at K-mart at Ovecnytrh.

Hotels
Hotel Intercontinental

Extremely close to the Jewish Quarter (for visitors who do not want to do too much walking on Shabbat).

Museums
Jewish Museum in Prague
Jachymova 3   (2) 2481-0099
                                       Fax: (2) 231-0681
Reservation centre, tel: 42 2 231-7191. Fax:42 2 231-7181

Restaurants
King Salamon
Siroka 8   (2) 786-4664
                                      Fax: (2) 786-4664
                              Email: Aaron@kosher.cz
                          Web site: www.Kosher.cz
Supervision: Rabbi Benjamin Halevy Rosenstein Bnei Brak Rabbi Karol Eprahim Sidon – Chief Rabbi of CZ..
Opposite Pinkas synagogue. Open 11am to 11pm.
Shalom, Maislova 18 1   (2) 2481-0929
Supervision: Chief Rabbi of Prague.
Hours: 11:30 am to 8 pm; January to March, 12 pm to 2 pm. Serves dinner Friday night. Meals for Shabbat have to be ordered and paid for in advance at the community's official travel agency.

Synagogues
Altneuschul
Cervena ul.7 1   (2) 231-0909
Jubilee Synagogue
Jerusalemska 7

Tours of Jewish Interest
Heritage Tours
                                       (2) 472-1068
Jewish Town Hall
Maislova 18 1
With Hebrew clock.
Wittmann Tours
Uruguayská 7, 120 00 Praha 2   (2) 251-235

Travel Agencies
Matana Travel Agency of the Jewish
Community of Prague
Maiselova 15 11000   (2) 232-1954
                    Fax: (2) 232-1049
              Email: matana@ms.qnet.cz
       Web site: http://www.tours.cz/matana/

Teplice

Synagogues
Community Centre
Lipova 25
Teplitz-Schönau, Teplitz-Schönau
                        (417) 26-580

Terezin

Museums
Theresienstadt, Theresienstadt
There is a new museum in the town dedicated
to the Jews who were deported from
Theresienstadt to Auschwitz. There is also a
cemetery in which 11,250 individual and 217
mass graves and the crematorium are placed.
34,000 people died in Terezin.

Usti Nad Labem

Community Organisations
Community Centre
Moskevska 26, Aussig, Aussig   (47) 520-8082

Denmark

Jews were allowed to settle in Denmark in 1622, earlier than in any other Scandinavian country. Thereafter, the community grew, with immigration largely from Germany. The Danish king allowed the foundation of the unified Jewish community of Copenhagen in 1684, and the Jews were granted full citizenship in 1849, earlier than in many other European countries.

In the early part of the twentieth century many refugees arrived from eastern Europe, and Denmark welcomed refugees from Nazi Germany. When the Germans conquered Denmark and ordered the Jews to be handed over, the Danish resistance managed to save 90 per cent of the community by arranging boats to take them to neutral Sweden. Some Jews did stay behind and were taken to the transit ghetto of Theresienstadt, where a number died.

The Royal Library (Amiliegaden 38, Copenhagen) houses a Jewish collection including the famous 'Bibliotheca Simonseniana' and part of the library of the late Professor Lazarus Goldschmidt. The library has a Jewish Department under the direction of Ulf Haxen. In the Library Museum there is a special division devoted to the Resistance Movement, and also a section dealing with 'The Persecution of the Jews'.

GMT + 1 hour	Total Population 6,237,000
Country calling code (45)	Jewish Population 8,000

Copenhagen

The Great Synagogue and the cemetery dating from 1693 are a couple of interesting sites. The Liberty Museum has a Jewish section.

Butchers
I. A. Samson
Roerholmsgade 3 1352   3313-0077
Fax: 3314-8277
Kosher grocery and provisions.
Kosher Delikatesse
87 Lyngbyvej 2100   3118-5777

Community Organisations
Jewish Community Centre
Ny Kongensgade 6 1472   3312-8868
Fax: 3312-3357

Embassy
Embassy of Israel
Lundevangsvej 4, Hellerup 2900   3962-6288

Mikvaot
12 Krystalgade 1172   3393-7662; 3332-9443

Jewish Community Centre
Ny Kongensgade 6 1472   3312-8868
Fax: 3312-3357

Synagogues
9 Oestbaneg 2100   3526-3540
Fax: 3929-2517

12 Krystalgade 1172
Daily and Shabbat services.

Orthodox
Machsike Hadass
Ole suhrsgade 12 1354   3315-3117
Holds regular daily and Shabbat services.

Hornbaek

Hotels
Hotel Villa Strand
Kystvej 12 3000   4396-9400
Fax: 4396-9137

Synagogues
Granavenget 8   4220-0731
Open from Shavuot to Succot.

Dominican Republic

Jewish settlement in the Dominican Republic is comparatively late - the oldest Jewish grave dates back to 1826. Descended from central European Jews, the community was not religious and many married Christians. A President, Francisco Henriquez y Carvajal (1916) traced his ancestry back to the early Jewish settlers.

Two synagogues and a rabbi who divides his time between them are features of Jewish life. There is also a Sunday school in Santo Domingo and a bi-monthly magazine is produced. There is a small Jewish museum in Sosua.

GMT – 4 hours	Total Population 7,961,000
Country calling code (1)	Jewish Population 300

Santo Domingo

Embassy
Embassy of Israel
Av. Pedro Henriquez Urena 80 1404
(809) 542-1635; 542-1548

Representative Organisations
Consejo Dominicano de Mujeres Hebreas
PO Box 2189   Fax: (809) 688-2058

Synagogues
Centro Israelita de la Republica Dominicana
Av. Ciudad de Sarasota 21   (809) 535-6042

Sosua

Contact Information
Felix G. Koch   (809) 571-2284
Welcomes all Jewish visitors.

Ecuador

Conversos (Marranos) comprised the earliest Jewish settlers in Ecuador. It was not until 1904 that East European Jews began to arrive, and numbers increased further following the Nazi take-over in Germany, as Ecuador granted refuge to more Jews than other neighbouring countries.

There are two central bodies for the Jewish community, one in Quito, the other in Guayaquil. A synagogue and other organisations such as WIZO and B'nai B'rith are based in Quito. There are no Jewish schools, but children do have access to Jewish education.

GMT – 5 hours	Total Population 11,700,000
Country calling code (593)	Jewish Population 1,000
Emergency Telephone (Police – 101) (Fire – 102) (Ambulance – 131)	

Quito

Community Organisations
18 de Septiembre 954, Casilla 17-03-800
(2) 502-734
Fax: (2) 502-733

Embassy
Embassy of Israel
Av. Eloy Alfaro 969, Casilla 2463
(2) 547-322 & 548-431

Egypt

The Jewish connection to Egypt is both ancient and important. The Bible relates the suffering and exodus of the Israelites from Egyptian slavery, and Judaism commands that the Exodus from Egypt should be remembered every day. After the Exodus, some Jews returned to Egypt, especially around the time of Alexander the Great. The Jews followed Greek culture, translated the Bible into Greek (the Septuagint) and Alexandria became a key Jewish centre.

Thereafter, the Jewish community declined, but a renaissance occurred in early medieval times, led by the Rambam, who lived in Cairo in the twelfth century. He wrote many of the classic texts still in use today. Spanish Jews arrived after the Inquisition, but Turkish rule led to further decline. From 1768 (Egyptian independence) to 1937 (the highest number of Jews in Egypt), the Jewish community expanded and flourished.

In 1945, riots broke out against Westerners and Jews. In 1948, Israeli independence led to more rioting, and many Jews emigrated. After the Six Day War, there were further outrages against Jews, and many more emigrated. Since then, Egypt has made peace with Israel (in 1979), but the present community is tiny and there are only synagogues in Cairo and Alexandria. The Ben Ezra synagogue in Cairo is worth a visit as it has recently been restored.

GMT + 2 hours	Total Population 63,271,000
Country calling code (20)	Jewish Population 100

Alexandria

Synagogues
Eliahu Hanavi
69 Nebi Daniel Street, Ramla Station
(3) 492-3974; 597-4438

Cairo

Community Organisations
13 Sebil el-Khazendar St., Midan el-Geish, Abassiya
(2) 824-613 & 824-885

Embassy
Israel Embassy
6 Ibn Malek St., Gizeh
(2) 845-260, 845-205 & 28862

Synagogues
Ben-Ezra
6 Harett il-Sitt Barbara, Mari Girges, Old Cairo
(2) 847-695

Meir Enaim, 55 No.13 Street, Maadi
This is a small American-Israeli congregation, which holds occasional services.
Shaarei Hashamayim
17 Adli Pasha Street
Downtown Cairo
(2) 749-025
Services are held on holidays. There is an interesting library across from the temple, which is only accessible with a key. Ask the guards.

Tourist information
Israel Government Tourist Office
6 Ibn Malek St., 4th Floor
(2) 729-734 & 730-997

El Salvador

It is believed that some Portuguese Conversos crossed the country a few hundred years ago. Other Jews came from Europe, but in smaller numbers than those settling in other Latin American countries. There were only 370 Jews in 1976, a number reduced during the civil war, when many emigrated. Some have returned now that the war is over.

An official community was set up in 1944 and a synagogue was opened in 1950, but now services are held in a house. El Salvador is one of the few countries to have an embassy in Jerusalem, rather than Tel Aviv.

GMT – 6 hours	Total Population 5,780,000
Country calling code (503)	Jewish Population 150

San Salvador

Community Organisations
Comunidad Israelita de El Salvador
06-182   981-388

Embassy
Colonia Escalon
85 Av. Norte, No 619   238-770; 239-221

Synagogues
Conservative
23 Blvd. del Hipodromo 626, Colonia San
Benito   237-366
Friday evening services only.

Estonia

The community has always been small, and is believed to have begun in the fourteenth century. However, most Jews arrived in the nineteenth century, when Czar Alexander II allowed certain groups of Jews into the area.

By 1939, the community had grown to 4,500 and was free from restraints. After the Soviet and Nazi occupations in the Second World War the Jews returned, mainly from the Soviet Union. Now that Estonia is independent, the Jewish community is able to practise freely. A newspaper appears every month and there is a radio programme, 'Shalom Aleichem', broadcast monthly.

GMT + 2 hours	Total Population 1,471,000
Country calling code (372)	Jewish Population 2,500
Emergency Telephone (Police – 02 or 002) (Fire – 01 or 001)	
(Ambulance – 03 or 003)	

Tallinn

Community Organisations
Jewish Community of Estonia
Karu Street 16, PO Box 3576 EE0090
                                                (2) 43-8566

Publishes a monthly, called 'Hashaher', in Russian and operates a radio programme on Radio 4 (Thurs., 22:15-23:00). Information on vegetarian restaurants available.

Synagogues
9 Magdalena Street, PO Box 3576 EE0090

Ethiopia

The Falashas (Ge'ez for 'stranger', applied to the Ethiopian Jews) of Ethiopia became known world-wide in the early 1980s, when they were airlifted to Israel en masse. The origins of the Beta Israel, as they call themselves, are unclear and little is known for certain. Historians have concluded that they may have become Jewish as early as the second or third century. The Jewish Ethiopians followed the Torah, but did not have access to the rabbinic commentaries, as they were cut off from the outside Jewish world.

The Jewish population was believed to have been about 50,000 in 1934. After the establishment of Israel, more interest was taken in the Ethiopian community and the Ethiopian civil war was the catalyst for Operation Moses, when 10,000 people were airlifted to Israel in 1984-85.

GMT + 3 hours	Total Population 58,243,000
Country calling code (251)	Jewish Population 1,000

Addis Ababa

Community Organisations
PO Box 50   (1) 111-725 & 446-471

Asmara

Synagogues
Via Hailemariam Mammo 34

Fiji

When Henry Marks moved to Fiji from Australia in 1881, he was the first recorded Jew on the island. Over the years, he developed a successful business across the region. He was only 20 when he emigrated.

Some Eastern Jews moved to Fiji but did not organise any official community. In recent years the Fiji Jewish Association has been created. The Israeli embassy organisesan annual seder for about 60 people.

GMT: + 12 hours	Total population: 797,000
Country calling code: (679)	Jewish population: under 100

Community Organisations
Fiji Jewish Association, P.O. Box 882, Suva

387-980 Fax: 387-946
email: contex@is.com.fj

Finland

When Finland was occupied by Russia in the nineteenth century, many Jewish conscripts in the Russian army settled in Finland after their discharge. They were still subject to several restrictions, but these ended after Finland's independence in 1917. In addition to these 'Cantonists', as they were known, immigrants came to Finland from eastern Europe. Finland proved a safe haven, as the government refused to hand over Finnish Jews to the Nazis, despite being allied to Germany.

The community is keen to preserve a sense of Jewish identity among the young generation, who are encouraged to experience Jewish life in Israel. The community is also keen to help other Jews in the newly independent Baltic states across the sea to the south of the country. There is a central body for Jewish Communities, and kosher food is available. There are also a school and synagogues.

GMT + 2 hours	Total Population 5,263,000
Country calling code (358)	Jewish Population 1,200
Emergency Telephone (Police – 10022) (Fire and Ambulance – 112)	

Helsinki

There is a Jewish cemetry containing an area dedicated to the Jews who fought in the Finnish army in various wars, including the Russo-Finnish war.

Embassy
Embassy of Israel
Vironkatu 5A 00170   (9) 135-6177
      Fax: (9) 135-6959

Restaurants
Kosher Deli
Malminkatu 24   (9) 685-4584
Hours: Tuesday to Wednesday, 1 pm to 5 pm; Thursday, 9 am to 5 pm; Friday, 9 am to 2 pm.
Community Centre
Malminkatu 26   (9) 6921297; 6941302
      Fax: (9) 694-8916
      Email: hjc@hjc.pp.fi
Kosher meals available. Telephone 694-1297 or 685-4584 to arrange.

Synagogues
Orthodox
Jewish Community Synagogue
Malminkatu 26 00100
      (9) 692-1297; 694-1302
      Fax: (9) 694-8916
      Email: jc@hjc.pp.fi
Services Monday and Thursday morning, 7:45 am, other weekdays 8 am; Friday evening, 7 pm (summer), 5 pm (winter); Shabbat and Sunday mornings, 9 am. All organisations, including Hazamir Choir, Jewish War Veterans, Keren Kayemet, Library, Maccabi, WIZO and the Youth Club, can be contacted at these numbers as well.

Turku
Synagogues
Brahenkatu 17   (2) 231-2557
      Fax: (2) 233 4689
The secretary is always pleased to meet visitors.

France

France now boasts the largest Jewish community in Europe. The Jewish connection with France is a long one: it dates back over a 1,000 years as there is evidence of Jewish settlement in several towns in the first few centuries of the Jewish diaspora. The community grew in early medieval times, and contributed to the economy of the region. Two great Jewish commentators, Rashi and Rabenu Tam both lived in France. However, French Jewry suffered both from the Crusaders and from other anti-semitic outbursts in the medieval period.

Napoleon heralded the emancipation of French Jewry and, as his armies conquered Europe, the emancipation of other communities began. Despite this, incidents such as the Dreyfus Affair highlighted the fact that anti-semitism was not yet dead. The worst case of anti-semitism in France occurred under the German occupation, when some 70,000 Jews were deported from the community of 300,000. After the war, France became a centre for Jewish immigration, beginning with 80,000 from eastern Europe, and then many thousands from North Africa, which eventually swelled the Jewish population to nearly 700,000.

The community is well served with organisations. Paris has 380,000 Jews alone, quite possibly more than in the whole of the UK. There are many kosher restaurants, synagogues in many towns throughout the country, newspapers, radio programmes, even a television programme and schools in several cities. In Carpentras and Cavaillon there are two synagogues which are considered to be national monuments.

GMT + 1 hour
Country calling code (33)
Emergency Telephone (Police – 17) (Fire – 18) (Ambulance – 15)
Total Population 58,333,000
Jewish Population 680,000

Agen

Synagogues
52 rue Montesquieu 47000   05.53.66.24.20

Aix-en-Provence

Butchers
C.C.V.A. Zouaghi
7 rue Sevigné 13100   04.42.59.93.94
Supervision: Grand Rabbinate of Marseille.

Synagogues
3 bis rue de Jerusalem 13100   04.42.26.69.39

Aix-les-Bains

Butchers
Eurocach
Av. d'Italie 73100

Berdah
29 Av. de Tresserve 73100   04.79.61.44.11

Hotels

Kosher

Auberge de La Baye
Chemin du Tir-Aux-Pigeons 73100
04.79.35.69.42
Strictly kosher. Tennis courts and swimming pool.

Mikvaot
Pavillon Salvador
rue du President Roosevelt 73100
04.79.35.38.08

Synagogues
Rue Paul Bonna 73100   04.79.35.28.08
Mikva on Premises

Amiens

Synagogues
38 rue du Port d'Amont 8000

Angers

Synagogues
12 rue Valdemaine 49100

Annemasse

Butchers
Yarden
59 rue de la Liberation, Gaillard 74240
04.50.92.64.05

Annency

Synagogues
18 rue de Narvik 74000   04.50.45.82.22

Antibes

Butchers
Ohayon, 28 Av. Admiral Courbet
04.93.67.25.08
Fax: 04.92.93.05.72
Krief, 3 rue Louis-Gallet 06160
04.93.74.73.30

Andre Sebbah
28 Av. Maiziers 06600   04.93.34.60.11

Restaurants
Pizza Beverley
Blvd. Charles Guilaument
Also holds Sephardi Services on Shabbat
Bamboo Grill
5 rue Alexandre III
Chez Andre, Chaim's Marches, 13 Av. Louis
Gallet, Juan les Pins   04.93.61.44.72
Mid-March to Mid-September

Synagogues
Villa La Monada, Chemin des Sables 06600
04.93.61.59.34

Arcachon

Synagogues
Cours Desbey

Open July & August only

Avignon

Butchers
Bensoussan
25 rue Ninon Vallin 84000   04.90.29.56.95
Supervision: Grand Rabbinate of Marseille.

Chelly
1-5 rue Chapeau Rouge 84000
04.90.82.47.50
Supervision: Grand Rabbinate of Marseille.

Mikvaot
7 rue des Sept-Baisers, Montfavet 84140

Synagogues
2 Place de Jerusalem 84000   04.90.85.21.24

Bar-le-Duc

Synagogues
7 Quai Carnot

Bayonne

Synagogues
35 rue Maubec 64100   05.59.55.03.95

Beauvais

Synagogues
Rue Jules Isaac 60000

Belfort

Community Organisations
27 rue Strolz 90000   03.84.28.55.41
Publishes 'Notre Communaute' (quarterly)

Synagogues
6 rue de l'As-de-Carreau 90000
03.84.28.55.41
Fax: 03.84.28.55.41

Benfeld

Community Organisations
6 rue du Grand Rempart 67230

Synagogues
7a rue de la Dome 67230

Besançon

Community Organisations
10 rue Grosjean 25000   03.81.80.82.82

Restaurants
M. Croppet, 18 rue des Granges
03.81.83.35.93

Thursdays Only

Synagogues
23c Quai de Strasbourg 25000

Beziers

Synagogues
19 Place Pierre-Semard 34500   04.67.28.75.98
Operates a Kosher Food Store

Biarritz

Synagogues
Rue Pellot 64200
July August and Yom Kippur

Bischeim-Schiltigheim

Synagogues
9 Place de la Synagogue 67800
                            02.38.33.02.87

Bitche

Synagogues
28 rue de Sarreguemines 57230
Services, Rosh Hashana & Yom Kippur

Bordeaux

Community Organisations
15 Pl. Charles-Gruet 33000   05.56.52.62.69

Mikvaot
213 rue Ste. Catherine 33000   05.56.91.79.39

Restaurants
Mazal Tov, 137 Crs Victor Hugo
05.56.52.37.03
Sabra, 144 Crs Victor Hugo   05.56.92.83.38

Synagogues
8 rue du Grand-Rabbin-Joseph-Cohen 33000
                            05.56.91.79.39

Boulay

Synagogues
Rue du Pressoir 57220   03.87.79.28.34

Boulogne-sur-Mer

Synagogues
63 rue Charles Butor

Bouzonville

Synagogues
Rue des Benedictins 57320

Brest

Synagogues
40 rue de la Republic 29200
Services, Friday, 7.30pm.

Caen

Butchers
M. Lasry
26 rue de l'Engannerie 14000   02.31.86.16.25
Open Thursday.

Synagogues
46 Av. de la Liberation 14000   02.31.43.60.54

Cagnes-sur-Mer

Synagogues
5 rue des Capucines 06800

Caluire et Cuire

Synagogues
107 Av. Fleming 69300   04.78.23.12.37

Cannes

Butchers
Marcel Benguigui
17 rue Marechal-Joffre 06400   04.93.38.46.59

Restaurants
Le Tovel
3 rue Gerard Monod 06400   04.93.39.36.25

Synagogues
Habad Lubavitch
22 rue Cdt Vidal (cnr Bd. de Lorraine) 06400
04.92.98.67.51
Habad Lubavitch
20 Blvd. D'Alsace 06400   04.93.38.16.54

Carpentras

Synagogues
                            04.90.63.39.97
Services are held on festivals in the ancient
synagogue in the Place de la Mairie, 84200,
classed as a national monument. Built in 1367
and rebuilt in 1741, it is worth a visit. Hours
10-12; 3-5.

Cavaillon

Synagogues
The remains of the old synagogue, built in 1774, are regarded as a French historical monument. Contact: 04.90.76.00.34
Fax: 04.90.71.47.06

Tours of Jewish Interest
Musees de Patrimoine de Cavaillon
52 Place de Castil-Blaze 84300 04.90.76.00.37
Fax: 04.90.71.47.06

Châlon-sur-Saône

Synagogues
10 rue Germiny 71100

Châlons-sur-Marne

Synagogues
21 rue Lochet 51000

Chambéry

Synagogues
44 rue St-Real
Services, Friday, 7pm and festivals.

Chateauroux

Contact Information
Michel Touati
3 Allee Emile Zola, Montierchaume, Deols
36130 02.54.26.05.47

Clermont-Ferrand

Synagogues
6 rue Blatin 04.73.93.36.59

Colmar

Contact Information
1 rue des Jonquilles
Haut-Rhin 68000 03.89.23.13.011

Synagogues
3 rue de la Cigogne 68000 03.89.41.38.29
Fax: 03.89.41.12.96

Compiègne

Synagogues
4 rue du Dr.-Charles-Nicolle 60200

Deauville

Synagogues
14 rue Castor 14800 02.31.81.27.06

Dieuze

Synagogues
Av. Foch 57260

Dijon

Butchers
Albert Sultan
4 petit rue Pouffier 03.80.73.31.38
Albert Levy
25 rue de la Manutention 03.80.30.14.42

Synagogues
5 rue de la Synagogue 03.80.66.46.47
Mikva on premises.

Dunkerque

Synagogues
19 rue Jean-Bart 59140

Elbeuf

Synagogues
29 rue Gremont 76500 02.35.77.09.11

Epernay

Synagogues
2 rue Placet 51200 03.26.55.24.44
Services, Yom Kippur only.

Epinal

Synagogues
Rue Charlet 88000 03.29.82.25.23

Evian-les-Bains

Synagogues
Adjacent to 1 av. des Grottes, 74500
04.50.75.15.63

Faulquemont-Créhange

Synagogues
Place de l'Hotel de Ville 57380
Services, festivals & High Holydays only.

Forbach

Synagogues
98 Av. St.-Remy 57600 03.87.85.25.57

Fréjus

Synagogues
98 Villa Ariane, rue du Progres, Frejus-Plage
83600   04.94.52.06.87

Grasse

Synagogues
82 Route de Nice 06130   04.93.36.05.33

Grenoble

Butchers
C. Cohen
19 rue Turenne 38000   04.76.46.48.14
Sebbag
6 rue Aubert-Dugayet 38000   04.76.46.40.78

Groceries
Aux Delices du Soleil
49 rue Thiers   04.76.46.19.60
David France
75 ave de Vizille   04.76.70.49.15
La Rose de Sables
15 place Gustave Rivet   04.76.87.80.94

Media

Radio

Radion Kol Hashalom
4 rue des Bains 38000   04.76.87.21.22

Religious Organisations
Rabbinate
4 rue des Bains 38000   04.76.47.63.72

Restaurants
Pizzeria Pinocchio
1 rue des bons Enfants 38000 04.76.46.88.66

Synagogues
Synagogue and Community Centre
4 rue des Bains 38000   04.76.46.15.14
11 rue André Maginot 38000   04.76.87.02.80
                   Fax: 04.76.87.27.14
             Email: rabbin38@aol.com
Mikva at same address.
Beit Habad
10 rue Lazare Carnot 38000   04.76.43.38.58

Grosbliederstroff

Synagogues
6 rue des Fermes 57520

Hagondange

Synagogues
Rue Henri-Hoffmann 57300

Haguenau

Mikvaot
7 rue Neuve

Restaurant
Maison les Cigognes
                         03.88.93.21.58

Synagogues
3 rue du Grand-Rabbin-Joseph-Bloch 67500
                         03.88.73.38.30

Hyeres

Synagogues
Chemin de la Ritorte 83400   04.94.65.31.97

Ingwiller

Synagogues
Cours du Chateau 67340

Insming

Synagogues
Rue de la Synagogue 57670

Izieu

Museums
The Izieu Children's Home
  01300
                recording 04.79.87.20.00
                  booking 04.79.87.20.08
                    Fax: 04.79.87.25.01
                  Email: izieu@alma.fr
Through photographs and audio-visual
displays, visitors can gain an understanding of
the horror of the fate of the 44 children who
lived here in 1944, and also of the 11,000
Jewish children who were sent from France to
death camps. This commemorative museum
was pivotal evidence in the Klaus Barbie trial
(the 'butcher of Lyons'). A guide is available in
English although the captions and videos are
all in French.

La Ciotat

Synagogues
1 Square de Verdun 13600   04.42.71.92.56
Services, Friday 7pm (Winter), 7.30pm
(Summer). Saturday 9am.

La Rochelle

Contact Information
Pierre Guedj
19 rue Bastion d'Evangile 17000
05.46.67.38.91

La Seyne-sur-Mer

Synagogues
5 rue Chevalier-de-la-Barre 83500
04.94.94.40.28

Butchers
Elie Benhamou
17 rue Baptistin-Paul 83500   04.94.94.38.60

Le Havre

Synagogues
38 rue Victor-Hugo 76600   02.35.21.14.59

Le Mans

Synagogues
4-6 Blvd. Paixhans 72000   02.43.86.00.96

Libourne

Synagogues
33 rue Lamothe 33500

Lille

Groceries

Kosher

Monoprix
Shopping Centre Euralille, rue du Molinel
59000

Synagogues
5 rue Auguste-Angellier 59000
03.20.30.69.86 or 03.20.85.27.37
Mikva on premises.

Limoges

Synagogues
25-27 rue Pierre-Leroux 87000
05.55.77.47.26

Lorient

Synagogues
18 rue de la Patrie 56100
Services, Friday nights, festivals & Holy-days only.

Luneville

Synagogues
5 rue Castara 54300

Lyon

Booksellers
Levi-Its'hak
3 Passage Cazenove   04.78.93.16.17
F.N.A.C.
rue de la Republique 69002
Decitre
Place Bellecour 69002
Menorah
(Ouaknine), 52 rue Montesquieu 69007
04.78.69.09.35
Mazal, 46 rue Jean-Claude-Vivant,
Villeurbanne 69100   04.78.52.85.94

Media
Le Bulletin
13 Quai Tilsitt 69002   04.78.37.13.43
La Voix Sepharade
317 rue Duguesclin 69007   04.78.58.18.74
Hachaar
18 rue St. Mathieu 69008   04.78.00.72.50
CIV News
4 rue Malherbe, Villeurbanne 69100
04.78.84.04.32
Radio Judaica Lyon (R.J.L.)
POB 7063 69341   04.78.03.99.20
FM 94.5
Orah Haim
17 rue Albert-Thomas, St.-Fons 69190
04.78.67.39.78

Sephardi
Neveh Chalom
Duguesclin 69007   04.78.58.18.54

Organisations
Beth Din, 34 rue d'Armenie, 3e
04.78.62.97.63
Fax: 04.78.95.09.47
Regional Chief Rabbi
13 Quai Tilsitt 69002   04.78.37.13.43
Consistoire Israelite de Lyon
13 Quai Tilsitt 69002   04.78.37.13.43
Fax: 04.78.38.26.57
Consistoire Israelite Sepharade de Lyon
Yaacov Molho Community Centre, 317 Rue
Duguesclin 69007   04.78.58.18.74
Fax: 04.78.58.17.49

Restaurants

Le Jardin d'Eden
14 rue Jean Jaune Villeurbanne
04.72.33.85.65

Mâcon

Synagogues
32 rue des Minimes 71000

Marignane

Synagogue
9 rue Pilote-Larbonne 13700

Marseille

Bakeries
Le Parve
72 av. Alphonse Daudet 130013
04.91.66.95.16
Supervision: Grand Rabbinate of Marseille.
Avyel Cash
28 rue St Suffren 13006   04.91.81.29.98
Supervision: Grand Rabbinate of Marseille.
Erets, 205 rue de Rome 13006
04.91.92.88.73
Supervision: Grand Rabbinate of Marseille.
Cacher Food
31 blvd Barry 13013   04.91.70.13.43
Supervision: Grand Rabbinate of Marseille.
Atteia et Fils
19 place Gaillardet 13013   04.91.66.33.28
Supervision: Grand Rabbinate of Marseille.
L'Entremets
206 avenue de la Rose 13013   04.91.70.72.19
Supervision: Grand Rabbinate of Marseille.
Motsi Mezonot 13380   04.91.07.13.95

Butchers
Dayan, 4 rue de la Glace 13001
04.91.54.03.70
Supervision: Grand Rabbinate of Marseille.
Attias
3 rue Halles Delacroix 13001   04.91.54.02.96
Supervision: Grand Rabbinate of Marseille.
Zennou Raphael
20 marché Capucins 13001   04.91.54.02.54
Supervision: Grand Rabbinate of Marseille.
Ayad, 8 cours Belsunce 13001   04.91.90.73.40
Supervision: Grand Rabbinate of Marseille.
Emouna
20 rue Max Dormoy 13004   04.91.34.98.84
Supervision: Grand Rabbinate of Marseille.
Guedj, 6 cours Julien 13006   04.91.48.44.24
Supervision: Grand Rabbinate of Marseille.

Dav Cacher
46 rue Negresko 13008   04.91.23.32.96
Supervision: Grand Rabbinate of Marseille.
Zouaghi
2 blvd Latil 13008   04.91.80.01.20
Supervision: Grand Rabbinate of Marseille.
Haddad Raphael
9 blvd G. Ganay 13009   04.91.75.04.56
Supervision: Grand Rabbinate of Marseille.
Ste Jamap
13 place Mignard 13009   04.91.71.11.70
Supervision: Grand Rabbinate of Marseille.
Raphael Cash
299 avenue de Mazargues 13009
04.91.76.44.13
Supervision: Grand Rabbinate of Marseille.
Zouaghi
206 blvd Paul Claudel 13009   04.91.74.30.01
Supervision: Grand Rabbinate of Marseille.
Yad Kel
143 blvd Paul Claudel 13010   04.91.75.03.57
Supervision: Grand Rabbinate of Marseille.
King Cacher
25 rue F. Mauriac 13010   04.91.80.00.01
Supervision: Grand Rabbinate of Marseille.
Eric Hadjedj
2 place Migranier 13010   04.91.35.10.27
Supervision: Grand Rabbinate of Marseille.
Sebanne
59 rue Alphonse Daudet 13013
04.91.66.98.76
Supervision: Grand Rabbinate of Marseille.

Embassy
Consulate General
146 rue Paradis 13006

Groceries
Avyel Cash
28 rue St Suffren 13006   04.91.37.95.25
Emmanuel
93 avenue Clot Bey 13008   04.91.77.46.08
Raphael Cash
299 avenue de Mazargues 13009
04.91.76.44.13
King Cacher
25 rue François Mauriac 13010
04.91.80.00.01
Les Délices d'Eden
Ctre Cial residénce Bellevue 13010
04.91.75.03.57
Taim Venaim
Montée de St Menet 13011   04.91.44.11.21
Delicash
94 blvd Barry 13013   04.91.06.39.04

Religious Organisations
Consistoire de Marseille
117 rue de Breteuil 13006   04.91.37.49.64;
04.91.81.13.57
Fax: 04.91.53.98.72

Restaurants

Dairy
Café Latin
11 rue Pisancon 13001   04.91.70.13.43
Supervision: Grand Rabbinate of Marseille.
Venice Beach
341 C. Kennedy 13007   04.91.22.15.75
Supervision: Grand Rabbinate of Marseille.
Pizza Le Prado
614 av. du Prado 13008   04.91.50.40.30
Supervision: Grand Rabbinate of Marseille.
Piz Mazal
8 blvd Gustave Ganay 13008   04.91.26.28.90
Supervision: Grand Rabbinate of Marseille.
Pizza Tova
Vert Bocage 13009   04.91.75.70.92
Supervision: Grand Rabbinate of Marseille.
Presto Pizza Cash
1 Cial résidence Bellevue 13010
04.91.75.19.00
Supervision: Grand Rabbinate of Marseille.
Pizza Berakha
5 rue Francois Mauriac 13010   04.91.74.05.41
Supervision: Grand Rabbinate of Marseille.
Pizza Menorah
86 rue A. Daudet 13013   04.91.66.68.75
Supervision: Grand Rabbinate of Marseille.
Cacher Food
31 blvd Barry 13013   04.91.70.13.43
Supervision: Grand Rabbinate of Marseille.

Meat
Sunset Plaza
24 rue Pavillion 13001   04.91.33.27.77
Supervision: Grand Rabbinate of Marseille.
Le Roman
1 place Gabriel Peri 13001   04.91.90.18.49
Supervision: Grand Rabbinate of Marseille.
Djerba Snack
7 rue Guy Mocquet 13001   04.91.42.41.81
Supervision: Grand Rabbinate of Marseille.
Erets, 205, rue de Rome 13006
04.91.92.88.73
Supervision: Grand Rabbinate of Marseille.
Natanya
17 rue du Village 13006   04.91.42.05.31
Supervision: Grand Rabbinate of Marseille.

China Tov
63 rue Negresco 13008   04.91.22.16.02
Supervision: Grand Rabbinate of Marseille.
Le Moriah
215 rue du Rouet 13008   04.91.78.59.12
Supervision: Grand Rabbinate of Marseille.
Byblos
38 blvd Barral 13008   04.91.22.87.87
Supervision: Grand Rabbinate of Marseille.
Le Sud
45 promenade de la plage 13008
04.91.77.90.91
Supervision: Grand Rabbinate of Marseille.
ORT, 3-9 rue des Forges 13010
04.91.79.61.65
Supervision: Grand Rabbinate of Marseille.

Melun

Synagogues
Cnr. rues Branly & Michelet 77000
01.64.52.00.05

Menton

Synagogues
Centre Altyner, 106 Cours du Centenaire
04.93.35.28.29

Merlebach

Synagogues
19 rue St.-Nicolas 57800

Metz

Butchers
Claude Sebbag
22 rue Mangin 57000   03.87.63.33.50
Supervision: Chief Rabbi of Moselle.

Groceries
Atac, 23 rue de 20e Corps Américain 57000
Galaries Lafayette
4 rue Winston Churchill 57000
03.87.38.60.60

Religious Organisations
Rabbi Bruno Fiszon
Chief Rabbi of Moselle 57000   03.87.75.04.44

Restaurants
Galil, 39 rue du Rabbin Elie-Bloch 57000
03.87.75.04.44
Supervision: Chief Rabbi of Moselle.

Synagogues
Main Synagogue and Community Centre
39 rue du Rabbin Elie-Bloch 57000
03.87.75.04.44
This street was renamed from rue de l'Arsenal, in memory of a youth movement rabbi deported and killed by the Nazis during the Second World War.
Oratoire Sepharade
39 rue du Rabbin Elie-Bloch 57000
2 rue Paul Michaux 57000
Adass Yechouroun
41 rue de Rabbin Elie-Bloch 57000

Montauban

Synagogues
14 rue Ste.-Claire 82000   05.63.03.01.37

Montbéliard

Synagogues
Rue de la Synagogue 25200

Montpellier

Butchers
Camille Bensoussan
Place Millenaire-Antigone 34000
04.67.66.03.22
Cooperative casher
18 rue Ferdinand Fabre 34000
Gilbert Bensoussan
41 rue de Lunaret 34000   04.67.72.67.94

Community Organisations
Centre Communautaire et Cultural Juif
560 blvd. d'Antigone 34000   04.67.15.08.76

Synagogues
Ben-Zakai
7 rue General-Laffon 34000   04.67.92.92.07
Mazal Tov
18 rue Ferdinand-Fabre 34000   04.67.79.09.82

Mulhouse

Butchers
Chez Nessim
Passage des Halles 68100   03.89.66.55.65

Synagogues
2 rue des Rabbins 68100   03.89.66.21.22
Fax: 03.89.56.63.49
Mikva on premises. The old cemetery is also worth a visit – enquire at centre.

Nancy

Community Organisations
19 Blvd. Joffre 54000   03.83.32.10.67

Museums
The Musee Historique Lorrain
64 Grand rue 54000
The museum has an important collection of sifrei Torah, prayer books and other ritual objects.

Restaurants
Restaurante Universitaire
19 Blvd. Joffre 54000   03.83.32.10.67
Open weekdays until noon.

Synagogues
17 Blvd. Joffre 54000   03.83.32.10.67

Nantes

Synagogues
5 Impasse Copernic 44000   02.40.73.48.92
Mikva on premises.

Nice

Booksellers
Librairie Tanya
25 rue Pertinax 06000   04.93.80.21.74

Kashrut Information
04.93.85.82.06
A list of kosher butchers and bakers can be obtained from the Chief Rabbi.

Mikvaot
22 rue Rossini   04.93.02.46.86

Rabbinate
Regional Chief Rabbinate of Nice, Cote d'Azur and Corsica
1 rue Voltaire 06000   04.93.85.82.06

Religious Organisations
Centre Consistorial and Synagogue
22 rue Michelet 06100   04.93.51.89.80
Publishes an annual calendar and guide to Nice and district.

Restaurants
Le Leviathan
1 ave Georges Clemenceau   04.93.87.22.64
Meat
Resto Mickael
18 rue Vernier 06000   04.93.83.89.34

Synagogues
Main Synagogue
7 rue Gustave-Deloye 06000   04.93.92.11.38

Nîmes

Community Organisations
5 rue d'Angouleme 30000   04.66.26.19.51

Synagogues
40 rue Roussy 30000   04.66.29.51.81
Mikva on premises.

Obernai

Synagogues
Rue de Selestat 67210

Orléans

Synagogues
14 rue Robert-de-Courtenay, (to the left of the
Cathedral) 45000
Kosher meat available every Wednesday,
4.30pm to 7.30pm. At Pithiviers near Orleans,
there is a monument to the Jewish victims of
Nazi persecution.

Paris

The city of Paris is divided into districts
(arrondissements) designated by the last two
digits of the postcode. In the categories below,
establishments are listed in numerical order
according to the postcode (that is, 01, 02, 03
and so on).
The historic centre of Paris Jewish life is found
in the Marais area (4th arrondissement).
Another more central area is that around rue
Richer (9th arrondissement) which although
not historic as such has many kosher
restaurants of varying styles.

Bakeries
Mezel, 1 rue Ferdinand Duval 75004
                              01.42.78.25.01
Supervision: Beth Din of Paris.
Marciano
14 rue des Rosiers 75004   01.48.87.48.88
Supervision: Chief Rabbi Mordechai
Rottenberg
Korcarz
29 rue des Rosiers 75004   01.42.77.39.47
                         Fax: 01.48.58.28.44
Supervision: Beth Din of Paris/Chief Rabbi
Mordechai Rottenberg.
Barbotte
229 rue du Fg St-Honoré 75008
Supervision: Beth Din of Paris.
Les Ailes
34 rue Richer 75009   01.47.70.62.53
Supervision: Beth Din of Paris.

Korcarz
25 rue de Trévise 75009   01.42.46.83.33
Supervision: Beth Din of Paris/Chief Rabbi
Mordechai Rottenberg.
Zazou, 20 rue du Fbg Montmartre 75009
                              01.47.70.81.32
Supervision: Beth Din of Paris.
Douieb
11 bis rue Geoffroy Marie 75009
                              01.47.70.86.09
Supervision: Beth Din of Paris.
Golan, 10 rue Geoffroy Marie 75009
                              01.48.00.94.71
Supervision: Beth Din of Paris.
Dahan, 7 rue Maillard 75011   01.43.79.43.55
Supervision: Beth Din of Paris.
Mendez
3 Ter rue de la Présent. 75011 01.43.57.02.03
Supervision: Beth Din of Paris.
Nathan de Belleville
67 blvd de Belleville 75011   01.43.57.24.60
Supervision: Beth Din of Paris.
Mat'amim
17 rue de Crimée 75019   01.42.40.89.11
                              01.42.40.89.23
Supervision: Beth Din of Paris.
Contini
116 avenue Simon Bolivar 75019
                              01.42.00.70.80
Supervision: Beth Din of Paris.
Le Relais Sucre
135 rue Manin 75019   01.42.41.20.98
Supervision: Beth Din of Paris.
Medayo
71 rue de Meaux 75019   01.40.03.04.20
Supervision: Beth Din of Paris.
Jaffa Pita
5 rue Dampierre 75019   01.46.07.27.77
Supervision: Chief Rabbi Mordechai
Rottenberg.
Aux Delices de Maxime
69 rue de Crimée 75019   01.40.36.44.76
Supervision: Beth Din of Paris.
Kadoche
2 avenue Corentin Cariou 75019
                              01.40.37.00.14
Supervision: Beth Din of Paris.
Charles Tr. Patissier
10 rue Corentin Cariou 75019 01.47.97.51.83
Supervision: Beth Din of Paris.
Eliyor
21 rue du Bisson 75020   01.43.49.12.66
Supervision: Beth Din of Paris.
Lilo, 20 rue Desnoyer 75020   01.47.97.63.20
Supervision: Beth Din of Paris.

Nani, 104 blvd de Belleville 75020
01.47.97.38.05
Supervision: Beth Din of Paris.
Zazou, 8 rue Rouvet 75020   01.40.36.67.61
Supervision: Beth Din of Paris.

Butchers
Lewkowicz
12 rue Des Rosiers 75004   01.48.87.63.17
Bensimon
40 rue des Rosiers 75004   01.42.77.38.28
Boucherie Goldstein
13 rue Ferdinand Duval 75004 01.42.77.00.82
Supervision: Chief Rabbi Mordechai
Rottenberg.
Tordjemann
40 rue St Paul 75004   01.42.72.93.22
Saada, 17 rue des Rosiers 75004
01.42.77.76.22

Adolphe
14 rue Richer 75009   01.48.24.86.33
Berbeche
46 Rue Richer 75009   01.47.70.50.58
Chez Claude
1 rue Saulnier 75009   01.48.24.71.22
La Rose Blanche
43 rue Richer 75009   01.48.24.84.65
Boucherie Goldstein
9 rue Rodier 75009   01.42.80.92.76
Supervision: Chief Rabbi Mordechai
Rottenberg.
La Charolaise R
51 rue Richer 75009   01.47.70.01.57
Charlot
33 Rue Richer 75009   01.45.23.10.34
Chez Andre
7 Rue Geoffroy Marie 75009   01.47.70.49.03
Chez Jacques
19 rue Bouchardon 75010   01.42.06.76.13
Chez Halak B. Y.
51 rue Richard Lenoir 75011   01.43.48.62.26

Chez Andre
69 bld de Belleville 75011   01.43.57.80.38
Chez Jojo
20 rue Louis Bonnet 75011   01.43.55.10.29
Maurice Zirah
91 rue de la Roquette 75011   01.43.79.62.53
Chez Lucien
180 rue de Charonne 75011   01.43.70.59.29
Boucherie Guy
266 rue de Charenton 75012   01.43.44.60.90
J V Temim
2 rue de Dr Goujon 75012   01.43.45.78.77
Chez Alain
8 rue Fagon 75013   01.42.16.80.25
B Berbeche
5 rue Vandrezanne 75013   01.45.88.86.50
B Berbeche
6 rue du Moulinet 75013   01.45.80.89.10
La Goulette
90 rue Didot 75014   01.43.95.01.48
B Claude
174 rue Lecourbe 75015   01.48.28.02.00
Kassab
88 bd Murat 75016   01.40.71.07.34
Sarl Gm Levy
83 rue de Lonchamp 75016   01.45.53.04.24
Ste Delicatess
209 av de versailles 75016   01.46.51.00.55
Berbeche
39 rue Jouffroy 75017   01.44.40.07.59
E Courses Elles
117 rue de Courcelles 75017   01.47.63.36.26
Krief, 104 rue legendre 75017 01.46.27.15.57
Berbeche
48 av de Clichy 75018   01.45.22.39.04
A Viandes Cacheres
6 av Corentin Cariou 75019   01.40.36.02.41
Hayot, 1 rue Edouard Pailleron 75019
01.42.45.72.22
Andre-Manin
135 rue Manin 75019   01.42.38.00.43

Maguen David
11/13 rue Curial 75019   01.40.37.46.00
Even Shapir
15 rue de Crimee 75019   01.42.02.43.00
Emsalem
18 rue Corentin Cariou 75019   01.40.36.56.64
Emsalem
17 Quai de la Gironde 75019   01.40.36.56.64
Chez Meyer
16 rue Menadier 75019   01.42.45.22.09
Berbeche
15/17 rue Henri Ribiere 75019   01.42.08.06.06
Boucherie Smadja
90 bd de Belleville 75020   01.46.36.25.36
Henrino
122 bd de Belleville 75020   01.47.97.24.52

Embassy
Embassy of Israel
3 rue Rabelais 75008

Groceries
Doueib
11 bis rue Geoffroy Marie 75009
                                01.47.70.86.09
Francois
45 rue Richer 75009   01.47.70.17.43

Le Haim
6 rue Paulin Enfert 75013
Chekel
14 av de Villiers 75017   01.48.88.94.97
Supervision: Beth Din of Paris.
Also sell delicatessen and sandwiches. Hours:
9 am to 8 pm. Nearest Metro: Villiers. Near
Champs-Elysées/Opéra.
Les Ailes Boutiques
15 rue des Fermiers 75017   01.44.15.93.93
Compt Pdts Aliment
111 av de Villiers 75017   01.42.27.16.91
Chochana
54 Av Secretan 75019
Elygel
116 Bld de Belleville 75020   01.47.97.09.73

Hotels
Hôtel Aida Opéra Comotel
17 rue du Conservatoire 75009
                                01.45.23.11.11
                        Fax: 01.47.70.38.73
                   Email: comotel@easyhet.fr
Supervision: Beth Din of Paris.
Kosher breakfast.

The Hotel ALPHA, with original decor, double glazed for your comfort and privacy. 30 delightful guest rooms with direct dial phone, safe deposit, bar and meeting room.

Shabbos meals served in the hotel

Kosher restaurant on premises

A few minutes walk away from department stores, Opera ...

11, rue Geoffroy Marie – 75009 PARIS

Under the supervision of the Beth Din of Paris

Tel: 0033.1.45.23.10.59
Fax: 0033.1.44.79.06.90

Hôtel Alpha
11 rue Geoffroy Marie 75009   01.45.23.10.59
                         Fax: 01.44.79.06.90
Supply kosher meals on Shabbat.
Hotel Touring
21 rue Buffault 75009   01.48.78.09.16
                       Fax: 01.48.78.27.74
                       Telex: 281 246

L'Hotel de Mericourt
50 rue Folie Mericourt 75011 01.43.38.73.63
                        Fax: 01.43.38.66.13
Situated in an area with many Kosher facilities.

Mikvaot
176 rue du Temple 75003   01.42.71.89.28
The mikvah is located in the centre of Paris,
near Place de la République, at the rear of the
building. The staff is English speaking.
19-21 rue Galvani 75017   01.45.74.52.80
Mayan Hai Source de Vie Haya Mouchka
2-4 rue Tristan Tzara 75018   01.40.38.18.29
                             01.46.36.11.09
1 rue des Annelets 75019   01.44.84.05.36
For men and women. Telephone is an answer
machine for women only.
75 rue Julien-Lacroix 75020   01.46.36.39.20
                             01.46.36.30.10
For men and women.

Religious Organisations
Communauté Israélite Orthodoxe de Paris
10 rue Pavée 75004   01.42.77.81.51
                        Fax: 01.48.87.26.29

Restaurants
Juliette
12/14 rue Duphot dans la cour 75001
                             01.42.60.18.10
                       Fax: 01.42.60.18.98
Supervision: Beth Din of Paris.

Yung Pana
41 rue d'Aboukir 75002   01.42.21.46.25
Supervision: Beth Din of Paris.
Ninou, 20/30 rue Léopold Bellon 75002
                             01.45.08.05.44
Supervision: Beth Din of Paris.
Natania
27 rue Poissonnière 75002   01.42.33.58.36
Supervision: Beth Din of Paris.
Restaurant Henri
13/15 Passage du Ponceau 75002
                             01.40.13.91.72
Supervision: Beth Din of Paris.
Chez Sarah
21 boulevard Saint-Martin 75003
                             01.42.78.08.88
Supervision: Beth Din of Paris.
La Petite Famille
32 rue des Rosiers 75003   01.42.77.00.50
Supervision: Beth Din of Paris.
Les Tables de la Loi
15 rue Saint-Gilles 75003   01.48.04.38.02
Supervision: Beth Din of Paris.
Café Ninette
24 rue Notre-Dame de Nazareth 75003
                             01.42.72.08.56
Supervision: Beth Din of Paris.
Tel Aviv Haketana
9 rue des Rosiers 75004   01.44.61.07.53
Supervision: Chief Rabbi Mordechai
Rottenberg.
La Pita
26 rue des Rosiers 75004   01.42.77.93.13
Supervision: Beth Din of Paris.
Yahalom
22 rue des Rosiers 75004   01.42.77.12.35
Supervision: Chief Rabbi Mordechai
Rottenberg.

Tutti Frutti
38 rue des Rosiers 75004   01.42.76.04.75
Supervision: Chief Rabbi Mordechai
Rottenberg.
Micky's Deli
23 bis rue des Rosiers 75004   01.48.04.79.31
Supervision: Chief Rabbi Mordechai
Rottenberg.
Koscher Pizza
1 rue des Rosiers 75004   01.48.87.17.83
Supervision: Chief Rabbi Mordechai
Rottenberg.
Contini
42 rue des Rosiers 75004   01.48.04.78.32
Supervision: Beth Din of Paris.
Chez Gaby
50 rue Broca 75005   01.43.31.04.14
Supervision: Beth Din of Paris.
Adolphe / Centre Rachi
39 rue Broca 75005   01.47.70.91.25
Supervision: Beth Din of Paris.
Centre Edmond Fleg
8 bis rue de l'Eperon 75006   01.46.33.43.31
Supervision: Beth Din of Paris.
Le Sabra
64 avenue Marceau 75008   01.40.70.03.23
Supervision: Beth Din of Paris.

La Table de David
64 avenue Marceau 75008   01.40.73.06.86
Supervision: Beth Din of Paris.
Sivane
36 rue de Berry 75008   01.49.53.01.21
Supervision: Beth Din of Paris.
Panino Café
31 rue St Georges 75009   01.48.78.78.78
Supervision: Beth Din of Paris.
Funny King
17 rue Montyon 75009   01.47.70.24.64
Supervision: Beth Din of Paris.
Adolphe
14 rue Richer 75009   01.47.70.91.25
Supervision: Beth Din of Paris.
Georges de Tunis
40 rue Richer 75009   01.47.70.24.64
Supervision: Beth Din of Paris.
Hotel Alpha
11 rue Geoffroy Marie 75009   01.45.23.10.59
Supervision: Beth Din of Paris.
Falafel Meny
8 rue Geoffroy-Marie 75009   01.42.46.76.46
Supervision: Beth Din of Paris.

Douieb
11 bis rue Geoffroy-Marie 75009
                       01.47.70.86.09
Supervision: Beth Din of Paris.
Zazou Burger
19 rue du Fbg Montmartre 75009
                       01.40.22.08.33
Supervision: Beth Din of Paris.
Yankees Cafe
31 rue du Fbg Montmartre 75009
                       01.42.46.52.46
Supervision: Beth Din of Paris.
Synagogue Beth El
10 rue Saulnier 75009   01.45.23.34.89
Supervision: Beth Din of Paris.
Centre Communautaire
5 rue Rochechouard 75009   01.49.95.95.92
Supervision: Beth Din of Paris.
Berberche Burger
47 rue Richer 75009   01.47.70.81.22
Supervision: Beth Din of Paris.
Hotel Lebron
4 rue Lamartine 75009   01.48.78.75.52
Supervision: Beth Din of Paris.
Casa Rina
18 rue du Fbg Montmartre 75009
                       01.45.23.02.22
Supervision: Beth Din of Paris.
Chez David
11 rue Montyon 75009   01.44.83.01.24
Supervision: Beth Din of Paris.
Azar & Fils
6 rue Geoffroy-Marie 75009 01.47.70.08.38
Supervision: Beth Din of Paris.
Snack Quick Delight
34 rue Richer 75009   01.45.23.05.12
Supervision: Beth Din of Paris.
La Grillade
42 rue Richer 75009   01.47.70.24.64
Supervision: Beth Din of Paris.
Le Gros Ventre
7/9 rue Montyon 75009   01.48.24.25.34
Supervision: Beth Din of Paris.
Les Ailes
34 rue Richer 75009   01.47.70.62.53
Supervision: Beth Din of Paris.
Dolly's Food
9 rue Cité Riverain 75010   01.48.03.08.40
Supervision: Beth Din of Paris.
Resto Flash
10 rue Lucien-Sampaix 75010 01.42.45.03.30
Supervision: Beth Din of Paris.

Les Cantiques
16 rue Beaurepaire 75010   01.42.40.64.21
Supervision: Beth Din of Paris.
Deliver.
Cash Food
63 rue des Vinaigriers 75010 01.42.03.95.75
Supervision: Beth Din of Paris.
Le Manahattan
231 boulevard Voltaire 75011 01.43.56.03.30
Supervision: Beth Din of Paris.
Le Cabourg
102 boulevard Voltaire 75011 01.47.00.71.43
Supervision: Beth Din of Paris.
Hours: 12 pm to 2:30 pm and 7 pm to 11 pm.
Nearest Metro: Voltaire.
La Fourchette d'Or
42 rue de l'orillon 75011   01.42.01.29.45
Supervision: Beth Din of Paris.
Le Lotus de Nissan
39 rue Amelot 75011   01.43.55.80.42
Supervision: Beth Din of Paris.
Yung Pana
115 boulevard Voltaire 75011 01.43.79.20.48
Supervision: Beth Din of Paris.
Le Haim
6 rue Paulin Enfert 75013   01.44.24.53.34
Supervision: Beth Din of Paris.
La Libanaise
13 rue des Sablons 75016   01.45.05.10.35
Supervision: Beth Din of Paris.
Eugenie
103 rue Jouffroy d'Abbans 75017
                       01.47.64.33.11
Supervision: Beth Din of Paris.
Mazel Tov
96 rue Nollet 75017   01.42.28.52.59
Supervision: Beth Din of Paris.
Nini, 24 rue Saussier-Leroy 75017
                       01.46.22.28.93
Supervision: Beth Din of Paris.
Jardins du Belvedere
111 avenue de Villiers 75017 01.42.27.16.91
Supervision: Beth Din of Paris.
Brasserie du Belvedere
109 avenue de Villiers 75017 01.47.64.96.55
Supervision: Beth Din of Paris.
Les Ailes
15 rue des Fermiers 75017   01.44.15.93.93
Supervision: Beth Din of Paris.
Fradji
42 rue Poncelet 75017   01.47.54.91.40
Supervision: Beth Din of Paris.

Tib's Café
128 boulevard de Clichy 75018
01.45.22.80.26
Supervision: Beth Din of Paris.
Alelouya
9 rue Charbonnière 75018   01.42.52.52.92
Supervision: Beth Din of Paris.
Chochana
54 avenue Secrétan 75019   01.42.41.01.16
Supervision: Beth Din of Paris.
Allo Sarina
38 rue Curial 75019   01.40.35.08.98
Supervision: Beth Din of Paris.
Mille Delices
52 avenue Secrétan 75019   01.40.18.32.32
Supervision: Beth Din of Paris.
Apropo
81 rue de Crimée 75019   01.42.03.10.10
Supervision: Beth Din of Paris.
Chez Marco
34 rue Curial 75019   01.40.05.05.99
Supervision: Beth Din of Paris.
Cotel Maaravi
69 avenue Armand-Carel 75019
01.42.06.13.00
Supervision: Beth Din of Paris.
Tib's Manin
161 rue Manin 75019   01.42.45.00.45
Supervision: Beth Din of Paris.
Elygel
116 boulevard de Belleville 75020
01.47.97.09.73
Supervision: Beth Din of Paris.
Chez François
5 rue Ramponeau 75020   01.47.97.40.06
Supervision: Beth Din of Paris.
Chez Rene et Gabin
92 boulevard de Belleville 75020
01.43.58.78.14
Supervision: Beth Din of Paris.
Le Petit Pelleport
135 rue Pelleport 75020   01.40.33.13.17
Supervision: Beth Din of Paris.
Le Relais
69 boulevard de Belleville 75020
01.43.57.83.91
Supervision: Beth Din of Paris.
Lumieres de Belleville
102 boulevard de Belleville 75020
01.47.97.51.83
Supervision: Beth Din of Paris.
Auberge de Belleville
110 boulevard de Belleville 75020
01.47.97.95.06
Supervision: Beth Din of Paris.

Chez Jeannot
112 boulevard de Belleville 75020
01.47.97.35.06
Supervision: Beth Din of Paris.

Dairy

Panini Folie
11 rue du Ponceau 75002   01.42.33.14.55
Supervision: Beth Din of Paris.
Hamman Café
4 rue des Rosiers 75004   01.42.78.04.46
Supervision: Beth Din of Paris.
Maestro Pizza
19 rue d'Anjou 75008   01.47.42.15.60
Supervision: Beth Din of Paris.
Cine Citta Café
7 rue d'Aguesseau 75008   01.42.68.05.03
Supervision: Beth Din of Paris.
Dizengoff Café
27 rue Richer 75009   01.47.70.81.97
Supervision: Beth Din of Paris.
King Salomon
46 rue Richer 75009   01.42.46.31.22
Supervision: Beth Din of Paris.
Cine Citta Café
58 rue Richer 75009   01.42.46.09.65
Supervision: Beth Din of Paris.
Ranch Pizza
2 passage du Jeu de Boules 75011
01.43.38.27.17
Supervision: Beth Din of Paris.
Paradiso
126 boulevard Voltaire 75011 01.48.06.79.33
Supervision: Beth Din of Paris.
Le New's
56 avenue de la République 75011
01.43.38.63.18
Supervision: Beth Din of Paris.
Coktail Café
82 avenue Parmentier 75011 01.43.57.19.94
Supervision: Beth Din of Paris.
Panino Café
121 rue du Château des Rentiers 75013
01.45.82.82.82
Supervision: Beth Din of Paris.
La Tour de Pizz
51 rue Bayen 75017   01.45.72.07.06
Supervision: Beth Din of Paris.
Pizza Curial
44 rue Curial 75019   01.40.37.15.00
Supervision: Beth Din of Paris.
Gin Fizz
157 boulevard Serrurier 75019
01.42.01.41.66
Supervision: Beth Din of Paris.

Dolphino Café
26 allée Darius milhaud 75019
                                01.42.01.20.30
Supervision: Beth Din of Paris.

Synagogues

Orthodox

Netzach Israël Ohel Mordehai
5 rue Sainte-Anastase 75003
15 rue Notre-Dame de Nazareth 75003
                                01.42.78.00.30
Groupe Rabbi Yehiel de Paris
25 rue Michel-Leconte 75003   01.42.78.89.17
Synagogue Tephilat Israël Frank-Forter
24 rue du Bourg-Tibourg 75004
                                01.46.24.48.94
Fondation Roger Fleishmann
18 rue des Ecouffes 75004   01.48.87.97.86
14 place des Vosges 75004   01.48.87.79.45
                        Fax: 01.48.87.57.58
21 bis rue des Tournelles 75004
                01.42.74.32.65; 01.42.74.32.80
                        Fax: 01.40.29.90.27
The secretary can be reached at
                                01.40.27.96.74
Adath Yechouroun
25 rue des Rosiers 75004   01.44.59.82.36
Agoudas Hakehilos Instit Yad Mordekhai
10 rue Pavée 75004   01.48.87.21.54
Oratoire Mahziké Adath Mouvement Loubavitch
17 rue des Rosiers 75004
Centre Rachi
30 boulevard du Port-Royal 75005
                                01.43.31.98.20
Séminaire Israélite de France
9 rue Vauquelin 75005   01.47.07.21.22
                        Fax: 01.43.37.75.92
Centre Edmond Fleg
8 bis rue de l'Epéron 75006   01.46.33.43.31
Houses the Union des Centres
Communautaires (UCC), which can be
contacted via the same telephone number.
Their fax number is 01.43.25.86.19.
Tikvaténou, the Jewish youth movement of the
Consistoire, is also located here, Tel:
01.46.33.43.24; Fax: 01.43.25.20.59.
E.E.I.F.
27 avenue de Ségur 75007   01.47.83.60.33
Hékhal Moché
218-220 rue du Faubourg St-Honoré 75008
                                01.45.61.20.25
Located behind the Golden Tulip Hotel and the
only one in the tourist centre of Paris.

Beth-Israël
4 rue Saulnier 75009   01.45.23.34.89
28 rue Buffault 75009   01.45.26.80.87
                        Fax: 01.48.78.44.02
44 rue de la Victoire 75009   01.40.82.26.26
                        Fax: 01.42.81.92.46
Synagogue Berit Chalom
18 rue Saint-Lazare 75009   01.48.78.45.32;
                                01.48.78.38.80
Kollel Rav Lévy
37 boulevard de Strasbourg 75009
Siège du Beth Loubavitch
8 rue Lamartine 75009   01.45.26.87.60
                        Fax: 01.45.26.24.37
5 rue Rochechouart 75009   01.49.95.95.92
                        Fax: 01.42.80.10.66
Beth-El
3 bis rue Saulnier 75009   01.47.70.09.23
                        Fax: 01.45.23.15.75
Adass Yereim
10 rue Cadet 75009   01.42.46.36.47
                        Fax: 01.48.74.35.35
Rachi Chull
6 rue Ambroise-Thomas 75009
                                01.48.24.86.95
Tiferet Yaacob
71 rue de Dunkerque 75009   01.42.81.32.17;
                                01.42.49.65.12
Beth-Eliaou
192 rue Saint-Martin 75010   01.40.38.47.53
                        Fax: 01.40.36.41.95
Rav Pealim (Braslav)
49 boulevard de la Villette 75010
                                01.42.41.55.44
A.U.J.
130 rue du Faubourg Saint-Martin 75010
                                01.40.05.98.34
UNAT La Fraternelle
13-15 rue des Petites-Ecuries 75010
                                01.42.46.65.02
4 rue Martel 75010
9 rue Guy-Patin 75010   01.42.85.12.74
Ozar Hatorath Shoul
40 rue de l'Orillon 75011   01.43.38.73.40
                        Fax: 01.43.38.36.45
Synagogue Don Isaac Abravanel
84-86 rue de la Roquette 75011
                                01.47.00.75.95
Adath Israël
36 rue Basfroi 75011   01.43.67.89.20
Ets Haim
18 rue Basfroi 75011   01.43.48.82.42
Ora Vesimha
37 rue des Trois-Bornes 75011
                                01.43.57.49.84

Névé Chalom
29 rue Sibué 75012   01.43.42.07.70
                              Fax: 01.43.48.44.50
Chivtei Israel
12-14 Cité Moynet 75012   01.43.43.50.12
                              Fax: 01.43.47.36.78
                  Email: ravatlan@club-internet.fr
Oratoire de la Fondation Rothschild (Maison de Retraite)
76 rue de Picpus 75012   01.43.44.72.98
                              Fax: 01.43.44.71.39
61-65 rue Vergniaud 75013   01.45.88.93.84
Avoth Ouvanim
59 avenue d'Ivry 75013
                    01.45.82.80.73; 01.45.85.94.39
19 rue Domrémy 75013
6 bis villa d'Alésia 75014   01.45.40.82.35
                              Fax: 01.45.40.72.89
Beith Chalom
25 villa d'Alésia 75014   01.45.45.38.71
                              Fax: 01.43.37.58.49
223 rue Vercingétorix 75014   01.45.45.50.51
Ohel Mordekhai
13 rue Fondary 75015   01.40.59.96.56
14 rue Chasseloup-Laubat 75015
                                   01.42.73.36.29
6 bis rue Michel-Ange 75016   01.44.14.71.23
                              Fax: 01.42.24.08.58
Ohel Avraham
31 rue Montevideo 75016   01.45.05.66.73
                              Fax: 01.40.72.83.76
23 bis rue Dufrénoy 75016
                    01.45.04.94.00; 01.45.04.66.73
5 bis rue Montevideo 75016   01.45.03.42.93
                              Fax: 01.40.72.83.76
10 rue Barye 75017
                    01.48.88.90.87; 01.40.53.91.57
Centre Rambam
19-21 rue Galvani 75017   01.45.74.52.80
Beth Hamidrach Lamed
67 rue Bayen 75017   01.45.74.52.80
42 rue des Saules 75018   01.42.64.65.00
80 rue Doudeauville 75018   01.42.62.77.63
Synagogue de Montmartre
13 rue Sainte-Isaure 75018   01.42.64.48.34
Rabbi David ou Moché
45 rue de Belleville 75019   01.40.18.30.63
                              Fax: 01.40.18.30.62
Beth Chalom
11-13 rue Curial 75019
                    01.40.37.65.16; 01.40.37.12.54
Ohaley Yaacov
11 rue Henri-Murger 75019   01.42.49.25.00

Heder Loubavitch
25 rue des Solitaires 75019   01.42.02.98.95
                              Fax: 01.42.02.04.62
Kollel Ysmah Moché
36 rue des Annelets 75019   01.43.63.73.94
Pah'ad David
11 rue du Plateau 75019   01.42.46.47.03
                              Fax: 01.42.46.47.56
Beth Loubavitch
25 rue Riquet 75019   01.40.36.93.90
Collel Hamabit
7 rue Rouvet 75019   01.40.38.13.59
Ohr Yossef
44-48 Quai de la Marne 75019
                                   01.42.45.74.20
                              Fax: 01.40.18.10.74
Ohr Tora
15 rue Riquet 75019   01.40.38.23.36;
                                   01.40.36.42.23
Synagogue Michkenot Israel
6 rue Jean-Nohain 75019   01.48.03.25.59
                              Fax: 01.42.00.26.87
Beth Loubavitch
53 rue Compans 75019   01.42.02.20.35
Chaare Tora
1 rue Henri-Turot 75019   01.42.06.41.12
                              Fax: 01.42.06.95.47
54 avenue Secrétan 75019   01.42.08.57.26
Synagogue Bet Yaacov Yossef
5 square des Cardeurs, 43 rue Saint-Blaise
75020   01.43.56.03.11
17 rue de la Cour-des-Noues 75020
                                   01.43.58.14.70
Ohr Chimchon Raphaël
5 passage Dagorno 75020   01.46.59.39.02
                              Fax: 01.46.59.14.99
50 bis rue des Prairies 75020   01.43.66.35.27
                              Fax: 01.43.66.97.18
Beth Loubavitch
93 rue des Orteaux 75020   01.40.24.10.60
Beth Loubavitch
47 rue Ramponeau 75020   01.43.66.93.00
Synagogue Achkenaze & Sephardi
49 rue Pali Kao 75020   01.46.36.30.10
Maor Athora
16 rue Ramponeau 75020   01.47.97.69.42
Synagogue Michkan-Yaacov
118 boulevard de Belleville 75020
                                   01.43.49.39.59
120 boulevard de Belleville 75020
                                   01.43.66.66.93

Paris Suburbs

Alfortville

Butchers
Tiness
12 rue Etienne Dollet 94140   01.49.77.95.79

Antony

Butchers
A.B.C.
96 av de la D Leclerc 92160   01.46.66.13.43

Synagogues

Orthodox

Community Centre and Synagogue
1 rue Sdérot, Angle 1, Rue Barthélémy 92160
01.46.66.19.17

Asnières

Mikvaot
82 rue du R.P. Christian-Gilbert 92600
01.47.99.26.59

Synagogues

Orthodox
73 bis rue des Bas 92600   01.47.99.32.55

Athis-Mons

Synagogues
55 rue des Coquelicots 92100   01.69.38.14.29

Aulnay-sous-Bois

Synagogues
80 rue Maximilien Robespierre 93600
01.48.69.66.93

Bagneux

Bakeries
Princiane
1 rue de l'Egalité, Parc de Garlande 92200
01.47.35.90.77
Supervision: Beth Din of Paris.

Butchers
Isaac, 188 av Aristide Briand 92220
01.45.47.00.21

Bagnolet

Bakeries
Sonesta
27 rue Adélaide Lahaye 93000
01.43.64.92.93
Fax: 01.43.60.51.26
Supervision: Beth Din of Paris.

Bobigny

Restaurants
Chez Charly et Cecile
2-24 rue Henri Barbusse 93000
01.48.43.79.00
Supervision: Beth Din of Paris.

Bondy

Synagogues

Orthodox

Maison Communautaire
28 avenue de la Villageoise 93140
01.48.47.50.79

Boulogne

Bakeries
Ariel, 143 avenue J.B. Clément 92100
01.46.04.24.42
Supervision: Beth Din of Paris.

Groceries
Ednale
28r Georges Sorel 92100   01.46.03.83.37

Synagogues

Orthodox
43 rue des Abondances 92100
01.46.03.90.63

Bussière

Mikvaot
Domaines de Melicourt 77750
01.60.22.54.85; 01.60.22.53.01

Champigny-sur-Marne

Synagogues

Orthodox

Synagogue Beth-David
25 avenue du général-de Gaulle 94500
01.48.85.72.29

Charenton

Butchers
Mazel Tov
14 rue Victor Hugo 94220   01.43.68.41.23

Chelles

Synagogues

Orthodox
14 rue des Anémones 77500   01.60.20.92.93

Choisy-le-Roi

Butchers
Chez Ilane
131 Marechal de Lattre de Tassigny 94600
01.48.52.27.74

Mikvaot
28 avenue de Newbum 94600
01.48.53.43.70; 01.48.92.68.68

Synagogues

Orthodox
28 avenue de Newburn 94600
01.48.53.48.27

Clichy-sous-Bois

Restaurants
Nathaneli
1 rue Poyer 92110   01.42.70.97.06
Supervision: Beth Din of Paris.

Clichy-sur-Seine

Synagogues

Orthodox
26 rue de Mozart (Espace Clichy) 92210
01.47.39.02.43

Créteil

Bakeries
Les Jasmins de Tunis
C.C. Kennedy 94000   01.43.77.50.66
Supervision: Beth Din of Paris.
Tov 'Mie
25 rue du Dr Paul Casalis 94000
01.42.07.94.81
Supervision: Beth Din of Paris.
Caprices et Delices
5 rue Edouard Manet 94000   01.43.39.20.20
Supervision: Beth Din of Paris.

La Nougatine
20 Esplanade des Abîmes 94000
01.49.56.98.56
Supervision: Beth Din of Paris.
Quick Chaud
26 allée Parmentier 94000   01.48.99.08.30
Supervision: Beth Din of Paris.

Butchers
La Ch Julien
Cte Commercial Kennedy, Loge 13 rue Gabriel
Peri 94000   01.43.39.20.43
Boucherie Patrick
2 rue Edouard Manet 94000   01.43.39.29.64
Boucherie Chalom
41 allee Parmentier 94000   01.48.99.15.45

Mikvaot
Rue du 8 Mai 1945 94000
01.43.77.01.70; 01.43.77.19.68

Restaurants
Fast Food Boucherie Chalom
41 allée Parmentier 94000   01.48.99.15.45
Supervision: Beth Din of Paris.
Daidou
9 Esplanade des Abîmes 94000
1.43.99.44.39
Supervision: Beth Din of Paris.
L'Aile et la Cuisse
C.C. Kennedy 94000   01.49.80.04.25
Supervision: Beth Din of Paris.
Promo Cacher
17 allée du Commerce 94000   01.49.80.04.25
Supervision: Beth Din of Paris.

Dairy

Le Laguna
8 rue d'Estienne-d'Orves 94000
01.42.07.10.38
Supervision: Beth Din of Paris.

Synagogues

Orthodox
Community Centre
rue du 8 Mai 1945 94051
01.43.77.01.70; 01.43.39.05.20
Fax: 01.43.99.03.60

Enghien

Mikvaot
47 rue de Malleville 95880   01.34.17.37.11

Synagogues

Orthodox
47 rue de Malleville 95880   01.34.12.42.34

Épinay

Butchers
Chalom
90 av Joffre 93800   01.48.41.50.64

Fontainebleau

Synagogues

Orthodox
38 rue Paul Seramy 77300   01.64.22.68.48

Fontenay-aux-Roses

Synagogues
Centre Moise Meniane
17 avenue Paul-Langevin 92660
       01.46.60.75.94

Fontenay-s/Bois

Mikvaot
Haya Mossia
177 rue des Moulins 94120
     01.48.77.53.90; 01.48.76.83.84

Garges-lès-Gonesse

Butchers
Abner, C C pal de la Dame Blanche 95140
01.39.86.43.63
Chez Harry
1 rue J B Corot 95140   01.39.86.53.81
Boucherie Berbeche
C C Pal de la Dame Blanche 95140
       01.39.86.53.81

Mikvaot
15 rue Corot 95140   01.39.86.75.64

Synagogues

Orthodox
Maison Communautaire Chaare Ra'hamim
14 rue Corot 95140   01.39.86.75.64

Issy-les-Moulineaux

Butchers
Cash Elysees
40 bis rue Ernest Renan 92130
       01.46.62.67.67

Synagogues

Orthodox
72 boulevard Gallieni 92130   01.46.48.34.49

La Courneuve

Synagogues
13 rue Saint-Just 93120   01.48.36.75.59

La Garenne-Colombes

Synagogues
Synagogue and Community Centre of
Courbevoie / La Garenne-Colombes
13 rue L.M. Nordmann 92250   01.47.69.92.17

La Varenne St-Hilaire

Synagogues
10 bis avenue du chateau 94210
01.42.83.28.75
Centre Hillel
30 rue St-Hilaire 94210   01.48.86.52.09

Le Blanc-Mesnil

Synagogues
65 rue Maxime-Gorki 93150   01.48.65.58.98

Le Chesnay

Mikvaot
39 rue de Versailles 78150
       01.39.54.05.65; 01.39.07.19.19

Le Kremlin-Bicêtre

Synagogues

Orthodox
41-45 rue J.F. Kennedy 94270
       01.46.72.73.64

Le Perreux-sur-Marne

Synagogues
Synagogue-Nogent/Le Perreux/Bry-Sur-
Marne
165 bis avenue du Gal-de Gaulle 94170
       01.48.72.88.65

Le Raincy

Mikvaot
67 boulevard du Midi 93340   01.43.81.06.61

Synagogues

Orthodox
Maison Communautaire
19 allée Chatrian 93340   01.43.02.06.11

Le Vésinet

Mikvaot
29 rue Henri Cloppet 78110
    01.30.53.10.45; 01.30.71.12.26

Synagogues

Orthodox

Maison Communautaire
29 rue Henri-Cloppet 78110   01.30.53.10.45

Les Lilas

Butchers
B Des Lilas
6 rue de la Republique 93260   01.43.63.89.15

Levallois

Restaurants
Delicates Eden
102 rue Rivay 92300   01.42.70.97.06
Supervision: Beth Din of Paris.

Maisons-Alfort

Mikvaot
92-94 rue Victor-Hugo 94700   01.43.78.95.69

Massy

Mikvaot
Allée Marcel-Cerdan 91300   01.42.37.48.24

Synagogues

Orthodox

Allée Marcel-Cerdan 91300   01.69.20.94.21

Meaux

Synagogues
11 rue P. Barennes 77100   01.64.34.76.58

Meudon-la-Forêt

Mikvaot
Rue de la Synagogue 92360
    01.46.32.64.82; 01.46.01.01.32

Synagogues

Orthodox

Maison Communautaire
rue de la Synagogue 92360   01.48.53.48.27

Montreuil

Bakeries
Le Relais Sucre
62 rue des Roches 93100   01.48.70.22.60
Supervision: Beth Din of Paris.
Gad Cachere
21 rue Gabriel Péri 93100   01.48.59.28.98
Supervision: Beth Din of Paris.
Korcarz
134 bis rue de Stalingrad 93100
             01.48.58.33.45
Supervision: Beth Din of Paris/Chief Rabbi
Mordechai Rottenberg.

Butchers
Andre Volailles
62 rue des Roches 93100   01.48.57.57.17
B Andre
64 rue des Roches 93100   01.48.57.57.17

Restaurants

Dairy

Pizza Monte Carlo
129 rue Marceau 93100   01.48.59.55.15;
01.48.59.01.34
Supervision: Beth Din of Paris.

Montrouge

Butchers
Boucherie Vivo
2 rue Camille Pelletan 92120   01.47.35.23.06

Mikvaot
Ismah-Israel
90 rue Gabriel-Péri 92120   01.42.53.08.54

Synagogues

Orthodox

Centre Communautaire Regional Malakoff-Montrouge
90 rue Gabriel-Péri 92120   01.46.32.64.82
          Fax: 01.46.56.20.49

Neuilly

Butchers
Neuilly Cacher
2/6 rue de Chartres 92200   01.47.45.06.06

Groceries
King David
14 rue Paul- Chatrousse 92200
             01.47.45.18.19

Restaurants
King David
14 rue Paul-Chatrousse 92200
01.47.45.18.19
Supervision: Beth Din of Paris.
Deliver. Hours: 8 am to 10 pm. Nearest Metro: Pont de Neuilly.

Synagogues

Orthodox
12 rue Ancelle 92200   01.47.47.78.76
Fax: 01.47.47.54.79

Nogent sur Marne
Restaurants

Dairy
Beteavone
24 rue Paul Bert 94130   01.48.73.48.48
Supervision: Beth Din of Paris.

Noisy-le-Sec
Synagogues
Orthodox
Beth Gabriel
2 rue de la Pierre Feuillère 93130
01.48.46.71.79

Pantin
Bakeries
Crousty Cash
27 avenue Anatole France 93100
01.48.40.89.74
Supervision: Beth Din of Paris.

Butchers
Levy Baroukh
5/7 rue Anatole France 93500
01.48.91.02.14
Chel Hida
177 avenue Jean Lolive 93500
01.48.40.08.29
Supervision: Chief Rabbi Mordechai Rottenberg.

Restaurants
Chez Jacquy
24 rue du Pré-Saint-Gervais 93500
01.48.10.94.24
Supervision: Beth Din of Paris.

Pavillons
Butchers
Societe Brami
36 av Victor Hugo 93320   01.48.47.15.76

Ris-Orangis
Synagogues
Orthodox
1 rue Jean-Moulin 91130   01.69.43.07.83

Roissy-en-Brie
Mikvaot
Rue Paul-Cézanne, C.Cial Bois Montmartre
77680   01.60.28.34.65;
01.60.29.09.44

Synagogues
Orthodox
Maison Communautaire
1 rue Paul-Cézanne, Centre Commercial Bois
Montmartre 77680   01.60.28.36.38

Rosny-sous-Bois
Synagogues
62-64 rue Lavoisier 93110   01.48.54.04.11
Fax: 01.69.43.07.83

Rueil-Malmaison
Synagogues
6 rue René-Cassin 92500   01.47.08.32.62

Saint-Denis
Synagogues
51 boulevard Marcel-Sembat, (à côté de la
Gendarmerie) 93200   01.48.20.30.87

Saint-Leu-La-Forêt
Mikvaot
2 rue Jules Vernes 95320   01.39.95.96.90;
01.34.14.24.15

Saint-Ouen-L'Aumône
Synagogues
Orthodox
Maison Communautaire
9 rue de Chennevières 95310
01.30.37.71.41

Sarcelles

Bakeries
Natania
34 blvd Albert Camus 95200
01.39.90.11.78
Supervision: Beth Din of Paris.
Louis D'or
90 avenue Paul Valéry 95200
01.39.90.25.45
Supervision: Beth Din of Paris.
Zazou, C.C. les Flanades 95200
01.34.19.08.11
Supervision: Beth Din of Paris.
Oh Delices
71 avenue Paul Valéry 95200   01.39.92.41.12
Supervision: Beth Din of Paris.

Butchers
Menorah
20 avenue Paul Valéry 95200   01.34.19.37.64
Supervision: Chief Rabbi Mordechai
Rottenberg.
Boucherie Du Coin
60 bd Albert Camus 95200   01.39.90.53.02
Hazeout
5 Av Paul Valery 95200   01.39.90.72.95

Mikvaot
Mayanot Rachel
14 avenue Ch.-Péguy 95200   01.39.90.40.17

Restaurants
Berbeche Burger
13 avenue Edouard-Branly 95200
01.34.19.12.02
Supervision: Beth Din of Paris.

Dairy
Marina
103 avenue Paul-Valéry 95200
01.34.19.23.51
Supervision: Beth Din of Paris.

Synagogues
Orthodox
Maison Communautaire
74 avenue Paul-Valéry 95200   01.39.90.59.59
Mikva on premises.

Sartrouville

Synagogues
Orthodox
**Synagogue Rabbi Shimon bar Yohai et
Rabbi Meir Baal Hannes**
1 rue de Stalingrad 78500   01.39.15.22.57

Savigny-Sur-Orge

Mikvaot
1 avenue de L'Armée-Leclerc 91600
01.69.24.48.25; 01.69.96.30.90

Sevran

Mikvaot
25 bis du Dr Roux 93270   01.43.84.25.40
Mikva Kelim.

Synagogues
Orthodox
Synagogue Mayan-Thora
25 bis rue du Dr. Roux, BP. 111 93270
01.43.84.25.40

St Germain

Butchers
Cash'Ruth
155 bis rue du P Roosevelt 78100
01.34.51.51.62

St Oüen

Butchers
Chez Paul
37 rue Charles Schmidt 93400 01.40.11.37.52

St-Brice-sous Forêt

Restaurants
Changat Palace
40 boulevard Albert-Camus 95350
01.39.92.29.73
Supervision: Beth Din of Paris.

Synagogues
Orthodox
Centre Communautaire Ohel Avraham
10 rue Pasteur 95350   01.39.94.96.10

Stains

Synagogues
8 rue Lamartine (face n°2), Clos St-Lazare
93240   01.48.21.04.12
Provisional address: 8 avenue Louis Bordes
(Ancien Conservatoire Municipal).

Thiais

Community Organisations
Community Centre Choisy-Orly-Thiais
Voie du Four, 128 avenue du Marechal de
Lattre de Tassigny 94320   01.48.92.68.68
                        Fax: 01.48.92.72.82

Trappes

Synagogues

Orthodox
7 rue du Port-Royal 78190   01.30.62.40.43

Velliers-sur-Marne

Synagogues
30 rue Léon-Douer, B.P. 15 94350
                              01.49.30.01.47
                        Fax: 01.49.30.85.40

Versailles

Butchers
La Versaillaise
112 rue de la Paroisse 78000   01.39.25.00.66

Synagogues
10 rue Albert-Joly 78000   02.39.07.19.19
                        Fax: 02.39.50.96.34
Mikva on premises.

Villejuif

Bakeries
Eden Eclair
30 rue Marcel Grosmenil 94800
                              01.47.26.42.96
Supervision: Beth Din of Paris.

Villeneuve-la-Garenne

Butchers
Chez Armand
6 rue Gaston Appert 92390   01.47.98.52.00

Mikvaot
42-44 rue du Fond-de-la Noue 92390
                              01.47.94.89.98

Synagogues

Orthodox
Maison Communautaire
44 rue du Fond-de-la-Noue 92390
                              01.47.94.89.98

Villiers-le-Bel

Mikvaot
1 rue Léon Blum 95400
                 01.39.94.45.51; 01.34.19.64.48

Synagogues

Orthodox
1 rue Léon-Blum, (Les Carreaux) 95400
                 01.39.94.30.49; 01.39.94.94.89

Vincennes

Butchers
Boucherie Des Levy
32 rue Raymond du Temple 94300
                              01.43.74.94.18
Hayache
146 Av de Paris 94300   01.43.28.16.04

Synagogues

Orthodox
Synagogue
30 rue Céline-Robert 94300   01.43.28.82.83

Vitry

Synagogues
133-135 avenue Rouget-de-l'Isle 94400
                 01.46.80.76.54; 01.45.73.06.58
                        Fax: 01.45.73.94.01

Yerres

Mikvaot
43/49 rue R. Poincar 91330
                 01.69.48.46.01; 01.69.48.44.67

Pau

Synagogues
8 rue des Trois-Freres-Bernadac 64000
05.59.62.37.85

Périgueux

Synagogues
13 rue Paul-Louis-Courrier 24000
05.53.53.22.52

Perpignan

Butchers
Gilbert Sabbah
3 rue P.-Rameil 66000   04.68.35.41.23

Cemetaries
Haut Vernet
Rivesaltes
Found near the camp from which thousands of
Jews were deported to Auschwitz.

Synagogues
54 rue Arago 66000

Phalsbourg

Synagogues
16 rue Alexandre-Weill 57370

Poitiers

Synagogues
1 rue Guynemer 86000

Reims

Memorials
War Memorial
Blvd. General Leclerc
With an urn containing ashes from a number
of Nazi death camps.

Synagogues
49 rue Clovis 51100   03.26.47.68.47

Rennes

Community Organisations
32 rue de la Marbaudais 35000
02.99.63.57.18
Services held telephone for times.

Roanne

Synagogues
9 rue Beaulieu 42300   04.77.71.51.56

Rouen

Synagogues
55 rue des Bons-Enfants 76100
02.35.71.01.44
The Jewish Youth Club can provide a board
residence for student travellers and holiday-
makers.

Saint-Avold

Cemetaries
The American Military Cemetery

Containing the graves of many Jewish soldiers
who fell in the Second World War.

Synagogues
Pl. du Marche 57500   03.87.91.16.16

Saint-Die

Synagogues
Rue de l'Eveche 88100
Services, festivals and Holy-days only.

Saint-Etienne

Synagogues
34 rue d'Arcole 42000   04.77.33.56.31

Saint-Fons

Synagogues
17 Av. Albert-Thomas 69190   04.78.67.39.78

Saint-Laurent-du-Var

Synagogues
Villa 'Le Petit Clos', 35 Av. des Oliviers 06700

Saint-Louis

Cemetaries
The Hegenheim Cemetery

This cemetery dates from 1673.

Community Organisations
19 rue du Temple 68300   03.89.70.00.48
Kosher products available.

Synagogues
3 rue de General Cassagnou 68300
Rue de la Synagogue 68300

Saint-Quentin

Synagogues
11 ter Blvd. Henri-Martin   03.23.08.30.72

Sarrebourg

Synagogues
12 rue du Sauvage

Sarreguemines

Synagogues
Rue Georges-V 57200   03.87.98.81.40
Mikva on premises.

Saverne

Synagogues
Rue du 19 Novembre 67700

Sedan-Charleville

Synagogues
6 Av. de Verdun 08200

Selestat

Synagogues
4 rue Ste.-Barbe 67600

Sens

Synagogues
14 rue de la Grande-Juiverie 89100
                              03.86.95.16.65

Strasbourg

With a Jewish population of 16,000, this city, contested by France and Germany throughout history, currently has an important Jewish community, with several kosher restuarants, butchers and even a kosher vineyard.

Bakeries
Meyer, 9 rue de la Nuee-Bleue 67000
                              03.88.32.73.79
Crousty Cash
4 rue Sellénick 67000   03.88.35.71.79
Levy, 4 rue Strauss, Durkheim 67000
                              03.88.35.68.21

Booksellers
Librairie Schne-Or
15 rue de Bitche 67000   03.88.37.32.37
Librairie Du Cedrat
19 rue du Marechal-Foch 67000

Butchers
David, 20 rue Sellenick 67000 03.88.36.75.01
Buchinger
13 rue Wimpheling 67000   03.88.61.06.98
Buchinger
63 Faubourg de Pierre 67000   03.88.32.85.03

Groceries
Franc Prix
13 rue du General-Rapp 67000
                              03.88.36.16.51
Yarden
3 rue Finkmatt 67000   03.88.22.49.76
Yarden
13 Blvd. de la Marne 67000   03.88.60.10.10
Franc Prix
31 Faubourg de Saverne 67000
                              03.88.32.04.40

Media

Newspapers
Echos-Unir
1a rue du Grand-Rabbin-Rene-Hirschler 67000
Monthly publication.

Mikvaot
1a rue du Grand-Rabbin-Rene-Hirschler 67000
                              03.88.14.46.50

Religious Organisations
Consistoire Israelite du Bas-Rhin
23 rue Sellenick 67000   03.88.25.05.75
                        Fax: 03.88.25.12.75
Regional Chief Rabbi
5 rue du General-de-Castelnau 67000
                              03.88.32.38.97

Restaurants
Restaurant Universitaire
11 rue Sellenick 67000   03.88.25.67.97
Le Wilson
25 Blvd. Wilson 67000   03.88.52.06.66
Le King
28 rue Sellenick 67000   03.88.52.17.71

Synagogues
Synagogue de la Paix
1a rue du Grand-Rabbin-Rene-Hirschler 67000
                              03.88.14.46.50
Ets Haim
28a rue Kageneck 67000
Adath Israel
2 rue St. Pierre-le-Jeune 67000
There are in all more than 15 synagogues in Strasbourg.

Vineyards

Kosher
Goxwiller, R. Koenig, 35 rue Principale 67000
                              03.88.95.51.93

Tarbes

Synagogues
Cite Rothschild
6 rue du Pradeau 65000

Thionville

Synagogues
31 Av. Clemenceau 57100   03.82.54.47.89

Toul

Synagogues
Rue de la Halle 54200

Toulon

Butchers
Abecassis
8 rue Vincent Courdouant 83000
04.94.94.39.86
Supervision: Grand Rabbinate of Marseille.
Fenech
15 avenue Colbert 83000   04.94.92.70.39
Supervision: Grand Rabbinate of Marseille.

Synagogues
Av. Lazare Carnot 83050   04.94.92.61.05
Mikva on premises.

Toulouse

Butchers
El Maalen David
7 rue des Chalets Bravo   05.61.63.77.39
05.61.62.32.74
Ghnassia
397 Route de St.-Simon 31000
05.61.42.05.81
Cacherout Diffusion
37 Blvd. Carnot 31000   05.61.23.07.59
Benichou
7 rue des Chalets 31000   05.61.63.77.39
Amsellem
6 rue de la Colombette 31000
05.61.62.97.55
Lasry, 8 rue Matabiau 31000
05.61.62.65.28

Community Orgnisations
Community Centre
14 rue du Rempart-St.-Etienne 31000
05.61.23.36.54

Groceries
Otguergoust
21 pl. V. Hugo 31000   05.61.21.95.36

Super Cach
Rondpoint de la Plaine Balma 31000
05.61.24.66.75
Novogel
14 rue E. Guyiaux 31300   05.61.57.03.19

Mikvaot
15 rue Francisque Sarcey 31000
05.61.48.89.84

Religious Organisations
Grand Rabbinet du Toulouse et des Pays de
la Garonne
17 rue Alsace-Lorraine 31000
05.61.21.51.14

Religious Orgnisations
Regional Chief Rabbi
17 rue Calvert 31500   05.61.21.51.14

Restaurants
Les 7 Epis Boulangers
3 Boulevard des Minimos 31200
05.61.11.43.11

Community Centre
14 rue du Rempart-St.-Etienne 31000
05.61.23.36.54
Students only.

Synagogues
Chaare Emeth
35 rue Rembrandt 31000   05.61.40.03.88

Ashkenazi
Adat Yechouroun
3 rue Jules-Chalande 31000   05.61.62.60.41

Sephardi
Adat Yechouroun
2 rue Palaprat 31000   05.61.21.69.56

Tours

Community Organisations
Community Centre
6 rue Chalmel 37000

Synagogues
37 rue Parmentier 37000   02.47.05.56.95

Troyes

Memorials

A statue of Rashi was unveiled at the Troyes
cemetery in 1990.

Mikvaot
1 rue Brunneval   03.25.73.34.44

Synagogues
5 rue Brunneval

Valence

Synagogues
1 Place du Colombier 26000   04.75.43.34.43

Valenciennes

Synagogues
36 rue de l'Intendance 59300   03.27.29.11.07

Vénissieux

Synagogues
12 Av. de la Division-Leclerc 69200
                                                   04.78.70.69.85

Verdun

Synagogues
Impasse des Jacobins 55100

Vichy

Synagogues
2 bis rue du Marechal Foch 03200

Vittel

Synagogues
Rue Croix-Pierrot 88800

Wasselonne

Synagogues
Rue des Bains 67310

Other Departments

Corsica

Contact Information
Jo Michel Reis
La Grande Corniche, Routes des Sanguinaires,
Ajaccio   9521-5752
There are between ten and fifteen families in
the town.

Synagogues
3 rue du Castagno
Bastia 20200
Services Shabbat morning and festivals. This
port town has a Jewish population of 25–35
families.

Guadeloupe

Synagogues
Bas du Fort, Gosier, Point-à-Pitre
                                                   90.90.99.09.
The synagogue, community centre and
restaurant/kosher store are all located here.

La Réunion

Contact Information
Leon Benamou
                                                   (262) 290-545

Hotels

Kosher

Hotel Astoria
16 rue Juliette Dodu
St. Denis 97400   (262) 200-558
                                     Fax: (262) 412-630

Synagogues
Communauté Juive de la Réunion
8 rue de l'Est, St Denis 97400   (262) 237-833
High Holy Day services and communal seder
held here.

Martinique

Synagogues
Maison Grambin
Plateau Fofo, Voie 1, Fort-de-France 97233
                                                   (596) 603-727
A community centre is also located here.

Tahiti

Religious Organisations
ACISPO
rue Moerenhout-Papeete
French Polynesia 4821   (689) 410-392
                                     Fax: (689) 420-909

Georgia

Georgia has had a very long history of Jewish settlement, dating back to two centuries before the destruction of the Second Temple, if the archaeological findings are correct. These earliest Jewish communities may have descended from the Babylonian exiles. Marco Polo in the thirteenth century noted the presence of Jews.

The Georgian Jews are also well informed about their religion, which is unusual in a former Soviet republic.

Synagogues are found in major towns, there is a school in Tbilisi (the capital) and there are some newsletters. It is worth noting that the non-Jewish population has traditionally been far less anti-Semitic than the populations of some other ex-Soviet republics.

GMT + 4 hours	Total Population 5,450,000
Country calling code (995)	Jewish Population 13,000

Batumi
Synagogues
6 9th March Street

Gori
Synagogues
Chelyuskin Street

Kulashi
Synagogues
170 Stalin Street

Onni
Synagogues
Baazova Street

Poti
Synagogues
Tskhakaya Street
23 Ninoshivili

Sukhumi
Synagogues
56 Karl Marx Street

Surami
Synagogues
Internatsionalaya Street

Tbilisi
Organisations
Jews of Georgia Assoc.
Tsarity Tamari Street 8 380012   (32) 234-1057

Synagogues
45-47 Leselidze Street

Ashkenazi
65 Kozhevenny Lane

Sephardi
Leselidze Street

Tshkinvali
Synagogues
Isapov Street

Tskhakaya
Synagogues
Mir Street

Vani
Synagogues
4 Kaikavadze Street

Germany

It may be a surprise to many that Germany comes immediately after France and the UK in the population table of Western European Jews. German Jews have contributed much to the culture of European Jews in general since their arrival in what is now Germany in the fourth century. The massive Jewish presence in Poland and other east European states stemmed from German Jews escaping persecution in the late Middle Ages, and they took the Medieval German language with them, which formed Yiddish, the old lingua franca of European Jews.

The Jews who stayed behind in Germany contributed much towards Jewish and German culture, with the Reform movement starting in nineteenth-century Germany, and Heine and Mendelssohn contributing to German poetry and music respectively. The enlightenment and modern orthodoxy also began in Germany.

The rise of Nazism destroyed the belief that the German Jews were more German than Jewish. Many managed to escape before 1939, but 180,000 were killed in the Holocaust (of the 503,000 who lived in Germany when Hitler came to power). Following the events of 1933-45, it seems incredible that any Jew should want to live in Germany again. However the community began to reform; mainly immigrants from eastern Europe, especially Russia. Now there are again Jewish shops in Berlin, and kosher food is available. There are many old synagogues which have been restored, and several concentration camps have been kept as monuments to history.

GMT + 1 hour
Country calling code (49)
Emergency Telephone (Police – 110) (Fire and Ambulance – 112)

Total Population 81,922,000
Jewish Population 60,000

Aachen

Representative Organisations
Bundesverband Jüdischer Studenten in Deutschland
Oppenhoffallee 50 (241) 75998

Alsenz

Sites
Synagogue, Kirchberg 1 (636) 23149
Fax: (636) 23149
Restored 18th century synagogue.

Amberg

Community Organisations
Community Centre
Salzgasse 5 (962) 113140

Andernach

Mikvaot
Rhine Valley
This Rhine Valley town contains an early 14th century mikva. Key obtainable from tourist office.

Annweiler

Tourist Sites
(623) 53333
The oldest cemetery in the Palatinate dating from 16th century.

Augsburg

Community Organisations
Community Centre
Halderstr. 8 (821) 517985
There is a Jewish museum in the restored Liberal synagogue.

Bad Kissingen

Hotels
Eden-Park
Rosenstrasse 5-7 97688   (971) 717-200
                                Fax: (971) 717-272
There is a restaurant on the premises that
serves kosher food and traditional meals.

Bad Kreuznach

Community Organisations
Community Centre
Gymnasialstr. 11   (671) 26991

Bad Nauheim

Hotels
Accadia, Lindenstr. 15/Frankfurterstr. 22
                                (603) 239068

Restaurants
Jewish Community
Karlstr. 34   (603) 231157
                                Fax: (603) 25605
Entrance from Friedensstr.

Synagogues
Community Centre
Karlstr. 34   (603) 25605; 171-951-1358
                              Fax: (603) 603-25605

Baden-Baden

Synagogues
Werderstr. 2 76530   (722) 139-1021
                              Fax: (722) 139-1024

Bamberg

Community Organisations
Community Centre
Willy-Lessing-Str. 7   (951) 23267

Bayreuth

Community Organisations
Community Centre
Munzgasse 2   (921) 65407

Berlin

Jewish life is beginning to grow again in Berlin,
formerly an important centre for German
Jewry. There are many sites which testify to
the tragedy that befell the community before
and during the war, such as the ruined
Oranienburgerstrasse Synagogue, which has
recently been turned into a Jewish centre. The
site of the Wannsee Conference, to the south
west of the city, (where the Holocaust was
officially planned), has been turned into a
museum.

Bed & Breakfasts
Guestrooms
Tucholskystrasse 40 Mitte 10117
                                (30) 281-3135
                          Fax: (30) 281-3122

Booksellers
Literaturhandlung
Joachimstaler-Str. 13 10719   (30) 882-4250
                          Fax: (30) 885-4713

Cemeteries
Adass Jisroel
Wittlicherstrasse 2
Weissensee 13088   (30) 925-1724
Established in in 1880, this historic cemetery is
used to this very day. Rabbi Esriel
Hildesheimer, Rabbi Prof. David Zvi Hoffmann,
Rabbi Eliahu Kaplan and many other wise and
pious Jews are buried here.

Community Organisations
Community Centre
Fasanenstr. 79-80, off the Kurfurstendamm
                                (30) 88028-250
                          Fax: (30) 88028-250
This has been built on the site of a famous
synagogue, destroyed by the Nazis
**Judischer Kulturverein (Jewish Cultural
Center)**
Oranienburgerstr. 26, Berlin-Mitte 10117
                  (30) 282-6669; 285-98052
                          Fax: (30) 285-98053
Hours: Monday-Thursday 11am to 5pm, Friday
11am to 2pm and 1 hour before evening and
Sunday events.

Embassy
Consulate General
Schinkel Street 10, PO Box 330531 14193
                                (30) 893-2203

Jewish Life in Berlin

The Jewish Restaurant in the center of Berlin Jewish and Israeli Dairy Specialities
40, Tucholsky St.

בית קפה

Kosher Food – Meat, Bread, Wines and meaty snacks.
Ritual Objects.
77/78, August St.

Also: Catering Service, Lunch-boxes, Guest Rooms. Special arrangements for touring "Jewish Berlin". Regular Services

Jewish Congregation Adass Jisroel
in Berlin, founded in 1869. Community Centre and Synagogue

40 Tucholsky St. (formerly 31, Artillerie St.)
10117 Berlin-Mitte
Tel: +4930/281 31 35 Fax: 281 31 22 Telex: 307220 ajb d

Groceries
Kolbo
Auguststrasse 77-78 Mitte 10117
(30) 281-3135
In addition to kosher food and wines, sifrei kodesh as well as general literature about Jewish subjects and klei kodesh can be obtained here.
Plazl, Passaver Str.4 10789   (30) 217-7506

Kashrut Information
Rabbinate of Adass Jisroel
Tucholskystrasse 40 Mitte 10117
(30) 281-3135
Fax: (30) 281-3122

Libraries
Jewish Library
Oranienburger Str. 28 10117   (30) 284-0122-7

Media

Magazines

Judische Korrespondez   (30) 282-6669
(Monthly review) Judischer Kulturverein.
(Jewish Cultural Ass.)

Judischer Korrespondenz
Oranienburgerstr. 26, Berlin-Mitte 10117
(30) 282-6669; 285-98052
Fax: (30) 285-98053
Monthly. Published in German and Russian.

Newspapers
Hadshot Adass Jisroel
Tucholsky str. 40 10117   (30) 281-3135
Published by Adass Jisroel and obtainable through their offices (see above for number).

Religious Organisations
Zentralrat der Juden in Deutschland
Oranienburger Str. 31 10117   (30) 282-8714
Fax: (30) 238-6607
Berlin Office.

Restaurants
Arche Noah Restaurant
Community Centre, Fasanenstr. 79-80 12
(30) 082-6138
Beth Café
Tucholskystrasse 40 Mitte 10117
(30) 281-3135
Fax: (30) 281-3122
Supervision: Rabbinate of Adass Jisroel.
Open daily, except Shabbat, from 11 am to 10 pm. Closes Friday two hours before Shabbat.

Café Oren
Oranienburger Str. 28 10117   (30) 282 82 28
Jewish Congregation Adass Jisroel
40 Tucholsky St. (formerly 31, Artillerie St.)
10117   (30) 281 31 35
                        Fax: 281 31 22
                    Telex: 3087220 ajb d
Rimon, Oranienburgerstr. 26,
Berlin-Mitte 10117   (30) 283-8403-2
Hours: Daily 10 am to 12 pm

Synagogues
Neue Synagogue Berlin
Centrum Judaicum, Oranienburger-Str. 29
1040   (30) 280-1250-1
Liberal
Pestalozzistr. 14, 1000 10625   (30) 313-8411
Orthodox
Adass Jisroel
Tucholskystrasse 40 Mitte 10117
                        (30) 281-3135
                    Fax: (30) 281-3122
Established 1869. Rabbinate, Kashrut
supervision and mohel can all be reached at
this number. Near its community centre, there
is a guest house, a kosher restaurant and a
shop which sells kosher products.

Tourist Information
Staatliches Israelisches Verkehrsbureau
Stollbergstrasse 6 15   (30) 883-6759
                    Fax: (30) 882-4093
Staatliches Israelisches Verkehrsbureau
Stollbergstrasse 6 15   (30) 881-9685
                    Fax: (30) 882-4093

Bochum
Synagogues
Alte Wittener Str. 18 44803   (234) 361563
                    Fax: (234) 360187

Bonn/Bad Godesberg
Embassy
Embassy of Israel
Simrock Allee 2, Postfach 200230 53173
                        (228) 934-6553
                    Fax: (228) 934-6555
                Email: botschaft@israel.de

Media
Newspapers
"Allgemeine Judische Wochenzeitung"
Rungsdorfer Str. 6 53173   (228) 351021
                        Fax: (228) 355469
                Email: ajw@comdok.de
Fortnightly.
Synagogues
Templestr. 2-4, cnr. Adenauer Allee 53113
                        (228) 213560
                    Fax: (228) 213560

Braunschweig
Community Organisations
Community Centre
Steinstr. 4   (531) 45536
Museums
The Jewish Museum
Ausstellungszentrum Hinter Aegiden 3300
                        (531) 484-2602
                    Fax: (531) 484-2607
            Email: blm@blm.bs.shuttle.de
Founded in 1746, this museum was formerly
the oldest Jewish museum in the world. It was
re-opened in 1987 under the auspices of the
Braunschweigisches Landesmuseum. Hours
Tues.-Sun: 10am to 5pm; Thurs. 10am to 8pm.

Bremen
Synagogues
Schwachauser Heerstr. 117   (421) 498-5104
                    Fax: (421) 498-4944

Chemnitz
Community Organisations
Community Centre
Stollberger Str. 28   (371) 32862

Coblenz
Community Organisations
Community Centre
Schlachthof Str. 5   (261) 42223

Cologne
Hotels
Leonet (80)
Rubensstr. 33   (221) 236016

Restaurants
Community Centre

(221) 240-4440
Fax: (221) 240-4440
Kosher meals available.

Synagogues
Roonstr. 50 50674 (221) 921-5600
Fax: (221) 921-5609
Web site: www.sgk.de
Daily services. There are a youth centre, Jewish museum and library at the same address.

Darmstadt
Community Organisations
Community Centre
Wilhelm-Glassing-Str. 26 (615) 128897

Dortmund
Representative Organisations
Landesverband der Judischen Kultusgemeinden von Westfalen
Prinz-Friedrich-Karl-Str. 12 44135
(231) 528495
Fax: (231) 5860372
Email: lvjuedwest@aol.com

Synagogues
Prinz-Friedrich-Karl-Str. 9 44135
(231) 528497

Dresden
Representative Organisations
Landesverband Sachsen der Judischen Gemeinden
Bautzner Str 20 01099
(351) 804-5491;802-2739
Fax: (351) 804-1445
A memorial to the six million Jews killed in the holocaust stands on the site of the Dresden Synagogue, burnt down by the Nazis in November 1938.

Synagogues
Fiedlerstr. 3 (351) 693317

Düsseldorf
Hotels
Gildors Hotel
Collenbachstr. 51 (211) 488005
Israeli owned.

Synagogues
Zietenstr. 50 (211) 461-9120
Fax: (211) 485156

Emmendingen
Synagogues
Lenzhausle am Schlossplatz (764) 157-1989

Erfurt
Community Organisations
Community Centre
Juri-Gagarin-Ring 16 (361) 24964

Essen
Community Organisations
Community Centre
Sedanstr. 46 (201) 273413

Essingen
Cemetery

Largest cemetery in the Palatinate, where Anne Frank's ancestors are buried, 16th Century. Key at the Mayor's Office.

Frankfurt-Am-Main
Tourist Information
Staatliches Israelisches Verkehrsbureau
Bettinstrasse 62, 5th Floor 60325
(69) 756-1920
Fax: (69) 756-9222
Staatliches Israelisches Verkehrsbureau
Kurfuerstendamm 202 100

Bakeries
Donath Werner
Raimundstr. 21 (69) 526202

Butchers
Aviv Butchery & Deli
Hanauer Landstr. 50 (69) 431539

Community Organisations
Community Centre
Westendstr. 43 (69) 74 07 21
This community produces a monthly magazine, "Judische Gemeinde-Zeitung Frankfurt".

Hotels
Hotel Excelsior & Monopol (200)
Mannheimer Str. 7-13, 6000 1 (69) 256080
Luxor Hotel
Am Allerheiligentor 2-4 (69) 293067 / 69
This hotel, which is under Jewish management, is within walking distance of the Freiherr-vom-Stein-Str. synagogue.

Mikvaot
Westend Synagogue
Freiherr-vom-Stein-Str. 30   (69) 726263

Museums
Jewish Museum
Untermainkai 14-15, 60311   (69) 212-35000
Fax: (69) 212-0705
Email: wolfgang.heiner@stadt-frankfurt.de
Sunday, Tuesday to Saturday 10.00am-5.00pm.
Wednesday 10.00am-8.00pm. Closed Monday.

Representative Organisations
Zentralwohlfahrtsstelle der Juden in Deutschland
Hebelstrasses 6 60318   (69) 94 43 71-15
Fax: (69) 49 48 17

Restaurants
Sohar's
Savignystrasse 66 60325   (69) 75 23 41
Fax: (69) 741 0116
Supervision: Rabbi Menachem Halevi Klein, Frankfurt Rabbinate.
Hours: Tuesday to Thursday and Sunday, 12 pm to 8 pm; Friday, 12 pm to Shabbat; Shabbat, 1:30 pm to 4 pm; Monday, closed. Special arrangements can be made by phone. Friday and Shabbat meals must be ordered in advance. Provide party service, airline catering and delivery to hotels. Fifteen minute walk from synagogue, fair centre and main train station.

Synagogues
Baumweg 5-7
(69) 069-439381 & 499-0758
Beth Hamidrash West End
Altkanigstr. 27   (69) 723805
Westend Synagogue
Freiherr-vom-Stein-Str. 30   (69) 726263
This is the city's main synagogue.

Freiburg
Community Organisations
Community Centre
Nussmannstr. 14   (761) 383096

Friedberg/Hessen
Tourist Sites
Judengasse 20
The ancient mikva, built in 1260 is located here. The town council has issued a special explanatory leaflet about it, and it is now scheduled as a historical monument of medieval architecture.

Fulda
Community Organisations
Community Centre
von Schildeckstr. 13   (66) 170252
Services first Friday of each month, half before dusk.

Fürth
Community Organisations
Community Centre
Blumenstr. 31   (91) 177-0879

Tourist Sites
Julienstr. 2
There is a beautifully restored synagogue as well as a historic mikva.

Gelsenkirchen
Community Organisations
Community Centre
Von-der-Recke-Str. 9   (20) 923143 & 206628

Hagen
Community Organisations
Community Centre
Potthofstr. 16   (2331) 711-3289

Halle/Saale
Community Organisations
Community Centre
Grosse Markerstr. 13   (345) 26963

Hamburg
Community Organisations
Community Centre
Schaferkampsallee 27 20357   (40) 440-9440
Fax: (40) 410-8430

Restaurants
(40) 440-94441
Fax: (40) 410-8430
Kosher food is available upon reservation.

Synagogues
Hohe Weide 34 20253   (40) 440-9440
Mikvah on premises.

Hanover
Community Organisations
Community Centre
Haecklstr. 10 810472

Synagogues
Haecklstr. 10 810472

Heidelberg

Restaurants
College Restaurant
Theaterstr.
Kosher meals available (by arrangement & in advance) Mon.-Fri at college restaurant, 100 yards from college.

Herford

Community Organisations
Community Centre
Keplerweg 11   (52) 212039

Hof/Saale

Community Organisations
Community Centre
An Wiesengrund 20   (92) 815-3249

Ichenhausen

Museums
Museum of Jewish History

Located in the fine baroque synagogue, not far from Ulm.

Ingenheim

Tourist Sites
Klingenerstr. 20
16th century cemetery can be visited. Key obtained from Klingenerstr. 20

Kaiserslautern

Community Organisations
Community Centre
Basteigasse 4   (63) 169720

Karlsruhe

Community Organisations
Community Centre
Knielinger Allee 11   (72) 172035

Kassel

Community Organisations
Community Centre
Bremer Str. 9   (56) 112960

Konstanz

Community Organisations
Community Centre
Sigismundstr. 19   (75) 312-3077

Krefeld

Community Organisations
Community Centre
Wiedstr. 17b   (21) 512-0648

Landau

Synagogues
Frank-Loebsche Haus, Kaufhausgasse 9

Leipzig

Community Organisations
Community Centre
Lahrstr. 10   (341) 291028

Lübeck

Synagogues
Synagogue & Community Centre
St Annen Str. 11 23552   (451) 798-2182
                    Fax: (451) 0451-798-2182
Supervised through the Hamburg community.

Magdeburg

Community Organisations
Community Centre
Graperstr. 1a   (391) 52665

Mainz

Community Organisations
Community Centre
Forsterstr. 2   (6131) 613990

Tourist Sites
Untere Zahlbacherstr. 11
The key to the 12th century Jewish cemetery can be obtained at the 'new' Jewish cemetery.

Mannheim

Community Organisations
Community Centre
                                (621) 153974

Marburg/Lahn

Community Organisations
Community Centre
Unterer Eichweg 17   (642) 132881

Minden

Community Organisations
Community Centre
Kampstr. 6   (57) 123437

Mönchengladbach

Synagogues
Community Centre
Albertusstr. 54 41363   (216) 123879
                Fax: (216) 114639

Mülheim/Ruhr-Oberhausen

Community Organisations
Community Centre
Kampstr. 7   (20) 835191

Munich

Community Organisations
Community Centre
Reichenbachstr. 27   (89) 271-2774; 271-8298

Museums
Judisches Museum Munchen
Maximilian Str. 36

Restaurants
Community Centre
                (89) 201-4565
Run by the community centre at
Reichenbachstrasse. Hours: 12pm – 2.30pm;
6pm – 9pm. Shabbat meals must be ordered
by Friday noon. Closed Sunday; August.

Synagogues
Reichenbachstr. 27
Mikva on premises.
Reichenbachstr. 27
Schulstrasse 30
Fri. evenings and Sabbath mornings only.
Possartstr. 15
Mikva on premises.
Schwabing Synagogue
Georgenstr. 71
Fri. evenings and Sabbath mornings only.

Münster

Community Organisations
Community Centre
Klosterstr. 8-9   (25) 144909

Neustadt/Rheinpfalz

Community Organisations
Community Centre
Ludwigstr. 20   (63) 212652

Nuremberg

Community Organisations
Community Centre
Johann-Priem-Str. 20   (91) 156250
For the Jewish Aged.

Odenbach

Tourist Sites
                (67) 532745
There is a historic synagogue with baroque
paintings in this small village near Bad
Kreuznach.

Offenbach

Community Organisations
Community Centre
Kaiserstr. 109   (69) 069-814874

Kashrut Information
Seligenstadter Strasse 153a   (69) 069-892198
                Fax: (69) 898396

Osnabrück

Community Organisations
Community Centre
In der Barlage 41 49078   (54) 148420
                Fax: (54) 143-4701

Paderborn

Community Organisations
Community Centre
Pipinstr. 32   (52) 512-2596

Potsdam

Community Organisations
Potsdam Community Centre
Heinrich-Mann-Allee 103 Haus 16
                (331) 872018

Regensberg

Community Organisations
Community Centre
Am Brixener Hof 2   (94) 157093; 21819

Rülzheim

Tourist Sites

The key to the early 19th century synagogue in
this village near Karlsruhe is obtainable from
the town hall.

Saarbrücken

Community Organisations
Community Centre
Lortzing Str. 8 66111   (68) 135152

Synagogues
Synagogengemeinde Saar
Postfach 102838 66028

Schwerin/Mecklenburg

Community Organisations
Judische Gemeinde zu Schwerin
Schlachterstr. 3-5   (38) 555-07345

Speyer

Tourist Sites
This town contains the oldest (11th c.) mikva in Germany, Judenbadgasse. To visit it, obtain the key from the desk at the Hotel Trutzpfuff, in Webergasse, just around the corner, or contact Prof. Stein at the Historical Museum. There are some early 19th c. village synagogues in the wine-growing region of the Palatinate.

Straubing

Community Organisations
Community Centre
Wittelsbacherstr. 2 94315   (94) 211387

Stuttgart

Religious Organisations
Israelitische Religionsgemeinschaft Wurttembergs
Hospitalstr. 36 70174   (711) 228360
         Fax: (711) 2283618

Restaurants
Community Centre

Rabbiner Konferenz of German Rabbis at same address.

Sulzburg

Tourist Sites

There is a beautifully restored early 19th c. synagogue here, some 20 miles from Freiburg. Keys obtainable from Mayor's office.

Trier

Community Organisations
Community Centre
Kaiserstr. 25   (65) 140530; 33295

Wachenheim

Tourist Sites
A large 16th c. cemetery. Key available from the Town Hall. First records of registration of Jews in the year 831.

Wiesbaden

Restaurants
Communal Offices
Friedrichstr. 33   (6121) 301870
Inquiries regarding kosher meals.

Synagogues
Friedrichstr. 33   (6121) 301870; 301282

Worms

Tourist Sites
The original Rashi Synagogue here, built in the 11th c. and the oldest Jewish place of worship in Europe, was destroyed by the Nazis in 1938. After the Second World War it was reconstructed and was reconsecrated in 1961. The building also contains a 12th c. mikva and a Jewish museum. There is also an ancient Jewish cemetery.

Wuppertal

Community Organisations
Community Centre
Friedrich-Ebert-Str. 73   (202) 300233

Würzburg

Mikvaot
Community Centre
Valentin-Becker-Str. 11 97072   (93) 151190
         Fax: (93) 118184
Appointments to be made.

Museums
The Synagogue and Museum of Jewish Culture
6 Muhlgasse
Recently restored.

Restaurants
Community Centre
Valentin-Becker-Str. 11 97072   (93) 151190
Fax: (93) 118184
Also guest rooms for tourists available.

Synagogues
Community Centre
Valentin-Becker-Str. 11 97072   (93) 151190
Fax: (93) 118184

Tourist Sites

There are old Jewish cemeteries in Wurzburg, Heidingsfeld and Hochberg.

Gibraltar

The first Jewish people in Gibraltar were Sephardi, who had crossed over the border from Spain before the Inquisition began in the fourteenth century. Many more followed in the ensuing centuries. When Britain took possession, Jews were banned, but later they were allowed in as traders and finally, in 1749, they were granted full permission to live there. The community began to flourish and the Jewish population, which now also included many North African Jews rose to 2,000.

At the end of the Second World War, some of the community returned after being evacuated to Britain. There are now fairly good Jewish facilities, namely four synagogues and newsletters.

GMT + 1 hour
Country calling code (350)

Total Population 28,000
Jewish Population 500

Bakeries
J. Amar, 47 Line Wall Road   73516

Butcher and Deli
Ambrosia Edery, 26 John Mackintosh Sqaure
75168
Fax: 42529

Community Organisations
Managing Board of Jewish Community
10 Bomb House Lane   72606
Fax: 40487

Contact Information
Solomon Levy J.P.
3 Convent Place, PO Box 190   77789; 42818
Fax: 42527
The president of the Jewish community, he is happy to provide information for Jewish travellers.

Cultural Organisations
Jewish Social & Cultural Club
7 Bomb House Lane   79636
Email: asuissa@gibnet.gi
Mailing address: Avner Suissa, 20 Lime Tree Lodge, Montagu Gardens, Gibraltar.

Delicatessens
Uncle Sam's Deli
62 Irish Town   51236; 51226
Fax: 42516
Email: dabamick@gibnet.gi.com
Provides kosher groceries and wine. Catering and takeaway service. Full Kosher service, glatt. Fully licensed.

Groceries
M. I. Abudarham
32 Cornwall's Lane   78506

Kashrut Information
There are no kosher hotels in Gibraltar, but the White's Hotel and Rock Hotel will provide vegetarian or fish diets. The Rock Hotel will provide kosher food if the parties consist of more than ten people.

Mikvaot
12 Bomb House Lane   77658
Fax: 72359

Restaurants
Jewish Club
Open daily from 10 am to 11 pm, except Shabbat, but arrangements can be made with this restaurant owner for Shabbat meals.
Leanse Restaurant
7 Bomb House Lane   41751

Synagogues
Abudarham
20 Parliament Lane   78506
Etz Hayim
Irish Town 75955
Nefusot Yehuda
65 Line Wall Road   73037
Shaar Hashamayim
19 Engineer Lane   78069

Greece

After the Hellenistic occupation of Israel (the Jewish revolt during this occupation is commemorated in the festival of Hanukah), some Jews were led into slavery in Greece, beginning the first recorded Jewish presence in the country. The next significant Jewish immigration occurred after the Inquisition, when many Spanish Jews moved to Salonika, which was a flourishing Jewish centre until the German occupation in the Second World War.

By the early 1940s, the Jewish population had grown to over 70,000, with 45,000 living in Salonika. With typical thoroughness, the Nazis deported not only the Jews from the Greek mainland, but also many communities from the Greek islands, including Crete. A local rabbi was a key member of the Greek resistance in the north of the country, and many local Christians did protect their Jewish neighbours in Athens. After the war, many of the survivors emigrated to Israel.

Today, there are eight Sephardi synagogues in Greece and, in Athens, a community centre and there is a Jewish museum. There are Jewish publications and a library in the community centre. In Aegina, Corfu and other Greek islands, ancient synagogues may be visited.

GMT + 2 hours	Total Population 10,490,000
Country calling code (30)	Jewish Population 5,000

Athens

The Jewish Museum in the city details the rise and fall of Greek Jewry.

Embassy
Embassy of Israel
Marathonodromou Street 1, Paleo Psychico,
POB 65140 15452   (1) 671-9530

Museums
36 Amalias Avenue   (1) 323-1577
Open 9am to 1pm Sun to Fri.

Representative Organisations
Central Board of the Jewish Communities of Greece
36 Voulis Street GR 105 57   (1) 324-4315-8
Fax: (1) 331-3852
Email: hhkis@netor.gr

Restaurants
Jewish Community Centre
8 Melidoni Street 10553   (1) 32-52875
Fax: (1) 32-20761
Kosher meals for groups can be organised via the Jewish Community Centre. The only 'kosher' restaurant in Athens.

Synagogues
Sephardi
Beth Shalom
5 Odos Melidoni   (1) 325-2773; 2823; 2875

Chalkis

Community Organisations
Community Centre
46 Kriezotou Street 34100   (221) 27297
Fax: (221) 76700

Kashrut Information
Community Centre
(221) 27297
Fax: (221) 76700

Synagogues
Kotsou Street
This synagogue has been rebuilt and renewed many times on its original foundations. tombstone inscriptions in the cemetery go back more than fifteen centuries.

Corfu

Community Organisations

Community Centre
5 Riz. Voulefton St. 49100   (661) 30591
Fax: (661) 31898

Hotels

King Alkinos Hotel
(661) 39300

Tourist Sites

Velissariou St.   (661) 38802
There was an ancient synagogue and cemetery here, destroyed by the Nazis.

Joannina

Tourist Sites

18 Josef Eliyia St. 45221   (651) 25195

Larissa

Synagogues

Community Centre
29 Kentavron St.

Rhodes

Tourist Sites

1 Simmiou St.   (241) 29406
The synagogue built in 1731, is in the old Jewish district. Visitors desiring to see around it should contact the caretaker, Lucia Sulan.

Salonika

Cultural Organisations

The Israelite Fraternity House
24 Vassileos Irakliou St.
Thessaloniki   (31) 221030

Yad le Zikaron
24 Vassileos Irakliou St.
Thessaloniki   (31) 275701

Libraries

The Centre for Historical Studies of Salonika Jews
24 Vassileos Irakliou St.
Thessaloniki   (31) 223231
Fax: (31) 229069

Synagogues

35 Sigrou
Thessaloniki 54630   (31) 031-524968

Trikkala

Synagogues

Odos Diacou
Kondili Philippou   25834

Verria

Synagogues

Situated in the ancient Jewish quarter.

Volos

Community Organisations

Community Centre
20 Pavlou Mela St.   (421) 25640
Community Centre
21b Vassani St. 38333   (421) 23079

Kashrut Information

20 Parodos Kondulaki
Small Jewish communities are to be found in Cavala & Carditsa. In Hania, the former capital of the island of Crete, there is an old synagogue in the former Jewish quarter, at the aforementioned addresses.

Guatemala

Conversos (Marranos) were the first recorded Jews in the contry, but, a few centuries later, the next Jewish immigration occurred with the arrival of German Jews in 1848. Later, some east European Jews arrived, but Guatemala was not keen to accept refugees from Nazism, and as a result passed some laws which, although not mentioning Jews directly, were aimed against Jewish refugees.

Even though these laws were in place, by 1939 there were 800 Jews in Guatemala. After the war an Ashkenazi community centre was built in 1965, but despite accepting some Jewish Cuban refugees, the community is shrinking due to assimilation and intermarriage.

There is a central Jewish organisation, the Consejo Central. Most Jews live in Guatemala City, and others in Quetzaltenango and San Marcos. WIZO and B'nai B'rith are both represented, and there is a Jewish school and kindergarten.

GMT – 6 hours

Country calling code (502)

Total Population 10,930,000

Jewish Population 1,200

Emergency Telephone (Police – 110) (Fire – 110) (Ambulance – 125)

Guatemala City

Embassy
Embassy of Israel
13 Av. 14-07, Zona 10   (2) 371305

Synagogues

Sephardi

Maguen David
7a Av. 3-80, Zona 2   (2) 232-0932

Haiti

Christopher Columbus brought the first Jew to Haiti – his interpreter, Luis de Torres, a Converso who had been baptised before the voyage. Thereafter, more settled, but the community was destroyed in an anti-European revolt in 1804. A hundred or so years later, Jews from the Middle East and some refugees from the Nazis settled in Haiti but many subsequently emigrated to Israel.

The remaining community has benefited from the help of the Israeli embassy, and services are held in the embassy or at a private address. There is no central Jewish organisation, and the community is too small to support other Jewish facilities.

GMT – 5 hours	Total Population 7,259,000
Country calling code (509)	Jewish Population Under 100

Port au Prince
Contact Information
Religious services are held at the home of the
Honorary Consul, Mr Gilbert Bigio.

Honduras

During the Spanish colonial period, some Conversos did live in Honduras, but it was only in the nineteenth century that any significant Jewish immigration occurred. In the early twentieth century, refugees from Nazism followed a handful of immigrants from eastern Europe. Honduras was one of the small number of countries to aid refugees from Nazism, and many Jews owe their lives to the help of Honduran Consulates which issued visas in wartime Europe.

Tegucigalpa (the capital) contains the largest Jewish population, but the only synagogue in the country is in San Pedro Sula (services are held in private homes in Tegucigalpa). There is also a Sunday school and WIZO branch.

GMT – 6 hours	Total Population 5,820,000
Country calling code (504)	Jewish Population Under 100

San Pedro Sula
Contact Information
530157
Services Friday and Shabbat at synagogue and
community centre.

Tegucigalpa
Contact Information
315908
Services usually held in private homes. Contact
secretary at above number.

Embassy
Israel Embassy
Palmira Building, 5th Floor   324232; 325176

Hungary

There were Jews living in Hungary in Roman times, even before the arrival of the Magyars (ancestors of the present-day Hungarians). The Jews suffered during the Middle Ages, when there was some anti-semitism, but conditions improved under Austro-Hungarian rule, and Judaism was recognised as being on a legal par with Christianity in 1896.

Hugary lost a considerable amount of territory after the First World War, and as a result many of its original Jewish communities (such as Szatmar) found themselves within other countries. Anti-semitism reached a peak in March 1944, when, during German occupation, most rural Jewish communities began to be transported to Auschwitz. Many of those who were deported survived, as Auschwitz was liberated later in 1944. The Budapest ghetto was liberated (largely intact) by the Red Army in January 1945.

Thus, after the war, Hungary had the largest Jewish community in central Europe. Inevitably, the community dwindled through emigration (especially after the 1956 uprising) and assimilation. Communism in Hungary was far more lenient than in other Warsaw Pact countries, and synagogues were allowed to operate. Since 1989, religious interest has increased, and the government has recently renovated the Dohany Synagogue, the second biggest synagogue in the world. The Jewish population is still the largest in the region, although most are not religious (save a tiny minority in the seventh district of Budapest).

GMT + 1 hour	Total Population 10,050,000
Country calling code (36)	Jewish Population 70,000
Emergency Telephone (Police – 107) (Fire – 105) (Ambulance – 104)	

Budapest

Bakeries
Kacinczy utca 28
Opening hours and availability are apparently variable.
Dob utca 20

Dairies
The Orthodox Central Synagogue
VII, Kazinczy utca 27
Kosher milk and cheese are available here three mornings a week

Embassy
Embassy of Israel
Fullank Utca 8, II 1026

Groceries
Koser Bott, Nyar utcal   (1) 322-9276
Osem products, bread etc.

The Orthodox Central Synagogue
VII, Kazinczy utca 27
Kosher milk and cheese are available here three mornings a week.

Hotels
King's Hotel
Niagy Dofar 27, Budapest VII 1074
                              (1) 267-9324
                         Fax: (1) 267-9324
Strictly kosher hotel and restaurant.

Media

Newspapers
Uj Elet (New Life)
Central Board Hotel

Mikvaot
VII Kazinczy utca 16

Museums

Hungarian Jewish Museum and Archives
Dohany u.2 1077   (1) 342-8949
Email: bpjewmus@mail.c3.hu
Web site: www.c3.hu/~bpjewmus

Organisations

Orthodox

Central Board of the Federation of Jewish Communities in Hungary
VII, Sip utca 12   (1) 342-1355
Fax: (1) 342-1790
Email: bzsh@mail.matav.hu

Conservative

The Central Rabbinical Council
VII, Sip utca 12   (1) 142-1180
Rabbi Schweitzer is Chief Rabbi of Hungary and Director of the Rabbinical Seminary.

Restaurants

Central Kitchen & Food Distribution
IX, Pava utca 9-11
Hannah, VII Dob Utca 35   (1) 142-1072
Hours: 11:30 am to 4 pm on weekdays. Cater meals paid in advance for Shabbat. Winter hours may vary.

Synagogue

Dohany Street Synagogue
VII Dohany Utca 4-6
Built in 1859, it is the largest in Europe and the second largest in the world. In its grounds lie buried the Hungarian Jewish victims of the Nazis. There is also a commemorative plaque to Hanna Senesh, the Jewish parachutist who was captured and tortured before being killed by the Nazis.

Heroes Synagogue
VII Wesselenyi utca 5

Orthodox

The Orthodox Central Synagogue
VII, Kazinczy utca 27   (1) 132-4331

Tourist information

Jewish Information Service
      (1) 166-5165
Fax: (1) 166-5165

Tours of Jewish Interest

Chosen Tours
      (1) 185-9499
Fax: (1) 166-5165
Tours of Jewish sites are provided by Chosen Tours by telephone arrangement.

Sopron

Museums

The Old Synagogue Museum
Uj utca 22-24 H-9400   (99) 311327
Fax: (99) 311347
Email: smuzeum@mail.c3.hu
A department of the Sopron Museum. Medieval Synagogue restored as a museum in 1976. Open from 1 May to 1 October, daily between 9am and 5pm. Closed Tuesdays.

Synagogues

Orthodox

Jewish Orthodox
Tomolom utca 22 H-9400   (99) 313558

Tourist Sites

Uj utca 11
A second medieval Synagogue which formerly housed the Museum is undergoing restoration. The ruins of the 1891 synagogue, out of use since 1956, can be seen at Pap-ret H-9400.

The Neologue Cemetery
Dating from the 19th c. There is a memorial wall dedicated to the 1600 local victims of the Holocaust.

India

The Jewish population of India can be divided into three components: the Cochin Jews, the Bene Israel and the Baghdadi Jews. The Cochin Jews are based in the south of India in Kerala. This community can be further divided into Black (believing themselves to be the original settlers arriving during the first century) and White (of European or Middle Eastern origin) Jews. Most of the community has emigrated, but there is still a synagogue in Cochin which is a major tourist attraction. The Bene Israel believe they are descended from Jewish survivors of a ship wrecked on its voyage from ancient Israel. They follow not only certain Jewish practices, such as kosher food and shabbat, but also adhere to certain Muslim and Hindu beliefs. In the eighteenth century, they settled in Bombay and now form the largest group of Indian Jews. Baghdadi Jews – immigrants from Iraq and the other Middle Eastern countries – arrived in India in the late eighteenth century, and followed British Colonial rather than local custom. Many emigrated to Israel in the 1950s and 1960s.

There is a central Council of Indian Jewry, based in Mumbai, where most of the Indian Jews live. Kosher food is available, and there are three Jewish schools in the city.

GMT + 5.5 hours	Total Population 944,580,000
Country calling code (91)	Jewish Population 5,000

Ahmedabad

Khamasa

Synagogues
Magen Abraham
Bukhara Mohalla, opp. Parsi Agiari 380001
(79) 535-5224

Calcutta

Representative Organisations
Jewish Association of Calcutta
1&2 Old Court House Corner   (33) 224861
General inquiries to this telephone number.

Synagogues
Bethel Synagogue
26/1 Pollack Street
Magen David Synagogue
109a Peplabi Rash, Bihari Bose Road,1,
(formerly Canning Street)
Neveh Shalome Synagogue
9 Jackson Lane, 1

Kochi *(formerly Cochin)*

Contact Information
Inquiries, Princess Street, Fort
(484) 24228; 24988

Synagogues
Chennamangalam
Jew Street, Chennamangalam
Built in 1614 & restored in 1916, this synagogue has been declared a historical monument by the Government of India. A few yards away is a small concrete pillar into which is inset the tombstone of Sara Bat-Israel, dated 5336 (1576).
Paradesi, Jew Town, Mattancherry 2
The only Cochin synagogue that is still functioning. Built 1568.

Mumbai *(formerly Bombay)*

Mumbai is home to the majority of Indian Jews. There are three Jewish schools, and the Council of Indian Jewry is in the city. Thane, some 22 miles away, is where much of the community lives. The synagogue on Curzon Street is a famous Jewish attraction.

Bakeries
ORT India
68 Worli Hill Estate, PO Box 6571 400018
(22) 496-2350; 8423
Fax: (22) 364-7308
Email: jhirad@giasbm01.vsnl.net.in
Supervision: www.ort.org.
The Jewish Education & Resource Centre
provides Kosher food from its Bakery and
Kitchen to all travellers who require the same.

Embassy
Israel Consulate
50 Kailash, G. Deshmukh Marg, 26
(22) 386-2793

Kashrut Information
Pearl Farm
A/1 Ground Floor, Sulabha, Dhobi Alley,
Maharashtra 400601
Arrangements for the provision of kosher food
can be addressed to this address.

Synagogues
Beth El Synagogue
Rewdanda, Allibag Tehsil, Raigad
Beth El Synagogue
Mirchi Galli, Mahatma Gandhi Road, Panvel
410206
Beth Ha-Elohim Syn
Penn
Etz Haeem Prayer Hall
2nd Lane, Umerkhadi 400009   (22) 377-0193
Gate of Mercy (Shaar Harahamim)
254 Samuel Street, Nr Masjid Railway Station
400003   (22) 345-2991
This is the oldest Bene Israel synagogue in
India, established in 1796 and known as the
Samaji Hasaji Synagogue or Juni Masjid until
1896 when its name was changed to Shaar
Harahamim.
Hessed-El Synagogue
Poynad, Alibag Tehsil
Knesseth Eliahu Synagogue
Forbes Street, Fort 400001   (22) 283-1502
Kurla Bene Israel Prayer Hall
275 S. G. Barve Road (C.S.T. Road), Kurla
400070   (22) 514-5014
Magen Aboth Synagogue
Alibag
Magen David Synagogue
opp. Richardson & Cruddas, Byculla 400008
Magen Hassidim Synagogue
8 Mohammaed Shahid Marg, (formerly
Moreland Road), Agripada 400011
(22) 309-2493

Rodef Shalom Synagogue
Sussex Road, Byculla 400027
Shaar Hashamaim Synagogue
Tembi Naka, opp. Civil Hospital, Thane 400601
(22) 853-4817
Shaare Rason Synagogue
90 Tantanpura Street, 3rd Road, Don Tad,
Israel Mohalla, Khadak 400009
Shahar Hatephilla Synagogue
Mhasla
Tifereth Israel Synagogue
92 K. K. Marg, Jacob Circle 400011
(22) 305-3713

Tour Agents
Tov Tours & Travels (India)
96 Penso Villa, 1st Floor, Dadar 400028
(22) 022-445-0134
Fax: (22) 022-437-1700
Tours of Jewish India

Tours of Jewish Interest
ORT India
68 Worli Hill Estate, PO Box 6571 400018
(22) 496-2350; 8423
Fax: (22) 364-7308
Email: jhirad@giasbm01.vsnl.net.in
Supervision: www.ort.org.
The Travel and Tourism Department arranges
tours in Mumbai & Raighad District.

New Delhi

Synagogues
Judah Hyam Synagogue
A/7 Nirman Vihar, Patparganj 110092
(11) 224-3136
The Judah Hyam Annexe houses a library and
centre for Jewish & inter-faith studies.
Judah Hyam Synagogue
2 Humayun Road 110003   (11) 463-5500

Pune *(formerly Poona)*

Synagogues
Ohel David Synagogue
Poona Camp (Cantonment) 411001
Succath Shelomo
93 Rasta Peth 411011
Inquiries to Hon. Sec. 247/1 Rasta Peth, Trupti
Apt., Pune 411011 or Dr S. B. David 9 Bund
Garden Road, Pune 411001

Iran

Iran, formerly known as Persia, has an ancient connection with Jews. The first Jewish communities in Persia date from First Temple times. King Cyrus, the Persian king who conquered Babylon, allowed the Jews to return to Israel from their exile. Not all returned, however, and some settled in Persia. The Persian community grew over time, suffering oppression after the Islamic conversion in 642.

However, the 1979 revolution quashed the hope for a more tolerant Iran, and many thousands of Jews decided to emigrate. Kosher food is difficult to obtain and is expensive. The tombs of Queen Esther and Mordechai (from the Purim story) are in Hamadan, south-west of the capital Tehran.

GMT + 3.5 hours	Total Population 69,975,000
Country calling code (98)	Jewish Population 25,000

Isfahan
Synagogues
Shah Abass Street

Tehran
Synagogues
Haim, Gavamossaltaneh Street
Meshedi, Kakh Shomali Avenue, opp.
Abrishami School
The Iraqi, Anatole France Street

Tourist Sites
Jewish Quarter of Tehran, Mahalleh, off Sirus Avenue

Irish Republic

The earliest Irish Jews (a small community) were expelled in 1290, along with the Jews from the rest of the British Isles. The community slowly grew again after the Jews were allowed to return and a few Marranos settled in Dublin. There was a strong community however and only in 1822 did a significant influx of Jews occur when immigrants came from England and eastern Europe.

Immigration continued and large numbers arrived from the Russian Empire after 1881. Some settled in Ireland intentionally but others believed that they had landed in America, deceived by their boat captains. In 1901, the community was 3,800 strong. The highest figure for the Jewish population of Ireland has been estimated at 8,000.

Robert Briscoe (1894-1969) who played an important role in the struggle for Irish independence was twice Lord Mayor of Dublin.

GMT + 0 hours

Country calling code (353)

Emergency Telephone (Police, Fire and Ambulance – 999 or 112)

Total Population 3,555,000

Jewish Population 1,300

Cork

Synagogues
10 South Terrace   (21) 870413
Services: Sabbath morning 10.30am and all Holy-days

Dublin

Bakeries
Deli Boutique
Corner of Orwell Road and Rathger Road,
Rathgar 6   (1) 496 7612

Butchers
B. Erlich, 35 Lower Clanbrassil Street 8
                                         (1) 454-2252
                                   Fax: (1) 490-6609
Supervision: Board of Shechita.

Embassy
Embassy of Israel
Carrisbrook House
122 Pembroke Road, Ballsbridge, Ballsbridge 4

Mikvaot
Adelaide Road 2   (1) 490-5348

Museums
Irish Jewish Museum
3-4 Walworth Road 8   (1) 453-1797
Phone for hours of opening.

Religious Organisations
Board of Shechita
1 Zion Road 6   (1) 492-3751
The Chief Rabbinate of Ireland
Herzog House, 1 Zion Road 6   (1) 492-3751
                                   Fax: (1) 492-4680

Synagogues
Dublin Hebrew Congregation
37 Adelaide Road 2   (1) 660-5279
Machzikei Hadass
77 Terenure Road North, Rathfarnham Road
                              (1) 490-8413 or 490-6130
Terenure Hebrew Congregation
Rathfarnham Road, Terenure, Terenure 6
The Jewish Home
Denmark Hill, Leinster Road West, Rathmines 6
                                         (1) 497-6258
                                   Fax: (1) 497-2018
Services are held Friday evening at start of Sabbath and Sabbath morning.

Progressive
7 Leicester Avenue, Rathgar, Po Box 3059 6
                                         (1) 490-7605
Services are held on Friday evening at 8.15pm, first Sabbath morning in the month and Sabbath morning at 10.30am

Israel

Some General Information

The Ministry of Tourism publishes a *Best of Israel Guide* detailing shops participating in the VAT refund scheme and recommended restaurants; and *Israel: a visitors' companion*. Available at 6 Wilson St., Tel Aviv. Fax: (03) 556-2339.

A visitor's visa is valid for a stay of three months from the date of arrival.

Student Travel to Israel

Throughout the long summer vacation student flights to Israel are operated by ISSTA (Israel Students' Tourist Association), in conjunction with various other national student travel bureaux. In London these are operated by the National Union of Students Travel Dept., 3 Endsleigh St., WC1. Tel: (0171) 387-2184. ISSTA has offices in Haifa, Jerusalem and Tel Aviv. WST Charters, Priory House, 6 Wright's Lane, W8 6TA, Tel: (0171) 938-4362, also specialises in Israel holidays for students and young people.

Individual arrangements for working on a kibbutz for a minimum period of one month can be made for any time of the year, except July and August, through Hechalutz b'Anglia, the Jewish Agency, 741 High Road, Finchley, N12 OBQ, Tel: (0171) 446-1477. Details of other kibbutz schemes are available from Kibbutz Representatives, 1A Accommodation Road, London NW11 8ED, Tel: (0181) 458-9235. Fax: (0181) 455-7930. Email: enquiries@kibbutz.org.uh. Airlines and most shipping lines offer reductions to students.

Disabled Persons

Friends of Yad Sarah, 43 Hanevi'im Street, Jerusalem, 95141, Tel: (02) 624-4242, Fax: (02) 624-4493 (Reg. Charity No. 294801), a volunteer operated home care organisation, lends free, regular and hi-tech medical rehabilitative equipment and provides a spectrum of home care supportive services. Services available to tourists. Head offices, Jerusalem; 77 branches in Israel.

Health Regulations

There are no vaccination requirements for tourists entering Israel.

Traffic Regulations

A valid International Driving Licence is recognised and preferred, although a valid national driving licence is also accepted, provided it has been issued by a country maintaining diplomatic relations with Israel and recognising an Israeli driving licence.

Traffic travels on the right and overtakes on the left. Drivers coming from the right have priority, unless indicated otherwise on the road signs, which are international. Distances on road signs are always given in kilometres (1 km is equal to 0.621 miles).

The speed limit is 50 km (approx. 31 miles) per hour in built-up areas; 80–90 km (approx. 50–56 miles) per hour on open roads.

Climate

With a long Mediterranean coastline, Israel's climate is similar to that of the French and Italian Rivieras. It may also be compared to that of Florida and southern California. Winters are mild and summers warm.

There are differences not only in temperature, but also in rainfall between the northern and southern regions of the country, as well as between the hills and valleys.

The rainless summer lasts from April to October. The winter season, November to March, is characterised by bright sunshine with occasional rain. During this period, Tiberias on the Sea of Galilee, Sdom on the Dead Sea and Eilat on the Red Sea are all absolutely ideal for winter holidays.

Kashrut

In Israel, kosher means under official rabbinical supervision. Kosher restaurants, hotels and youth hostels are by law required to display a kashrut certificate.

Hotel Rates

Rates vary slightly from resort to resort according to season.

Youth Hostels

There are 31 youth hostels in Israel for students, youth groups and adults, which are supervised by the Israel Youth Hostels Association (a member of the International Youth Hostels Federation). All hostels offer the standard facilities: dormitories, kosher dining rooms. Most hostels also have a guest house section, with double and family rooms, and private facilities. Most are air-conditioned. Attractive travel packages are offered by the Youth Travel Bureau, P.O.B. 6001, Jerusalem, 91060, Tel: (02) 655-8432.

The Israel Youth Hostels Association offices are at Convention Hall Bldg., P.O.B. 1075, Jerusalem, 91060, Tel: (02) 655-8400.

Shopping, Bank & Office Hours

Shops and offices are open from Sunday to Thursday inclusive, from 8am to 1pm and from 4pm to 7pm. Shopping hours on Friday are from 8:30am to 2pm. In Haifa, most shops are closed on Tuesday afternoons. Banks are open Sunday, Tuesday and Thursday from 8:30am to 12:30pm. Branches of most banks are also open from 4 to 6pm. On Monday and Wednesday, they are open from 8:30am to 12:30pm only. On Friday and the eve of holidays and festivals, they open at 8:30am and close at 12 noon. Government offices are generally open to the public Sunday to Thursday inclusive from 8am to 1pm.

Tours

Regular scheduled tours, using air-conditioned coaches, are operated by Egged and other companies on week-days to all parts of the country, starting from Jerusalem, Tel Aviv and Haifa. Egged's intercity toll-free information number is 177-022-5555.

Among the most important sites visited are the Western Wall; the Old City of Jerusalem; Mount Scopus; the Mount of Olives; Rachel's Tomb in Bethlehem; the Tomb of the Patriarchs (Cave of Machpela) in Hebron; Jericho and the Dead Sea. Tours starting in Jerusalem also visit Beersheba, Masada, Sdom, Ein Gedi and the Galilee.

From Tel Aviv, regular tours go south to the Dead Sea and Elat, and north to the Galilee and the Golan Heights, as far as Banias.

From Haifa, regular tours go north to the Galilee, and south to all places visited by tours from Jerusalem and Tel Aviv.

Air tours, operated by Arkia, Israel's internal airline (Sde Dov airport, Tel Aviv), cover all of Israel. In addition a number of smaller companies operate flights and tours to all parts of the country on a charter basis.

It is now possible to fly to Cairo from Israel, as well as to enter Egypt by land. Full details are available from all Government Tourist Information Offices in Israel and Israel Government Tourist Offices abroad.

Information about coach and air tours inside Israel is available from all Government Tourist Information Offices in Israel.

Transport in Israel

Buses are the most popular means of transport, both for urban and inter-urban journeys.

The Israel Railway runs from Naharia in the north to Beersheba in the south, and fares are lower than on the buses. All passenger trains have a buffet car. Taxis are quick and convenient. All urban taxis have meters, which drivers must use.

Certain taxi companies operate a 'Sherut' service in and between the main cities on weekdays, and some independent taxi owners operate similar services seven days a week. Individual seats are sold at fixed prices, with up to seven people sharing a taxi. In some cities and towns, 'Sherut' taxis follow the main bus routes, charging slightly higher fares than the buses.

Israel Embassy (UK) Travel Information:
http://www.israel-embassy.org.uk/london

Electrical Equipment

Israel's electrical current is 220 volts, A.C., single phase, 50 cycles.

Radio

You can hear the news in English four times a day on Israel Radio at 576, 1170 and 1458 kHz: 7 am; 1 pm; 5 pm; 8 pm. BBC World Service at 1322 kHz.: 1400, 1700 and 2015 GMT. Voice of America at 1260 kHz: 5–6 am and 8–9 am, 5 pm, 5:30 pm, 11 pm.

Average Temperature (Celsius)

	Jerusalem	Tel Aviv	Haifa	Tiberias	Eilat
January	12	15	14	17	17
March	16	18	17	17	22
May	22	22	21	26	29
July	23	24	25	30	35
September	23	26	26	30	32
November	16	19	19	21	21

Rainy Days

	Jerusalem	Tel Aviv	Haifa	Tiberias	Eilat
January	12	14	15	12	1
March	8	8	9	5	2
May	2	1	1	1	0
July	0	0	0	0	0
September	0	1	1	0	0
November	7	8	5	5	1

GMT + 2 hours   Total Population 5,800,000
Country calling code (972)   Jewish Population 4,700,000
Emergency Telephone (Police – 100) (Fire – 102) (Ambulance – 101)
Please note this applies to Haifa, Jerusalem and Tel Aviv only.

Tourist Information
JCT – Jewish Culture Tours, CH-8017
Forch/Switzerland   +41 (0) 980 32 71
           Fax: +41 (0) 980 00 99
        Email: RayGuggenheim@compuserve.com

Afula

Restaurants
La Cabania, Ha'atzmaut Square (6) 659-1638
San Remo, 4 Ha'atzmaut Square (6) 652-2458

Akko

One of the most atmospheric locations in Israel is the old city of Akko (Acre). It boasts old and ancient buildings, mighty ramparts and walls, relics of Crusaders days (a city with a complex of subterranean buildings), a small fishing harbour, a bazaar and the muezzin's repetitive call throughout the day and night. The town has a tumultuous history dating back to 1500 BC according to ancient Egyptian texts. It has been besieged repeatedly by Romans, Arabs, Crusaders, Turks, Napoleon and the British. Skipping ahead several hunderd years, in May 1948, the Israeli army marched into old Akko and claimed it as part of Israel. Noteworthy is the Citadel, built on the ruins of the Crusaders' city in 1780. During the British mandate it was used as a high-security prison to imprison Jewish resistance fighters pre-1948. The ideological head of the Irgun, Vladimir Jabotinsky, was held prisoner here. In 1947, the Jewish underground fighters orchestrated a mass breakout from the prison to free a number of senior terrorist leaders who had been condemned to death. One of them was Menachem Begin, a member of the Stern Group, who was later to become president of Israel. Leon Uris described the breakout in his popular novel Exodus. There is a museum called the Israeli Museum of Heroes which is dedicated to this period in Israeli history.

Hotels
Palm Beach
P.O. Box 2192 24101   (4) 981-5815
           Fax: (4) 991-0434
Supervision: Kashrut by local Rabbi.
Hotel, Restaurant and Convention Centre

Kosher
Argaman Motel
Sea Shore   (4) 991-6691/7
Palm Beach Club Hotel
Sea Shore   (4) 981-5815

Museums
Akko Municipal Museum
Old City

Restaurants
Vegetarian
Amirei Hagalil
Akko-Safed Road, nr. Moshav Amirim 20115
        (4) 698-9815/6

Tourist Information
Eljazar Street, opposite Mosque (4) 999-1764

Youth Hostels
Acre Youth Hostel   (4) 991-1982
        Fax: (4) 991-1982

Arad

Arad, the town nearest to the Dead Sea, was founded in 1962 as a base for scientists working in connection with Dead Sea industries and for archaeologists engaged in researching desert and Dead Sea sites. Because there is no pollen in the air and the air is extremely clean, it is suitable for asthmatics. The Margoa Arad Hotel has a clinic catering specifically for them. For visitors Arad makes an ideal base for touring the northern Negev, the Dead Sea and the wild Judean hills. The Visitor Information Center is well informed on local antiquities and desert walks. Round the edge of the town are several Bedouin encampments where, despite the unrelieved aridity of the area, sheep and goats are somehow grazed. The Bedouin, who have very good relations with the locals, find casual work in the town. Tel Arad, which is outside of the modern city, was once the settlement of a Canaanite royal family and today is an interesting archaeological site.

Hotels
Kosher
Arad, 6 Hapalmach Street   (7) 995-7040
Margoa
Mo'av Street, POB 20 89100   (7) 995-1222
        Fax: (7) 995-7778
      Email: margoa@mail.inter.net.il
Supervision: Kushrut: Rabbinat Arad.
Reservations Telephone: Mrs Anne Boussidan 995-1203. Mrs Avigail Cohen 995-1212
Nof Arad, Moav Street   (7) 997-5056/8

Youth Hostels
Blau-Weis (7) 995-7150
This organisation is located in the centre of town.

Ashdod
As with much of this country, Ashkelon and Ashdod changed hands frequently. There were various Crusader vs Muslim battles over the city and the Crusaders basically destroyed the area in the twelfth century. When Ashdod became resettled in this century, it was initially a hostile Arab village, which housed a British army base; during the 1948 War of Independence, the Egyptians advanced this far into Israel before being forced to retreat. Ashdod is mostly a pretty beachfront with a few modest hotels and a small-town feel to it. Ashkelon, which is 9 miles south of Ashdod, also has a pleasant beachfront but is more interesting for tourists because of the Ashkelon National Park, a popular picnic area with remnants from several periods. Crusader ruins lie on the sand. This part of the country is very close to the desert and south and makes a good stopover for day trips.

Hotels

Kosher

Miami, 12 Nordau Street (8) 852-2085

Tourist Information
4 Haim Moshe Shapira Street, Rova Daled
(8) 864-0485/090

Avihail
Museums
Bet Hagedudim (History of Jewish Brigade W.W.I) 988-22212
Fax: 986-21619

B'nei Berak
Hotels
Wiznitz, 16 Damesek Elizier Street
(3) 777-1413

Restaurants
Chapanash, 6 Jabotinsky Street

Bat Yam
Hotels
Kosher

Mediterreanean Towers
2 Hayam Street 59303 (3) 555-3666

Beersheba
The patriarch Abraham settled in Beersheba and purchased a well for the price of seven lambs (be'er sheva means the well of seven and well of the oath). Later, Beersheba was named the southern limit of the land of Israel. Today it is the fifth-largest city in Israel with 120,000 citizens. The town's most interesting feature is the continuing Bedouin presence. The Bedouin market is held every Thursday but it has been affected negatively by tourism and modernization. Permanent Bedouin encampments can be seen south of town.

Hotels
Desert Inn (7) 642-4922

Museums
Man in the Desert Museum
Situated 5 miles north-east of the city.
Negev Museum
Ha'atzmaut Street, cnr of Herzl Street

Restaurants
Bulgarian, 112 Keren Kayemet Street
(7) 623-8504

Bet Shean
Bet Shean is one of the most important excavation sites in Israel (known to archaeologists as Tel al Husn, the Hill of Strength). Twenty-eight layers of civilization have been uncovered at this spot, including Egyptian, Canaanite, Philistine, Jewish, Hellenistic, Scythian, Roman, Arab and Frankish Crusader settlements. The town gained real importance, however, only when the Romans came in the 2nd century BC and made it into the capital of a ten state federation.In the middle of the town, a large site contains remnants of a Roman theatre. There are also remains from a well-preserved Byzantine amphitheatre discovered in late 1986. The amphitheatre seated up to 6,000 spectators. Nearby Mount Gilboa is known throughout the country for its wild flowers. A bit further west is the Bet Alpha synagogue [ruins] which dates back to 518 CE, discovered in 1928. The floor of the synagogue is striking, made up of beautiful mosaics divided into three panels. One depicts religious emblems and the Ark of the Covenant. Another shows a zodiac circle with the astrological signs named in Hebrew, the moon and the stars, four women symbolising the seasons, and a youth riding a horse-drawn chariot. The third represents the sacrifice of Isaac. The work is dated with an

Aramaic inscription: 'This floor was laid down in the year of the reign of Emperor Justinus'. Justinus ruled Palestine from 518 to 527 CE.

Museums
Bet Shean Museum
1 Dalet Street

Caesarea

Caesarea is an exciting archaeological site with city remains from Herodian, Roman, Byzantine and Crusader periods. In 22 BC Herod built a port, amphitheatre, theatre and hippodrome which could hold up to 38,000 spectators. It surpassed the Colosseum's dimensions in Rome. It has been restored and in the summer hosts a festival of music with live concerts. South of Caesarea is the Sdot Yam kibbutz which has a small archeological museum and was home to Hannah Sennesh – a young Haganah fighter who parachuted into Nazi Germany in the attempt to save Jews but was caught, tortured and killed by the Nazis. The kibbutz also maintains an attractive vacation village with a beach for bathing. Caesarea's Dan Golf Hotel possesses the only 18-hole golf course in Israel.

Hotels

Kosher

Dan Caesarea Golf Hotel   (6) 636-2266/268

Restaurants
Caesarean Self Service
Paz Petrol Station   (6) 633-4609

Dan

The ancient city of Dan, standing on the largest of the three sources of the Jordan River, marked the northern border of the Jews' Biblical Land of Israel. It is now located within a beautiful 100-acre nature preserve with various streams and paths.

Museums
Bet Ussishkin

Dead Sea

The Hebrew name for the Dead Sea is Yam Hamelech or Sea of Salt because the water has an extremely high level of salt that makes life impossible in these waters. The sea is 50 miles (80 km) long and up to 11 miles (18 km) wide, covers a surface area of 390 square miles (1,010 sq. km) and is as much as 1,305 feet deep (399 m). It is so salty that the human body floats like a cork and you can sit in the water reading a newspaper. You travel more than 3,200 feet (1000 m) in altitude along this stretch of road so watch out for ears popping. There are various spas and mudbaths around the Dead Sea with signs posted directing visitors where to go. Included is the Neve Zohar, a lakeside spa with sulphur baths, the Ein Gedi and En Boqeq resorts with thermal baths that specialize in the treatment of eczema and other skin diseases and, of course, the various high class hotels clustered together in one part of the Sea.

Hotels
Caesar
The Caesar Resort Hotel on the shores of the Dead Sea introduces the latest in design and comfort with refreshing new style of vacationing and convention facilities. Contact the Caesar Group sales office in Tel Aviv for information,
          (03) 696-8383; Fax: (03) 696-9896.

Degania Alef

Museums
Bet Gordon

Eilat

Israel's southernmost city and its only port on the Red Sea. Eilat is all tourist centre and resort playground, although it is also residential and has both religious and non-religious residents. Founded for its port potential, its main import is mineral oil; in fact it was Egypt's blockade of the Gulf of Eilat on May 22, 1967 that triggered the Six Day War. A deep blue sea, rich with reefs and exotic fish, surrounded by red granite mountains and a climate warm all year round, the Gulf of Aqaba is a tourist haven which is also one of the most fragile ecosystems in the world. Shared by four nations, Israel, Jordan, Egypt and Saudi Arabia, the Gulf is expected to explode with activity in the next few years as the peace process holds the promise of opening a door for both tourism and industry. Eilat feels like a land apart, separated from the rest of Israel not just by the Negev desert but by attitude. It feels more like a beach town, alive with a taste for pleasure and action.With the opening of Eilat's Arava border-crossing with Jordan, Petra makes a superb excursion. The amazing desert capital of the Nabateans, with its temples, treasury, tombs, amphitheatre and monastery all cut out of pink sandstone cliffs, can be visited with an overnight stop. Inclusive trips from Eilat are bookable through all hotels.Trips to the Sinai are also very accessible and cheap.

Hotels

Kosher

Americana Eilat
PO Box 27
North Beach   (7) 633-3777

Caesar
North Beach   (7) 633-3111
     Fax: (7) 633-2624

Carlton Coral Sea
Coral Beach   (7) 633-3555

Dalia
North Beach   (7) 633-4004

Edomit, New Tourist Center   (7) 637-9511
Etzion, Hatmarim Street   (7) 637-4131
Galei Eilat
PO Box 1866
North Beach   (7) 636-7444
     Fax: (7) 633-0627

Lagoona
North Beach   (7) 633-3666

Marina ClubPO Box 4277
North Beach   (7) 633-4191
     Fax: (7) 633-4206

Moriah Plaza Eilat
North Beach   (7) 636-1111
     Fax: (7) 633-4158

Neptune
PO Box 295
North Beach   (7) 636-9369
     Fax: (7) 633-3767

Paradise
N.L.
North Beach 88000   (7) 633-5050

Queen of Sheba
North Beach   (7) 633-4121

Red Rock
PO Box 306
North Beach 88102   (7) 637-3171

Sonesta Suites
N.L., Harava Road   (7) 637-6222
Sport
North Beach   (7) 633-3333

Museums
Museum of Modern Art
Hativat Hanegev Street

Restaurants
Arizona, on Main Road to Tel Aviv
     (7) 667-2710
Bar-B-Que, Hatemarim Blvd.
     (7) 667-3634; 667-5793
Café Royal
King Solomon's Palace Hotel
North Beach   (7) 667-6111
Chinese Restaurant
Shulamit Gardens Hotel
North Beach   (7) 667-7515
Dolphin Baguette
Tourist Centre
Egged, Central Bus Station   (7) 667-5161
El Morocco, Tourist Centre
Golden Lagoon
New Lagoona Hotel
North Beach   (7) 667-2176
Hakerem, Elot Street, cnr. Hatemarim Blvd.
     (7) 667-4577
Halleluyah, Building 9, Tourist Centre
     (7) 667-5752
Metamei Teman
Hatemarim Blvd., Mini Golf   (7) 667-4402
Neve Elat
Hatemarim Blvd.
Neviot, North Shore   (7) 697-1081
Off the Wharf
King Solomon's Palace Hotel
North Beach   (7) 667-9111
Panorama, New Commercial Centre
     (7) 667-1965

Tours of Jewish Interest
Orionia   (7) 667-2902
Pirate   (7) 667-6549

Youth Hostels
Eilat   (7) 637-0088

Ein Harod
Museums
Bet Sturman & Art Institute

Galilee

Hotels

Kosher

Ayelet Hashahar
Katzrin 12200   (6) 693-2611
Ein Gedi
Katzrin   (7) 659-4222/726
Kfar Hittim
N.L.,, DN. Galil Tachton   (6) 679-5921
Rakefet
N.L.,
Gush Segev, Western Galilee   (6) 980-0403

Restaurants
Lev Hagolan
30 Dror. Street Katzrin   (6) 961-6643
Orcha
Commercial Centre Katzrin   (6) 696-1440

Youth Hostels
Karei Deshe (Tabgha)
Yoram   (6) 672-0601
       Fax: (6) 672-4818

11 miles north of Tiberias

Golan Heights

Leisure
Hamat Gader

The Golan Heights rise steeply fron the Sea of Galilee to the Mount Avital plateau. The Hamat Gader were thought to be the nicest spa baths in the whole Roman world, according to the Byzantine empress Eudocia. There are impressive ruins including the extensive Roman and Byzantine spa, which served as a grand bathing resot for six centuries, and an ancient synagogue. Four mineral springs and a freshwater spring emerge at Hamat Gader and so it is used today as a modern bathhouse. There is also an alligator farm where dozens of alligators and crocodiles can be seen lazing around.

Restaurants
Hamat Gader Restaurant
Hamat Gader   (6) 675-1039

Gush Etzion

The Gush Etzion bloc recently celebrated its thirtieth anniversary of Jewish renewal. There are a few historical sites to see here. There is a new Gush Etzion Judaica Center, where a beautiful selection of Judaica is displayed and a Kfar Etzion multi-media programme, an audio-video show that describes the history of the Gush. In addition, 15 minutes from Efrat, the largest settlement in the Gush area with over 2,000 families, is Herodian, King Herod's favorite summer palace with a whole underground tunnel complex built by Bar Kochba to fight the Romans. The tunnels were only discovered recently and are quite fun to walk through although the drive is through Arab villages and should be done either during the holidays like Sukkot and Pesach, when the area is open and well-travelled, or with organised tours.

Museums
Gush Etzion Museum
Kfar Etzion

Restaurants
Cravings Café
Dekel Shopping Center, Efrat   (2) 993-3188
Pizzeria Efrat
Te'ena Shopping Center, Efrat   (2) 993-1630
Trocadero, Judaica Center, Gush Etzion
Junction   (6) 22613

Hadera

Museums
The K'han Museum
74 Hagiborim Street, POB 3232 38131
     (6) 632-2330; 632-4562
     Fax: (6) 634-5776
Hours: Sunday to Thursday, 8 am to 1 pm; Friday, 9 am to 12 pm; Sunday and Tuesday, 4 pm to 6 pm.

Haifa
This city is built on three levels, each with its distinctive and highly special character. Mount Carmel (Har Hacarmel), the top level, which offers some magnificent views, is mostly residential and recreational; Hadar Hacarmel, the central level, is also residential, but it also contains the city's main commercial district. The third level contains the port area, Israel's largest, and another business district. Over recent years the beach front to the south of the port has been attractively refurbished. Like

Jerusalem and Tel Aviv, Haifa has a university, and it is also the home of the Technion, Israel's Institute of Technology. The city's theatre and symphony orchestra are well-known, and its array of unusual museums are worth a visit. They include the National Maritime Museum, the Grain Museum, the Mané Katz Museum and the Illegal Immigration Museum. Haifa is also a tourist resort, with miles of bathing beaches and acres of woodland parks and well-tended gardens. It is also the scene of international flower shows, folklore-festivals, conventions and other events.

Hotels

Kosher

Dan Carmel, 87 Hanassi Avenue (4) 838-6211
Dan Panorama
107 Hanassi Avenue   (4) 835-2222
Dvir, 124 Yefe Nof Street   (4) 838-9131/7
Nesher, 53 Herzl Street   (4) 864-0644
Nof, 101 Hanssi Avenue   (4) 835-4311
Shulamit
15 Kiryat Sefer Street 34676   (4) 834-2811
                            Fax: (4) 825-5206
Yaarot Hacarmel
Mt. Carmel   (4) 822-9144/9

Museums

Bet Pinchas Biological Insititute
124 Hatishbi Street   (4) 837-2886; 837-2390
                            Fax: (4) 837-7019
            Email: biolinst@netvision.net.il
Includes nature museum, zoo and botanical garden. Entrance via Gan Ha'em. Hours: Sunday to Thursday, winter, 8 am to 4 pm, July to August, 8 am to 7 pm; Friday and holiday eves, 8 am to 2 pm; Saturday, 9 am to 5 pm; winter, 9 am to 4 pm.
Dagon Grain Museum
Plumer Square   (4) 866-4221
                            Fax: (4) 866-4211
Free admission. Tours Sunday to Friday, 10:30 am.
Israel Oil Industry Museum
Shemen Factory, 7 Tovim Street,
POB 136 31000   (4) 865-4237
                            Fax: (4) 862-5872
Israel Railways Museum
Haifa Railway Station (east)
Mane Katz Museum
89 Panorama Road   (4) 838-3482
                            Fax: (4) 836-2985
Moshe Shtekelis Museum of Pre-History
124 Hatishbi Street, Entrance from Gan Ha'em

Museum of Clandestine Immigration & Naval Museum
204 Allenby Road 35472   (4) 853-6249
                            Fax: (4) 851-2968
Museum of Haifa
26 Shabbtai Levi Street   (4) 852-3255
Includes museums of Ancient Art, Modern Art and Music & Ethnology. Hours: Sunday, Monday, Wednesday, Thursday, 10 am to 4 pm; Tuesday, 4 pm to 7 pm; Friday and holidays, 10 am to 1 pm; Saturday, 10 am to 2 pm.
Reuben & Edith Hecht Museum
Haifa University 31905   (4) 825-7773
                            Fax: (4) 824-0724
          Email: mushecht@research.haifa.ac.il
Hours: Sunday, Monday, Wednesday, Thursday, 10 am to 4 pm; Tuesday, 10 am to 7 pm; Friday, 10 am to 1 pm; Saturday, 10 am to 2 pm. Admission free.
Technoda, National Museum of Science and Technology
opp. 15 Balfour Street   (4) 867-1372
The National Maritime Museum
198 Allenby Road   (4) 853-6622
                            Fax: (4) 853-9286
Hours: Sunday, Monday, Wednesday, Thursday, 10 am to 4 pm; Tuesday, 4 pm to 7 pm; Friday and holidays, 10 am to 1 pm; Saturday, 10 am to 2 pm.
Tikotin Museum of Japanese Art
89 Hanassi Avenue, Mount Carmel
                                   (4) 838-3554
                            Fax: (4) 837-9824
Hours: Sunday, Monday, Wednesday, Thursday, 10 am to 4 pm; Tuesday, 4 pm to 7 pm; Friday and holiday eves, 10 am to 1 pm; Saturday, 10 am to 2 pm.

Restaurants

Banker's Tavern
2 Habankim Street   (4) 852-8439
Lunch only. Closed Shabbat.
Ben Ezra, 71 Hazayit Street   (4) 884-2273
Egged, Central Bus Station   (4) 851-5221
Self-service
Gan Rimon, 10 Habroshim Street
                                   (4) 838-1392
Lunch only.
Ha'atzmaut, 63 Derech Ha'atzmaut
                                   (4) 852-3829
Hamber Burger
61 Herzl Street   (4) 866-6739
Hamidrachov
10 Nordau Street   (4) 866-2050
Paznon, Hof Carmel   (4) 853-8181

Rondo, Dan Carmel Hotel, 87 Hanassi Blvd.
(4) 838-6211
Technion, Neve Shaanan   (4) 823-3011
Self service. Lunch only.
The Chinese Restaurant of Nof
Nof Hotel, 101 Hanassi Blvd.   (4) 838-8731
The Second Floor
119 Hanassi Blvd.   (4) 838-2020
Tsemed Hemed
Herbert Samuel Square   (4) 824-2205

Dairy

Milky Pinky (Milk Bar)
29 Haneviim Street   (4) 866-4166

Meat

Mac David, 131 Hanassi Boulevard
(4) 838-3684
Mac David, 1 Balfour Street

Tourist Information
106 Sderot Hanassi   (4) 837-4010
What's on in Haifa
(4) 864-0840

Tours of Jewish Interest
(4) 867-4342
Bahai shrine and gardens, Druse villages,
Muchraka, the Moslem village of Kabair, the
Carmelite monastery and Elijah's cave, Weds,
9:30am.   (4) 867-4342
Mt Carmel, Druse villages, Kibbutz Ben Oren
and Ein Hod artists' colony: Suns, Mons, Tues,
Thurs, Sats, 9:30am.

Youth Hostels
Carmel   (4) 853-1944
Fax: (4) 853-2516
Shlomi, Hanita Forest   (4) 980-8975

Hanita

Museums
Tower & Stockade Period Museum

Haon

Holiday Villages
Kibbutz Haon
Jordan Valley   (6) 675-7555/6

Hazorea

Museums
Wilfrid Israel House of Oriental Art

Herzlia

Hotels

Kosher

Dan Accadia
Herzlia on Sea   (9) 959-7070
Fax: (9) 959-7092
Email: danhtls@danhotels.co.il
Holiday Inn
Crown Plaza   (9) 954-4444
Fax: (9) 954-4675
Tadmor, 38 Basel Street   (9) 952-5000
Fax: (9) 957-5124
The Sharon, Herzlia on Sea   (9) 957-5777
Fax: (9) 957-2448

Restaurants
Dona Flor
22 Hagalim Blvd.
Herzlia Pituach   (9) 950-9669

Tadmor Hotel School
38 Basel Street 46660   (9) 957-2321

Tourist Information
English Speaking Residents Association
PO Box 3132 46104   (9) 950-8371
Fax: (9) 954-3781
Email: esra@trendline.co.il

Jaffa

Yaffo or Jaffa, the Arab part of Tel Aviv, in
contrast to Tel Aviv, can look back on 3,000
years of history. It is probably the oldest
working port in the world. Its name is
supposed to date back to Yaphet, the third
son of Noah. Cedar from Lebanon was shipped
here to be used in King Solomon's temple. Its
narrow old streets and well-renovated old
town with art galleries, jewellery shops and
excavations have more picturesque charm than
Tel Aviv. In addition, the spectacular view of
the Tel Aviv skyline and the fresh fish
restaurants make the old harbour a very
worthwhile visit.

Museums
The Antiquities Museum of Tel Aviv-Jaffa
10 Mifratz Shlomo Street, Old Jaffa 68038
(3) 682-5375 Fax: (3) 681-3624
Hours: Sunday, Monday, Tuesday, Thursday,
9am to 2pm; Wednesday, 9am to 6pm;
Saturday, 10am to 2pm.

Tours of Jewish Interest
Tel Aviv-Yafo Tourism Association.
Clock Square, nr. Yefet Street, Ramat Gan
Walk takes 2.5 hours, starting at Clock Square
near Yefet Street, in the centre of Jaffa. Free.

Jerusalem

To sense the mystery of Jerusalem, start with
Mount Scopus just before dawn. Watch the
red ball of a new day's sun ascend the mists
from behind the Mountains of Moab and set
afire the Judean Desert which laps at the city's
skirts. Near sunset, look down again from near
the same vantage point on the city itself, when
the light catches the gold of the Dome of the
Rock, scattering its rays across Jerusalem's
many hills.

But Jerusalem is also a city of people, a
collection of villages separated by faith and
custom. Enter the Old City by Jaffa Gate and
turn right on to Armenian Patriarchate Road,
where you will find the Cathedral of St. James
and an Armenian community living in its own
little world.

By contrast, spend a Friday morning in Mea
Shearim, the walled city of Ultra-Orthodoxy,
where the ghetto way of life is maintained
with fierce pride. Friday all is abustle.
Youngsters scamper out of school in a babble
of Yiddish. Men, young and old, eyes averted
from the passing tourists, hurry to the mikva,
for here males as well as females take the
ritual cleansing bath.

But also in Jerusalem, you must touch
history, not the spurious history of this tomb
or that stone, but the reality, say, of such as
Hezekiah's Tunnel, hewn by the Judean king's
workmen through the rock of Jerusalem nearly
2,700 years ago so that water would be
available in the city in time of war. The tunnel,
still a conduit for water through which intrepid
Jerusalem explorers frequently wade for 600
yards of its winding course, starts close by the
spring of Gihon in the Kidron Valley, on the
edge of the ancient City of King David, southwest of the Old City, with its excavations.

Jerusalem has pavement cafes in the part of
Ben-Yehuda Street which is closed to traffic.
There are also many stalls selling a variety of
foods to be enjoyed as one strolls, and they
are well patronised. There is an enormous
variety of national and ethnic foods available.
The many restaurants offer everything from
kosher Chinese to kosher Argentine.

When night falls, as it does quite early
compared with the slow dusk of the West, it
seems that most of the inhabitants have gone
to bed. Many have, because the day's early
start, despite the traditional afternoon siesta,
dampens any inclination for late nights. But
there is a night-life of sorts.

Accommodation Information
Good Morning Jerusalem
9 Coresh Street 94146 (2) 623-3459
Fax: (2) 625-9330
Email: gmjer@netvision.net.il
Web site: www.accommodation.co.il
Lists rooms and apartments available for
tourists.

Bed & Breakfasts
Kosher
A Little House in the Colony
4/a Lloyd George Street
German Colony 93110 (2) 563-7641
Fax: (2) 563-7645
Email: melonit@netvision.net.il
16 rooms, air-conditioning, Israeli breakfast,
cafeteria, small garden.

Le Sixteen
16 Midbar Sinai Street
Givat Hamivtar 97805 (2) 532-8008
Fax: (2) 581-9159
Email: le16@virtual.co.il or
danan16@netvision.net.il
Web site: www.virtual.co.il/travel/BnB/le16
Member of the Jerusalem Home
Accommodation Association. Can provide
guest studios with kosher dairy kitchenettes.

Contact Information
Jewish Student Information Centre
Ohel Avraham, 1/15 Hameshor'rim Street,
Old City (2) 628-2634
Fax: (2) 628-8338
Email: jseidel@netmedia.net.il
Jewish Student Information Centre
Hebrew University Off-Campus Center
5/4 Etzel Street, French Hill (2) 581-4939
Email: jseidel@netmedia.net.il

Guest Houses

Bet Shmuel
6 Shamma Street 94101
(2) 620-3473; 620-3465
Fax: (2) 620-3467
Single and family guest rooms with a capacity
of 240 beds; conference facilities and banquet
services; restaurant and coffee shop;
international culture and education centre with
an ideal central location.

Holiday Villages

Youth Recreation Centre Holiday Village
Yefei Nof
Jerusalem Forest   (2) 641-6060

Hotels

Kosher

Ariel, 31 Hebron Road   (2) 568-9999
Fax: (2) 673-4066
Caesar, 208 Jaffa Road   (2) 500-5656
Fax: (2) 538-2802
Email: caesarjm@netvision.net.il
Supervision: Jerusalem Rabbinate.
150 comfortably furnished rooms.
Central, 6 Pines Street   (2) 538-4111
Fax: (2) 5381-480
Four Points Paradise Jerusalem
4 Wilnai Street 96110   (2) 655-8888
Fax: (2) 651-2266
Supervision: Jerusalem Rabbinate.
The hotel is located in the prestigious hotel
area at the entrance to the city and is within
walking distance of the Israel Museum and the
Knesset.
Hyatt Regency Jerusalem
32 Lehi Street   (2) 533-1234
Fax: (2) 581-5947
Email: hyattjrs@trendline.co.il
Web site: www.hyattjer.co.il
Jerusalem Gate
43 Yirmiyahu Street   (2) 538-3101
Jerusalem Hilton
Givat Ram   (2) 653-6151
Jerusalem Renaissance
6 Wolfson Street 91033   (2) 652-8111
Jerusalem Tower
23 Hillel Street   (2) 620-9209
King David, 23 King David Street (2) 620-8888
Fax: (2) 620-8880
King Solomon
32 King David Street   (2) 569-5555
Kings, 60 King George Street (2) 620-1201
Fax: (2) 620-1211

Knesset Tower
4 Wolfson Street   (2) 651-1111
Lev Yerushalayim
18 King George Street   (2) 530-0333
Mount Zion, 17 Hebron Road   (2) 568-9555
Fax: (2) 673-1425
Email: hotel@mountzion.co.il
Supervision: Jerusalem Rabbinate.
Palatin, 4 Agripas Street   (2) 623-1141
Radisson Moriah Plaza Jerusalem
39 Keren Hayessod Street 94188 (2) 569-5695
Fax: (2) 623-2411
Supervision: Jerusalem Rabbinate.
Ramat Rachel Hotel 90900   (2) 670-2555
Fax: (2) 673-3155
Email: resv@ramatrachel.co.il
Web site: www.ramatrachel.co.il
The only kibbutz hotel in Jerusalem.
Reich
1 Hagai Street
Bet Hakerem   (2) 652-3121
Ron, 44 Jaffa Road   (2) 622-3122
Fax: (2) 625-0707
Sheraton Jerusalem Plaza
47 King George Street   (2) 629-8683
Fax: (2) 623-1667
Supervision: Jerusalem Rabbinate, Kosher
Lamehadrin.
Sonesta Jerusalem
2 Wolfson Street   (2) 652-8221
Windmill, 3 Mendele Street   (2) 566-3111
Fax: (2) 561-0964
Zion, 10 Dorot Rishonim   (2) 625-9511
Fax: (2) 625-7585
Zion, 4 Luntz Street   (2) 623-2367
Zion, 47 Lieb Jaffe Street   (2) 671-7557

Museums

Ammunition Hill Memorial & Museum,
Ramat Eshkol   (2) 582-8442
Bible Lands Museum
25 Granot Street, POB 4670 91046
(2) 561-1066
Fax: (2) 563-8228
Email: biblelnd@netvision.net.il
The home of one of the most important
collections of ancient artifacts displaying rare
works of art from the dawn of civilisation to
the Byzantine period. Gift shop, special
exhibitions,weekly lectures and concerts.
Hours: Sunday, Monday, Tuesday, Thursday,
9:30 am to 5:30 pm; Wednesday, April to
October, 9:30 am to 9:30 pm, November to
March, 1:30 pm to 9:30 pm; Friday and
holiday eves, 9:30 am to 2 pm; Saturday and
holidays, 11 am to 3 pm. Daily guided tours.

Kosher restaurant.
G.U.Y.'s Gallery
12 Hebron Road 92261 (2) 672-5111
Fax: (2) 672-5166
Judaica, Israeli art, Archaeology
Herzl Museum
Herzl Blvd., Mount Herzl
Isaac Kaplan Old Yishuv Court Museum
6 Or Hachaim Street, POB 1604 91016
(2) 627-6319
Fax: (2) 628-4636
The museum is located in the heart of the
Jewish Quarter in the Old City of Jerusalem in
a sixteenth-century building. It displays
Ashkenazi and Sephardic life styles from the
beginning of the nineteenth century. Hours:
Sunday to Thursday, 9 am to 2 pm.
Israel Museum, Hakirya
  Includes Bezalel National Museum, Samuel
Bronfman Biblical & Archaeological Museum,
Shrine of the Book & the Rockefeller Museum
in East Jerusalem.
L.A. Mayer Museum for Islamic Art
2 Hapalmach Street (2) 566-1291/2
Fax: (2) 561-9802
Museum of Musical Instruments
Rubin Academy of Music, 7 Smolenskin Street
Museum of Natural History
6 Mohilever Street
Museum of the History of Jerusalem
Tower of David, Jaffa Gate (2) 628-3273
Nahon Museum of Italian Jewish Art
27 Hillel Street 94581
(2) 624-1610; 625-3480
Founded in 1981, this museum collects and
preserves objects pertaining to the life of the
Jews in Italy from the Middle Ages to the
present day. The main attraction is the ancient
synagogue of Conegliano Veneto, a township
some 60 km from Venice. Hours: Sunday to
Tuesday, 9 am to 2 pm; Wednesday, 9 am to
5 pm; Thursday, 9 am to 1 pm. For guided
tours contact the numbers above.
S.Y. Agnon's House
16 Klausner Street
Talpiot 93388 (2) 671-6498
Fax: (2) 673-8285
Hours: Sunday to Thursday, 9 am to 1 pm.

Shocken Insititute
6 Balfour Street
**Siebenberg House of Archaeological
Museum**
6 Hagittit Street
Jewish Quarter (2) 628-2341

The Sir Isaac & Lady Wolfson Museum
Hechal Shlomo, 58 King George Street
(2) 624-7908
Fax: (2) 623-1810
Tourjeman Post Museum
1 Hel Hahandassa Street (2) 628-1278
**Yad Vashem, The Holocaust Martyrs' and
Heroes' Remembrance Authority**
Har Hazikaron, PO Box 3477 91034
(2) 675-1611
Fax: (2) 643-3511
Email: info@yad-vashem.org.il

Organisations

Friends of Yad Sarah
43 Hanevi'im Street, 95141 (2) 624-4242
Fax: (2) 624-4493
A volunteer operated home care organisation
for disabled persons incorporating lends free,
regular and hi-tech medical rehabilitive
equipment and providing a spectrum of home
care, supportive services. These services also
being available to tourists. In addition to this
Head Office in Jerusalem, there are 77
branches throughout Israel.
Travelers Aid of Israel
PO Box 2828 (2) 582-0126
Fax: (2) 624-3228
Legal counselling, social and human services,
immigrant assistance, interest free loans,
stranded travelers, medical assistance, crime
victim assistance, homelessness, emergency
assistance.

Religious Organisations

The Young Israel Movement in Israel
20 Strauss Street 91371 (2) 623-1631
Fax: (2) 623-1363

Restaurants

Casa Italiana
6 Yoel Salamon Street
Clafouti, 2 Hasoreg Street (2) 624-4491
Dagrill, 21 King George Street (2) 622-2922
Feferberg's
53 Jaffa Road (2) 625-4841
Ye Olde English Tea Room
68 Jaffa Road (2) 537-6595

Dairy

Alumah, 8 Yavetz Street (2) 625-5014
Supervision: Jerusalem Rabbinate, Kosher
Lamehadrin.
Natural food. Take-away available.
Bagel Nash, 14 Ben-Yehuda Street
(2) 622-5027

Besograyim, 45 Ussishkin Street (2) 624-5353
Dagim Beni, 1 Mesilat Yesharim Street
(2) 622-2403
Daglicatesse
1 Rachel Imenu   (2) 563-2657
La Pasta, 16 Rivlin Street   (2) 622-7687
Mamma Mia
38 King George Street 94262   (2) 624-8080
                          Fax: (2) 623-3336
Supervision: Jerusalem Rabbinate.
Located in the centre of town in an old (1899)
restored building. Air conditioned. All credit
cards accepted. Hours: Sunday to Thursday, 12
pm to midnight, Friday 12 pm to 4 pm;
Saturday, from the end of Shabbat..
Of Course!, Zion Confederation House, Emile
Botta Street   (2) 624-5206
Off The Square
8 Ramban Street
Supervision: Jerusalem Rabbinate, Kosher
Lamehadrin.
Poire et Pomme
The Khan Theatre, 2 Remez Square
                          (2) 671-9602
Primus, 3 Yavetz Street   (2) 624-6565
Rimon, 4 Lunz Street   (2) 622-2772
Theatre Lounge
Jerusalem Theatre, 20 Marcus Street
                          (2) 566-9351
Zeze, 11 Bezalel Street   (2) 623-1761

Meat

Burger Ranch
18 Shlomzion Hamalka Street   (2) 622-2392
Burger Ranch
3 Lunz Street   (2) 622-5935
El Gaucho, 22 Rivlin Street   (2) 622-6665
El Marrakesh
4 King David Street   (2) 622-7577
El Morocco, 43 Yirmiyahu Street, Centre One
                          (2) 500-1670
                          Fax: (2) 538-3496
Supervision: Rabbi Meir Kruyzer.
Marvad Haksamim
16 King George Street
Norman's Steak 'n Burger
27 Emek Refaim Street   (2) 566-6603
                          Fax: (2) 673-1768
                  Email: rmjb@netvision.net.il
                  Web site: www.normans.co.il
Supervision: Jerusalem Rabbinate.
American steakhouse. Reservations
recommended. Easy walking distance from
main hotels. Hours: Sunday to Thursday,
12 pm to 11 pm; Friday, closed; Saturday,
from after Shabbat.

Shaul's Shwarma Centre
14 Ben-Yehuda Street   (2) 622-5027
Shemesh, 21 Ben-Yehuda Street (2) 622-2418
Shipodei Hagefen
74 Agrippas Street   (2) 622-2367
Yemenite Step
12 Yoel Salamon Street   (2) 624-0477
Yo-si Peking
5 Shimon Ben-Shetach Street   (2) 622-6893

Pizzerias

Pizzeria Rimini
15 King George Street   (2) 622-6505
Pizzeria Rimini
43 Jaffa Road   (2) 622-5534
Pizzeria Rimini
7 Paran Street
Ramat Eshkol
Pizzeria Trevi
8 Leib Yaffe Street   (2) 672-4136

Vegetarian

Village Green
1 Bezalel Street   (2) 625-1464
Also catering and takeaway.
Village Green
10 Ben Yehuda Street   (2) 625-2007
                          Fax: (2) 625-7972
Also catering and takeaway.

Synagogues
Great Synagogue
260 King George Street
Yeshurun, 44 King George Street (Ashkenazi)

Tourist Information
ISSTA, 5 Eliashar Street   (2) 622-5258
Ministry of Tourism
24 King George Street   (2) 675-4811
The Israel Youth Hostels Association
Convention Hall Building, P.O.B. 1075 91060
                          (2) 655-8400
**Tourist Coordinators for the Administered
Territories**
Allenby Bridge   Fax: (2) 694-2294
**Tourist Coordinators of the Administered
Territories**   Fax: (2) 624-0571

Tours of Jewish Interest
American P'eylim Student Union
10 Shoarim Street   (2) 653-2131
Free tours of Jewish Quarter and free
accommodation, in the hostel quarters.
Knesset (Parliament)   (2) 654-4111
Sunday & Thursday 8.30 am and 2.30 pm

Society for the Protection of Nature in Israel: Israeli Nature Trails
13 Helen Hamalka Street, PO Box 930
(2) 624-9567

Youth Hostels
Bet Bernstein
1 Keren Hayesod Street   (2) 625-8286
80 rooms.
Davidka, 67 HaNevi'im Street   (2) 538-4555
26 rooms.
Ein Karem   (2) 641-6282
97 rooms. 10 minutes from the Louise
Waterman-Wise Hotel in Bayit Vegan
Jerusalem Forest   (2) 675-2911
140 rooms.
Moreshet Yahadut   (2) 628-8611
Old city. 75 rooms.
The Israel Youth Hostels Association
Convention Hall Building,
POB 1075, 91060   (2) 655-8400
Youth Travel Bureau
POB 6001, 91060   (2) 655-8432
There are 31 youth hostels in Israel for
students, youth groups and adults, which are
supervised by the Israel Youth Hostels
Association (a member of the International
Youth Hostels Federation). All hostels offer the
standard facilities of dormitories, kosher dining
rooms, etc. Most hostels also have a guest
house section, with double and family rooms
and private facilities. Most are air-conditioned.

Katzrin

This is the largest Jewish town (6,000 Jews and
growing) in the Golan and serves as its
administrative capital. The town makes a good
base for exploring the local antiquities. Ancient
Katzrin was a Talmudic city and, today, there
stands a reconstructed synagogue and village
made to resemble life as it was in Talmudic
times. Gamla, which is 10 km southeast of
Katzrin, is known as the Masada of the north.
Some 9,000 Jewish Zealots had set up a town
in Gamla and were eventually besieged by the
Romans in 67 CE. According to Josephus
Flavius, rather than be captured, they, like their
counterparts in Masada, committed suicide.
The ruined city contains the remains of an old
castle and nearby are Gamla Falls, a 51 metre
waterfall.

The Gamla winery is nearby and offers tours.
Other sites in the area are Gilgal Refa'im
(Ghost's Circle), ancient stone circles 156 m in
diameter, and Khasfin, an abandoned Syrian
village built on the ruins of the Jewish town of
Hisfiyya. It was mentioned in Maccabees as
Kaspin and a church dating back to 400 CE has
been found there.

Hotels
Kosher
Ayelet Hashahar
12200   (2) 693-2611
Ein Gedi   (2) 659-4222 or 4726
Gesher Haziv
Western Galilee   (4) 982-5715
Hagoshrim, Ha'on Camping Village,
Sea of Galilee   (4) 675-7555/6
Hagoshrim, Upper Galilee   (4) 695-6231
Kfar Giladi
Upper Galilee   (4) 694-1414/5
                                Fax: (4) 695-1248
Kiriat Anavim
Judea Hills   (4) 534-8999
Ma'ale Hachamisha
Judea Hills   (4) 534-2591

Museums
Golan Archaeological Museum

Restaurants
Lev Hagolan
30 Dror Street   (2) 961-6643
Orcha, Commercial Centre   (2) 696-1440

Kfar Etzion
Museums
Gush Etzion Museum

Kfar Giladi
Museums
Bet Hashomer

Kfar Vitkin
Youth Hostels
Emer Hefer   (9) 866-6032
25 miles north of Tel Aviv.

Kibbutz Hardof
Restaurants
Vegetarian Organic
Vegetarian Restaurant   (4) 950-1104
                                Fax: (4) 986-6835

Kibbutz Yotvata

Leisure
Biblical Wildlife Reserve Hai Bar Arava
The reserve is situated 37 miles north of Eilat.
Biologoists have settled every breed of animal
that is mentioned in the Bible. Animals include
herd of Somalian wild asses, oryx antelope,
ibex, ostriches, desert foxes, lynx, hyenas and
the last desert leopard in the Negev, living out
her days on the preserve. Guided tours start at
9 and 10.30 am, noon and 1.30 pm.

Restaurants

Dairy
Dairy Restaurant (7) 635-7449

Korazim

Holiday Villages
Amnon Bay Recreation Centre (6) 693-4431
Vered Hagalil Guest Farm (6) 693-5785
Fax: (6) 693-4964
Email: vered@veredhagalil.co.il

Lod

Tourist Information
Ministry of Tourism
Ben Gurion International Airport (3) 971-1485

Lohamei Hagetaot

Museums
Ghetto Fighters' House, Holocaust &
Resistance Museum
D.N. Western Gallilee 25220 (4) 995-8080
Fax: (4) 995-8007
Email: simstein@gfh.org.il
Hours: Sunday-Thursday 9.00am-4.00pm.
Friday 9.00am-1.00pm. Saturday and holidays
10.00am-5.00pm. Kosher dining room and
cafeteria

Maagan

Holiday Villages
Maagan Holiday Village
Sea of Galilee (6) 675-3753

Maayan Harod

Youth Hostels
Hankin (6) 658-1660
7 miles east of Afula.

Mahanayim

Tourist Information
Zomet Mahanayim (6) 693-5016

Metula

Hotels

Kosher
Hotel Hamavri (6) 694-0150
Sheleg Halevanon
P.O.B. 13 (6) 694-4015/7

Moshav Shoresh

Hotels
Shoresh Apartment Hotel
Harey Yehuda (2) 533-8338
Fax: (2) 534-0262

Naharia

Naharia is a fairly modern city, founded in
1934 by Jews fleeing from Germany. It lies 20
miles north of Haifa on the coast and boasts
beautiful white beaches. Four miles north of
this city, on the Lebanese border, is Rosh
Hanikra, which has an extensive system of
caves which the sea has washed out of the
soft chalk. There is also a lookout point with
an adjacent restaurant which reveals a
gorgeous panorama of the coast.

Hotels
Astar, 27 Gaaton Blvd. (4) 992-3431
Beit Hava
Shavei Zion 25227 (4) 982-0391
Carlton, 23 Ha'agaaton Blvd (4) 992-2211
Eden, N.L.,, Meyasdim Street (4) 992-3246/7
Frank, 4 Haaliya Street (4) 992-0278
Panorama, 6 Hamaapilim Street (4) 992-0555
Rosenblatt, 59 Weizmann Street (4) 992-0069

Leisure
Rosh Hanikra
Rosh Hanikra is situated 4 miles north of
Naharia, on the Lebanese border, and has an
extensive system of caves which the sea has
washed out of the soft chalk. There is also a
lookout point with an adjacent restaurant
which reveals a gorgeous panarama of the
coast.

Museums
Naharia Municipal Museum
Hagaaton Boulevard

Restaurants
Cafe Tsafon
10 Gaaton Blvd.   (4) 992-2567

Tourist Information
Israel Camping Union
P.O.B. 53   (4) 992-5392

Nazareth

Restaurants
Iberia, Rassco Centre, Nazareth Elite
                                  (6) 655-6314
Nof Nazareth
23 Hacarmel Street, Nazareth Elite
                                  (6) 655-4366

Negev

Making the desert flourish is an old Zionist dream dating back to David Ben-Gurion who tried to push settlement in the south, and who himself went to live on a kibbutz in the Negev after he retired from politics. While it is amazing to see kibbutzim growing produce in the middle of the desert and the pockets of green shock the eye on the drive down south through the arid countryside, it really never became as popular as Ben-Gurion had hoped. Most of landscape is still barren with scorched rock and bare granite mountains surrounded by dry valleys.

Sde Boker (Sede Boqer)
This desert kibbutz was home to Israel's first prime minister David Ben-Gurion and his wife Paula. Every year hundreds of thousands of visitors make their way to his simple wooden hut in the Negev.Entry to the site is free, as Ben-Gurion stipulated in his will. It is open from 8:30 am to 5 pm in the summer (to 4 pm from October to March), Sunday to Thursday. Fridays and holiday eves it is open from 8:30 am to 2 pm and on Shabbat and holidays from 9 am to 2:30 pm.

En Gedi
En Gedi is the largest oasis in this region. Recreational activities include swimming in the Dead Sea, relaxing in the spa, and hiking in the nearby nature reserves that include hikes in Nahal David and Nahal Arugot. The kibbutz which houses the resort was set up in the 1950s by the children of concentration camp survivors. It is now a beautiful landscape with lush florid greenery startling the visitor with its contrast to the stark, barren red desert rock around it.

Masada

Masada's history and the preservation of the site are fascinating and worth a trip even in the scorching heat of the summer, although then it is advised to either walk up at 4 am or take a cable car.About 9 miles south of En Gedi, and rising up vertically from the plain 1,440 feet (440 m) on each side, this mighty mountain top has a significant place in Jewish history, to the extent that Israeli soldiers used to be sworn in saying 'Masada shall not fall again'.

Youth Hostels
Bet Noam
Mitzpeh Ramon   (7) 658-8433
                            Fax: (7) 658-8074

Bet Sara
Ein Gedi   (7) 658-4165
1.5 miles north of Kibbutz Ein Gedi on Dead Sea.
Blau-Weiss
Arad   (7) 995-7150
Centre of town.
Eilat   (7) 637-0088
Hevel Katif: Hadarom   (7) 684-7597
                            Fax: (7) 684-7680
For more detailed information, apply either to the Israel Youth Hostels Assoc. or to the nearest Israel Government Tourist Office.
Isaac H. Taylor
Masada   (7) 658-4349
28 miles from Arad.

Netanya

Holiday Villages

Kosher
Green Beach Holiday Village   (9) 865-6166
                            Fax: (9) 835-0075

Hotels
Arches
4 Remez Street 42271   (9) 860-9860
                            Fax: (9) 860-9866
                  Email: arches-hotel@correy.com
Bagel Nash, 10 Ha'atzmaut Street
                                  (9) 861-6920
Blue Bay
37 Hamelachim Street 42228   (9) 860-3603
                            Fax: (9) 833-7475
Gal Yam, 46 Dizengoff Street (9) 862-5033
Galei Hasharon
42 Ussishkin Street 42273   (9) 882-5125
Galei Zans, 6 Ha'melachim Street
                                  (9) 862-1777
Galil, 18 Nice Blvd.   (9) 862-4455

Ginot Yam, 9 David Hamelech Street
(9) 834-1007
Goldar, 1 Usishkin Street   (9) 833-8188
Supervision: Rabbinate of Netanya.
Grand Yahalom
15 Gad Makhnes Street   (9) 862-4888
Green Beach
PO Box 230   (9) 865-6166
Fax: (9) 835-0075
Hagozal, 95 Herzl Street   (9) 833-5301
Jeremy, N.L., 11 Gad Machnes Street
(9) 862-2651
King Koresh
6 Harav Kook Street   (9) 861-3555
King Solomon
18 Hamaapilim Street   (9) 833-8444
Fax: (9) 861-1397
MacDavid, 7a Ha'atzmaut Street (9) 861-8711
Margoa (new)
9 Gad Makhnes Street   (9) 862-4434
Maxim, 8 King David Street   (9) 862-1062
Metropol Grand
17 Gad Makhnes Street   (9) 862-4777
Milky Way, 6 Herzl Street   (9) 832-4638
Orly, 20 Hamaapilim Street   (9) 833-3091
Palace, N.L., 33 Gad Machnes Street
(9) 862-0222
Fax: (9) 862-0224
Park, 7 David Hamelech Street   (9) 862-3344
Residence, 18 Gad Machnes Street
(9) 862-3777
The Seasons Hotel
1 Nice Boulevard   (9) 860-1555
Fax: (9) 862-3022
Email: seasons@netmedia.net.il
Supervision: Rabbinate of Netanya.
Buses nearby.
Topaz, 25 King David Street   (9) 862-4555
Zli-Esh, 6 Shaar Hagai Street   (9) 832-4295

Museums
Netanya Museum of Biology & Archaeology

Synagogues
Congregation Agudath Achim
45 Jabotinsky Street
New Synagogue of Netanya
7 MacDonald Street   (9) 861-4591
Ohel Shem Civic Auditorium
Cultural Centre, 4 Raziel Street   (9) 833-6688
Young Israel of Northern Netanya
cnr. Shlomo Hamelech, & Yehuda Hanassi
Streets

Tourist Information
Kikar ha'Atzmaut   (9) 882-7286

Neve Zohar

Museums
Bet Hayotser
Dead Sea area

Petach Tikva

Museums
Bet Yad Labanim
30 Arlosov Street

Ra'anana

Restaurants
Dana, 198 Achuza   (9) 790-1452
Lady D, 158 Achuza   (9) 791-6517
Limosa, 5 Eliazar Jaffe   (9) 790-3407
Pica Aduma, 87 Achuza   (9) 791-0508

Ramat Gan

Museums
Bet Emmanuel Museum
18 Chilbat Zion Street
Pierre Gildesgame Maccabi Museum
Kfar Hamaccabiah

Ramat Hanegev

Tourist Information
Zomet Mashabay Sadeh   (7) 655-7314

Ramat Yohanan

Youth Hostels
Yehuda Hatzair   (4) 844-2976
Fax: (4) 844-2976
11 miles north-east of Haifa.

Rehovot

This was home to Zionist leader Chaim
Weizmann (1874-1952), Israel's first president.
In his honour, the world-famous Weizmann
Institute research centre was founded in 1944.
Tours, including the house where he lived and
died, and his garden, can be arranged.

Restaurants
Rehovot Chinese Restaurant
202 Herzl Street   (8) 947-1616

Rosh Hanikra

Youth Hostels

Rosh Hanikra   (4) 998-2516
Near the grottos.

Rosh Pina

Rosh Pina, which means cornerstone, is close to the city of Safed and was settled with Rothschild funds, by Jews from Safed in 1878. The original settlement has been preserved and consists of a main street, restored pioneer dwellings and the old synagogue. In addition, many of the old buildings are inhabited by some 60 artists whose work can be seen and purchased.

Youth Hostels

Hovevei Hateva   (6) 693-7086
16 miles north of Tiberias

Safed

Set at an altitude of more than 2,600 feet in the midst of magnificent landscapes, Safed is the fourth holy city of the Talmud after Jerusalem, Tiberias and Hebron, and was once the spiritual centre of Jewish mystics and kabbalists.

Its altitude and purity of air, its completely restored Old City with its narrow, cobblestone streets, myriad old synagogues and its large artist's colony, all combine to make Safed a popular summer resort. In this town, the different sects – hassidic and non-religious, artistic hippies and newly-religious – all mingle without the tension felt in larger cities like Jerusalem. It has a small-town atmosphere.

Hotels

Kosher

David, Mount Canaan   (6) 692-0062
Nof Hagalil
Mount Canaan   (6) 692-1595
Pisgah, Mount Canaan   (6) 692-0105
Rimon Inn, Artists Colony   (6) 692-0665/6
Ron, Hativat Yiftah Street   (6) 697-2590

Museums

Bet Hameiri Institute(History & Heritage of Safed)
Israel Bible Museum
Museum of Printing Art
Artists' Colony

Tourist Information
50 Jerusalem Street   (6) 692-0961/633

Youth Hostels
Bet Benyamin   (6) 692-1086
                    Fax: (6) 697-3514
In southern part of town.

Tel Aviv

Tel Aviv (Hill of Spring) started as a Jewish suburb of Arab Jaffa in 1909. Growth was encouraged in the area by the Balfour Declaration in 1917. The anti-Jewish Jaffa riots of 1921 and the advent of Nazism in Germany also encouraged more development of the empty sand dunes. When in 1948 Israel declared independence, Tel Aviv became the temporary site for the provisional government and its population grew by sixty per cent. It is now the second largest city after Jerusalem and the majority of the country's population lives on a narrow strip along the coast, ranging from Ashkelon up to Naharia.

With skyscrapers, crowded streets and traffic and car pollution, Tel Aviv is like any other western metropolis with its upscale shopping districts and poor run-down neighbourhoods. Tel Aviv's outdoor cafes are reminiscent of Europe. Another big draw to the city is its coastline and beaches. There is a five mile stretch of beaches, some of which are only a 10-minute walk from Dizengoff – the main central avenue. There is also a Promenade, paved in swirling patterns, stretching from North Tel Aviv, the border of the yuppified Ramat Aviv, and extending nearly into Yaffo.

Accommodation Information
Kibbutz Hotels Chain: Head Office
1 Smolanskin Street, P.O.B. 3193 61031
                     (3) 524-6161
             Fax: (3) 527-8088
      Email: batya@kibbutz.co.il
      Web site: www.kibbutz.co.il

Contact Information
Jewish Student Information Centre
Tel Aviv University Off-Campus Center, 82/10 Levanon Street, Ramat Aviv
      Email: jseidel@netmedia.net.il

Hotels

Kosher

Adiv, 5 Mendele Street   (3) 522-9141
Ambassador, 56 Herbert Samuel Street
                     (3) 510-3993

Ami, 152 Hayarkon Street (3) 524-9141/5
Armon Hayarkon
268 Hayarkon Street (3) 455-271/3
Avia, Ben Gurion Intl. Airport Area
(3) 536-0221
Fax: (3) 536-0036
Basel, 156 Hayarkon Street (3) 520-7711
Bell, 12 Allenby Street (3) 517-7011
Carlton Tel Aviv
10 Eliezer Peri Street (3) 520-1818
Fax: (3) 527-1043
City, 9 Mapu Street (3) 524-6253
Dan Panorama
10 Y. Kaufman Street (3) 519-0190
Dan Tel Aviv
99 Hayarkon Street (3) 520-2505
Fax: (3) 524-9755
Deborah, 87 Ben-Yehuda Street (3) 544-822
Florida, 164 Hayarkon Street (3) 524-2184
Grand Beach
250 Hayarkon Street (3) 546-6555
Howard Johnson – Shalom
216 Hayarkon Street (3) 524-3277
Fax: (3) 523-5895
Maxim, 86 Hayarkon Street,
P.O.B. 3442 63903 (3) 517-3721/5
Fax: (3) 517-3726
Metropolitan
11-15 Trumpeldor Street 63803 (3) 519-2727
Fax: (3) 517-2626
Email: reserve@metrotlv.co.il
Monopol, N.I. on the promenade, 4 Allenby
Street (3) 655-906
Moriah Plaza Tel Aviv
155 Hayarkon Street (3) 527-1515
Ora, N.L., 35 Ben Yehuda Street (3) 650-941
Ramada Continental
121 Hayarkon Street (3) 527-2626
Ramat Aviv, 151 Derech Namir. (3) 699-0777
Fax: (3) 699-0997

Sheraton Tel Aviv
115 Hayarkon Street (3) 521-1111
Fax: (3) 523-3322
Email: shtelviv@netvision.net.il
Tal, 287 Hayarkon Street (3) 544-2281
Tayelet, N.L. on the promenade, 6 Allenby
Street (3) 510-5845
Tel Aviv Hilton
Independence Park 63405 (3) 520-2222
Fax: (3) 527-2711
Email: fom_tel-aviv@hilton.com
Wiznitz
16 Damesek Eliezer Street Bnei-Brak
(3) 777-141/3
Yamit Towers
79 Hayarkon Street (3) 517-1111

Vegan
Holyland Hotel
49 Bograshov Street Byat (3) 287-382

Museums
Bet Bialik, 22 Bialik Street (3) 525-3403
Fax: (3) 525-4530
Bet Eliahu-Hahagana
23 Rothschild Blvd. 65122 (3) 560-8624
Fax: (3) 566-6131
Bible Center (Beth Tanach)
16 Rothschild Boulevard (3) 517-7760
Fax: (3) 510-7661
Eretz Israel Museum
2 Haim Levanon Street 69975 (3) 641-5244
Fax: (3) 641-2408
Goldmann Museum of the Diaspora (Beth Hatefutsoth)
Klausner Street, Ramat Aviv (3) 646-2020
Fax: (3) 646-2134
Web site: www.bh.org.il

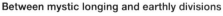

Israel

Haaretz Museums
17 Ben-Gurion Boulevard
Includes eight smaller museums at Ramat Aviv, as well as the Israel Theatre Museum.
Helena Rubenstein Pavilion for Contemporary Art
6 Tarsat Blvd   (3) 528-7196
          Web site: www.tamuseum.co.il
Jabotinsky Institute
38 King George Street   (3) 528-7320
                                       Fax: (3) 528-5587
                            Email: jabo@actcom.co.il
              Web site: www.jabotinsky.org
Hours: Sunday to Thursday, 8 am to 4 pm.
Tel Aviv History Museum
27 Bialik Street
Tel Aviv Museum of Art
27 Shaul Hamelech Boulevard 64283
                                       (3) 696-1297
                                   Fax: (3) 695-8099
              Web site: www.tamuseum.co.il
Hours: Sunday, Monday, Wednesday, Thursday, 10 am to 6 pm. Tuesday 10 am to 10 pm. Friday and Saturday, 10 am to 2 pm
Public transport: buses 9, 18, 28, 70, 82, 91.
Parking facilities.

Restaurants
Hamakom, 1 Lilienbaum Street   (3) 510-1823
Shaul's Inn
11 Elyashiv Street, Kerem Hatemanim
                                       (3) 517-3303
                                   Fax: (3) 517-7619
Supervision: Chief Rabbinate of Tel Aviv.
Oriental and Yemenite food. Popular and exclusive sections. Hours: 12 pm to 12 am.
Dairy
Hungarian Blintzes
35 Yirmiyahu Street   (3) 605-0674
Meat
Twelve Tribes
Sheraton Hotel, 115 Hayarkon Street
                                       (3) 521-1111
Prestigious restaurant. Innovative cuisine with Mediterranean flavours.

Synagogues
Bilu, 122 Rothschild Blvd.
Great, 314 Dizengoff Street
Ihud Shivat Zion
86 Ben-Yehuda Street
Central European rite.
Tiferet Zvi
Hermann Hacohen Street

Ashkenazi
Main Synagogue
110 Allenby Road
Progressive
Kedem, 20 Carlebach Street
Sephardi
Ohel Mis'ad
5 Shadal Street

Tourist Information
Shop # 6108, 6th Floor, New Central Bus Station   (3) 639-5660
                                   Fax: (3) 639-5659
ISSTA, 109 Ben Yehuda Street
The Ministry of Tourism
6 Wilson Street, Tel Aviv   (3) 556-2339
The Ministry of Tourism publishes a guide called 'The Best of Israel', detailing shops participating in the VAT refund scheme and recommended restaurants. A visitor's visa is valid for a stay of three months from the date of arrival.
The Ministry of Tourism: "Best of Israel Guide"
6 Wilson Street   (3) 556-2339

Travel Agencies
Interom Tourism Ltd.   (3) 924-6425
                                   Fax: (3) 579-1720

Tiberias
Tiberias is one of the four cities mentioned in the Talmud. In 1904 Jewish resettlement began. By the First World War the tourism business, which characterises it today, was already going strong because of its Jewish and Christian history and its hot springs. During the War of Independence there was much fighting over the city, and a memorial garden was built in the old Jewish quarter of Tiberias to commemorate the soldiers killed in 1948.

Hotels
Kosher
Ariston, 19 Herzl Blvd.   (6) 679-0244
Astoria, 13 Ohel Ya'akov Street (6) 672-2351/2
Caesar   (6) 672-3333
                                   Fax: (6) 679-1013
Carmel Jordan River
Habanim Street   (6) 671-4444
                                   Fax: (6) 672 2111
Daphna, Ussiskin Street   (6) 679-2261/4
Eshel, Tabur Haaretz Street   (6) 669-0562

Gai Beach, Derech Hamerchatzaot
(6) 679-0790
Galei Kinnereth
1 Kaplan Street   (6) 672-8888
Galilee, Elhadef Street, PO Box 616
(6) 679-1166/8
Gan Esther, Hadishon Street   (6) 672-9946
Ganei Hamat
Habanim Street, nr. Hot Springs (6) 679-2890
Golan, 14 Achad Ha'am Street (6) 679-1901/4
Hamat Gader Restaurant   (6) 675-1049
Kinar, N.E. Sea of Galilee   (6) 673-2670
Lavi Kibbutz Hotel
Lower Galilee 15267   (4) 679-9450
Fax: (4) 679-9399
Email: lavi@lavi.co.il
Web site: www.lavi.co.il
Glatt Kosher, Shomer Shabbat. Unique atmosphere of religious kibbutz.
Lido Kenneret
Gdud Barak Street   (6) 672-1538
Moriah Plaza Tiberias
Habanaim Street   (6) 679-2233
Pagoda
Lido Beach, PO Box 253 14102   (6) 672-5513
Quiet Beach
Gedud Barak Street   (6) 679-0125
Ramot-Resort Hotel
Sea of Galilee   (6) 673-2636
Sironit Beach
Hamerchazaot Road   (6) 672-1449
Tzameret Inn
Plus 2000 Street   (6) 679-4951
Washington, 13 Seidel Street (6) 679-1861/3

Museums
Tiberias Hot Springs Lehmann Museum
Hammat Tiberias National Park

Tourist Information
HaBanim Street, The Archaeological Park
(3) 672-5666

Youth Hostels
Taiber   (6) 675-0050 Fax: (6) 675-1628
2.5 miles south of Tiberias.

Zichron Ya'achov
The road to Haifa is populated with various Rothschild-funded settlements. The largest is Zichron Yaakov, 38 km south-east of Haifa, which was named for James or Jacob Rothschild (1792–1868). It was initially a kibbutz and one of the first Zionist settlements in Israel, having been founded in the mid-1880s. Today it is in the process of rapid growth, its new-found popularity resulting from its proximity to the large Matam industrial park outside of Haifa. Zichron Yaakov is home to the Carmel Oriental Wine Cellars – the second largest in Israel.

West of Zichron Yaakov is Beth Daniel, which affords a wonderful view of the Carmel Coast. It was built as a refuge for musicians by Lillian Friedlander in 1938 in memory of her son Daniel. Concerts are held here and it also has a guest house.

Hotels
Kosher
Baron's Heights & Terraces
N.L. PO Box 332   (6) 630-0333
Fax: (6) 630-0310

Museums
Nili Museum & Aaronson House
40 Hameyasdim Street

Tours of Jewish Interest
American P'eylim Student Union
10 Shoarim Street   (6) 653-2131
Free tours of Jewish Quarter and free accommodation, in the hostel quarters.
Jerusalem Youth Centre
9 Shonei Halachot Street   (6) 628-5623
Free accommodation.
Knesset (Parliament)   (6) 654-4111
Sun. & Thurs. between 8.30am and 2.30pm.

Italy

Italy has an ancient connection with the Jews, and was home to one of the earliest Diaspora communities. Before the Roman invasion of ancient Israel, Judah Maccabee sent a representative to Rome in the first century. There were Jewish communities in Italy after the destruction of the Second Temple, as Italy was the trading hub of the Roman empire. After Christianity became the official religion in 313, restrictions began to be placed on the Jewish population, forcing the community to migrate from town to town across the country.

In the medieval period, there was a brief flourishing of learning, but the Spanish conquered southern Italy in the fifteenth century, expelling the Jews from Sicily, Sardinia and eventually Naples. The first ghetto was established in Italy by Pope Paul IV. Conquest by Napoleon led to the emancipation of Italian Jewry, and full equal rights were granted in 1870.

Ironically, the Italian Fascist party contained some Jewish members, as Mussolini was not anti-semitic and, even under pressure from Hitler, did not instigate any major anti-semitic policy. The situation changed after Germany's occupation of the north in 1943. Eventually, almost 8,000 Italian Jews were killed in Auschwitz, although the local population hid many of those who survived.

Today there is a central organisation which provides services for Italian Jews. B'nai B'rith and WIZO are represented, and there are kosher restaurants in Rome, Milan and other towns. There are also Jewish schools. There has been an Israeli ambassador to the Vatican.

GMT + 1 hour   Total Population 57,226,000
Country calling code (39)   Jewish Population 30,000
Emergency Telephone (Police – 112) (Fire – 115) (Ambulance – 116)

Ancona

Community Organisations
Community Offices
Via Fanti 2 bis   (71) 202638

Mikvaot
Via Astagno

Asti

Museums
Via Ottolenghi 8 Torino
                        (141) 539281; 0141-594271

Synagogues
Via Ottolenghi 8 Torino

Bologna

Cafeterias
Comunita Ebraica Bologna
Via Gombruti 9 40123   (51) 232-066
                                     Fax: (51) 229-474
Supervision: Rav Moshe Saadoun.
Lunch Sunday to Friday; dinner Friday; closed mid-July and August.

Community Organisations
Comunita Ebraica Bologna
Via Gombruti 9 40123   (51) 232-066
                                     Fax: (51) 229-474

Mikvaot
Mikveh Chaya Mushkah
Via Oreste Regnoli 17/1   (51) 623-0316

Synagogues
Via Mario Finzi

Casale Monferrato

Synagogues
Community Offices
Vicolo Salomone Olper 44   (142) 71807
The synagogue, built in 1500 and rebuilt in
1866, also contains a Jewish museum. Casale-
Monferrato is on the Turin-Milan road, and can
be reached by turning off it about 13 miles
beyond Chivasso.

Ferrara

Community Organisations
Community Offices
Via Mazzini 95   (532) 760372

Mikvaot
Via Mazzini 95   (532) 247004

Synagogues
Via Mazzini 95   (532) 247004

Florence

Bakeries
Kosher Bakery
Forno dei Ciompi, Piazza, Dei Ciompi

Bread
Forno dei Ciompi
Piazza dei Ciompi   (55) 241-256

Kosher
Falsettini, Mercato Coperto S. Amobrogio
                                  (55) 248-0740

Butchers
Bruno Falsettini
Mercato Coperto di S., Ambrogio,
Firenze   (55) 248-0740
Gionvannino
Via Macci 106, Firenze   (55) 248-0734

Community Organisations
Community Offices
Via Luigi Carlo Farini 4, Firenze   (55) 245252
                          Fax: (55) 241811

Delicatessens
Giovannio, Via dei Macci, 106
                                  (55) 248-0734

Hotels
Ariston, Via Fiesolana, 42   (55) 247-6980
Arizona, Via Farini, 2   (55) 245321
Capitol, Viale Amendola, 34   (55) 234-3203
Geneve, Via della Mattonaia, 43
                                  (55) 247-7923

Monna Lisa, Borgo Pinti, 27   (55) 247-9751
Regency, 3, piazza d'Azelgio   (55) 245247
Located in the square, near the synagogue.

Mikvaot
Via Luigi Carlo Farini 4, Firenze
                          (55) 245252 & 243164

Museums
Jewish Museum
Via Luigi Carlo Farini 4, Firenze
                                  (55) 234-6654
                          Fax: (55) 241811
                          Email: comebrfi@fol.it
There is a religious and artistic souvenir shop.

Restaurants
Kosher Vegetarian
Ruth's
Via Farini 2/A, Firenze   (55) 248-0888
Kosher.

Synagogues
Via De BanchiFirenze   (55) 212-474
Via Luigi Carlo Farini 4, Firenze   (55) 245252

Orthodox
Via Farini, 4
          Web site: seehttp.www.fol.it/sinagoga
Different seating areas for men and women.
Saturday morning service open from 8:30am
until 11:15am. After service public Kiddush.
Services on Shabbat and holidays, not daily.

Genoa

Community Organisations
Community Offices
Via Bertora 6 16122

Synagogues
Via Bertora 6   (10) 839-1513
                          Fax: (10) 846-1006
Services every evening & Shabbat morning.

Gorizia

Synagogues
Via Ascoli 19, Gradicia   (3831) 532115

Leghorn

Butchers
Corucci
Banco 25, Mercato Centrale, Livorno
                                  (0586) 884596

Mikvaot
Community Offices
Piazza Benamozegh 1, Livorno   (0586) 896290

Museums
Jewish Museum
via Micali 21, Livorno

Synagogues
Community Offices
Piazza Benamozegh 1, Livorno   (0586) 896290
Fax: (0586) 896290

Mantua
Synagogues
Community Offices
Via G. Govi 11, Mantova   (379) 321490

Merano
Museums
Jewish Museum and Synagogue
Via Schiller 14   (0473) 236127
Fax: (0473) 237520
Hours: Tuesday and Wednesday 3-6pm.
Thursday 9-12am. Friday 3-5pm.

Synagogues
Community Offices
Via Schiller 14   (473) 236127

Milan
Community Organisations
Community Offices
Sally Mayer 2   (2) 483-02806
Fax: (2) 483-04660

Documentation Centres
Contemporary Jewish Documentation
Centre
Via Eupili 8   (2) 316338
Fax: (2) 336-02728

Groceries
Eretz, Largo Scalabrini 5   (2) 423-6891
Fax: (2) 423-4753
Hours: 9 am to 7:30 pm. Nearest metro: buses,
50, 95, 13, 61, subway 1 (red), stop, Bande-
Nere.

Mikvaot
Central Synagogue
Via Guastalla 19   (2) 551-2101

Persian
Angelo Donati Beth Hamidrash
Via Sally Mayer 4-6

Restaurants
Pizzeria Carmel
viale San Gimignano 10   (2) 416-368
Supervision: Rav S. Behor.
Hours: 12 pm to 2:30 pm and 5:30 pm to
10:30 pm. Nearest public transportation: buses
58, 61, 50, 95, subway 1.

Synagogues
Beth Shelomo
Galleria Vittorio Emanuele, Via Ugo Foscolo 3 .
(2) 8646-6118
Fax: (2) 236-2771/475256
Services are held on Friday evening, Shabbat,
Sunday morning and Holy days.
Central Synagogue
Via Guastalla 19   (2) 551-2101
Merkos L'Inyonei Chinuch
Via Carlo Poerio 35 20129   (2) 295-31213
New Home for Aged
Via Leone XIII   (2) 498-2604
Services on Sabbaths and festivals. Kosher food
available upon reservation
New Synagogue
Via Eupili 8
Service on Sabbaths and festivals

Lubavitch
Ohel Yacob, Via Benvenuto Cellini 2
(2) 545 5076

Orthodox; Sephardi
Via Guastalla 19   (2) 551-2029
Fax: (2) 551-92699
Rabbi Dr Laras is the Chief Rabbi

Persian
Angelo Donati Beth Hamidrash
Via Montecuccoli 27   (2) 415-1660
Angelo Donati Beth Hamidrash
Via Sally Mayer 4-6
Angelo Donati Beth Hamidrash
Via Tuberose 14   (2) 415-1660

Tourist Information
Uffizio Nazionale Israeliano del Turismo
Via Podgora 12/b 20122   (27) 602-1051
Fax: (27) 760-124-77

Modena

Butchers
Macelleria Duomo
Mercato Coperto (Covered Market), Stand 25
(59) 217269

Synagogues
Community Offices
Piazza Mazzini 26   (59) 223978

Naples

Synagogues
Community Offices
Via Cappella Vecchia 31, Napoli
(81) 764-3480

Ostia Antica

Sites
Here can be found the partially restored
excavated remains of a fourth-century
synagogue built on the site of another one
which stood there 300 years earlier. This is the
oldest synagogue in Europe. Ostia Antica is
about 40 minutes by train from Rome (Termini
or Pyramid stations). To reach the synagogue,
cross the footbridge on leaving station. The
entrance to the excavations is straight ahead.

Parma

Synagogues
Community Offices
Vicolo Cervi 4

Perugia

Synagogues
P. della Republica 77   (75) 21250

Pisa

Synagogues
Community Offices
Via Palestro 24   (50) 542580
Services are held on festivals and Holy-days.
During the week the resident beadle will be
glad to show visitors round the synagogue,
which is famed for its beauty. It is very near
the Teatro Verdi.

Riccione

Hotels
Vienna Touring Hotel: The Hotel Nevada
(54) 160-1245
In the summer, kosher food is obtainable.
Provides vegetarian food and particularly
welcomes Jewish guests.

Rome

About half of Italian Jewry (some 15,000
people) live in Rome. As there has been a
very long period of Jewish settlement, a
Nusach Italki has developed (or Italain prayer
ritual), which is practised in some synagogues
in the town. Kosher restuarants and kosher
food are available. Titus' Arch, depicting the
destruction of Jerusalem by the Romans is in
the city, and Jews were forbidden to walk
under it. The catacombs include a number of
Jewish tombs.

Bakeries
Limentani Settimio
Via Portico d'Ottavia 1

Bed & Breakfasts
Pension Carmel
via Goffredo Mameli 11 00153
(06) 580-9921
Kosher pension situated in the old district of
Trastevere, ten minutes from the main
synagogue.

Butchers
Massari, Piazza Bologna 11   (06) 429120
Sion Ben David
Via Filippo Turati 110   (06) 733358
Terracina, Via Portico d'Ottavia 1b
(06) 654-1364

Embassy
Embassy of Israel
Via Michelle Mercati 14 00197   (06) 322-1541
Embassy of Israel to The Holy See
Via M. Mercati 12 00197   (6) 3619-8690
Fax: (6) 3619-8626

Groceries
Sabra, Via S. Ambrogio 6

Media

Newspapers
Shalom, Lungotevere Cenci 9   (06) 687-6816
Monthly.

Museums

The Jewish Museum
Lungotevere Cenci 9
The main synagogue building contains a permanent exhibition covering the 2000 year history of the Italian Jewish community. Another link with this long history is the Rome Ghetto almost adjoining. It can be reached by taking buses 44, 56, 60 or 75, near the neighbouring Ponte Garibaldi. It is a maze of narrow alleys dating from Imperial Roman times, within which, until 1847, all Roman Jews were confined under curfew. A striking monument has been erected to the memory of 335 Jewish and Christian citizens of Rome who were massacred in 1944 by the Nazis. names Fosse Ardentine, it lies just outside the Porta San Paolo, a few yards from the main synagogue.

Religious Organisations

The Italian Rabbinical Council
Headquarters, Lungotevere Sanzio 9
(06) 580-3667; 580-3670

Representative Organisations

Unione Comunita Ebraiche Italiane (Union of Italian Jewish Communities)
Lungotevere Sanzio 9
(06) 580-3667; 580-3670
Fax: (06) 589-9569
Information on Italian Jewry, its monuments and history may be obtained from here.

Restaurants

Da Lisa International Restaurant
Via Joscolo 16-18   (06) 7049-5456
                            Fax: (06) 860-3619
Tavola Calda
via Livorno, Piazza Bologna   (06) 440-4862

Kosher

La Migliori Specialita Mediorientiali
Via Livorno, 9-10   (06) 440-4862
                            Fax: (06) 440-4862

Pizzeria

Zi Fenizia
via Santa Maria del Pianto 64-65 00186
                            (06) 689-6976
Kashrut certificate is for meat – they do not use any cheeses in their pizzas.

Synagogues

Via Catalana 1
Rabbi Dr. Toaff is the Chief Rabbi of Rome.

Orthodox

Lungotevere Cenci (Tempio) 9 (Orthodox Italian service)   (06) 684-00652
                            Fax: (06) 684-00655

Orthodox; Ashkenazi

Via Balbo 33

Tours

Guides

G. Palombo, Via val Maggia 7
                    (06) 810-3716; 993-2074
Ruben E. Popper
12 Via dei Levii   (06) 761-0901
                            Fax: (06) 761-0901
Telephone number is afternoons only.

Senigallia

Synagogues

Via dei Commercianti

Siena

Synagogues

Vicolo delle Scotte 14   (577) 284647
The committee has issued a brochure in English, giving the history of the synagogue which dates back to medieval times. The Synagogue dates from 1750. Services are held on the Sabbath and High Holy-days. Further information from Burroni Bernardi, Via del Porrione. M. Savini, via Salicotta 23. Tel: 283140 (close to the synagogue)

Spezia

Synagogues

Via 20 Settembre 165

Trieste

Community Organisations

Community Offices
Via San Francesco 19   (40) 371466

Synagogues

Via Donizetti 2   (40) 631898

Tour Information

Smile Service
via Martiri della Liberta' 17 34134
                            (40) 372-8464
                            Fax: (40) 372-6630
This service agency organises tours around the Jewish sites of Friuli Venezia-Giulia.

Turin

Booksellers
Libreria Claudiana
Via Principe Toncmaso 1
Torino 10125   (11) 669-2458

Community Organisations
Community Centre
P.tta Primo Levi 12
Torino 10125   (11) 658-585
Synagogue and mikva on premises.

Restaurants
Luna
via C.L. Berthollet 23
Torino 10125   (11) 650-2053

Urbino

Synagogues
Via Stretta

Venice

Community Organisations
Community Ofiices
Ghetto Nuovo 2899   (41) 715012

Groceries
David's
Ghetto Nuovo 2880
Jewish articles & religious appurtenances are
available from here.

Mordehai Fusetti
Ghetto Nuovo, Ghetto Vecchio 1219
                                 (41) 714024
Jewish articles & religious appurtenances are
available from here.

Guest Houses
Jewish Rest Home
Cannaregio 30121
Ghetto Nuovo 2874   (41) 716002
                            Fax: (41) 714394
Kosher meals and accommodation can be had
here. Early booking is advised.

Hotels
Buon Pesce, S. Nicolo 50.   (41) 760533
Open Apr. to Oct. Danieli (tel) 26480; Europa
& Regina (tel) 700477

Libraries
Jewish Library
Ghetto Nuovo 2899   (41) 718833

Mikvaot
Jewish Rest Home
Ghetto Nuovo 2874   (41) 715118

Museums
Jewish Museum
Schola Tedesca
Ghetto Nuovo 2902 b   (41) 715359
Guided visits to the synagogue (in English)
start every hour from the Museum. There is
also a kosher cafeteria.

Restaurants
Bar Ristorante Ebraico
Sottoportico di Ghetto Vecchio   (41) 715284
Beit Chabad
Cannaregio
Ghetto Nuovo 2884   (41) 716214
                            Fax: (41) 716214
Restaurants, books and Judaica available from
here.

Meat
Gam-Gam
Cannaregio 1122
Old Jewish Ghetto   (41) 715-284
Supervision: Rabbi G. Garelick – Lubavitch, R.
Della Rocca – Jewish Community of Venice.
Glatt Kosher. Shabbat arrangements available.
Open lunch and dinner.

Synagogues
Chabad
Cannaregio
Ghetto Nuovo 2915   (41) 716214

Sephardi
Schola Levantina
Ghetto Vecchio   (41) 715012
Sabbath services are held here during winter.

Schola Spagnola
Ghetto Vecchio
Sabbath services are held here during summer.

Vercelli

Community Organisations
Community Offices
Via Oldoni 20

Synagogues
Via Foa 70

Verona

Community Organisations
Community Centre
Via Portici 3   (45) 800-7112
            Fax: (45) 596627
            Email: s. l@intesys. it

Synagogues
Via Portici 3

Viareggio

Contact Information
Mr Sananes, via Pacinotti 172/B (584) 961-025
Private office: Tirreno Tour Srl, 26 Viale
Carducci, Tel: 30777, during daytime.

Sardinia

There is no Sardinian Jewish community
today, but the island is of more than
passing Jewish interest. In 19 C.E. the
Emperor Tiberius exiled Jews to Sardinia.
There was a synagogue at Cagliari, the
island's capital, at least as early as 599, for
in that year a convert led a riot against it.
Sardinia eventually came under Aragonese
rule, and when the edict of expulsion of
the Jews from Spain was issued in 1492,
the Jews of the island had to leave. Since
then there has been no community there.

Sicily

Although there are very few Jews in Sicily
today, there is a long and varied history of
Jewish settlement on the island stretching
back to at least the sixth century C.E. and
possibly – according to some scholars – to
the first or second centuries.

By the late Middle Ages, the community
numbered 40,000. In 1282, Sicily passed
under Spanish rule. A century or so later,
there was a wave of massacres of Jews,
and another in 1474. These culminated in
the introduction of the Inquisition in
1479, and the expulsion of the Jews in
1492.

Jamaica

During the time of Spanish colonisation, Jamaica witnessed many Conversos arriving
from Portugal. After the British took over in 1655, many of these could practise Judaism
openly. Soon, other Jews, mainly Sephardim, followed from Brazil and other nearby
countries. The community received full equality in 1831 (before a similar step was taken
in England).

The Jews played an important role in Jamaican life and, in 1849, the House of
Asembly did not meet on Yom Kippur! However, assimilation and intermarriage took its
toll and in 1921 the Ashkenazi and Sephardi synagogues combined. There is now only
one synagogue on the island, but there are remains of old synagogues in Kingston, Port
Royal and other towns.

Community life includes WIZO, B'nai B'rith, and a school (the Hillel Academy).

GMT – 5 hours   Total Population 2,491000
Country calling code (1)   Jewish Population 300
Emergency Telephone (Police – 119) (Fire – 110) (Ambulance – 110)

Kingston

Synagogues
Shaare Shalom
Duke & Charles Street   (809) 927-7948
         Fax: (809) 978-6240

Services, Friday, 5:30 pm (May to October), 5
pm (November to April). Shabbat, 10 am;
festivals, 9 am all year round.

Japan

After Japan became open to Western ideas and Westerners in the mid-nineteenth century, a trickle of Jewish immigrants from the Russian Empire, the UK and the USA began to make their homes there. Many were escaping anti-semitism and by 1918 there were several thousand in the country.

The Japanese, despite being allied to Nazi Germany, did not adopt the anti-semitic attitude of the Nazis. The post-war American occupation of the country brought many Jewish servicemen, and the community was also augmented by Jews escaping unrest in China. In recent years, there have been some Jewish 'gaijin', or 'foreign workers'.

In Tokyo there is a synagogue which provides meals on shabbat, a Sunday school, and the Executive Board of the Jewish Community of Japan, which is the central body.

GMT + 9 hours	Total Population 125,351,000
Country calling code (81)	Jewish Population 2,000
Emergency Telephone (Police – 110) (Fire and Ambulance – 119)	

Hiroshima

Tourist Sites

Holocaust Education Centre
866 Nakatsuhara, Miyuki, Fukuyama 720
(849) 558001
Fax: (849) 558001
Email: hecjpn@urban.ne.jp
Web site:
http://www.urban.ne.jp/home/hecjpn/
Open Tuesday, Wednesday, Friday and Saturday, 10:30 am to 4:30 pm.

Kobe

Synagogues

Orthodox

Ohel Shelomoh
12/12 Kitanocho, 4-chome, Chuo-ku, Port PO Box 639 651-0191 (78) 221-7236; 231-6633
Fax: (78) 242-7254; 231-6633

Nagasaki

There are no Jews living in Nagasaki. The old Jewish cemetery is located at Sakamoto Gaijin Bachi. The site of the first synagogue in Japan is Umegasaki Machi.

Okinawa

While there is no native Jewish community on Okinawa, there are normally 200–300 Jews serving with the US military on the island. Regular services are conducted by the Jewish chaplain at Camp Smedley, D. Butler, and visitors are welcome.

Tokyo

Community Organisations

Beth David Synagogue
8-8 Hiroo, 3-chome, Shibuya Oku 150
(3) 3400-2559
Fax: (3) 3400-1827

Embassy

Israel Embassy
3 Niban-cho, Chiyodaku (3) 3264-0911

Synagogues

Beth David Synagogue
8-8 Hiroo, 3-chome, Shibuya Oku 150
(3) 3400-2559
Fax: (3) 3400-1827
Services are held Friday evening at 6:30 pm (7 pm during summer); Shabbat morning, 9:30 am; and on Holy-days and festivals. Advance notification requested. Mikvah on premises.

Kazakhstan

Essentially, this community began when the Soviets rescued several thousand Jews at the time of the Nazi invasion of the Soviet Union in 1941. Others joined after the war. The community is mainly based in Alma-Ata, the capital, and also in Karaganda and Chimkent. Some 2,000 Bukharan and Tat Jews also live in the country.

The central organisation is the Mitzvah Association, which heads various Jewish groups. It even has a chair on the All-Peoples Assembly of Kazakhstan. There is a high rate of emigration to Israel.

GMT + 6 hours
Country calling code (7)

Total Population 17,027,000
Jewish Population 12,000

Alma-Ata
Synagogues
Tashkentskaya Street, 1a 480057
(3272) 306-898

Chimkent
Synagogues
Sephardi
Svobody Street, 47th Lane

Kenya

Kenya could have been the site of the first Jewish state for two thousand years, but when this offer, the 'Uganda Plan', was made to the Zionists in 1903, it was rejected. There were, however, some Jews living in Kenya at that time, and a synagogue was built in 1912. Many more Jews came here after the war as Holocaust survivors, and recently some Israelis have worked on a short-term basis in the country.

Kenya was an ally to Israel in its rescue of the Jews from Entebbe in Uganda. Jews have contributed much to the hotel industry and professional life of the country.

Regular services are held every Saturday in the Nairobi Hebrew Congregation, and there is a Community Centre next to the synagogue. The centre, the Vermont Memorial Hall, offers educational and social events.

GMT + 3 hours
Country calling code (254)
Emergency Telephone (Police, Fire and Ambulance 999)

Total Population 27,799,000
Jewish Population 400

Nairobi
Community Organisations
Community Centre
Vermont Memorial Hall
Open Mon., Tues., Fri 9am to 1pm; Wed 2.30pm to 5.30pm; Services Friday evening at 6.30pm; Sat morning at 8am. All Festivals. Kosher chickens available.

Synagogues
cnr. University Way & Uhuru Highway, PO Box 40990   (2) 222770, 219703
Rosh Kehilla
Vaizman Aharoni

Kyrgyzstan

Jews migrated to Kyrgyzstan after the Russian Revolution and after the Second World War.

Currently, religious activity is almost negligible. In addition to the synagogue in Bishkek, the capital, there are a number of small Bukharan prayer houses.

GMT + 5 hours	Total Population 4,669,000
Country calling code (996)	Jewish Population 3,500

Bishkek
Synagogues
193 Karpinsky Street

Latvia

The Jews in the medieval principalities of Courland and Livonia represent the earliest Jewish settlement in Latvia. Tombstones from the fourteenth century have been found. After the Russian take-over, Jews were only allowed to live in the area if they were considered 'useful', or had lived there before the Russians took control, because the area was outside the 'Pale of Settlement' that the Russian Empire had designated for the Jews.

The Jews contributed much to Latvia's development, but this was never recognised by the government, which tried to restrict their influence in business matters. Religious Jewish life was also strong. When the Nazis invaded Latvia, 90 per cent of the 85,000 Jews were systematically murdered by them and their Latvian collaborators.

The bulk of today's community originates from immigration into Latvia after the war, although 3,000 Holocaust survivors did return to Latvia. Before the collapse of communism, there was much Jewish dissident activity. There is a Jewish school and a Jewish hospital. There are some Holocaust memorial sites, in Riga (the capital) and also in the Bierkernieki Forest, where 46,000 Holocaust victims were shot.

GMT + 2 hours	Total Population 2,504,000
Country calling code (371)	Jewish Population 15,000

Daugavpils
Synagogues
Suvorov Street
Gogol Street

Liepaja
Community Organisations
Jewish Community
Kungu Street 21   (34) 25336

Rezhitsa
Synagogues
Kaleru Street

Riga
Embassy
Embassy of Israel
Elizabetes Street 2 LV1340

Synagogues
6/8 Peitavas Street   (2) 21-0827
Fax: (2) 22-4549

Lithuania

The history of Lithuania Jewry is as old as the state of Lithuania itself. There were Jews in the country in the fourteenth century, when Grand Duke Gedeyminus founded the state. The community eventually grew, and produced many famous yeshivas and great commentators, such as the Vilna Gaon. The community began to emigrate (particularly to South Africa) at the beginning of the nineteenth century, yet in 1941 there were still 160,000 Jews in the country. Ninety-five per cent of these were murdered in the Holocaust, by the local population as well as the Nazis.

The remaining post-war community included some who had hidden or had managed to survive by other means and some Jews from other parts of the Soviet Union. Interestingly, the Lithuanian Soviet Socialist Republic was more tolerant of Jewish activity than some of the neighbouring republics, such as Latvia. Now that Lithuania is independent, Jewish life is free once more.

There are synagogues in Vilnius (known to many as Vilna), the capital, and Kaunas. There is also a school and it is possible to study Yiddish. There are tours available to show the old Jewish life in Lithuania. The grave of the Vilna Gaon can be visited.

GMT + 2 hours
Country calling code (370)
Emergency Telephone (Police – 02) (Fire – 01) (Ambulance – 03)

Total Population 3,728,000
Jewish Population 6,000

Tourist Information
Jews in the Baltic States
JCT - Jewish Culture Tours
CH-8017 Forch/Switzerland
+41 (0)1 980 32 71
Fax: +41 (0)1 980 00 09

Druskininkai
Community Organisations
Jewish Community
9/15 Sporto Street   54590

Kaunas
Community Organisations
Jewish Community
26 B Gedimino Street   (7) 203717
Fax: (7) 7201135
Hours of opening: Sunday to Thursday 3-6pm

Synagogues
11 Ozheshkienes Street

Klaipeda
Community Organisations
Jewish Community
3 Ziedu Skersqatvis   (6) 93758

Panevezys
Community Organisations
Jewish Community
6/22 Sodu Street 5300   (54) 68848

Shiauliai
Community Organisations
Jewish Community
24 Vyshinskio   (1) 26795

Vilnius
Otherwise known as Vilna, this town used to be known as the 'Jerusalem of Lithuania'. There was a very important Jewish community in the town before the Holocaust. The town still has the largest community of Lithuanian Jews, and there are many sites of historical interest, including the Vilna Gaon's grave and the State Jewish Museum.

Bakeries
Matzah Bakery
39 Pylimo Street   (2) 61-2523

Community Organisations

Jewish Community of Lithuania
Ground Floor, Pylimo St. 4 2001   (2) 61-3003
Fax: (2) 22-7915
Email: root@lzb.vno.osf.lt
Opening hours: Monday to Friday 10 a.m. 6.00 p.m.

Jewish Community of Vilnius
4 Pylimo 2001   (2) 63-2951
Fax: (2) 63-2951

Cultural Organisations

The Israel Centre of Cultures and Art in Lithuania
4 Pylimo, 2nd Floor 2001
(2) 61-1736 or 652139

Museums

State Jewish Museum
4 Pylimo, 1st Floor 2001   (2) 63-2951

Synagogues

Main Synagogue
39 Pylimo Street   (2) 61-2523

Luxembourg

The small community in Luxembourg faced massacres and expulsions during medieval times and Jews only began to resettle here several hundred years later. Napoleon heralded the rebirth of the community when he annexed Luxembourg, and by 1823 a synagogue had been built, but the community remained small, although, another synagogue was built in 1899 Later many refugees from the Nazis arrived in the country, bringing the number of Jews to nearly 4,000. After the Nazi take-over, 750 Luxembourg Jews were killed, but many others were saved by the local population.

GMT + 1 hour

Country calling code (352)

Emergency Telephone (Police – 113) (Fire and Ambulance – 112)

Total Population 412,000

Jewish Population 600

Esch-sur-Alzette

Synagogues
52 rue de Canal
Minyan services held on Friday evenings.

Luxembourg City

Embassy
Consulate General
38 BD Napoleon 1er L-2210   446-557
Fax: 453-676

Groceries
Calon, rue de Reins 3

Kashrut Information
34 rue Alphonse munchen 2172   452366

Synagogues
45 Av. Monterery   452914
Fax: 250430

Macedonia

At the southern end of the former Yugoslavia, this new country has an ancient Jewish heritage dating back to Roman times. The Jews took advantage of the area's favourable commercial position, lying between Turkey and Western Europe, and the remains of a synagogue at Stobei is evidence of a once thriving Jewish community.

Iberian Jews escaping the Inquisition settled in the area, and brought with them Sephardi customs and the Ladino language (based on Spanish). The fate of the 8,000 Macedonian Jews under Bulgarian occupation during the Second World War is in stark contrast to the fate of the Bulgarian Jews – the Macedonian Jews were deported to their deaths, yet the Bulgarian Jews were saved by the defiance of the king and the common people. Only ten per cent of the Macedonian community survived, of whom many have emigrated to Israel.

Today's community is mainly based in the capital Skopje, but there are no synagogues and there is little access to Jewish life. However, the community does have contact with Jews in Serbia and Greece.

GMT + 1 hour

Country calling code (389)

Emergency Telephone (Police – 92) (Fire – 93) (Ambulance – 94)

Total Population 2,000,000

Jewish Population 100

Skopje
Community Organisations
Community Offices
Borka Talevski Street 24   (91) 237-543

Malaysia

There are now only a handful of Jewish families in the Malaysian island-state of Penang (Pulau Pinang), all resident in the capital of Georgetown. The synagogue is now closed. There is a cemetery in Jalan Yahudi (Jewish St.).

GMT + 8 hours

Country calling code (60)

Total Population 20,103,000

Jewish Population – under 100

Mexico

Marranos were the first Jews in the country, and some achieved high positions in early Spanish colonial Mexico. When Mexico became independent of Spain, Jews gradually began to enter the country, coming from German and other European communities.

It was during the twentieth century that most Jewish immigrants entered Mexico. The communities grew on a parallel level, rather than together, with two languages, Yiddish and Ladino.

GMT – 6 hours
Country calling code (52)
Emergency Telephone (Police, Fire and Ambulance 080)

Total Population 92,720,000
Jewish Population 40,700

Acapulco

Hotels
The Hyatt Regency
Costera Miguel Alemani 39869   (74) 691-234
Fax: (74) 843-086
Email: hyatta@netmex.com
The hotel has a synagogue and a mikve.

Restaurants

Meat

The Hyatt Regency
Costera Miguel Alemani 39869   (74) 691-234
Fax: (74) 843-086
Email: hyatta@netmex.com
The hotel has a synagogue and a mikve.

Cuernavaca

Synagogues
Madero 404   (73) 20516; 20179

Guadalajara

Community Organisations
Comunidad Israelita de Guadalajara
Juan Palomar y Arias 651   (36) 416-463

Mexico City

There are almost 40,000 Jews in Mexico City, the vast majority of Mexican Jewry. With 23 synagogues, kosher restuarants and Jewish schools, the city is well equipped with Jewish facilities. Polanco is a Jewish area in the city with some synagogues. The first synagogue, dating from 1912, is in the downtown area.

Butchers
Fuente de Templanza 17, Tecamachalco
Mehadrin.
Carniceria Sary
Santa Ana 64, Tecamachalco
Mehadrin.
Pollos Mugrabi
Platon 133, Polanco
Mehadrin.

Embassy
Israel Embassy
Sierra Madre 215, PO Box 11000 10
(5) 201-1500
Fax: (5) 201-1555

Groceries
Casa Amiga, Horacio 1719, Col. Polanco
(5) 540-1455
Super Teca Kosher
Acuezunco 15, San Miguel
(5) 905-589-9823, 9860 or 3225

Media

Books

Imagen David
La Fontaine 229   (5) 203-9964
Maguen David
La Fontaine 229   (5) 203-9964
Revista, La Fontaine 229   (5) 203-9964

Newspapers

CDI, Centro Deportivo, Plaza de toros of Cuatro Caminos   (5) 557-3000
Spanish weekly.
Di Shtime, Pedro Moreno 149   (5) 546-1720
Yiddish weekly.

Mexico

Foro de Vida Judia en el Mundo
Aviacion Commercial 16, Col. Polanco 15700
(5) 571-1114
Spanish monthly.
Kesher, Ap. Postal 41-969, Lomas de
Chapultepec   (5) 203-0517
Spanish monthly.
La Voz de la Kehila
Acapulco 70, 2nd Floor   (5) 211-0501
Spanish monthly.

Mikvaot
Av. de los Bosques 53, Tecamachalco
(5) 589-5530
Banos Campeche 58   (5) 574-2204
Platon 413   (5) 520-9569
Bernard Shaw 110, Polanco (5) 203-9964
Tevila Cuernavaca
Priv. de Antinea 4, Col. Delicias
(5) 15 08 41; 18 16 55

Organisations
Comunidad Monte Sinai
Tennyson 134, Polanco   (5) 280-9956
T.O.V., Fuente de Concordia 73, Col.
Tecamachalco   (5) 389-8756; 8766
Fax: (5) 589-9101

Religious Organisations
Comite Central   (5) 520-9393; 540-7376
Comunidad Maguen David

Email: mdavid@ort.org.mx
Contact for any religious questions.
Jerusalem de Mexico
Anatore France 359, Local C, Polanco
(5) 531-2269

Restaurants
Aladinos, Ingenieros Militares 255
(5) 395-2949
Buffet, Madero 402, Cuernavaca, Mor
.   (5) 251-3251
Buffet C.D.I.
(5) 557-3000
Sundays only.
Centro Social Monte Sinai
Fuente de la Huerte 22   (5) 589-8322
Macabim, 5 de Febrero (5) 709-1446
Sabre Kosher
San Jeronimo 726   (5) 709-3368
Tauqueria Piny
Ejercito Nacional y Emerson (5) 250-5168
Wendys, Homero & Sofocles, Col. Polanco
(5) 395-3083

Dairy
Sabrocito, Fuete de Juventud 72
(5) 589-0513
Mehadrin.
Wendy's, Homero 1507, Col. Polanco
(5) 395-3083
Mehadrin.
Zahavi Pizza
Pasaje Moliere Loc. 6-1 Polanco   (5) 280-5608
Mehadrin.

Synagogues
Agudas Achim
Montes de Oca 32, Condesa 06140
(5) 553-6430
Alianza Monte Sinai
Tennyson No 134, Col. Polanco 11560
(5) 280-6369 ;6375
Fax: (5) 281-3969
Bet Midrash Tecamachalco
Fuente de Marcela 23, Col. Tecamachalco
(5) 251-8454
Bircas Shumel
Plinio 311, Polanco   (5) 280-2769
Cuernavaca, Prolongacion Antinea Lote 2,
Delicias
Eliahu Elfasi
Fuente de Templanza 13, Col. Tecamachalco
(5) 294-9388
Shabbat services only.
Jajam Elfasi
Fuente Del Pescador 168, Col. Tecamachalco
Shabbat services only.
Kolel Aram Zoba
Sofocles 346, Col. Polanco
(5) 280-2669; 4886;
Kolel Maor Abraham
Lafontaine 344, Col. Polanco   (5) 545-2482
Midrash Latorah
Cerrada de Los Morales 8, Col. Polanco 11510
(5) 280-0875; 3526
Rabbi Zrihen, formerly of London, will be
happy to welcome and assist visitors.
Monte Sinai
Fuente de Sulpicio, Tecamachalco
Nidche Israel
Acapulco 70, Condesa   (5) 211-0575
Or Damesek, Seneca 343 (5) 280-6281
Ramat Shalom
Fuente del Pescador 35, Tecamachalco
(5) 251-3854
Shaare Shalom
Av. de Los Bosques 53, Tecamachalco
(5) 251-0973

Shuba Israel
Edgar Alan Poe 43, Col. Polanco
(5) 545-8061 & 280-1036

Conservative

Bet El, Horacio 1722, Polanco los Morales
(5) 281-2592
Fax: (5) 281-2467
Email: comunidad.betel@bigfoot.com
Beth Israel
Virreyes 1140, Lomas   (5) 520-8515
English speaking.

Orthodox

Beth Itzhak
Eujenio Sue 20, Polence

Sephardi

Maguen David
Bernard Shaw 110, Polanco   (5) 203-9964
Sephardi Synagogue
Monterey 359   (5) 564-1197;1367

Monterrey

Community Organisations
Centro Israelita de Monterrey
Canada 207, Nuevo León   (83) 461-128

Tijuana

Contact Information
JCC Chabad House
Centro Social Israelita de Baja California
Av. 16 Septiembre, Baja California 3000
(66) 862-692; 862-693
Fax: (66) 341-532
Email: chabadtj@telnor.net
Mikva on premises.

Restaurants

Meat

JCC Chabad House
Centro Social Israelita de Baja California
Av. 16 Septiembre, Baja California 3000
(66) 862-692; 862-693
Fax: (66) 341-532
Email: chabadtj@telnor.net
Supervision: Rabbi Mendel Polichenco, Chabad.
For information on services and kosher
products, contact Rabbi Polichenco
Tel: 388-154

Synagogues
Tijuanua Hebrew Congregation
Amado Nervo 207
Baja California

Moldova

When the Jews first entered what is now Moldova, the area was known as Bessarabia, and was on an important trade route between Turkey and Poland. By the time of Russian rule in 1812, there was a permanent Jewish community. The Russians included the area in the 'Pale of Settlement', which held the majority of the Jews of their empire. By the end of the nineteenth century, there were over 200,000 Jews in the region. However, the twentieth century started with the infamous progrom in the capital Kishinev, where 49 Jews were killed and much damage was done to Jewish property. Emigration began to increase. The area fell under Romanian control between 1918 and 1940, but the community continued to lead a normal life until the Second World War, when many thousands of the pre-war community of over 250,000 were killed during the German occupation.

After the war, some survivors continued to live in Moldova, and Jews from other parts of the Soviet Union joined them. There is an umbrella society for Moldovan Jews, and there are synagogues and schools. The Lubavitch movement is active in building up religious life.

GMT + 2 hours
Country calling code (373)

Total Population 4,450,000
Jewish Population 18,000

Kishinev

Religious Organisations
Yeshiva of Kishinev
Sciusev 5 277001   (2) 264-362; 264-331
Aside from Jewish studies, a mikva and kosher food can be found on premises

Synagogues
Yakimovsky per. 8 277000   (2) 221-215

Teleneshty

Synagogues
4 28th June Street

Tiraspol

Contact Information
336-495
Fax: 322-208
Details of the Jewish Community from Dr Vaisman.

Monaco

Some French Jews lived in Monaco before 1939 and the government issued them with false papers during the war; this saved them from the Nazis. This tiny country has attracted retired people from France, North Africa and the United Kingdom.

There is an official Jewish body, the Association Culturelle Israelite de Monaco, and there is a synagogue, a school and a kosher food shop. Half of the total Jewish population are Ashkenazi and the other half are Sephardi and 60 per cent of the community is retired.

GMT + 1 hour	Total Population 32,000
Country calling code (377)	Jewish Population 1,000

Monte Carlo
Synagogues
15 Av. de la Costa, opp. Balmoral Hotel MC
98000   (32) 9330-1646

Services, Friday even. at 6.30pm and Sat. morning at 8.45am and Sat. afternoon at 5.30pm
Association Culturelle Israelite de Moisra
19 Avenue de la Costa, 9800. (32) 9330-1646

Morocco

Moroccan Jewry has a long history, stretching back to before Roman times, of acceptance, followed by attacks and then isolation under Islam, when Jews were made to wear a special costume, as 'dhimmis', or 'subordinates'. The community grew through immigrants from Iberia in the Middle Ages, but Jews did not achieve full equality until the French arrived in 1912. During the Second World War, and the Vichy regime, the king, Mohammed V, refused to allow the Jews to be deported. After the war, many emigrated, and although, since 1956, Jews have been allowed to become full citizens of the newly independent Morocco, the community has continued to decline.

The Jews today are fairly comfortable, both economically and in the sense that there is little anti-semitism, and even anti-Zionism is not widespread. There are synagogues and kosher restaurants in Casablanca. An interesting aspect to the country is the large number of tombs venerated by the community.

GMT + 0 hours	Total Population 27,021,000
Country calling code (212)	Jewish Population 6,500
Emergency Telephone (Fire – 15) (Ambulance – 19)	

Agadir
Mikvaot
Av. Moulay Abdallah, cnr. rue de la Foire
(8) 842339

Organisations
Community Offices
Imm. Arsalane Av. Hassan II   (8) 840091
Fax: (8) 822268

Synagogues
Av. Moulay Abdallah, cnr. rue de la Foire
(8) 846793

Casablanca

Mikvaot
32 rue Officier de Paix Thomas   (2) 276688

Organisations
Community Offices
rue Abbon Abdullah   (2) 270976 & 222861
Fax: (2) 266953
Council of Moroccan Jewish Communities
rue Abbon Abdullah

Restaurants
Bon Delice, 261 Blvd. Ziraoui, opp. Lycee
Lyautey
La Truffe Blanche
57 rue Taher Sebti   (2) 277263

Synagogues
Benisty, 13 rue Ferhat Hached
Bennaroche, 24 rue Lusitania
Em Habanim, 14 rue Lusitania
Ne'im Zemiroth
29 rue Jean-Jacques Rousseau

El Jadida

Organisations
Community Offices
PO Box 59

Essaouira (formerly Mogador)

Organisations
Community Offices
2 rue Ziri Ben Atyah

Synagogues
2 rue Ziri Ben Atyah

Fez

Hotels
La Boutique
rue de Beyrouth
Mrs Mamane will be pleased to assist all
Jewish visitors.

Mikvaot
Talmud Torah
rue Dominique Bouchery

Organisations
Community Offices
rue Dominique Bouchery

Restaurants
Community Offices
rue Dominique Bouchery

Synagogues
Beth El, rue de Beyrouth
Sadoun, ruelle 1, blvd. Mohammed V.
Talmud Torah
rue Dominique Bouchery

Kenitra

Mikvaot
58 rue Sallah Eddine

Organisations
Community Offices
58 rue Sallah Eddine

Synagogues
rue de Lyon

Marrakech

Organisations
Community Offices
PO Box 515   (4) 448754

Restaurants
Le Viennois
Hotel Mansour Eddabbi, Ave de France
                                          (4) 448222
                                     Fax: (4) 448168

Supervision: local rabbi.

Synagogues
Villa Oliviery, Blvd. Zerktouni (Gueliz)
Bitton, rue de Touareg
El Fassines

Cadoch and Mikvah
Lazama, rue Talmud Torah

Meknes

Mikvaot
5 rue de Ghana   (5) 21968 or 22549
Tourists will be assisted if telephoning 24
hours in advance of their requests.

Synagogues
5 rue de Ghana   (5) 21968 or 22549
Tourists will be assisted if telephoning
24 hours in advance of their requests.

Oujda

Organisations
Community Offices
Texaco Maroc, 36 Blvd. Hassan Loukili

Rabat

Mikvaot
3 rue Moulay Ismail

Organisations
Community Offices
1 rue Boussouni

Synagogues
3 rue Moulay Ismail

Safi

Synagogues
Beth El, rue de R'bat
Mursiand, rue de R'bat

Tangier

Hotels
El Minzah (140)
85 rue de la Liberte   (9) 935-885
                                  Fax: (9) 934-546

La Grande Villa de France
rue de Belgique
Les Almohade (150)
Av. des F. A. R.
Rambrant, Av. Pasteur   (9) 378-7071
Rif, Av. d'Espagne

Mikvaot
Shaar Raphael
27 Blvd. Pasteur   (9) 231304

Organisations
Community Centre
1 rue de la Liberte   (9) 31633 or 21024

Synagogues
Shaar Raphael
27 Blvd. Pasteur   (9) 231304
Temple Nahon
rue Moses Nahon

Tourist Sites
rue des Synagogues, off rue Siaghines
There are a number of synagogues in the old
part of the town in this street.

Tetuan

Organisations
Community Offices
16 rue Moulay Abbas

Synagogues
Benoualid, The old Mellah
Pintada, The old Mellah
Yagdil Torah
Adj. Community Centre

Mozambique

The small community in Mozambique originally consisted of South African Jews who were forced out of South Africa for supporting the British at the beginning of the twentieth century. A synagogue was opened in 1926, and there is a cemetery in Alto Maha. The biggest Jewish community is in Lourenço Marques.

GMT + 2 hours | Total Population 17,796,000
Country calling code (258) | Jewish Population Under 100

Maputo

Organisations
Jewish Community of Maputo
PO Box 232   (1) 494413

Onumoz
PO Box 1915   (1) 42 30 17
      Fax: (1) 42 33 82

Myanmar (formerly Burma)

The first Jews came to Myanmar in the early eighteenth century from Iraq and other Middle Eastern countries. A synagogue was built in 1896, and the Jewish population swelled to 2,000 before 1939, but most of these escaped to Britain and India before the Japanese invasion in the Second World War. Not many returned after the war (only a few hundred), and the community began to decline through intermarriage and conversion. The handful of remaining Jews are elderly and services are held only on the High Holy Days when a minyan is made up with help from the Israeli embassy.

However, not all of Myanmar's Jews came from the Middle East. There is an autochthonous group of Jews in the north of the country who have their own prayer house and who believe that they are descended from the tribe of Menashe.

GMT + 6.5 hours | Total Population 45,922,000
Country calling code (95) | Jewish Population Under 100
Emergency Telephone (Police – 199) (Fire – 191) (Ambulance – 192)

Yangon *(formerly Rangoon)*

Embassy
Embassy of Israel
49 Pyay Road, Yangon
      (1) 222-290; 222-709; 222-201
      Fax: (1) 222-463
      Email: emisrael@datserco.com.mm

Synagogues
Musmeah Yeshua
85 26th Street   (1) 75062

Namibia

Namibian Jewry began at the time when the country was a German colony, before the First World War. The cemetery at Swakopmund dates from that settlement. Keetmanschoop also had a congregation, but this no longer exists. The Windhoek synagogue is still in use, and was founded in 1924. Services are held on shabbat and festivals.

South Africa provides some help for the community, such as a cantor on festivals, and the Cape Board of Jewish Education assists with Hebrew education. From approximately 100 Jewish families in the 1920s and 1930s, the number has dwindled to about 11.

GMT + 2 hours   Total Population 1,500,000
Country calling code (264)   Jewish Population Under 100
Emergency Telephone

Windhoek
Synagogues
Cnr. Tal & Post Streets, PO Box 563

Netherlands

Although some historians believe that the first Jews in Holland lived there during Roman times, documentary evidence dates back only from the twelfth century.   The contemporary settlement occurred when Portuguese Conversos (Marranos) found refuge from the Inquisition in Holland.   Religious freedom was advocated in the early seventeenth century and Jews contributed much to the Netherlands' 'golden age' of prosperity and power.

By the time of Napoleon, the community had grown to 10,000 (the largest in western Europe), mainly by incoming Jewish traders from eastern Europe. The Jews were emancipated in 1796, but the community began to decline slowly during the nineteenth century. Of the 140,000 Jews (including 30,000 German Jewish refugees) in Holland in 1939, the Germans transported 100,000 to various death camps in Poland, but the local Dutch population tended to behave sympathetically towards their Jewish neighbours, hiding many. Anne Frank and her family are the most famous of the hidden Jews from Holland. Amsterdam witnessed the only strike of the war, called as a protest against the Jewish deportations.

Today, there are three Jewish councils in the Netherlands, representing the Ashkenazi, Reform and Orthodox communities. There are many synagogues in Amsterdam, as well as synagogues in other towns. There are kosher restaurants in Amsterdam, which also has many historical sites – Anne Frank House, the Portuguese Synagogue, lit by candlelight, and the Resistance Museum.

GMT + 1 hour	Total Population 15,575,000
Country calling code (31)	Jewish Population 30,000
Emergency Telephone (Police, Fire and Ambulance – 112)	

Contact Information

(20) 644-3868

For information on synagogues, services and kosher food outside Amsterdam, Rotterdam and The Hague, contact Chief Rabbinate of Holland.

Amersfoort

Synagogues
Drieringensteeg 2   (33) 720943

Amsterdam

Bakeries
Maasstraat 16   (20) 662-4827
Jerusalem Bakery
Scheldestr. 55   (20) 679-4764
Theeboom, Bolestein 45-47   (20) 642-7003
Hours: Sunday-Friday 9.00-1700, closed on Tuesday. Trams: 12, 25.
Tweede, Sweelinckstr. 5   (20) 662-7086

Booksellers
Joachimsthal's Boekhandel
Van Leijenberghlaan 116 1082 DB
(20) 442-0762
Fax: (20) 404-1843
Email: jachims@xsyall.nl
Open Sunday to Thursday 9.30 am. to 6 pm.
Friday 9.30 am. to 5 pm.
Samech Books
Gunterstein 69   (20) 642-1424
Fax: (20) 642-1424
Email: samech@dds.nl.

Butchers
Marcus Ritueel
Ferd. Bolstr. 44   (20) 671-9881
Meyer, Scheldestr. 63   (20) 664-0036

Chocolate Shops
Chocolate shop Bonbon Jeannette
Hall Central Station Amsterdam, Stationsplein 15 1012 AB   (20) 421-5194
Fax: (20) 421-5194
Their bitter and dairy chocolates and bonbons are kosher and are sanctioned by the Chief Rabbinate for the Netherlands. Open daily, 8 am to 9 pm.

Chocolate shop Bonbon Jeannette
Europaplein 87 1078 GZ   (20) 664-9638
                                Fax: (20) 675-6543
Their bitter and dairy chocolates and bonbons
are kosher and are sanctioned by the Chief
Rabbinate for the Netherlands. Hours: Monday
to Friday, 9 am to 6 pm; Sunday, 9 am to 5
pm; closed Mondays in July and August.
Nearest means of public transport: tram 4 and
buses 15, 71, 220 and 315.

Delicatessens
Mouwes Koshere Delicatessan
Kastelenstraat 261 1082   (20) 661-0180

Hotels
Hotel Arsenal
Frans van mierisstr. 97   (20) 679-2209
Pre-packed kosher breakfasts available for
guests.
Hotel Doria
Damstraat 3   (20) 638-8826
                                Fax: (20) 638-8726
                        Email: doria@euronet.nl
Hotel Golden Tulip
Barbizon Centre, Stadhouderskade 7
                                 (20) 685-1351

Libraries
Bibliothecha Rosenthaliana
Singel 423
A fine collection of Judaica and Hebraica in the
university library.
Livraria Montezinos & Ets Haim Library
Mr. Visserplein 3
Open for research only Mon.-Thurs. 9am to
12.30pm

Media

Newspapers
"Nieuw Israelitisch Weekblad"
Rapenburgerstr. 109   (20) 623-5584

Mikvaot
Mr. Visserplein 3, Heinzestr. 3   (20) 662-0178

Museums
Anne Frank House
Prinsengracht 263   (20) 556-7100
                                Fax: (20) 620-7999
                        Web site: www.annefrank.nl
Several exhibitions, including the original
hiding place of Anne Frank, where she wrote
her diary. Open daily from 9am to 5pm. April

1st to September 1st daily from 9am to 9pm. May 4th 9am to 7pm. January 1st and December 25th 12 noon to 5pm.

The Jewish Historical Museum
Jonas Daniel Meijerplein 2-4   (20) 626-9945
Fax: (20) 624-1721
Housed in a complex of 4 former synagogues. Sandwich shop serving kosher food although not under rabbinical supervision. Open daily from 11am to 5pm.

The Resistance Museum
Lekstr. 61
Housed in the Synagogue building

Organisations
Ashkenazi Community Offices
van der Boechorststr. 26 10108
(20) 646-0046
Fax: (20) 646-4357
Community Centre
van der Boechorststraaat 26 10108
(20) 644-0180

Restaurants
Carmel
Amstelveensewag 224 1075 XT
(20) 675-7636
 Hours: 12 pm to 11:30 pm, Sunday to Thursday. Cater Shabbat meals for groups if ordered in advance. Transport: trams 6, 16, bus 15, 63, 170, 171, 172.
Jewish Youth Centre
De Lairessestraat 13   (20) 676-7622
Email: jjc@dds.nl
Supervision: Amsterdam Rabbinate.
Due to reopen in 1999. Café/Restaurant, party room, conference room.
Mrs B. Hertzberger
Plantage Westermanlaan 9 1018 DK
(20) 623-4684
Supervision: Rabbinate of Amsterdam.
5 minutes from Portuguese Synagogue. Friday night and Shabbat meals only. Reservation in advance. Also lunchboxes for groups.
Museum Café
Jewish Historical Museum, Jonas Daniel Meijerplein 2-4   (20) 626-9945
Hours 11am to 5pm daily
Sandwichshop Sal. Meijer
Scheldestraat 45 1078 GG   (20) 673-1313
Fax: (20) 642-9020

Vegetarian
Bolhoed, Prinsengacht 60-62   (20) 626-1803
Hours: 12 pm to 10 pm daily. Serve organic vegetarian and vegan food.

Snackbar
Vlaams Friteshuis (Vleminckx)
Voetboog Str.33, (alleyway off Spui)
(020) 624-6075
This vendor sells only fries (chips), cooked in vegetable oil. A variety of sauces are available and included in the price. The chips are served in a paper cone.

Synagogues
Buitenveldert
van der Boechorststr. 26 10108
Jacob Obrechtplein
Gerard Doustr. 238
Services: Saturday and Festival mornings
Kehilas Ja'Akow (E. Europe)
Gerrit van der Veenstraat 26 1077 ED
(20) 676-3602
Kehilas Ja'Akow (E. Europe)
Lekstr. 61
Nieuwe Kerkstraat 148 (East European)
Straat van Messina 10   (20) 676-6400
Shabbat service at 9.30 hours.
The Portuguese Synagogue
Mr. Visserplein 3   (20) 624-5351
Fax: (20) 625-4680
This synagogue has been completely restored, and is open April – October: Sun – Fri 10am to 12.30pm and 1pm to 4pm; November to March Sun 10am to 12pm; Mon.-Thurs. 10am to 12pm and 1pm to 4pm; Fri 10 am to 12.30pm and 1pm to 3pm

Ashkenazi
Ashkenazi Rabbinate of Amsterdam
van der Boechorststr. 26, PO Box 7967 10108
(20) 646-0046
Fax: (20) 646-4357
Contact hours Monday 2-6pm. Wednesday 3-6pm.
Beth Shalom Home for Aged
Kastelenstraat 80, Amsterdam
Services: Friday, Festival evening, Saturday morning/afternoon/evening. Open to the general public
General Hospital Amstelveen (C.I.Z.)
Laan van de Helende Meesters 8
(20) 347-4747
Fax: (20) 347-4917
Email: role@zha.nl.
The synagogue is a part of the 'Jewish Wing' of the General Hospital. Services: Saturday and Festival mornings. Open to the general public.

Liberal

Jacob Soetendorpstr. 8 1079   (20) 642-3562
Fax: (20) 642-8135

The Liberal Synagogue

Houses the Judith Druk Library and the Centre for Jewish Studies.

Sephardi

Portuguese Synagogue & Community Centre
Texelstr. 82   (20) 624-5351

Tourist Sites
Portuguese Cemetery
Ouderkerk-on-the-Amstel
10 miles south-east of Amsterdam (Manasseh ben Israel is buried here).

Arnhem

Synagogues
Pastoorstr. 17a   (26) 442-5154

Liberal

Liberal Congregation Inquiries
Regentesselaan 18, Apeldoorn 7316 AE
(55) 522-2332

Bussum

Synagogues
Kromme Englaan 1a   (35) 691-4882

Delft

Synagogues
Beth Studentiem
Hillel House, Jewish Students Centre, Technical
University, Koornmarkt 9   (15) 212-0300

Eindhoven

Religious Organisations
Synagogue Inquiries
(40) 241-2710

Synagogues
H. Casimirstr. 23   (40) 751-1253

Enschede

Synagogues
Prinsestr. 16   (53) 432-3479; 435-3336

Liberal

Liberal Congregation Inquiries
Haaksbergen   (53) 435-1330

Groningen

Synagogues
Postbus 550 9700 AN   (50) 312-3151

Haarlem

Synagogues
Kenaupark 7   (23) 332-6899; 324-2051

Hilversum

Synagogues
Synagogue, Laanstr. 30   (35) 621-2044
Inter-Provincial Chief Rabbinate also based at
this address. Rabbi's J. S. Jacobs, S. Evers and
A. L. Heintz Tel: 035-623-9238

Leiden

Organisations
Jewish Students Centre
Levendaal 8   (71) 513-0382

Synagogues
Levendaal 14-16   (71) 512-5793
Fax: (71) 512-5793

Maastricht

Synagogues
Capucijnengang 2
Est. 1840

Rotterdam

Butchers
Piket, Walen-burgerweg 97   (10) 467-2856
Wednesdays only. Kosher groceries available
Wednesday and Thursday pm.

Synagogues
Joodse Gemeente Rotterdam
A B N Davidsplein 2   (10) 466-9765
Fax: (10) 467-5713

Mikva on premises.

Liberal

Molenhoek Hillegersberg   (20) 644-2619
Inquiries to Secretary on 010-461-3211

The Hague

Embassy
Embassy of Israel
Buitenhof 47 2513 AH

Synagogues

Corn. Houtmanstr., 11 Bezuidenhout
(70) 347-3201
Mikva on premises, appointments should be
made 24hrs in advance by telephoning
350-7621.
Beis Jisroel
Doorniksestraat 152 2587 AZ   (70) 358-6363
Fax: (70) 347-9002

Liberal
Liberal Synagogue
Prinsessegracht 26   (70) 365-6893
Fax: (70) 360-3883

Tourist Sites
Spinoza House
Paviljoensgracht
Spinoza House is of special interest, as is the
18th c. Portuguese Synagogue in the
Prinsessegracht, which is now used by the
Liberal congregation.

Tilburg
Synagogues
Liberal Synagogue Brabant
(70) 365-6893
Inquiries to 013-467-5566

Utrecht
Bakeries
De Tarwebol
Zadelstr. 19   (30) 231-4887
Delicatessens
Milk and Honey
Poorstr. 93   (30) 273-3114
Synagogues
Springweg 164 3511 VZ   (30) 231-4742
Fax: (30) 272-2091
Email: heintz@globalxs.nl
Liberal
Liberal Synagogue
(20) 644-2619
Inquiries to 030-603-9343
Zwolle
Synagogues
Samuel Hirschstr. 8, Postbox 1468 8001
(38) 211412

Netherlands Antilles

The first Jew in Aruba was Moses Salomo Levy Maduro (1753). A Jewish community
was officially recognised in 1946.

A Samuel Cohen served as an interpreter to the Dutch army which captured Curaçao
from the Spaniards in 1634. A congregation was founded in 1651. The Jews of Curaçao
enjoyed excellent relations with the Dutch West India Company who owned the island
until the end of the eighteenth century.

GMT – 4 hours   Total Population 207,000
Country calling code (599)   Jewish Population Under 100

Aruba
Synagogues
Adrian Lacle Boulevard, Oranjestad
(9) 23272
Services Friday, 8pm

Curaçao
Kashrut Information

There is no kosher restaurant in Curacao, but
kosher food is available at some out-of-town
supermarkets.

Organisations

Israel Consulate
Blauwduifweg 5, Willemstad   (9) 736-5068
Fax: (9) 737-0707
Email: midalya@ibm.net

Synagogues

Ashkenazi Orthodox

Congregation Shaarei Tsedek
Leliweg 1a, PO Box 498   (9) 375738

Sephardi, Reconstructionist

United Netherlands Portuguese Congregation
PO Box 322   (9) 461-1067
Fax: (9) 465-4141
Sabbath services are Friday at 6.30pm (second Friday in the month is a family service), Saturday at 10am. Holy-day services at same times.

Travel Agencies

S. E. L. Maduro & Sons, Inc.
Maduro Plaza, Dokweg 19   (9) 376700
Fax: (9) 376131

New Zealand

New Zealand Jewry is almost as old as the European presence in the country. The year 1829 marks the beginning of Jewish settlement, and Jews played a prominent role in the development of the country in the nineteenth century, especially in trading with Australia and Britain. Auckland Jewish community was founded in 1841, followed by Wellington in 1843. The first two mayors were Jewish and there was a Jewish Prime Minister, Sir Julius Vogel, in the nineteenth century.

British Jews emigrated to New Zealand in the twentieth century, but New Zealand restricted immigration from Nazi Europe.

Today the community has six synagogues, four on the North Island and two on the South Island. Auckland and Wellington have Jewish day schools, WIZO and B'nai B'rith are both present, and the 'Kosher Kiwi Guide' is published in Auckland. There has been recent Jewish immigration from South Africa, and the community, although small, is set to continue to provide a Jewish life.

GMT + 12 hours
Country calling code (64)

Total Population 3,602,000
Jewish Population 5,000

Auckland

Bakeries

Manhattan Bagels
(9) 309-9098

Caterers

Shelleys Catering
13 Collingswood Street, Freemans Bay
(9) 360-2989
Fax: (9) 486-0158
Shelleys provide kosher meals for all New Zealand flights.

Representative Organisations

Auckland Jewish Council
PO Box 4315   (9) 309-9444
Fax: (9) 373-2283

Synagogues

Orthodox

Auckland Hebrew Congregation
108 Greys Avenue, PO Box 68-224
(9) 373-2908
Fax: (9) 303-2147
Email: jay-el@ihug.co.nz

Progressive

Beth Shalom Synagogue
180 Manukau Road, Epsom 3   (9) 524-4139
Fax: (9) 524-7075
Email: bshalom@ihug.co.nz

Christchurch

Representative Organisations
Christchurch Jewish Council
(3) 358-8769

Synagogues
406 Durham Street (3) 365-7412

Dunedin

Synagogues
Progressive Congregation
cnr. George & Dundas Streets

Wellington

Community Organisations
Wellington Jewish Community Centre
80 Webb Street (4) 384-5081
Fax: (4) 384-5081
Email: bethel@ihug.co.nz
There are no kosher restaurants in Wellington.
Visitors who want kosher meals & kosher food
should contact the centre office of the
Community Centre or the Kosher Co-op, on
384-3136.

Delicatessens
Dixon Street Delicatessen
(4) 384-2436
Fax: (4) 384-8692
Not kosher but provides kosher bagels, bread
rolls and challahs.

Embassy
Israel Embassy
D.P. Tower, 111 The Terrace, PO Box 2171
(4) 472-2368
Fax: (4) 499-0632

Groceries
Kosher Co-op
80 Webb Street (4) 384-3136

Media

Newspapers

New Zealand Jewish Chronicle
PO Box 27-156 (4) 384-4229
Fax: (4) 384-4229
Email: mregan@voyager.co.nz
Edited by Mike Regan, this monthly is the
official publication of the Zionist Federation of
New Zealand.

Mikvaot
Wellington Jewish Community Centre
80 Webb Street (4) 384-5081
Fax: (4) 384-5081
Email: bethel@ihug.co.nz

Representative Organisations
Wellington and New Zealand Regional
Jewish Council
54 Central Terrace 5 (4) 475-7622

Synagogues

Orthodox

Beth-El Synagogue
80 Webb Street (4) 384-5081
Fax: (4) 384-5081
Email: bethel@ihug.co.nz

Progressive

Temple Sinai
147 Ghuznee Street (4) 385-0720
Fax: (4) 385-0572

Norway

The only way Jews could enter Norway before the nineteenth century was with a 'Letter of Protection', as Danish control limited the amount of Jewish entry. The situation changed in the 1840s, when a Norwegian liberal poet, Henrik Wergeland, argued for the admission of Jews into the country, and the parliament eventually agreed. There were only some 650 Jews in the country after emancipation in 1891, mainly in Oslo and Trondheim. By 1920 the community numbered 1,457 and by the time of the Nazi invasion there were 1,800. Despite attempts by the Norwegian resistance to smuggle Jews to Sweden, 760 Jews were transported to Auschwitz. The 800 Jewish survivors were joined after the war by 500 Displaced Persons, especially invited by the Norwegian government.

Shechita is forbidden but there is a kosher food shop in Oslo. B'nai B'rith and WIZO are present, and there is also a Jewish magazine. An old-age home was built in 1988. Trondheim, in the north of the country, has the northernmost synagogue in world.

GMT + 1 hour

Country calling code (47)

Emergency Telephone (Police – 112) (Fire – 110) (Ambulance – 113)

Total Population 4,348,000

Jewish Population 1,500

Oslo

Embassy
Embassy of Israel
Drammensveien 82c 0271   2244-7924
                        Fax: 2256-2183
                 Email: israel@online.no

Restaurants
Kosher Food Centre
Waldemar Thranesgt. 0171   2260-9166
Supervision: Rabbi Michael Melchior.
There are no kosher hotels or restaurants in Oslo but there is the Kosher Food Centre. Open 4 pm to 6 pm Tuesday and Thursday, and 12 pm to 2 pm on Friday. Closed Shabbat.

Vegetarian
Frisksport Vegeta Vertshus
Munkedamsveien 3b 0161
                    2283-4020; 2283-4232
                        Fax: 6690-0162
                Email: arewr@online.no
Hours: 11 am to 11 pm, 7 days a week. Large salad and hot dish buffet all day. Lacto-ovo-vegetarian food.

Synagogues
Bergstien 13-15 0172   2269-6570
                        Fax: 2246-6604

Tourist Sites
Ostre Gravlund Cemetery
There is a Jewish war memorial erected here.

Trondheim
Synagogues
Ark. Christiesgt. 1

Panama

There were some Jews, most of them pretending to be Christians, who came to Panama during colonial times. Panama was an important crossroads for trade and, as a result, many Jews passed through the country on their journeys in the region. In 1849, the first Jewish community began, with Jews on their way to the Californian Gold Rush settling in Panama. They were joined by Jews from the Caribbean, and later by central European Jews. Synagogues were founded in 1876 in Panama City and in 1890 in Colon. The economic boosts produced by the building of the Panama Canal and the First World War led to an increased number of Middle Eastern Jews settling in the country.

This influx has resulted in the present community being approximately 60 per cent Sephardi and 40 per cent Ashkenazi. There are B'nai B'rith and WIZO in the country, and there are a number of synagogues and kosher restaurants. There have even been two Jewish presidents this century – the only country apart from Israel where this has happened.

GMT – 5 hours
Country calling code (507)
Emergency Telephone (Police – 104 Fire – 103)

Total Population 2,677,000
Jewish Population 7,000

Panama City

Butchers
Shalom Kosher
Plaza Bal Harbour, Paitilla   264-4411
Super Kosher
Calle San Sebastian, Paitilla
263-5253;263-5254
Fax: 263-2067
Supervision: Shevet Ahim Rabinate.
Also Kosher supermarket, bakery and restaurant. Open from 8.30 am to 8.30 pm Sunday to Thursday. Friday until 4.30 pm

Chocolatier
Chocolatier
Calle 53, Urb., Marbella   264-4712

Contact Information
PO Box 6629 5   228-6311
Fax: 228-6796

Embassy
Israel Embassy
Edificio Grobman, Calle Manuel Maria Icaza,
5th Floor, apdo 6357 5   264-8022
Fax: 642-706

Mikvaot
Beneficiencia Israelita Beth El
Calle 58E, Urb., Obarrio   223-3383
Sociedad Israelita Shevet Ahim
Calle 44-27   225-5990
Fax: 227-1268

Organisations
Consejo Central Comunitario Hebrew de Panama
Apt. 3309, 4   263-8411
Fax: 264-7936
Jewish Centre Centro Cultural Hebreo De beneficiencia
Calle 50 Final, PO Box 7166, 5   226-0455
Fax: 226-0869
(K) Restaurant open daily for lunch and supper. Closed Saturdays.

Religious Organisations
Chief Rabbi Sion Levy
Calle 44-40, Bella Vista 85, Apartado, 6222, 5
227-2828

Restaurants
Candies Bazaar
Via Argentina, 155 L-2   269-4857
Pita Pan, Plaza Bal Harbour, Paitilla 264-2786

Synagogues

Ashkenazi

Beneficiencia Israelita Beth El
Calle 58E, Urb., Obarrio   223-3383

Reform

Kol Sherith Israel
Av. Cuba y Calle 36, No. 34-16, Apartado
4120 5   225-4100
                          Fax: 225-6412

Sephardi Orthodox

Sociedad Israelita Shevet Ahim
Calle 44-27   225-5990
                          Fax: 227-1268
Daily services.

Paraguay

Jewish settlement in this land-locked country came late for this area of South America. The few who came over from Western Europe at the end of the last century rapidly assimilated into the general population. The first synagogue was founded early in the twentieth century by Sephardis from Palestine, Turkey and Greece. Ashkenazis arrived in the 1920s and 1930s from eastern Europe and some 15,000 came to the country to escape Nazism, intending to move on into Argentina. Some of these, however, settled. Paraguay, in more recent times, has accepted Jews from Argentina who were fleeing from the military regime.

Today there are three synagogues, a Jewish school and a Jewish museum in Asunción. There is a high rate of intermarriage, but children of mixed marriages do receive a Jewish education.

GMT – 5 hours

Country calling code (595)

Total Population 4,960,000

Jewish Population 1,000

Emergency Telephone (Police – 441 111) (Fire – 494 799) (Ambulance – 204 799)

Asunción

Embassy

Israel Embassy
Calle Yegros No. 437 C/25 de Mayo, Edificio
San Rafael, Piso 8, PO Box 1212
          (21) 495-097; 496-043; 496-044
                        Fax: (21) 496-355

Organisations

Consejo Representativo Israelita de
Paraguay
General Diaz, 657, PO Box 756   (21) 41744

Synagogues

General Diaz, 657

Peru

The original Jews in Peru arrived with the first Europeans, as many Marranos, or secret Jews, were leaders in the Spanish army which invaded the country in 1532. After the Inquisition was set up in 1570, the Jews were persecuted, and many were burned alive. After 1870, groups of Jews came over from Europe, but tended to disappear into the general population. In 1880, a group of North African Jews settled in Iquitos and worked in the rubber industry. More Jewish immigration occurred after the First World War, and, later, Nazi refugees entered the country. By the end of the Second World War the Jewish population had reached 6,000, but this subsequently declined.

Almost all of the present Jewish population are Ashkenazi. There is a central community organisation, the Asociacion Judia del Peru, and there are synagogues. Two Jewish newspapers are produced and most Jewish children go to the Colegio Leon Pinelo school, which is well known for its high standards. There is a cemetery at Iquitos, built by the nineteenth-century community. The community is shrinking owing to intermarriage and assimilation.

GMT – 5 hours

Country calling code (51)

Emergency Telephone (Police – 105) (Fire -116) (Ambulance – 470 5000)

Total Population 23,944,000

Jewish Population 3,000

Lima

Caterers
Salon Majestic
965 Pueblo Libre, 21   (14) 463-0031
                         Fax: (14) 461-8912
Supervision: Rabbi Abraham Benhamu and Rabbi Yaacov Kraus.
Catering for special groups and parties by prior arrangement only.

Embassy
Israel Embassy
Natalio Sanchez 125 6 Piso, Santa Beatris, apartado 738   (14) 433-4431
                         Fax: (14) 433-8925

Groceries
Minimarket Kasher
Av. Gral. Juan A. Pezet 1472, San Isidro, 27
                              (14) 264-2187
Supervision: Rabbi Kraus.

Hotels
Hostal Regina
Av. 2 de Mayo 1421, San Isidro, 27
             (14) 441-2541; 442-8870
                         Fax: (14) 421-2044
Shabbat observers may wish to stay here as there is only a short walk to the Centro Sharon.

Hotel Libertador
Los Eucaliptos 550, San Isidro, 27
                              (14) 421-6666
                         Fax: (14) 442-3011
Shabbat observers may wish to stay here as there is only a short walk to the Centro Sharon.

Kashrut Information
Rabbinate
Av. de Mayo 1815, San Isidro 27
                              (14) 264-0678
There is no kosher restaurant in Lima. Visitors who want kosher meals should contact Rabbi Kraus.

Media
Newspapers

J.T.A. – Publicationes Memora S. A.
Psje. Malvas 135, Brena, 5   (14) 424-0534
Daily publication.
Shofar, Husares de Junin 163, Jesus Maria, 11
                              (14) 241412, 312410
Monthly.

Mikvaot
Union Israelita
Ave. Gral. Juan A. Pezet 1472, San Isidro, 27
                              (14) 264-2187
Sociedad Israelita Sefardi; Beit Jabad

Museums
Museum of the Inquisition
Junin 548
Dungeon and torture chamber of the headquarters of the Inquisition for all Spanish South America. In front of the Congress.

Organisations
Asociacion Judia de beneficencia y Culto de 1870
Jose Galvez 282, Miraflores, 18
(14) 451089 or 445-5148
Fax: (14) 445-5148

Religious Organisations
Chief Rabbi
(14) 424-505
Rabbi Benhamu is the Chief Rabbi of Peru.

Synagogues
Beit Jabad, Salverry 3095, San Isidro, 27
(14) 264-6060
Fax: (14) 442-9441

Orthodox
Centro Social y Cultural Sharon
Av. 2 de Mayo 1815, San Isidro, 27
(14) 440-0290
Sociedad de beneficencia Israelita Sefardi
Enrique Villar 581, Santa Beatriz, 1
(14) 442-4505 or 471-7230
Union Israelita del Peru
Jose Quinones 290, Miraflores 18
(14) 441-3461
Services are held at the Centro Sharon

Tourist Sites
Pilatos House
Ancash 390
17th c. private mansion, now used by the National Institute of Culture. On the 2nd floor was the synagogue of the Marrano Jews.

Philippines Republic

Conversos (Marranos or secret Jews) who came with the Spanish in the sixteenth century were the first Jewish presence in the region. In the late nineteenth century, western European Jews came to trade in the area, and after the Americans occupied the country in 1898, more Jews arrived from a variety of places, including the USA and the Middle East. The first synagogue was built in 1924. The Philippines accepted refugees from Nazism, but the Japanese occupied the islands during the war and the Jewish population was interned. After the war many of the community emigrated. However, a new synagogue opened in 1983, and services are also held in the US Air Force bases around the country.

GMT + 8 hours
Country calling code (63)

Total Population 69,282,000
Jewish Population 250

Manila

Embassy
Israel Embassy
Trafalgar Plaza 23rd Floor
105 H.V. dela Costa Street, Salcedo Village,
Makati City, Metro Manils 1200
(2) 892-5329/30/31/34
Fax: (2) 894-1027
Email: israelembphl@netasia.net

Mikvaot	**Synagogues**
Jewish Association of the Philippines (Beth Yaacov Synagogue)	Jewish Association of the Philippines (Beth Yaacov Synagogue)
H. V. de la Costa Street, Salcedo Village, Makati, Metro Manila 1200	H. V. de la Costa Street, Salcedo Village, Makati, Metro Manila 1200
(2) 815-0263, 0265	(2) 815-0263, 0265
Fax: (2) 818-9990	Fax: (2) 818-9990
Kosher requirements by arrangement.	Services: Fri at 6.30pm, Sat at 9.30am

Poland

After just five years of German occupation in the Second World War, the thousand-year-old Jewish settlement in Poland, one of the largest Jewish communities in the world, had been almost totally eradicated. The Jews first came to Poland, in order to escape anti-semitism in Germany, in the early Middle Ages. They were initially welcomed by the rulers, and the Jews became greatly involved in the economy of the country.

Before the Second World War most Jews lived in the east and south of the country, under Russian and Austrian domination respectively until 1918. After 1918, Poland became an independent country once more, with over 3,000,000 Jews (300,000 in Warsaw). The community continued to flourish before 1939, with Yiddish being the main language of the Jews. The community was destroyed in stages during the war, as Poland became the centre for the Nazi's destruction of European Jewry. After the war, the borders shifted again, and the 100,000 or so survivors mostly tried to emigrate. The few who remained endured several progroms even after the events of the Holocaust.

Today the community is comparatively small, and most of the members are elderly, but there is a functioning synagogue in Warsaw and many Jewish historical sites are scattered throughout the country. The Polish Tourist Board publishes information about the Jewish heritage in Poland.

GMT + 1 hour	Total Population 39,000,000
Country calling code (63)	Jewish Population 8,000
Emergency Telephone (Police – 997) (Fire – 998) (Ambulance – 999)	

Bielsko-Biala

Organisations
Elzbieta Wajs, Ul Mickiewicza 26 43-300
(2) 22438

Bytom

Organisations
Ul Smolenia 4 41902   (3) 813510

Cracow

Booksellers
Jordan, 2 Szeroka Street, Miodowa 41
(12) 217166

Galleries
Hadar, 13 Florianska Street   (12) 218992

Organisations
Zwiazek Wyznania Mojzeszowego
Ul Skawinska 2   (12) 662347

Restaurants

Meat

Na Kazimierzu
ul. Szeroka 39 31-053   (12) 229-644
Fax: (12) 219-909
Billed as the 'only kosher restaurant in Cracow and the south of Poland'. Hours: 12 pm to 12 am everyday. Traditional Shabbat courses are available on Shabbat.

Synagogues
Remuh, Ul Szeroka 40

Gliwice

Contact Information
Ul Dolnych Walow 9 44100   (32) 314797

Katowice

Contact Information
Ul Mlynska 13 40098   (32) 537742

Legnica

Contact Information
Ul Chojnowska 37 59220   (76) 22730

Lodz

Organisations
Jewish Chabad
     (42) 331221, 336825
Jewish Congregation
Zachodnia 78   (42) 335156

Lublin

Once a major Jewish town in eastern Europe, Lublin today has fewer than a hundred Jews. Pre-war Lublin was a centre for Torah study, and a large yeshivah was built only a few years before World War Two, and is now used as a college. Majdanek Concentration Camp lies within the city's boundary, clearly visible from a major road leading south east. There is a particularly moving memorial in the camp, consisting of the ashes from the camp's crematoria.

Contact Information
Ul Lubartowska 10 20080   (81) 22353

Rzeszów

Synagogues
ul. Bonicza, edge of Pl. Ofiara Getta

Szczecin

Contact Information
Ul Niemcewicza 2 71553   (91) 221674

Warsaw

Before the war, Warsaw had approximately 300,000 Jews. Now there are only a couple of thousand, mostly elderly. There are many historical sites which can be visited, such as surving fragments of the Ghetto and a several memorials in the ghetto area. The Jewish cemetery, untouched by the Nazis, is very imposing, and is still in use.

     The Warsaw Ghetto fighters are included in the inscription to Tomb of the Unknown Soldier in the centre of the city.

Embassy
Embassy of Israel
Ul I Kryzwickiego 24

Organisations
The Jewish Historical Institute
3/5 Tlomackie Street 00090   (22) 827-9221
     Fax: (22) 827-8372
     Email: zihinb@ikp.atm.com.pl
This establishment has a remarkable collection of Judaica. It includes a library of documents on the manuscripts stolen by the Germans from all over Europe.
Zwiazek Gmin Wyznaniowych Zydowskich w RP
Ul. Twarda 6 00-950   (22) 620-4320
     Fax: (22) 620-1037

Restaurants
Ekologica Restaurant
Rynek 13, Nowy Miasto
Menora, Plac Grzybowski 2   (22) 203754
Panorama, Al Witsoa 31   (22) 642-0666
Salad Bar, Ul Tamka 37   (22) 635-8463

Synagogues
Vadd Hakehilla
6 Twarda Street   (22) 204324

Tours of Jewish Interest
Shalom Tours
     (22) 220-3037
     Fax: (22) 220-0559

Wrocklaw

Museums
Historical Museum
Slezna Street 37   (71) 678236

Portugal

Portuguese Jewry had a parallel history to Spanish Jewry until the twelfth century, when the country emerged from Spain's shadow, and Jews worked with the Portuguese kings in developing the country. However, they were heavily taxed and had to live in special areas, although they were free to practise their religion as they pleased. As a result, the community flourished.

Persecution began during the period of the Black Death, and the Church was a key instigator of the riots which broke out against the Jews. During the Inquisition in neighbouring Spain, many Jews fled to Portugal, but were expelled in 1496. Many Jews converted in order to remain in the country and help with the economy. These became the Portuguese 'Conversos' and some of their descendants are converting back to Judaism today.

Over the last century and a half, Jews have begun to re-enter the country, and many others have used it as an escape route to America. Most of the community are now Sephardi, and there is a Sephardi synagogue in Lisbon. There is also a central Jewish organisation which is a binding force for Jews in the country.

GMT + 0 hours	Total Population 9,808,000
Country calling code (351)	Jewish Population 900
Emergency Telephone (Police, Fire and Ambulance – 115)	

Algarve

Community Organisations
Jewish Community of Algarve
Rua Infante Dom Henrique 12
3°B, Portimão 8500   (82) 416-710
                            Fax: (82) 416-515

Belmonte

Organisations
Jewish Community of Belmonte
Apt. 18, Bairo de Santa Maina, 6250 Belmonte
                            (75) 912465
                            Fax: (75) 912465

Faro

Museums
Faro Jewish Cemetery and Museum

1838-1932. Only remaining vestige of the first post-Inquisition Jewish presence in the Algarve. Open weekday mornings from 9:30 am to 12:30 pm. Situated opposite entrance to Faro Hospital. Enquiries to Ralf Pinto, Jewish Community of Algarve.

Lisbon

Community Organisations
Communal Offices
Rua Alexandre Herculano 59 1250
                            (1) 385-8604
                            Fax: (1) 388-4304

Embassy
Embassy of Israel
Rua Antonio Enes 16 1000
     (1) 570-251; 570-145; 570-374; 570-478

Kosher Meals
Mrs R. Assor
Rua Rodrigo da Fonseca 38.1'D   (1) 386-0396
                            Fax: (1) 395-3725
                            Email: iassor@mail.telepac.pt
Kosher meals and delicatessen are obtainable if prior notice is given. For kosher meats, contact the communal offices.

Organisations
Jewish Club & Centre
Rua Rosa Araujo 10   (1) 572041

Synagogues
Jewish Community
Rua Alexandre Herculano 59 1250
(1) 385-8604
Fax: (1) 388-4304
Services on Fri. eve. & Sat. morning.

Ashkenazi
Avenida Elias Garcia
100-1'-1050

Tomar

The ancient synagogue in Rua de Joaquim Jacinto (built 1492–1497) has been re-opened as a museum. A Marrano. Luis Vasco, is the custodian and guide. Tomar is north of Lisbon, near Fatima.

Oporto
Synagogues
Rua Guerra Junqueiro 340

Puerto Rico

The Jewish community in Puerto Rico is barely 100 years old, with the first Jews arriving in 1898, after the beginning of American rule. During the Second World War, many Jewish American servicemen went to the island, along with refugees from Nazism. A Jewish Community Centre dates from the early war years. After the war the community grew with an influx of Cuban and US Jews.

San Juan, the capital, has the largest Jewish population, and there are two synagogues. There is also a Hebrew school, held in the community centre. The first Chief Justice of Puerto Rico was Jewish.

GMT – 4 hours	Total Population 3,736,000
Country calling code (1 787)	Jewish Population 2,500

San Juan-Santurce
Kashrut Information

Frozen kosher poultry and delicatessen are available at some Pueblo supermarkets.

Synagogues
Shaare Zedeck
903 Ponce de Leon Av., 00907
(787) 724-4157

Reform
Temple Beth Shalom
San Jorge Av. & Loiza St., 00907

Romania

Romanian Jewry began at the time the Romans gave the country its name and language. In the fifteenth century, community life had begun to be organised, and settlement had spread to the town of Iasi and some Moldavian towns. Jews were welcomed from Poland and other east European countries, despite the opposition of the Church. Over the years, the community grew in size with further immigration, but emigration became the dominant factor after 1878, when the Treaty of Berlin, which demanded equal rights for Jews, was not implemented in Romania. Following Romania's acquisition of large area of Transylvania from Hungary after 1918, the Jewish population increased once more. The Jews were finally emancipated, but harsh discriminatory decrees were passed in 1937; 385,000 of the 800,000 Romanian Jews were killed in the Holocaust.

It is ironic that Romanian Jewry was able to function relatively normally under the harsh Ceaușescu regime. He was the only Warsaw Pact leader not to sever relations with Israel in 1967, and he allowed Jewish practices to continue, even permitting the Chief Rabbi, Dr Moses Rosen, to have a seat in the parliament. This freedom also tolerated emigration to Israel, which was seen by Ceaușescu as advantageous to Romania. Post-1989, the community still has its central body, the Federation of Jewish Communities, and there are kosher cafeterias in several cities. The community is ageing, but many synagogues are still functioning, and there are also Jewish newspapers and a Yiddish theatre. The Choral Synagogue in Bucharest is of particular interest to visitors.

GMT + 2 hours
Country calling code (40)
Emergency Telephone (Police – 955) (Ambulance – 961) (Fire – 981)

Total Population 22,650,000
Jewish Population 14,000

Arad

Hotels
Hotel Parc, Bd. Dragulina 25   (57) 280-820

Organisations
Community Offices
10 Tribunal Dobra Street   (57) 281310
Home for the Aged
22, 7 Episcopei Street

Restaurants
Ritual, 22, 7 Episcopei Street   (57) 280731

Synagogues
Muzeul Judetean
Piata George Enescu 1   (57) 280114
Neologa, 10 Tribunal Dobra Street
Talmud Torah
10 Tribunal Dobra Street

Orthodox
12 Cozia Street

Bacau

Organisations
Community Offices
11 Alexandru cel Bun Street   (34) 134714

Restaurants
11 Alexandru cel Bun Street

Synagogues
Avram A. Rosen Synagogue
31 V. Alecsandri Street
Cerealistilor
29 Stefan cel Mare Street

Borsec

Hotels

Kosher

Transylvania Hotel
c/o Interom Tours   972-3-924-6425
                      Fax: 972-3-579-1720

Synagogues
c/o Interom Tours   (972) 3924-6425
                      Fax: (972) 579-1720

Botosani

Mikvaot
67 7 Aprilie Street

Organisations
Community Offices
220 Calea Nationala   (31) 0315-14659

Restaurants
69 7 Aprilie Street   (31) 0315-15917

Synagogues
Great, 1a Marchian Street
Mare, 18 Muzicantilor Street
Yiddish, 10 Gh. Dimitrov Street

Brasov

Organisations
Community Offices
27 Poarta Schei Street   (68) 143532

Restaurants
27 Poarta Schei Street   (68) 144440

Synagogues
27 Poarta Schei Street

Bucharest

Community Organisations
Federation of Jewish Communities of
Romania
Str. Sf. Vinen 9-11, Sector 3   (1) 313-2538
                          Fax: (1) 312-0869

Documentation Centres
Romanian Jewish History Research Centre
12 Juliu Barasch Street   (1) 323-7246

Embassy
Embassy of Israel
6 Burghelea Street   (1) 613-2634/5/6

Mikvaot
5 Negustori Street

Museums
Museum of the Jewish Community in
Romania
3 Mamoulari Street   (1) 615-0837
Hours: Wednesday and Sunday, 9 am to 1 pm.

Religious Organisations
Chief Rabbi of Romania
Strada Sf. Vineri 9   (1) 613-2538
                      Fax: (1) 312-0869

Representative Organisations
Federation of Romanian Jewish
Communities
24 Popa Rusu Street   (1) 211-8080
The Federation publishes a bi-monthly, 'Revista
Realitatea Evreiasca'.

Restaurants
Jewish Community
18 Popa Soare Street   (1) 322-0398
This restaurant is operated by the Jewish
Community.

Synagogues
Choral Temple
Strada Sf. Vineri 9   (1) 147-257
Credinta, 48 Vasile Toneanu Street
Ieshua Tova
9 Nikos Beloiannis Street   (1) 659-5675
Near the Lido and Ambassador hotels.

Sephardi

Great Synagogue
9-11 Vasile Adamache Street   (1) 615-0846

Theatres
Jewish State Theatre
15 Iuliu Barasch Str., Sector 3 74212
                      (1) 323-4530;4035
                     Fax: (1) 323-2746
                     Email: harry@tes.ro
                     Web site: www.tes.ro

Cluj Napoca

Mikvaot
16 David Fransisc Street

Organisations
Community Offices
25 Tipografiei Street   (64) 11667

Restaurants
5-7 Paris Street   (64) 11026

Synagogues
Beth Hamidrash Ohel Moshe
16 David Fransisc Street
Sas Hevra, 13 Croitorilor Street

Templul Deportatilor
21 Horea Street

Constanta

Organisations
Community Office
3 Sarmisagetuza Street   (41) 611598

Synagogues
Great Temple
2 C. A. Rosetti Street
Small, 3 Sarmisagetuza Street
Talmud Torah
3 Sarmisagetuza Street

Dorohoi

Organisations
Community Office
95 Spiru Haret Street   (31) 611797

Restaurants
14-18 Dumitru Furtuna Street

Synagogues
Great, 4 Piata Unirii Street

Galati

Organisations
Community Office
9 Dornei Street   (36) 413662

Restaurants
9 Dornei Street   (36) 413662

Synagogues
Meseriasilor
11 Dornei Street

Iasi (Jassy)

Mikvaot
15 Elena Doamna Street

Organisations
Community Office
15 Elena Doamna Street   (32) 114414

Restaurants
15 Elena Doamna Street   (32) 1117883

Synagogues
Great, 7 Sinagogilor Street
Schor, 5 Sf. Constantin Street

Oradea

Mikvaot
5 Mihai Viteazu Street

Organisations
Community Office
4 Mihai Viteazu Street   (59) 134843

Restaurants
5 Mihai Viteazu Street   (59) 131383

Synagogues
Great, 4 Mihai Viteazu Street
Neolog, 22 Independentei Street
Sas Hevra, 4 Mihai Viteazu Street

Piatra Neamt

Organisations
Community Office
7 Petru Rares Street   (33) 623815

Synagogues
Leipziger, 12 Meteorului Street
Old Baal Shem Tov
7 Meteorului Street
Old historical monument.

Radauti

Organisations
Community Office
11 Aleea Primaverii, Block 14, Apt.1
(30) 461333

Synagogues
Great, 2, 1 Mai Street
Vijnitzer, 49 Libertatii Street

Satu Mare

Satu Mare is the Romanian name for the
Hungarian town of Szatmar, where the famous
Hassidic sect originated. It is in the north-west
of Romania, very near the border with
Hungary. Before World War One, the town was
in Hungary itself but Hungary lost Transylvania
(as well as other territory) after that war.

Organisations
Community Office
4 Decebal Street   (61) 743783

Synagogues
Great, 4 Decebal Street

Sighet

Organisations
Community Office
8 Basarabia Street   (62) 511652

Synagogues
Great, 8 Basarabia Street

Suceava

Organisations
Community Office
8 Armeneasca Street   (30) 213084

Synagogues
Gah Chavre, 4 Dimitrie Onciu Street

Timisoara

Mikvaot
55 Resita Street

Organisations
Community Office
5 Gh. Lazar Street   (56) 132813

Restaurants
10 Marasesti Street   (56) 136924

Synagogues
Cetate, 6 Marasesti Street
Fabric, 2 Splaiul Coloniei
Iosefin, 55 Resita Street

Tirgu Mures

Organisations
Community Office
10 Brailei Street   (65) 115001

Synagogues
21 Aurel Filimon Street

Tushnad

Hotels

Kosher

Olt Hotel, c/o Interom Tours
                                 972-3-924-6425
                          Fax: 972-3-579-1720

Vatra Dornei

Organisations
Community Office
54 M Eminescu Street   (30) 371957

Synagogues
Vijnitzer, 14 Luceafarul Street

Russian Federation

In early Russian history, Jews were not allowed to settle and the few who did were later expelled by various Czars. After 1772, Russia acquired a large area of Poland and, with it, a large number of Jews. There were still restrictions against the Jews, and eventually they were allowed to settle only in the 'Pale of Settlement', an area in the west of the Russian Empire. Some 2,000,000 Jews emigrated from the Empire between 1881 and 1914, escaping anti-semitism.

Jews were only allowed into Russia itself in the mid-nineteenth century, and by 1890 there were 35,000 Jews in Moscow. Most were expelled the following year. The community grew after the Second World War, drawing Jewish immigration from Belarus and Ukraine to cities such as Moscow and Leningrad. Birobidjan was a failed experiment to give the Jews their own 'Autonomous District', and those who moved there (in the far east, near China) later moved away. Under Communism, the community was restricted in both religious practices and emigration to Israel, but since 1991 there has been a revival in Jewish learning. There are synagogues functioning in many cities, and there are now 100 Jewish schools.

GMT + 2 to 12 hours	Total Population 148,126,000
Country calling code (7)	Jewish Population 450,000
Emergency Telephone (Police – 02) (Fire – 01) (Ambulance – 03)	

Astrakhan

Synagogues
30 Babushkin Street

Birobidjan

Synagogues
9 Chapaev Street, Khabarovsk Krai

Bryansk

Synagogues

Lubavitch
Synagogue of Bryansk
27a Uritskovo Street 241000   (0832) 445-515

Klintsy

Synagogues
82 Lermontov Street

Daghestan

Buynaksk

Synagogues
Narodov Vostoka Street

Derbent

Synagogues
94 Tagi-Zade Street

Lubavitch
Jewish Community of Derbent
23 Kandelaky Street 368600   (8724) 021-731

Makhachkala

Synagogues
111 Yermoshkin Street

Ekaterinburg

Synagogues
14 Kuibyshev Street

18/2 Kirov Street

Irkutsk

Synagogues
17 Karl Liebknecht Street

Kazan

Synagogues

Lubavitch
Synagogue of Kazan
15 Profsouznaya Street 420111
                             (8432) 329-743

Kostrama

Synagogues
Synagogue of Kostrama
16a Sennoi Peroulok 156026   (0942) 514-388

Krasnoyarsk

Synagogues
Synagogue of Krasnoyarsk
65 Surikova Street 660049   (3912) 223-615
                             Fax: (3912) 440-137
                         Email: jckras@hotmail.com

Kursk

Synagogues
3 Bolshevitskaya Street

Moscow

Some 200,000 Jews live in Moscow, and since the collapse of the USSR in 1991, the community has experienced a revival. The Synagogue on Arkhipova Street was built in 1891 and was used under the Soviet regime. The Lubavitch movement has its own centre, and there has been an upsurge of interest in Jewish education. The city can also boast a Jewish theatre.

Contact Information
Rabbi Pinchas Goldschmidt
Chief Rabbi of Moscow
                         (95) 923-4788; 924-2424

Embassy
Embassy of Israel
Bolshaya Ordinka 56

Museums
Poliakoff Synagogue
Bolshaya Brennaya 6

Restaurants

Meat

King David Club
Bolshoi Spasoglinishchevsky per. (Arkhipova St) 6, door code 77   (95) 925-4601
                             Fax: (95) 924-4243
                         Email: ail@ail.msk.ru
Supervision: Rabbi Pinchas Goldschmidt, Chief Rabbi of Moscow.
This Kosher Food Center serves as a glatt kosher restaurant and a mini hotel. Catering services are available as are lunchboxes.

Synagogues
2nd Korenyovsky Lane, Moscow Oblast,
Malakhovka
Moscow Choral Synagogue
Bolshoi Spasoglinishchevsky per.
(Arkhipova St) 10   (95) 924-2424
Poliakoff Synagogue
Chabad Center, Bolshaya Brennaya 6
                                     (95) 202-7696
                                Fax: (95) 202-7645

Lubavitch
Chabad Lubavitch
4 Novoisushevsky Peroulok 103055
                                     (95) 218-0001
                                Fax: (95) 219-9707
                          Email: lazar@glasnet.ru
Chabad Lubavitch Synagogue
6 Balshaya Bronya Street. 103104
                                     (95) 202-4530
                                Fax: (95) 291-6483
Darkei Shalom Synagogue
1 Novovladikinsky Peroulok 103055
                                     (95) 903-0782
                                Fax: (95) 903-2218

Nalchik
Synagogues
73 Rabochaya Street, cnr. Osetinskaya

Nizhny Novgorod
Synagogues

Lubavitch
Nizhny Novgorod Synagogue
5a Gruzinskaya Street 603000
                                   (8312) 336-345
                              Fax: (8312) 303-759

Novosibirsk
Synagogues
23 Luchezarnaya Street

Lubavitch
Synagogue of Novosibirsk
14 Koministisheskaya   (3832) 210-698

Penza
Synagogues
15 Krasnaya Street

Perm
Synagogues
Kuibyshev Street
Pushkin Street

Rostov-na-Donu
Synagogues

Lubavitch
Synagogue of Rostov-na-Dou
18 Gazetny Peroulok 344007
                                   (8632) 624-759
                              Fax: (8632) 624-119

Sachkhere
Synagogues
145 Sovetskaya Street
105 Tsereteli Street

Samara
Synagogues
3 Chapaev Street

Lubavitch
Synagogue of Samara
84 Tshepayovskaya Street 443099
                                   (8462) 334-064
                              Fax: (8462) 382-576
                  Email: chabad@transit.samara.ru

Saratov
Synagogues
2 Kirpichnaya Street
Posadskov Street

Lubavitch
Synagogue of Saratov
208 Posadskovo Street 410005
                                   (8452) 249-592

St Petersburg
With 100,000 Jews, St.Petersburg is witnessing
a similar Jewish revival to Moscow. There are
opportunities to pray, learn and eat kosher in
relative freedom – this was not the case (in
general) before 1991 in the USSR. Americans
and Israelis are the main motivators behind the
revival, but St Petersburg Jewry are also keen
to learn about their religion, now that they
have the freedom to do so.

Mikvaot
2 Lermontovsky Prospekt   (812) 113-8974

Representative Organisations
St Petersburg Jewish Association
Ryleev St, 29-31, a/b 103   (812) 272-4113

Restaurants
Dining Room at Shamir School
Ligovskiy Prospekt 161-8   (812) 116-1003

Synagogues
The Choral Synagogue of St Petersburg
2 Lermontovsky Prospekt 190121
    (812) 113-6209
Email: mendel@newzner.spb.su
This is the second street past the Kirov Opera
& Ballet Theatre.

Tour Information
Zekher Avoteinu
Jewish Tourist and Genealogical Agency, Pr.
Strachek 212, #46 198262   (812) 184-1248
    Fax: (812) 184-1248
The agency has prepared an exciting program
to inform visitors about Jewish history and life
in St Petersburg and perhaps to give insight to
the genealogy of ancestors.

Tshelyabinsk

Synagogues

Lubavitch
Synagogue of Tshelyabinsk
PO Box 16187 454091   (3512) 333-618
    Fax: (3512) 303-759

Tula

Synagogues
15 Veresaevskaya Street

Vladikavkaz
(formerly Ordzhonikidze)

Synagogues
Revolutsiya Street

Yekatrinburg

Synagogues

Lubavitch
Yekatrinburg Synagogue
118/93 Shekmana Street 620144
    (3432) 236-440
    Fax: (3432) 293-054

Singapore

As Singapore developed into an important south-east Asian trading centre in the mid-nineteenth century, some Jewish traders from India and Iraq set up a community there in 1841. A synagogue was built in 1878, and another in 1904. By the time of the Japanese occupation in the Second World War, the community had grown to 5,000, and included eastern European Jews. The Japanese imprisoned the community and took their property. After the war, emigration to Australia and the USA reduced numbers, but in recent years Israelis who work in the country and other Jews have moved in. Ninety per cent of the community are Sephardi.

One of the two synagogues is used regularly, and there is a mikva and a newsletter. In 1955 David Saul Marshall was appointed the country's first chief minister.

GMT + 8 hours
Country calling code (65)
Emergency Telephone (Police – 999) (Fire and Ambulance – 995)

Total Population 3,384,000
Jewish Population 300

Contact Information
Rabbi Abergel

Email: mordehai@singnet.com.sg
Contact either of these people for more detailed information on the community and availability of kosher products.

Embassy
Israel Embassy
58 Dalvey Road S-1025   235-0966
Fax: 733-7008

Representative Organisations
Jewish Welfare Board
Robinson Road, PO Box 474

Synagogues

Orthodox
Chesed-El
2 Oxley Rise S-0923   732-8832
Services, Monday only, Shacharit and Mincha/Maariv.

Maghain Aboth
24 Waterloo Street   336-0692
Mikva on premises. Daily and Shabbat services held, except for Monday. Because Singapore has equatorial times, Mincha/Maariv falls between 6:30 and 6:45 pm throughout the year. Shacharit: weekdays, 7 am; Shabbat, 9 am. Every Shabbat lunch is served for the community. Breakfast is currently served every morning after services.

Reform
United Hebrew Congregation (Singapore)
65 Chulia Street, OCBC Centre, #31-00 East Lobby 049513   536-8300
Established in 1995, the congregation's members are mostly Ashkenazi from English-speaking countries. The congregation conducts a full set of High Holy Day services with a rabbi and cantor, celebrations for other holidays, monthly Shabbat dinners and services, and educational and social events.

Slovak Republic

Slovakia has passed through the control of various countries over the centuries, finally gaining independence after the peaceful splitting of Czechoslovakia in 1992. Before 1918 the region was part of Hungary and many in southern Slovakia, near the Hungarian border, still speak Hungarian.

In 1939, the Jewish population in the Slovak area of Czechoslovakia numbered 150,000 but the Hungarians once again occupied the south of the country, and assisted the Germans in deporting Jews to Auschwitz and other camps. Many survivors emigrated after the war, but some remained, and are now rediscovering their Jewish heritage. Since independence, B'nai B'rith and Maccabi have been established, but anti-semitism has re-emerged. There are kosher restaurants in Bratislava and Kosice, and Jewish education is beginning once more.

GMT + 1 hour
Country calling code (421)
Emergency Telephone (Police – 158) (Fire – 150) (Ambulance – 155)

Total Population 5,350,000
Jewish Population 6,000

Bratislava

Known in German as Pressburg, Bratislava was a key centre of Judaism when Slovakia was under Hungarian rule before World War One. Bratislava was especially famous for the number of Jewish scholars living there, including the Chatam Sofer. The underground tomb of the Chatam Sofer and other rabbis in Bratislava make an unusual and interesting place to visit.

Bed & Breakfasts
Chez David
Zamocka 13
Pressburg 81101
(7) 544-13 824; 544-13 943
Fax: (7) 544-12 642
Supervision: Rabbi Baruch Myers, the Jewish Religious Community.

Mikvaot
Zamocka 13
Pressburg 81101
(7) 544-13 824; 544-13 943
Fax: (7) 531-2642
Kosher food is obtainable here as well. (Open for lunch only.)

Museums
The Museum of Jewish Culture
Zidovska Street, Pressburg, Pressburg

Underground Mausoleum
Pressburg
Contains the graves of 18 famous rabbis, including the Chatam Sofer. The key is available from the community offices.

Representative Organisations
Central Union of Jewish Religious Communities in the Slovak Republic
Kozia ul. 21, Bratislava 81447
(7) 531-2167; 531-8357
Fax: (7) 531-1106
Email: uzzno@netax.sk

Restaurants
Chez David
Zamocka 13
Pressburg 81101   (7) 544-13 824; 544-13 943
Fax: (7) 544-12 642
Supervision: Rabbi Baruch Myers, the Jewish Religious Community.

Synagogues
Heydukova 11-13, Pressburg
Services held Mon. Thurs. – Sat.

Galanta
Mikvaot
Partizanska 907

Synagogues
Partizanska 907
Daily services held.

Kosice

Restaurants
Community Centre
Zvonarska Ul 5
Kaschau 04001   (95) 622-1047

Synagogues
Puskinova Ul 3, Kaschau
Beth Hamidrash
Zvonarska Ul 5, Kaschau
Daily services held.

Piestany

Cemeteries

Old Cemetery
Janosikova Ul 606

Synagogues
Hviezdoslavova 59
Shabbat and festival services held.

Presov

Community Organisations
Community Centre
Sverthova 32   (91) 31271
                            Fax: (91) 31271
Synagogue and museum on premises.

Trnava

Monument
Monument to Deportees
Halenarska Ul 32
In the courtyard of the former synagogue.

Synagogues
Kapitulska Ul 7

Slovenia

Maribor was the centre for medieval Jewish life in what is now Slovenia. Expulsion followed after the Austrian occupation in the late Middle Ages, but, in 1867, the Jews in the Austrian empire were emancipated and some returned to Slovenia. The community was never large. During the Second World War the members of the small Jewish community either escaped to Italy, fought with the Yugoslav partisans, or were deported.

There is a Jewish Community of Slovenia, connected to the Croatian community, but none of the synagogues in this small country are functioning at present. There is one synagogue in Maribor that is classed as an historic monument and dates from the Middle Ages. There are also, other sites from medieval times, such as the cemeteries in Ljubljana (the capital) and Murska Sobota. The nearest functioning synagogue is across the Italian border in Trieste.

GMT + 1 hour	Total Population 1,942,000
Country calling code (386)	Jewish Population Under 100
Emergency Telephone (Police – 113) (Fire – 112) (Ambulance – 94)	

Ljubljana

Community Organisations
Jewish Community of Slovenia and
Ljubljana
PO Box 569 61101   (61) 221-836

South Africa

Although some believe that Jews were present in the country at around the time of the first European settlement in the area (the seventeenth century), the community only really began in the nineteenth century, when religious freedom was granted. The year 1841 marked the first Hebrew Congregation in Cape Town, and the discovery of diamonds in the Transvaal later on in the century prompted another wave of Jewish immigration.

The main immigration of Jews into South Africa occurred at the end of the nineteenth century, when many thousands left eastern Europe, the majority from Lithuania. Some 40,000 had arrived by 1910. Although the country did not accept refugees from the Nazis, about 8,000 Jews managed to enter the country after their escape from Europe.

Today the community is affluent and is on good relations with Nelson Mandela's government. There is a South African Board of Deputies, and many international Jewish associations are present in the country. There are kosher hotels and restaurants, and Jewish museums. Kosher wine is produced at the Zaandwijk Winery.

GMT + 2 hours
Country calling code (27)
Emergency Telephone (Police – 10111) (Fire – 731892) (Ambulance – 10177)

Total Population 42,393,000
Jewish Population 92,000

Cape Province

Cape Town

Bed & Breakfast

Kosher

Dinah's Guest House
6 Molteno Road
Oranjezicht 8001   (21) 241-568
                          Fax: (21) 241-598
                   Email: dinas@grm.co.za
             Web site: www.tourcape.co.za
Supervision: Cape Beth Din.
SA Tourism Board accredited kosher guest house. Walking distance to Gardens Synagogue (Orthodox), close to city centre, with 'meet and greet' facility from airport.

Butchers
Checkers
Sea Point 8001   (21) 439-6159
                          Fax: (21) 439-5630
Supervision: Cape Beth Din.
Also bakery.

Claremont Kosher Butchers
Marine Drive, Paarden Eiland, Claremont,
Claremont   (21) 683-2920
Supervision: Cape Beth Din.
Also serve light lunches, Monday to Friday, 9 am to 3 pm (meat).

Pick 'N Pay
Claremont   (21) 683-2900
Supervision: Cape Beth Din.

Pick 'N Pay
Sea Point 8001   (21) 438-2049
Supervision: Cape Beth Din.
Also bakery.

Pick 'N Pay
Constantia   (21) 794-5690
Supervision: Cape Beth Din.

Shoprite
Rondebosch   (21) 689-4563
Supervision: Cape Beth Din.

Delicatessens
Goldies
64 Regent Road
Sea Point 8001   (21) 434-1116
Supervision: Cape Beth Din.
Sit-down deli and take-away. Meat and pareve. Hours: Sunday to Thursday, 7 am to 8 pm; Friday, to 5 pm.

Reingold's Deli & Butchery
Plumstead   (21) 762-8093
Supervision: Cape Beth Din.

Hotels

Kosher

Belmont Hotel
Holmfirth Road
Sea Point 8005   (21) 439-1155
                        Fax: (21) 434-9451
Supervision: Cape Beth Din.

Cape Sun, Strand Street   (21) 238-844
Supervision: Cape Beth Din.
Only serves breakfast.

Libraries
Jacob Gitlin Library
Albow Bros. Centre, 94 Hatfield street 8001
(21) 453-311

Mikvaot
Arthur's RoadSea Point
            (21) 434-3148; 525-684; 082-452-5757

Museums
Jewish Museum
84 Hatfield StreetGardens   (21) 451-546
Sunday, 10 am to 12:30 pm; Tuesday &
Thursday, 2 pm to 5 pm.

Religious Organisations
**Union of Orthodox Synagogues Cape
Council**
191 Buitenkant Street 8001   (21) 461-6310
                        Fax: (21) 461-8320
            Email: uoscape@iafrica.com
Beth Din located at same address and phone
number.

Representative Organisations
**South African Jewish Board of Deputies
Cape Council**
Leeusig House, 3rd floor, 4 Leeuwen Street
8001   (21) 423-2420
                        Fax: (21) 423-2775
            Email: sajbodcc@iafrica.com

Restaurants

Dairy

Dovidil's Pizza
74 Regent Road
Sea Point 8001   (21) 434-1267
                        Fax: (21) 439-7280
Supervision: Cape Beth Din.
Hours: Sunday to Thursday, 11 am to 11 pm;
Friday, to 3 pm; Saturday night after Shabbat.

The Pickle Barrel
Dean Street Arcade, Dean Street, Newlands,
                            (21) 686-3633
Supervision: Cape Beth Din.
Deli and take-away also available. Pre-packed
cold meat available for take-away. Hours:
Monday to Wednesday, 8 am to 6 pm;
Thursday, to 10:30 pm; Friday, to 4 pm;
Sunday, 10 am to 11 pm.

Meat

Garden of Eden
359a Main Road
Sea Point 8001   (21) 439-1632
Supervision: Cape Beth Din and permanent
mashgiach.
Has a relaxed atmosphere of a Mediterranean
street café. Deli and take-away service
available. Hours: Sunday to Thursday, 9:30 am
to 11:30 pm; Friday, to 4 pm; Motzei Shabbat.
On the main bus and taxi route.

Kaplan Student Canteen
University of Cape Town   (21) 650-2688
Supervision: Cape Beth Din.
Lunches, take-away and orders. Meat and
pareve. Open Monday to Friday. Closed
December/January for varsity holidays and
during summer vacation.

Marrakesh
315 Main Road
Sea Point 8001   (21) 434-0455
                        Fax: (21) 434-0829
Supervision: Cape Beth Din.
Situated in the centre of Cape Town's Jewish
area, within walking distance ofl major hotels,
guest houses and four synagogues. All meat
glatt kosher. Open 6 days a week for lunch
and dinner.

The Pie Works
15 Regent Road, Sea Point   (21) 439-4484
Supervision: Cape Beth Din.
Hours: Sunday to Thursday, 8:30 am to 9 pm;
Friday, to 4 pm.

Synagogues

Orthodox

Camps Bay
Chilworth Road Camps Bay   (21) 438-8082
                        Fax: (21) 438-8082
Cape Town Hebrew Congregation
84 Hatfield Street, Gardens, Gardens
                            (21) 451-405

Claremont Hebrew Congregation
16 Carisbrook Avenue, Claremont
(21) 619-007
Fax: (21) 683-3011

Constantia
Old Rendal Road
Constantia 7806

Green & Sea Point Hebrew Congregation
Marais Road Sea Point
(21) 439-7543
Fax: (21) 434-3760

Milnerton
29 Fitzpatrick Road
Cambridge Estate 7441
(21) 697-1913
Fax: (21) 461-8320

Muizenberg
Camp Road, Muizenberg
(21) 788-1488

Schoonder Street Shul
10 Yeoville Road, Vredehoek
(21) 452-239
Fax: (21) 461-1510

Wynberg Hebrew Congregation
5 Mortimer Road
Wynberg 7800
(21) 797-5029
Fax: (21) 761-4669

Reform

Temple Israel
Salisbury Road Wynberg
(21) 797-3362
Temple Israel
Upper Portswood Road
Green Point
(21) 434-9721

East London

Synagogues

Orthodox

Shar Hashomayim
56 Park Avenue 5201
(431) 430-181

Kimberley

Synagogues
United Hebrew Institutions
20 Synagogue Street 8301
(531) 825-652

Oudtshoorn

Synagogues
United Hebrew Institutions
291 Buitenkant Street
(443) 223-068
There is a Jewish section in the C.P. Nel
Museum.

Paarl

Synagogues
New Breda Street
(2211) 24087
Community centre and Talmud Torah at same
address.

Port Elizabeth

Museums
Raleigh Street Synagogue
(41) 554-458

Synagogues

Orthodox
**Port Elizabeth Hebrew Congregation United
Synagogue**
55 Roosevelt Street
Glendinningvale 6001
(41) 331-332
Fax: (41) 333-293

Progressive
Temple Israel
Upper Dickens Street
(41) 336-642

Free State

Bloemfontein

Religious Organisations
United Hebrew Institutions
Community Centre, 2 Fairview, PO Box 1152
9300
(51) 312-207
Mornings.

Representative Organisations
O.F.S. & Northern Cape Zionist Council
Community Centre, 2 Fairview
PO Box 564, 9300
(51) 480-817
Fax: (51) 480-104

Synagogues

Orthodox
United Hebrew Synagogue
16 Waverley Road
(51) 436-7609
Fax: (51) 436-6447

Gauteng

Benoni

Religious Organisations
United Hebrew Institutions
32 Park Street
(11) 845-2850

Brakpan
Religious Organisations
United Hebrew Institutions
11 Heidelberg Road, Parkdene   (11) 744-4822

Germiston
Religious Organisations
United Hebrew Institutions
President Street   (11) 825-2202

Johannesburg
It seems appropriate that the largest city in South Africa should have the largest Jewish community in the country. About 60 per cent of the country's Jews live there (a community of some 60,000), and the headquarters of many of South African Jewry's institutions are housed there.

Bakeries
Friends Bakery
Ridge Road, Glenhazel   440-5094/5

Booksellers
Chabad House Books
Fairmount Shopping Centre, George Street,
Fairmount   (11) 485-1957
Fax: (11) 648-1139

Kollel Bookshop
8a Gardens Centre, Pick 'n Pay Hypermarket,
Grant Avenue, Norwood   (11) 728-1822
Fax: (11) 128-1813

Ohr Someyach Books
2 Syleslyn Place
15 Northfield Avenue, Glenhazel 2192
(11) 887-1437
Fax: (11) 887-7092
Email: ohr@netactive.co.za

Butchers
Bolbrand Poultry Shoppe
74-76 George Avenue
Sandringham 2192
(11) 640-4080; 640-4170
Supervision: Beth Din.

Checkers
Emmerentia, Balfour Park 2196
(11) 880-6962
Supervision: Beth Din.

Gardens Kosher
Braides Avenue 2052   (11) 483-3357
Fax: (11) 728-3660
Supervision: Beth Din.

Kinneret Butchery
Saveways
Fairmount Shopping Centre, Sandringham
(11) 640-6592
Supervision: Beth Din.

Maxi Discount Kosher Butcher
74 George Avenue
Sandringham 2192   (11) 485-1485; 485-1486
Fax: (11) 485-2991
Supervision: Beth Din.

Nussbaums
434 Louis Botha Avenue
Highlands North 2192   (11) 485-2303
Supervision: Beth Din.

Pick 'N Pay
Gallo Manor
Supervision: Beth Din.
Rishon Butchery
Balfour Park Shopping Centre
Atholl Road, Balfour Park 2090   (11) 786-5396
Supervision: Beth Din.

Yumpolski's
5 Durham Street
Raedene 2192   (11) 485-1045
Fax: (11) 485-1082
Supervision: Beth Din.

Community Organisations
Chabad House
27 Aintree Avenue
Savoy Estate, Yeoville 2090   (11) 440-6601
Fax: (11) 440-6600
Email: chabad@netactive.co.sa

Delicatessens & Bakeries
Feigel's Kosher Delicatessan
Bramley Gardens Shopping Centre, shop 1,
280 Corlett Drive   (11) 887-9505/6
Supervision: Beth Din.
Hours: Friday, 7:30 am to 4:30 pm; Sunday, 8 am to 1 pm; Monday to Thursday, 10 am to 5 pm.
Feigel's Kosher Delicatessan
Shop 3
Queens Place, Kingswood Road, Glenhazel
2192   (11) 887-1364
Supervision: Beth Din.

Kosher King
74 George Avenue
Sandringham   (11) 640-6234
Supervision: Beth Din.
Hours: Monday to Thursday, 8:30 am to 5 pm; Friday, 8 am to 3 pm; Sunday, 9 am to 1 pm.

Mamale's Deli
Shop No 38
Morning Glen Shopping Centre, Bowling
Avenue, Gallo Corner Avenue, Gallo Manor
2052   (11) 804-2068
Supervision: Beth Din.

Neil's Bakery
Fairmount Shopping Centre, 10 Bradfield Drive,
Fairmount   (11) 640-2686
Supervision: Beth Din.
Hours: Monday to Thursday, 7:30 am to 5 pm;
Friday, to 2:30 pm; Sunday, to 1 pm.

Pick 'N Pay
cnr. Grant Avenue & 6th StreetNorwood
                        (11) 483-3357
Supervision: Beth Din.
Closed on Shabbat and Yom Tov.

Saveways Spar Supermarket
Fairmount Shopping Centre
cnr. Livingston St & Sandler Avenue,
Fairmount 2192   (11) 640-6592; 3056
Supervision: Beth Din.
Hours: Monday to Thursday, 8 am to 6 pm;
Sunday and public holidays, 8 am to 1 pm.

Shirley's Bakery & Deli
442 Louis Botha Avenue
Highlands North 2192   (11) 640-2629
Supervision: Beth Din.

Shoshana's Bakery
1 Glenstar Centre, Kingswood Avenue,
Glenhazel   (11) 885-1039
Supervision: Beth Din.

Shula's
42 Kenmere Road, cnr. Hunter Street, Yeoville
                        (11) 487-1072
Supervision: Beth Din.

The Pie Works
74 George Avenue
Sandringham 2192   (11) 485-2447
Supervision: Beth Din.
Hours: weekdays, 8 am to 5 pm; Friday, to 4
pm; Sunday, to 2 pm.

The Pie Works
Shop 35 Greenhill Road
Emmerentia 2195   (11) 486-1502
                     Fax: (11) 486-0580
Supervision: Beth Din.
Hours: weekdays, 8 am to 5 pm; Friday, to 4
pm; Sunday, to 2 pm.

Hotels

Courtleigh Hotel
38 Harrow Road, Berea   (11) 487-1577
                     Fax: (11) 648-6743
             Email: kosher@global.co.za
Supervision: Beth Din.

Libraries

Kollel Library
22 Muller Street
Yeoville 2198   (11) 648-1175

Media

Magazines

Jewish Affairs
Building 1, Anerley Office Park, 7 Anerley Road,
Parktown   (11) 486-1434
                     Fax: (11) 646-4940
             Email: sajbod@iafrica.com
Quarterly journal of the South African Jewish
Board of Deputies.

Jewish Heritage
PO Box 3 7179
Birnham Park 2015   (11) 880-1830

Jewish Tradition
24 Raleigh Street
PO Box 27701, Yeoville 2143   (11) 648-9136
                     Fax: (11) 648-4014
Publication of the Union of Orthodox
Synagogues.

South African Jewish Observer
PO Box 29189
Sandringham 2131
                          (11) 640-4420
                     Fax: (11) 640-4442
Publication of the Mizrachi organisation of
South Africa.

The South African Jewish Times
Publico House, 30 Andries Street, Wynberg
                          (11) 887-6500
                     Fax: (11) 440-5364

Mikvaot

Goldberg Centre, 24 Raleigh Street, Yeoville
                          (11) 648-9136

**Beth Harer (Glenhazel Area Hebrew
Congregation)**
PO Box 28836
Sandringham, Glenhazel 2131   (11) 640-5061

Religious Organisations

**The Southern African Union for Progressive
Judaism**
357 Louis Botha Avenue
Highlands North   (11) 640-6614

Union of Orthodox Synagogues of South Africa
Goldberg Centre, 24 Raleigh Street, Yeoville
(11) 648-9136
Fax: (11) 648-4014
The Office of the Chief Rabbi as well as the Beth Din are located here. Beth Din fax: 648-2325. There are more than 50 Orthodox synagogues in Johannesburg alone. Contact these offices for more details.

Restaurants
Aviv
444b Louis Botha Avenue
Highlands North 2192
(11) 640-4572
Fax: (11) 640-4081
Supervision: Beth Din.
Food store on premises as well. Hours: Sunday to Thursday, 9 am to 11 pm; Friday, to 4:30 pm; Motzei Shabbat, to 1 am.

D.J.'s Take Away
Balfour Park Shopping Centre
Shop No. 121, Balfour Park 2090
(11) 440-1792
Supervision: Beth Din.

Haifa Haktanah
576 Louis Botha Avenue, Gresswold
(11) 887-1059
Supervision: Beth Din.
Hours: Monday to Thursday, 10 am to 10 pm; Friday, t 4 pm; Motzei Shabbat, 1 hour after Shabbat till late.

King Solomon
Gallaghers Corner
cnr. Louise Botha Avenue & 9th Street, Orange Grove
(11) 728-3000
Fax: (11) 728-3305
Supervision: Beth Din.
Hours: Monday, 4:30 pm to late; Tuesday to Thursday and Sunday, 11:30 am to 2:30 pm, 5:30 pm to late; Motzei Shabbat, late.

On The Square
Cradock Avenue
Rosebank 2196
(11) 880-4153
Supervision: Beth Din.
Hours: Sunday to Thursday, 10 am to 3 pm; 6 pm to 10 pm; Motzei Shabbat, 1 hour after Shabbat to 12 am.

Shula's
173 Oxford Road
Rosebank 2196
(11) 880-6969
Fax: (11) 880-6605
Supervision: Beth Din.
Pareve and milk restaurant. Hours: Sunday to Thursday, 7 am to 11 pm; Friday, to 4 pm; Motzei Shabbat to 1 am.

The Only Kosher Nandos
27 Aintree Avenue Savoy
885-1496

Milchik
MacDavids
Northfield Shopping Centre, Northfield Avenue, Glenhazel
(11) 440-2214
Supervision: Beth Din.

Synagogues
Chabad of the North Coast
5 Ocean Way, Umhlanga
(31) 561-2487

Tour Information
Celafrica Tours
PO Box 357
Highlands North 2037
(11) 887-5262
Fax: (11) 885-3097
Email: celpro@hixnet.co.za
Web site: www.celafrica.com
The company specialises in kosher tours to southern Africa, for people needing kosher food and Shabbat arrangements.

Israel Government Tourist Office
5th Floor, Nedbank Gardens
33 Bath Avenue, PO Box 52560, Rosebank 2132
(11) 788-1700
Fax: (11) 447-3104

Krugersdorp
Religious Organisations
United Hebrew Institutions
Cilliers Street, Monument, PO Box 1008 1740
(11) 954-1367
Fax: (11) 953-4905

Pretoria
Embassy
Israel Embassy & Consulate-General
3rd Floor, Dashing Centre, 339 Hilda Street, Hatfield
(12) 421-2227

Groceries
One Stop Superliner
217 Bronkhorst Street, Baileys Muckleneuk, Brooklyn 0181
(12) 463-211

Kashrut Information
Pretoria Council of BOD
| | (12) 344-2372 |
| Fax: | (12) 344-2059 |

Museums
Sammy Marks Museum
Swartkoppies Hall (12) 833 239

Restaurants
JAFFA Old Age Home
42 Mackie Street, Baileys Muckleneuk 0181
(12) 346-2006
Fax: (12) 346-2008
Email: jaffa@smartnet.co.za
Hotel as well. Prior booking necessary. Kosher catering, resident mashgiach.

Synagogues
Adath Israel
441 Sibelius Street, Lukasrand 0181
(12) 344-1511
Fax: (12) 343-0287

Progressive
Temple Menorah
315 Bronkhorst Street, New Muckleneuk, PO Box 1497 (12) 467-296

Springs
Religious Organisations
United Hebrew Institutions
Charterland Avenue, Selcourt 1559   818-2572

KwaZulu-Natal
Durban
Butchers
Pick 'N Pay
Musgrave Centre, Berea 4001   (31) 214-208
Bakery as well.

Community Organisations
Durban Jewish Club
44 Old Fort Road 4001   (31) 337-2581
Fax: (31) 337-9600
Email: velna@eastcoast.co.za
Mailing address: P.O.Box 10797, Marine Parade 4056.

Representative Organisations
Council of KwaZulu-Natal Jewry
44 Old Fort Road 4001   (31) 337-2581
Fax: (31) 337-9600
Email: velna@eastcoast.co.za
Mailing address: P.O.Box 10797, Marine Parade, 4056

Synagogues
Orthodox
Durban Hebrew Congregation
cnr. Essenwood & Silverton Roads, PO Box 50044, Musgrave Road 4062   (31) 214-755
Fax: (31) 211-964

Progressive
Durban Progressive Jewish Congregation
369 Ridge Road   (31) 286-105
Fax: (31) 292-429

Umhlanga
Contact Information
Chabad of Umhlanga
POBox 474 4320   (31) 562-487
Fax: (31) 561-5845

South Korea

Before the Korean War (1950-53), there were a handful of Jews in the country who had escaped from Russia. During the Korean War, a larger community came to South Korea – US army soldiers. There is still an American detachment based in the country, and among them are some Jews. They have been joined by individuals coming to the country to work. Services are held at the US army base in Seoul, and the US army have their own Jewish chaplain in the country.

GMT + 9 hours
Country calling code (82)
Emergency Telephone (Police – 112) (Fire and Ambulance – 119)

Total Population 45,314,000
Jewish Population 150

Seoul

Synagogues
South Post Chapel
Building 3702, Youngsan Military Reservation
(2) 793-3728
Fax: (2) 796-3805

Civilians welcome to participate in all Jewish activities, inc. kosher le-Pesach sedarim, meals and services.

Spain

Spain has an ancient connection with the Jews, and the term 'Sephardi' originates from the Hebrew word for Spain. Great Jewish figures arose in the Spanish community, such as Ibn Ezra and the Ramban. However, the situation changed when the Christians gained the upper hand, and blood libels began. In 1492, almost 100 years after a particularly violent period of persecution, the Jews were expelled from Spain. Many thousands were baptised but practised Judaism in secret (the Conversos, or Marranos), and many were caught and burnt at the stake.

Jewish life began again in the nineteenth century. The Inquisition ended in 1834 and by 1868 Spain had promulgated religious tolerance. Synagogues could be built after 1909, and Spain accepted many thousands of Jewish refugees before and during the Second World War and helped to save a few thousand Hungarian Jews. The government has recently revoked the expulsion order in a symbolic act. Rambam's synagogue in Cordoba can be visited, and there are several other old synagogues in the country.

GMT + 1 hour
Country calling code (34)
Emergency Telephone (Police – 092 or 091) (Fire – 080) (Ambulance – 092)

Total Population 39,647,000
Jewish Population 14,000

Alicante

Organisations
Communidad Israelita
Apdo. 189, Playa de San Juan 03540
(96) 515-1572

Synagogues
Avda Santander, 3, Playa de San Juan

Avila

The Mosen Rubi Church, cnr. Calle Bracamonte and Calle Lopez Nunez, was originally a synagogue, built in 1462.

Barcelona

The ancient community of the city lived in the area of the Calle el Call. The cemetery was in Montjuich (Mountain of the Jews). Most of the tombstones are in the Provincial Archaeological Museum.

Mikvaot
Calle de l'Avenir 24 08071
(93) 200-6148, 8513

Organisations
Calle de l'Avenir 24 08021
(93) 200-6148, 8513
Fax: (93) 200-6148
Email: cib_bcn@mx3.redesth.es
Community Centre
Calle de l'Avenir 24 08071
(93) 200-6148 or 8513

Restaurants

Vegetarian
Calle Canuda 41
Closed during August.

Synagogues
Calle Porvenir 24   (93) 200-6148, 8513
The first synagogue to be built in Spain since the Inquisition.
Sinagoga Atid, Castanyer 27 08022
(93) 417-3704
Fax: (93) 417-3704

Travel Agencies
Jewish Travel Agency
Viajes Moravia, Consejo de Ciento 380
(93) 246-0300

Bembibre
The synagogue here was converted into a church.

Benidorm
Kashrut Information
(96) 522-9360

Besalu
The Juderia is by the River Fluvia. A mikva was recently discovered there.

Burgos
Calle Fernan Gonzalez
The Juderia was in the area of Calle Fernan Gonzalez

Caceres
Part of the Juderia still exists. The San Antonio Church on the outskirts of the town is a 13th century former synagogue.

Cordoba
Tourist Sites
Calle de los Judios 20
This is an ancient synagogue (declared as a monument). Near by, a statue of Maimonides has been erected in the Plazuela de Maimonides. The entrance to the ancient Juderia is near the Almodovar Gate.

El Escorial
San Lorenzo Monastry
The library of San Lorenzo Monastry contains a magnificent collection of medieval Hebrew Bibles and illuminated manuscripts. On the walls of the Patio of Kings, in the Palace of Philip II, are sculpted effigies of six Kings of Judah.

Estella
The Santa Maria de Jus Castillo Church was once a synagogue.

Girona
The Jewish quarter of Girona, known as the Call, is located in the heart of the old town. Its main street exists today, and it is known as Carrer de la Força. The Jewish Quarter of Girona is one of the best-preserved to be found in Europe today.

During the Middle Ages, the Jewish community of Girona achieved considerable importance. It was there that the most important Cabbala school in Western Europe was developed, largely under the guidance of Rabbi Mossé ben Nahman, or Ramban, perhaps its best known representative.

The Bonastruc ça Porta Center houses the Museum of Catalan-Jewish Culture and the Nahmanides Institute for Jewish Studies, on the site where the 15th- century synagogue was located.

In the municipal archives there is an important collection of fragments of Hebrew manuscripts dating from the 13th and 14th centuries. The Archaeological Museum contains more than 20 medieval gravestones with Hebrew inscriptions, found in the old Jewish cemetery. Since January 1995, Girona has held the status of Secretary of the Red de Juderías de España, a network of towns and cities within Spain whose common aim is to foster popular knowledge and awareness of Jewish culture in Spain.

Organisations
Bonastruc ca Porta Center
c/ Sant Llorenc s/n 17004   (97) 221-6761
                          Fax: (97) 221-6761
Opening hours; Winter 10am to 6pm. Summer 10am to 9pm; Sundays and Holidays 10am to 2pm

Granada
The Juderia ran from the Corral del Carlon to Torres Bermejas.

Hervas
The village of Gredos Mountains is 150 miles west of Madrid and its well-preserved Juderia has been declared a National Monument. The main street has been renamed as Calle de la Amistad Judeo Cristiana.

Madrid
Embassy
Embassy of Israel
Calle Velasquez 150, 7th Floor 28002
                          (91) 411-1357

Libraries
Calle Balmes 3   (91) 445-9843, 9835

Mikvaot
Calle Balmes 3   (91) 445-9843, 9835

Museums
Museo Arquelogico
Calle de Serrano 13
See casts of Hebrew inscriptions from medieval buildings.

Organisations
Community Centre
Calle Balmes 3   (91) 445-9843, 9835

Restaurants
Community Centre
Calles Balmes 3   (91) 446-7847
For groups only.

Souvenir Shops
Sefarad Handicrafts
Jose Antonio Av. 54
                 (91) 548-2577, 547-6142
Jewish religious articles and Spanish handicrafts are on sale here.

Synagogues
Calle Balmes 3   (91) 445-9843, 9835
The capital's first synagogue since the Expulsion of Jews in 1492 was opened in December 1968. The building also houses the Community Centre, as well as Mikvah, Library, Classrooms, an assembly Hall and the office of the community. Nearest underground station: Metro Iglesias.
Lubavitch Synagogue
Chabad House, Calle Jordan 9, Apt. 4 Dcha. 28010   (91) 445-9629

Tourist Information
Ogicina Nacional Israeli de Turismo
Gran via 69, Ofic 801 28013   (91) 559-7903
                          Fax: (91) 542-6511

Malaga
Butchers
Carmiceria Kosher
Calle Somera 14 29001   (95) 260-4201

Mikvaot
Calle Somera 12 29001

Tour Sites
There is a statue of the 11th-century Hebrew poet, Shlomo Ibn-Gabirol, a native of Malaga, in the gardens of Alcazaba Castle, in the heart of the city.

Marbella
Bakeries
La Tahona   (95) 282-2781

Groceries
Joelle Kanner
                          (95) 277-4074
Kosher poultry and wine.

Media
Publications
"Edificio Marbella 2000"
Paseo Maritima

"Focus"
PO Box 145 29600
Community Journal

Mikvaot
Beth El, 21 Calle Jazmines, Urbanizacion El
Real, Km. 184
(95) 277-4074, 0757 or 282-4983

Organisations
Community Centre
Paseo Maritima

Synagogues
Beth El, 21 Calle Jazmines, Urbanizacion El
Real, Km. 184
(95) 277-4074, 0757 or 282-4983
About 2 miles from the town centre to the
east. Services held at the following times;
Friday eve. (winter) 7.00pm (summer) 8.30pm;
Shabbat morn. & all festivals 10am.

Melilla *(N. Africa)*
Kashrut Information
Calle General Mola 19

Synagogues
Barrio Poligono
There are nine other synagogues in the Barrio
Poligono. These are open on festivals and High
Holy-days only.

Isaac Benarroch
Calle Marina 7
Jacob Almonznino
Calle Luis de Sotomayor 4
Salama
Calle Alfonso XII 6
Solinquinos
Calle O'Donnell
Yamin Benarroch
Calle Lopez Moreno 8

Montblanc
The Jewish quarter was in the Santa Clara
district, where the church was once a
synagogue.

Santiago de Compostela
The cathedral has 24 statues of Biblical
prophets framed in the so-called 'Holy-Door'.

Segovia
The Alcazar contains the 16th century 'Tower
of the Jews'. Calle de la Juderia Vieja and Calle
de la Juderia Nueva are the sites of the
medieval Jewish quarters, where the former
synagogue now houses the Corpus Christi
Convent.

Seville
Essential Information
Seville Cathedral
The cathedral preserves in its treasures two
keys to the city presented to Ferdinand III by
the Jews.

Historic Information
The Columbus Archives
3 Queipo de Llano Av.
Also known as the Archives of the West Indies,
preserving the account books of Luis de
Santangel, financier to King Ferdinand and
Queen Isabella.

Jewish Cemetery
There is a Jewish cemetery in part of the city's
Christian burial ground in the Macarena
district.

Juderia
Arco & Torreon of the Juderia
Calle de la Juderia
This was the gate connecting the Alcazar and
the Jewish quarter.

Synagogues
Barrio de Santa Cruz
The old synagogue, now the church of Los
Venerables Sacerdotes is the Barrio de Santa
Cruz.
Comunidad Israelita de Sevilla
Calle Bustos Tavera 8 41003

Tarazona
Juderia
The Juderia is near the bishop's palace.

Tarragona
Tarragona Cathedral, Calle de Escribanias
Viejas has, in its cloister, a seventh-century
stone inscribed in Latin and Hebrew. Some
very old coins are preserved in the Provincial
Archaeological Museum. The gate to the
medieval Juderia still stands at the entrance to
Calle de Talavera.

Torremolinos

Synagogues
Beth Minzi, Calle Skal La Roca 16
(95) 383952
Calle Skal La Roca is a small street at the seaward end of the San Miguel pedestrian precinct, almost opposite the Police Station. Sephardi and Ashkenazi services are held on Sabbath morning at 9.30am and Friday evening services are held at 6.30pm in winter and 8.30pm in summer.

Toledo

Though it now has no established community, Toledo is the historical centre of Spanish Judaism. Well worth a visit are two ancient former synagogues. One is the El Transito (in Calle de Samuel Levi), founded by Samuel Levi, the treasurer of King Pedro I, in the 14th century. It has been turned by the Spanish Government into a museum of Sephardi culture. The other, now the Church of Santa Maria la Blanca, is the oldest Jewish monument in Toledo, having been built in the 13th century. It stands in a quiet garden in what was once the heart of the Juderia, not far from the edge of the Tagus River. Also of interest is the house of Samuel Levi, in which El Greco, the famous painter, lived. The house is now a museum of his works.

Plaza de la Juderia, half-way between El Transito and Santa Maria la Blanca, was part of the city's two ancient Jewish quarters, where many houses and streets are still much as they were 500 years ago.

Tortosa

Museums
The Musem of Santa Domingo Convent
This preserves the sixth-century gravestone of 'Meliosa, daughter of Judah of blessed memory'.

Tudela

Juderia
The remains of the Juderia are near the cathedral. There is memorial stone to the great Jewish traveller, Benjamin of Tudela.

Valencia

Synagogues
Calle Asturias 7-4'
(96) 334-3416
Services: Friday eve. & festivals.

Office, Av. Professor Waksman 9
(96) 339901

Vitoria

Jewish History
Campo de Judizmendi
The monument here commemorates the ancient Jewish cemetery.

Zaragoza

Mikvaot
126 – 132 Calle del Coso
This city was once a very important Jewish centre. A mikva has been discovered in the basement of the modern building found at this address.

Balearic Islands

Majorca

Jewish Cemetery
Santa Eugenia
Majorca's population today numbers about 300, although fewer than 100 are registered in the Jewish community. Founded in 1971, it was the first Jewish community to be officially recognised since 1435. The Jewish Cemetery is at Santa Eugenia, some 12 miles from Palma.

Jewish History
Church of San Miguel
This church also stands on the site of a former synagogue. It is not far from the Calle de la Plateria, once a part of the Palma Ghetto.
Montezion Church
The church was the Great Synagogue of this capital in the 14th century.
Palma Cathedral
The cathedral contains some interesting Jewish relics, including a candelabrum with 365 lights, which was originally in the synagogue. In the 'Tesoro' room are two unique silver maces, over 6 feet long, converted from Torah 'rimonim'.
Santa Clara Church
The church stands on the site of another pre-Inquisition synagogue.

Kashrut Information
(971) 283799

Synagogues
Calle Monsenor Palmer   (971) 700243
This synagogue was dedicated to the
community in June 1987. Services are held on
Fridays and Holy-days. A communal Seder is
also held.

Canary Islands

The first Jewish immigrants to the Canary
Islands were Conversos from Spain seeking
refuge from the Inquisition.

La Palmas de Gran Canaria

Synagogues
Calle Leon y Castillo 238, 1st Floor
                                    (928) 248497

Tenerife

Kashrut Information
General Mola 4, Santa Cruz 38006
                                    (922) 274157
Welcomes all Jewish visitors

Organisations
Comunidad Israelita de Tenerife
                          (922) 247296, 247246

Sri Lanka

Evidence for Jewish settlement was recorded about 1,000 years ago by Muslim travellers. There was a small Jewish community when the Dutch took the island as a colony. This attracted Jews from southern India to the island because of the possibilities of trade.

There was a plan put forward when the island came under British rule for mass Jewish immigration. The Chief Justice, Sir Alexander Johnston, appeared to consider the idea a serious one, but the British government did not act on it. A coffee estate was founded in 1841 near Kandy by Jews from Europe.

There is no communual organisation on the island.

GMT + 5.5 hours   Total Population 17,500,000
Country calling code (94)   Jewish Population Under 100
Emergency Telephone (Police – 433333) (Fire and Ambulance – 422222)

Colombo
Kashrut Information
82 Rosmead Place 7   (1) 695642
                        Fax: (1) 446543

Surinam

Surinam's Jewish community began when the first Jews settled in the seventeenth century, escaping from persecution in Brazil. Jews came later from Britain, after the country had passed into British hands. Surinam welcomed more Jewish refugees from the Caribbean, and the country became a Dutch colony in 1668, bringing Sephardi Jews from Amsterdam. Eventually, half the white population in the country was Jewish, and there was a 'Joden Savann' (Jewish savannah), where the Jews owned large sugar plantations. They called the plantations by Hebrew names and built a synagogue in 1685. The community began to decline in the nineteenth century. Recently, many have emigrated to Israel.

Today, there are two synagogues in Paramaribo, the capital. The Ashkenazi synagogue has a sandy floor, which is symbolic of the 40 years in the desert and was also supposed to have hidden the footsteps of the Marranos as they carried out their Judaism in secret.

GMT – 3 hours	Total Population 432,000
Country calling code (597)	Jewish Population 200

Paramaribo

Kashrut Information
Commewijnestr. 21   (692) 400236
Fax: (692) 71154

Organisations
Jewish Community
PO Box 1834   (692) 11998

Synagogues
Neveh Shalom
Keizerstr. 82
Services are held every Shabbat in each synagogue alternately.
Sedek Ve Shalom
Herenstr. 20

Tourist Sites
Sights to see include Joden Savann (Jewish Savannah), one of the oldest Jewish settlements in the Americas.

Sweden

Sweden was under the influence of the Lutheran church until the late eighteenth century and was therefore opposed to Jewish settlement. Aaron Isaac from Mecklenburg was the first Jew admitted into the country, in 1774. The emancipation of Jews in Sweden was a slow process; Jews had limited rights, as they were designated a 'foreign colony'. After a gradual lifting of restrictions in the nineteenth century, Jews were fully emancipated in 1870, although ministerial office was closed to them until 1951.

This freedom heralded the growth of the community, and many eastern European Jews found refuge in Sweden at the beginning of this century. The initial refusal to accept Jews fleeing the Nazis changed to sympathy as evidence for the Holocaust mounted, and in 1942 many Jews and other refugees were allowed into the country, followed, in 1943, by almost all of Danish Jewry. Sweden also accepted Hungarian and Polish Jews after the war.

There is an Offical Council of Jewish Communities in Sweden, and many international Jewish groups, such as WIZO and B'nai B'rith, are represented. There are three synagogues in Stockholm, including the imposing Great Synagogue built in 1870; and there are synagogues in other large towns. Although shechita is forbidden, kosher food is imported, and there are some kosher shops.

GMT + 1 hour
Country calling code (46)
Emergency Telephone (Police, fire and Ambulance – 112)

Total Population 9,000,000
Jewish Population 18,000

Borås

Organisations
Jewish Community of Boras & Synagogue
Varbergsvagen 21, Box 46 50305
(33) 124892
Email: s. rytz@vertextrading.se

Gothenburg

Groceries
Dr. Allardsgata 4   (31) 824-051

Media

Radio
Thursdays at 9pm on 94.4 MHz.

Organisations
Jewish Community Centre and Community Offices
Ostra-Larmgatan 12 S-411 07   (31) 177245
Fax: (31) 7119360

Synagogues

Conservative
Ostra Larmgatan 12 S-411 07   (31) 177245
Fax: (31) 711-9360

Orthodox
Storgatan 5

Helsingborg

Organisations
Jewish Centre
Springpostgranden 4

Lund

Organisations
Community Centre & Students Club (Jusil)
Winstrupsgatan 1   (46) 148052
Services on festivals and High Holy-days only.
Institute for Jewish Culture
Winstrupsgatan 1   (46) 148052
Services on festivals and High Holy-days only.

Synagogues

Orthodox

Winstrupsgatan 1   (46) 148052
Services on festivals and High Holy-days only.

Malmö

Mikvaot
Kamrergatan 11   (40) 118860

Organisations
Jewish Community Centre
Kamrergatan 11   (40) 611 6460; 8860
                          Fax: (40) 234-469
Also houses old-age home and Community
offices.

Synagogues

Orthodox
Foreningsgatan

Stockholm

Bakeries
Kosher Bakery
Nybrogatan 7   (8) 678-8128
Has a full range of cakes, bread, sandwiches,
salads and dairy meals. Restaurant on
premises. Take-away can be arranged.

Booksellers
Community Centre
Judaica House, Nybrogatan 19, PO Box 5053
10242   (8) 663-6566, 662-6686

Caterers
                                    (8) 678-8127
Take-aways can be arranged, kosher deli also
caters for any function and is arranging
Shabbat meals for tourists.

Hillelschool Kitchen
                                    (8) 662-3948
During school term time, dairy and vegetarian
lunch is available at the School lunch room.
The Judaica House
Nybrogatan 19   (8) 663-6566; 662-3948
Offers a meat menu Monday to Friday, 11:30
am to 1:30 pm. Food can also be ordered for
take-aways.

Delicatessens
Kosher Deli
Riddargatan 7   (8) 678-8127
Has an extensive range of kosher meats,
poultry and delicatessen as well as cheeses,
salads and provisions. Meat sandwiches. Take-
away can be arranged. Kosher Deli also caters
for any function and arranges Shabbat meals
for tourists.

Embassy
Embassy of Israel
Torstenssongatan 4, 11456, PO Box 14006
S-104 40   (8) 663-1465
                                Fax: (8) 662-5301

Kashrut Information
Community Centre, Judaica House, Nybrogatan
19, PO Box 5053 10242   (8) 663-6566
There are no kosher restaurants in Stockholm,
but (K) lunches are under the Rabbi Edelmann's
supervision at the Community Centre during
the summer. Dinners can be arranged at the
Community Centre for groups.

Jewish Museum
Hälsingegatan 2, Stockholm
Central Location Tel: +46-(0)8-310143 Fax: +46-(0)8-318404
Email: judiska.museum@swipnet.se

*At the Jewish Museum in Stockholm, the only one of its kind in the Nordic
countries, you will be informed about the history of the Swedish Jews and
their adaptation to the Swedish society, their contribution to Swedish culture,
art, literature, trade, industry and Jewish life in Sweden today.*

Open: Every day except Saturdays 12 noon-16.00

Libraries

Wahrendorffsgatan 3, PO Box 7427 10391
(8) 679-2900
Fax: (8) 611-2413
Email:
jewish.community.stockholm@swipnet.se
Raoul Wallenberg Room also on premises,
named after the Swedish diplomat who saved
scores of thousands of Hungarian Jews from
the Nazis, was arrested by the Russians in
Budapest in 1945 and disappeared.

Mikvaot

Community Centre
Judaica House, Nybrogatan 19
PO Box 5053 10242   (8) 663-6566, 662-6686

Museums

Jewish Museum
Halsingegatan 2   (8) 310143

Organisations

Community Centre
Judaica House, Nybrogatan 19,
PO Box 5053 10242   (8) 663-6566, 662-6686
Jewish Community of Stockholm
Wahrendorffsgatan 3, PO Box 7427 10391
(8) 679-2900

Restaurants

Kosherian
Judaica House, Nybrogatan 19,
PO Box 5053 10242   (8) 663-6580
Offers a weekday cold meat buffet as well as
burgers, sausages, meat sandwiches and small
dishes.

Dairy

Community Centre
Nybrogatan 19 10242
Coffee, cakes and sandwiches (dairy) are
available at the Community Centre during
opening hours. The Community Centre can
also arrange catering for visiting groups.

Souvenir Shops

Menorah: Community Centre Shop
Nybrogatan 19 11439   (8) 663-6566

Synagogues

Conservative

Great Synagogue
Wahrendorffsgatan 3b, P.O.Box 7427 S-103 91
(8) 679-2900
Fax: (8) 611-2413/679-5042
Email:
jewish.community.stockholm@swipnet.se

Orthodox

Adas Jeshurun
Riddargatan 5, PO Box 5053 10242
(8) 611-9161
Adas Jisroel
St. Paulsgatan 13 S11846   (8) 644-1995
Daily Services.
Adat Jeshurun
Riddargatan 5, PO Box 5053 S-10242
(8) 611-9161
Adat Jisrael
St Paulsgatan 13 S-118 46   (8) 644-1995

Tourist Information

Israeliska Statens Turistbyra
Sveavagen 28-30, 4 tr., Box 7554, 10393
Stockholm 7   (8) 21-3386/7
Fax: (8) 21-7814

Travel Agencies

Menorah
PO Box 5053 10242   (8) 667-6770
Fax: (8) 663-7676

Uppsala

Organisations

Jewish Students Club.
Dalgatan 15   (8) 125453

Switzerland

By the late eighteenth century, when the Helvetic Confederation was formed, there were three small communities. Freedom of movement was allowed, and full emancipation was granted in 1866. Theodor Herzl held the first World Zionist Conference in Basle in 1897.

Although Switzerland accepted some refugees from Nazism, many were refused, and most of the refugee Jewish population emigrated soon after the war. The community today has a central body, and is made up of various factions, from ultra-Orthodox to Reform. The major towns have synagogues, and kosher meat is imported. There are several hotels with kosher facilities. Over half of the community live in the German-speaking area, the French-speaking area has the second largest number, and a few are in the southern, Italian-speaking area.

GMT + 1 hour

Country calling code (41)

Emergency Telephone (Police – 117) (Fire – 118) (Ambulance – 144)

Total Population 7,224,000

Jewish Population 18,000

Arosa

Hotels
Levin's Hotel Metropol

(81) 377-4444

Fax: (81) 377-2100

Mikva on premises. Own Kosher bakery.

Baden

Synagogues
Parkstrasse 17   (56) 221-5128 or 222-9436

Fax: (56) 221-5153

Email: dr.jos.bollag@zugernet.ch

Friday nights: Winter 18.30; Summer 19.30.

Festivals: mornings 8.45am.

Basel

Bakeries
Bakery Schmutz

Austrasse 53   (61) 272-4765

IGB & IRG   (61) 272-6365

Booksellers
Victor Goldschmidt

Mostackerstrasse 17   (061) 261 61 91

Butchers
Genossenschaftsmetzgerei

Friedrichstrasse 26 CH-4009   (61) 301-3493

Fax: (61) 381-6939

Supervision: Both Basl Rabbinates.

Also sells groceries and wine. Open 7.30am-12.00 noon, 3pm-6.30. Closed Friday afternoon.

H. Hess, Leimenstrasse 41   (61) 272-8835

Hotels
Hotel Drei Konige

(61) 261-5252

Fax: (61) 261-2153

Offers kosher meals on request.

Hotel Euler

(61) 272-4500

Fax: (61) 271-5000

Offers kosher meals on request.

Media

Newspapers

Judische Rundschau Maccabi

Leonhardstrasse 37   (61) 272-8589

Mikvaot
Thannerstrasse 60   (61) 301-2200

Eulerstr. 10 4051   (61) 301-6831

Museums
Jewish Museum of Switzerland
Kornhausgasse 8 4051   (61) 261-9514
Hours: Monday and Wednesday, 2 pm to 5
pm; Sunday, 11 am to 5 pm. Free entrance.

Restaurants
Restaurant Topas
Leimenstrasse 24 4051   (61) 206-9500
Fax: (61) 206-9501
Email: pessach@access.ch
Supervision: Rabbi Dr I.M. Levinger, Basel
Jewish Community.
Hours: 11:30 am to 2 pm Sunday to Friday.
6:30 pm to 9 pm Sunday to Thursday. Friday
night, Shabbat lunch and holidays by
reservation before 2 pm of preceding day.

Take-Away
Hess Kosher sausage-king
(61) 272-8835
Offers kosher meals on request at Hotel Euler.

Synagogues
Leimenstrasse 24   (61) 279-9850
Fax: (61) 279-9851
Email: igb@igb.ch
Rabbi Dr. I.M. Levinger: 279-9840; 271-6024
Israelitische Gemeinde Basel
Leimenstrasse 24   (61) 271-6024
Israelitische Religionsgemeinschaft
Ahornstrasse 14   (61) 301-4898
Rabbi Telephone: 302-5391

Bern

Embassy
Embassy of Israel
Alpenstrasse 32 3006

Synagogues
Synagogue & Community Center
Kapellenstrasse 2   (31) 381-4992
Rabbiner Michael Dick: 031-381-7303

Biel/Bienne

Synagogues
Ruschlistrasse 3   (32) 331-7251

Bremgarten / Aargau

Contact Information
Ringstr. 37 5620   633-6626

Synagogues
Luzernstr. 1

Davos

Mikvaot
Etania Rest Home
(81) 416-5404
Fax: (81) 416-2592

Synagogues
Etania Rest Home
Richtsattweg 3, 7270   416-5404
Mikva on premises. Rooms and kosher meals
available.

Endingen

Contact Information
J. Bloch
Buckstr. 2 5304   (56) 242-1546
Can arrange visits to the old synagogues and
cemetery.

Engelberg

Hotels
Hotel Marguerite
6390 Engelberg   (41) 637-2522
Fax: (41) 637-2926
Supervision: Agudas Achim, Zurich.
Mikva on premises.

Fribourg

Synagogues
9 avenue de Rome   (26) 322-1670

Geneva

Butchers
Boucherie Charcuterie Kascher
Bitton 21, rue de Montchoisy   (22) 736-3168

Embassy
**Permanent Mission of Israel to the United
Nations**
9 Chemin Bonvent
Cointrin 1216

Media
Newspapers
Shalom European Jewish Times
rue St Leger 10 1205   (22) 347-8088

Mikvaot
(22) 786-4671

Restaurants

Le Jardin, 10, rue St-Leger (22) 317-8910
Fax: (22) 317-8990
Arrangements can be made so that lunches and dinners can be delivered to any hotel downtown.

Meat

Heimishe Kitchen
Avenue de Miremont 1 1206 (22) 346-0892
Fax: (22) 346-0830
Supervision: Machsike Hadas.
This is located on the first floor of an apartment building and there is no sign outside the building.

Synagogues

The Geneva Synagogue (Ashkenazi)
Place de la Synagogue

Liberal

Machsike Hadass
12 Quai du Seujet (22) 732-3245

Orthodox

Machsike Hadass
2 place des Eaux Vives (22) 735-2298

Sephardi

Hekhal Haness
54 ter route de Malagnou (22) 736-9632

Kreuzlingen

Contact Information
Louis Hornung
Schustr. 7 (71) 671-1630

Lausanne

Community Organisations
Communauté Israélite de Lausanne
3 avenue de Georgette, case postale 336 1001
(21) 312-6733
Fax: (21) 320-9383

Groceries
Kolbo Shalom
7 avenue Juste-Olivier (21) 312-1265

Mikvaot
1 avenue Juste-Olivier (21) 729-9820

Restaurants
Community Centre
3 avenue de Georgette 1003 (21) 312-6731
Serves lunch only, from 12 pm to 2 pm.

Synagogues

Orthodox

1 avenue Juste-Olivier (21) 320-9911
Corner of J. Olivier and av. Florimont

Lengnau

Contact Information
(56) 241-1203
For visits to the old synagogue and cemetery.

Lucerne

Butchers
Judische Metzgerei
Bruchstrasse 26 (41) 240-2560

Mikvaot
Bruchstrasse 51 (41) 320-4750

Synagogues
Bruchstrasse 51 (41) 240-6400

Lugano

Hotels
Hotel Dan, Via Fontana 1   (91) 985-7030

Kashrut Information
via Olgiati 1   (91) 922-9955
Mon.-Thurs. 5.30pm-7pm

Mikvaot
Via Maderno 11   (91) 932-6134

Synagogues
Via Maderno 11   (91) 932-6134

Montreux

Synagogues
Synagogue in Montreux
25 avenue des Alpes

St Gallen

Synagogues
Frongartenstrasse 18   (71) 223-5923

St Moritz-Bad

Hotels
Bermann's Hotel Edelweiss
          (81) 833-5533
Fax: (81) 833-5573

Solothurn

Contact Information
R. Dreyfus, Grenchenstr. 8   (32) 623-2327

Vevey

Restaurants
Kosher Meals at Les Bergers du Leman
          (21) 923-5355/54

Synagogues
Synagogue in Vevey
3 blvd. Plumhof   (21) 923-5354

Winterthur

Synagogues
Rosenstrasse 5   (52) 232-8136

Yverdon

Contact Information
Dr Maurice Ellkan
1400 Cheseaux-Noreaz   (24) 425-1851

Zug

Restaurants
Restaurant Glashof
Baarerstr. 41 6301   (42) 221-248
Prepared kosher meals are available.

Zurich

Bakeries
Ruben Bollag
Brauerstrasse 110 8004   (1) 242-8700
          Fax: (1) 291-4684
Ruben Bollag
Waffenplatzstrasse 5, (near Bahnhof Enge)
8002   (1) 202-3045

Booksellers
Morasha
Seestrasse 11 8002   (1) 201-1120

Butchers
Zukon AG
Amelstrasse 8, 8003   (1) 451-8384
Supervision: Israelitische Religionsgesellschaft
Zurich Ashkenas.

Hotels
Hotel International
          (1) 311-4341
Offers kosher meals on request

Media
Israelitisches Wochenblatt/Revue Juive
Rudigerstr 10, Postfach 8027   (1) 206-4200
          Fax: (1) 206-4210
          Email: iwzh@webshuttle.ch

Mikvaot
Freigutstrasse 37   (1) 201-7306
Appointment by phone between 9a.m. &
11a.m.
          (1) 202-0127
Appointment by phone between 9a.m. &
11a.m.

Periodicals
Jewish City Guide of Switzerland
Spectrum Press International, Im Tannegg 1,
Friesenbergstrasse 221 8055
          (1) 462-6411; 462-6412
          Fax: (1) 462-6462
Published quarterly in English and German, a
guide to Jewish communities throughout
Switzerland.

Restaurants

Fein & Schein
Schontalstrasse 14, Corner/Ecke Hallwylstrasse
(1) 241-3040
Fax: (1) 241-2112
Supervision: IRGZ Rabbi Daniel Levy.
Restaurant Shalom
G. van Dijk, Lavaterstrasse 33-37 8002
(1) 201-1476
Fax: (1) 201-1496

Synagogues

Manessestrasse 198 8045 (1) 202-8784
Lowenstrasse – Ecke, crnr: Nuschelerstrasse
Freigutstrasse 37 (1) 201-4998
Beth Hamidrash, Chasidei Gur
(1) 242-3899
Chabad Minjan Esra
(1) 386-8403
Israel, Religionsgesellschaft
Freigutstrasse 37 8002 (1) 201-6746

Israelitische Cultusgemeinde
(1) 201-1659
Judische Gemeinde Agudas Achim
Erikastrasse 8 8003
Minjan Bels (Chassidic)
Weststrasse 151
Minjan Brunau
Mutschellenstrasse 11-15 (1) 202-5167
Minjan Machsikei Hadass (chassidic)
Anwandstrasse 60 (1) 241-3798
Rabbi Schmerler: 01-242-9046
Minjan Wollishofen
Etzelstrasse 6 8038 (1) 201-1691

Tourist Information

Offizielles Israelisches Verkehrsbureau
Lintheschergasse 12 8021 (1) 211-2344/5
Fax: (1) 212-2036
Email: igto@access.ch

Taiwan

The US Army brought the first Jews to Taiwan in the 1950s, when an American base, now closed, was set up in the country. In the 1970s, some Jewish businessmen began to work on the island, serving two- or three-year contracts with their companies. Most are Americans, although there are some Israelis and other nationalities. Services are held on shabbat in a hotel, and there is a Jewish community centre and opportunities exist for Jewish learning.

GMT + 8 hours	Total Population 21,000,000
Country calling code (886)	Jewish Population Under 100
Emergency Telephone (Police – 110) (Fire and Ambulance – 119)	

Taipei

Restaurants

Meat

Y.Y.'s Steakhouse
Chungshan North Road, Section 3, cnr. The Huei St.
There are no kosher restaurants in Taipei, but this Steakhouse has a separate kitchen and dining room, where kosher meat meals are served on separate crockery, with separate cutlery. No milk products are available in this section.

Synagogues

Orthodox

Ritz Hotel, 41 Min Chuan East Road
(2) 597-1234
Shabbat and festival services are held here.

Tajikistan

One of the former Soviet Republics, Tajikistan has a small Jewish population but after the fall of the Soviet Union, many Jews emigrated to Israel. The community is a mix of 40 per cent Bokharans and 60 per cent Soviet Jews from other parts of the former USSR who migrated to Tajikistan during the Second World War. The Bokharan Jews are believed to be descendants of Persian Jewish exiles. Dushanbe, the capital and Shakhrisabz are provided with synagogues, and Dushanbe also has a library.

GMT + 5 hours	Total Population 5,935,000
Country calling code (7)	Jewish Population 1,800

Dushanbe

Synagogues

Ashkenazi
Proletarsky Street

Bokharan
Nazyina Khikmeta Street 26

Shakhrisabz

Synagogues
23 Bainal Minal Street

Thailand

Thai Jewry began with Jews escaping Russia and eastern Europe in the 1920s and 1930s, but most of these emigrated after 1945. The present, largely Sephardi community arrived in the 1950s and 1960s. They came mainly from Syria and Lebanon, but also from Europe, America and Israel. Many work in the jewellery trade.

Bangkok has Ashkenazi, Sephardi and Lubavitch synagogues. The community centre is based in the Ashkenazi synagogue. The Lubavitch synagogue offers several communual activities, including seders at Passover, which attract a large attendance.

GMT + 7 hours

Country calling code (66)

Total Population 58,703,000

Jewish Population 250

Bangkok

Bakeries
Kosher Store and Bakery
223 Soi Sai, Nam Thip 2 (Soi 22), Banglampoo
(2) 663-8719

Embassy
Israel Embassy
'Ocean Tower II' 25th floor, 75 Sukumvit Soi 19
10110 (2) 260-4854/9
Fax: (2) 260-4860

Kashrut Information
(2) 234-0606
(2) 318-1577
(2) 237-1697

Organisations
Jewish Community of Thailand Community Centre
Beth Elisheva Building, 121 Soi Sai, Nam Thip 2, Sukhumvit Soi 22 (2) 258-2195
Fax: (2) 663-0245
Email: ykantor@ksc15.th.com
Friday night and Shabbat services with Kiddush & Shabbar meal. Holidays services. Call to confirm.

Restaurants
Ohr Menachem – Chabad House
108/1 Ram Buttri Rd, Kaosarn Road,
Banglampoo (2) 282-6388
Fax: (2) 629-1153
Supervision: Rabbi Y. Kantor.

Synagogues
Beth Elisheva
121 Soi Sai, Nam Tip 2 (Soi 22)
Sukhumvit Road (2) 258-2195
Fax: (2) 663-0245
Email: ykantor@ksc15.th.com
Close to Imperial Qeens Park, Jade Pavilion and Sheraton Grande Hotel

Orthodox
Even Chen Synagogue
The Bossotel Inn, 55/12-14 Soi Charoenkrung,
42/1 New Road (Silom Road) (2) 630-6120
Fax: (2) 237-3225
Synagogue club and kosher restaurant under supervision of Rabbi Y. Kantor. Daily morning & evening minyan. Regular Friday evening & Shabbat morning, afternoon and evening services. Light kosher meal after services, by advance reservation.

Tunisia

There is written proof of ancient Jewish settlement in Carthage in the year 200, when the region was under Roman control. The community was successful and was left in peace. Under the Byzantine Empire, conditions for the Jews did worsen, but after the Islamic conquest, the 'golden age' of Tunisian Jewry occurred. There was prosperity and many centres of learning were established. This did not continue into the Middle Ages, as successive Arab and Spanish invasions led to discrimination. Emancipation came from the French, but the community suffered under the Nazi-influenced Vichy government. After the war, many emigrated to Israel or to France and the community is still shrinking.

There are several synagogues in the country, together with kindergartens and schools. Tunisia is not as extreme in its attitude towards Israel as some Arab states, and there has been communication between the two countries at a high level. The Bardo Museum in Tunis has an exhibition of Jewish ritual objects.

GMT + 1 hour
Country calling code (216)

Total Population 9,156,000
Jewish Population 1,900

Jerba

There are Jews in two villages on this small island off the Tunisian coast. There is also a magnificent synagogue, El Ghriba, many hundreds of years old, in the village of Er-Riadh (Hara Sghira). Jewish silversmiths are prominent in Hournt souk on rue Bizerte.

Sfax

Synagogues
Azriah, 71 rue Habib Mazoun
Near the Town Hall.

Tunis

Kashrut Information
26 rue de Palestine   (1) 282406; 283540

Organisations
Community Offices
15 rue de Cap Vert   (1) 282469, 287153

Synagogues
Beth Yacob, 3 rue Eve, Nohelle   (1) 348964
Grande, 43 Av. de la Liberte
Lubavitch Yeshiva
73 rue de Palestine   (1) 791429

Turkey

After the Expulsion of the Jews from Spain in 1492, at a time when Jews were not tolerated in most of the Christian countries of Western Europe, what was then the Ottoman (Turkish) Empire was their principal land of refuge. In 1992 they celebrated the 500th anniversary of the establishment of the community. Under the national constitution, their civil rights were reconfirmed. In recent years, many Jews have emigrated to Israel, Western Europe and the United States.

GMT + 2 hours
Country calling code (90)
Emergency Telephone (Police – 155) (Fire – 110) (Ambulance – 112)

Total Population 61,797,000
Jewish Population 20,000

Ankara

Embassy
Embassy of Israel
Mahatma Gandhi Sok 85
Gaziosmanpasa

Synagogues
Birlik Sokak
Samanpazari   (312) 311-6200
This Synagogue is not easy to find. Off Anafartalar Caddesi in Samanpazari, there is a stairway down at the right of the TC Ziraat Bankasi. The synagogue is several buildings along the street on the left, behind a wall. Services every morning. Sabbath morning services begin at 7 or 7.30am depending on the time of year.

Bursa

Synagogues
Gerush Synagogue
Kurucesme Caddesi   (224) 368-636
Services on Friday evening, Shabbat morning and festivals. This Synagogue is in the old Jewish quarter. There are 180 Jews in this town.

Istanbul

Community Organisations
Buyuk Hendek
Sokak No 61 Galata   (212) 293-7566
Secretary General: Lina Filiba

Embassy
Consulate General
Valikonag Caddesi No 73   (212) 255-1040
                          Fax: (212) 225-1048
             Email: isrcon@comnet.com.tr

Hotels
Merit Antique
Ordu Cad 226 Lalelil   (212) 513-9300
                          Fax: (212) 512-6390
With kosher restaurant.

Religious Organisations
Chief Rabbinate
Yemenici Sokak 23, Beyoglu, Tunel 80050
                               (212) 293-8794/5
                          Fax: (212) 244-1980

Synagogues
Askenazi Synagogue
Yuksekkaldinm Sok No 37 Galata
                               (212) 243-6909
Saturdays only.
Beth Israel
Efe Sok No 4 Sisli   (212) 240-6599
Every day.
Caddesbostan Synagogue
Tasmektep Sok Goztepe   (212) 356-5922
Every day.
Etz Ahayim Synagogue
Muallim Naci Cad No 40 & 41 Ortakoy
                               (212) 260-1896
Every day.
Hemdat Israel Synagogue
Izettin Sok No 65 Kadikoy   (212) 336-5293
Every day.
Hesed Leavraam Synagogue
Pancur Sok No 15 Buyukada   (212) 382-5788
June-September including High Holy days.

Italian Synagogue
Sair Ziya Pasa Yokusu No 27, Karakoy, Galata
(212) 293-7784
Neve Shalom Buyuk Hendek Sok
No 61 Galata   (212) 293-7566
Saturdays only.

Izmir

Butchers
Kosher Meat
(232) 148-395
Tuesday and Thursday or inquire at the synagogue.

Community Organisations
Jewish Community Council
Azizler Sokak 920/44 Guzelyurt (232) 123-708
Fax: (232) 421-1290

Synagogues
Beth Israel
265 Mithatpasa StreetKaratas
Shaar Ashamayan
1390 Sokak 4/2, Bikur Holim, Esrefpasa
Caddesi, Alsancak

Ukraine

The Ukraine has had a long and complicated history, with areas of the present country being under the rule of various other countries, from Austria to Romania. The history of the Jews who live in the modern-day, independent Ukraine is both long and tragic. From settlement in Kiev in the tenth century, before the concept of a Ukrainian national identity had been formed, the Jewish community grew and was joined by many Jews from central Europe. The Chmielnicki massacre of 1648 was the worst event to befall the Jews before the Holocaust, and much destruction occurred in the west of the country.

Throughout the nineteenth century, the Ukraine was mainly under Russian domination. After 1918, the Ukraine attempted to become independent, and many Jews were killed in the fighting. The Ukraine absorbed some of south-eastern Poland in 1939 and, after the German invasion of the Soviet Union, the Jewish community suffered terrible losses in the Holocaust.

The community today remains fairly large, and is slowly emerging from the atheist Soviet times. Most Jews live in towns, and Kiev (the capital) is a major centre. There are now Jewish schools, and kosher food can be obtained. In a similar way to Belarus, there are many inspiring places to visit – graves of famous Hasidic masters and the monument to the Babi Yar massacre (near Kiev) are frequent destinations. There have been memorials erected (mainly after the fall of Communism) all over the country to events which happened during the Holocaust.

GMT + 2 hours
Country calling code (380)
Emergency Telephone (Police – 02) (Fire – 01) Ambulance – 03)

Total Population 51,608,000
Jewish Population 310,000

Berdichev

Synagogues
4 Dzherzhinskaya Street
(4143) 23938 / 20222
Kosher kitchen on premises.

Beregovo

Synagogues
17 Sverdlov Street

Bershad

Synagogues
25 Narodnaya Street

Chernigov

Synagogues
34 Kommunisticheskaya Street

Chernovtsy

Synagogues
24 Lukyana Kobylitsa Street   54878

Chmelnitsy

Synagogues
58 Komminnestnaya Street

Dnepropetrovsk

Synagogues
Synagogue of Dnepropetrovsk
7 Kotsubinskovo St. 320030   (562) 342-120
Fax: (562) 342-137
Email: dnepr@jewcom.dp.ua

Donetsk

Synagogues
Synagogue of Donetsk
36 Oktabriskaya Street 340000   (622) 357-725
Fax: (622) 938-155

Kharkov

Synagogues
48 Kryatkovskaya Street
Synagogue of Kharkov
12 Pushkinskaya Street 310057   (572) 126-526
Fax: (572) 452-140
Email: chabad@kharkov.com

Orthodox

Orthodox Union Project Reunite
Surnskaya 45   (572) 408-378
Fax: (572) 439-209

Kherson

Synagogues
Synagogue of Kherson
27 Gorkovo Street 325025   (552) 223-334
Fax: (552) 325-367

Kiev

Embassy
Embassy of Israel
Lesi Ukrainki 34, GPE-S 252195

Synagogues
Central Synagogue of Kiev
29 Shchekovitzkaya Street   (44) 417-3583

Reform
Reform Congregation
7 Nemanskaya Street   (44) 295-6539

Korosten
Synagogues
8 Shchoksa Street

Kremenchug
Synagogues
50 Sverdlov Street

Lviv
Situated on the edge of shifting imperial boundaries, this city has been under Austrian, Polish and Soviet control. It has had as many names as its number of rulers – Lwów in Polish and Lemberg in German. Now called Lviv in Ukrainian, there are 6,000 Jews in the city, once a major Jewish centre in Galicia. A couple of synagogues are still functioning, and a number of monuments have been erected commemorating the Holocaust. Many Jews on 'heritage tours' use the town as a base to explore the region, and guides (generally Yiddish-speaking) are available.

Synagogues
4 Brativ Mikhnovskykh Street 290018
(32) 330-524
Fax: (32) 333-536
Email: bald@link.lviv.ua
Kosher kitchen available: 33-35-35. Tour guide and transportation also available.

Nikolayev
Synagogues
Synagogue of Nikolayev
13 Karl Libknechta Street 327001
(512) 358-310
Fax: (512) 353-072

Odessa
A famous port city, from which many Jews emigrated to various countries during the 19th and 20th centuries. There is a synagogue in the town, which still has a substantial Jewish population (about 45,000).

Synagogues
Main Synagogue
Corner of ul. Eureiskaya and ul.f Richeliev.
Synagogue of Odessa
21 Osipovo St. 270011
(482) 218-890
Fax: (482) 247-296

Simferopol
Synagogues
Synagogue of Simferopol
24 Mironovo Street
(652) 276-932

Slavuta
Synagogues
Kuzovskaya Street 2
(447) 925-452
The first edition of Tanya was printed here by the Shapira family whose tombs are in the cemetery.

Zaparozhe
Synagogues
Synagogue of Zaparozhe
22 Turgeneva Street. 330063
(612) 642-961

Zhitomir
Synagogues
59 Lubarskaya Street
(412) 373-468
Reb Ze'ev Wolf disciple of Dov Baer is buried in the Smolanka cemetery.
Synagogue of Zhitomire
7 M. Berdishevskaya St. 262001
(412) 226-608
Fax: (412) 373-428

United Kingdom

Well over half the 300,000 (1991) Jews of Britain live in London. Numbering about 210,000, they are spread throughout the metropolis, with the largest concentration in north-western districts like Golders Green, Hendon, Edgware and Hampstead Garden Suburb. There are also large communities in North London (Stamford Hill) and in the East (Redbridge). Once it was in Stepney that the biggest part of London Jewry lived and, in spite of many changes there, Aldgate and Whitechapel should be visited, not only for the many reminders of their Jewish heyday, but also for the bustling life which is still to be seen there.

The City

There are many historically interesting sites in the City, that square mile of Central London which adjoins the East End. The Bank of England, is a useful starting point.

One of the numerous streets which converge on this busy hub is Poultry, leading quickly to Cheapside. The first street on the right is Old Jewry. Here, and in the neighbourhood, the earliest community lived before England expelled all its Jews in 1290. There were synagogues in this street and in Gresham and Coleman Streets, not far from historic Guildhall, which is itself a 'must' for tourists.

Inside the Royal Exchange, situated opposite the Bank of England in Threadneedle Street, there is a series of murals including one by Solomon J. Solomon, R.A., of 'Charles I Demanding the Five Members', and a portrait of Nathan Mayer Rothschild, who founded the London house of the famous banking firm. There was a time when the south-east corner of the Royal Exchange was known as 'Jews' Walk'.

The Rothschild headquarters is not far away, in St. Swithin's Lane. To reach this handsome building (which has in its entrance-hall more Rothschild portraits, as well as a large tapestry of Moses striking the rock), cross carefully from the Royal Exchange to the Lord Mayor's Mansion House and then turn left into King William Street.

Cornhill, which stretches eastwards from the Bank, leads to Leadenhall Street and its shipping offices and, after a short walk, to Creechurch Lane and the Cunard building, on the back of which is an interesting plaque. 'Site of the First Synagogue after the Resettlement 1657–1701. Spanish and Portuguese Jews' Congregation' is the inscription. Here the post-Expulsion Jews whom Oliver Cromwell welcomed to England set up their house of prayer. In 1701 they built a synagogue in Bevis Marks (close by), modelling it on the famous Portuguese Synagogue in Amsterdam. It has been scheduled by the Royal Commission on Ancient Historical Monuments as 'a building of outstanding value', and is considered one of the most beautiful pieces of synagogue architecture extant. In it are some benches from the Creechurch Lane Synagogue.

London's chief Ashkenazi place of worship, the Great Synagogue, stood, until it was bombed during the Second World War, in Duke's Place, which adjoins Bevis Marks. The 'Duke's Place Shool' (as it was called) was the country's best-known synagogue, the scene of many great occasions and a popular choice for weddings. On the wall of International House, which has replaced it, there is a plaque informing the visitor that the synagogue stood there 'from 1690 and served the community continuously until it was destroyed in September, 1941'.

After the Second World War and until the 1970s, the Great Synagogue was in Adler

Street, named after the two Chief Rabbis of that name, Rabbi Nathan Marcus Adler and his son, Rabbi Dr. Hermann Adler. Duke's Place leads to Aldgate High Street where, on the opposite side, Jewry Street marks another centre of the pre-Expulsion community. At the time of Richard I's coronation many Jews, escaping from rioting mobs, moved here from Old Jewry.

The East End

Further eastwards, along Aldgate High Street, is Middlesex Street, which becomes the crowded Petticoat Lane every Sunday morning. The cheerful and cheeky language of the stall-holders has made 'The Lane' famous throughout the world. On week-days an offshoot, Wentworth Street, continues the market.

Eastwards again, to Whitechapel, which has changed almost out of all recognition since the days before the Second World War, when it had a teeming Jewish population. Just beyond Aldgate East Underground station, two familiar spots remain: Whitechapel Art Gallery and Whitechapel Library.

The library's extensive Yiddish collection has been transferred to the Taylorian Library, Oxford University's modern-language library. The next turning on the left is Osborne Street, which leads to Brick Lane. A large and sombre building in Brick Lane (at the corner of Fournier Street) represents more than anything else the changes that have taken place in the East End over the years. The Huguenots built it as a church, the Jews turned it into a synagogue (the Machzike Hadass), and now the Bengalis, who have replaced the Jews, have converted it into a mosque.

The former synagogue in Princelet Street (No. 19) is being converted into a museum by the Spitalfields Trust, which is collaborating with the Jewish Museum to develop the building to show the history of the different immigrant groups which have inhabited the Spitalfields area during the past 300 years. For further information about activities at the Princelet Street Building, contact the Jewish Museum.

In Brune Street, it is possible to see the building of the former Soup Kitchen for the Jewish Poor that was established in 1902. Its work of distributing food to the small elderly Jewish community still resident in the area is now undertaken by Jewish Care, the largest Jewish social service organisation in Britain.

Further along Whitechapel Road, outside Whitechapel Underground station, stands a drinking fountain. It was erected in 1911 'in Loyal and Grateful Memory of Edward VII Rex et Imperator from subscriptions raised by Jewish inhabitants of East London'.

Brady Street is the site of an old cemetery, opened for the New Synagogue in 1761 and subsequently used also by the Great Synagogue. The cemetery became full in the 1790s, and it was decided to put a four-foot-thick layer of earth over part of the site, using this for further burials. This created a flat-topped mound in the centre of the cemetery. The cemetery is perhaps the only one where, because of the two layers, the headstones are placed back to back. Among those buried here are: Solomon Hirschel, who was Chief Rabbi from 1802 to 1842, and Nathan Meyer Rothschild (1777–1836), the banker. To view the cemetery, contact the United Synagogue Burial Society (0181-343 3456).

In Mile End there are three more old cemeteries: two Sephardi and one Ashkenazi. Behind 253 Mile End Rd., where the Sephardi Home for the Aged (Beth Holim) was located before moving to Wembley, is the first Resettlement cemetery, the oldest existing Anglo-Jewish cemetery, opened in 1657.

Abraham Fernandez Carvajal, regarded as the founder of the modern Anglo-Jewish community, is buried here, and also Haham David Nieto, one of the greatest of Sephardi spiritual leaders. At 329 Mile End Road, the Nuevo Beth Chaim, opened in 1725, contains the grave of Haham Benjamin Artom. This is among the 2,000 graves remaining on the site. Some 7,500 were transferred to a site in Brentwood, Essex, during the 1970s. The earliest Ashkenazi cemetery, acquired in 1696, is in Alderney Road, and here the founders of the Duke's Place Synagogue, Moses and Aaron Hart and others, and also the 'Baal Shem of London' (the Cabbalist, Haim Samuel Falk), lie buried. In Beaumont Grove, on the south side of Mile End Road, is the Stepney B'nai B'rith Clubs and Settlement, managed in co-operation with Jewish Care, which caters primarily for the needs of the 7,500 Jews still living in the East End.

In Commercial Road, Hessel Street, another Jewish market centre, is now occupied by Bengali traders. Henriques Street is named after Sir Basil Henriques, a leading welfare worker and magistrate, and founder of the Bernhard Baron St. George's Jewish Settlement, who died in 1961. On the same side, three turnings along, is Alie Street. At the Jewish Working Men's Club here in July, 1896, Theodor Herzl addressed a meeting which was effectively the launching of the Zionist movement in Britain.

West Central

Chief Rabbi Hermann Adler (1891–1911) is honoured at the Central Court, the Old Bailey (Underground station: St. Paul's), where a mural over the entrance to Court No. 1, entitled 'Homage to Justice,' includes the figure of Dr. Adler. By the City Boundary High Holborn is the Royal Fusiliers City of London Regiment Memorial. The names of the 38th, 39th and 40th (Jewish Batallions) are inscribed on the monument together with all other batallions which served in the First World War. At the western edge of the City, Chancery Lane Station, Holborn, is a useful centre for several points of interest. To the east, Furnival Street has the Jewish Chronicle office. Northward, Gray's Inn Road leads to Theobald's Road. There, at No. 22, a plaque on the wall recalls that it is the birthplace of Benjamin Disraeli. Further to the north is Great Russell Street, which runs along part of the south side of the British Museum. When visiting the Museum, one should certainly see its collection of illuminated haggadot, in particular its copy of the fifteenth century Ashkenazi Haggadah. No. 77 Great Russell Street was the headquarters of the Zionist organisations from 1919 to 1964. Westward, in Chancery Lane, the Public Record Office has in its vast collection many documents of Jewish historical value, including the petitions to Cromwell.

Commonwealth House, 1-19 New Oxford Street, is the new centre of British Jewry's communal activities, housing the Board of Deputies and a range of other offices.

B'nai B'rith-Hillel House, the student centre, is at 1-2 Endsleigh Street, in Bloomsbury, at the heart of the University neighbourhood, and the Council of Christians and Jews in Gordon Street is close by. In the building of University College in Gower Street, the Jewish Studies Library houses the Altmann, Mishcon and Mocatta Libraries and the Margulies Yiddish Collection. The School of Oriental and African Studies in the University precinct includes Judaica and Israelitica in its library.

West End

In the Marble Arch district, in the part of Hyde Park known as 'The Dell', a Holocaust Memorial Garden was dedicated in June 1983. The garden plot was given over by the British Government to the Board of Deputies, which commissioned Mr. Richard Seifert to design the memorial centre-piece rocks bearing a quotation from the Book of Lamentations. Also in the Marble Arch area, you will find an important associate of the United Synagogue (the amalgamated Western and Marble Arch Synagogues in Great Cumberland Place), the West End Great, as well as the West London (Reform) Synagogue (Upper Berkeley Street) and the magnificent Victorian New West End Synagogue in St. Petersburg Place, just off Bayswater Road. The Jewish Memorial Council and Bookshop is in Enford Street.

The British Zionist Federation was inaugurated at the Trocadero Restaurant in Piccadilly Circus in January 1899. At 175 Piccadilly was the London bureau of the Zionist Organisation, set up in August 1917. Here, Dr. Chaim Weizmann and other Zionist leaders worked, and here, in November 1917, the Balfour Declaration was delivered by Lord Rothschild. The Westminster Synagogue in Rutland Gardens, Knightsbridge, houses the Czech Memorial Scrolls Centre, where there is a permanent exhibition telling the story of the salvaging from Prague in 1964 of 1,564 Torah Scrolls confiscated by the Nazis during the Second World War, and of their restoration and the donation of many to communities throughout the world. The exhibition is open from 10 am to 4 pm on Tuesdays and Thursdays, and at other times by appointment.

In St. John's Wood are three more interesting synagogues: the New London (Abbey Road) and the St. John's Wood (Grove End Road), where the Chief Rabbi, who lives in near-by Hamilton Terrace, generally worships. The third synagogue of great interest in St. John's Wood is the Liberal Jewish, opposite Lord's Cricket Ground, recently rebuilt and renovated.

Stamford Hill

Of London's many synagogues, one remarkable group is the series of Chasidic 'shtiblech' in Stamford Hill (and the yeshivot which are attached to some of them). Cazenove Road contains several of these, and it is here and in the vicinity that the long coats and wide hats of chasidim and the curled sidelocks of their children are to be seen. The Lubavitch Foundation headquarters and the Yesodey Hatorah Schools are in Stamford Hill.

AJEX House at East Bank, Stamford Hill houses an interesting military museum. In this district, also, are North African, Adeni, Indian and some Persian Jews and their synagogues.

North-East

The migration of the Jews from the East End took many of them eventually to the London borough of Redbridge where today the greatest density of London's Jews reside. To obtain a flavour of this large Jewish community one should visit the Redbridge Youth and Community Centre, Sinclair House, Woodford Bridge Road, Ilford, Essex. Sinclair House is a large modern, purpose-built Jewish community centre and it is the base for a number of organisations and the focal point of many Israeli and Zionist communal events. It also houses the Clayhall Synagogue, the Redbridge Jewish Programmes Material Project and community representative councils.

North-West

The Jewish Museum has moved from Woburn House and opened at new premises in Albert Street, Camden Town. It houses Britain's major collection of ritual articles and Anglo-Judaica.

The starting point for visiting North-West London is Golders Green. Jews first settled here during the First World War, and the Golders Green Synagogue (United) in Dunstan

Road, was opened in 1922. Walk down Golders Green Road from the Underground station for half a mile or so, and you will come to Broadwalk Lane on the right-hand side, where the Lincoln Institute is. This is the home of Ohel David, a congregation of Indian Jews, many of whom came to England when India was partitioned in 1947. Their forebears went to India from Baghdad.

On the opposite side of the road, at the end of a short turning called The Riding, is the Golders Green Beth Hamedrash – formerly known as 'Munk's' after its founder in the 1930s, Rabbi Dr. Eli Munk. This very Orthodox congregation, mainly of German origin, adheres to the religious principles of Rabbi Samson Raphael Hirsch. There are many other strictly Orthodox congregations in Golders Green, including chasidic groups.

Any of the buses travelling along Golders Green Road away from the Underground station will take you to Bell Lane, in Hendon. A few hundred yards down on the left-hand side is Albert Road, where you will find the London School of Jewish Studies (formerly Jews' College) – established in 1855 as an Institute of Higher Education and associated with London University for many years. A group of Persian Jews holds Shabbat morning services there. Its 70,000-volume library is open to the public.

Also in Hendon in Egerton Gardens, a turning opposite Barnet Town Hall in The Burroughs, 10–15 minutes walk from Bell Lane, is Yakar, which provides a wide variety of adult educational and cultural programmes and has a lending library. Several minyanim are held here on Shabbat and festivals. Further information is available on (0181) 202 5552.

Return to Golders Green Underground station from Hendon Central, either by Underground or by bus. Once there, take a bus northwards along Finchley Road for two miles or so, getting off at East End Road, which is more or less opposite the bus stop. On the right-hand side is the Sternberg Centre, the largest Jewish community centre in Europe. The Georgian former manor house contains Leo Baeck College, with its library of 18,000 books, which trains Reform and Liberal rabbis; the offices of the Reform Synagogues of Great Britain, and the London Museum of Jewish Life, now the second centre of the Jewish Museum. In addition to permanent displays, the museum also mounts special exhibitions and runs walking tours and educational programmes. There is a Holocaust memorial, as well as a biblical garden, a bookshop and a dairy snack bar.

GMT	Total Population 58,144,000
Country calling code (44)	Jewish Population 300,000
Emergency Telephone (Police, Ambulance, Fire – 999)	

Avon

Bristol

Bristol was one of the principal Jewish centres of medieval England. Even after the Expulsion from England in 1290 there were occasional Jewish residents or visitors. A community of Marranos lived here during the Tudor period. The next Jewish settlement in Bristol was around 1754 and its original synagogue opened in 1786. The present building dates from 1871 and incorporates fittings from the earlier building. The Jewish house at Clifton College (known as Polack's House) was founded in 1878 and is the only remaining Jewish house in a public school.

Delicatessens
British Hebrew Congregation
Bristol   (0117) 970-6938
Open alternate Sundays at 10 am.

Organisations
Hillel House
45 Oakfield Road
Clifton, Bristol BS8 2BA   (0117) 946-6589

Restaurants
Vegetarian

Cherries
122 St Michaels Hill
Bristol BS2 8BU   (0117) 929-3675

Millwards Vegetarian Restaurant
40 Alfred Place
Kingsdown, Bristol BS2 8HD   (0117) 924-5026

Synagogues
British Hebrew Congregation
9 Park Row
Bristol BS1 5LP   (0117) 925-5160
Synagogue has kosher delicatessan, alternate
Sundays, 10am. Friday night services: Winter
7.30pm Summer 8.30pm; Saturdays 9.45am

Progressive

**Bristol & West Progressive Jewish
Congregation**
43 Bannerman Road
Easton, Bristol BS5 0RR   (0117) 954-1937
                              Fax: (0117) 942-4837
          Email: freedman@fishpond.demon.co.uk

Bedfordshire
Luton
Synagogues
PO Box 215, Luton LU1 1HW   (01582) 25032
Fri night and Sabbath morn. services. Office
open 9.30am to 12.30pm on Sundays.

Berkshire
Maidenhead
Maidenhead is a growing Jewish area. The
synagogue, membership 500+ families, covers
the Berkshire and Buckinghamshire areas.

Synagogues
Reform
**Constituent of Reform Synagogues of Great
Britain**
9 Boyn Hill Avenue
Maidenhead SL6 4ET   (01628) 673012
                              Fax: (01628) 671058
                 Email: mheadsyn@aol.com
Services; Fri 8.30pm; Sat 10.30am

Reading
Jewish settlement began in 1886. The
Orthodox synagogue was opened in 1900 and
has been in continuous use since. This
flourishes today and has the distinction of
being the only Orthodox synagogue in
Berkshire.

Synagogues
Goldsmid Road
Reading RG1 7YB   (01734) 571018
          Email: secretary@rhc.datanet.co.uk
     Web site: www.datanet.co.uk/enterprise/rhc/
**Thames Valley Progressive Jewish
Community**
6 Church Street, Reading RG   (01734) 867769

Buckinghamshire
Milton Keynes
Butchers
Gilbert's Kosher Foods
Kestrel House
Mount Avenue, Milton Keynes MK1 1LJ
                              (01908) 646-787
                         Fax: (01908) 646-788
Supervision: London Board of Shechita.

Cambridgeshire
Cambridge
Kosher Food
                              (01223) 352145
There is a kosher canteen during term time
serving lunch most weekdays and Friday night
and Shabbat meals.

Organisations
Syn/Student Centre
3 Thompsons Lane, Cambridge CB5 8AQ
(01223) 354783 or 368346 answer phone
Daily morning and evening service during term
time. Friday evening and Saturday morning
during vacations, other services by
arrangement.

Synagogues
Reform
Beth Shalom Reform Synagogue
                              (01223) 365614

Cleveland

Middlesbrough

Restaurants

Vegetarian

Filberts
47 Borough Road
Middlesbrough TS1 4AF   (01642) 245-455

Synagogues
Park Road South
Middlesbrough TS5 6LE   (01642) 819034

Cumbria

Grasmere

Hotels

Vegetarian

Lancrigg Vegetarian Country House Hotel
Easedale
Grasmere LA22 9QN   (01539) 435317

Devon

Exeter

In pre-Expulsion times, Exeter was an important Jewish centre. The synagogue was built in 1763, while the cemetery in Magdalen Road dates from 1757.

Restaurants
Brambles
31 New Bridge Street
Exeter EX4 3AH   (01392) 74168

Herbies
15 North Street
Exeter EX4 3QS   (01392) 258473

Synagogues
Synagogue Place
Mary Arches Street, Exeter EX4 3BA
                         (01392) 51529

Plymouth

The congregation was founded in 1752 and a synagogue erected ten years later. This is now the oldest Ashkenazi synagogue building in England still used for its original purpose. It is a scheduled historical monument. In 1815 Plymouth was one of the four most important provincial centres of Anglo-Jewry.

Libraries
Holcenberg Collection
Plymouth Central Library
Drake Circus, Plymouth PL4 8AL
A Jewish collection of fiction and non-fiction books, mainly lending copies.

Restaurants

Vegetarian

Plymouth Arts Centre Vegetarian Restaurant
38 Looe Street
Plymouth PL4 0EB   (01752) 202-616
Hours: lunch, Monday to Saturday, 12 pm to 2 pm; dinner, Tuesday to Saturday, 5 pm to 8 or 9 pm.

Synagogues

Ashkenazi

Catherine Street
Plymouth PL1 2AD   (01752) 301995
          Email: plymouthshul@ndirect.co.uk
Services: Fri., 6pm; Sat., 9:30am. The congregation offers free use of minister's modern flat as holiday accommodation in return for conducting Orthodox Friday evening and Saturday morning services.

Torquay

Bed & Breakfasts
Brookesby Hall Hotel
Hesketh Road
Meadfoot Beach, Torquay TQ1 2LN
                         (01803) 292-194
Strictly vegetarian/vegan. 14 rooms. Bus stop 200 yards away.

Synagogues
Old Town Hall
Abbey Road, Torquay TQ1 1BB
                         (01803) 607724
Covering also Brixham and Paignton. Services first Sabbath of every month and festivals 10.30am

Dorset

Bournemouth

The Bournemouth Hebrew Congregation was established in 1905, when the Jewish population numbered fewer than 20 families. Today, the town's permanent Jewish residents number 3,500 out of a total population of some 151,000. During the holiday season, however, there are many more Jews in Bournemouth, for it is an extremely popular resort with kosher hotels, guest houses and other holiday accommodation.

Delicatessens

Louise's Deli
164 Old Christchurch Road
Bournemouth BH1 1NU   (01202) 295-979
Supervision: Kedassia.

Hotels

Kosher

New Ambassador Hotel
Meyrich Road
East Cliff, Bournemouth BH1 3DP
(01202) 555-453
Fax: (01202) 311-077
Web site: www.saqnet.co.uk/users/newamb
Supervision: London Beth Din.
112 rooms, all with bathroom en suite.

Normandie Hotel
Manor Road
East Cliff Drive, Bournemouth BH1 3HL
(01202) 552-246
Fax: (01202) 291-178
Supervision: Kedassia.
71 rooms.

Mikvaot

Orthodox

Bournemouth Hebrew Congregation
Synagogue Chambers
Wootton Gardens, Bournemouth BH1 1PW
(01202) 557-443

Organisations

Bournemouth Jewish Representative Council
Bournemouth BH1   (01202) 762101

Synagogues

Orthodox

Bournemouth Hebrew Congregation
Synagogue Chambers
Wootton Gardens, Bournemouth BH1 1PW
(01202) 557-433

Reform

Bournemouth Reform Synagogue
53 Christchurch Road
Bournemouth BH1 3PN   (01202) 557736

Essex

Basildon

Contact Information

M. Kochmann
3 Furlongs
Basildon SS16 4BW   (01268) 524947

Synagogues

Affiliated

Basildon Hebrew Congregation
3 Furlongs
Basildon SS16 4BW   (01268) 524947
Fax: (01268) 271358

Chigwell

Synagogues
Limes Avenue
Limes Farm Estate, Chigwell IG7 5NT

Harlow

Synagogues

Reform
Constituent of Reform Synagogues of Great Britain
34 Greenhills
Harlow CM20 3SX   (01279) 416138
Syn: Harberts Road, CM20 4DT

Hornchurch

Synagogues

Affiliated
Elm Park Synagogue
Woburn Avenue
Elm Park, Hornchurch RM12 4NG
                              (01708) 449305

Loughton

Synagogues
Loughton, Chigwell & District Synagogue
Borders Lane
Loughton IG10 1TE   (0181) 508-0303
Friday evening. 8pm; Sat Morn. 9.30am

Romford

Synagogues
25 Eastern Road
Romford RM1 3NH   (01708) 741690

Trowbridge RoadRomford RM
Inq: Miss D. Meid, 4 Portmadoc House,
Broseley Road, RM3 9BT   (01708) 48904

Southend-on-Sea

Jews began settling in the area in the late nineteenth century, mainly from the East End of London. The first temporary synagogue was built in 1906. The Jewish population is 4,500.

Booksellers
Dorothy Young
21 Colchester Road
Southend-on-Sea SS2 6HW   (01702) 331218
Religious articles, Israeli giftware, etc., also stocked. Jewish software ordered. Call for appointment.

Delicatessens
Westcliff Kosher Bagel
Hamlet Court Road
Westcliff, Southend-on-Sea SS
                              (01702) 435-678
Supervision: Southend & Westcliff Kashrut Committee.

Hotels
Cobham Lodge Hotel
2 Cobham Road
Westcliff, Southend-on-Sea SS0 8EA
                              (01702) 346-438
Guests can be reached on 332-377.
Unsupervised. Telephone for brochure and tariffs.

Kosher
Redstone's Hotel
Pembury Road
Westcliff, Southend-on-Sea SS0 8DS
                              (01702) 348-441
Supervision: Unsupervised.

Organisations
Southend & District Representative Council
Southend-on-Sea SS0   (01702) 343192
Synagogues
Southend and Westcliff Hebrew Congregation
Finchley Road
Southend-on-Sea SS0 8AD   (01702) 344900

Southend and Westcliff Hebrew Congregation
99 Alexandra Road
Southend-on-Sea SS0 8AD   (01702) 344900

Southend Reform Synagogue
851 London Road
Westcliff, Southend-on-Sea SS0
                              (01702) 75809

Gloucestershire

Cheltenham

The congregation was established in 1824 and the present synagogue opened in 1839. However, after two generations, the congregation declined and the synagoque was closed in 1903. At the outbreak of the Second World War, the synagogue was re-opened following the influx of Jewish newcomers to the town. The congregation has its own cemetery on Elm Street, purchased in 1824.

Restaurants

Vegetarian

The Barleycorn
317 High Street
Cheltenham GL50 3HN   (01242) 241070

Synagogues

St James Square, Cheltenham GL
                              (01242) 525032

Hampshire

Aldershot

Contact Information
H.M. Forces
25 Enford Street
Aldershot W1H 2DD   (0171) 724-7778
                     Fax: (0171) 706-1710
Inquiries to Senior Jewish Chaplain.

Portsmouth & Southsea

The Portsmouth community was founded in 1746. Its first synagogue was in Oyster Row, but the congregation moved to a building in White's Row which it continued to occupy for almost two centuries. A new building was erected in 1936. The cemetery is in a street which was once known as Jews' Lane. It is the oldest in the provinces still used for the interment of Jews.

Synagogues
Synagogue Chambers
The Thicket
Southsea, Portsmouth & Southsea PO5 2AA
                              (01705) 821494

Southampton

Libraries
Hartley Library
University of Southampton
Southampton SO
Houses both the Parkes Library and the Anglo-Jewish Archives.

Synagogues
Moordaunt Road
The Inner Avenue, Southampton SO2 0GP
Services Sat. morn 10am

Southampton & District Jewish Society
Hillel House
5 Brookvale Road, Portswood
Southampton SO2 1QN

Hertfordshire

Hemel Hempstead
Synagogues
Morton House
Midland Road
Hemel Hempstead HD1 1RP   (01923) 232007

St Albans
Synagogues
Oswald Road
St Albans AL1 3AQ   (0181) 565-4872
St Albans Masorti Synagogue
PO Box 23
St Albans AL1 4PH   (01727) 860642
    Email: jonathanfreedman@compuserve.com

Watford
Synagogues
16 Nascot Road
Watford WD1 3RE   (01923) 222755
Covers also Carpenders Park, Croxley Garden, Garston, Kings Langley and Rickmansworth.

Welwyn Garden City
Synagogues
Barn Close
Handside Lane, Welwyn Garden City AL8 6ST
                              (01582) 762829
With Ladies' Guild.

Humberside

Grimsby

Synagogues
Sir Moses Montefiore Synagogue
Heneage Road
Grimsby DN32 9DZ   (01472) 351404

Hull

In Hull, as in other English port towns, a Jewish community was formed earlier than in inland areas. The exact date is unknown, but it is thought to be the early 1700s. There were enough Jews in Hull to buy a former Roman Catholic chapel, damaged in the Gordon Riots of 1780, and turn it into a synagogue. A cemetery is believed to have been acquired in the late 1700s. Hull was then the principal port of entry from northern Europe, and most Jewish immigrants came through it. In 1851 the Jewish community numbered about 200. Today, it numbers some 350 families. Both the Old Hebrew Synagogue in Osborne Street and the Central Synagogue in Cogan Street were destroyed in air raids during the Second World War. The two Orthodox congregations merged in 1994 and moved to the new Pryme Street building in the western suburbs, where most of the community now live.

Museums
Hull Synagogue Museum
Linnaeus Street, Hull HU3 2PD   (01482) 26848
                    Fax: (01482) 568756
Correspondence to: 771 Anlaby Road
HU3 2PD.

Synagogues
Hull Hebrew Congregation
30 Pryme Street, Anlaby, Hull HU10 6SH
                    (01482) 653242

Reform
Reform Synagogue
Great Gutter Lane, Willerby, Hull HU10 7JT
                    (01482) 656469

Kent

Canterbury

Restaurants
Vegetarian
Teapot Mother Earth
34 St Peter's Street
Canterbury CT16 1BK   (01227) 463-175

Synagogues
The Old Synagogue
King Street, Canterbury
The Old Synagogue, an Egyptian-style building of 1847 stands in King Street and is now used by the Kings School for recitals.

Margate

Synagogues
Godwin Road
Cliftonville, Margate CT9 2HA
                    (01843) 223219

Ramsgate

Synagogues
Montefiore Endowment
Hereson Road, Ramsgate
Montefiore Mausoleum & Synagogue
33 Luton Avenue, Broadstairs, Ramsgate
                    (01843) 862507

Rochester

Synagogues
Magnus Memorial Synagogue
366 High Street
Rochester ME1 1DJ   (01634) 847665
Grade 2, listed building known as The Chatham Memorial Synagogue.

Lancashire

Blackpool

Delicatessens
Lytham Delicatessen
53 Warton Street, Lytham St Annes
Blackpool FY1   (01253) 735861

Synagogues

Orthodox
United Hebrew Congregation
Synagogue Chambers
Leamington Road, Blackpool FY1 4HD
(01253) 28164

Reform
Reform Jewish Congregation
40 Raikes Parade
Blackpool FY1 4EX (01253) 23687

Lancaster
Bed & Breakfast
Lancaster University Jewish Society
Interfaith Chaplaincy Centre
University of Lancaster, Bailrigg Lane
Lancaster LA1 4YW (01524) 65201 ext. 4075
Jewish rooms and kosher kitchen.

Orthodox
Fairview
32 Hornby Road
Caton, Lancaster LA2 9QS (01524) 770118

St Annes-on-Sea
Synagogues
Orchard Road
St Annes On Sea FY8 1PJ (01253) 721831
Services 7.30am and 8pm

Leicestershire
Leicester
There has been a Jewish presence here since the Middle Ages, but the first record of a 'Jews' Synagogue' dates from 1861 in the Leicester Directory.

Libraries
Jewish Library and Bookshop
Community Hall
Highfield Street, Leicester LE2 0NQ
(0116) 273-7620

Mikvaot
Synagogue Building
Highfield Street, Leicester LE2 0NQ

Restaurants
The Chaat House
108 Belgrave Road
Leicester LE4 5AT (0116) 266-0513

Vegetarian
Blossoms
17b Cank Street
Leicester LE1 5YP (0116) 253-9535
The Ark
St Martins Square, Leicester (0116) 262-0909
The Good Earth
19 Free Lane
Leicester LE1 1JX (0116) 262-6260

Synagogues
Community Centre
Highfield Street
Leicester LE2 0NQ (0116) 270-6622
Mikva on premises.
Progressive Jewish Congregation
Leicester (0116) 283-2927

Lincolnshire
Lincoln
Lincoln was one of the centres of medieval Jewry. One of England's oldest stone houses in the city is known as Aaron the Jew's House. The site of the old Jewry is remembered now at Jews' Court. In the cathedral is a recent token of ecclesiastical apology for the thirteenth-century incidence of the blood libel retold in Chaucer. Jews returned to the area in the nineteenth century. The current community is of very recent date.

Community Organisations
Lincoln Jewish Community
c/o Edna Creed
Plot 62, Hales Lane, Chapel Heath, Navenby, Lincoln LN5 0TP

Organisations
Lincolnshire Jewish Community (Associate ULPS)
c/o Mr D Gould
2 Barleyfield Close, Heighington, Lincoln LN4 1TX (01522) 793-994

London

Central London

Booksellers

Jewish Memorial Council and Bookshop
25 Enford Street
London W1H 2DD   (0171) 724-7778
                                  Fax: (0171) 706-1710

Butchers

Gold Bros.
222 Jubilee StreetLondon E1
(0171) 790-1572
Supervision: London Board of Shechita.

Contact Information

Central Enquiry Desk
Board of Deputies
Commonwealth House, 1-19 New Oxford
Street, London WC1A 1NF
                    (0171) 543-5421/5422
                    Email: bod@ort.org

JCI (Jewish Community information)
Commonwealth House
1-19 New Oxford Street, London WC1N 1NF
                    Fax: (0171) 543-0010
                    Email: jci@bod.org.uk
A comprehensive service of communal
information. For information please contact
the Board of Deputies Central Enquiry Desk on
0171 543 5421/2. For administration please
contact 0171 543 5423.

Delicatessens

Munch Box
41 Greville Street London EC1
                    (0171) 242-5487
Supervision: London Beth Din.

Embassy

Embassy of Israel
2 Palace Green
Kensington W8 4QB   (0171) 957-9500
                    Fax: (0171) 957-9555
                    Email: isr-info@dircon.co.uk
Web site: www.israel-embassy.org.uk/london/

Israeli Consulate-General
15a Old Court Place
Kensington W8 4QB   (0171) 957-9500
                    Fax: (0171) 957-9577
    Web site: www.israel-embassy.org.uk/london
Nearest tube station: High Street Kensington.
Consular office hours: Monday to Thursday, 10
am to 1 pm; Friday, 10 am to 12 pm. Postal
address: Consulate Section, Embassy of Israel,
2 Palace Green, London W8 4QB

Hotels

Andrews Hotel
12 Westbourne Street
Hyde Park W2 2TZ   (0171) 723-4514
                    Fax: (0171) 706-4143
Hebrew spoken. Kosher, but no supervision.
Walking distance to all synagogues in this
area.

Libraries

The Jewish Studies Library
University College London Library
Gower Street, London WC1E 6BT
                    (0171) 387-7050
                    Fax: (0171) 380-7373
In addition to materials purchased for the
College's Department of Hebrew Studies it
incorporates the Mocatta Library, Altmann
Library, William Margulies Yiddish Library and
the Library of the Jewish Historical Society of
England. Applications to use or view the
collections should be made in advance in
writing to the Librarian.

Media

Newspapers

Jewish Chronicle
25 Furnival Street
London EC4A 1JT   (0171) 415-1500
                    Fax: (0171) 405-9040
                    Email: jconline@jchron.co.uk
Established 1841. Weekly publication.

Museums

Institute of Contemporary History and Wiener Library
4 Devonshire Street
London W1N 2BH   (0171) 636-7247
                   Fax: (0171) 436-6428
                   Email: lib@wl.u-net.com
With 50,000 books and periodicals, and over 1,000,000 press cuttings, etc., the library serves as a research institute and reference centre for 20th- century history (especially German), modern Jewish history and anti-semitism, minorities, refugees, fascism, etc. Hours: Mon. to Fri., 10am to 5.30pm

Jewish Museum
Raymond Burton House
129-131 Albert Street, Camden NW1 7NB
                        (0171) 284-1997
                   Fax: (0171) 267-9008
The Museum has been awarded Designated status by the Museums and Galleries Commission in recognition of its outstanding collections of Jewish ceremonial art, which are amongst the finest in the world. The Museum's attractive premises include a History Gallery, Ceremonial Art Gallery and a Temporary Exhibitions Gallery offering a varied programme of changing exhibitions. Open Sunday to Thursday 10am to 4pm. Closed Jewish Festivals and public holidays. Group visits by prior arrangement. Admission £3.00, children £1.50, family ticket £7.50.

Organisations

Union of Liberal and Progressive Synagogues
The Montagu Centre
21 Maple Street, London W1P 6DS
                        (0171) 580-1663
                   Fax: (0171) 436-4184
                   Email: montagu@ulps.org

Restaurants

Meat

Hillel Restaurant
Yoffi's
B'nai B'rith-Hillel Foundation, 1-2 Endsleigh Street, London WC1H 0DS   (0171) 388-0801
                   Fax: (0171) 916-3973
                   Email: hillel@ort.org
Supervision: London Beth Din.
Hours: Monday to Thursday, 12 pm to 2:30 pm; Friday night Shabbat meal available if booked and paid in advance by Thursday 11 am. Please phone for details of summer months opening. Re-opens for students and all other visitors mid-September.

Reubens
79 Baker Street
London W1M 1AJ   (0171) 486-0035
                   Fax: (0171) 486-7079
Supervision: Sephardi Kashrut Authority.
Open daily except for Shabbat; open Friday until two hours before sundown.

Tourist Information

Israel Government Tourist Office
UK House
180 Oxford Street, London W1N 9DJ
                        (0171) 299-1111
                   Fax: (0171) 299-1112
                   Email: igto-uk@dircon.co.uk

Visitorcall – The Phone Guide to London
London Tourist Board
26 Grosvenor Gardens, Victoria SW1W 0DU
                        (0839) 123-456
Features over 30 lines of recorded information services.

Travel Agencies

Goodmos Tours
Dunstan House
14a St Cross Street, London EC1N 8XA
                        (0171) 430-2230
                   Fax: (0171) 405-5049
                   Email: Telex: 21676

East London

Bakeries

Galillee Bakery
388 Cranbrook RoadIlford IG2
                        (0181) 924-5333
Supervision: London Beth Din.

Mr Bagels Factory
1 Kings Yard
Carpenters Road, London E15 2HD
(0181) 533-7553
Supervision: Sephardi Kashrut Authority.

Bed & Breakfasts
Harold Godfrey Hillel House
25 Louisa Street
Stepney E1 4NF
Summer accommodation in London at affordable prices. 20 rooms, kosher, dairy only kitchens, easy access to London tourist attractions and theatre, across from Stepney Green Tube station (District line). Enquiries and bookings to: Evelyn Bacharach, Kingscliffe, 1a Antrim Grove, London NW3 4XS, Tel: 0171 722-0420, Fax: 0181 203-8727.

Butchers
Ilford Kosher Meats
7 Beehive Lane, Ilford IG2   (0181) 554-3238
Supervision: London Board of Shechita.
La Boucherie
145 High Street
Barkingside IG6 2AJ   (0181) 551-9215
Fax: (0181) 551-9977
Supervision: London Board of Shechita.

N. Goldberg
12 Claybury Broadway, Redbridge
(0181) 551-2828
Supervision: London Board of Shechita and Kedassia.
Stanley Cohen
93b Upper Clapton Road, Clapton E5
(0181) 806-5035
Supervision: London Board of Shechita.

Groceries
Brownsteins Delicatessen
24a Woodford Avenue
Gants Hill IG2 6XG   (0181) 550-3900
Selection of groceries and delicatessen sold are under the supervision of various religious authorities. Hours: Monday to Thursday, 7:30 am to 6 pm; Friday and Sunday, 7 am to 2 pm. Orders delivered.

Hotels
Kadimah Hotel
146 Clapton Common
Clapton E5 9AG   (0181) 800-5960
Fax: (0181) 800-6237
Supervision: London Beth Din.

Kosher
Menorah Hotel & Caterers
54-54a Clapton Common, Clapton E5
(0181) 806-4925; 6340

Media

Directories

Jewish Year Book
Vallentine Mitchell
Newbury House, 900 Eastern Avenue, Newbury Park, Ilford IG2 7HH   (0181) 599-8866
Fax: (0181) 599-0984
Annual directory.

Internet

Brijnet
11 The Lindens
Prospect Hill, Waltham Forest, Walthamstow E17 3EJ   (0181) 520-3531
Email: rafi@brijnet.org
Web site: shamash.org/ejin/brijnet

Newspapers

Essex Jewish News
900 Eastern Avenue
Newbury Park, Ilford IG2 7HH
(0181) 599-8866
Fax: (0181) 599-0984
Quarterly publication serving East London and Essex.

Mikvaot

Ilford Mikvah Federation of Synagogues
463 Cranbrook Road, Ilford
(0181) 554-2551 (Evenings: 554-8532)
Correspondence to 367 Cranbrook Road

Synagogues

Macabi King of Falafel
59 Wentworth Street E1   (0171) 247-6660
Supervision: Beth Din of the Federation of Synagogues.

Take Away

Carmel Freezer Centre
145 Clapton Common, Clapton E5
(0181) 800-4033
Supervision: London Beth Din.

Travel Agencies

Longwood Travel
182 Longwood Gardens
Ilford IG5 0EW   (0181) 551-4466
Fax: (0181) 551-5588

North London

Bakeries

Marlene's Kosher Bakery and Delicatessen
6 Hendon Lane, Finchley N3   (0181) 349-1674

Parkway Patisseries Ltd.
326-328 Regents Park Road, Finchley N3
(0181) 346-0344
Supervision: London Beth Din and Kedassia.
Hours: Sunday, 7:30 am to 1:30 pm; Monday to Thursday, to 5:30 pm; Friday, to 1 hour before Shabbat.

Renbake Patisserie Ltd.
Unit A
8-10 Timber Wharf Road, Stamford Hill
N16 6DB   (0181) 800-2525
Fax: (0181) 880-2023
Supervision: London Beth Din and Kedassia.

Bed & Breakfasts

Pension Strom
22 Rookwood Road
Stamford Hill N16 6SS   (0181) 800-1151
Breakfast only. Other meals to order.

Butchers

A. Perlmutter
1-2 Onslow Parade
Hampden Square, Southgate N14 5JN
(0181) 361-5441/2
Fax: (0181) 361-5442
Supervision: London Board of Shechita.

D. Gilbert
880 High Road
Finchley N12 9RH   (0181) 445-2224
Supervision: London Board of Shechita.

Greenspans
9-11 Lyttelton Road, London N2 0DW
(0181) 455-9921; 455-7709
Fax: (0181) 455-3484
Supervision: London Board of Shechita.

Jack Schlagman
112 Regents Park Road, Finchley N3
(0181) 346-3598
Supervision: London Board of Shechita.

Mehadrin Meats
25a Belfast Lane
Stamford Hill N16
                    (0181) 806-7686; 806-3002
Supervision: Kedassia.

Miss G. Ismach
230 Regents Park Road, Finchley N3
                    (0181) 346-6554
Supervision: London Board of Shechita.

Groceries
The World of Kosher
25 Station Parade
Cockfosters Road, Cockfosters EN4 0DW
                    (0181) 441-3621
Supervision: Federation of Synagogues.

Kashrut Information
**Joint Kashrus Committee of the Union of
Orthodox Hebrew Congregations, Adath
Yisroel Synagogues and Golders Green Beth
Hamedrash**
67 Amhurst Park
Stamford Hill N16   (0181) 802-6226/7
                    Fax: (0181) 809-7092

**Joint Kashrus Committee-Kedassia (Union of
Orthodox Hebrew Congregations)**
140 Stamford Hill
Stamford Hill N16 6QT   (0181) 802-6226
                    Fax: (0181) 809-7092

Kashrut Division London Beth Din
735 High Road
Finchley N12 0US   (0181) 343-6255
                    Fax: (0181) 343-6254
            Web site: www.kosher.org.uk
Kashrut hotline: 0181-343-6259.

London Beth Din
735 High Road
Finchley N12 0US
                    (0181) 343-6255
            (Kashrut hotline: 343-6259)
                    Fax: (0181) 343-6254
            Web site: www.kosher.org.uk
Publishes 'The Really Jewish Food Guide', which
contains a list of all the establishments it
certifies as well as guidance for the shopper in
buying general consumer products.

National Council of Shechita Boards
401-405 Nether Street
Finchley N3 1YR   (0181) 349-9153
                    Fax: (0181) 346-2209

The London Beth Din
735 High Road
Finchley N12 0US   (0181) 343-6270
                    Fax: (0181) 343-6257
            Email: www.kosher.org.uk

Libraries
British Library, Oriental & Indian Collections
96 Euston Road
London NW1 2DB   (0171) 412-7646
                    Fax: (0171) 412-7641/7858
            Email: oioc-enquiries@bl.uk
The Hebrew section contains over 70,000
printed books, ca. 3,000 manuscripts and
some 10,000 Genizah fragments. Oriental
reading room open to holders of readers'
passes: Monday – Saturday, 9.30 to 17.00.
Hebrew manuscripts on permanent display in
the John Ritblat Gallery.

Mikvaot
Adath Yisroel Synagogue Mikvah
40a Queen Elizabeth's Walk
cnr. 28 Gazebrook Rd., Stamford Hill N16 0HH
                    (0181) 802-2554

Craven Walk Mikvah
72 Lingwood Road
Stamford Hill N16   (0181) 800-8555
Evening Telephone #: 0181-809-6279

**Mikveh of the Reform Synagogues of Great
Britain**
The Sternberg Centre
80 East End Road, Finchley N3 2SY
                    (0181) 349-2568
                    Fax: (0181) 343-0901
            Email: beitdin@refsyn.org.uk

Satmar Mikvah
62 Filey Avenue
Stamford Hill N16   (0181) 806-3961

Stamford Hill and District Mikvah
Margaret Road
Stamford Hill N16   (0181) 806-3880
Other Telephone #: 0181-809-4064 or 0181-
800-5119

The Sternberg Centre for Judaism
80 East End Road
Finchley N3 2SY   (0181) 349-4731
                    Fax: (0181) 343-0901
            Email: admin@refsyn.org.uk
            Web site: www.refsyn.org.uk
Hours: 9.30 – 5.30 Monday to Thursday, Friday
9.30 – 3.30 /4.

Union of Orthodox Hebrew Congregations
140 Stamford Hill
Stamford Hill N16 6QT   (0181) 802-6226
                    Fax: (0181) 809-7097

Museums

Jewish Military Museum and Memorial Room
AJEX House
East Bank, Stamford Hill N16 5RT
          (0181) 800-2844; 802-7610
                    Fax: (0181) 800-1117
Memorabilia, artefacts, medals, letters, documents, pictures and uniforms all illustrating British Jewry's contribution to the Armed Forces of the Crown from the Crimea to the present day. By appointment, Sunday to Thursday, 11 am to 4 pm.

Ben Uri Art Society & Gallery
126 Albert Street
London NW1 7NE   (0171) 482-1234
                    Fax: (0171) 482-1414
                    Email: benuri@ort.org
The aim of the Society, which is a registered charity founded 1915, is to promote Jewish art as part of the Jewish cultural heritage, The Gallery provides a showcase for exhibitions of contemporary art as well as for the Society's own collection of over 700 works by Jewish artists, including David Bomberg, Mark Gertler, Jacob Epstein, Reuven Rubin and Leon Kossof.

The Jewish Museum
80 East End Road
Finchley N3 2SY   (0181) 349-1143
                    Fax: (0181) 343-2162
Permanent exhibitions traces history London Jewry with reconstructions of a tailoring and furniture workshop. Holocaust education is also a major feature of the Museum's work and the Museum's displays include a moving

exhibition on London-born Holocaust survivor, Leon Greenman.

Organisations

140 Stamford Hill
Stamford Hill N16 6QT   (0181) 802-6226/7

Administration Office of Assembly of Masorti Synagogues
1097 Finchley Road
Golders Green NW11 0PU   (0181) 201-8772
                    Fax: (0181) 201-8917
                    Email: Masorti@ort.org

United Synagogue
Adler House
735 High Road, Finchley N12 0US
          (0181) 343-8989
                    Fax: (0181) 343-6262

Orthodox

London Beth Din
735 High Road
Finchley N12 0US   (0181) 343-6270
                    Fax: (0181) 343-6257

Union of Orthodox Hebrew Congregations
140 Stamford Hill
Stamford Hill N16 6QT   (0181) 802-6226
                    Fax: (0181) 809-7902

Reform

Reform Synagogues
The Sternberg Centre for Judaism
80 East End Road, Finchley N3 2SY
          (0181) 349-4731
                    Fax: (0181) 343-0901
                    Email: admin@refsyn.org.uk
                    Web site: www.refsyn.org.uk

THE JEWISH MUSEUM
London's Museum of Jewish Life

The Jewish Museum – Camden Town
129–131 Albert Street, London NW1 7NB. Tel: 0171-284 1997
Attractive galleries on Judaism and Jewish history in Britain.
One of the world's finest collections of Jewish ceremonial art.

The Jewish Museum – Finchley
80 East End Road, London N3 2SY. Tel: 0181-349 1143
Lively social history displays and Holocaust Education Gallery

---

Restaurants

Uncle Shloime's
204 Stamford Hill
Stamford Hill N16   (0181) 802-9355
Supervision: Kedassia.

Dairy

Tasti Pizza
23 Amhurst Parade
Amhurst Park, Stamford Hill N16 5AA
                    (0181) 802-0018; 455-0004
Supervision: London Beth Din and Kedassia.

Take Away

Take 16
16 Paget Road, London N16   (0181) 802-6331
                    Fax: (0181) 880-1117
Supervision: Kedassia.

Travel Agencies

Peltours
11-19 Ballards Lane
Finchley N3 1UX   (0181) 346-9144
                    Fax: (0181) 343-0579
                    Email: sales@peltours.com

Northwest London

Bakeries

Carmelli Bakery
128 Golders Green Road
Golders Green NW11   (0181) 455-2074
Supervision: London Beth Din and Kedassia.

Cousins Bagel Bakery
109 Golders Green Road
Golders Green NW11   (0181) 201-9694
Supervision: Sephardi Kashrut Authority.

Creme de la Creme
5 Temple Fortune Parade
Bridge Lane, Golders Green NW11 1QN
                    (0181) 458-9090
Supervision: London Beth Din.

Daniel's Bagel Bakery
12-13 Hallswelle Parade
Finchley Road, Golders Green NW11
                    (0181) 455-5826
Supervision: London Beth Din.
Hours: Sunday to Wednesday, 7 am to 9 pm;
Thursday, to 10 pm; Friday, to 1 1/2 hours
before Shabbat. Nearest tube station: Golders
Green; buses, 82, 102, 260.

David Bagel Bakery
38 Vivian Avenue, Hendon NW4
                    (0181) 203-9995
Supervision: Kedassia.

Dino's Bakery
106 Brent Street
Hendon NW4 2HH   (0181) 203-6623
Supervision: London Beth Din and Kedassia.

Dino'z Bakery
11 Edgwarebury Lane
Edgware HA8 8LH   (0181) 958-1554
                    Fax: (0181) 958-2554
Supervision: Kedassia.

Hendon Bagel Bakery
55-57 Church Road, Hendon NW4
                    (0181) 203-6919
                    Fax: (0181) 203-8843
Supervision: Kedassia.

J. Grodzinski
6 Edgwarebury Lane, Edgware HA8
                    (0181) 958-1205
Supervision: London Beth Din and Kedassia.

Keene's Patisserie
Unit 6, Mill Hill Ind. Est.
Flower Lane, Mill Hill NW7 2HU
                    (0181) 906-3729
Supervision: London Beth Din.

M & D Grodzinski Hot Bread Shop
223 Golders Green Road
Golders Green NW119ES   (0181) 458-3654
                    Fax: (0181) 905-5382
Supervision: London Beth Din and Kedassia.
Hours: Sunday, Monday, Wednesday 6 am to
11 pm. Tuesday 6 am to 9 pm. Thursday 6 am
to 1 am. Friday three- quarters of an hour
before Shabbat in the winter or 6 pm in the
summer.

Parkway Patisserie Ltd.
30a North End Road
Golders Green NW11   (0181) 455-5026
Supervision: London Beth Din and Kedassia.
Hours: Sunday, 7:30 am to 1:30 pm; Monday
to Thursday, to 5:30 pm; Friday, to 1 hour
before Shabbat.

The Cake Company
Basement, 3-4 Sentinel Square
Hendon NW4 2EL   (0181) 202-2327
Supervision: London Beth Din.

Woodberry Down Bakery
47 Brent Street, Hendon NW4
                    (0181) 202-9962
Supervision: London Beth Din.

Bed & Breakfast
26 Highfield Avenue
Golders Green NW11 9ET   (0181) 455-7136

Bed & Breakfasts

3 Elm Close
Hendon NW4 2PH   (0181) 202-0642
Breakfast only. Other meals by arrangement.

Kacenberg's
1 Alba Gardens
Golders Green NW11 9NS   (0181) 455-3780
                          Fax: (0181) 381-4250
Shabbat meals available. Strictly Orthodox.

Booksellers

J. Aisenthal
11 Ashbourne Parade
Finchley Road, Temple Fortune NW11 0AD
                          (0181) 455-0501

Joseph's Bookstore
2 Ashbourne Parade
1257 Finchley Road, Temple Fortune NW11
0AD   (0181) 731-7575
                          Fax: (0181) 731-6699

Torah Treasures
4 Sentinel Square
Brent Street, Hendon NW4 2EL
                          (0181) 202-3134
                          Fax: (0181) 202-3161
Seforim, Judaica and gifts.

Butchers

Frohwein's
1095 Finchley Road
Temple Fortune NW11   (0181) 455-9848
Supervision: Kedassia.

H. Gross & Son
6 Russell Parade
Golders Green Road, Golders Green NW11
                          (0181) 455-6662
Supervision: London Board of Shechita.

Ivor Silverman
358 Uxbridge Road
Hatch End HA4 4HP   (0181) 428-6564
Supervision: London Board of Shechita.

Ivor Silverman
4 Canons Corner
London Road, Stanmore HA8 8AE
                  (0181) 958-8682; 958-2692
                          Fax: (0181) 958-1725
           Email: ivorsilverman@compuserve.com
Supervision: London Board of Shechita.

L. Botchin
423 Kingsbury Road, Kingsbury NW9
                          (0181) 204-2236
Supervision: London Board of Shechita.

La Boucherie
4 Cat Hill
East Barnet EN4 8JB   (0181) 449-9215
                          Fax: (0181) 441-1848
Supervision: London Board of Shechita.

Louis Mann
23 Edgwarebury Lane, Edgware HA8
                          (0181) 958-3789
Supervision: London Board of Shechita.

Menachem's
15 Russell Parade
Golders Green Road, Golders Green NW11
                          (0181) 201-8629
Supervision: London Board of Shechita.

R. Wolff
84 Edgware Way
Edgware HA8 8JS   (0181) 958-8454
Supervision: London Board of Shechita.

Kosher

J.M. Glass of D. Glass & Co
100 High Road
Bushey Heath, Herts, Bushey WD2 3JE
(0181) 420-4443
Supervision: London Board of Shechita.

Fishmongers

Leveyuson
47a Brent Street, Hendon NW4
(0181) 202-7834
Supervision: London Board of Shechita.

Sam Stoller
28 Temple Fortune Parade
Finchley Road, Golders Green NW11
(0181) 455-1957; 458-1429
Supervision: Sephardi Kashrut Authority.

Groceries

B Kosher
91 Bell Lane, Hendon NW4   (0181) 202-1711
Opposite Vincent Court.

Carmel Fruit Shop
40 Vivian Avenue, Hendon NW4
(0181) 202-9587
Fresh fruit and vegetables as well as a good
supply of kosher products, cakes and biscuits.

Kosher King
235 Golders Green Road
Golders Green NW11   (0181) 455-8329/1429

Kosher Paradise
10 Ashbourne Parade
Temple Fortune NW11   (0181) 455-2454

Maxine's
20 Russell Parade
Golders Green Road, Golders Green NW11
(0181) 458-3102

Pelter Stores
82 Edgware Way, Edgware HA8
(0181) 958-6910
Supervision: Federation Kashrus Board.

Yarden
123 Golders Green Road
Golders Green NW11   (0181) 458-0979
Free delivery on orders over £25. Hours:
Sunday, Wednesday, Thursday, 8 am to 10 pm;
Monday, Tuesday, 8 am to 9 pm; Friday, 8 am.

Hotels

13 Brook Avenue
Edgware HA8 9XF   (0181) 958-4409

Central Hotel
35 Hoop Lane
Golders Green NW11 8BS   (0181) 458-5636
Fax: (0181) 455-4792
Private bathrooms and parking.

Croft Court Hotel
44 Ravenscroft Avenue
Golders Green NW11 8AY   (0181) 458-3331
Fax: (0181) 455-9175
Supervision: Kedassia.
Twenty rooms.

Hampstead House Residential Hotel
12 Lyndhurst Gardens
Hampstead NW3 5NR   (0171) 794-6036

Woodstock Guesthouse
68 Woodstock Avenue
Golders Green NW11 9RJ   (0181) 209-0637;
455-4120

Kosher

Pension Strom
147-149 Golders Green Road
Golders Green NW11 9BN   (0181) 458-7127/9
Fax: (0181) 905-5143
Supervision: Beth Din of the Federation of
Synagogues.

Kashrut Information

Federation Kashrus Board (Federation of Synagogues)
65 Watford Way
Hendon NW4 3AQ   (0181) 202-2263
    Fax: (0181) 203-0610

Federation of Kashrus Board
65 Watford Way
Hendon NW4 3AQ   (0181) 202-2263
    Fax: (0181) 203-0610

Media

Listings

The Diary
32 Bell Lane
London NW4 2AD   (0181) 922-5437
    Fax: (0181) 922-8709

Newspapers

London Jewish News
28 St Albans Lane
Golders Green NW11 7QE   (0181) 731-8031
    Fax: (0181) 381-4033

Radio

Jewish Spectrum Radio
558 AM
PO Box 12591, London NW2 2ZP
    (0181) 905-5533
    Fax: (0181) 209-0055

Spectrum Radio
PO Box 12591
London NW2 2ZP   (0181) 905-5533
    Fax: (0181) 209-1565

558 AM

Mikvaot

Edgware & District Communal Mikvah
Edgware United Synagogue Grounds, 22
Warwick Avenue Drive, Edgware HA8
    (0181) 958-3233
North West London Communal Mikvah
10a Shirehall Lane, Hendon NW4
    (0181) 202-1427 (Evenings:202-8517/5706)

Orthodox

Kingsbury United Synagogue
Kingsbury Road
Kingsbury NW9 8XR   (0181) 204-8089

Organisations

65 Watford Way
Hendon NW4 3AQ   (0181) 202-2263

Masorti (Conservative in the USA)

Assembly of Masorti Synagogues
1097 Finchley Road
Golders Green NW11 0PU   (0181) 201-8772
    Fax: (0181) 201-8917
    Email: Masorti.uk@ort.org
    Web site: www.ort.org/masorti

Orthodox

Federation of Synagogues
65 Watford Way
Hendon NW4 3AQ   (0181) 202-2263
    Fax: (0181) 203-0610

Restaurants

Amor
8 Russell Parade
Golders Green NW11   (0181) 458-4221
Supervision: Kedassia.

CROFT COURT HOTEL
44 Ravenscourt Avenue, London NW11 8AY
Telephone: 0181 458 3331 Fax: 0181 455 9175

*The hotel is situated in Golders Green and is well positioned for easy access
into the West End. All rooms have en suite facilities and are equipped with direct
dial telephone, tea and coffee facilities, colour television and hairdryer.
Safe and fax facilities are available. We serve a cooked breakfast and
mouth-watering traditional Shabbat meals.*

We also have facilities to cater for private parties, Barmitzvah, Batmitzvah,
STRICTLY KOSHER   *Anniversary, Sheva Berachot, Engagements.*

Aviv Restaurant
87 High Street, Edgware   (0181) 952-2484
Supervision: Beth Din of the Federation of
Synagogues.
Elite
225 Golders Green Road
Golders Green NW11 9PN   (0181) 455-8195

Folman's Restaurant
134 Brent Street NW4   (0181) 202-5592
Supervision: Beth Din of the Federation of
Synagogues.
Sami's, 157 Brent Street NW4
      (0181) 203-8088
Supervision: Beth Din of the Federation of
Synagogues.

Dairy

Café on the Green
122 Golders Green Road
Golders Green NW11 8HB   (0181) 209-0232
Supervision: London Beth Din.
Chalav Yisrael. Open Motzei Shabbat in winter.

Cassit
225 Golders Green Road
Golders Green NW11 9PN   (0181) 455-8195
Supervision: Beth Din of the Federation of
Synagogues.

Croft Garden Restaurant
44 Ravenscroft Avenue
Golders Green NW11 8AY   (0181) 458-3331
      Fax: (0181) 455-9175
Supervision: Kedassia.

Milk n' Honey
124 Golders Green Road
Golders Green NW11 8HB   (0181) 455-0664
Supervision: Kedassia.
Vegetarian/dairy restaurant/coffee
shop/airconditioned. Menus in English and
Hebrew. Also take-away available.

Orli Café, 96 Brent Street NW4
      (0181) 203-7555
Supervision: Kedassia.
Tasti Pizza
252 Golders Green Road
Golders Green NW11   (0181) 209-0023
Supervision: London Beth Din and Kedassia.

Fish

Folman's
134 Brent Street, Hendon NW4
      (0181) 202-5592
Supervision: Federation of Synagogues Kashrut
Board.
Kosher fish restaurant and take-away.

Meat

Blooms World-Famous Kosher Restaurant
130 Golders Green Road
Golders Green NW11 8HB
      (0181) 455-1338; 3033
      Fax: (0181) 455-1338
Supervision: London Beth Din.
Free delivery service, air conditioned. Open
untill 1.00am Sunday to Thursday; Friday
lunchtime and Saturday nights 1 hour after
Shabbos untill 4.00am.

Catskills
1-4 Belmont Parade
Finchley Road, Temple Fortune NW11
      (0181) 458-1999
Supervision: London Beth Din.
Kosher deli, diner, restaurant. Open Motzei
Shabbat in winter.

⚓ Café on the Green ⚓

London's most exciting Kosher Dairy Restaurant

LONDON BETH DIN SUPERVISION

122 Golders Green Road, London NW11 8HB
Tel: 0181-209 0232

Dizengoff Ltd
118 Golders Green Road
Golders Green NW11 8HB
(0181) 458-7003; 458-9958
Fax: (0181) 381-4902
Email: s.shurkin@virgin.net
Supervision: Sephardi Kashrut Authority.
Hours: Sunday to Thursday, 11 am to
midnight; Friday, to 4 pm; Saturday night,
winter only.

Kaifeng
51 Church Road
Hendon NW4 4DU   (0181) 203-7888
Fax: (0181) 203-8263
Web site: www.kaifeng.co.uk
Supervision: London Beth Din.
Luxury Chinese restaurant with take-away and
delivery service. Weekday lunches, 50% off
menu prices. Free delivery with minimum order
of £25. Hours: Sunday to Thursday, 12:30 pm
to 2:30 pm, 6 pm to 11 pm; Open Saturday
evening, September to April.

Marcus's
5 Hallswelle Parade
Finchley Road, Golders Green NW11 0DL
(0181) 458-4670
Supervision: London Beth Din.

Sami's Restaurant
157 Brent Street
Hendon NW4 4DJ   (0181) 203-8088
Fax: (0181) 203-1040
Supervision: Federation of Synagogues Kashrut
Board.
Glatt kosher middle eastern cuisine. Mashgiach
temidi. .

Solly's
148a Golders Green Road
Golders Green NW11   (0181) 455-0004
Supervision: London Beth Din.

Solly's Exclusive
146-150 Golders Green Road
Golders Green NW11   (0181) 455-2121
Supervision: London Beth Din.

The White House Kosher Restaurant
10 Bell Lane, Hendon NW4   (0181) 203-2427
Fax: (0181) 203-2527
Supervision: London Beth Din.

Synagogues
Radlett & Bushey Reform
118 Watling Street
Radlett WD7 7AA   (0181) 953-8889

Radlett United Synagogue
PO Box 28
Radlett WD7 7PN

Take Away
Kosher King
223 Golders Green Road
Golders Green NW11   (0181) 455-1429

N. Reich
10 Princes Parade
Golders Green Road, Golders Green NW11
(0181) 455-2613
Supervision: Kedassia.

Tours of Jewish Interest
Skyros Holistic Holidays
92 Prince of Wales Road
London NW5 3NE
(0171) 267-4424/284-0365
Fax: (0171) 284-3063
Organises holidays on the island of Skyros in
the Sporades group of islands in Greece.

Travel Agencies
LestAir Services
1 The Grove
Edgware HA8 9QA   (0181) 958-9340
Promoting Jewish Heritage Tours to the Czech
Republic, Poland, Hungary, Byelorus, Latvia
and Lithuania and can be contacted for
detailed information and guidance.

Peltours
240 Station Road
Edgware HA8 7AU   (0181) 958-1144
Fax: (0181) 958-5515

Sabra Travel Ltd.
9 Edgwarebury Lane
Edgware HA8 8LH   (0181) 958-3244-7

Travelink Group Ltd.
50 Vivian Avenue
London NW4 3XH   (0181) 931-8000
Fax: (0181) 931-8877

South London

Butchers
L. Kelman
49 Streatham Hill, Streatham SW2
(0181) 674-3626
Supervision: London Board of Shechita.

S. Samuels
30 Red Lion Street, Richmond
(0181) 940-3060; 940-6282
Supervision: London Board of Shechita.

Mikvaot

South London Mikvah
42 St Georges Road
Wimbledon SW19 4ED   (0181) 944-7149
                            Fax: (0181) 944-7563

Restaurants

Vegetarian

Hockney's
98 High Street
Croydon CR0 1ND   (0181) 688-2899

West Central London

Media

Listings

Board of Deputies
Commonwealth House
5th Floor, 1-19 New Oxford Street, London
WC1A 1NF   (0171) 534-0010
Email: info @bod.org.uk

West London

Bakeries

Keene's Patisserie
192 Preston Road, Wembley HA9
                            (0181) 904-5952
Supervision: London Beth Din.
Parkway Patisserie Ltd.
204 Preston RoadWembley HA9
                            (0181) 904-7736
Supervision: London Beth Din and Kedassia.
Hours: Sunday, 7:30 am to 1:30 pm; Monday
to Thursday, to 5:30 pm; Friday, to 1 hour
before Shabbat.

Butchers

J. Kelman
198 Preston Road
Wembley HA9 9NQ   (0181) 904-7625
                            Fax: (0181) 904-0897
Supervision: London Board of Shechita.

M. Lipowicz
9 Royal Parade, Ealing W5   (0181) 997-1722
Supervision: London Board of Shechita.

Kashrut Information

Sephardi Kashrut Authority
2 Ashworth Road
Maida Vale W9 1JY   (0171) 289-2573
                            Fax: (0171) 289-2709

Organisations

Spanish & Portuguese Jews' Congregation
Vestry Office
2 Ashworth Road, Maida Vale W9 1JY
                            (0171) 289-2573
                            Fax: (0171) 289-2709
                Email: shah@sandpsyn.demon.uk

Orthodox

Spanish and Portuguese Jews Congregation
Vestry Office
2 Ashworth Road, Maida Vale W9 1JY
                            (0171) 289-2573
                            Fax: (0171) 289-2709

Travel Agencies

Magic of Israel
47 Shepherds Bush Green
Shepherds Bush W12 8PS   (0181) 743-9000

Manchester

The Manchester Jewish community is the
second largest in the United Kingdom,
numbering about 35,000. There was no
organised community until 1780. A cemetery
was acquired in 1794. The present Great
Synagogue claims with justice to be the direct
descendant of this earliest community. The
leaders of Manchester Jewry in those early
days had without exception come from the
neighbouring relatively important Jewish
community of Liverpool. After the Continental
revolutions of 1848, the arrival of 'liberal' Jews
began. One of them, a Hungarian rabbi and
soldier of the Revolution, Solomon Schiller-
Szinessy, became minister of a Reform
synagogue established in 1856. In 1871 a
small Sephardi group from North Africa and
the Levant drew together and formed a
congregation, which extended to fill two
handsome synagogues. However, one has now
been turned into a Jewish museum.

Synagogues

Orthodox

Cheetham Hebrew Congregation
453-455 Cheetham Hill Road
Manchester M8 9PA   (0161) 740-7788

Heaton Park Hebrew Congregation
Ashdown
Middleton Road, Manchester M8 6JX
                            (0161) 740-4766

Prestwich Hebrew Congregation
Bury New Road
Manchester M25 9WN   (0161) 773-1978
                           Fax: (0161) 773-7015

United Synagogue
Meade Hill Road
Manchester M8 4LR   (0161) 740-9586

Reform

Cheshire Reform Congregation Menorah Synagogue
Altrincham Road
Manchester M22 4RZ   (0161) 428-7746

Manchester Reform Synagogue
Jackson's Row
Manchester M2 5NH   (0161) 834-0415

Cheshire

Butchers
Hymark Kosher Meat Ltd
39 Wilmslow Road, Cheadle, Cheshire,
Manchester SK   (0161) 428-3400
Supervision: Manchester Beth Din.
Meat department only.

Caterers
Sheila Mendelson Catering
81-87 Silverdale Road, Gatley
Manchester SK8 4QR   (0161) 428-1477
Supervision: Manchester Beth Din.

Synagogues

Orthodox

Hale & District Hebrew Congregation
Shay Lane
Hale Barns, Cheshire, Manchester WA15 8PA
                           (0161) 980-8846

Yeshurun Hebrew Congregation
Coniston Road, Gatley, Cheshire
Manchester SK8 4AP   (0161) 428-8242

Fallowfield

Synagogues
South Manchester
Wilbraham Road, Fallowfield
Manchester M14 6JS   (0161) 224-1366
                           Fax: (0161) 225-8033

Manchester (Central)

Bakeries
State Fayre Bakeries
Unit 1, Empire Street, Manchester M3
                           (0161) 832-2911
Supervision: Manchester Beth Din.

Butchers
J.A. Hyman (Titanic) Ltd
123/9 Waterloo Road Manchester M8
                           (0161) 792-1888
Supervision: Manchester Beth Din.
Suppliers of meat and poultry, cooked meats
and delicatessen products.
Lloyd Grosberg (J. Kreger)
102 Barlow Moor Road
Manchester M20   (0161) 445-4983
Supervision: Manchester Beth Din.

Delicatessens
Hyman's Delicatessen
41 Wilmstow Road, Cheadle, Manchester
                           (0161) 491-1100
Supervision: Manchester Beth Din.

Groceries
State Fayre
77 Middleton Road Manchester M8
                           (0161) 740-3435
Supervision: Manchester Beth Din.

Kashrut Information
Manchester Beth Din
435 Cheetham Hill Road
Manchester M8 0PF   (0161) 740-9711
                           Fax: (0161) 721-4249
They certify all the following restaurants,
bakeries, butchers, delicatessans, caterers,
groceries and hotels. Contact them to ensure
that the establishment is still certified.

Libraries
Central Library
St Peter's Square
Manchester M2 5PD   (0161) 234-1983; 1984
Large collection of Jewish books for reference
and loan, including books in Hebrew. Contact
the Social Sciences Library.

Mikvaot
Naomi Greenberg South Manchester Mikvah
Hale Synagogue, Shay Lane, Hale Barns,
Manchester   (0161) 904-8296
Use is by appointment only.

Museums

Manchester Jewish Museum
190 Cheetham Hill Road
Manchester M8 8LW
(0161) 834-9879; 832-7353
Exhibitions, Heritage trails, Demonstrations &
Talks. Calendar of events available on request.
Educational visits for schools and adult groups
must be booked in advance. Open Mon.-
Thurs., 10.30am to 4pm Sundays 10.30am to
5pm Admission charge.

Restaurants

Antonio's
JCLC, Corner Bury Old Road & Park Road,
Manchester (0161) 795-8911
Supervision: Manchester Beth Din.

Travel Agencies

ITS: Israel Travel Service
427/430 Royal Exchange
Old Bank Street, Manchester M2 7EP
(0161) 839-1111
Fax: (0161) 839-0000
Email: all@its_travel.u-net.com
Freephone 0800 0181 839

Peltours Ltd
27-29 Church Street
Manchester M4 1QA (0161) 834-3721
Fax: (0161) 832-9343
Email: Telex: 667893 PELTOUR G.

Prestwich

Bakeries

Crusty Corner
24 Bury New Road
Manchester M25 (0161) 773-7997
Supervision: Manchester Beth Din.

Swiss Cottage Patisserie
118 Rectory Lane
Manchester M25 (0161) 798-0897
Supervision: Manchester Beth Din.

Booksellers

B. Horwitz
20 King Edwards Buildings
Bury Old Road, Prestwich, Manchester M7 4QJ
(0161) 740-5897
Open 9.30am-5.30pm Monday to Friday;
10.00am-1.00pm Sunday; 9.00am-2.00pm
Fridays during winter.

B. Horwitz Judaica World
2 Kings Road
Manchester M25 0LE (0161) 773-4956
Fax: (0161) 773-4956
Email: melachim11@aol.com

Butchers

A1 Kosher Meats
445 Bury New Road, Prestwich
Manchester M25 (0161) 773-6601
Supervision: Manchester Beth Din.

Kosher Foods
49 Bury New Road, Prestwich
Manchester M25 (0161) 773-1308
Supervision: Manchester Beth Din.
Sells groceries as well.

Meat at Abramsons
61 Bury Old Road, Prestwich
Manchester M25 (0161) 773-2020
Supervision: Manchester Beth Din.

Vidal's Kosher Meats
75 Windsor Road , Prestwich
Manchester M25 (0161) 740-3365
Supervision: Manchester Beth Din.

Delicatessens

Deli King
Kings Road, Prestwich
Manchester M25 8LQ (0161) 798-7370
Fax: (0161) 798-5654
Supervision: Manchester Beth Din.
Hours: Sunday to Friday, 8:30 am to 6 pm. .

Haber's
8 Kings Road, Prestwich
Manchester M25 0LE (0161) 773-2046
Fax: (0161) 773-9101
Supervision: Manchester Beth Din.

Jehu Delis and Take Away
5 Parkhill
Bury Old Road, Prestwich
Manchester M25 (0161) 740-2816
Supervision: Manchester Beth Din.

Groceries

State Fayre
53 Bury Old Road
Manchester M25 (0161) 773-7630
Supervision: Manchester Beth Din.

Media

Newspapers

Jewish Telegraph
Telegraph House
11 Park Hill, Bury Old Road, Prestwich
Manchester M25 0HH   (0161) 740-9321
                          Fax: (0161) 740-9325

Mikvaot

Manchester & District Mikva (Machzikei Hadass)
Sedgley Park Road, Prestwich
Manchester M25   (0161) 773-1537; 773-7403

Restaurants

Meat

J.S. Kosher Restaurant
7 Kings Road, Prestwich
Manchester M25 0LE   (0161) 798-7776
Supervision: Manchester Beth Din.
Glatt kosher.

Synagogues

Orthodox

Higher Prestwich
445 Bury Old Road, Prestwich

Manchester M25 1QP   (0161) 773-4800

Holy Law South Broughton Congregation
Bury Old Road, Prestwich
Manchester M25 0EX
                          (0161) 792-6349/721-4705

Sedgley Park (Shomrei Hadass)
Park View Road. Prestwich
Manchester M25 5FA   (0161) 773-6092

Sale

Synagogues

Sale & District Hebrew Congregation
14 Hesketh Road, Sale
Manchester M33 5AA   (0161) 973-2172

Salford

Bakeries

Brackman's
43 Leicester Road, Salford
Manchester M7   (0161) 792-1652
Supervision: Manchester Beth Din.

Broughton Bakery
18 Trafalgar Street, Cambridge Industrial Area
Salford, Manchester M7   (0161) 839-5224
Supervision: Manchester Beth Din.

Jack Maurer Patisserie
70 St James' Road, Salford, Manchester M7
                          (0161) 792-3751
Supervision: Manchester Beth Din.

Vera Issler Patisserie
3 Waterpark Road, Salford, Manchester M7
                          (0161) 792-2778
Supervision: Manchester Beth Din.

Booksellers

Hasefer Book Store
18 Merrybower Road, Salford, Manchester M7
                          (0161) 740-3013
                          Fax: (0161) 721-4649

J. Goldberg
11 Parkside Avenue
Salford, Manchester M7 0HB
                          (0161) 740-0732

Jewish Book Centre
25 Ashbourne Grove
Salford, Manchester M7 4DB
                          (0161) 792-1253
Hours: Sunday to Thursday, 9 am to 9 pm;
Friday, to 1 am.

Butchers

Halberstadt Ltd
55 Leicester Road, Salford, Manchester M7
                          (0161) 792-1109
Supervision: Manchester Beth Din.
Open full day Tuesday, Wednesday, and
Thursday. Open half day Sunday, Monday and
Friday.

Caterers

I&M Kosher Banqueting Caterers
Unit 17, Cambridge Industrial Estate, Salford,
Manchester M7   (0161) 832-2167
Supervision: Manchester Beth Din.

Simon's Catering
105 Leicester Road, Salford, Manchester M7
                          (0161) 740-3905
Supervision: Manchester Beth Din.

Groceries

S. Halpern
59 Leicester Road, Salford, Manchester M7
                          (0161) 792-1752
Supervision: Manchester Beth Din.

Hotels

Fulda's Hotel
144 Old Bury Road
Salford, Manchester M7 4QY
(0161) 740-4748
Fax: (0161) 740-4551
Supervision: Manchester Beth Din.
Four star hotel open all year. Glatt kosher.
Within easy access of motorways, and uniquely
placed in the heart of the Manchester Jewish
community in Broughton Park. Within easy
walking distance of numerous synagogues and
shopping facilities. .

Mikvaot

Manchester Communal Mikvah
Broome Holme
Tetlow Lane, Salford, Manchester M7 0BU
(0161) 792-3970
During opening hours only. For appointments
for Friday night and YomTov evenings: 740-
4071; 740-5199. For tevilat kelim, 795-2272.

Organisations

Machzikei Hadass
17 Northumberland Street
Salford, Manchester M7 0FE
(0161) 792-1313

Synagogues

Orthodox

Adass Yeshurun
Cheltenham Crescent
Salford, Manchester M7 0FE
(0161) 792-1233

Adath Yisroel Nusach Ari
Upper Park Road
Salford, Manchester M7 0HL
(0161) 740-3905

**Central & North Manchester (incorporating
Hightown Central and Beth Jacob)**
Leicester Road
Salford, Manchester M7 4GP
(0161) 740-4830

Congregation of Spanish and Portuguese
18 Moor Lane
Kersal, Salford, Manchester M7 0WX
(0161) 773-2954

Higher Crumpsall & Higher Broughton
Bury Old Road
Salford, Manchester M7 4PX
(0161) 740-1210

Kahal Chassidim
62 Singleton Road
Salford, Manchester M7 0LU
(0161) 740-1629

Machzikei Hadass
17 Northumberland Street
Salford, Manchester M7 0FE
(0161) 792-1313

Manchester Great & New Synagogue
Stenecourt
Holden Road, Salford, Manchester M7 4LN
(0161) 792-8399

North Salford
2 Vine Street
Manchester M7 0NX
(0161) 792-3278

Ohel Torah
132 Leicester Road
Manchester M7 0EA
(0161) 740-6678

Travel Agencies

Goodmos Tours (Man) Ltd.
23 Leicester Road
Manchester M7 0AS
(0161) 792-7333
Fax: (0161) 792-7336
Email: goodmos836@aol.com

West Didsbury

Synagogues

Orthodox

Sha'are Sedek Synagogue & Talmud Torah
Old Landsdowne Road
Manchester M20 8NZ
(0161) 445-5731

**Withington Congregation of Spanish &
Portuguese Jews**
8 Queenston Road
Manchester M20 2WZ
(0161) 445-1943
Fax: (0161) 434-8094

Whitefield

Butchers

Park Lane Kosher Meats
142 Park Lane
Manchester M45 7PX
(0161) 766-5091
Supervision: Manchester Beth Din.
Hours: Sunday 8.30am – 1.00pm; Monday &
Friday 8.00am – 1.00pm; Tuesday, Wednesday
& Thursday 8.00am – 6.00pm.

Delicatessens
Cottage Deli
83 Park Lane, Whitefield, Manchester
(0161) 766-6216
Supervision: Manchester Beth Din.

Mikvaot
Whitefield Mikvah
Park Lane
Manchester M45 7PB (0161) 796-1054
Ansaphone. Evenings only: 792-0306. Use is by appointment only.

Synagogues

Orthodox

Hillock Hebrew Congregation
Ribble Drive
Manchester M45
(0161) 766-1162

Whitefield Hebrew Congregation
Park Lane
Manchester M45 7PB (0161) 766-3732
Fax: (0161) 767-9453

Reform

Sha'arei Shalom North Manchester Reform Synagogue
Elms Street
Manchester M45 8GQ (0161) 796-6736

Withington

Caterers
Renée Hodari Specialist Kosher Caterers
36 Brooklawn Drive
Manchester M20 9GZ (0161) 445-7170
Supervision: Manchester Beth Din.

Merseyside

Liverpool
There is evidence of an organised community before 1750, believed to have been composed of Sephardi Jews and to have had some connection with the West Indies or with Dublin, although some authorities believe they were mainly German Jews. This small community, which was known to John Wesley, the religious reformer, declined at first, but was reinforced by a new wave of settlers, mostly from Europe in about 1770. The largely Ashkenazi Jews were to some degree intending emigrants for the USA and the West Indies who changed their minds and stayed in

Liverpool. By 1807 the community had a building in Seel Street, the parent of today's synagogue in Princes Road, one of the handsomest in the country.

Booksellers
Liverpool Jewish Bookshop
Harold House
Dunbabin Road, Liverpool L15 6XL
(0151) 475-5671
Full range of Jewish books, artifacts and gifts.
Sundays 11.00am to 1.00pm.

Kashrut Information
Liverpool Kashrut Commission (inc. Liverpool Shechita Board)
c/o Shifrin House
433 Smithdown Road, Liverpool L15 3JL
(0151) 733-2292

Media

Newspapers

Jewish Telegraph
Harold House
Dunbabin Road, Liverpool L15 6XL
(0151) 475-6666
Fax: (0151) 475-2222
Email: telegraph@jaytel.demon.co.uk

Mikvaot
Childwall Hebrew Congregation
Dunbabin Road
Liverpool L15 6XL (0151) 722-2079

Organisations
Merseyside Jewish Representative Council
433 Smithdown Road
Liverpool L15 3JL (0151) 733-2292

Restaurants
JLGB Centre
Liverpool (0151) 475-5825; 475-5671
Open Sun, Tues., Thurs. 6.30-11.00pm.
Licensed bar. Out-of-town visitors welcome.
Also take-away service.

Harold House
Dunbabin Road
Liverpool L15 6XL (0151) 475-5825/5671
Fax: (0151) 475-2212
Supervision: Liverpool Kashrut Commission.

Vegetarian

Munchies Eating House
Myrtle Parade, Liverpool (0151) 709-7896

Synagogues

Allerton Hebrew Congregation
cnr. Mather & Booker Avenues
Allerton, Liverpool L18 9TB   (0151) 427-6848

Greenbank Drive Hebrew Congregation
Greenbank Drive
Liverpool I 17 1AN   (0151) 733-141/

Old Hebrew Congregagtion
Princes Road
Liverpool L8 1TG   (0151) 709-3431

Orthodox

Childwall Hebrew Congregation
Dunbabin Road
Liverpool L15 6XL   (0151) 722-2079

Progressive

Liverpool Progressive Synagogue
28 Church Road North
Liverpool L15 6TF   (0151) 733-5871

Southport

Groceries

Tesco
Town Lane, Kew, Southport PR
Kosher bread range only.

Organisations

Jewish Representative Council
Southport   (01704) 538276

Synagogues

Southport Hebrew Congregation
Arnside Road
Southport PR9 0QX   (01704) 532964
    Fax: (01704) 514002
Mikveh on premises.

Reform

New (Reform) Synagogue
Portland Street
Southport PR8 1LR   (01704) 535950

Middlesex

Ruislip

Synagogues
Shenley Avenue
Ruislip Manor, Ruislip HA4 6BP
    (01895) 632934

Staines

Synagogues

Staines & District Synagogue
Westbrook Road
South Street, Staines TW18 4PR
    (01784) 254604
Includes Slough and Windsor Synagogue.

Stanmore

Take Away

Steve's Kosher Delicatessen
5 Canons Corner, Stanmore   (0181) 958-9446

Norfolk

Norwich

The present community was founded in 1813,
Jews having been resident in Norwich during
the Middle Ages, and connected with the
woollen and worsted trade, for which the city
was at that time famous. A resettlement of
Jews is believed to have been completed by
the middle of the eighteenth century. Today's
congregation serves a large area, having
members in Ipswich, Great Yarmouth,
Lowestoft and Cromer.

Restaurants

Vegetarian

Eat Naturally
11 Wensum Street
Norwich NR3 1LA   (01603) 660-838

The Treehouse
14 Dove Street
Norwich NR2 1DE   (01603) 763-258
Open 10.00am – 5.00pm Monday to
Wednesday. 10.00am – 9.30pm Thursday to
Saturday. Closed Sunday.

Synagogues
3a Earlham Road
Norwich NR2 3RA   (01603) 503434

**Progressive Jewish Community of East
Anglia**
c/o Frimette CarrNorwich NR
    (01603) 714162

Northamptonshire

Northampton

Synagogues
Overstone Road
Northampton BB1 3JW   (01604) 33345
Services on Friday night.

Nottinghamshire

Newark

Museums
Beth Shalom Holocaust Memorial Centre
Laxton
Newark NG22 0PA   (01623) 836-627
                    Fax: (01623) 836-647

Nottingham

Jews settled in Nottingham as early as medieval times, and centres of learning and worship are known to have existed in that period. The earliest known record of an established community dates from 1822 when a grant of land for burial purposes was made by the Corporation; in 1825 the then Chief Rabbi appointed the community's first *shochet*. The community grew apace as a result of the late nineteenth century pogroms in eastern Europe and during the 20 years preceding and following the Second World War, growing to some 1,700 by the 1950s. Today the known Jewish population is estimated at 1,00, about two-thirds of whom are members of the Orthodox synagogue.

Restaurants

Vegetarian

Krisha Restaurant
144 Alfreton Road
Redford, Nottingham NG7 3NS
                    (0115) 970-8608

Maxine's Salad Table
56 Upper Parliament Street
Nottingham NG1 2AG   (0115) 947-3622

Rita's Café
15 Goosegate
Hockley, Nottingham NG1 1FE
                    (0115) 948-1115

The Vegetarian Pot
375 Alfreton Road
Redford, Nottingham NG7 5LT
                    (0115) 970-3333

Synagogues
Shakespeare Street
Nottingham NG1 4FQ   (0115) 947-2004

Nottingham Progressive Jewish Congregation
Lloyd Street
Sherwood, Nottingham NG5 4BP
                    (0115) 962-4761

Oxfordshire

Oxford

There was an important medieval community, and the present one dates back to 1842. The Oxford Synagogue and Jewish Centre, opened in 1974, serves both the city and the university. It is available for all forms of Jewish worship.

Community Organisations
L'Chaim Society
Albion House, Little Gate, Oxford
                    (01865) 794-462
The Synagogue and Jewish Centre
21 Richmond Road
Oxford OX1 2JL   (01865) 553-042
          Email: joel_kaye@oxfe.ac.uk
Call for information about services. A kosher meals service operates during term time.

Staffordshire

Stoke-on-Trent

Synagogues
Birch Terrace
Hanley, Stoke On Trent ST1 3JN
                    (01782) 616417

Surrey

Guildford

Synagogues
Guildford & District Synagogue
York Road
Guildford GU1 4DR   (01483) 576470

Tourist Sites

Enquiries about the recent discovery of a medieval synagogue in the town may be addressed to the Guildford Museum.

Sussex

Brighton and Hove

The first known Jewish resident of Brighton lived there in 1767. The earliest synagogue was founded in Jew Street in 1789. Henry Solomon, vice-president of the congregation, was the first Chief Constable of the town. He was murdered in 1844 by an insane youth. His brother-in-law, Levi Emanuel Cohen, founded the *Brighton Guardian*, and was twice elected president of the Newspaper Society of Great Britain. Other nineteenth-century notables living in Brighton and Hove included Sir Isaac Lyon Goldsmid and numerous members of the Sassoon family. The town's Jewish population today is about 8,000.

Community Organisations
Lubavitch Chabad House
15 The Upper Drive
Brighton and Hove BN3 6GR   (01273) 321-919

Delicatessens
Cantor's of Hove
20 Richardson Road
Hove, Brighton and Hove BN3 5BB
(01273) 723-669

Media

Newspapers
Sussex Jewish News
PO Box 1623
Brighton and Hove BN   (01273) 504-455

Mikvaot
Prince Regent Swimming Pool Cmplx.
Church Street, Brighton and Hove BN1 1YA
(01273) 321-919

Organisations
Hillel House
18 Harrington Road
Brighton and Hove BN1 6RE   (01273) 503-450
Closed during summer vacation. Friday evening meals available.

Religious Organisations
Brighton and Hove Joint Kashrus Committee
5 The Paddock
The Droveway, Hove, Brighton and Hove BN
(01273) 506574

Synagogues
Brighton & Hove Hebrew Congregation
Middle Street Synagogue
66 Middle Street, Brighton and Hove BN1 1AL
Hove Hebrew Congregation
79 Holland Road
Brighton and Hove BN3 1JN   (01273) 732085
West Hove Synagogue
31 New Church Road
Brighton and Hove BN3 4AD   (01273) 888855
Fax: (01273) 888810

Progressive
Progressive Synagogue
6 Landsdowne Road
Brighton and Hove BN3 1FF   (01273) 737223
9.30am to 1pm

Reform
New (Reform)
Palmeira Avenue
Brighton and Hove BN3 3GE   (01273) 735343

Eastbourne

Synagogues
22 Susans Road
Eastbourne BN21 3HA   (01435) 866928
Fax: (01435) 865783

Hastings

Contact Information
Hastings District Jewish Society
c/o Mrs Ilse Eton
6 Gilbert Road, St Leonards on Sea, Hastings
TN27 0RH   (01424) 436551

Tyne & Wear

Gateshead
A community with many schools, *yeshivot* and training institutions.

Bakeries
Stenhouse
215 Coatsworth Road
Gateshead NE8 1SR   (0191) 477-2001

Booksellers
J. Lehmann
28-30 Grasmere Street
Gateshead NE8 1TS   (0191) 477-3523
Also has wholesale and mail order
20 Cambridge Terrace, NE8 1RP
                           (0191) 490-1692
                       Fax: (0191) 477-5955

Butchers
K.L. Kosher Butcher
83 Rodsley Avenue
Gateshead NE8   (0191) 477-3109
Kosher.

Mikvaot
180 Bewick Road
Gateshead NE8 1UF   (0191) 477-3552

Synagogues
138 Whitehall Road
Gateshead NE8 1TP   (0191) 477-3012
A community with many schools, 'yeshivot' and
training institutions.

180 Bewick Road
Gateshead NE8 1UF   (0191) 477-0111
Mikva on premises. For appt: 477-3552

Newcastle
The community was established before 1831,
when a cemetery was acquired. Jews have
lived in Newcastle since 1775. There are about
1,200 Jews in the city today.

Bed & Breakfast
Vegetarian
Old School House
Kirkwhelpington
Newcastle NE19 2RT   (01830) 40226

Groceries
Zelda's Delicatessen
Unit 7 Kenton Park Shopping Centre
Newcastle NE3 4RU   (0191) 213-0013
Supervision: Newcastle Kashrus Committee,
Rabbi Yehuda Black.
Delicatessen, fresh meat, poultry and bread
also sold here. Closed Mondays. Credit cards
accepted. Buses: 10, 31 from city centre.

Kashrut Information
Kashrus Committee
Lionel Jacobson House
Graham Park Road, Gosforth, Newcastle NE3
4BH   (0191) 284-0959

Media
Newspapers
The North-East Jewish Recorder
24 Adeline Gardens
Gosforth, Newcastle NE3 4JQ
                           (0191) 285-1253

Organisations
Representative Council of North-East Jewry
24 Adeline Gardens
Newcastle NE3 4JQ
                           (0191) 285-1253

Restaurants
Vegetarian
The Red Herring
3 Studley Terrace
Fenham, Newcastle NE4 7PG
                           (0191) 272-3484

Synagogues
Newcastle Reform Synagogue
The Croft
off Kenton Road, Gosforth, Newcastle NE3 4RF
                           (0191) 284-8621

United Hebrew Congregation
Graham Park Road
Newcastle NE3 4BH
                           (0191) 284-0959
Mikva on premises.

Sunderland
Mikvaot
11 The Oaks East
Ryhope Road, Sunderland SR2 8EX
                           (0191) 565-0224

Organisations
11 The Oaks East
Ryhope Road, Sunderland SR2 8EX
                           (0191) 565-0224

Synagogues
Communal Rav.
11 The Oaks East
Ryhope Road, Sunderland SR2 8EX
                           (0191) 565-0224

Sunderland Hebrew Congregation
Ryhope Road
Sunderland SR2 7EQ   (0191) 522-7560

Whitley Bay

Synagogues
2 Oxford Street
Whitley Bay NE26
(0191) daytime: 01670 367053, evening: 0191 252-1367
Visitors required for services.

West Midlands

Birmingham

This Jewish community is one of the oldest in the Provinces, dating from at least 1730. Birmingham was a centre from which Jewish pedlars covered the surrounding country week by week, returning home for Shabbat.

The first synagogue of which there is any record was in The Froggery in 1780. There was a Jewish cemetery in the same neighbourhood in 1730, and Moses Aaron is said to have been born here in 1718. The synagogue of 1780 was extended in 1791, 1809 and 1827. A new and larger synagogue, popularly known as 'Singers Hill', opened in 1856. Today's Jewish population stands at about 2,300.

Booksellers
Lubavitch Bookshop
95 Willows Road
Birmingham B12 9QF   (0121) 440-6673
                    Fax: (0121) 446-4199

Caterers
B'tayavon
20 Hampton Court
George Road, Birmingham B15 1PU
                    (0121) 456-2172

Golda
161 Vice Roy Close
Bristol Road, B5 7HX, Birmingham B13 8LA
                    (0121) 440-7574
                    Fax: (0121) 440-1925

Contact Information
Lubavitch Centre
95 Willows Road
Birmingham B12 9QF   (0121) 440-6673
Bookshop on premises.

Delicatessens
A. Gee
75 Pershore Road
Birmingham B5 7NX   (0121) 440-2160
Kosher butcher, baker and deli.

Kashrut Information
Shechita Board
Singers Hill
Ellis Street, Birmingham B1 1HL
                    (0121) 643-0884

Mikvaot
Birmingham Central Synagogue
133 Pershore Road
Birmingham B5 7PA   (0121) 440-4044

Representative Organisations
Representative Council of Birmingham & Midland Jewry
37 Wellington Road
Birmingham B15 2ES   (0121) 236-1801
Evenings: 440-4142
                    Fax: (0121) 236-9906

Synagogues
Bimingham Hebrew Congregation
Singer's Hill
Ellis Street, Birmingham B1 1HL
                    (0121) 643-0884

Central Synagogue
133 Pershore Road
Birmingham B5 7PA   (0121) 440-4044

Progressive Synagogue
4 Sheepcote Street
Birmingham B16 8AA   (0121) 643-5640

Tourist Information
Israel Information Centre & Bookshop
Singers Hill
Blucher Street, Birmingham B1 1QL
                    (0121) 643-2688
                    Fax: (0121) 643-2688

Coventry

Synagogues
Coventry Hebrew Congregation
Barras Lane
Coventry CV1 3BW   (01203) 220168

Reform
Coventry Jewish Reform Community
Coventry CV   (01203) 672027
The Jewish presence in Coventry dates back to 1775, if not earlier.

Solihull

Synagogues
Solihull & District Hebrew Congregation
3 Monastery Drive
Solihull B91 1DW   (0121) 707-5199
                         Fax: (0121) 706-8736
          Email: rabbiypink@compuserve.com
Services: Friday evening 6.30 winter, 8.00 pm
summer; Sat 9.45am, Sun 9am

Wolverhampton

Synagogues
Fryer Street
Wolverhampton WV1 1HT
Est. over 150 years ago. Membership 15
families. Services Fri. even. & some Sabbath
morns.

Yorkshire

Bradford
The Jewish community, although only about
140 years old, has exercised much influence on
the city's staple industry: wool. Jews of
German descent developed the export trade of
wool yarns and fabrics.

Synagogues

Orthodox
Bradford Hebrew Congregation
Springhurst Road
Shipley, Bradford BD18 3DN
                         (01274) 581189
Services 10am monthly on Shabbat
Mevarchim, High holy-days & certain festivals.

Reform
Bradford Synagogue
Bowland Street
Manningham Lane, Bradford BD1 3BW
                         (01274) 728925
Service Friday 6pm; Sat 11am; Festivals, 6pm &
11am

Harrogate

Guest Houses
Amadeus Vegetarian Hotel
115 Franklin Road
Harrogate HG1 5EN   (01423) 505-151
                         Fax: (01423) 505-151
Totally vegetarian and non-smoking. Meals for
resident guests only, Saturday nights only.
Vegetarian café nearby open Friday evenings.
10 minutes walk from railway station.

Synagogues
St Mary's Walk
Harrogate HG2 0LW
Friday 6pm in Winter and 7pm in Summer.
Sabbath 9.30am

Harrogate Hebrew Congregation
St Mary's Walk, Harrogate   (01423) 871713
                         Fax: (01423) 879143
Services: Saturday 9.30 a.m. 1st Friday evening
in month – Winter 6 p.m. / Summer 7 p.m.

Leeds
The Leeds Jewish community is the second
largest in the provinces, and numbers about
12,000. The community dates only from 1804,
although a few Jews are known to have lived
there in the previous half-century. The first
synagogue was built in 1860, when there were
about 60 Jewish families.

Bakeries

Orthodox
Chalutz Bakery
378 Harrogate Road
Leeds LS17 6PY   (0113) 269-1350
Supervision: Leeds Kashrut Commission.
Hours: Monday to Thursday, 8 am to 6 pm;
Friday, to 1 hour before Shabbat; Saturday,
from 1 hour after Shabbat to 2 pm Sunday.

Butchers
The Kosherie
410 Harrogate Road
Leeds LS17 6PY   (0113) 268-2943
                         Fax: (0113) 269-6979
          Email: famouskosherie.demon.co.uk
Supervision: Leeds Beth Din.

Community Organisations
The Club
Lubavitch Centre
168 Shadwell Lane, Leeds LS17 8AD
(0113) 266-3311
Fax: (0113) 237-1130
Supervision: Leeds Kashrut Authority and Leeds Beth Din.
A community centre which provides educational activities. Restaurant on premises which is currently not open. Call to see if it has re-opened.

Delicatessens
Fisher's Deli
391 Harrogate Road
Leeds LS17 6DJ (0113) 268-6944
Supervision: Leeds Beth Din.
Butcher and deli.

Gourmet Foods
Sandhill Parade
584 Harrogate Road, Leeds LS17 8DP
(0113) 268-2726
Supervision: Leeds Beth Din.
Butcher and deli.

Hotels
Beegee's Guest House
18 Moor Allerton Drive
off Street Lane, Moortown, Leeds LS17 6RZ
(0113) 293-5469
Fax: (0113) 275-3300
Near all synagogues.
Hansa's
72 North Street, Leeds LS2 7PN
(0113) 244-4408
Vegetarian restaurant as well.

Libraries
Jewish Library
Porton Collection; Central Library, Municipal Buildings, Leeds LS1 3AB (0113) 247-8282

Media
Newspapers
Jewish Telegraph
1 Shaftesbury Avenue, Leeds LS8 1DR
(0113) 266-6000
Fax: (0113) 266-6006
Email: telegraph@jaytel.demon.co.uk

Mikvaot
411 Harrogate Road
Leeds LS17 7BY (0113) 237-1096
(answerphone)

Religious Organisations
Beth Din
Etz Chaim Synagogue
Leeds LS17 6BY (0113) 269-6902
Fax: (0113) 237-0893
Information about kosher food and accommodation may be obtained here.

Representative Information
Leeds Jewish Representative Council
c/o Shadwell Lane Synagogue
Leeds LS17 (0113) 269-7520
Fax: (0113) 237-0851
Publishes Year Book.

Synagogues
Orthodox
Beth Hamedrash Hagadol
399 Street Lane
Leeds LS17 6HQ (0113) 269-2181

Chassidishe
c/o Donisthorpe Hall
Shadwell Lane, Leeds LS17 6AW

Etz Chaim
411 Harrogate Road
Leeds LS17 7BY (0113) 266-2214

Shadwell Lane Synagogue (United Hebrew Congregation)
151 Shadwell Lane
Leeds LS17 8DW (0113) 269-6141
Fax: (0113) 237-0851

Shomrei Hadass
368 Harrogate Road
Leeds LS17 6QB (0113) 268-1461

Reform
Sinai
Roman Avenue, off Street Lane, Leeds LS8 2AN
(0113) 266-5256

Sheffield
Synagogues
Sheffield Jewish Congregation and Centre
Wilson Road
Sheffield S11 8RN (0114) 266-3567
Fax: (0114) 266-3567

Reform
Sheffield & District Reform Jewish Congregation
PO Box 675
Sheffield S11 8T8 (0114) 230-1054
Service alternate Friday evenings

York

Tours of Jewish Interest
Yorkwalk
3 Fairway, Clifton, York Y030 5QA
(01904) 622303
Fax: (01904) 656244
Introduced new walk called 'The Jewish Heritage Walk', recalling the Jewish contribution to York's history. The tour includes the Minster with its magnificent religious art. The walk finishes at Clifford's Tower, the site of a dreadful Jewish massacre in 1190.

Channel Islands

Alderney
On the Corblets Road at Longy, there is a memorial to the victims of the Nazis during their occupation of the English Channel Islands during the Second World War. It bears plaques in English, French, Hebrew and Russian.

Jersey

Synagogues
Jersey Jewish Congregation
La Petite Route des Mielles
St Brelade, Jersey JE3 8FY
Shabbat morning service, 10:30 am; Holy days, 7 pm and 10 am.

Contact Information
Armon
3 Clos des Chataigniers, Rue de la Croix, St Ouen, Jersey JE3 2HA
Honorary secretary of the Jersey Jewish Congregation.

Isle of Man

Douglas

Synagogues
Hebrew Congregation
Douglas (01624) 24214
There are more than 70 Jews on the island.

Northern Ireland

Belfast
There were Jews living in Belfast in the year 1652, but the present community was founded in 1869.

Synagogues
49 Somerton Road BT15 3LH (01232) 777974
Services: Sat., Sun., Mon., & Thurs.; am.

Organisations
Vegetarian Society of Ulster
66 Ravenhill Gardens
Ulster BT6 8QG (01232) 457888

Restaurants
Jewish Community Centre
49 Somerton Road
Ulster BT15 3LH (01232) 777-974
Open Sunday 6.30 pm to 9.30 pm.

Scotland

Aberdeen

Restaurants

Vegetarian

Jaws Wholefood Café
5 West North Street AB1 3AT (01224) 645676
10am to 3pm Mon.-Sat; 10am to 9pm Thurs. & Fri

Synagogues
74 Dee Street AB1 2DS (01224) 582135

Dundee

Synagogues
St Mary Place DD1 5RB (01382) 223557

Dunoon

Synagogues
Argyll & Bute Jewish Community
(01369) 705118

Edinburgh

The Town Council and Burgess Roll minutes of 1691 and 1717 record applications by Jews for permission to live and trade in Edinburgh. Local directories of the eighteenth century contain Jewish names.

Butchers

3 Hallhead Road EH16 5QT

(0131) 667-1521

Regular deliveries from suppliers in Glasgow and Manchester. Further information from Hon. Sec.

Kashrut Information

3 Hallhead Road EH16 5QT (0131) 667-1521

Restaurants

Vegetarian

Anna Purna
45 St Patrick Sq. EH   (0131) 662-1807
Black Bo's
Blackfriars Street EH   (0131) 557-6136
Henderson's
94 Hanover Street EH2 1DR
(0131) 225-2131
Fax: (0131) 220-3542
Kalpna Restaurant
2 St Patrick Sq. EH8 9EZ   (0131) 667-9890
Hours: Lunch 10.00am to 2.00pm. Dinner 5.30pm to 11.00pm.
Pierre Lapin
West Nicholson Street EH   (0131) 668-4332

Synagogues

4 Salisbury Road EH16 5AB
(0131) 667-3144

Glasgow

The Glasgow Jewish community dates back to 1823. The oldest synagogues building is the Garnethill Synagogue, now also the home of the Scottish Jewish Archives, which opened in 1879. The community grew rapidly from 1891 with many Jews settling in the Gorbals. In recent years the community has gradually spread southwards and is now mainly situated in the Giffnock and Newton Mearns areas.

Booksellers

J & E Levingstone
47/55 Sinclair Drive G42 9PT
(0141) 649-2962
Fax: (0141) 649-2962
Religious requisites also stocked.

Delicatessens

Michael Morrison and Son
52 Sinclair Drive G42 9PY   (0141) 632-0998
Not under official supervision. Stockist of many Glatt Kosher items.

Media

Newspapers

Jewish Telegraph
43 Queen Square G41 2BD   (0141) 423-9200
Fax: (0141) 423-9200
Email: telegraph@jaytel.demon.co.uk

Restaurants

Meat

Kaye's Restaurant
Maccabi Youth Centre, May Terrace G46
(0141) 620-3233
Kosher.

Synagogues

Orthodox

Garnethill
127 Hill Street G3 6UB   (0141) 322-4151
Langside
125 Niddrie Road G42 8QA   (0141) 423-4062
Lubavitch   (0141) 638-6116
Netherlee & Clarkston
Clarkston Road at Randolph Drive G44
(0141) 637-8206
Newton Mearns
14 Larchfield Court G77 5BH
(0141) 639-4000
Queen's Park
Falloch Road G42 9QX   (0141) 632-1743

Reform

Glasgow New Synagogue
147 Ayr Road, Newton Mearns G77 6RE
(0141) 639-4083

Booksellers

Well of Wisdom
Giffnock Synagogue
Giffnock G46   (0141) 638-2030

Delicatessens

Giffnock Kosher Deli
200 Fenwick Road
Giffnock G46   (0141) 638-8267

Marlenes Kosher Deli
2 Burnfield Road
Giffnock G46 7QB   (0141) 638-4383

Hotels

Forres Guest House
10 Forres Avenue
Giffnock G46 6L
(0141) 638-5554 (mobile: 0410 864-151)
Email: june.d@ukonline.co.uk

Guest House
26 St Clair Avenue
Giffnock G46 7QE   (0141) 638-3924
Kosher, but not supervised.

Mikvaot

Giffnock & Newlands Synagogue
Maryville Avenue
Giffnock G46 7NE   (0141) 577-8250

Organisations

Glasgow Jewish Representative Council
222 Fenwick Road
Giffnock G46 6UE   (0141) 620-1700
Fax: (0141) 638-2100

Synagogues

Orthodox

Giffnock & Newlands
Maryville Avenue
Giffnock G46 7NE   (0141) 638-6600

St Andrews

Contact Information

Jewish Student's Society
c/o Sec., Students' Union
University of St Andrews, Kirkcaldy KY16 9UY

Wales

Cardiff

Mikvaot

Wales Empire Pool Building, Wood Street
CF1 1PP   (01222) 382296

Restaurants

Vegetarian

Munchies Wholefood Co-op
60 Crwys Road, Cathays CF2 4NN
(01222) 399677

Self-catering

210 Lake Road East CF2 5NR   (01227) 58614

Synagogues

Reform

Cardiff New Synagogue
Moira Terrace CF2 1EJ   (01222) 614915

Orthodox

Cardiff United Synagogue
Brandreth Road, Penylan
(01222) 473728/491795

Llandudno

Synagogues

28 Church Walks LL30 2HL   (01492) 572549
No resident minister, but visiting ministers
during summer months. Friday night services
held throughout year, 6.16pm (winter) and
8pm (summer)

Newport

Synagogues

Newport Mon Hebrew Congregation
3 Queens Hill Crescent NP9 5HH
(01633) 262308

Swansea

Restaurants

Vegetarian

Chris's Kitchen
The Market SA1 3PE   (01792) 643455
8.30 am to 5.30 pm Mon.-Sat

Synagogues

Ffynone
17 Ffynone Drive SA1 6DB   (01792) 473333

Contact Information

70 Gabalfa Road
Sketty SA2 8NE   (01792) 205263

95 Cherry Grove
Sketty SA2 8AX   (01792) 202106
Both are happy to help and advise students
coming to University College.

United States of America

GMT -5 to 11 hours
Country calling code (1)

Total Population 270,000,000
Jewish Population 5,600,000

Kashrut Information

As there is no unified Jewish ecclesiastical control in America, or a Chief Rabbinate as exists in other countries of the world, there is little 'official' supervision of kashrut. Instead, there are a proliferation of hashgachot by individual rabbis and companies who engage in kashrut supervision on a commercial level. More than 170 such symbols and organisations are known to exist in the US today. They tend to have differing degrees of reliability. The 'big three' national symbols are OU, Kof-K and Circle-K. 'K' alone is an unregistered trademark and unreliable as a mark of proper kosher supervision. Travellers are recommended to check with a local rabbi or religious organisation to learn the local reliable supervising bodies. Agudat Israel (address and phone number below) will provide, free of charge, a list of people in most major US cities who can provide reliable information about kashrut.

Religious Organisations

Although most of these organisations are based in New York, they can provide you with information about their constituent synagogues and the relevant details (addresses, phone numbers, minyan times) across the country

Orthodox

Agudat Israel World Organization, 84 William Street, NY, 10038   (212) 797-9600
Fax: (212) 269-2843
Lubavitch Movement, 770 Eastern Parkway, Brooklyn, NY, 11213   (718) 221-0500
Fax: (718) 221-0985
National Council of Young Israel National Office, 3 West 16th Street NY, 10011   (212) 929-1525
Fax: (212) 727-9526
Email: nyci@youngisrael.org
www.youngisrael.org
Southern Regional Office, 1035 NE 170th Terrace, Miami, FL, 33162   (305) 770-3993
Email: ncyi.south@youngisrael.org

Washington, DC Office, 1101 Pennsylvania Avenue, Suite 1050, Washington, DC, 20004
(202) 347-4111
Fax: (202) 347-8341
West Coast Regional Office, 1050 Indiana Avenue, Venice, CA 90291   (310) 396-3935
Fax: (310) 581-0904
email: ncyi.west@youngisrael.org
Union of Orthodox Jewish Congregations of America, 333 Seventh Avenue, NY, 10001
(212) 563-4000
Fax: (212) 613-8333

Conservative

United Synagogue of America
155 Fifth Avenue, NY 10010   (212) 533-7800
World Council of Synagogues can be found at the same location.

Reform

Union of American Hebrew Congregations
838 Fifth Ave, NY, 10021   (212) 650-4085
Fax: (212) 650-4169

Progressive

World Union for Progressive Judaism, 838 Fifth Ave, NY, 10021   (212) 650-4090
Fax: (212) 650-4090
Email: 5448032@mcimail.com

Sephardic

Union of Sephardic Congregations, 8 West 70th Street, NY, 10023   (212) 873-0300

Alabama

Birmingham

Contact Information
Rabbi Meir Rosenberg
3225 Montevallo Road 35213
(205) 879-1464
Visitors requiring information about kashrut, temporary accommodation, etc., should contact Rabbi Rosenberg.

Delicatessens
Browdy's
2607 Cahaba Road 35223   (205) 879-6411

Libraries
Hess Library
3960 Montclair Road 35213

Mikvaot
Knesseth Israel
3225 Montevallo Rd 35213   (205) 879-1464
Supervision: (O).

Synagogues

Conservative

Beth-El
2179 Highland Avenue 35205
                                   (205) 933-2740

Orthodox

Knesseth Israel
3225 Montevallo Road 35223   (205) 879-1464
                              Fax: (205) 879-5774

Reform

Emanu-El
2100 Highland Avenue 35205
                                   (205) 933-8037

Huntsville
Synagogues
Conservative
Etz Chayim
7705 Bailey Cove Road 35802

Mobile
Synagogues
Reform
Spring Hill Avenue Temple
1769 Spring Hill Avenue 36607

Montgomery
Community Organisations
Jewish Federation
PO Box 20058 36120   (205) 277-5820

Synagogues
Maxwell Air Force Base
Building 833, Chaplain's School

Conservative

Agudath Israel
3525 Cloverdale Road 36111
Mikvah attached

Orthodox

Etz Ahayem (Sephardi)
725 Augusta Road 36111

Reform

Beth Or
2246 Narrow Lane 36106
Maxwell Air Force Base
Building 833, Chaplain's School

Alaska
Anchorage
Synagogues
Orthodox
Congregation Shomrei Ohr
1210 E. 26th 99508   (907) 279-1200
                            Fax: (907) 279-0800

Reform

Beth Sholom
7525 E. Northern Lights Blvd 99504
                            (907) 338-1836
                       Fax: (907) 337-4013
                 Email: sholom@alaska.net

Arizona
Mesa
Synagogues
Conservative
Beth Sholom Congregation
316 Le Seuer Street 85204   (602) 964-1981

Phoenix
Community Organisations
Jewish Federation of Greater Phoenix
32 W. Coolidge, Suite 200 85013
                                   (602) 274-1800

Kashrut Information
Rabbi David Rebibo
Phoenix Hebrew Academy, 515 E. Bethany
Home Rd. 85012   (602) 277-7479
Visitors requiring kashrut information should
contact Rabbi Rebibo.

Media

Newspapers

Jewish News of Greater Phoenix
1625 E. Northern 106 85020 (602) 870-9470
Fax: (602) 870-0426
Email: jngphx@aol.com

Shalom Arizona
32 W. Coolidge, Suite 200 85013
(602) 274-1800

Museums

Sylvia Plotkin Judaica Museum
10460 N. 56th St
Scottsdale 85253 (602) 951-0323
Fax: (602) 951-7150
Email: tbeth@primenet.com
Hours: Most Sundays 12-3 p.m., Tuesday-
Thursday 10-3, Friday evenings after services.
Advanced notice required for groups of 10 or
more.

Restaurants

Meat

Segal's Kosher Foods
4818 North 7th Street 85014 (602) 285-1515
Fax: (602) 277-5760
Supervision: Greater Phoenix Vaad Hakashrut.
Strictly kosher full service restaurant serving
lunch and dinner Monday through Thursday
and Shabbat take-out on Friday. Kosher bakery
within premises.

Meat and Dairy

J.J.'s Kosher
1331 E. Northern Av. 85015 (602) 371-0999

Synagogues

Tri-Cities Jewish Community Center
1965 E. Hermosa Temp, AZ 85282
(602) 897-0588

Conservative

Congregation Beth El
1118 W. Glendale 85021 (602) 944-3359

Orthodox

Chabad-Lubavitch Center
2110 E. Lincoln Drive 85020 (602) 944-2753
Congregation Beth Joseph
515 E. Bethany Home Road 85012
(602) 277-7479
Congregation Shaarei Tzedek
7608 N. 18th Avenue 85021 (602) 944-1133

Valley of the Sun Jewish Community Center
1718 W. Maryland Avenue 85015
(602) 249-1832
Young Israel of Phoenix
745 E Maryland Avenue 85014
(602) 265-8888

Reform

Temple Beth Ami
4545 N. 36th Street, No. 211 85018
(302) 956-0805
Temple Chai
4645 E. Marilyn Avenue 85032
(602) 971-1234
Temple Kol Ami
15030 N. 64th Street, 204 85254
(602) 951-9660

Scottsdale

Delicatessens

Cactus Kosher
8005 E. Indian School Road 85251
(602) 970-8441
Supervision: Greater Phoenix Vaad Hakashrut.
Delicatessen which also offers take-out and
catering for area hotel delivery.

Synagogues

Conservative

Beth Emeth of Scottsdale
5406 E. Virginia Avenue 85254
(602) 947-4604
Beth Joshua Congregation
6230 E. Shea Blvd. 85254 (602) 991-5404
Har Zion
5929 E. Lincoln Drive 85253 (602) 991-0720

Reform

Temple Solel
6805 E. MacDonald Drive 85253
(602) 991-7414

Sierra Vista

Synagogues

Temple Kol Hamidbar
228 North Canyon Drive
(602) 458-8637 (Ans. phone only)

Sun City and West

Synagogues

Conservative

Beth Emeth of Sun City
13702 Meeker Blvd., Sun City West 85373
(602) 584-1957

Reform

Beth Shalom of Sun City
12202 101st Avenue, Sun City 85351
(602) 977-3240

Tempe

Community Organisations
Tri-City Jewish Community Center
1965 E. Hermosa Drive 85282 (602) 897-0588

Synagogues

Orthodox

Chabad-Lubavitch Center
23 W. 9th Street 85281
(602) 966-5163

Reform

Temple Emanuel
5801 Rural Road 85283
(602) 838-1414

Tucson

Community Organisations
Jewish Federation of Southern Arizona
3822 E. River Rd. 85718
(520) 577-9393

Groceries
Feig's Kosher Foods
5071 E. 5th Street 85711
(520) 325-2255
Supervision: Rabbi A. Oleisky.
Fresh glatt beef, lamb and veal, full service
deli, groceries. Hours: Monday to Thursday,
8 am to 5:45 pm; Friday, to 3:45 pm; Sunday,
to 1:45 pm.

Synagogues

Conservative

Congregation Bet Shalom
3881 E. River Road 85718
Anshei Israel
5550 E. 5th Street 85711

Orthodox

Congregation Chofetz Chayim
5150 E. 5th Street 85711
(520) 747-7780
Fax: (520) 745-6325

Young Israel
2443 E. 4th Street 85719
Young Israel of Tucson
2443 E 4th Street 85710
(520) 326-8362

Reform

Temple Emanuel
225 N. County Club Road 85716

Arkansas

El Dorado

Synagogues

Reform

Beth Israel
1130 E. Main Street

Helena

Synagogues
Temple Beth-El
406 Perry Street 72342
Founded 1875.

Hot Springs

Synagogues
House of Israel
300 Quapaw Avenue. 71901
(501) 623-5821
Fax: (501) 622-3500
Email: houseofi@direclynx.net
Supervision: (R).
Hot Springs is known for its curative waters.
The Leo Levi Memorial Hospital (for joint
disorders, such as arthritis) was founded by
B'nai B'rith, as was the adjacent Levi Towers, a
senior citizen housing project.

Little Rock

Bakeries
Andre's
11121 Rodney Parham Rd 72212

Community Organisations
Jewish Federation of Arkansas
2821 Kavanaugh, Garden Level 72205 3868
(501) 663-3571
Fax: (501) 663-7286
Email: jfalr@aristotle.net
Monday to Thursday 9.00am to 5.00pm. Friday
9.00am to 4.00pm.

Mikvaot
Agudath Achim
7901 W. 5th St. 72205

Synagogues
Reform
B'nai Israel
3700 Rodney Parham Rd. 72212
(501) 225-9700
Fax: (501) 225-6058
Email: elevy@snider.net

California

As the general population of California continues to increase, the Jewish community is growing as well. Places of worship abound, from Eureka in the north to San Diego in the south, but the major part of the community lives in the Los Angeles metropolitan area.

Alameda
Synagogues
Reform
Temple Israel
3183 Mecartney Road 94501

Anaheim
Synagogues
Conservative
Temple Beth Emet
1770 W. Cerritos Avenue 92804
(714) 772-4720

Arcadia
Synagogues
Congregation Shaarei Torah
550 S. 2nd Avenue 91006   (818) 445-0810

Arleta
Synagogues
Reform
Temple Beth Solomon of the Deaf
13580 Osborne Street 91331   (818) 899-2202
Fax: (818) (TDD) 896-6721

Bakersfield
Synagogues
Conservative
B'nai Jacob
600 17th Street 93301

Reform
Temple Beth El
2906 Loma Linda Drive 93305

Berkeley (See also Oakland)
Mikvaot
Mikvah Taharas Israel
2520 Warring St. 94704-3111   (510) 848-7221
Fax: (510) 849-0536
Email: vaad@flash.net
Available for use by Men. Women by appointment.

Museums
Judah L. Magnes – Jewish Museum of the West
2911 Russell St. 94705   (510) 549-6950
Fax: (510) 849-3650
Among the latest institutions of its kind west of New York. It includes the Western Jewish History Center & the Blumenthal Library. Open Sun-Thurs. 10-4.
Judah L. Magnes Museum
2911 Russell St. 94705   (510) 549-6950
Fax: (510) 849-3673
Email: magnes-pr@eb.jfed.org
Open Sunday to Thursday 10am to 4pm.
Closed Jewish and US Federal holidays.

Restaurants
Café Olam, UC Berkeley Hillel
2736 Bancroft Way   (510) 665-1818
Supervision: The Vaad Kakashrus of Northern California.
Noah's Bagels
1883 Solano Avenue, Solano   (510) 525-4447
Supervision: The Vaad Kakashrus of Northern California.

Synagogues
Conservative
Netivot Shalom
1414 Walnut Street

Egalitarian

Hillel Foundation
2736 Bancroft Way 94704   (510) 845-7793
Traditional egalitarian services on Friday
evening.

Jewish Renewal

Aquarian Minyan
c/o Goldfarb, 2020 Essex 94703
Kehilla
PO Box 3063 94703

Orthodox

Beth Israel
1630 Bancroft Way 94703
Chabad House
2643 College Avenue 94704

Reform

Temple Beth El
2301 Vine Street 94708

Beverly Hills

Note: Beverly Hills, Hollywood and Los Angeles
are contiguous communities and in many cases
have overlapping bodies.

Synagogues

Orthodox

Beth Jacob
9030 Olympic Boulevard 90211
Young Israel of Beverly Hills
8701 Pico Blvd 90035   (310) 275-3020
Young Israel of North Beverly Hills
9350 Civic Center Drive
North Beverly Hills 90210   (310) 203-0170

Orthodox Sephardi

Magen David
322 N. Foothill 90210

Reform

Temple Emanuel
8844 Burton Way 90211   (310) 274-6388
                             Fax: (310) 271-7976

Burlingame

Synagogues
Peninsula Temple Sholom
1655 Sebastian Drive 94010   (415) 697-2266
                             Fax: (415) 697-2544

Carmel

Synagogues
Congregation Beth Israel
5716 Carmel Valley Road 93923
                             (408) 624-2015

Castro Valley

Synagogues
Shir Ami
4529 Malabar Avenue 94546   (415) 537-1787

Costa Mesa

Organisations
Jewish Federation of Orange County
250 E. Baker Street 92626   (714) 755-5555
                             Fax: (714) 755-0307
                             Email: info@jfoc.org

Daly City

Synagogues

Conservative

B'nai Israel
1575 Annie Street 94015   (415) 756-5430

Davis

Synagogues

Reform

Davis Jewish Fellowship
1821 Oak Avenue 95616

Downey

Synagogues
Temple Ner Tamid
10629 Lakewood Boulevard 90241
                             (310) 861-9276

Eureka

Synagogues
Beth El
Hodgson & T Streets, PO Box 442 95502
                             (707) 444-2846

Fairfax

Bakeries
BH International Bakery
7113 Beverly BlvdLa Brea   (213) 939-6497
Supervision: Kehillah of Los Angeles.
Pareve and dairy. Chalav Yisrael.

Fremont

Synagogues

Reform

Temple Beth Torah
42000 Paseo Padre Pkwy 94539
(415) 656-7141

Fresno

Community Organisations
Jewish Federations Office
1340 W. Herndon, Suite 103 93711

Synagogues

Conservative

Beth Jacob
406 W. Shields Avenue 93705

Orthodox

Chabad House
6735 N. ILA 93711

Reform

Temple Beth Israel
6622 N. Maroa Avenue 93704
This temple has its own etrog tree, planted
from a sprig brought to the USA from Israel.

Gardena

Synagogues

Conservative

Southwest Temple Beth Torah
14725 S. Gramercy Place 90249

Hancock Park

Synagogues

Orthodox

Young Israel of Hancock Park
225 South La Brea   (213) 931-4030

Hollywood

Kashrut Information
Kosher Information Bureau
15365 Magnolia Blvd, Sherman Oaks 91403
(818) 762-3197

Laguna Hills

Delicatessens
The Kosher Bite
23595 Moulton Parkway 92653
(949) 770-1818
Fax· (949) 770 5321
Supervision: Rabinical Council of Orange
County.
Monday 9am-5pm.Tuesday to Thursday 9am to
7pm. Friday 9am-3pm. Sunday 8am to 2pm.

Lakewood

Synagogues

Conservative

Temple Beth Zion Sinai
6440 Del Amo Blvd. 90713   (562) 429-0715
Fax: (562) 429-0715

Long Beach

Community Organisations
**Jewish Federation of Greater Long Beach &
W. Orange County**
3801 E. Willow St. 90815   (310) 426-7601

Media

Newspapers

Jewish Community Chronicle
3801 E. Willow St. 90815 1791

Mikvaot
3847 Atlantic Avenue 90807

Synagogues

Conservative

Beth Shalom
3635 Elm Avenue 90807
Congregation Shalom of Leisure World
1661 Golden Rain Road
Northwood Clubhouse No. 3, Seal Beach, Seal
Beach 90740

Orthodox

Congregation Lubavitch
3981 Atlantic Avenue 90807
Young Israel of Long Beach
PO Box 7041 90807-0041   (310) 527-3163

Reform

Temple Beth David
6100 Hefley Street
Westminster

Temple Israel
338 E. 3rd Street 90812

Los Alamitos

Bakeries
Fairfax Kosher Market & Bakery
11196-98 Los Alamitos Blvd 90720
(714) 828-4492

Los Angeles

Los Angeles is America's, and the world's, second largest Jewish metropolis, with a Jewish population of around 600,000. Fairfax Avenue and Beverly Blvd together form the crossroads of traditional Jewish life while a growing Orthodox enclave centres around Pico and Robertson Blvds.

Important note: Area telephone codes have recently been split to 310 and 213 for central Los Angeles. We have endeavored in all cases to correct our information, but cannot guarantee the veracity of those who did not send in updates.

Bakeries
Aviv Bakery
15030 Ventura Blvd (818) 789-3176
Supervision: RCC.
Back East Bialy Bakery
8562 W. Pico Blvd (310) 276-1531
Supervision: Kehillah of Los Angeles.
Beverly Hills Patisserie
9100 W. Pico Blvd (310) 275-6873
Supervision: RCC.
BH International Bakery
9211 W. Pico Blvd (310) 859-8927
Supervision: Kehillah of Los Angeles.
Pareve and dairy. Chalav Yisrael.
BH International Bakery
7304 1/4 Santa Monica (213) 874-7456
Supervision: Kehillah of Los Angeles.
Pareve and dairy. Chalav Yisrael.
Eilat Bakery
457 1/2 N. Fairfax Avenue (213) 653-5553
Supervision: Kehillah of Los Angeles.
Chalav Yisrael.
Eilat Bakery #2
9233 W. Pico Blvd (310) 205-8700
Supervision: Kehillah of Los Angeles.
Chalav Yisrael.
Famous Bakery
350 N. Fairfax Avenue (213) 933-5000
Supervision: Kehillah of Los Angeles.
Chalav Yisrael.

Le Palais, 8670 W. Pico Blvd (310) 659-4809
Supervision: RCC.
Noah's New York Bagels
1737 Santa Rita Road #400, Pleasanton 94566
(510) 485-1921
Email: noah@noahs.com
Supervision: California Rabbinical Council.
All stores in Southern California are under RCC supervision; for the location of a store near you, call the above number.
Renaissance Bakery
22872 Ventura Blvd (818) 222-0110
Supervision: RCC.
Schwartz Bakery
441 N. Fairfax (213) 653-1683
Supervision: RCC.
Schwartz Bakery
8616 W. Pico Blvd (310) 854-0592
Supervision: RCC.
Yummy Pita Bakery
1437 S. Robertson Blvd. (310) 557-2122
Supervision: Kehillah of Los Angeles.
Restaurant as well. Chalav Yisrael.

Booksellers
House of David
9020 W. Olympic Blvd, Beverly Hills 90211
(310) 276-9414
Probably the most complete selection of books of Jewish interest can be found here.

Butchers
City Glatt, 7667 Beverly Blvd (213) 933-4040
Supervision: Kehillah of Los Angeles.
Sells Kehillah brand meats.
Doheny Kosher Meats
9213 W. Pico (310) 276-7232
Supervision: RCC.
Non-glatt.
Elat Market
8730 W. Pico (310) 659-7070
Supervision: RCC.
Non-glatt meat, deli and fish only.
Kosher Club
4817 W. Pico Blvd (213) 933-8283
Supervision: RCC.
Market as well.
Royal Palate Foods
960 E. Hyde Park Blvd (310) 330-7700
Supervision: RCC.
Roz Kosher Meat
12422-24 Burbank Blvd (818) 760-7694
Supervision: RCC.
Market as well.

Star Meats, 12136 Santa Monica Blvd
(310) 447-1612
Supervision: RCC.
Valley Glatt
12450 Burbank Blvd   (818) 766-4530
Supervision: Kehillah of Los Angeles.
Sells Kehillah brand meats.

Community Organisations
Jewish Federation of Greater Los Angeles
6505 Wilshire Blvd 90048   (310) 852-7758
Fax: (310) 852-8723
Los Angeles Jewish Community Buildings
6505 Wilshire Blvd 90048
Los Angeles West Side Community Center
5870 W. Olympic Blvd. 90036
This address also houses the Jewish Center's
Association of Los Angeles and includes a
'hands-on' museum for children.

Delicatessens
Micheline's
2627 S. LaCienega Blvd   (310) 204-5334
Supervision: RCC.
Catering and take out.
Pico Kosher Deli
8826 W. Pico Blvd 90035   (310) 273-9381
Fax: (310) 273-8476
Supervision: RCC.
Hours: Sunday to Thursday, 10 am to 9 pm;
Friday, 9 am to 3 pm; Shabbat, closed. Major
credit cards accepted.

Embassy
Consulate General
Suite 1700, 6380 Wilshire Blvd 90048
(213) 852-5523
Fax: (213) 852-5555
Email: israinfo@primenet.com
Web site: http://www.israelemb.org/la

Fishmongers
Fairfax Fish
515 N. Fairfax Avenue   (213) 658-8060
Supervision: Kehillah of Los Angeles.

Groceries
Kotlar's Pico Market
8622 W. Pico Blvd   (310) 652-5355
Supervision: RCC.
Market, fish and butcher.
La Brea Kosher Market
410 N. La Brea Avenue   (213) 931-1221
Supervision: Kehillah of Los Angeles.
Little Jerusalem
8917 W. Pico Blvd   (310) 858-8361
Supervision: RCC.
Market, fish and butcher.

Pico Glatt Kosher Mart
9427 W. Pico Blvd   (310) 785-0904
Supervision: Kehillah of Los Angeles.
PS Kosher Food Services
9760 W. Pico Blvd 90035   (310) 553-8804
Fax: (310) 553-8989
Email: psfood@juno.com
Kitchens located at Yeshiva University.
Western Kosher Market
444 N. Fairfax Avenue   (213) 655-8870
Supervision: Kehillah of Los Angeles.

Kashrut Information
Board of Rabbis of Southern California
5700 Wilshire Blvd, Suite # 2511 90036
(323) 761-8600
Fax: (323) 761-8603
Kosher Information Bureau
(818) 792-3197
Fax: (818) 980-6908
Rabbi Bukspan
6407 Orange Street 90048   (310) 653-5083
Rabbinical Council of California
1122 S. Robertson Blvd 90035 (310) 271-4160
Fax: (310) 271-7147

Kosher Kitchens
Cedars Sinai Hospital
8700 Beverly Blvd   (310) 855-4797
Supervision: RCC.

Media
Newspapers
Heritage Southwest Jewish Press
Weekly publication, coming out on Fridays.
Israel Today

Jewish Calendar Magazine

Jewish Journal

Weekly publication, coming out on Fridays.
Jewish News

Yisrael Shelanu

Mikvaot
Los Angeles Mikva
9548 W. Pico Blvd., 90035

Museums

Museum of Tolerance (Beit Hashoah)
9786 West Pico Blvd 90035   (310) 553-9036
Fax: (310) 553-4521
Web site: www.wiesenthal.com
High-tech, hands-on museum that focuses on
two themes through interactive exhibits: the
dynamics of racism and prejudice, and the
history of the Holocaust – the ultimate
example of man's inhumanity to man.
Simon Wiesenthal Museum of Tolerance
9876 West Pico Boulevard 90035
(310) 553-8403
Web site: www.wiesenthal.com

Organisations

Jewish Social Action Organisation
Simon Wiesenthal Center, 9760 W. Pico Blvd.
90035   (310) 553-9036
Fax: (310) 553-4521
Email: webmaster@wiesenthal.com
Web site: www.wiesenthal.com

Restaurants

Berookhim Royal Catering
6170 Wilbur Ave   (310) 458-9993
Berookhim Royal Catering
324 Marguerita Ave   (310) 458-9993

Beverly Hills Cuisine
9025 Wilshire Blvd   (310) 247-1239
Supervision: RCC.
Beverly/Fairfax & Downtown
7231 Beverly Blvd   (310) 936-1653
Classic Restaurant
1420 Westwood Blvd   (310) 234-9191
Supervision: RCC.
Coffee Brake
1507 S. Robertson Blvd   (310) 277-6741
Grill at the Beverly Carlton
9400 W. Olympic   (310) 282-0945
Hillel Restaurant
108 E. 8th Street   (213) 488-9939
Supervision: RCC.
Judy's, 129 N. La Brea Avenue (213) 934-7667
Supervision: RCC.
Mosaique, 8146 W. Third St.   (310) 951-1133
Nessim's, 8939 W. Pico Blvd   (310) 204-5334
Supervision: RCC.
New York Sandwich
600 W. 9th St.   (310) 623-4623

Red Ox
1271 S California Blvd., Walnut Creek 94596
(510) 256-6500
Supervision: Vaad Hakashrus of Northern
California.
Glatt kosher.
Rib Tickler
533 N. Fairfax Ave.   (310) 655-6333
Rimini Restaurant
9400 W. Olympic Blvd   (310) 552-1056
Supervision: RCC.
Simone, 8706 W. Pico Blvd   (310) 657-5552
Supervision: RCC-Mehadrin.

Dairy

Café Elite, 7115 Beverly Blvd   (213) 936-2861
Supervision: Kehillah of Los Angeles.
Chalav Yisrael.
Fish Grill, 7226 Beverly Blvd   (213) 937-7162
Supervision: Kehillah of Los Angeles.
Chalav Yisrael. Sit down or take out.
Milk N'Honey
8837 W. Pico Blvd   (310) 858-8850
Supervision: RCC.
Milky Way, 9108 W. Pico Blvd
(310) 859-0004
Supervision: Kehillah of Los Angeles.
Chalav Yisrael.
Smoothie Queen
8851 W. Pico Blvd   (310) 273-3409
Supervision: Kehillah of Los Angeles.
Chalav Yisrael.

Fish

Tami's Fish House
553 B, Fairfax Avenue   (310) 655-7953
The Fishing Well
W. Pico Blvd   (310) 859-9429
Supervision: RCC.

Meat

Chick'N Chow
9301 W. Pico Blvd 90035   (310) 274-5595
Fax: (310) 274-9693
Supervision: Kehillah of Los Angeles.
Glatt kosher eat in, take out, delivery. Hours:
11:30 am to 10 pm.
Cohen Restaurant
316 E. Pico Blvd 90015   (213) 742-8888
Fax: (213) 742-0066
Supervision: RCC.
Dizengoff Restaurant
8103 1/2 Beverly Blvd   (213) 651-1465
Supervision: Kehillah of Los Angeles.
Sit down or take out.
Elat Burger
9340 W. Pico Blvd   (310) 278-4692
Supervision: RCC.
Elite Cuisine
7119 Beverly Blvd   (213) 930-1303
Supervision: Kehillah of Los Angeles.
Sit down or take out.
Glatt Hut, 9303 W. Pico Blvd (310) 246-1900
Supervision: RCC.
Grill Express
501 N. Fairfax Avenue   (213) 655-0649
Supervision: RCC.
Habayit Restaurant
11921 W. Pico Blvd   (310) 488-9877
Haifa Restaurant
8717 W. Pico Blvd   (310) 550-2704
Kabob & Chinese Food
9180 W. Pico Blvd   (310) 274-4007
Supervision: Kehillah of Los Angeles.
Kabob & Chinese Food
11330 Santa Monica   (310) 914-3040
Supervision: Kehillah of Los Angeles.

La Gondola Ristorante Italiano
6405 Wilshire Blvd 90048 (213) 852-1915
Fax: (213) 852-0853
Web site: www.thegondola.com
Supervision: Kehillah of Los Angeles.
Use all Lubavitch meats. Hours: Monday to
Thursday, 11:30 am to 3 pm, 5 pm to 10 pm;
Sunday, 5 pm to 10 pm; Saturday night after
Shabbat in the winter. Located next to Beverly
Hills, there is a delivery service to the hotels. .
Magic Carpet Restaurant
8566 W. Pico Blvd 90035 (310) 652-8507
Fax: (310) 652-3568
Supervision: Kehillah of Los Angeles.
Motty's Place
7308 Beverly Blvd (213) 935-8087
Supervision: Kehillah of Los Angeles.
Museum Cafeteria
9760 W. Pico Blvd, 4th Floor (310) 553-9036
Supervision: Kehillah of Los Angeles.
Pareve and meat.
Nagila Meating Place
9407 W. Pico Blvd (310) 788-0119
Supervision: Kehillah of Los Angeles.
Olé, 7912 Beverly Blvd (213) 933-7254
Supervision: Kehillah of Los Angeles.
Hours: 12 pm to 9 pm, five days a week;
closed Friday and Saturday.
Pat's, 9233 W. Pico Blvd (310) 205-8705
Supervision: Kehillah of Los Angeles.
Sit down restaurant and catering.
Shalom Hunan Restaurant
5651 Wilshire Blvd (213) 934-0505
Supervision: RCC.
Sharon's II
306 E. 9th Street (213) 622-1010
Supervision: RCC.
Shula & Esther
5519 N. Fairfax Ave (310) 951-9651
Simon's La Glatt
446 N. Fairfax (213) 658-7730
Supervision: RCC.
Westside Grille
9411 W. Pico Blvd (310) 843-9829
Yiddishe Mama
9216 W. Pico Blvd (310) 385-0101
Supervision: Kehillah of Los Angeles.

Pizzerias

Kosher Pizza Nosh
8644 W. Pico Blvd (310) 276-8708
Nagila Pizza
9016 W. Pico Blvd (213) 550-7735
Supervision: Kehillah of Los Angeles.
Chalav Yisrael.

Pizza Delight
435 N. Fairfax Avenue 90036 (323) 655-7800
Fax: (323) 653-3299
Supervision: Kehillah of Los Angeles.
Chalav Yisrael.
Pizza Mayven
140 Labrea Ave (310) 847-0353
Pizza Mayven
140 N. La Brea Area (310) 857-0353
Pizza World
365 S. Fairfax Avenue 90036 (213) 653-2896
Supervision: Kehillah of Los Angeles.
An Italian/Mexican dairy restaurant. Chalav
Yisrael.
Rami's Pizza
17736 1/2 Sherman Way (818) 342-0611
Supervision: RCC.
Shalom Pizza
8715 W. Pico Blvd (310) 271-2255
Supervision: RCC.

Synagogues

Conservative

Adat Shalom
3030 Westwood Blvd. 90034
Beth Am
1039 S. La Cienega Blvd. 90035
Sinai Temple
10400 Wilshire Blvd. 90024

Orthodox

B'nai David Congregation
8906 W. Pico Blvd. 90035
Breed St. Shule
247 N. Breed St. 90033
This synagogue is of historial interest.
Chabad House
741 Gayley Avenue
West Los Angeles 90025
Etz Jacob
7659 Beverly Blvd. 90036
Mogen David
9717 W. Pico Blvd. 90035
Ohel David, 7967 Beverly Blvd.
Ohev Shalom
525 S. Fairfax Avenue 90036
Young Israel of Century City
9317 West Pico Blvd
Century City 90035 (310) 273-6954
Young Israel of Hancock Park
225 South La Brea (213) 931-4030
Young Israel of Los Angeles
660 N Spaulding Avenue 90036
(213) 655-0300/0322

Orthodox Sephardi

Kahal Joseph
10505 Santa Monica Blvd. 90025
Temple Tifereth Israel
10500 Wilshire Blvd., 90024

Reconstructionist

Kehillat Israel
16019 Sunset Blvd., Pacific Palisades 90272
(310) 459-2328
Fax: (310) 573-2098
Kehillat Israel has a modern sanctuary in the round. It is the largest reconstructionist synagogue in the United States.

Reform

Beth Chayim Chadishim
6000 W. Pico Blvd. 90035
Leo Baeck Temple
1300 N. Sepulveda Blvd. 90049
Stephen S. Wise Temple
15500 Stephen S. Wise Drive
Bel Air 90024

Temple Akiba
5249 S. Sepulveda Blvd., Culver City 90230
Temple Isaiah
10345 W. Pico Blvd. 90064
University Synagogue
11960 Sunset Blvd. 90049
Wilshire Blvd. Temple
3663 Wilshire Blvd., 90010

Northridge

Synagogues

Orthodox

Young Israel of Northridge
17511 Devonshire Street 91324
(818) 368-2221

Oakland

Delicatessens

Holy Land Restaurant
677 Rand Avenue 94610   (510) 272-0535
Glatt kosher.
Oakland Kosher Foods
677 Rand Avenue 94610   (510) 272-0535
Glatt kosher.

Mikvaot

Beth Jacob Synagogue
3778 Park Blvd 94610   (510) 482-1147
Fax: (510) 482-2374
Email: bjc-office@eb.jfed.org

Organisations

Berkeley/Richmond JCC
1414 Walnut St., Berkeley 94709
Contra Costa JCC
2071 Tice Valley Blvd., Walnut Creek 94595
Jewish Federation of the Greater East Bay
401 Grand Avenue #500 94610

Synagogue

Beth Jacob Synagogue
3778 Park Blvd 94610   (510) 482-1147
Fax: (510) 482-2374
Email: bjc-office@eb.jfed.org

Synagogues

Conservative

B'nai Shalom
74 Eckley Lane, Walnut Creek 94596
Beth Abraham
327 MacArthur Blvd. 94610
Beth Sholom
642 Dolores, San Leandro 94577

Independent

B'nai Israel of Rossmoor
c/o Fred Rau, 2601 Ptarmigan #3, Walnut Creek 94595
Beth Chaim
PO Box 23632, Pleasant Hill 94523

Orthodox

Beth Jacob
3778 Park Blvd 94610

Reform

B'nai Tikvah
25 Hillcroft Way, Walnut Creek 94596
Beth Emek
PO Box 722, Livermore 94550
Beth Hillel
801 Park Central, Richmond 94803
Temple Isaiah
3800 Mt. Diablo Blvd., Lafayette 94549
Temple Sinai
2808 Summit 94609

Palm Springs

Community Organisations

Jewish Federation of Palm Springs Desert Area
611 S. Palm Canyon Drive 92264
(760) 325-7281

Restaurants

Dairy

New York Sandwich
125 E. Tahquitz   (760) 323-7883

Synagogues

Conservative

Temple Isaiah
332 W. Alejo Road 92262
Jewish community centre at this location too.

Orthodox

Chabad of Palm Springs
425 Avenue, Ortega, Palm Springs
(619) 325-0774

Daily Services
Desert Synagogue
1068 N. Palm Canyon Drive 92262
(760) 327-4848

Palo Alto

Community Organisations

Albert L. Schultz Community Center
655 Arastradero Road 94306   (415) 493-9400

Groceries

Garden Fresh
1245 W. El Camino Road, Mount View 94040
(415) 961-7795

Mollie Stone's Markets
164 South California Avenue   (415) 323-8361
Near Stanford University.

Synagogues

Orthodox

Congregation Chabad
3070 Louis Road 94308   (415) 429-8444
Palo Alto Orthodox Minyan
260 Sheridan Avenue 94306   (415) 948-7498

Pasadena

Synagogues

Conservative

Pasadena Jewish Temple and Center
1434 North Altadena Drive, Pasadena 91107
(626) 798-1161

Sacramento

Community Organisations

Jewish Federation of Sacramento
2351 Wyda Way 95825   (916) 486-0906
Fax: (916) 486-0816
Email: jfed@juno.com
Web site: www.jewishsac.org

Groceries

Bob Butcher Block & Deli
6426 Fair Oaks Blvd, Carmichael 95608

Restaurants

Farah's Catering & Fine Foods
2319 El Camino Avenue 95821
(916) 971-9500
Supervision: Rabbi Rosen, Kenesset Israel.

Synagogues

Conservative

Mosaic Law
2300 Sierra Blvd. 95825   (916) 488-1122

Orthodox

Kenesset Israel Torah Center
1024 Morse Avenue 95864   (916) 481-1159

Reform

B'nai Israel
3600 Riverside Blvd. 95818   (916) 446-4861
Beth Shalom
4746 El Camino Avenue 95608
(916) 485-4478

San Bernardino

Synagogues

Emanu El
3512 N. E Street 92405   (909) 886-4818
Fax: (909) 885-5892
Email: rabbihcohn@compuserve.com
This congregation is the oldest in southern
California. The 'Home of Eternity' cemetery,
8th St. & Sierra Way, presented by the
Mormons, is one of the oldest Jewish
cemeteries in western US.

San Carlos

Accommodation Information

Jewish Travel Network
PO Box 283 94070   (650) 368-0880
Fax: (650) 599-9066
Email: jewishtn@aol.com
International hospitality exchange. Bed and
breakfast and home exchanges.

San Diego Area

Community Organisations

United Jewish Federation of San Diego County
4797 Mercury Street 92111-2101
(619) 571-3444
Fax: (619) 571-0701

Delicatessens

Eva's Fresh & Natural
6717 El Cajon Blvd 92115   (619) 462-5018
Fax: (619) 453-5659
Supervision: Vaad of San Diego.
Dairy and vegetarian food. Fleishig dinners are available to go only upon request in advance.

Media

Directories

Jewish Directory
4797 Mercury Street 92111-2101
(619) 571-3444
Fax: (619) 571-0701

Newspapers

Heritage
3443 Camino Del Rio S., Suite 315 92108
(619) 282-7177

San Diego Jewish Times
4731 Palm Avenue, La Mesa 91941
(619) 463-5515

Mikvaot

5170 La Dorna   (619) 287-6411
Call to arrange an appointment.

Restaurants

City Delicatessen
6th Avenue & University Avenue 92103
(619) 295-2747
Fax: (619) 295-2129
Kosher style restaurant and bakery featuring Jewish specialties. Open late. All credit cards accepted.

Dairy

Lang's
6165 El Cajon Blvd 92115
(619) 287-7306; 800-60-LANGS
Fax: (619) 582-1545
Email: lanasbakery@cari.net
Supervision: Vaad HaRabbanim of San Diego.
Kosher pareve bakery, dairy deli and foods.

Shmoozers Vegetarian & Pizzeria
6366 El Cajon Blvd 92115   (619) 583-1636
Supervision: Vaad HaRabbanim of San Diego.
Hours: Sunday to Thursday, 11:30am to 9pm; Friday, to 2pm; Saturday, Motzei Shabbat to 11pm.

Meal

Western Glatt Kosher & N.Y. Deli
7739 Fay Avenue, La Jolla 92037
(619) 454-6328

Synagogues

Conservative

Adat Ami / Beth Tefilah
123 Camino de la Reina, Suite N100 92108
(619) 220-8888

Beth El
8660 Gilman Drive, La Jolla 92037
(619) 452-1734

Congregation Beth Am
5050 Black Mtn. Road 92130   (619) 481-8454
Fax: (619) 481-6068

Ner Tamid
16981 Via Tazon, Suite G 92127
(619) 592-9141

Temple Beth Sholom
208 Madrona Street, Chula Vista 91910
(619) 420-6040

Temple Judea
1527 Roma Drive, Vista 92083 (619) 724-8318

Tifereth Israel
6660 Cowles Mountain Blvd 92119
(619) 697-6001

Orthodox

Beth Eliyahu Torah Center
5012 Central Avenue, Bonita 91902
(619) 472-2144

Beth Jacob Congregation
4855 College Avenue 92115   (619) 287-9890
Fax: (619) 287-0578

Chabad House
6115 Montezuma Road 92115 (619) 265-7700
Supervision: Vaad of San Diego.

Chabad of La Costa
1980 La Costa Avenue, Carlsbad 92009
(760) 943-8891
Fax: (760) 943-8892
Email: chabad@inetworld.net

Chabad of La Jolla
3232 Governor Drive, Suite N 92122
(619) 455-1670

Chabad of Rancho Bernardo
16934 Old Espola Road, Poway 92064
(619) 451-0455
Congregation of Adat Yeshurun
8950 Villa La Jolla Drive, Suite 1224, La Jolla
92037 (619) 535-1196
Young Israel of San Diego
7920 Navajo Road, Suite 102 92119
(619) 589-1447

Reconstructionist
Dor Hadash
4858 Ronson Court, Suite A 92111
(619) 268-3674

Reform
Beth Israel
2512 3rd Avenue 92103 (619) 239-0149
Etz Chaim
PO Box 1138, Ramona 92065 (619) 789-8117
Temple Adat Shalom
15905 Pomerado Road, Poway 92064
(619) 451-1200
Temple Emanu-El
6299 Capri Drive 92120 (619) 286-2555
Temple Solel
552 S. El Camino Real, Encinitas 92024
(619) 436-0654

Tourist Sites
Balboa Park
The largest public park in San Diego, includes
the House of Pacific Relations, which comprises
30 cottages for various ethnic groups. These
include the Cottage of Israel, which mounts
exhibitions throughout the year, portraying the
history and traditions of the Jewish people,
biblical and modern Israel. Open Sun. 1:30 pm
to 4:30 pm, except on Holy-days and major
festivals.

San Fernando Valley
Bakeries
Continental Kosher Bakery
12419 Burbank Blvd (818) 762-5005
Sam's Kosher Bakery
12450 Burbank Blvd, Suite H (818) 769-8352
Supervision: RCC.

Catering
Hadar Restaurant and Catering
12514 Burbank Blvd 91607 (818) 762-1155
Supervision: RCC.

Community Organisations
North Valley Center
16601 Rinaldi Street, Granada Hills 91344
Valley Cities Center
13164 Burbank Blvd., Van Nuys 91401
West Valley Center
22622 Vanowen Street
West Hills 91307

Groceries
Ventura Market
18357 Ventura Blvd (213) 873-1240
Supervision: RCC.
Butcher, market and deli.

Ice Cream Parlors
Carvel's Ice Cream
25948 McBean Parkway, Valencia
(805) 259-1450
Supervision: KOF-K.

Kashrut Information
The Kashrus Information Bureau
12753 Chandler Blvd, N. Hollywood 91607
(818) 762-3197

Mikvaot
Teichman Mikvah Society
12800 Chandler Blvd, N. Hollywood 91607
(818) 506-0996

Restaurants
Apropo Falafel
6800 Reseda Blvd (818) 881-6608
Flora Falafel
12450 Burbank Blvd, N. Hollywood
(818) 766-6567
Supervision: RCC.
Golan, 13075 Victory Blvd (818) 763-5375
Supervision: RCC.

Dairy
Orly Dairy Restaurant & Pizza
12454 Magnolia Blvd (818) 508-5570

Meat
Drexler's Kosher Restaurant
12519 Burbank Blvd, N. Hollywood
(818) 984-1160
Falafel Express
5577 Reseda Bl (818) 345-5660
Falafel Village
16060 Ventura Blvd (818) 783-1012
Supervision: RCC.
Sharon's, 18608 1/2 Ventura Blvd, Tarzana
(818) 344-7472
Supervision: RCC.

Sportsman Lodge
Sherman Oaks   (818) 984-0202
Tiberias
18046 Ventura Blvd, Encino   (818) 343-3705
Supervision: RCC.

Pizzerias
La Pizza, 12515 Burbank Blvd. (818) 760 8198
Pacific Kosher Pizza
12460 Oxnard   (818) 760-0087

Synagogues

Conservative
Beth Meier Congregation
11725 Moorpark, Studio City
Ner Maarev Temple
5180 Yarmouth Avenue, Encino 91316
Shomrei Torah
Valley Circle, West Hills   (818) 346-0811
Temple Aliyah
24400 Aliyah Way
Woodland Hills 91367

Temple B'nai Hayim
4302 Van Nuys Blvd, Sherman Oaks
Temple Emanu-El
1302 N. Glenoaks Avenue, Burbank 91504
Temple Ramat Zion
17655 Devonshire Avenue, Northridge
Valley Beth Shalom
15739 Ventura Blvd, Encino 91316

Orthodox
Adat Ari El Synagogue
5540 Laurel Canyon Blvd, N. Hollywood 91607
There are eleven beautiful stained-glass
windows, designed by Mischa Kallis, depicting
significant dates in the religious calendar.
Chabad House
4915 Hayvenhurst, Encino 91346
Shaarey Zedek
12800 Chandler Blvd, N. Hollywood 91607
                                    (818) 763-0560
                               Fax: (818) 763-8215

Reform
Beth Emet
320 E. Magnolia Blvd, Burbank 91502
Shir Chadash
17000 Ventura Blvd, Encino
Temple Ahavat Shalom
11261 Chimineas Avenue, Northridge
Temple Judea
5429 Lindley Avenue, Tarzana

San Francisco
Embassy
Consulate General
Suite 2100, 456 Montgomery Street 94104

Groceries
Gourmet Kosher Meals
Cong. Adath Israel, 1851 Noriega St., 94122
Supervision: Orthodox Rabbinical Council.
Grill Middle Eastern Cuisine
430 Geary Street   (415) 749-0201
Jacob's Kosher Meats
2435 Noriega Street 94122   (415) 564-7482
Jerusalem
420 Geary (at Mason) 94108   (415) 776-2683
Supervision: Cong. Thilim.
Kosher Meats Israel & Cohen Kosher Meats
5621 Geary Blvd 94121   (415) 752-3064
Kosher Nutrition Kitchen
Montefiore Senior Center, 3200 California Av.,
Supervision: Orthodox Rabbinical Council.
Tel Aviv Strictly Kosher Meats
2495 Irving Street 84122   (415) 661-7588
Supervision: Orthodox Rabbinical Council.

Libraries
Holocaust Library & Research Center
601 14th Avenue 94118   (415) 751-6040

Mikvaot
Mikva, 3355 Sacramento Street 94118
                                    (415) 921-4070

Museums
Jewish Com. Museum
121 Steuart St 94105   (415) 543-8880

Organisations
**Jewish Com. Fed. of San Francisco, the
Peninsula, Marin & Sonoma Counties**
121 Steuart St. 94105   (415) 777-0411
                               Fax: (415) 495-6635
Publishes 'Resource guide to the Bay Area' and
'Resource guide to Jewish life in Northern
California'.

Restaurants
King David
614 Pine Street, At Grant Avenue 94210
                                    (415) 693-9172
                               Fax: (415) 693-9173
Glatt Kosher.

Meat

Sabra
419 Grant Avenue, Chinatown (415) 982-3656
Fax: (415) 982-3650
Supervision: Vaad Hakashrus of Northern CA.
Bishul Yisrael, Pat Yisrael and Mashgiach
Temidi. Free delivery to the financial district for
groups of 10 or more. Catering available.
This Is It
430 Geary Street 94210   (415) 749-0201
Middle Eastern cuisine.

Vegetarian

Lotus Garden
532 Grant Avenue 94108   (415) 397-0130

Synagogues

Conservative

B'nai Emunah
3595 Taraval Street 94116   (415) 664-7373
Fax: (415) 664-4209
Email: emuna@jps.net
Beth Israel-Judea
625 Brotherhood Way 94132 (415) 586-8833
Beth Sholom
14th Avenue & Clement Street 94118
(415) 221-8736
Ner Tamid
1250 Quintara Street 94116   (415) 661-3383

Orthodox

Adath Israel
1851 Noriega Street 94122   (415) 564-5565
Anshey Sfard
1500 Clement Street 94118   (415) 752-4979
Chabad House
11 Tillman Place 94108   (415) 956-8644
Chevra Thilim
751 25th Avenue 94121   (415) 752-2866
Keneseth Israel
655 Sutter Street, Suite 203 94102
(415) 771-3420
A downtown synagogue offering meals over
Shabbat.
Torat Emeth
768 27th Avenue 94121   (415) 386-1830
Young Israel of San Francisco
1806 A Noriega Street 94122   (415) 387-1774

Reform

Emanu-El
Arguello Blvd. & Lake Street 94118
(415) 751-2535

Sha'ar Zahav
290 Dolores Street 94103   (415) 861-6932
Email: shaarzahav@jgc.apc.org
Sherith Israel
2266 California Street 94118   (415) 346-1720

Sephardi

Magain David
351 4th Avenue 94118   (415) 752-9095

Tourist Information

Jewish Com. Information & Referral
121 Steuart St 94105   (415) 777-4545

San Jose

Booksellers

Alef Bet Judaica
14103-0 Winchester Blvd, Los Gatos 95032
(408) 370-1818
Fax: (408) 725-8269
Email: nurit@best.com

Community Organisations

Jewish Federation of Greater San Jose
14855 Oka Road, Los Gatos 95030
(408) 358-3033
Fax: (408) 356-0733

Delicatessens

Willow Glen Kosher Deli
1185 Lincoln Avenue 95125   (408) 297-6604
Under Orthodox Rabbinical supervision. Glatt
kosher.

Restaurants

White Lotus
80 North Market Street   (408) 977-0540

Synagogues

Conservative

Congregation Beth David
19700 Prospect Road, Saratoga 95070
(408) 257-3333
Congregation Emeth
PO Box 1430, Gilroy 95021   (408) 847-4111

Orthodox

Ahavas Torah
1537-A Meridian Avenue 95125
(408) 266-2342
Fax: (408) 264-3139
Web site: www.ahava.org
Almaden Valley Torah Center
1281 Juli Lynn Drive 95120   (408) 997-9117
Congregation Am Echad
1504 Meridian Avenue 95125 (408) 267-2591

Reform

Congregation Shir Hadash
16555 Shannon Road, Los Gatos 95032
(408) 358-1751
Fax: (408) 358-1753
Web site: www.shirhadash.org
Temple Beth Sholom
2270 Unit D, Canoas Garden Avenue 95153
(408) 978-5566
Temple Emanu-El
1010 University Avenue 95126
(408) 292-0939

Traditional

Congregation Sinai
1532 Willowbrae Avenue 95125-4450
(408) 264-8542
Fax: (408) 264-4316
Email: rebej@compuserve.com or
sinai_sj@juno.com

San Rafael (Marin County)

Synagogues

Reform

Rodef Sholom
170 N. San Pedro Rd 94903

Santa Barbara

Synagogues

Orthodox

Young Israel of Santa Barbara
1826 C Cliff Drive 93109   (805) 966-4565

Reform

Congregation B'nai B'rith
900 San Antonio Creek Road 93111

Santa Monica

Synagogues

Orthodox

Chabad House
1428 17th Street 90404
Young Israel of Santa Monica
21 Hampton Avenue   (213) 399-8514
Mailing address is: PO Box 5725, 90405. Shul
is actually located at 21 Hampton Avenue

Reform

Beth Sholom
1827 California Avenue 90403

Santa Rosa

Synagogues

Conservative

Beth Ami
4676 Mayette Avenue 95405   (707) 545-4334
Dairy kitchen on premises.

Reform

Shomrei Torah
Services at United Methodist Church, 1717
Yulupa Av. 95405   (707) 578-5519

Saratoga

Synagogues

Conservative

Congregation Beth David
19700 Prospect Road at Scully 95070-3352
(408) 257-3333

Stockton

Stockton is one of the oldest communities
west of the Mississippi River, founded in the
days of the California Gold Rush. Temple Israel
was founded as Congregation Ryhim Ahoovim
in 1850 and erected its first building in 1855.

Synagogues

Reform

Temple Israel
5105 N. El Dorado St 95207
Stockton is one of the oldest communities
west of the Mississippi River, founded in the
days of the California Gold Rush. Temple Israel
was founded as Congregation Ryhim Ahoovim
in 1850 and erected its first building in 1855.

Thousand Oaks

Synagogues

Conservative

Temple Etz Chaim
1080 E. Janss Rd 91360   (805) 497-6891
Fax: (805) 497-0086
Kosher catering. Synagogue contains unique
artistic Aron Kodesh and Holocaust memorial.

Tiburon

Synagogues

Congregation Kol Shafar
215 Blackfield Dr 94920   (415) 388-1818

Tustin

Synagogues
Congregation B'nai Israel
655 S. "B" St 92680   (714) 259-0655

Vallejo

Synagogues

Unaffiliated

Congregation B'nai Israel
1256 Nebraska St. 94590   (707) 642-6526

Venice

Hotels

Kosher

Pacific Jewish Center
720 Rose Avenue 90291   (310) 392-8749
                        Fax: (310) 392-8740
                  Email: pjc613@juno.com
Office location: 2432-C Lincoln Blvd., Santa
Monica, CA 90405

Mikvaot
Pacific Jewish Center
720 Rose Avenue 90291   (310) 392-8749
                        Fax: (310) 392-8740
                  Email: pjc613@juno.com
Office location: 2432-C Lincoln Blvd. Santa
Monica, CA 90405

Organisations

Orthodox

**National Council of Young Israel West Coast
Regional Office**
1050 Indiana Avenue 90291   (310) 396-3935
                        Fax: (310) 581-0904
            Email: ncyi.west@youngisrael.org

Religious Organisations
Young Israel West Coast Regional Office
1050 Indiana Avenue 90291   (310) 396-3935
                        Fax: (310) 581-0904
            Email: ncyi.west@youngisrael.org

Restaurants
Pacific Jewish Center
720 Rose Avenue 90291   (310) 392-8749
                        Fax: (310) 392-8740
                  Email: pjc613@juno.com
Office location: 2432-C Lincoln Blvd. Santa
Monica, CA 90405

Synagogues

Orthodox

Jewish Pacific Center
505 Ocean Front Walk & 720 Rosa Avenue
90291   (310) 392-8749
Mikva and an elementary day school with
summer camp facilities for visitors. It also
offers a full range of kosher food, bakery
products and meat, as well as accommodation.
Pacific Jewish Center
505 Ocean Front Walk 90291   (310) 392-8749
                        Fax: (310) 392-8740
                  Email: pjc613@juno.com
Office location: 2432-C Lincoln Blvd. Santa
Monica, CA 90405
**Young Israel Torah Learning Center of
Venice**
949 Sunset Avenue 90021   (310) 450-7541

Ventura

Community Organisations
Jewish Community Centre
259 Callens Road   (805) 658-7441

Synagogues

Reform

Temple Beth Torah
7620 Foothill Road 93004   (805) 647-4181

Walnut Creek

Synagogues

Conservative

Congregation B'nai Shalom
74 Eckley Lane 94595
Contra Costa Jewish Community Center
2071 Tice Valley Blvd 94595

Reform

Congregation B'nai Tikvah
25 Hillcroft Way 94595

Whittier

Synagogues

Conservative

Beth Shalom Synagogues Center
14564 E. Hawes Street 90604 (310) 914-8744

Colorado

Boulder

Organisations
Lubavitch of Boulder County
4900 Sioux Drive 80303   (303) 494-1638
Offering home hospitality

Synagogues
Hillel Foundation
2795 Colorado Avenue, University of Colorado
(303) 442-6571

Conservative
Congregation Bonai Shalom
1527 Cherryvale Rd, 80303   (303) 442-6605
Fax: (303) 442-7545
Email: ronaci@aol.com
Offering home hospitality

Reform
Congregation Har Hashem
3950 Baseline Road 80303   (303) 499-7077
Jewish Renewal Community of Boulder
5001 Pennsylvania 80303   (303) 271-3541
Meets third Friday of each month.

Colorado Springs

Synagogues

Conservative & Reform
Temple Shalom
1523 E. Monument Street 80909
(719) 634-5311
Reform services are held on Fri. evening &
Conservative services on Sat. morning

Orthodox
Chabad House
3465 Nonchalant Circle 80909
(719) 596-7330

Denver

Bakeries
New York Bagel Boys
6449 E Hampden Avenue 80231
(303) 759-2212
Supervision: Vaad Hakashrus of Denver.
The Bagel Store
942 South Monaco 80224   (303) 388-2648
Supervision: Vaad Hakashrus of Denver.
A bakery serving bagels, challah, rye bread,
wheat bread, pumpernickel bread, donuts,
rugelach, mandelbrot, honey cakes, poppyseed
rolls, etc.

Delicatessens
East Side Kosher Deli
5475 Leetsdale Drive 80222   (303) 322-9862
Fax: (303) 331-3290
Email: eskd1@juno.com
Supervision: Vaad Hakashrus of Denver.
Glatt Kosher. Deli, restaurant, grocer, butcher
shop and caterer. Closed on Saturday and
Friday afternoon.
East-Side Kosher Deli, Inc.,
5475 Leetsdale Drive 80222   (303) 322-9862
New York Deli News
7105 East Hampden   (303) 759-4741

Groceries
Cub Foods, 4600 Leetsdale Drive
(303) 232-1110
With Kosher section.
Cub Foods, 1985 Sheridan Blvd, Edgewater
(303) 232-8972
With Kosher section.
King Soopers
6470 East Hampden Avenue   (303) 758-1210
With kosher section.
King Soopers
890 S.Monaco Parway   (303) 333-1535
With Kosher section.
Safeway, 7150 Leetsdale drive (& Quebec)
(303) 377-6939
With Kosher section.
Safeway, 6460 E. Yale (& Monaco)
(303) 691-8870
With Kosher section.

Kashrut Information
Rabbi Mordecai Twerski
295 South Locust Avenue 80224
(303) 377-1200
Vaad Hakashrus
1350 Vrain 80204   (303) 595-9349
Vaad Hakashrus of Denver
1350 Vrain 80204   (303) 595-9349
Rabbi Yechezkel Feldberger, Rabbinic
Administrator Moshe Heisler, Hakashrus
Administrator

Media

Newspapers
Intermountain Jewish News
1275 Sherman Avenue, Suite 214 80203
(303) 861-2234
Miriam Goldberg Editor and Publisher Rabbi
Hillel Goldberg PhD Executive Editor Weekly
American Jewish newspaper of the
intermountain region.

Mikvaot
Mikvah of Denver
1404 Quitman 80204   (303) 893-5315
Rifky Beren Ritual bath for observance of Torah family purity laws

Mikveh
1404 Quitman 80204   (303) 893-5315

Organisations
Allied Jewish Federation of Colorado
300 S. Dahlia Street 80222   (303) 321-3399
                                    Fax: (303) 322-8328
Com. Center
4800 E. Alameda Avenue 80222
Com. Ctr Kosher Childrens Camp
4800 E. Alameda Avenue 80222
Jewish Family & Children's Service
1335 S. Colorado Blvd, Building C-800 80222
                                    (303) 759-4890
Rocky Mountain Rabbinic Council
6445 East Ohio Avenue 80224
                                    (303) 388-4441
Synagogue Council of Greater Denver
PO Box 102732 80250   (303) 759-8484

Religious Organisations
Synagogue Council of Greater Denver
PO Box 102732 80250   (303) 759-8484

Restaurants
Korney's Kosher Deli
4800 Baseline, (Baseline & Foothills), Meadows Shopping Center
Supervision: Vaad Hakashrus of Denver.

Dairy
Mediterranean Health Cafe
2817 East 3rd Avenue 80206
                                    (303) 399-2940
Supervision: Vaad Hakashrus of Denver.
Kosher/dairy/vegetarian food. Chalav Yisrael and Pat Yisrael available. Hours: Sunday, 12 pm to 8 pm; Monday to Thursday, 11 am to 8 pm; Friday, to 2 pm.

Pizzerias
Johnny's Pizza
934 S. Monaca Parkway   (303) 399-6666
Supervision: Vaad Hakashrus of Denver.

Library of Holocaust Testimonies

Have You Seen My Little Sister?
Janina Fischler-Martinho

Memoirs from Occupied Warsaw 1940–1945
Helena Szereszewska
Translated by Anna Marianska

An End to Childhood
Miriam Akavia

I Light a Candle
Gena Turgel

The Children Accuse
Maria Peleg-Mariawska

My Heart in a Suitcase
Anne Fox

A Cat Called Adolf
Trude Levi

A Child Alone
Martha Blend

Breathe Deeply My Son
Henry Wermuth

My Lost World – A Survivor's Tale
Sara Rosen

My Private War
One Man's Struggle to Survive the Soviets and the Nazis
Jacob Gerstenfeld-Maltiel

From Dachau to Dunkirk
Fred Pelican

Synagogues

Beth Shalom
2280 East Noble Place, Littleton 80121
(303) 794-6643
Rabbi F E Greenspahn, Cantor Birdie Becker,
Lionel Menin President, Tammi Stitelman
Religious School Director. A congregation
serving the southern metropolitan area.
Provides religious services religious school
(weekend and afternoon) social and
educational activities, and rabbinic services.

Conservative

Rodef Shalom
450 S. Kearney 80224

Orthodox

Bais Medrash Kehillas Yaakov
295 S. Locust Street 80222   (303) 377-1200
Congrgation Zera Abraham
1560 Winona Court 80204   (303) 825-7517
Southeast Center for Judiasu
900 E Chenango Avenue, #100
(303) 220-7200

Reconstructionist

B'Nai Havurah
6445 East Ohio Avenue 80224
(303) 388-4441
Hebrew Educational Alliance (HEA)
6445 East Ohio#200 80224   (303) 331-6950

Reform

Congregation Emanuel
51 Grape Street 80220   (303) 388-4013
Fax: (303) 288-6328
Email: emanuel@ix.netcom.com
Temple Micah
2600 Leyden Street 80207   (303) 388-4239
Temple Sinai
3509 South Glencoe Street 80237
(303) 759-1827

Traditional

B.M.H. Congregation
560 S. Monaco Pkwy 80222

Littleton

Synagogues

Conservative

Beth Shalom
2280 E. Noble Place 80121   (303) 794-6643

Pueblo

Synagogues

United Hebrew Congregation
106 W. 15th Street 81003

Reform

Temple Emanuel
1325 Grand Avenue 81003

Connecticut

Bridgeport

Delicatessens

Chai Café at the JCCS
4200 Park Avenue   (203) 374-5556
Supervision: Vaad Hakashrus of Fairfield
County.
Glatt kosher deli serves a wide variety of eat in
and take out products. Some grocery items are
sold. Dairy items are packaged. Weekly and
Shabbat take out specials. Large selection of
fresh meat and poultry.

Media

Newspapers

Bridgeport Jewish Ledger
c/o Jewish Federation, 4200 Park Avenue
(203) 372-6504

Radio

WVOF Radio
c/o Fairfield University, Fairfield 06430
(203) 254-4111
Jewish public affairs show on Sundays at 7pm
on 88.5FM

Mikvaot

Mikveh Israel
1326 Stratfield Road, Fairfield 06432

Organisations

**Jewish Center for Community Services of
Eastern Fairfield County**
4200 Park Avenue 06604   (203) 372-6567
Fax: (203) 374-0770
Serving Bridgeport, Easton, Fairfield, Monroe,
Shelton, Stratford, Trumbull and Westport

Religious Organisations

Bridgeport Va'ad
1571 Stratfield Road, Fairfield 06432
(203) 372-6529

Restaurants

Cafe Shalom
c/o Abel, Community Center   (203) 372-6567

Dairy

Brooklawn Bakery & Pizza Shop
1718 Capitol Avenue   (203) 384-0504
Supervision: Vaad Hakashrus of Fairfield
County.
Separate pareve and dairy sections.

Synagogues

Conservative

B'nai Torah
5700 Main St.,, Trumbull 06611
Congregation Beth El
1200 Fairfield Woods Rd, Fairfield 06430
Rodeph Sholom
2385 Park Avenue 06604

Orthodox

Agudas Achim
85 Arlington Street 06606
Ahavath Achim
1571 Stratfield Road, Fairfield 06432
Bikur Cholim
Park & Capitol Avenues 06604
Shaare Torah Adath Israel
3050 Main Street 06606

Reconstructionist

Congregation Shirei Shalom
PO Box 372, Monroe 06468

Reform

Temple B'nai Israel
2710 Park Avenue 06604

Danbury

Organisations
Jewish Federation
105 Newtown Road 06810   (203) 792-6453
                        Fax: (203) 748-5099
Issuing monthly publication.

Synagogues

Conservative

Congregation B'nai Israel
193 Clapboard Ridge Road 06811
                             (203) 792-6161

Reform

United Jewish Center
141 Deer Hill Avenue 06810   (203) 748-3355

Fairfield

Bakeries
Carvel Ice Cream Bakery
1838 Black Rock Turnpike   (203) 384-2253
Supervision: Vaad Hakashrus of Fairfield
County.
All products in the store are under supervision,
except for those Snapple drinks not marked
with an OK.
The Original Bagel King of Fairfield
22670 Black Rock Turnpike   (203) 368-3365
Supervision: Vaad Hakashrus of Fairfield
County.
Wide variety of bagels and challah. The uncut
bagels and uncut challah are supervised.

Hamden

Restaurants
Abel's
2100 Dixwell Avenue 06514

Hartford

Booksellers
Israel Gift Shop Hebrew Book Store
262 S. Whitney Street 06105   (860) 232-3984

Kashrut Information
Kashrut Commission
162 Brewster Road 06117   (860) 563-4017

Media

Guides
"All Things Jewish"
333 Bloomfield Avenue 06117
                             (860) 232-4483

Mikvaot
Mikva, 61 Main Street 06119

Organisations
Jewish Federation of Hartford
333 Bloomfield Avenue 06117
                             (860) 232-4483
Publishes 'All Things Jewish'.

Synagogues

Conservative

B'nai Sholom
26 Church St, Newington 06111
Beth El
2626 Albany Avenue, West Hartford 06117

Beth Tefilah
465 Oak St, East Hartford 06118
Emanuel Synagogue
160 Mohegan Dr, West Hartford 06117
                              (860) 234-1275
                      Fax: (860) 231-8890
                 Email: emansyn@ziplink.net

Orthodox
Agudas Achim
1244 N. Main St, West Hartford 06117
Beth David
20 Dover Road, West Hartford 06119
                              (860) 236-1241
Chabad House of Greater Hartford
798 Farmington Avenue 06119
Contact for kosher meal & Shabbat
arrangements.
Teferes Israel
27 Brown St, Bloomfield 06002
United Synagogue of Greater Hartford
840 N. Main St, West Hartford 06117
Young Israel of Hartford
1137 Troutbrook Drive 06119
                              (860) 523-7804
Young Israel of West Hartford
2240 Albany Avenue, West Hartford 06117

Reform
Beth Israel
701 Farmington Avenue, West Hartford 06119
Temple Sinai
41 W. Hartford Road, Newington 06011

Manchester
Synagogues

Conservative
Temple Beth Sholom
400 Middle Turnpike E 06040
                              (860) 643-9563

Meriden
Synagogues
B'nai Abraham
127 E. Main St 06450

Middletown
Synagogues
Adath Israel
48 Church St 06457

New Britain
Synagogues
B'nai Israel
265 W. Main St 06051   (860) 224-0479

Orthodox
Tephereth Israel
76 Winter Street 06051

New Haven
Bakeries
Westville Kosher Bakery
1460 Whalley Avenue 06515   (203) 397-0839

Contact Information
Young Israel House at Yale University
    Web site: www.yale.edu/hillel/orgs/yihy.html

Delicatessens
Fox's Deli
1460 Whalley Avenue 06515   (203) 387-2214
Zackey's
1304 Whalley Avenue 06515   (203) 387-2454

Groceries
Westville Kosher Meat Market
95 Amity Road 06525   (203) 389-1723

Mikvaot
86 Hubinger Street 06511   (203) 387-2184

Organisations
Jewish Federation of Greater New Haven
360 Amity Road, Woodbridge Ct., 06525
                              (203) 387-2424

Synagogues

Conservative
Beth-El Keser Israel
85 Harrison Street 06515   (203) 389-2108

Orthodox
Beth Hamedrosh Westville
74 West Prospect Street 06515
                              (203) 389-9513
Young Israel of New Haven
292 Norton Street 06511   (203) 776-4212
          Web site: www.youngisrael.org/yinh

New London
Organisations
Jewish Federation of Eastern Connecticut
28 Channing Street 06320   (203) 442-8062

Norwalk

Bakeries
The Original Bagel King of Norwalk
250 Westport Avenue   (203) 846-2633
Supervision: Vaad Hakashrus of Fairfield County.
Wide variety of bagels and challah. The uncut bagels and uncut challah are supervised.

Organisations
Jewish Federation of Greater Norwalk
Shorehaven Road 06855   (203) 853-3440

Norwich

Synagogues

Orthodox
Brothers of Joseph
Broad & Washington Avs., 06360
                              (203) 887-3777
Mikva attached.

Stamford

Bakeries
Carvel Ice Cream Bakery
810 East Main Street   (203) 324-0944
Supervision: Vaad Hakashrus of Fairfield County.
All products in the store are under supervision, except for those Snapple drinks not marked with an OK.
Cerbone Bakery
605 Newfield Avenue   (203) 348-9029
Supervision: Vaad Hakashrus of Fairfield County.

Delicatessens
Delicate-Essen at the JCC
1035 Newfield Avenue 06902 (203) 322-0944
                    Fax: (203) 322-5160
Supervision: Vaad Hakashrus of Fairfield County.
Glatt kosher sit down café serving hot and cold sandwiches, soups and grilled items.
Hours: Monday to Thursday, 9 am to 8 pm; Friday, to 2 pm; Sunday, to 4 pm.
Nosherye
JCC Building, 1035 Newfield Av., 06905
                              (203) 321-1373

Groceries
Delicate-Essen
111 High Ridge Road 06905   (203) 316-5570
                    Fax: (203) 316-5573
Supervision: Vaad Hakashrus of Fairfield County.
Full selection of grocery items. Glatt kosher butcher and take-out products available. Open six days a week.

Media

Magazines
United Jewish Federation
39 Regent Court 06907   (203) 322-2840

Organisations
United Jewish Federation
1035 Newfield Avenue 06905 (203) 321-1373

Synagogues

Orthodox
Young Israel of Stamford
69 Oak Lawn Avenue 06905   (203) 348-3955

Waterbury

Bakeries
Ami's Hot Bagels
111 Tomaston Avenue   (203) 596-9020
Supervision: Vaad Hakashrus of Fairfield County.
Bagels, sandwiches and spreads are all supervised. All products are dairy.

Organisations
Jewish Federation of Greater Waterbury
73 Main Street, South Woodbury 06798
                              (203) 263-5121

West Hartford

Synagogues

Orthodox
Young Israel of West Hartford
2240 Albany Avenue 06117   (860) 828-5199

Westport

Synagogues
Young Israel of Wesport & Norwalk
215 Post Road West 06880   (203) 226-6901

Woodbridge

Libraries
Center Cafe & Jewish Library
360 Amity Road 06525   (203) 387-2424

Restaurants

Dairy

Center Cafe & Jewish Libraries
JCC of Greater New Haven, 360 Amity Road
06525   (203) 387-2424
Kosher dairy café offering breakfast, lunch and
light snacks.

Delaware

Dover

Synagogues

Conservative

Congregation Beth Sholom of Dover
PO Box 223 19903

Newark

Synagogues

Reconstructionist

Temple Beth El
101 Possum Park Rd 19711

Wilmington

Community Organisations
Jewish Community Center
101 Garden of Eden Road 19803
                    (302) 478-5660
                    Fax: (302) 478-6068

Synagogues

Conservative

Beth Shalom
18th St. and Baynard Blvd 19802

Orthodox

Adas Kodesh Shel Emeth
Washington Blvd & Torah Drive 19802
                    (302) 762-2705
                    Fax: (302) 762-3236
                    Web site: www.akse.org

Reform

Beth Emeth
300 W. Lea Blvd. 19802

District of Columbia

Washington

Delicatessens
Hunan Deli, "H" Street   (202) 833-1018
Posins Bakery & Deli
5756 Georgia Avenue   (202) 726-4424
Bakery is under Conservative hashgacha.

Embassy
Embassy of Israel
3514 International Drive 20008

Eruv Information
Eruv in Georgetown   (202) 338-ERUV

Galleries
The National Portrait Gallery
"F" Street between 7th & 8th Sts.,
Houses more than 100,000 portraits including
Albert Einstein, Golda Meir and George
Gershwin

Kashrut Information
Rabbinical Council of Greater Washington
7826 Eastern Avenue 20012

Libraries
Jewish War Veteran, USA Memorial
1811 R. Street N.W. 20009   (202) 265-6280
Has a large collection of Judaica

Media

Directories

Jewish Com. Council of Greater Washington
American Israel Public Affairs Com., 500 N.
Capitol St., N.W., Suite 412 20001

Newspapers

The Jewish Week
1910 "K" Street 20006

Museums
**B'nai B'rith Klutznick National Jewish
Museum**
1640 Rhode Island Av. 20036   (202) 857-6583
                    Fax: (202) 857-1099
                    Email: hmillerm@bnaibrith.org
**Jewish War Veterans, Usa National
Memorial**
1811 R. Street N.W. 20009   (202) 265-6280
John F. Kennedy Center
2700 "F" Street
Israeli lounge donated by the people of Israel

Lillian & Albert Small Museum
3rd & "G" Sts. N.W. 20008
Housed in Washington's oldest synagogue
building, Adas Israel, built in 1876
Smithsonian Institute
The Natural History Building, 10th &
Constitution Avs. N.W. 20001
Contains a collection of Jewish ritual articles.
The Isaac Polack Building
2109 Pennsylvania Av. N.W.
Built in 1796, The Isaac Polack Building was
the home of the first Jew to settle in
Washington

South West

United States Holocaust Memorial Museum
100 Raoul Wallenberg Place 20024-2150
(202) 488-0400
Fax: (202) 488-2606
Email: group_visit@ushmm.org
Web site: www.ushmm.org
Hours: 10.00am to 5.30pm. The Museum is
accessible to people with disabilities

Organisations
Israel Embassy
3514 International Drive 20008
(202) 364-5500
Fax: (202) 364-5423
Email: ask@israelemb.org
Jewish Community Centre
16th Street at Q
Supervision: Va'ad Hakashrut of Washington.
Kosher restaurant on site (dairy and fish) with
Hechser.
**Jewish Historical Society of Greater
Washington**
701 3rd Street N. W. 20001-2624
(202) 789-0900
Fax: (202) 789-0485
Email: jewishhistoricalsoc.com
Also the Lillian & Albert Small Jewish Museum.

Orthodox

**National Council of Young Israel
Washington DC Office**
1101 Pennsylvania Avenue, Suite 1050 20004
(202) 347-4111
Fax: (202) 347-8341

Religious Organisations
Young Israel Washington DC Office
1101 Penn Avenue, Suite 1050 20004
(202) 347-4111
Fax: (202) 347-8341

Restaurants

Pizzerias
Nuthouse Pizza
(301) 942-5900

Synagogues

Reform
Temple Micah
2829 Wisconsin Avenue N.W. 20007
(202) 342-9175

Florida

Aventura

Synagogues
Orthodox
Young Israel of Aventura
2956 Aventura Blvd, 2nd Floor 33180
(305) 931-5188

Belle Glade

Synagogues
Conservative
Temple Beth Sholom
224 N.W. Avenue, "G" 33430   (202) 996-3886

Boca Raton

Delicatessens
Deli Maven
8208 Glades Road 33434   (407) 477-7008

Organisations
**Jewish Federation of South Palm Beach
County**
9901 Donna Klein Blvd 33428-1788
(407) 852-3100
**The Richard and Carole Siemens Jewish
CAmpus of the Jewish Federation of South
Palm Beach County**
9901 Donna Klein Blvd 33428-1788
(407) 852-3100

Restaurants

Dairy
Eliat Cafe
Delmar Shopping Village, 7158 N. Beracasa
Way 33434   (407) 368-6880
The Cafe
Cultural Arts Building, 9801 Donna Klein Blvd
33428-1788   (407) 852-3204
Breakfast – dairy; Lunch – meat.

Meat

Falafel Armon
22767 State Road 7 33428   (407) 477-0633
Orchids Garden
9045 La Fontana Blvd, #B-9 33434
(561) 482-3831
Fax: (561) 482-5951
Supervision: ORB.
Hours: Monday to Thursday, 11:30 am to
9 pm; Sunday, 3 pm to 9 pm.

Synagogues

Orthodox

Young Israel of Boca Raton
7200 Palmetto Circle Blvd 33433
(561) 391-5509

Clearwater

Organisations

Jewish Federation of Pinellas County
13191 Starkey Road, Suite 8, Largo
33773-1438   (727) 530-3223
Fax: (727) 531-0221
Email: pinellas@jon.cjfny.org

Synagogues

Conservative

Beth Shalom
1325 S. Belcher Road 33764   (727) 531-1418
Fax: (727) 531-0798

Orthodox

Young Israel of Clearwater
2385 Tampa Road
Suite 1, Palm Harbor 34684   (727) 789-0408
Young Israel of Clearwater
2385 Tampa Road, Suite 1 & 2
Palm Harbor 34684   (727) 789-0408

Reform

B'nai Israel
1685 S. Belcher Road 34624   (727) 531-5829
Temple Ahavat Shalom
1575 Curlew Road, Palm Harbor 34683
(727) 785-8811

Daytona Beach

Organisations

**Jewish Federation of Volusia & Flagler
Counties**
733 S. Nova Road, Ormond Beach 32174
(904) 672-0294
Fax: (904) 673-1316

Synagogues

Conservative

Temple Israel
1400 S. Peninsula Drive 32118
(904) 252-3097

Reform

Temple Beth El
579 N. Nova Road, Ormond Beach 32174
(904) 677-2484

Deerfield Beach

Synagogues

Orthodox

Young Israel of Deerfield Beach
1880 H West Hillsboro Blvd 33112
(954) 698-0328

Delray Beach

Groceries

Meat Market
Oriole Kosher Market
7345 West Atlantic Ave., 33446

Synagogues

Conservative

Temple Anshei Shalom of West Delray
Oriole Jewish Center, 7099
W. Atlantic Avenue 33446   (561) 495-1300
Temple Emeth
5780 W. Atlantic Avenue 33446
(561) 498-3536

Orthodox

Anshei Emuna
16189 Carter Road 33445   (561) 499-9229

Reform

Temple Sinai
2475 W. Atlantic Avenue 33445
(561) 276-6161
Fax: (561) 276-3485
Email: sinai1@juno.com

Fort Lauderdale

Delicatessens

East Side Kosher Restaurant & Deli
6846 W. Atlantic Blvd, Margate 33063

Organisations

Jewish Federation of Greater Fort Lauderdale
8358 W. Oakland Park Blvd 33321
(305) 748-8400
Fax: (305) 748-6332

Restaurants

David Shai King
5599 N. University Drive, Lauderhill 33321
(305) 572-6522

Synagogues

Orthodox

Young Israel of Hollywood-Ft. Lauderdale
3291 Stirling Road
Hollywood 33312
(954) 966-7877
Fax: (954) 962-5566

Fort Meyers

Synagogues

Reform

Temple Beth El
16225 Winkler Road Ext 33908
(941) 433-0018

Fort Pierce

Synagogues

Temple Beth-El Israel
4600 Oleander Drive 34982   (407) 461-7428

Hollywood & Vicinity

Media

Newspapers

The Jewish Community Advocate of South Broward
2719 Hollywood Blvd 33020   (305) 922-8603

Mikvaot

Mikveh/Young Israel of Hollywood – Ft. Lauderdale
3291 Stirling Road
Ft. Lauderdale, 33312
(954) 966-7877; 963-3952
Fax: (954) 962-5566

Organisations

Jewish Federation of South Broward
2719 Hollywood Blvd 33020   (305) 921-8810

Restaurants

Meat

Pita Plus
5650 Stirling Road 33021   (305) 985-8028

Pizzerias

Jerusalem Pizza II
5650 Stirling Road 33021   (305) 964-6811

Synagogues

Conservative

B'nai Aviv
200 Bonaventure Blvd.Weston
Century Pines Jewish Center
13400 S.W. 10 St, Pembroke Pines
Hallandale Jewish Center
416 N.E. 8 Av, Hallandale
Temple Beth Ahm Israel
9730 Stirling Rd
Temple Beth Shalom
1400 N. 46 Avenue, Hollywood
Temple Judea of Carriage Hills
6734 Stirling Rd, Hollywood
Temple Sinai
1201 Johnson St, Hollywood

Orthodox

Chabad Ocean Synagogue
4000 S. Ocean Drive, Hallandale
Chabad of Southwest Broward
11251 Taft St, Pembroke Pines
Congregation Ahavat Shalom
315 Madison St, Hollywood
Congregation Levi Yitzchok-Lubavitch
1295 E. Hallandale Beach Blvd, Hallandale
(954) 458-1877
Fax: (954) 458-1651
Email: chai@dialisdn.com
Young Israel of Hollywood/Ft. Lauderdale
3291 Stirling Rd, Ft. Lauderdale
(954) 966-7877
Fax: (954) 962-5566
Email: red@icanect.net
Young Israel of Pembroke Pines
13400 S.W. 10 St, Pembroke Pines

Reform

Temple Beth El
1351 S. 14 Av, Hollywood
Temple Beth Emet
10801 Pembroke Road, Pembroke Pines
Temple Solel
5100 Sheridan St, Hollywood

Sephardi
B'nai Sephardim
3670 Stirling Rd, Ft. Lauderdale

Jacksonville
Mikvaot
Etz Chaim
10167 San Jose Blvd 32257   (904) 262-3565

Organisations
Jacksonville Jewish Federation
8505 San Jose Blvd 32217   (904) 448-5000
Kosher Nutrition Center
5846 Mt. Carmel Terrace. 32216
(904) 737-9075

Kendall
Synagogues
Orthodox
Young Israel of Kendall
7880 SW 112th Street 33156   (305) 232-6833

Key West
Synagogues
Conservative
B'nai Zion
750 United Street 33040-3251
(305) 294-3437

Lakeland
Synagogues
Temple Emanuel
600 Lake Hollingsworth Drive 33803
(813) 682-8616

Miami/Miami Beach
Accommodation Information

The following hotels offer kosher catering and Passover facilities, but visitors are advised to check before booking.
Some of the above hotels are open all year round. The others close for varying lengths of time between the end of Pesach and November 20.

Community Organisations
Greater Miami Jewish Federation
4200 Biscayne Blvd 33137   (305) 576-4000
Fax: (305) 573-8115
Has information and referral service, ext. 283.

Embassy
Consulate General
Suite 1800, 100N Biscayne Blvd 33132

Hotels
Alexander
5225 Collins Avenue 33140
Carriage House
5401 Collins Avenue 33140
Crown Hotel
Ocean Front Block 40-41 Street 33140
(305) 531-5771
Supervision: OU.
Doral, 4833 Collins Avenue 33140
Eden Roc
4525 Collins Avenue 33140
Embassy
1051 N. Miami Beach Blvd 33168
(305) 538-7550
Under Kashrut supervision.
Fountainbleau-Hilton
4441 Collins Avenue 33140
Harbor House Hotel Apartments
10275 Collins Avenue 33154
Marco Polo
19201 Collins Avenue 33160
Sans Souci Hotel
31st Street & Collins Avenue 33140
(305) 531-8261
Under Kashrut supervision.
Sasson Ocean Resort
2001 Collins Avenue 33139   (305) 531-0761
Under Kashrut supervision.
Shawnee Beach Resort
4343 Collins Avenue 33140
Sheraton Bal Harbor
9701 Collins Avenue 33154
Sherry Frontenac
6565 Collins Avenue 33141   (305) 866-1637
Under Kashrut supervision.

Media
Directories
Jewish Life in Dade County
4200 Biscayne Blvd 33137   (305) 576-4000
Fax: (305) 573-8115

Mikvaot
Adas Dej Mikveh
225 37th Street 33140   (305) 538-0070
B'nai Israel & Greater Miami Youth Synagogue Mikveh
16260 S. W. 288th Street, Naranja 33033
(305) 264-6488

Boca Raton Synagogue Mikveh
7900 Montoya Circle South, Boca Raton 33433
(305) 538-0070
Daughters of Israel
2530 Pinetree Drive 33140   (305) 672-3500
Miami Beach Mikveh
2530 Pinetree Drive 33140   (305) 672-3500
Mikveh Blima of North Dade
Miami Gardens Drive 33179   (305) 949-9650
Mikveh Blima of North Dade, Inc.,
1054 N.E. Miami Gardens Drive 33179
(305) 949-9650

Rabbi Meisel's Mikveh
Washington Av. & 2nd Street 33139
(305) 673-4641
For men only
Shul of Bal Harbour Mikvah
9500 Collins Avenue, Surfside 33154
(305) 868-1411

Museums
Jewish Museum of Florida
301 Washington Avenue, Miami Beach
33139-6965   (305) 672-5044
Fax: (305) 672-5933
Email: mzeriuitz@ad.com
Web site: www.jewishmuseum.com
Open Tuesday to Sunday 10.00am to 5.00pm.
Closed Mondays and Jewish holidays.

Organisations
Orthodox
National Council of Young Israel Southern Regional Office
1035 NE 170th Terrace 33162
(305) 770-3993
Email: ncyi.south@youngisrael.org

Religious Organisations
Young Israel Southern Regional Office
173575 NE 7th Avenue 33162
(305) 770-3993
Fax: (305) 770-3993
Email: ncyi.south@youngisrael.org

Restaurants
Aviva's Kitchen
16355 W. Dixie Hwy., 33160   (305) 944-7313
Beethoven Restaurant
Sasson Hotel, 2001 Collins Ave., 33139
(305) 531-0761
Crown Buffet & Dairy Bar
Crown Hotel, 4041 Collins Av., 33140
(305) 531-5771

Gitty's Hungarian Kitchen
6565 Collins Avenue
Sherry Frontenac Hotel 33141 (305) 865-4893
Pinati Restaurant
2520 Miami Gardens Drive 33180
(305) 931-8086
Pita King
343 East Flagler 33131   (305) 358-0386
Pita Plus
20103 Biscayne Blvd 33180   (305) 935-0761
Shalom Haifa
1330 N.E. 163 Street 33162   (305) 945-2884
South Beach Pita
Washington Avenue 33139   (305) 534-3706
The Noshery (Seasonal dairy)
Saxony Hotel, 3201 Collins Ave., 33140
(305) 538-6811
Wing Wan II
1640 N.E, 164 Street 33162   (305) 945-3585

Dairy
Bagel Time
3915 Alton Road 33140   (305) 538-0300
Supervision: Star-K.
Eat in or take out. Hours: Sunday to Friday,
6:30 am to 4 pm.
Ocean Terrace Restaurant & Grille
4041 Collins Avenue 33140   (305) 531-5771
Shemtov's Pizza
514 41st Street 33140   (305) 538-2123
Fax: (305) 534-4213

Meat
China Kikor Tel Aviv
5005 Collins Avenue 33140   (305) 866-3316
Embassy Peking Tower Suite
4101 Pine tree Drive, Tower 41 33140
(305) 538-7550
Fax: (305) 538-7570
Supervision: NK.
Jerusalem Peking
4299 Collins Avenue 33140   (305) 532-2263

Pizzerias
Jerusalem Pizza
761 N.E. 167th Street 33162   (305) 653-6662
Sarah's Kosher Pizza
2214 N.E. 123 Street 33181   (305) 891-3312
Sarah's Kosher Pizza
1127 N. E. 163 Street 33162   (305) 948-7777
Yonnie's Kosher Pizza
19802 W. Dixie Hwy. 33180   (305) 932-1961

Synagogues

Conservative

Beth Raphael
1545 Jefferson Avenue 33139
(305) 538-4112
This synagogue is dedicated to the six million martyrs of the Holocaust. On an outside marble wall, a large six-light menorah burns every night in their memory. Six hundred names, representing each city, have been inscribed on the marble. There is also a notable Holocaust Memorial at Dade Av. and Meridian Av.

Orthodox

Young Israel of Greater Miami
990 NE 171st Street, North Miami Beach
33162
(305) 651-3591
Young Israel of Miami Beach
4221 Pine Tree Drive 33140
(305) 534-3206
Young Israel of Sky Lake
1850 NE 183rd Street, North Miami Beach
33179
(305) 945-8712/8715

Tours of Jewish Interest

Jewish Travel and Education Network – JTEN
(305) 931-1782
Offers organised tours of Miami and Miami Beach.

Orlando

Delicatessens

Market Place Deli, Hyatt Orlando
6375 W. Irlo Bronson Highway
(407) 396-1234
Has frozen kosher food only.

Groceries

Amira's Catering and Specialty
1351 E. Altamonte, Altamonte Springs
(407) 767-7577
Cold cuts, side dishes, frozen meals, groceries.
Kosher Korner
8464 Palm Parkway, Vista Center 32836
(407) 238-9968
Fax: (407) 238-2008
Supervision: Florida Kosher Services.
Complete kosher grocery and takeout.
Packaged frozen glatt meat. Will deliver to hotels. Two minutes from downtown Disney

Hotels

Catalina Inn – Lower East Side Restaurant
3401 MacLeod Road 32805
(407) 648-4830
Supervision: OU.

Organisations

Jewish Federation of Greater Orlando
851 N. Maitland Avenue 32751
P.O.B.
1508 Maitland 32794-1508
(407) 645-5933

Restaurants

Kinneret Kitchens
517 South Delany
(407) 422-7205
Senior Citizens dining room. Meals: d, Mon.-Fri at 5pm. Call at least 24 hours in advance to reserve a meal.

Meat

The Lower East Side at Catalonia Inn Hotel
(407) 648-4830
Glatt kosher.

Synagogues

Conservative

Congregation Beth Shalom
13th & Center Streets, Leesburg 32748
(407) 742-0238
Congregation Ohev Shalom
5015 Goddard Avenue 32804 (407) 298-4650
Congregation Shalom (Williamsburg)
c/o Sydney Ansell, 11821 Soccer Lane
32821-7952
Congregation Shalom Aleichem
PO Box 424211, Kissimmee 34742-4211
Southwest Orlando Jewish Congregation
11200 S. Apopka-Vineland Road 32836
Temple Israel
4917 Eli Street 32804
(407) 647-3055

Orthodox

Ahavas Yisroel
708 Lake Howell Road, Maitland 32741

Reform

Congregation of Liberal Judaism
928 Malone Drive 32810
(407) 645-0444

Palm City

Synagogues

Conservative

Treasure Coast Jewish Center-Congregation Beth Abraham
3998 S.W. Leighton Farms Avenue. 34990
(407) 287-8833

Palm Coast

Synagogues
Temple Beth Shalom
40 Wellington Drive, POB 350557 32135-0557
(904) 445-3006

Pembroke Pines

Synagogues

Orthodox
Young Israel of Pembroke Pines
13400 SW 10th Street 33027   (954) 433-8666

Pensacola

Synagogues

Conservative
B'nai Israel
1829 N. 9th Avenue 32503

Reform
Beth El
800 N. Palafox Street 32501

Rockledge

Organisations
Jewish Federation of Brevard
108A Barton Avenue   (407) 636-1824

Sarasota

Organisations
Sarasota-Manatee Jewish Federation
580 S. McIntosh Road 34232-1959
(941) 371-4546
Fax: (941) 378-2947
Email: smjf@jon.cjfny.org

Sky Lake

Synagogues

Orthodox
Young Israel of Sky Lake
1850 NE 183rd Street, North Miami Beach
33179   (305) 945-8712/8715

St Augustine

Synagogues
First Sons Of Israel
161 Cordova Street 32084

St Petersburg

Groceries
Jo-El's Specialty Foods
2619 23rd Avenue N. 33713   (813) 321-3847
Also has delicatessen and butcher shop. Hours:
Monday to Thursday, 9 am to 5 pm; Friday, to
4 pm; Sunday, to 1 pm.

Synagogues

Conservative
B'nai Israel
301 59th Street N. 33710
Beth Chai
Beth Shalom
1844 54th Street S. 33707

Reform
Beth-El
400 Pasadena Avenue S. 33707
(813) 347-6136

Sunny Isles

Synagogues

Orthodox
Young Israel of Sunny Isles
17395 North Bay Road, North Miami Beach
33160   (305) 935-9095

Surfside

Synagogues
The Shul of Bal Harbor, Bay Harbor &
Surfside
9540 Collins Avenue 33154   (305) 868-1411

Tamarac

Synagogues
Young Israel of Taramac
8565 W McNab Road 33321   (954) 726-3586

Tampa

Mikvaot
Bais Tefilah
14908 Pennington Road 33624
(813) 963-2317
Mikva, Orthodox pre-school on premises.

Organisations
Tampa Jewish Federation
13009 Community Campus Drive 33625-4000
(813) 960-1840
Fax: (813) 265-8450

Tampa Jewish Federation
13009 Community Campus Drive 33625-4000
(813) 264-9000
Fax: (813) 265-8450

Synagogues

Conservative

Kol Ami
3919 Moran Road 33618   (813) 962-6338
Rodeph Shalom
2713 Bayshore Blvd. 33629   (813) 837-1911
Temple David
2001 Swann Avenue 33606   (813) 254-1771

Orthodox

Hebrew Academy
14908 Penington Road 33624 (813) 963-0706
Young Israel of Tampa
3721W Tacon Street 33629   (813) 832-3018
Young Israel of Tampa
3721 W. Tacon Street 33629   (813) 832-3018

Reform

Schaarai Zedek
3303 Swann Avenue 33609   (813) 876-2377

Vero Beach

Synagogues
Temple Beth Shalom
365 43rd Street   (407) 569-4700

West Palm Beach

Community Organisations
Chabad House
4800 23rd St. N 33407   (561) 640-8111

Organisations
Jewish Federation of Palm Beach County
4601 Community Drive 33417 (561) 478-0700
Fax: (561) 478-9696

Synagogues

Orthodox

Palm Beach Synagogue
235 Sunrise Avenue, PO Box 3225 33480
(561) 687-5001; 820-9652

Georgia

Athens

Synagogues

Reform

Congregation Children Of Israel
Dudley Drive 30606   (404) 549-4192

Atlanta

Bakeries
Bernie the Baker
3015 N. Druid Hills Road, N.E. 30329
(404) 633-1986
Supervision: Atlanta Kashrut Commission.
Pat Yisrael.
Kg's Bakery & Stuff
2088 Briarcliff Road 30329   (404) 321-1166
Supervision: Atlanta Kashrut Commission.
Pat Yisrael.

Bed & Breakfasts
Bed & Breakfast Atlanta
1608 Briarcliff Road, Suite 5 30306
(404) 875-0525
Fax: (404) 875-8198
Email: www.bedandbreakfast.com
Kosher and Shomer Shabbat accommodation.

Caterers
Bijan Catering
3130 Raymond Drive, N.E. 30360
(770) 457-4578
Supervision: Atlanta Kashrut Commission.

Community Organisations
Jewish Federation
1753 Peachtree Road, NE 30309
(404) 873-1661
Fax: (404) 874-7043
Publishes an annual community guide.

Delicatessens
Chai Peking
2205 La Vista Road, N.E. 30329
(404) 327-7810
Fax: (404) 327-7811
Supervision: Atlanta Kashruth Commission.
Harris Teeter
1799 Briarcliff Road, 2nd level 30329
(404) 607-1189
Supervision: Atlanta Kashrut Commission.
Kosher fish, meat and deli.

Kroger Kosher Fish, Meat & Deli
2205 La Vista Road, N.E. 30329
(404) 633-8694
Supervision: Atlanta Kashrut Commission.
Select departments only.
Quality Kosher
2153 Briarcliff Road 30329
(404) 636-1114 or 1-800-305-6328
Fax: (404) 636-8675
Supervision: Atlanta Kashrut Commission.
Glatt and non-glatt butcher, deli and grocery.
Open 7.30am-6pm Monday to Thursday.
7.30am-3pm Friday and Sunday.

Embassy
Consulate General
Suite 440, 1100 Spring Street, NW 30309-2823

Kashrut Information
Atlanta Kashrut Commission
1855 La Vista Road, N.E. 30329
(404) 634-4063
A non-profit organisation dedicated to
promoting kashrut through education,
research and supervision. Publishes a monthly
kashrut newsletter.

Mikvaot
Beth Jacob
1855 La Vista Road 30329   (404) 633-0551

Restaurants

Dairy

Broadway Café
2168 Briarcliff Road 30329   (404) 329-0888
Fax: (404) 329-9888
Supervision: Atlanta Kashrut Commission.
Seafood, vegetarian, and vegan foods.
Wall Street Pizza
2470 Briarcliff Road, N.E. 30329
(404) 633-2111
Supervision: Atlanta Kashrut Commission.
Delivery available.

Meat

Quality Kosher
5942 Roswell Road, Hammond Square 30342
Supervision: Atlanta Kashrut Commission.

Synagogues

Orthodox

Young Israel of Toco Hills
2074 La Vista Road
Toco Hills 30329   (404) 315-1417
Fax: (404) 315-1417
Email: youngisrael@toll-free.com

Augusta
Bakeries
Sunshine Bakery
1209 Broad Street 30902

Delicatessens
Parti-Pal
Daniel Village 30904
Strauss
965 Broad Street 30902

Synagogues

Orthodox

Adas Yeshuron
935 Johns Road, Walton Way 30904

Columbus
Synagogues

Conservative

Shearith Israel
2550 Wynnton Road 31906

Reform

Temple Israel
1617 Wildwood Avenue 31906

Macon
Synagogues

Conservative

Sherah Israel
1st & Plum Streets 31201   (912) 745-4571
Fax: (912) 745-5892

Reform

Beth Israel
892 Cherry Street 31201

Savannah
Contact Information
Rabbi Avigdor Slatus
5444 Abercoen Street 31405   (912) 354-5272
Fax: (912) 354-5272
Visitors requiring information about kashrut,
temporary accommodation, etc., should
contact Rabbi Slatus.

Mikvaot
Mickve Israel
Bull & Gordon Sts. 31401
The oldest synagogue in Georgia, having been
founded before 1790

Savannah Jewish Federation
5111 Abercorn Street 31405   (912) 355-8111
Fax: (912) 355-8116
Email: savannah.federation@jon.cjfny.org

Synagogues

Conservative
Agudath Achim
9 Lee Blvd. 31405

Orthodox
B'nai B'rith Jacob
5444 Abercorn Street 31405   (912) 354-7721
Fax: (912) 354-9923

Hawaii

Hilo

Synagogues

Unaffiliated
Temple Beth Aloha
PO Box 96720   (808) 969-4153

Honolulu

Bed & Breakfasts
Bed & Breakfast Honolulu (Statewide)
3242 Kaohinani Drive 96817
(808) 595-7533; 800-288-4666
Fax: (808) 595-2030
Email: BnBsHI@aloha.net
Web site: planet-hawaii.com/bnb-honolulu
Not specifically kosher, but within walking
distance of Orthodox services for the High Holy
Days.

Groceries
Down To Earth
King's Street, Near University Av.,
Foodland Supermarket Beretania
1460 S. Beretania St.

Organisations
Jewish Federation of Hawaii
44 Hora Lane 96813   (808) 941-2424

Synagogues

Conservative
Congregation Sof Ma'arav
2500 Pali Highway 96817   (808) 595-3678

Orthodox
Chabad of Hawaii
2nd floor conference room, 1777 Ala Moana
Blvd., 96822   (808) 735-8161
Fax: (808) 735-4130

Kihei

Synagogues
Jewish Congregation of Maui
PO Box 6101, Maui 96732   (808) 243-2499

Reform
Congregation Gan Eden
P.O. Box 555, Kihei Road 96753
(808) 879-9221
Fax: (808) 874-8570

Kona

Synagogues
Kona Beth Shalom Kailua-Kona
(808) 322-9144

Waikiki

Synagogues

Orthodox
Chabad, Alana Hotel, Park Plaza, 1956 Ala
Moana Blvd.   (808) 735-8161

Idaho

Boise

Synagogues

Conservative
Ahavath-Beth Israel
1102 State Street 83702

Illinois

Buffalo Grove

Restaurants

Dairy
Dunkin Donuts
1169 Old McHenry Road, 60089
(847) 821-0044
Supervision: Chicago Rabbinical Council.

Champaign-Urbana

Community Organisations
Champaign-Urbana Jewish Federation
503 E. John St, Champaign 61820
(217) 367-9872

Synagogues

Reform
Sinai Temple
3104 Windsor Road, Champaign 61821
(217) 352-8140

Chicago

Chicagoland (Greater Chicago) consists of the City of Chicago and the collar counties of Cook, Dupage, Kane, Lake and McHenry Counties. The Jewish community is spread throughout Chicagoland, with the main concentrations being in West Rogers Park (City of Chicago), Skokie (Cook County), Buffalo Grove and Highland Park (Lake County).

Greater Chicago has a Jewish population of about 261,000. For a history of the Jews of Chicago see: I. Cutter: *The Jews of Chicago: from Shtetl to Suburbs.*

Entries in this section are arranged in the sequence that Chicagoland residents think of the area. There are three basic divisions in Chicagoland:

a. City of Chicago (telephone area code 312 and 773) includes West Rogers Park and the California/Dempster Avenue areas
b. North and Northwest Suburbs (includes Cook, Lake and McHenry counties; telephone area codes 773, 815 and 847) includes Buffalo Grove, Deerfield, Evanston, Highland Park, Northbrook, and Skokie.
c. South and West Suburbs (includes DuPage and Kane counties' telephone area codes 630 or 708) includes Flossmoor and Olympia Fields.

Bakeries
Gitel's Bakery
2745 W. Devon
City of Chicago 60659 (773) 262-3701
Supervision: Chicago Rabbinical Council.

North Shore Bakery
2919 W. Touhy
City of Chicago 60645 (773) 262-0600
Supervision: Chicago Rabbinical Council.

Tel Aviv Bakery
2944 W. Devon
City of Chicago 60659 (773) 764-8877
Supervision: Chicago Rabbinical Council.

Booksellers
Chicago Hebrew Book Store
2942 W. Devon
City of Chicago 60645

Rosenblum's World of Judaica, Inc.
2906 W. Devon Ave
City of Chicago 60659 (773) 262-1700
Fax: (773) 262-1930
Email: afox@rosenblums.com
Web site: www.rosenblums.com

Spertus College Museum Store
618 S. Michigan Avenue
City of Chicago 60605 (888) 322-1740
Fax: (888) 922-6406
Email: sijs@spertus.edu
Hours: Sunday to Wednesday 10am to 5pm.
Thursday 10am to 8pm. Friday 10am to 3pm.
Closed Saturday.

Butchers
Jacob Miller & Sons
2727 W. Devon
City of Chicago 60659 (773) 761-4200
Supervision: Chicago Rabbinical Council.

Romanian Kosher Sausage
7200 N. Clark
City of Chicago 60625 (773) 761-4141
Supervision: Chicago Rabbinical Council.

Community Organisations
Jewish Federation of Metropolitan Chicago
1 S. Franklin Street
City of Chicago 60606 (312) 346-6700
Chicago Board of Rabbis (multi-denominational) is located here as well.

Delicatessens
Good Morgan Fish
2948 W. Devon
City of Chicago 60645 (773) 764-8115
Supervision: Chicago Rabbinical Council.

Kosher Karry
2828 W. Devon
City of Chicago 60659 (773) 973-4355
Supervision: Chicago Rabbinical Council.
Sells groceries as well.

Moshe's New York Kosher
2900 W. Devon
City of Chicago 60659 (773) 338-3354
Supervision: Chicago Rabbinical Council.
Sells groceries as well.

Embassy

Consulate General
Suite 1308
111 East Wacker Drive, City of Chicago 60601

Groceries

Kol Tuv
2938 W. Devon
City of Chicago 60659   (773) 764-1800
Supervision: Chicago Rabbinical Council.

Media

Newspapers

Chicago Jewish News
2501 West Peterson Avenue
City of Chicago 60659

JUF News
1 S. Franklin Street
City of Chicago 60606   (312) 346-6700

Museums

Spertus Museum
Spertus Institute of Jewish Studies
618 S. Michigan Avenue, City of Chicago
60605   (312) 322-1747
Fax: (312) 922-3934
Email: musm@spertus.edu
Hours: 10-5.00pm Sunday to Thursday. 10-3.00pm Friday. Closed Saturday.

Religious Organisations

Chicago Mikva Association
3110 W. Touhy Avenue
City of Chicago 60645

Chicago Rabbinical Council
3525 W. Peterson Avenue
Suite 315, City of Chicago 60659
                               (312) 588-1600
Fax: (312) 588-2141
Information about kashrut and related matters
may be obtained from the Council, which
issues an annual directory.

Restaurants

Dairy

Dunkin Donuts
3132 W. Devon
City of Chicago 60659   (773) 262-4561
Supervision: Chicago Rabbinical Council.

Jerusalem Kosher Restaurant
3014 W. Devon
City of Chicago 60659   (773) 262-0515
Supervision: Chicago Rabbinical Council.

Tel Aviv Kosher Pizza & Dairy Restaurant
6349 N. California
City of Chicago 60659   (773) 764-3776
Supervision: Chicago Rabbinical Council.

Meat

Great Chicago Food & Beverage Co.
3149 W. Devon
City of Chicago 60659   (773) 465-9030
Fax: (773) 465-9011
Email: gcfbken@aoi.com
Supervision: Chicago Rabbinical Council.

Jeweler's Club
5 S. Wabash
City of Chicago 60603   (312) 849-9898
Supervision: Chicago Rabbinical Council.

Mi Tsu Yun
3010 W. Devon
City of Chicago 60659   (773) 262-4630
Supervision: Chicago Rabbinical Council.

Synagogues

Orthodox

K.I.N.S of West Rogers Park
2800 W. North Shore Avenue
City of Chicago 60645

Lake Shore Drive Synagogue
70 E. Elm street
City of Chicago 60611

Loop synagogue
16 S Clark street
City of Chicago 60603

Young Israel of Chicago
4931 North Kimball Street
City of Chicago 60625

Evanston

Bakeries

King David's Bakery
1731 W. Howard St. 60202   (847) 475-0270
Supervision: Chicago Rabbinical Council.

Glenview

Bakeries

The Glenview Breadsmith
2771 Pfingsten 60025   (847) 509-9955
Supervision: Chicago Rabbinical Council.

Highland Park

Butcher
Shaevitz Kosher Meats
712 Central Avenue   (847) 432-8334

Delicatessens
Selig's Kosher Deli
209 Skokie Valley Road, 60035
                          (847) 831-5560
Supervision: Chicago Rabbinical Council.
Sells groceries as well.

Synagogues

Conservative

North Surburban Synagogue Beth El
1175 Sheriden Road, 60035   (847) 432-8900

Lincolnwood

Delicatessens

Dairy
Wally's Milk Pail
3320 W. Devon
City of Chicago 60645   (773) 673-3459
Supervision: Chicago Rabbinical Council.
Sells groceries as well.

Northbrook

Synagogues

Orthodox
Young Israel of Northbrook
3545 West Walters Road, 60062
                          (708) 480-9462

Peoria

Community Organisations
Jewish Federation
Town Hall Building, 5901 N. Prospect Road
61604   (309) 689-0063

Synagogues

Orthodox

Agudas Achim
5614 N. University 61604   (309) 692-4848

Rock Island

Community Organisations
Jewish Federation of the Quad Cities
209 18th Street 61201   (309) 793-1300
Fax: (309) 793-1345

Rockford

Community Organisations
Jewish Federation
1500 Parkview Avenue 61107   (815) 399-5497

Synagogues

Conversative

Ohave Sholom
3730 Guildford Road 61107

Reform

Temple Beth El
1203 Comanche Drive 61107   (815) 398-5020

Skokie

Booksellers
Hamakor Gallery Ltd.
4150 Dempster 60076   (847) 677-4150
Fax: (847) 677-4160
Email: gallery@jewishsource.com
Web site: www.jewishsource.com

Delicatessens
Chaim's Kosher Deli & Supermarket
4954 Dempster 60077   (847) 675-1005
Fax: (847) 675-0028
Supervision: Chicago Rabbinical Council.
Bakery and grocery shop as well.

Hungarian Kosher Foods
4020 W. Oakton St. 60076   (847) 674-8008
Supervision: Chicago Rabbinical Council.
Butcher shop and sells groceries as well.

Media

Newspapers

Chicago Jewish Star
PO Box 268 60076

Restaurants

Dairy

Bagel Country
9306 Skokie Blvd. 60077   (847) 673-3030
Supervision: Chicago Rabbinical Council.

Da'Nali's
4032 Oakton 60076   (847) 677-2782
Supervision: Chicago Rabbinical Council.

Slice of Life
4120 W. Dempster 60076   (847) 674-2021
Supervision: Chicago Rabbinical Council.

Meat

Bugsy's Charhouse
3353 Dempster 60076   (847) 679-4030
Email: gcfbken@aol.com
Supervision: Chicago Rabbinical Council.

Falafel King
4507 W. Oakton 60076   (847) 677-6020
Supervision: Chicago Rabbinical Council.

Hylife
4120 W. Dempster, Skokie 60076
(847) 674-2021
Supervision: Chicago Rabbinical Council.

Ken's Diner
3353 Dempster 60076   (847) 679-4030
Fax: (847) 835-3354; 3835- Deli
Email: gcfbken@aoi.com
Supervision: Chicago Rabbinical Council.

Synagogues

Orthodox

Young Israel of Skokie
3708 North Dempster 60076   (847) 329-0990
Shul is located in the Timber Ridge School,
Samoset and Davis

West Rogers Park

Synagogues
Young Israel of West Rogers Park
2716 West Touhy Avenue
City of Chicago 60645   (773) 743-9400

Indiana

Bloomington

Synagogues

Chabad House
516 E. 17th Street 47408   (812) 332-6784

Reform

Congregation Beth Shalom
3750 E. Third 47401   (812) 334-2440

East Chicago

Synagogues

Conservative

Beth Sholom
4508 Baring Avenue 46312

Orthodox

B'nai Israel
3517 Hemlock Street 46312

Evansville

Synagogues

Conservative

Adath Israel
3600 E. Washington Avenue 47715

Reform

Tempe, Washington Avenue Temple, 100
Washington Avenue 47714

Fort Wayne

Synagogues

Conservative

B'nai Jacob
7227 Bittersweet Moors Drive 46804
    (219) 672-8459

Reform

Achduth Vesholom
5200 Old Mill Road 46807   (219) 744-4245

Gary

Synagogues
Temple Israel
601 N. Montgomery Street 46403
    (219) 938-5232

Hammond

Synagogues

Conservative

Beth Israel
7105 Hohman Avenue 46324

Reform

Temple Beth-El
6947 Hohman Avenue 46324

Highland

Organisations
Jewish Federation of North West Indiana
2939 Jewett Street, Highland 46322
    (219) 972-2251
    Fax: (219) 972-4779
Serving Lake Porter and LaPorte Counties

Indianapolis

Organisations
Bureau of Jewish Education
6711 Hoover Road 46260   (317) 255-3124
Anglo-Jewish visitors are invited to get in
touch with the Executive Vice President.
Jewish Federation of Greater Indianapolis
6705 Hoover Road 46260
    (317) 317-726-5450
    Fax: (317) 205-0307
    Email: hnadler@jewishinindy.org

Synagogues

Conservative

Beth-El Zedeck
600 W. 70th Street 46260   (317) 253-3441
    Fax: (317) 259-6849
    Email: bez-613@aol.com
Shaarey Tefilla Congregation
5879 Central Avenue 46220-2509
    (317) 253-4591
    Fax: (317) 253-8529

Orthodox

B'nai Torah
6510 Hoover Road 46260   (317) 253-5253
Etz Chaim (Sephardi)
826 64th Street 46260   (317) 251-6220

Reform

Indianapolis Hebrew Congregation
6501 N. Meridian Street 46260
    (317) 255-6647

Lafayette

Synagogues

Orthodox
Sons of Abraham
661 N. 7th Street 47906

Reform
Temple Israel
620 Cumberland Street 47901

Michigan City

Synagogues
Sinai Temple
2800 S. Franklin Street 46360   (219) 874-4477

Muncie

Synagogues
Temple Beth El
525 W. Jackson Street, cnr. Council Street
47305   (317) 288-4662

South Bend

Contact Information
Rabbi Y. Gettinger
Hebrew Orthodox Congregation, 3207 S. High
Street 46614   (219) 291-4239; 291-6100
Visitors requiring information about kashrut,
temporary accommodation, etc., should
contact Rabbi Gettinger. Or contact Michael
Lerman, 1-800-348-2529.

Kashrut Information
Hebrew Orthodox Congregation
3207 S. High Street 46614   (219) 291-4239
                              Fax: (219) 291-6100

Mikvaot
                              (219) 291-6240

Organisations
Jewish Federation of St. Joseph Valley
105 Jefferson Center, Suite 804 46601
                              (219) 233-1164
                              Fax: (219) 288-4103

Synagogues

Conservative
Sinai, 1102 E. Laselle Street 46617

Orthodox
Hebrew Orthodox Congregation
3207 S. High Street 46614

Reform
Beth-El
305 W. Madison Street 46601 (219) 234-4402

Terre Haute

Delicatessens
Kosher Meat & Sandwiches
410 W. Western Avenue 47807

Valparaiso

Synagogues

Conservative
Temple Israel
PO Box 2051 46383

Whiting

Synagogues

Orthodox
B'nai Judah
116th Street & Davis Avenue 46394

Iowa

Cedar Rapids

Synagogues

Reform
Temple Judah
3221 Lindsay Lane S.E. 52403
                              (319) 362-1261

Davenport

Synagogues
Temple Emanuel
12th Street & Mississippi Avenue 52803
Davenport is part of the Rock Island, Illinois
area, which is divided by the Mississippi River.
See the Rock Island entry.

Des Moines

Delicatessens
Pickle Barrel
1241 6th Avenue 50314
The Nosh
800 First Street 50265

Organisations
Jewish Community Relations COm.
910 Polk Blvd 50312
Jewish Family Services
910 Polk Blvd 50312

Jewish Federation of Greater Des Moines
910 Polk Blvd 50312   (515) 277-6321

Synagogues

Conservative
Tifereth Israel
924 Polk Blvd. 50312

Orthodox
Beth El Jacob
954 Cummins Parkway 50312

Reform
Temple B'nai Jeshurun
5101 Grand Avenue 50312   (515) 274-4679
                            Fax: (515) 274-2072
                       Email: rabbifink@aol.com

Dubuque
Synagogues
Beth El
475 W. Locust Street 52001

Fort Dodge
Synagogues

Conservative
Beth El
501 N. 12th Street 50501   (515) 572-8925

Iowa City
Synagogues

Conservative & Reform
Agudas Achim
602 E. Washington Street 52240
                            (319) 337-3813

Sioux City
Groceries
Sam's Food Market
1911 Grandview 51104

Organisations
Jewish Federation
525 14th Street 51105   (712) 258-0618

Synagogues

Conservative
Beth Sholom
815 38th Street 51105

Orthodox
United Orthodox
14th & Nebraska Streets 51105

Kansas
Lawrence
Synagogues
Lawrence Jewish Community Center
917 Highland Drive 66046   (785) 841-7636

Overland Park
Media

Newspapers
Kansas City Jewish Chronicle
7375 W. 107th Street 66204
Weekly publication.

Synagogues

Orthodox
Congregation Beth Israel Abraham & Voliner
9900 Antioch 66212   (913) 341-2444
                            Fax: (913) 341-2467
Kehilath Israel Synagogue
10501 Conser 66212   (913) 642-1880
                            Fax: (913) 642-7332

Reform
Congregation Beth Torah
6100 W 127th Street 66209   (913) 498-2212
                            Fax: (913) 498-1071

Prairie Village
Butchers
Jacobsons Strictly Kosher Foods
5200 W95th Street 66207

Synagogues

Conservative
Ohev Shalom
5311 W. 75th Street 66208   (913) 642-6460
                            Fax: (913) 642-6461
Orthodox rite but mixed seating.

Topeka
Organisations
Topeka Lawrence Jewish Federation
4200 Munson Street 66604

Synagogues

Reform

Beth Sholom
4200 Munson Street 66604   (785) 272-6040

Wichita

Groceries

Dillon's
13th Street & Woodlawn Street 67208
Dillon's
21st Street & Rock Road 67208
Dillon's
Foodbarn Woodlawn & Central Sts., 67208
The Bread Lady
20205 Rock Road, #80 2607

Synagogues

Orthodox

Hebrew Congregation
1850 N. Woodlawn 67208

Reform

Congregation Emanu-El
7011 E. Central Street 67206

Kentucky

Lexington

Organisations
Central Kentucky Jewish Federation
340 Romany Road 40502   (606) 268-0775

Synagogues

Conservative

Lexington Havurah
PO Box 54958 40551
Ohavay Zion
2048 Edgewater Ct. 40502

Reform

Adath Israel
124 N. Ashland Avenue 40502

Louisville

Organisations
Jewish Community Federation
3630 Dutchman's Lane 40205

Synagogues

Conservative

Adath Jeshurun
2401 Woodbourne Avenue 40205

Orthodox

Anshei Sfard
3700 Dutchman's Lane 40205
Mikvah attached.

Reform

Temple Shalom
4615 Lowe Road 40220   (502) 459-4738
Fax: (502) 451-9750
Email: rsmiles@pipeline.com
The Temple
5101 Brownsboro Road 40241

Traditional

Keneseth Israel
2531 Taylorsville Road 40205

Paducah

Synagogues

Reform

Temple Israel
330 Joe Clifton Drive 42001

Louisiana

Alexandria

Groceries
100 Park Place 71301   (318) 445-9367
Kosher food by arrangement.

Libraries
Meyer Kaplan Memorial Library (Judiaca)
c/o B'nai Israel, 1908 Vance Street 71301

Synagogues

Conservative

B'nai Israel
1907 Vance Street 71301

Reform

Gemiluth Chassodim
2021 Turner Street 71301

Baton Rouge

Organisations
Jewish Federation of Greater Baton Rouge
P.O.B. 80827 70898   (504) 291-5895

Synagogues

Reform

B'nai Israel
3354 Kleinert Avenue 70806

Beth Shalom
9111 Jefferson Highway 70809

Lafayette

Synagogues
Temple Sholom
603 Lee Avenue, P.O.Box 53711 70505
(318) 234-3760
There is a fine Judaica library at the University
of Southwestern Louisiana.

New Orleans

Delicatessens
Kosher Cajun Deli & Grocery
3250 N. Hullen Street, Metrairie 70002
(504) 888-2010
Fax: (504) 888-2014
Under strict rabbinical supervision. Hours:
Monday to Thursday, 10 am to 7 pm; Friday
and Sunday, to 3 pm. We also deliver to
Hotels.

Groceries
Casablanca
3030 Seven Avenue, Metrairie 70002-4826
(504) 888-2209
Touro Infirmary
1401 Foucher Street 70115   (504) 897-8246
Glatt kosher meals available

Home Hospitality
Dr & Mrs Saul Kahn
4000 Clifford Drive, Metrairie 70002
(504) 831-2230
Fax: (504) 522-8981
We are a Bed & Breakfast establishment
keeping glatt kosher, the Kahns say, 'Having
guests from all over the world enriches our
lives.'

Hotels
The Pontchartrain Grand Heritage Hotel
2031 St Charles Avenue 70140
(800) 777-6193
Fax: (800) 529-1165
Kosher food available on request.
The Pontchartrain Grand Heritage Hotel
2031 St Charles Avenue 70140
(504) 524-0581
Kosher food available on request.

Media

Newspapers
The Jewish News
3500 N. Causeway Blvd, #1240
Metaire 70002

Mikvaot
Beth Israel
7000 Canal Blvd 70124

Organisations
Jewish Federation of Greater New Orleans
3500 N. Causeway Blvd., #1240
Metairie 70002   (504) 828-2125
Fax: (504) 828-2827

Synagogues

Orthodox
Anshe Sfard
2230 Carondelet Street 70130
(504) 422-4714

Shreveport

Community Organisations
Jewish Federation
2032 Line Avenue 71104   (318) 221-4129

Synagogues

Conservative
Agudath Achim
9401 Village Green Drive 71115
(318) 797-6401

Reform
B'nai Zion
245 Southfield Road 71105

Maine
Auburn

Synagogues

Conservative
Congregation Beth Abraham
Main Street & Laurel Avenue 04210
(207) 783-1302

Temple Shalom
74 Bradman Street 04210

Bangor

Bakeries
The Bagel Shop
1 Main Street 04451   (207) 947-1654

Synagogues

Conservative
Congregation Beth Israel
144 York Street 04401

Orthodox

Beth Abraham
145 York Street 04401

Lewiston

Community Organisations
Lewiston-Auburn Jewish Federation
74 Bradman Street 04210   (207) 786-4201

Old Orchard Beach

Kashrut Information
Eber Weinstein
187 E. Grand Avenue 04064   (207) 934-7522
Eddie Hakim
    (207) 934-7223
Harold Goodkovski
    (207) 934-4210

Synagogues

Orthodox

Beth Israel
49 E. Grand Avenue 04064   (207) 934-2973
Daily minyan, May 28 to Yom Kippur, Shabbat
& Yom Tov minyan all year round.

Portland

Butchers
Penny Wise Super Market
182 Ocean Avenue 04130
Take-out counter at a local supermarket.

Mikvaot
Shaarey Tphiloh
76 Noyes Street 04103

Organisations
Jewish Fed.-Com. Council of Southern Maine
57 Ashmont Street 04103   (207) 773-7254

Synagogues

Conservative

Beth El
400 Deering Avenue 04103   (207) 774-2649

Orthodox

Etz Chaim
267 Congress Street 04101
Shaarey Tphiloh
76 Noyes Street 04103
Mikvah & Hebrew Day School on premises.

Maryland

Bethesda, Bowie, Chevy Chase, Gaithersburg,
Greenbelt, Hyattsville, Kensington, Laurel,
Lexington Park, Olney, Potomac, Rockville,
Silver Spring & Wheaton and Temple Hills are
all part of Greater Washington, DC.

Annapolis

Synagogues

Conservative

Congregation Kol Ami
1909 Hidden Meadow Lane 21401

Reform

Temple Beth Shalom
1461 Baltimore-Anaapolis Blvd., 21012

Baltimore

Synagogues

There are more than 50 synagogues in the
Baltimore metropolitan area. Visitors are
advised to contact one of the community
organisations in the area to find the
synagogue nearest them.

Bakeries
Brooklyn Bakery
222 Riesterstown Road 21208
Supervision: Kof-K.
Dunkin Donuts
1508 Reisterstown Road 21208
    (410) 653-8182
Supervision: Rabbi Salfer.
Dunkin Donuts
7000 Reisterstown Road 21215
    (410) 764-6846
Supervision: Rabbi Salfer.
Goldman's Kosher Bakery
6848 Reistertown Road, Farstaff Shopping
Center 21215   (410) 358-9625
    Fax: (410) 358-5859
    Email: mcohn@home.com
Pariser's Kosher Bakery
6711 Reisterstown Road 21215
Schmell-Azman
7006 Reisterstown Road 21215
    (410) 484-7373
Supervision: Star K.
Seven Mile Market
4000 Seven Mile Lane 21208
    (410) 653-2000; 2002
Supervision: Star K.

Delicatessens

Danielle's
401 Reistertown Road 21208
Knish Shop
508 Reisterstown Road 21208 (410) 484-5850
Knish Shop
508 Reisterstown Road 21208
Liebes Kosher Deli Carry Out
607 Reisterstown Road 21208 (410) 653-1977
Only glatt kosher meats. Hours: Sunday to
Wednesday, 8:30am to 6pm; Thursday, late
night Friday, to 1 hour before sundown.

Groceries

Mirakle Market
6836 Reistertown Road 21215 (410) 358-3443
Seven Mile Market
4000 Seven Mile Lane, Pikesville 21208
(410) 653-2000

Shlomo Meat & Fish
4030 Falstaff Road 21215 (410) 358-9633
Wasseman & Lemberger
610 Reistertown Road (301) 486-4191
Will deliver to DC on Monday.
Wasserman & Lemberger
70006-D Reistertown Road 21208
(410) 486-4191

Kashrut Information

Ha Star-K Kosher Certification
11 Warren Road 21208 (410) 484-4110
Fax: (410) 653-9294
Email: starkii@aol.com
Jewish Information Service
5750 Park Heights Avenue 21215
(410) 466-4636
Fax: (410) 664-0551
Email: jfs@jfs.org
Open daily from 10.0am to 2.0pm for help on
almost anything.

Mikvaot

Mikva of Baltimore Inc.,
3207 Clarks Lane 21225 (410) 664-5834

Museums

The Jewish Museum of Maryland
15 Lloyd Street 21202 (410) 732-6400
Fax: (410) 732-6451
Email: info@jhsm.org
This newly-enlarged complex of museum
buildings is unlike anything else in the United
States, comprising two historic synagogues
(Lloyd Street Synagogue, built in 1845, and
B'nai Israel, built in 1876) and an adjoining
research center and museum featuring
changing exhibits and regional Judaica.

Organisations

Associated Jewish Community Federation of Baltimore
101 W. Mount Royal Avenue 21201
(410) 727-4828
The Baltimore Jewish Council
Gay & Water Sts.,
The Jewish Historical Society of Maryland
15 Lloyd Street 21202 (410) 732-6400

Restaurants

The Brasserie
Pomona Square, 1700 Reisterstown Road
(410) 484-0476
Supervision: Star K.

Dairy

I Can't Believe It's Yogurt
1430 Reisterstown Road (410) 484-4411
Supervision: Rabbi Salfer.

Meat

Chapps Kosher Chinese
Pomona Square Shopping Center, 1700
Reisterstown Rd., 21208
Kosher Bite
6309 Reisterstown Road 21215
Royal Restaurant
7006 Reisterstown Road 21208

Pizzerias

Tov Pizza
6313 Reisterstown Road 21215
(301) 358-5238
Supervision: Kof-K.

Tours of Jewish Interest

Holocaust Memorial
Gay & Water Sts.

Bethesda

Organisations

United Jewish Appeal Federation of Greater Washington
7900 Wisconsin Avenue 20814
(301) 652-6480

Bowie

Synagogues

Conservative

Nevey Shalom
12218 Torah Lane 20715 (301) 262-4020

Reform

Temple Solel
2901 Mitchelville Road 20716
(301) 249-2424

Chevy Chase

Synagogues

Conservative

Ohr Kodesh
8402 Freyman Drive 20815   (301) 589-3880
Fax: (301) 495-4801
Email: okcjmm@erols.com

Reform

Temple Shalom
8401 Grubb Road 20815   (301) 587-2273

College Park

Libraries
The National Archives
8601 Adelphi Road 20740
Containing historical Jewish documentation

Cumberland

Restaurants

Dairy

The Bagel Shop
1 Main Street 04401   (207) 947-1654
Closed Shabbat. Restaurant, deli, bakery and take-out.

Synagogues

Conservative

Beth Jacob
1 Columbia Street 21502

Reform
B'Er Chayim
107 Union Street 21502

Gaithersburg

Synagogues

Conservative

Kehilat Shalom
9915 Apple Ridge Road 20886
(301) 869-7699
Fax: (301) 977-7870
Email: kehilat@tiac.net
Web site: www.kehilatshalom.org

Greenbelt

Synagogues
Mishkan Torah
Westway and Ridge Road 20770
(301) 474-4223

Hagerstown

Delicatessens
Celebrity Deli
6700 Adelphi Road 20782   (301) 927-5525

Synagogues

Reform
B'nai Abraham
53 E. Baltimore Street 21740   (301) 733-5039

Hyattsville

Synagogues

Conservative

Beth Torah Congregation
6700 Adelphi Road 20782   (301) 927-5525

Kensington

Synagogues

Reform
Temple Emanuel
10101 Connecticut Avenue 20895
(301) 942-2000
Fax: (301) 942-9488

Laurel

Synagogues

Reconstructionist
Oseh Shalom
8604 Briarwood Drive 20708   (301) 498-5151

Lexington Park

Synagogues

Conservative
Beth Israel
Bunker Hill Drive 20650   (301) 862-2021

Olney

Synagogues
B'nai Shalom
18401 Burtfield Drive 20832   (301) 774-0879

Pocomoke

Synagogues
Temple Israel
3rd Street 21851

Potomac

Restaurants

Meat
Hunan Gourmet
350 Fortune Terrace   (301) 424-0191

Synagogues

Conservative
Har Shalom
11510 Falls Road 20854   (301) 299-7087

Orthodox
Beth Sholom of Potomac
11825 Seven Locks Road 20854
                             (301) 279-7010
Young Israel of Ezras Israel of Potomac
11618 Seven Locks Road 20854
                             (301) 299-2827

Rockville

Groceries
Katz Supermarket
4860 Boiling Brook Parkway   (301) 468-0400

Restaurants

Meat
Moshe Dragon Glatt Kosher Chinese Restaurant
4840 Boiling Brook Parkway   (301) 468-1922
Royal Dragon
4840 Boiling Brook Parkway   (301) 468-1922

Meat and Dairy
Kat'z Kafe, 4860 Boiling Brook Parkway
                             (301) 468-0400

Synagogues

Conservative
B'nai Israel
6301 Montrose Road 20852
Beth Tikvah
2200 Baltimore Road 20853

Orthodox
Magen David Sephardic Congregation
11215 Woodglen Drive 20852 (301) 770-6818
                        Fax: (301) 881-0498

Reform
Temple Beth Ami
800 Hurley Avenue 20850   (301) 340-6818

Salisbury

Synagogues

Conservative
Beth Israel
Camden Avenue & Wicomico Street 21801

Silver Spring & Wheaton

Bakeries
The Wooden Shoe Pastry Shop
11301 Georgia Avenue 20902
Virtuoso
11230a Lockwood Avenue 50901
                             (301) 593-6034
Wooden Shoe Bakery   (301) 942-9330

Booksellers
Lisbon's Hebrew Books & Gifts
2305 University Blvd West 20902
                             (301) 933-1800
                        Fax: (301) 933-7466
                Email: slisbon@idsonline.com
The Jewish Bookstore
11252 Georgia Avenue 20902
                             (301) 942-2237
                        Fax: (301) 933-5464

Delicatessens
Shalom
2307 University Blvd 20902

Groceries
Shalom Meat Market
2307 University Blvd West   (301) 946-6500
Shaul & Hershel Meat Market
                             (301) 949-8477

Guest Houses
Hebrew Sheltering Society
11524 Daffodil Lane 20902   (301) 649-3141;
                        649-4425; 649-2799
For people unable to afford accommodation,
will get 3 free nights stay at the shelter.

Mikvaot
Mikva, 8901 Georgia Avenue 20910
                             (301) 565-3737

Restaurants

Dairy
The Nut House
11419 Georgia Avenue 20902
                             (301) 942-5900

Synagogues

Conservative

Har Tzeon-Agudath Achim
1840 University Blvd. W 20902
Shaare Tefila
11120 Lockwood Drive 20901
Temple Israel
420 University Blvd. E 20901   (301) 439-3600

Orthodox

Silver Spring Jewish Center
1401 Arcola Avenue 20902   (301) 649-4425
South-East Hebrew Congregation
10900 Lockwood Drive 20902
Woodside Synagogue Ahavas Torah
9001 Georgia Avenue 20910
Young Israel of White Oak
PO Box 10613
White Oak 20914   (301) 369-1531
Young Israel Shomrai Emunah of Greater Washington
1132 Arcola Avenue 20902   (301) 593-4465
Young Israel Shomrei Emunah
1132 Arcola Avenue 20902

Temple Hills

Synagogues

Conservative

Shaare Tikva
5405 Old Temple Hills Road 20748
     (301) 894-4303

Massachusetts

Acton

Synagogues

Independent

Beth Elohim
10 Hennessy Drive 07120   (978) 263-8610

Amherst

Synagogues
Jewish Community
742 Main Street 01002   (413) 256-0160

Andover

Synagogues

Reform

Temple Emanuel
7 Haggett's Pond Road 01810   (978) 470-1563

Arlington

Bakeries
Dough-C-Donuts
1460 Massachusetts Avenue 02174
     (617) 643-4550
Supervision: Vaad Harabonim of
Massachusetts.

Athol

Synagogues

Conservative

Temple Israel
107 Walnut Street 01331   (978) 249-9481

Attleboro

Synagogues

Reconstructionist

Agudas Achim Congregation
901 N. Main Street 02703   (508) 222-2243
     Email: rgaild@juno.com

Ayer

Synagogues

Independent

Congregation Anshey Sholom
Cambridge Street 01432   (508) 772-0896

Belmont

Synagogues

Reform

Beth El Temple Center
2 Concord Avenue 02178   (781) 484-6668

Beverly

Synagogues

Conservative

B'nai Abraham
200 E. Lothrop Street 01915   (978) 927-3211

Boston (Greater Boston)

Embassy
Consulate General
1020 Statler Office Blvd 02116

United States of America / Massachusetts

Kashrut Information

Synagogue Council of Massachusetts
1320 Centre Street, Newton Centre
02459-2400   (617) 244-6506
Fax: (617) 964-7055
Email: syncouncil@aol.com.
The Kashruth Commission
177 Tremont Street 02111   (617) 426-2139
Fax: (617) 426-6268
Vaad Harabonim of Massachusetts
177 Tremont Street 02111   (617) 426-2139
Fax: (617) 426-6268

Media

Directories

Synagogue Council of Massachusetts
1320 Centre Street, Newton Centre
02459-2400   (617) 244-6506
Fax: (617) 964-7055
Email: syncouncil@aol.com.

Guides

Jewish Guide to Boston and New England
15 School Street 02108   (617) 267-9100
Fax: (617) 267-9310

Newspapers

Boston Jewish Times
15 School Street 02108   (617) 267-9100
Fax: (617) 367-9310
The Jewish Advocate
15 School Street 02108   (617) 367-9100
Fax: (617) 367-9310

Mikvaot

Daughters of Israel
101 Washington Street, Brighton 02135

Organisations

Jewish Community Relations Council of Greater Boston
1 Lincoln Plaza, Suite 308 02111
(617) 330-9600
Represents 34 community organisations in the area.

Religious Organisations

Rabbinical Council of New England
177 Tremont Street 02111   (617) 426-2139
Fax: (617) 426-6268
Rabbinical Court
177 Tremont Street 02111   (617) 426-2139
Fax: (617) 426-6268

Restaurants

Dairy

Milk Street Cafe
The Park at Post Office Square, Zero Post Office
Square   (617) 350-PARK
Supervision: Orthodox Rabbinic Council of Greater Boston.
Dairy foods and sealed meat sandwiches from meat corporate catering kitchens. In the summer, 4 carts in the park with hot dogs and BBQ beef; deli wraps and sandwiches; Italian specialties – pizza and calzone; and ice cream and frozen desserts.
Milk Street Cafe
50 Milk Street   (617) 542-FOOD
Fax: (617) 451-5FAX
Supervision: Orthodox Rabbinic Council of Greater Boston.
Hours: Monday to Friday, 7 am to 3 pm.

Meat

B.U. Hillel
233 Bay State Road 02215   (617) 353-3663
Supervision: Vaad Harabonim of Massachusetts.
Hillel Foundation
Boston University, 233 Bay State Road
02215-1499   (617) 353-7200
Fax: (617) 353-7660
Supervision: Rabbi Joseph Polak and Vaad HaRabanim of Massachusetts.
Hours: 11:30 am to 1:15 pm; 5 to 7 pm.
Shabbat meals need to be pre-paid. For information: 353-2947.

Synagogues

Conservative

Hillel B'nai Torah
120 Corey St, W. Roxbury 02132
(617) 323-0486
Temple B'nai Moshe
1845 Commonwealth Avenue, Brighton 02135
(617) 254-3620

Orthodox

Chabad House
491 Commonwealth Avenue 02215
(617) 523-0453
Congregation Kadimah-Toras Moshe
113 Washington Street, Brighton 02135
(617) 254-1333
Lubavitch Shul of Brighton
239 Chestnut Hill Avenue, Brighton 02135
(617) 782-8340

The Boston Synagogue
(at Charles River Park), 55 Martha Road 02114
(617) 523-0453
Fax: (617) 723-2863

Zvhiller Beis Medrash
15 School Street 02108   (617) 227-8200
Web site: www.rebbe.org

Reform
Temple Israel
Plymouth Street & Longwood Avenue 02115
(617) 566-3960

Tours of Jewish Interest
BostonWalks and The Jewish Friendship Trail
(617) 489-5020
Email: rossocp@gis.net

Braintree
Bakeries
Sara's Kitchen
South Shore Plaza 01501   (617) 843-8803
Supervision: Vaad Harabonim of
Massachusetts.

Synagogues
Conservative
Temple Bnai Shalom
41 Storrs Avenue 02184   (781) 843-3687

Bridgewater
Bakeries
J & E Baking Company
10 Bedford Park, Unit #5 02324
(508) 279-0990
Supervision: Vaad Harabonim of
Massachusetts.
Shomer Shabbat.

Brighton
Restaurants
B-B-N J.C.C. Dining Hall
50 Sutherland Road 02146   (617) 278-2950
Supervision: Vaad Harabonim of
Massachusetts.
J.C.H.E. Dining Hall
30 Wallingford Road 02146   (617) 254-9001
Supervision: Vaad Harabonim of
Massachusetts.

Brockton
Synagogues
Conservative
Temple
479 Torres Street 02401   (508) 583-5810

Orthodox
Agudath Achim
144 Belmont Avenue 02401   (508) 583-0717

Reform
Temple Israel
184 W. Elm Street 02401   (508) 587-4130

Brookline
Bakeries
Catering by Andrew
404A Harvard Street 02148   (617) 731-6585
Supervision: Vaad Harabonim of
Massachusetts.
Shomer Shabbat.
Taam Tov Bakery
305A Harvard Street 02146   (617) 566-8136
Supervision: Vaad Harabonim of
Massachusetts.
Shomer Shabbat. Pareve.

Kashrut Information
Jewish Commercial Center
Harvard Street
Harvard Street is the Jewish commercial
Center, with art & bookshops, as well as many
kosher butcher's shops and bakeries.

Restaurants
Ruth's Kitchen
401 Harvard Street   (617) 734-9810

Meat
Cafe Shiraz
1030 Commonwealth Avenue 02215
(617) 566-8888
New private function rooms for group parties.
Glatt kosher Persian and Middle Eastern
cuisine. Alcohol served. Catering available.
Wheelchair accessible. Hours: Monday to
Thursday, 5 pm to 10 pm; Saturday, 45
minutes after sundown to midnight; Sunday, 4
pm to 10 pm.
Rami's
324 Harvard Street 02146   (617) 738-3577
Supervision: Vaad Harabonim of
Massachusetts.
Glatt kosher.

Rubin's
500 Harvard Street 02146   (617) 566-8761
Supervision: Vaad Harabonim of
Massachusetts.
Glatt kosher.
Shalom Hunan
92 Harvard Street 02146   (617) 731-9760
Supervision: Vaad Harabonim of
Massachusetts.
Glatt kosher.

Pizzerias

Victor's Pizza
1364 Beacon Street 02146   (617) 730-9903

Synagogues

Conservative

Kehillath Israel
384 Harvard St 02146   (617) 277-9155

Orthodox

Beth David
64 Corey Road 02146   (617) 232-2349
Beth Pinchas (Bostoner Rebbe)
1710 Beacon Street 02146   (617) 734-5100
Chai Odom
77 Englewood Av 02146   (617) 734-5359
Young Israel of Brookline
62 Green Street 02146   (617) 734-0276

Reform

Ohabei Shalom
1187 Beacon St 02146   (617) 277-6610
Temple Sinai
50 Sewall Av, Coolidge Corner 02146
(617) 277-5888

Sephardic

Sephardic Congregation
1566 Beacon St 02146   (617) 566-8171

Burlington

Synagogues

Reform

Temple Shalom Emeth
14-16 Lexington Street 01803   (781) 272-2351

Cambridge

Kashrut Information

Hillel House
Harvard University, 52 Mt. Auburn St 02138
(617) 495-4696
Fax: (617) 864-1637
Email: imulliga@camailz.harvard.edu
Kosher meals are obtainable, by previous
arrangement.
Hillel House
312 Memorial Drive 02139
Under Rabbinical supervision

Restaurants

Harvard Hillel Dining Hall
52 Mt. Auburn Street 02138
(617) 495-4695; 495-4696
Supervision: Vaad Harabonim of
Massachusetts.
Dining Hall: 876-3535

Meat

M.I.T. Hillel
40 Massachusetts Avenue 02139
(617) 253-2982
Fax: (617) 253-3260
Email: hillel@mit.edu
Supervision: Vaad Harabonim of
Massachusetts.

Synagogues

Conservative

Temple Beth Shalom of Cambridge
8 Tremont Street 02139   (617) 864-6388

Canton

Synagogues

Beth Abraham
1301 Washington Street 02021
(781) 828-5250

Reform

Temple Beth David of the South Shore
1060 Randolph Street 02021   (617) 828-2275

Chelmsford

Synagogues

Congregation Shalom
Richardson Road 01824   (978) 251-8090

Chestnut Hill

Bakeries
Cheryl Ann's Bakery
1010 West Roxbury Parkway 02167
           (617) 469-9241
Supervision: Vaad Harabonim of
Massachusetts.

Clinton

Synagogues

Independent
Shaarei Zedeck
Water Street 01510   (978) 365-3320

East Dedham

Bakeries
Cookies Express
252 Bussey Street 02026   (617) 461-0044
Supervision: Vaad Harabonim of
Massachusetts.
Shomer Shabbat.

East Falmouth

Synagogues

Reform
Falmouth Jewish Congregation
7 Hatchville Road 02536   (508) 540-5081

Easton

Synagogues

Traditional
Temple Chayai Shalom
238 Depot Street 02334   (508) 238-6385
Mail address: P.O.Box 404, N. Easton 02356

Everett

Synagogues
Tifereth Israel
34 Malden Street 02149   (617) 387-0200

Fall River

Organisations
Fall River Jewish Community Council
Room 327, 56 N. Main St., 02720

Synagogues

Conservative
Beth El
385 High Street 02720   (508) 674-9761

Orthodox
Adas Israel
1647 Robeson Street 02720   (508) 674-9761

Fitchburg

Synagogues

Independent
Agudas Achim
40 Boutelle Street 01420   (978) 342-7704

Framingham

Bakeries
Boston Cookie
Framingham Mall, Route 30 01701
           (508) 872-1052
Supervision: Vaad Harabonim of
Massachusetts.
Bread Basket Bakery
151 Cochituate Road 01701   (508) 875-9441
Supervision: Vaad Harabonim of
Massachusetts.

Synagogues

Conservative
Beth Sholom
50 Pamela Road 01701   (508) 877-2540

Orthodox
Chabad House
74 Joseph Road 01701   (508) 877-5313

Reform
Beth Am
300 Pleasant Street 01701   (508) 872-8300
         Fax: (508) 872-9773
    Email: tempbetham@aol.com

Gloucester

Synagogues

Conservative
Ahavat Achim
86 Middle Street 01930   (978) 281-0739
         Fax: (978) 281-0739

Greenfield

Synagogues
Temple Israel
27 Pierce Street 01301   (413) 773-5884

Haverhill

Synagogues

Orthodox

Anshe Sholom
427 Main Street 01830   (508) 372-2276

Reform

Temple Emanu-El
514 Main Street 01830   (508) 373-3861

Hingham

Synagogues
Congregation Sha'aray Shalom
112 Main Street 02043   (781) 749-8103

Holbrook

Synagogues

Conservative

Temple Beth Shalom
95 Plymouth Street 02343   (617) 767-4922

Holliston

Synagogues
Temple Beth Torah
2162 Washington Street 01746
                              (508) 429-6268

Holyoke

Synagogues
Sons of Zion
378 Maple Street 01040   (413) 534-3369

Orthodox

Rodphey Sholom
1800 Northampton Street 01040
                              (413) 534-5262

Hull

Synagogues

Conservative

Temple Beth Sholom
600 Nantasket Avenue 02045 (781) 925-0091
Temple Israel of Nantasket
9 Hadassah Way 02045   (617) 925-0289
Summer only.

Hyannis

Synagogues

Reform

Cape Cod Synagogue
145 Winter Street 02601   (508) 775-2988

Hyde Park

Synagogues

Conservative

Temple Adas Hadrath Israel
28 Arlington Street 02136   (617) 364-2661

Lawrence

Organisations
Jewish Com. Council of Greater Lawrence
580 Haverhill Street 01841   (617) 686-4157

Synagogues

Orthodox

Anshai Sholum
411 Hampshire Street 01843   (508) 683-4544

Leominster

Synagogues

Conservative

Congregation Agudat Achim
268 Washington Street 01453
                              (508) 534-6121

Lexington

Synagogues
Temple Emunah
9 Piper Road 02173   (781) 861-0300
                       Fax: (781) 861-7141

Orthodox

Chabad Center
9 Burlington Street 02173   (781) 863-8656

Reform

Temple Isaiah
55 Lincoln Street 02173   (781) 862-7160

Lowell

Bakeries
Donut Shak, 487 Westford Street
                              (508) 937-0178
Supervision: Vaad Harabonim of
Massachusetts.

Bed & Breakfast
The Very Victorian Sherman-Berry House
c/o Montefiore Synagogue, 48 Academy Drive
(508) 970-2008

Mikvaot
Mikvah, 48 Academy Drive   (508) 970-2008

Synagogues
Conservative
Temple Beth El
105 Princeton Blvd. 01851   (508) 453-7744

Orthodox
Montefiore Synagogue
460 Westford Street 01851   (508) 459-9400

Reform
Temple Emanuel of Merrimack Valley
101 W. Forest Street 01851
(508) 454-1372

Lynn
Synagogues
Orthodox
Ahabat Shalom
151 Ocean Street 01902   (617) 593-9255
Houses the Eliot Feuerstein Library.
Anshai Sfard
150 S. Common Street 01905 (617) 599-7131
Chevra Tehilim
12 Breed Street 01902   (617) 598-2964

Malden
Bakeries
Brick Oven Bakery
237 Ferry Street 02148   (781) 322-3269
Supervision: Vaad Harabonim of
Massachusetts.

Synagogues
Conservative
Ezrath Israel
245 Bryant Street 02148   (617) 322-7205

Orthodox
Beth Israel
10 Dexter Street 02148   (617) 322-5686
Young Israel of Malden
45 Holyoke Street 02148   (617) 961-9817

Reform
Tifereth Israel
539 Salem Street 02148   (617) 322-2794

Traditional
Agudas Achim
160 Harvard Street 02148   (617) 322-9380

Marblehead
Community Organisations
Jewish Federation of the North Shore
4 Community Road 01945   (617) 598-1810

Synagogues
Conservative
Temple Sinai
1 Community Road 01945   (617) 631-2244

Orthodox
Orthodox Congregation of the North Shore
4 Community Road 01945   (617) 598-1810

Reform
Temple Emanu-El
393 Atlantic Avenue 01945   (617) 631-9300

Marlboro
Synagogues
Conservative
Temple Emanuel
150 Berlin Road 01752
(508) 485-7565; 508-562-5105

Medford
Bakeries
Donuts with a Difference
35 Riverside Avenue 02155   (781) 396-1021
Supervision: Vaad Harabonim of
Massachusetts.

Restaurants
Tufts Hillel
474 Boston Avenue 02155   (781) 627-3242
Supervision: Vaad Harabonim of
Massachusetts.

Synagogues
Conservative
Temple Shalom
475 Winthrop Street 02155   (781) 396-3262

Melrose

Synagogues

Reform

Temple Beth Shalom
21 E. Foster Street 02176   (617) 665-4520

Milford

Synagogues

Conservative

Beth Shalom
49 Pine Street 01757   (508) 473-1590

Millis

Synagogues
Ael Chunon
334 Village Street 02054   (508) 376-5984

Milton

Synagogues
Temple Shalom
180 Blue Hill Avenue 02186   (617) 698-3394

Orthodox

B'nai Jacob
100 Blue Hill Parkway 02187   (617) 698-0698

Natick

Synagogues

Conservative

Temple Israel
145 Hartford Street 01760

Orthodox

Chabad Lubavitch Center
2 East Mill Street 01760   (508) 650-1499

Needham

Synagogues

Conservative

Temple Aliyah
1664 Central Avenue 02492   (781) 444-8522
Fax: (781) 449-7066

Reform

Temple Beth Shalom
670 Highland Avenue 02494   (781) 444-0077
Fax: (781) 449-3274
Email: tbshalom@fcl-us.net

New Bedford

Organisations
Jewish Federation of Greater New Bedford
467 Hawthorn Street, N. Dartmouth 02747
(508) 997-7471

Synagogues

Conservative

Tifereth Israel
145 Brownell Avenue 02740   (508) 997-3171

Orthodox

Ahavath Achim
385 County Street 02740   (508) 994-1760

Newburyport

Synagogues
Congregation Ahavas Achim
Washington & Olive Streets 09150
(508) 462-2461

Newton

Bakeries
Lederman's Bakery
1223 Centre Street 02159   (617) 527-7896
Supervision: Vaad Harabonim of
Massachusetts.

Tuler's Bakery
551 Commonwealth Avenue 02159
(617) 964-5653
Supervision: Vaad Harabonim of
Massachusetts.
Pareve. Shomer Shabbat.

Cafeterias
**Orthodox Rabbinical Council of
Massachusetts**   (617) 558-6475
Provides snack bar for Jewish Community
Center of Greater Boston.

Organisations
Jewish Community Center of Greater Boston
333 Nahanton Street 02159   (617) 558-6522
Kosher snack bar provided. See below.
Synagogue Council of Massachusetts
1320 Center Street, Newton Center 02159
(617) 244-6506

Restaurants
Golda Meir House
160 Stanton Avenue, Dining Hall 02166
(617) 969-1764
Supervision: Vaad Harabonim of
Massachusetts.   Kitchen: 965-0770

Dairy

J.C.C. Campus Snack Bar
333 Nahanton Street 02159   (617) 965-7410
Supervision: Vaad Harabonim of
Massachusetts.

Synagogues

Orthodox

Congregation B'nai Jacob (Zvhiller-Mezbuz Rebbe)
955 Beacon Street   (617) 227-8200
Web site: www.rebbe.org

North Adams

Synagogues

Conservative

Congregation Beth Israel
265 Church Street 01247   (413) 663-5830
Fax: (413) 663-5830
Email: cbi@bcn.net

Northampton

Synagogues
B'nai Israel
253 Prospect Road 01060   (413) 584-3593

Norwood

Synagogues
Temple Shaare Tefilah
556 Nichols Street 02062   (617) 762-8670

Onset

Hotels
Bridge View Hotel
12 S. Water Street 02558   (508) 295-9820
Welcomes Jewish guests. Self-catering flatlets available. Kosher meat and other products available.

Synagogues

Orthodox

Beth Israel
cnr. of Onset Avenue & Locust Street, PO Box 24 02558   (508) 295-9185
Services 3 times daily from last Sat. in June to Labour Day. Services are also held on the Holy days. Efficiency apartments available near synagogue. Further information from Burt Parker.

Peabody

Bakeries
Anthony's Bakery
4 Lake Street 01906   (508) 535-5335
Supervision: Vaad Harabonim of Massachusetts.

Synagogues

Conservative

Temple Ner Tamid
368 Lowell Street 01960   (508) 532-1293

Independent

Congregation Tifereth Israel
Pierpont Street 01960   (508) 531-8135

Reform

Beth Shalom
489 Lowell Street 01960   (508) 535-2100

Traditional

Congregation Sons of Israel
Park & Spring Streets 01960   (508) 531-7576

Pittsfield (Berkshires)

Organisations
Jewish Federation of the Berkshires
235 East Street 01201   (413) 442-4360

Plymouth

Synagogues

Reform

Congregation Beth Jabob
8 Pleasant Street 02361   (508) 746-1575

Quincy

Synagogues

Conservative

Adas Shalom
435 Adams Street 02169   (617) 471-1818
Temple Beth El
1001 Hancock Street 02169   (617) 479-4309

Orthodox

Beth Israel
33 Grafton Street 02169   (617) 472-6796

Randolph

Bakeries
Zeppy's Bakery
937 North Main Street 02368   (617) 963-9837
Supervision: Vaad Harabonim of
Massachusetts.

Booksellers
Davidson's Hebrew Book Store
1106 Main Street 02368

Synagogues

Conservative

Temple Beth Am
871 N. Main Street 02368   (617) 963-0440

Orthodox

Young Israel – Kehillath Jacob of Mattapan
& Randolph
374 N. Main Street 02368   (617) 986-6461
Young Israel of Mattapan-Randolph
374 N Main Street 02368

Revere

Delicatessens
Myer's Kosher Kitchen
168 Shirley Avenue 02151

Restaurants
Chelsea-Revere J.C.C.
65 Nahant Avenue 02151   (617) 584-8395
Supervision: Vaad Harabonim of
Massachusetts.

Synagogues

Independent

B'nai Israel
1 Wave Avenue 02151   (617) 284-8388

Orthodox

Ahavas Achim Anshei Sfard
89 Walnut Way 02151   (617) 289-1026
Tifereth Israel
43 Nahant Avenue 02151   (617) 284-9255

Salem

Synagogues

Conservative

Temple Shalom
287 Lafayette Street 01970   (508) 741-4880

Sharon

Mikvaot

Orthodox

Young Israel of Sharon
9 Dunbar Street 02067   (781) 784-6112
Operated by the Mikvah Organisation of the
South Shore, Chevrat Nashim Mikvah

Religious Organisations
Eruv Society
                                (614) 784-6112
Eruv maintained by Sharon County Eruv
Society

Synagogues

Conservative

Adath Sharon
18 Harding Street 02067   (617) 784-2517
Temple Israel
125 Pond Street 02067   (781) 784-3986

Orthodox

Chabad Center
101 Worcester Road 02067   (617) 784-8167
Young Israel of Sharon
9 Dunbar Street 02067
                           (617) 784-6112/5391

Reform

Temple Sinai
100 Ames Street 02067   (617) 784-6081

Somerville

Bakeries
La Ronga
599 Somerville Avenue 02143 (617) 625-8600
Supervision: Vaad Harabonim of
Massachusetts.
Pareve. Bread and rolls with KVH emblem only.

Synagogues

Independent

B'nai B'rith of Somerville
201 Central Street 02145   (617) 625-0333

Springfield & Longmeadow

Groceries
Waldbaum's Food Mart
355 Belmont Avenue 01108   (413) 732-3866

Mikvaot
Mikveh Association
1138 Converse Street 01106

Organisations

Jewish Community Center
1160 Dickinson Street 01108   (413) 739-4715
Fax: (413) 739-4747
Kosher Coffee Corner.
Jewish Federation of Greater Springfield
1160 Dickinson Street 01108   (413) 737-4313

Synagogues

Conservative

B'nai Jacob
2 Eunice Dr, Longmeadow 01106
(413) 567-3163
Temple Beth El
979 Dickinson Street 01108   (413) 733-4149
Fax: (413) 739-3415
Daily a.m. and p.m. services.

Orthodox

Beth Israel
1280 Williams St, Longmeadow 01106
(413) 567-3210
Congregation Kodimoh
124 Summer Avenue 01108   (413) 781-0171
The largest Orthodox congregation in New
England.
Kesser Israel
19 Oakland Street 01108   (413) 732-8492
Lubavitcher Yeshiva Synagogue
1148 Converse St, Longmeadow 01106
(413) 567-8665

Reform

Temple Sinai
1100 Dickinson Street 01108   (413) 736-3619

Stoughton

Bakeries

Green Manor
31 Tosca Drive 02072   (617) 828-3018
Supervision: Vaad Harabonim of
Massachusetts.
Shomer Shabbat.
Ruth's Bake Shop
987 Central Street 02021   (617) 344-8993
Supervision: Vaad Harabonim of
Massachusetts.

Restaurants

Dairy

Café Choopar Striar J.C.C.
445 Central Street 02072   (413) 341-2016
Supervision: Vaad Harabonim of
Massachusetts.

Synagogues

Conservative

Congregation Adhavath Torah
1179 Central Street 03083   (617) 344-8733

Dairy

**Striar Jewish Community Center on the
Fireman Campus**
445 Central Street 02072   (617) 341-2016

Sudbury

Synagogues

Independent

Congregation B'nai Torah
Woodside Road 01776   (508) 443-2082

Reform

Congregation Beth El
Hudson Road 01776   (508) 443-9622

Swampscott

Bakeries

Newman's
252 Humphrey Street 01901   (617) 592-1550
Supervision: Vaad Harabonim of
Massachusetts.

Synagogues

Conservative

Beth El
55 Atlantic Avenue 01907   (617) 599-8005
Temple Israel
837 Humphrey Street 01907   (617) 595-6635

Vineyard Haven

Synagogues

Martha's Vineyard Hebrew Center
Center Street 02568   (508) 693-0745

Wakefield

Synagogues

Conservative

Temple Emmanuel
120 Chestnut Street 01880   (617) 245-1886

Waltham

Synagogues
**American Jewish Historical Society
(Brandeis University campus)**
2 Thornton Road 02154   (617) 891-8110
                              Fax: (617) 899-9208

Conservative

Beth Israel
25 Harvard Street 02154   (617) 894-5146

Watertown

Bakeries
Tabrizi Bakery
56A Mt. Auburn Street 02172
                              (617) 926-0880
Supervision: Vaad Harabonim of
Massachusetts.

Wayland

Synagogues

Reform

Templr Shir Tikva
141 Boston Post Road 01778   (508) 358-5312

Wellesley Hills

Synagogues
Beth Elohim
10 Bethel Road 02181   (617) 235-8419

Westboro

Synagogues
B'nai Shalom
117 E. Main Street, PO Box 1019 01581-6019
                              (508) 366-7191

Westwood

Synagogues
Beth David
40 Pond Street 02090   (617) 769-5270

Winchester

Synagogues
Temple Shir Tikvah
PO Box 373 01890   (617) 792-1188

Winthrop

Bakeries
Fabiano Bakery
7 Somerset Avenue 02152   (617) 846-5946
Supervision: Vaad Harabonim of
Massachusetts.

Synagogues

Orthodox

Tifereth Abraham
283 Shirley Street 02152   (617) 846-5063
Tifereth Israel
93 Veteran's Road 02152   (617) 846-1390

Worcester

Contact Information
**Agudath Israel of America Hachnosas
Orchim Committee**
69 S. Flagg Street 01602
Contact Rabbi Reuven Fischer.
Rabbi Hershel Fogelman
22 Newton Avenue   (617) 752-5791
Visitors requiring information about kashrut,
temporary accommodation, etc., should
contact Rabbi Fogelman.

Mikvaot
Mikva, Huntley Street 01602   (508) 755-1257

Organisations
Jewish Federation
633 Salisbury Street 01609   (508) 756-1543

Synagogues

Orthodox

Young Israel of Worcester
889 Pleasant Street 01602   (508) 754-3681

Michigan

Ann Arbor

Mikvaot
Chabad House Mikva
715 Hill Street 48104

Organisations
Jewish Federation/UJA
2939 Birch Hollow Drive 48108
                              (734) 679-0100
                         Fax: (734) 679-0109
                    Email: jccfed@aol.com

Benton Harbour (St Joseph)

Synagogues

Conservative

Temple B'nai Shalom
2050 Broadway 49022

Detroit

Synagogues

With tens of synagogues in the Bloomfield, Oak Park and Southfield areas, visitors are recommmended to contact one of the local religious organisations listed for the nearest synagogue.

Delicatessens

Sarah's Glatt Kosher Deli
15600 W. Ten Mile Road, Southfield 48075
(313) 443-2425

Groceries

Sperber's Kosher Karry-Out
25250 W. Ten Mile Road, Oak Park 48237
(313) 443-2425

Kashrut Information

Council of Orthodox Rabbis
17071 W. Ten Mile Road, Southfield 48075
(313) 559-5005/06

Media

Newspapers

Jewish News
Franklin Road, Southfield 48034

Organisations

B'nai B'rith Hillel Foundations
Wayne State University, 667 Charles Grosberg Religious Ctr. 48202
Hot lunch, sandwiches, salads, soups served during academic year (Sept. – April).
Council of Orthodox Rabbis of Detroit (Vaad Harabonim)
17071 W. Ten Mile Road, Southfield 48075
(313) 559-5005/06
Jewish Community Center of Metr. Detroit
6600 W. Maple Road, W. Bloomfield 48322
(810) 661-1000
Fax: (810) 661-3680
With tens of synagogues in the Bloomfield, Oak Park and Southfield areas, visitors are recommended to contact one of the local religious organisations listed for the nearest synagogue.
Jewish Federation of Metr. Detroit
Telegraph Road, Bloomfield Hills 48303

Machon L'Torah (The Jewish Network of Michigan)
W. 10 Mile Road 48237

Restaurants

Center Branch
Jimmy Prentis Morris Building, 15110 W. Ten Mile Road, Oak Park 48237 (810) 967-4030

East Lansing

Organisations

B'nai B'rith Hillel Foundation
Michigan State University, 402 Linden St., 48823
(517) 332-1916
Fax: (517) 332-4142
Kosher meals available during academic year.

Synagogues

Conservative & Reform

Shaarey Zedek
1924 Coolidge Road 48823

Flint

Organisations

Flint Jewish Federation
619 Wallenberg Street 48502 (810) 767-5922

Synagogues

Conservative

Congregation Beth Israel
5240 Calkins Road 48532 (810) 732-6310

Orthodox

Chabad House
5385 Calkins 48532 (810) 230-0770

Reform

Temple Beth El
501 S. Ballenger Highway 48532
(810) 232-3138

Grand Rapids

Synagogues

Conservative

Congregation Ahavas Israel
2727 Michigan Street N.E. 49506

Orthodox

Chabad House of Western Michigan
2615 Michigan Street N.E. 49506

Reform

Temple Emanuel
1715 E. Fulton Street 49503

Jackson

Synagogues
Temple Beth Israel
801 W. Michigan Avenue 49202

Kalamazoo

Synagogues

Conservative
Sons of Moses
2501 Stadium Drive 49008

Lansing

Synagogues

Reconstructionist
Kehillat Israel
2014 Forest Road 48910   (517) 882-0049

Oak Park

Synagogues

Orthodox
Young Israel of Oak Park
15140 West Ten Mile Road 48237
                                (810) 967-3655

Saginaw

Synagogues

Conservative
Temple B'nai Israel
1424 S. Washington Avenue 48601

Reform
Congregation Beth El
100 S. Washington Avenue 48607

South Haven

Synagogues

Orthodox
First Hebrew Congregation
249 Broadway 49090   (616) 637-1603

Southfield

Synagogues
Young Israel of Southfield
27705 Lahser Road 48034   (248) 358-0154
                         Fax: (248) 358-0154
                   Email: rabg@aol.com

West Bloomfield

Museums
Holocaust Memorial Center
6602 W. Maple Road 48322-3005
                            (810) 661-0840
                       Fax: (810) 661-4204
              Email: info@holocaustcenter.org
                 Web site: holocaustcenter.org
First free-standing holocaust museum in U.S.
Consists of museum, library-archive, garden.
Services include tours, lectures, oral history
program, exhibits, speakers' bureau. No
admission fee.

Synagogues

Orthodox
Young Israel of West Bloomfield
6111 West Maple Road 48322
                (810) 661-4183/855-8722/626-7651

Minnesota

Duluth

Organisations
Jewish Federation & Com. Council
1602 E. 2nd Street 55812   (218) 724-8857

Synagogues

Conservative & Reform
Temple Israel
1602 E. 2nd Street 55812

Orthodox
Adas Israel
302 E. Third Street 55802

Minneapolis

Butchers
Fishman's Kosher
4000 Minnetonka Blvd 55416
                            (612) 926-5611
Glatt butcher and take-out certified by the
local Orthodox vaad.

Contact Information
Rabbi Perez
 55416   (612) 926-3185
Contact for kosher establishments in the area
and for eruv information.

Mikvaot
Knesseth Israel
4330 W. 28th Street 55416   (612) 920-2183
                       Fax: (612) 920-2184

Organisations
Jewish Com. Center of Greater Minneapolis
4330 Cedar Lake Rd. S. 55416

Synagogues

Orthodox
Congregation Bais Yisroel
4221 Sunset Blvd 55416   (612) 926-7867
Knesseth Israel
4330 W. 28th Street 55416   (612) 920-2183

Rochester

Hospitality
Lubavitch Bais Chaya Moussia Hospitality Center
730 2nd Street S.W. 55902   (507) 288-7500
Fax: (507) 286-9329
Email: rstrav@rconnect.com
Also provides Shabbat dinners and hospital visitations. Mikva on premises.

St Paul

Groceries
L'chaim
655 Snelling Avenue 55116

Restaurants

Dairy
Old City Cafe
1571 Grand Avenue   (612) 699-5347
Supervision: Upper Midwest Kashrus.
Dairy/vegetarian. Hours: Sunday, 10 am to 9 pm; Monday to Thursday, 11 am to 9 pm; Friday, to 2 pm. Corner of Grand and Snelling Avenues, both of which are buslines. .

Mississippi

Greenville

Synagogues

Reform

Hebrew Union Congregation
504 Main Street 38701

Greenwood

Synagogues

Orthodox

Ahavath Rayim
Market & George Streets, PO Box 1235
38935-1235   (601) 453-7537

Natchez

Synagogues

Reform

B'nai Israel
Washington & S. Commerce Streets, PO Box 2081 39120
Oldest synagogue in Mississippi

Tupelo

Synagogues

Conservative

B'nai Israel
Marshall & Hamlin Streets 38801

Missouri

Ft. Leavenworth

synagogues

Reform

Ft. Leavenworth Jewish congregation
Main Post Chapel, Pope Avenue 64114
(816) 523-5757

Kansas City

Media

Newspapers

Kansas City Jewish Chroncicle
7375 W. 107th Street, Overland Park 66204
Note: Please consult under Kansas, Overland Park and Prairie Village, since Kansas City spans both Missouri and Kansas.

Organisations
Jewish Federation of Greater Kansas City
5801 W. 115th Street, Suite 201, Overland Park 66211

Restaurants
Sensations
1148 W. 103 Street 64114

synagogues

Conservative

Congregation Beth Shalom
9400 Wornall road 64114   361-2990
Fax: 361-4495

Reform

Temple B'nai Jehudah
712 E. 69th Street 64131   363-1050
                                       Fax: 363-8610
The New reform Temple
7100 Main 64114   523-7809

St Joseph

Synagogues

Conservative

Temple B'Nai Sholem
615 S. 10th Street 64501   (816) 279-2378
                            Fax: (816) 361-4495

St Louis

Bakeries
Schnuck's Nancy Ann Bakery
Olive & Mason   (314) 434-7323

Butchers
Diamant's Kosher Meat Market
618 North & South Road   (314) 721-9624
S. Kohn's
10405 Old Olive St. Road 63141
                                 (314) 569-0727
                            Fax: (314) 569-1723
Sol's, 8627 Olive   (314) 993-9977

Groceries
Lazy Suzan Imaginative Cartering
110 Millwell Drive   (314) 291-6050
Simon Kohn's Kosher Meat & Deli
10424 Old Olive   (314) 569-0727
Sol's Kosher Meat Market
8627 Olive   (314) 993-9977

Kashrut Information
The Vaad Hoeir
4 Millstone Campus 63141

Libraries
The Brodsky Jewish Community Library
12 Millstone Campus Drive 63146

Mikvaot
Mikva, 4 Millstone Campus 63146
                                 (314) 569-2770

Organisations
Jewish Federation of St. Louis
12 Millstone Campus Drive 63146
                                 (314) 432-0020
                            Fax: (314) 432-1277
                     Email: stljf@jon.cjfny.org

**The Vaad Hoeir (United Orthodox Jewish
Community of St. Louis)**
4 Millstone Campus 63141   (314) 569-2770
Recognised Orthodox religious authority for
the city.

Restaurants

Dairy
NoBull Cafe
10477 Old Olive   (314) 991-9533

Meat
Diamant's, 618 North & South Rd.
                                 (314) 712-9624
Simon Kohn's
10424 Old Olive   (314) 569-0727

Synagogues

Orthodox
Young Israel of St Louis
8101 Delmar Blvd 63130   (314) 727-1880

Tours of Jewish Interest
Jewish Tercentenary
Forest Park
Home to the Monument & Flagpole

Montana

Billings

Synagogues

Reform

Congregation Beth Aaron
1148 N. Broadway 59101   (406) 248-6412

Great Falls

Synagogues
Aitz Chayim
PO Box 6192 59406   (406) 542-9521
                 Email: aaron@weissman.com

Missoula

Synagogues
Har Shalom
PO Box 7581 59807   (406) 523-5671

Nebraska

Lincoln

Synagogues

Conservative

Tifereth Israel
3219 Sheridan Blvd. 68502

Reform

South Street Temple B'nai Jeshurun
20th & South Streets 68502

Omaha

Mikvaot
Com. Mikva
323 S. 132nd Street 68154

Organisations
Jewish Federation of Omaha
333 S. 132nd Street   (402) 334-8200

Synagogues
B'nai Israel
PO Box 24161 68124

Conservative

Beth El
14506 California Street 68154

Orthodox

Beth Israel
1502 N. 52nd Street 68104

Reform

Temple Israel
7023 Cass Street 68132

Nevada

Las Vegas

Delicatessens
Casba Glatt Kosher
2845 Las Vegas Blvd   (702) 791-3344
Jerusalem Kosher Restaurant & Deli
1305 Vegas Valley 89109   (702) 791-3668
Rafi's Place
6135 West Sahara 89102   (702) 253-0033
Sara's Place
4972 S. Maryland

Kashrut Information
Community Relations
                             (702) 732-0556

Restaurants

Meat

Jerusalem Glatt Kosher Restaurant
1305 Vegas Valley Dr., 89109
                             (702) 696-1644
                        Fax: (702) 696-0919

Synagogues

Conservative
Midbar Kodesh Temple
33 Cactus Garden, Henderson (702) 454-4848
                        Fax: (702) 454-4847
Shabbat Services: weekly, Fri. 7:30pm, Sat.
9.00am and all holidays Special Services: USY
1st Fri.; Young Family 3rd Fri.; Jr. Congregation
1st Sat. Education: Mommy & Me Mon., Wed.:
Children's programs daily; Pre-K, Judaic
Enrichment Program Mon., Wed., Fri.; Hebrew
school & B'nai Mitzvah Tues., Thurs., Sat.;
Confirmation, and Adult Education programs.
Organizations: Katan, Kadima, Jr. & Sr. USY.
Temple Beth Shalom
1600 E. Oakley Blvd.   (702) 384-5070
                        Fax: (702) 383-3246
Shabbat Service: Fri. 7:30pm (at the Hebrew
Academy); Sat. 9:30am; Daily minyon Mon-Fri.
7:30am; Sat, Sun & holidays 9:00am (at the
synagogue). Education: Adult, Religious and
Hebrew schools, Jews by Choice, Confirmation,
Summer Camp program. Organizations: Senior,
Men's Club, Sisterhood, USY.

Orthodox
Congregation Or-Bamidbar
2959 Emerson Ave.   (702) 369-1175
Shabbat Service: Mon-Fri. 7:00am; Sat.
8:30am; Sun. 9:00am; Mincha & Ma'ariv daily
at sunset. Education: Hebrew School, Sun. 12-
2pm; Judaism Class, Wed. 8pm.
Congregation Shaarei Tefilla
1331 S. Maryland Pkwy.   (702) 384-3565
                Email: aishnevada@aol.com
Mikvah open to the public. Daily minyon &
Shabbat Service: Sun. 9am; Mon-Fri. 7:00am;
Mincha/Maariv 4:30pm. Education: Hebrew
reading crash course; Chumash with Rashi;
Rambam; Mishnyous.
Young Israel Synagogue of Las Vegas
1724 Winners Cup 89117   (702) 360-8909
Shabbat Service: Sat. 9am, Sun. 9am.
Beginners minyon for ages 10-15. Education:
Adult; Bar/Bat Mitzvah training. Organizations:
Sisterhood, NCSY. Radio-talk show: 1230am,
Tues. at 8pm.

Reconstructionist

Valley Outreach Synagogue
Luthern Church, 2 S. Pecos Rd.,, Henderson
(702) 436-4900
Fax: (702) 436-4901
Shabbat Service: 1st Fri. of month 8pm.
Education: Adult Education, Community-wide
Interfaith Education, B'nai Mitzvah Religious,
Prayerbook Study Group. Organizations: Choir,
Chauvrot, Modern Chevra Kaddisha, Bowling
League, Social Action, Couple Activities, Mixed
Doubles, Inter-married Group.

Reform

Bet Knesset Bamidbar
Desert Vista Community Center, 10360 Sun
City Blvd., Sun City   (702) 391-2750
Shabbat Service: 2nd & 4th Fri. 7:30pm.
Congregation Ner Tamid
2761 Emerson Ave.   (702) 733-6292
Fax: (702) 733-8553
CNT Event Hotline: (702) 263-5960. Shabbat
Service: Fri. 7:30pm. Education: Religious and
Hebrew Schools. Confirmation; Pre-school;
Adult Education. Organizations: Sisterhood,
Brotherhood, Golden Chai, Singles, Outreach
(Interfaith), Chauvrot, Jr & Sr Choirs, NTTY and
TNT.
Temple Adat Chavarim
Bonner School, 765 Crestdale Lane
(702) 647-7254
Shabbat Service: Fri. 7:30pm; Tot Shabbat,
7pm. Education: Religious and Hebrew school,
Adult education. Programs: Tot Shabbat, Adult
& Children's Choirs, Youth Group.
Temple Bet Emet
Presbyterian Church, 8601 Del Webb Blvd.,
Sun City   (702) 255-2348
Shabbat Service: 1st & 3rd Fri. 7:30pm.
Temple Beth Am
9001 Hillpointe Road   (702) 254-5110
Fax: (702) 254-0997
Shabbat Service: Fri. 7:30pm; Sat. 10:30am;
Sat. Torah Study 9:30am. Education: Pre-
school, full-day, kindergarten, religious &
hebrew schools, confirmation and growth &
learning center. Adult education.
Organizations: Sisterhood, Men's Club, Youth
Group, Cub Scouts, Chauvrot, B'nai B'rith
Youth, Choirs.

Reform-Traditional

Adat Ari El
3310 S. Jones Blvd.   (702) 221-1230
Fax: (702) 221-1385
AAE Event Hotline: (702) 390-8142. Shabbat
Service: Fri. 7:30pm. Torah Tots: Fri. 7pm.
Education: Adult, Religious and Hebrew
School. Sisterhood: Men's Club, Young Adult
Achedet Group. Organizations: Choir; Youth
Group.

Traditional

Chabad of Southern Nevada
1254 Vista Drive   (702) 259-0770
Fax: (702) 877-4700
Email: chabadlv@aol.com
Web site: www.mazornet.com/chabadiv
Daily services. Mikvah on premises (call (702)
224-0184).
Chabad of Summerlin
2620 Regatta Dr. #117   (702) 259-0770
Shabbat Service: Fri. 6:00pm; Sat. 10:00am.
Special children's service, 11:00am; Sun.
8:30am is the B-L-T service (Bagels, Lox,
Tefillah).

Traditional Conservative

Temple Emanu-El
(702) (Wally Klein) 248-6515 or (Mae
Futterman) 255-1666
Shabbat Service: Fri. 7:30pm. Organizations:
Sisterhood, Chavurah.

Reno

Synagogues

Conservative

Temple Emanu-El
1031 Manzanita Lane at Lakeside Dr. 89509
(702) 825-5600
This is the oldest active congregation in
Nevada.

Reform

Temple Sinai
3405 Gulling Road 89503   (702) 747-5508
Fax: (702) 747-5508
Email: myrabbi@aol.com

New Hampshire

Bethlehem

Synagogues

Conservative

Bethlehem Hebrew Congregation
Strawberry Hill 03574
Temple Israel
66 Salmon Street 03104   (603) 622-6171

Orthodox

Lubavitch
7 Camelot Place 03104   (603) 647-0204
Machzikei Hadas
Lewis Hill Road 03574
Summer only.

Manchester

Media

Newspapers

The Reporter
698 Beech Street 03104   (603) 627-7679
                              Fax: (603) 627-7963
Lists further communities in Amherst, Concord,
Derry, Dover, Durham, Hanover, Keene,
Laconia and Nashua.
The Reporter
698 Beech Street 03104   (603) 627-7679
                              Fax: (603) 627-7963
Lists further communities in Amherst, Concord,
Derry, Dover, Durham, Hanover, Keene,
Laconia and Nashua.

Organisations
Jewish Federation of Greater Manchester
698 Beech Street 03104   (603) 627-7679
                              Fax: (603) 627-7963

Synagogues

Conservative

Temple Israel
66 Salmon St 03104   (603) 622-6171

Orthodox

Lubavitch
7 Camelot Place 03104   (603) 647-0204

Reform

Adath Yeshurun
152 Prospect Street 03104   (603) 669-5650

Portsmouth

Synagogues

Conservative

Temple Israel
200 State Street 03801   (603) 436-5301
The Curator of the Historic Waterfront
Neighbourhood reports that the creation of a
Jewish (Russian immigrants) home at
Strawberry Banke. Tel: 603-433-1100 Fax: 603-
433-1115

New Jersey

Aberdeen

Synagogues

Orthodox

Bet Tefilah
479 Lloyd Road 07747   (908) 583-6262

Atlantic City

Organisations
**Federation of Jewish Agencies of Atlantic
City**

Synagogues

Conservative

Beth El
500 N. Jerome Ave, Margate 08402
                              Fax: (609) 823-1810
Beth Judah
6725 Ventnor Av, Ventnor 08406
Chelsea Hebrew Congregation
4001 Atlantic Av 08401
Community Synagogue
Maryland & Pacific Avs 08401

Orthodox

Rodef Shalom
3833 Atlantic Av 08401

Reform

Beth Israel
2501 Shore Rd, Northfield 08225
Temple Emeth Synagogue
8501 Ventnor Av, Margate 08402

Bayonne

Community Organisations
Jewish Community Centre
1050 Kennedy Blvd 07002   (201) 436-6900

Synagogues

Conservative

Temple Emanuel
735 Kennedy Blvd 07002

Orthodox

Ohab Sholom
1016-1022 Ave. C 07002
Ohav Zedek
912 Ave. C 07002
Uptown Synagogue
49th St. & Ave C 07002

Reform

Temple Beth Am
111 Avenue B 07002

Belmar

Synagogues

Orthodox

Sons of Israel Congregation
PO Box 298 07719

Bergenfield

Butchers

Glatt World
89 Newbridge Road   (201) 439-9675
Supervision: RCBC.

Bordentown

Synagogues

Non-affiliated

Congregation B'nai Abraham
59 Crosswicks Street 08505
Founded in 1918.

Bradley Beach

Synagogues

Orthodox

Congregation Agudath Achim
301 McCabe Avenue 07720

Bridgeton

Organisations
Jewish Federation of Cumberland County

Synagogues

Conservative

Congregation Beth Abraham
330 Fayette Street 08302

Burlington

Synagogues
B'nai Israel
212 High Street 08332

Cherry Hill

Bakeries
Pastry Palace Kosher Bakery
State Highway 70 08034   (609) 429-3606

Butchers
Cherry Hill Kosher Market
907 W. Marlton Pike 08002   (609) 428-6663
                              Fax: (609) 216-0752

Media

Newspapers
The Jewish Community Voice
2393 W. Marlton Pike 08002

Mikvaot
Sons of Israel
720 Cooper Landing Road 08002
                              (609) 667-9700

Organisations
Jewish Federation of Southern New Jersey
2393 W. Marlton Pike 08002   (609) 665-6100

Restaurants

Meat

Maxim's
404 Route 70 East 08034   (609) 428-5045
Supervision: Tri-County Vaad.
Glatt kosher middle eastern cuisine.

Synagogues

Conservative

Beth El
2901 W. Chapel Avenue 08002
Beth Shalom
1901 Kresson Road 08003
Congregation Beth Tikva
115 Evesboro-Medford Road, Marlton

Reform

Congregation M'kor Shalom
850 Evesham Road   (609) 424-4220
                              Fax: (609) 424-2890

Temple Emmanuel
1101 Springdale Road

Cinnaminson
Synagogues
Conservative

Temple Sinai
New Albany Road, & Route 130 08077

Clark
Synagogues
Temple Beth O'r
111 Valley Road 07066   (609) 381-8403

Clifton
Media
Newspapers

Jewish Community News
199 Scoles Avenue 07012

Organisations
Jewish Federation of Greater Clifton-Passaic
199 Scoles Avenue 07012   (201) 777-7031
                          Fax: (201) 777-6701
                Email: yymuskin@jon.cjfny.org

Restaurants
Jerusalem II Pizza
224 Brook Avenue 07055   (201) 778-0960
Kosher Konnection
200 Main Avenue 07055   (201) 777-1120

Synagogues
Conservative

Clifton Jewish Center
18 Delaware Street 07011

Reform

Beth Shalom
733 Passaic Avenue 07012

Colonia
Synagogues
Conservative

Ohev Shalom
220 Temple Way 07067   (908) 388-7222

Cranbury
Synagogues
Jewish Congregation of Concordia
c/o Club House 08512   (609) 655-8136

Cranford
Contact Information
Rabbi Hoffberg   (201) 276-9231
Contact for kosher hospitality.

Synagogues
Conservative

Temple Beth El
338 Walnut Avenue 07016

Deal
Booksellers
Nathan's Judaica Bookstore
256 Norwood Avenue 07723   (908) 531-8657

Restaurants
Deal Gardens   (908) 531-4887
Lhangmao
214 Roosevelt Avenue, Oakhurst 07755

Pizzerias

Jerusalem II Pizza
106 Norwood Avenue 07723   (908) 531-7936

Synagogues
Orthodox

128 Norwood Avenue 07723   (908) 531-3200
Ohel Yaacob Congregation
6 Ocean Avenue, P.O. Box 225 07723-0225
                          (732) 531-0217
                     Fax: (732) 531-2405

East Brunswick
Butchers
East Brunswick Kosher Meats
1020 State Highway 18 08816
                          (908) 257-0007

Synagogues
Conservative

E. Brunswick Jewish Center
511 Ryders Lane 08816   (908) 257-7070

Orthodox

Young Israel of E. Brunswick
193 Dunham Corner Road 08816
                          (908) 254-1860
Young Israel of East Brunswick
195 E Dunhams Corner Road 08816
                          (908) 254-1860

Reform

Temple B'nai Shalom
Old Stage Road & Fern Road 08816
(908) 251-4300

Edison

Butchers
Edison Kosher Meats
State Highway 27, and Evergreen Rd
(201) 549-3707

Community Organisations
Jewish Community Center of Middlesex County
1775 Oak Tree Road 08820

Synagogues

Conservative

Beth El
91 Jefferson Blvd 08817

Elizabeth

Contact Information
Rabbi Elazar Teitz
35 North Avenue 07208
Contact for information about kosher rooms, temporary accommodation, etc.

Delicatessens
Superior Deli & Restaurant
150 Elmora Avenue 07202

Groceries
Kosher Express
155 Elmora Avenue 07202

Mikvaot
Mikva, 35 North Avenue 07208

Restaurants

Dairy

Dunkin' Donuts
186 Elmora Avenue 07202

Meat

New Kosher Special
163 Elmora Avenue 07202   (908) 353-1818

Pizzerias

Jerusalem Restaurant
150 Elmora Avenue 07202

Elmwood Park

Organisations
Elmwood Park Jewish Center
100 Gilbert Ave.,   (201) 797-7320/797-9749

Englewood

Groceries
Kosher By the Case & Less
255 Van Nostrand Avenue 07631
(201) 568-2281
Supervision: RCBC.
The Menageries
41 East Palisade Avenue 07631
(201) 569-2704
Supervision: RCBC.
Dairy and meat.

Mikvaot
Mikva, 89 Huguenot Avenue   (201) 567-1143

Restaurants

Dairy

J.C. Pizza at Jerusalem V
24 W. Palisade Avenue 07631   (201) 569-5546
Supervision: RCBC.

Synagogues

Conservative

Temple Emanu-El
147 Tenafly Road 07631   (201) 567-1300

Orthodox

Ahavath Torah
240 Broad Avenue 07631   (201) 568-1315
Fax: (201) 568-2991
Shomrei Emunah
89 Huguenot Avenue 07631

Fair Lawn

Bakeries
New Royal Bakery
19-09 Fair Lawn Avenue 07410
(201) 796-6565
Supervision: RCBC.
Pat Yisrael.

Bagels

Hot Bagels
6-07 Saddle River Road 07410
(201) 796-9625
Supervision: RCBC.
Dairy. Only the bagels are under supervision.

Hot Bagels
13-38 River Road 07410   (201) 791-5646
Supervision: RCBC.
Dairy. Only the bagels are under supervision.

Butchers
Food Showcase
24-28 Fair Lawn Avenue 07410
    (201) 475-0077
Supervision: RCBC.
Sells food provisions as well.

Groceries
Kosher Express
22-16 Morlot Avenue 07410   (201) 791-8818
Supervision: RCBC.
Petak's Glatt Kosher Fine Foods
19-03 Fair Lawn Avenue 07410
    (201) 797-5010
Supervision: RCBC.
Glatt kosher caterers as well.

Restaurants

Dairy
J.C. Pizza of Fairlawn
14-20 Plaza Road 07410   (201) 703-0801
Supervision: RCBC.

Synagogues
Bris Arushon
2204 Fairlawn Ave.   (201) 791-7200

Fort Lee
Synagogues

Orthodox
Young Israel of Fort Lee
1610 Parker Avenue 07024   (201) 592-1110

Freehold
Restaurants
Fred and Murry's
Pond Road Shopping Center, Route 9 07728
    (908) 462-3343
Not glatt kosher or shomer Shabbat, but has
Conservative supervision.

Synagogues

Orthodox
Agudath Achim
Broad & Stokes Streets 07728

Congregation Agudath Achim
Freehold Jewish Center, Broad & Stokes Streets
07728   (732) 462-0254
Fax: (732) 462-0127
Email: rabgreene@aol.com

Hackensack
Organisations
**Jewish Federation of Community Services of
Bergen County**
170 State Street 07601

Synagogues

Conservative
Temple Beth El
280 Summit Avenue 07601

Haddonfield
Butchers
Sarah's Kosher Kitchen
63 Ellis Road

Hasbrouck Heights
Synagogues

Reform
Temple Beth Elohim
Bourlevard & Charlton Aves.   (201) 393-7707

Highland Park
Booksellers
Highland Park Sefarim & Judaica
227 Raritan Avenue

Groceries
B&E Kosher Meat Market
76 Raritan Avenue   (908) 846-3444
Berkley Bakery
405 Raritan Avenue 08904
Dan's Deli & Meat Market
515 Raritan Avenue 08904
Kosher Catch
239 Raritan Avenue   (908) 572-9052
Mystic Gourmet
229 Raritan Avenue 08904

Mikvaot
Park Mikva
112 S. 1st Avenue 08904

Synagogues

Conservative

Highland Park Conservative Temple & Center
201 S. 3rd Av 08904   (908) 545-6482

Orthodox

Congregation Ahavas Achim
(908) 247-0532
Congregation Etz Ahaim (Sephardi)
230 Denison St 08904   (732) 247-3839
Fax: (732) 545-3191
Email: etzahaim@earthlink.net
Web site: home.earthlink.net/netzahaim
Congregation Ohav Emeth
415 Raritan Avenue 08904   (908) 247-3038

Hillside

Synagogues

Conservative

Shomrei Torah Ohel Yosef Yitzchok
910 Salem Avenue 07205   (908) 289-0770

Orthodox

Congregation Sinai Torath Chaim
1531 Maple Avenue 07205   (908) 923-9500

Hoboken

Synagogues

Conservative

United Synagogue of Hoboken
830 Hudson Street & 115 Park Avenue 07030
(201) 659-2614
Fax: (201) 659-7944

James Burg

Synagogues
Rossmoor Jewish Congregation Meeting Room 08831   (609) 655-0439

Lakewood

Organisations
Ocean County Jewish Federation
301 Madison Avenue 08701   (201) 363-0530

Restaurants
Kosher Experience
Kennedy Blvd., 08701
Supervision: Rabbi Chumsky.
Closed on Shabbat and all holidays and festivals.

Meat

R. & S. Kosher Restaurant and Deli
416 Clifton Avenue 08701   (732) 363-6688
Glatt kosher meat only. Hours: Sunday to Thursday, 12:30 pm to 9 pm; Friday, 8 am to 2:30 pm. On Friday, take-out only.

Synagogues

Conservative

Ahavat Shalom
Forest Avenue & 11th Street 08701

Orthodox

Lakewood Yeshiva
Private Way & 6th Street 08701
Sons of Israel
Madison Avenue & 6th Street 08701

Reform

Beth Am
Madison Avenue & Carey Street 08701

Lawrenceville

Synagogues

Orthodox

Young Israel of Lawrenceville
2556 Princeton Pike 08648   (609) 883-8833

Linden

Synagogues

Conservative

Mekor Chayim Suburban Jewish Center
Deerfield Road & Academy Terrace 07036
(908) 925-2283

Orthodox

Congregation Anshe Chesed
100 Orchard Terrace at St George Av 07036
(908) 486-8616

Livingston

Delicatessens
Super Duper Bagels
498 S. Livingston Avenue 07052
(201) 533-1703
Supervision: Vaad Hakashrus of the Council of Orthodox Rabbis Metrowest.

Restaurants

Moshavi
515 S. Livingston Avenue 07039
(201) 740-8777
Supervision: Vaad Hakashrus of the Council of
Orthodox Rabbis Metrowest.

Pizzerias

Jerusalem Pizza
16 East Mt. Pleasant Avenue 07039
(201) 533-1424
Supervision: Vaad Hakashrus of the Council of
Orthodox Rabbis Metrowest.

Synagogues

Orthodox

Etz Chaim Synagogue
Mt Pleasant Avenue
Synagogue of the Suburban Torah Center
85 W. Mount Pleasant Avenue 07039
(973) 994-0122; 994-2620
Fax: (973) 535-3898

Makwah

Synagogues
Temple Beth Haverim
280 Remjo Valley Road   (201) 512-1983

Manalapan

Restaurants

Meat

Kosher Chinese Express
335 Route 9 South 07726   (908) 866-1677
Fax: (908) 866-1621
Glatt kosher and Shomer Shabbat.

Metuchen

Synagogues

Conservative

Neve Shalom
250 Grove Avenue 08840   (732) 548-2238

Millville

Organisations
Jewish Federation of Cumberland County

Synagogues

Conservative

Beth Hillel
3rd Avenue & Oak Street 08332

Morris Plains

Restaurants

Kosher Delicatessen

Jonathan's Deli Restaurant
2900 Route 10 West 07950   (973) 539-6010
Fax: (973) 539-6011

Morristown

Kashrut Information
Baila Mandel   (973) 267-4184
Ahavath Yisrael operates a kosher food buying
service for the community, dealing only in
strictly kosher products.
Congregation of Ahavath Yisrael
9 Cutler Street 07960   (973) 267-4184
Fax: (973) 898-1711
Email: sofernj@aol.com
This synagogue operates a kosher food buying
service for the community, dealing only in
strictly kosher products.
Rabbinical College of America
226 Sussex Avenue 07960   (973) 267-9404
Fax: (973) 267-5208
Email: rca226@aol.com

Synagogues

Conservative

Morristown Jewish Center
177 Speedwell Avenue 07960   (973) 538-9292

Reform

Temple B'nai Or
Overlook Road 07960

Mount Freedom

Synagogues

Orthodox

Mount Freedom Jewish Center
1209 Sussex Turnpike 07970

New Brunswick

Bakeries
Sam's Club, 290 State Highway 18
(908) 613-9323
Supervision: Kof-K.
This store only.

Synagogues

Orthodox

Chabad House Friends of Lubavitch
8 Sicard St 08901   (908) 828-9191

Reform

Anshe Emeth Memorial Temple
222 Livingston Av 08901   (908) 545-6484

Unaffiliated

Congregation Poile Zedek
145 Neilson St 08901   (908) 545-6123

Newark

Booksellers

Hebrew Bookstore
1923 Springfield Avenue, Maplewood 07040
                                 (201) 763-4244/5

Delicatessens

Arlington Kosher Deli, Restaurant & Caterers
Arlington Shopping Center, 744 Route 46W,
Parsippany 07054   (201) 335-9400
David's Deco-Tessen
555 Passaic Avenue, West Caldwell 07006
                                 (201) 808-3354
                        Fax: (201) 808-5806
Kosher Inn, Newark Airport – International
Building, Terminal B   (201) 961-3300 ext 237
Supervision: Rabbi Eliezer Lipa Weingarten,
Cong. Beth Eliyahu of Shomrei Emunah.
Located after ticket check-point between gates
55 and 58.
Reuben's Deli Delite
500 Pleasant Valley Way, West Orange 07052
                                 (201) 731-6351

Groceries

Zayda's Super Value Meat Market & Deli
309 Irvington Avenue, South Orange 07079
                                 (201) 762-1812

Media

Newspapers

The Metrowest Jewish News
901 Route 10, Whippany 07981
                                 (201) 887-3900
Weekly publication owned by Jewish Fed. of
Metrowest.

Mikvaot

Mikvah of Essex County
717 Pleasant Valley Way, West Orange 07052
Sarah Esther Rosenhaus Mikvah Institutue
93 Lake Road 07960

Organisations

United Jewish Federation of Metrowest
901 Route 10, Whippany 07981
                                 (201) 884-4800
                        Fax: (201) 884-7361

Restaurants

Jerusalem West
16 E. Mt. Pleasant Avenue 07039
                                 (201) 533-1424
Metro Glatt/Delancy Street
515 Livingston Avenue 07039   (201) 992-9189
                        Fax: (201) 992-6430
Fax number for take-out orders

Meat

Pleasantdale Kosher Meat
470 Pleasant Valley Way, West Orange 07052
                                 (201) 731-3216

Synagogues

With dozens of synagogues in the district,
visitors are advised to contact a local or
national religious organisation to locate the
most convenient synagogue.

North Brunswick

Synagogues

Conservative

Congregation B'nai tikvah
1001 Finnegans Lane 08902   (908) 297-0696

Paramus

Organisations

Jewish Center of Paramus
304 Midland Ave.,   (201) 262-7691

Parlin

Synagogues

Conservative

Ohav Shalom
3018 Bordertown Avenue 08859
                                 (201) 727-4334

Parsipanny

Synagogues
Adath Shalom Synagogue

Passaic

Delicatessens

B&Y Kosher Korner Inc.,
200 Main Avenue 07055   (201) 777-1120

Organisations

Meat

Jewish Federation of Greater Clifton-Passaic

Restaurants
Main-Ly Chow
227 Main Avenue 07055   (201) 777-4900

Pizzerias

Jerusalem II Pizza of Passaic
224 Brook Avenue 07055

Synagogues

Orthodox

Young Israel of Passaic-Clifton
200 Brook Avenue 07055   (201) 778-7117

Paterson
Synagogues

Conservative

Temple Emanuel
151 E. 33rd Street 07514

Perth Amboy
Synagogues
Beth Mordechai
224 High Street 08861   (732) 442-2431

Orthodox

Shaarey Teflioh
15 Market Street 08861   (732) 826-2977

Piscataway
Synagogues

Reform

B'nai Shalom
25 Netherwood Avenue 08854
   (908) 885-9444

Plainfield
Synagogues

Conservative

Beth El
225 E. 7th Street 07060   (201) 755-0043

Orthodox

United Orthodox Synagogue
526 W. 7th Street 07060

Reform

Temple Sholom
815 W. 7th Street 07063   (201) 756-6447

Princeton
Synagogues

Traditional

Jewish Center
435 Nassau Street 08540   (609) 921-0100
   Fax: (609) 921-7531

Rahway
Synagogues

Conservative

Temple Beth Torah
1389 Bryant Street 07065   (609) 576-8432

Ridgewood
Synagogues
Temple Israel
475 Grove Street   (201) 444-9320

River Edge
Synagogues

Reform

Temple Sholom
385 Howland Avenue 07661

Roselle
Media

Guides

Shalom Book
843 St Georges Avenue 07203
   (908) 298-8200
   Fax: (908) 298-8220

Organisations
Jewish Federation of Central New Jersey
843 St Georges Avenue 07203
   (908) 298-8200
   Fax: (908) 298-8220

Rumson
Synagogues

Conservative

Congregation B'nai Israel
Hance & Ridge Roads 07760   (908) 842-1800

Scotch Plains

Organisations
Jewish Community Center of Central New Jersey
1391 Martine Avenue 07076   (908) 889-1830

Synagogues

Conservative

Congregation Beth Israel
1920 Cliffwood Street 07076   (908) 889-1830
Fax: (908) 889-5523

Somerset

Synagogues
Temple Beth El
1945 Amwell Road 08873   (201) 873-2325

South River

Community Organisations
Jewish Federation of Greater Middlesex County
230 Old Bridge Turnpike
Middlesex County 08882   (732) 432-7711
Fax: (732) 432-0292
Email: jfednj@aol.com

Synagogues

Traditional

Congregation Anshe Emeth
88 Main Street 08882   (201) 257-4190
See also Edison

Spotswood

Synagogues

Reform

Monroe Township Jewish Center
11 Cornell Avenue 08884   (201) 251-1119

Teaneck

Bakeries
Butterflake Bake Shop
448 Cedar Lane 07666   (201) 836-3516
Supervision: RCBC.
Pat Yisrael.
Gruenbaum Bakeries
477B Cedar Lane 07666   (201) 836-3128
Supervision: RCBC.
Pat Yisrael.

Royal Too Bakery
172 West Englewood Avenue 07666
(201) 833-0114
Supervision: RCBC.
Pat Yisrael.
Sammy's New York Bagels
1443 Queen Anne Road 07666
(201) 837-0515
Supervision: Kof-K.
Pat Yisrael.

Bagels
Hot Bagels
976 Teaneck Road 07666   (201) 833-0410
Supervision: RCBC.
Dairy. Only the bagels are under supervision.

Booksellers
Zoldan's Judaica Center
406 Cedar Lane 07666   (201) 907-0034

Butchers
Glatt Express
1400 Queen Anne Road 07666
(201) 837-8110
Supervision: RCBC.
Sells food provisions as well.
Marketplace at Teaneck
647 Cedar Lane 07666   (201) 692-1290
Supervision: RCBC.
Sells food provisions as well.

Delicatessens
Chopstix
172 West Englewood Avenue 07666
(201) 833-0200
Fax: (201) 833-8326
Supervision: RCBC.
Glatt kosher Chinese take-out. Hours: Sunday to Thursday, 11:30 am to 10 pm; Friday, closing times vary – please call. We accept major credit cards.
Ma'adan
446 Cedar Lane 07666   (201) 692-0192
Supervision: RCBC.
Take-out.

Groceries
Dovid's Fresh Fish Market
736 Chestnut Avenue 07666   (201) 928-0888
Supervision: RCBC.

Mikvaot
Mikveh
1726 Windsor Road 07666   (201) 837-8220

Restaurants

Dairy

Jerusalem Pizza
496 Cedar Lane 07666   (201) 836-2120
Supervision: RCBC.
Plaza Pizza & Restaurant
1431 Queen Anne Road 07666
                             (201) 837-9500
Supervision: RCBC.
Shelly's
482 Cedar Lane 07666   (201) 692-0001
                        Fax: (201) 692-1890
          Email: shellys@noahsark.net
Supervision: RCBC.
Chalav Yisrael. Hours: Monday to Thursday,
10:30 am to 9:30 pm; Sunday, 9 am to 10 pm.
Ten minutes from the George Washington
Bridge.

Meat

Fliegels
456 Cedar Lane 07666   (201) 692-8060
Supervision: RCBC.
Hunan Teaneck
515 Cedar Lane 07666   (201) 692-0099
                        Fax: (201) 692-1907
Supervision: RCBC.
Glatt kosher Chinese and American cuisine. Eat
in or take out. Mashgiach temidi. Hours:
Sunday to Thursday, 11:30 am to 9:45 pm;
Friday, to 4 pm; Saturday night, after Shabbat
until midnight..
Mabat Steak House
540 Cedar Lane 07666   (201) 836-4115
Supervision: RCBC.
Glatt kosher.
Noah's Ark
493 Cedar Lane 07666   (201) 692-1200
                        Fax: (201) 692-1890
          Email: info@noahsark.net
Supervision: RCBC.
Chassidishe shechita meats. Hours: Monday to
Thursday, 10:30 am to 10:30 pm; Friday, 8 am
to 4 pm; Sunday, 9:30 am to 10:30 pm;
Saturday during winter, after Shabbat to
midnight. Ten minutes from the George
Washington Bridge.

Synagogues

Conservative

Beth Sholom
Rugby Rd. & Rutland Av 07666

Jewish Center of Teaneck
70 Sterling Place 07666   (201) 833-0515
                        Fax: (201) 833-0511
          Email: execdir@aol.com

Orthodox

Congregation Beth Aaron
950 Queen Anne Rd 07666   (201) 836-6210
                        Fax: (201) 836-0005
          Email: mail@bethaaron.org
          Web site: www.bethaaron.org
Congregation Bnai Yeshurun
641 W. Englewood Avenue 07666
                             (201) 836-8916
                        Fax: (201) 836-1888
Rinat Yisrael
389 W. Englewood Av 07666
Roemer Synagogue
Whittier School, W. Englewood Av., 07666
Young Israel of Teaneck
868 Perry Lane 07666   (201) 833-4419

Reform

Beth Am
510 Claremont Av 07666
Temple Emeth
1666 Windsor Rd 07666

Tenafly

Restaurants

Dairy

P.K. Café & Pizza at the JCC
411 East Clinton Avenue   (201) 894-0801
Supervision: RCBC.

Trenton

Organisations
**Jewish Federation of Mercer & Bucks
Counties**
999 Lower Ferry Road 08628   (609) 883-5000

Union

Organisations
Jewish Federation of Central New Jersey
Green Lane 07083   (201) 351-5060

Synagogues

Conservative

Beth Shalom
2046 Vauxhall Road 07083
Temple Israel
2372 Morris Avenue 07083   (201) 686-2120

Vineland

Organisations
Jewish Federation of Cumberland County
629 Wood Street, Suite 202-204 08360
(609) 696-4445
Also serves the Bridgeton & Cumberland
County areas

Synagogues

Conservative

Beth Israel
1015 E. Park Avenue 08630

Orthodox

Ahavas Achim
618 Plum Street 08360
Sons of Jacob Congregation
321 Grape Street 08360   (609) 692-4232
Fax: (609) 691-4985
Monday to Friday 6.45 a.m. Saturday 9.00 a.m.
Sunday 7.30 a.m. For evening service, please
call synagogue.

Warren

Organisations
Jewish Federation of Central New Jersey
Suburban Services Office, 150 Mt. Bethel Rd.,
07059   (908) 647-0232
Fax: (908) 647-3115

Synagogues

Reform

Mountain Jewish Community Center
104 Mount Horeb Road 07060
(908) 356-8777

Washington Township

Synagogues
Temple Beth Or
56 Ridgewood Rd.,   (201) 664-7422

Wayne

Organisations
Jewish Federation of New Jersey
1 Pike Drive 07470   (973) 595-0555

Synagogues

Conservative

Shomrei Torah
30 Hinchman Avenue 07470

Reform

Temple Beth Tikvah
950 Preakness Avenue 07470

West New York

Synagogues

Orthodox

Congregation Shaare Zedek
5308 Palisade Avenue 07093   (201) 867-6859

West Orange

Booksellers
Lubavitch Center of Essex County
456 Pleasant Valley Way 07052
(201) 731-0770

Groceries
Gourmet Galaxy
659 Eagle Rock Avenue 07052
(201) 736-0060
Supervision: Vaad Hakashrus of the Council of
Orthodox Rabbis Metrowest.
Dairy and meat available.

Mikvaot
Essex County Ritualarim
717 Pleasant Valley Way 07052
(201) 731-1427; 669-0462

Restaurants

Meat

Eden Wok
478 Pleasant Valley Way 07052
(201) 243-0115
Supervision: Vaad Hakashrus of the Council of
Orthodox Rabbis Metrowest.
Chinese food.

Synagogues

Orthodox

**Congregation Ahawas Achim B'nai Jacob
and David**
700 Pleasant Valley Way 07052
(201) 736-1407

Westfield

Synagogues

Reform

Temple Emanu-El
756 E. Broad Street 07090   (908) 232-6770
Fax: (908) 233-3959

Willingboro

Synagogues
Adath Emanu-El
299 John F. Kennedy Way 08046

Woodbridge

Synagogues

Conservative

Adath Israel
424 Amboy Avenue 07095   (732) 634-9601
                    Fax: (732) 634-1593

Wykoff

Synagogues

Reform

Temple Beth Rishon
585 Russell Ave.,   (201) 891-4466

New Mexico

Alberquerque

Kashrut Information
JFGA   (505) 821-3214

Media

Newspapers

The Link
5520 Wyoming Blvd 87109   (505) 821-3214
                    Fax: (505) 821-3351

Organisations
Jewish Federation of Greater Alberquerque
5520 Wyoming Blvd N.E. 87109
                             (505) 821-3214
                    Fax: (505) 821-3351
                    Email: andrewl@jon.cjfny.org

Las Cruces

Synagogues

Reform

Temple Beth El
702 Parker Road, at Melendres

Los Alamos

Synagogues
Jewish Center
2400 Canyon Road 87544   (505) 662-2440

Rio Rancho

Synagogues

Reform

Rio Rancho Jewish Center
2009 Grande Blvd. 87124   (505) 892-8511

Santa Fe

Contact Information
                             (505) 986-2091
For information about home hospitality,
Shabbat and Mikva

Groceries
Alfalfa's
Jewel Osco
Kaune Food Town

Kosher Food Town
Wild Oats, Market Place
Marketplace Natural Grocery

Wild Oats

Challah

Wolfe's Bagels Comissary
Alberquerque

Organisations
Chabad Jewish Center
1428 Don Gaspar Avenue 87505
                             (505) 983-2000
Kosher food, special holiday services and
events.

Synagogues

Conservative & Reform

Temple Beth Shalom
205 E. Barcelona Road 87501   (505) 982-1376
Rabbi Bentley Tel 505-983-7446

Orthodox

Pardes Yisroel
1308 Don Diego Avenue 87505
                             (505) 989-7711
Mailing address: PO Box 2745, 87504. Mikvah
on premises. Shabbat home hospitality. Kosher
meals. Rabbi Weinberg is Halakhic advisor.

Reform

Congregation Beit Tikvah
PO Box 2112 87504
Temple Beth Shalom
205 E. Barcelona Road 87501   (505) 982-1376
Also Conservative service Shabbat morning.
Religious pre-school on premises.

New York

New York City encompasses so much territory and so much activity that it can sometimes be easy to forget that there is also a whole state named New York. The Empire State stretches from New York City in the south to the Canadian border at Quebec and Ontario provinces in the north; from the New England border with Connecticut, Massachusetts and Vermont in the east to Pennsylvania and the Great Lakes of Erie and Ontario in the southwest and west.

Within this 50,000 square mile expanse lie metropolis, suburb, small town, large city, village, vast state parks and preserves, seashores, islands, high mountains and rolling foothills, and abundant natural wilderness.

To New York City residents, anything outside the five boroughs (Manhattan, Queens, Brooklyn, the Bronx, and Staten Island) is either upstate or Long Island. But within those areas are numerous large and thriving Jewish communities. The cities of Buffalo, Rochester, Binghamton, Syracuse, and Schenectady, the suburban counties of Westchester and Rockland, and the Long Island counties of Nassau and Suffolk count hundreds of thousands of Jews among their residents.

Jewish settlement began in New York in early September 1654 when twenty-three Sephardic and Ashkenazi Jews disembarked at the harbour of New Amsterdam from the French ship *St Catherine*. They had escaped the Spanish Inquisition in Recife, Brazil to settle in the Dutch colony. Though Governor Peter Stuyvesant forbade their admission to his jurisdiction, the travellers' protests to his bosses at the Dutch West India Company were accepted and the Jews were allowed to settle. Ten years later, in 1664, four British men-of-war appropriated New Amsterdam in the name of King Charles II of England, who, in turn, made a gift of it to his brother, James, Duke of York. Hence the name, New York.

Jewish immigration was sparse for the next 150 years, but it increased dramatically, especially in New York City between 1880 and 1924, as more than two million Jews made their way to 'der goldene medinah' (the golden door) from eastern and central Europe.

From that original group of 23 Jews in 1654, some made their way up the Hudson river as far as Albany (now the state capital). Two of them, Asser Levy and Jacob de Lucena, became Hudson river traders and also dealt in real estate in the Albany and Kingston areas. South of Albany, in nearby Newburgh, Jewish merchants established a trading post in 1777, but no Jewish community existed there until 1848.

New York's first Jewish community outside of New York City was the town of Sholom in the Catskill mountains in Ulster county. Founded by twelve families, it no longer exists. The oldest existing community is Congregation Beth El, founded in 1838 in Albany and later merged with Congregation Beth Emeth.

Westchester (just north of New York City) county's present Jewish population of close to 150,000 dates from 1860.

Rockland

Southeast of the Catskills, in Rockland county just north of New York City, are a number of communities with large Hasidic and orthodox populations. New Square, a corruption of the name Skvir, was founded by the Skvirer Hasidim and is incorporated as a separate village within the town of Ramapo. With such an administrative and legal designation,

New Square has its own zoning rules, its own village council, its own mayor, etc., and is run on strictly orthodox precepts. Monroe, Monsey and Spring Valley have very large orthodox and Hasidic communities. Though observant Jews are predominant, these communities are also home to non-Jews and less observant Jews. There are a number of villages in the area which have been incorporated with the express purpose of keeping orthodox and Hasidim out, through regulations such as zoning to prevent synagogues from being built too close to residences and through the prohibition of having a synagogue in one's house.

New York City
Nowhere in the United States is there a city richer in Jewish heritage than New York. From the city's beginnings as a Dutch trading post in the seventeenth century up to the present day, Jews have flocked to New York, made it their home, and left an indelible mark on the city's heritage, language, culture, physical structure, and day to day life. There are more Jews in the New York metropolitan area than in any other city in the world, and more than in any country except Israel. So, without a great deal of effort, just being in this largest urban Jewish community in history affords you the opportunity to be a tourist without concern about the ease of observing kashrut and Shabbat.

New York City is the largest Jewish community in the world outside Israel. The estimated Jewish population of New York City proper is just over one million. Another million or so live in the immediate suburbs which include not only New York, but New Jersey and Connecticut as well. Roughly one-third of American Jews live in and around New York City and virtually every national Jewish organisation has its headquarters here.

New York City neighbourhoods with large Jewish populations are the upper west and upper east sides of Manhattan (modern orthodox and secular Jewish), Borough Park, Williamsburg (orthodox and Hasidic) and Brighton Beach (Russian) in Brooklyn, Forest Hills (Israelis and Russians), Kew Gardens, Kew Garden Hills (orthodox) in Queens, Riverdale in the Bronx, and Staten Island.

In this largest urban Jewish community in history, the Jewish traveller is overwhelmed with choices of where to eat, where to find a minyan, what to see of Jewish interest and so on. And the variety of kosher restaurants makes choosing a pleasure: Chinese, Moroccan, Italian (both meat and dairy), traditional European, Indian, Japanese and seafood.

Though Jews from numerous countries of origin live together throughout New York's Jewish communities, many groups tend to congregate in their own neighbourhoods or sections of neighbourhoods.

Ever since the fateful year of 1654 Jews have been coming to New York City. Sometimes a few, sometimes more, and sometimes by the boatload, as was the case between 1880 and 1924 when some two million Jews entered the United States. Today, nearly one-third of all American Jews live in and around New York City. And though one might argue cause and effect, New York City is still the commercial, intellectual and financial centre of the country.

Synagogues
Hundreds if not thousands of synagogues, chavurot and shtiblech lie within the city, representing the myriad expressions of Judaism: Orthodox, Hasidic, Conservative, Reform and Reconstructionist.

Complete lists of synagogues in all five boroughs can be obtained from the various umbrella organisations listed in the beginning of the section on the USA .

The 1,300-seat, Moorish-style Central Synagogue (Reform) at 652 Lexington Avenue in Manhattan is the city's oldest synagogue on an original site and is an official New York City landmark; the oldest Ashkenazi congregation, founded in 1825, is B'nai Jeshrun (Conservative) at 270 West 89th Street; Shearith Israel, the Spanish and Portuguese synagogue on Central Park West at 70th Street, is one of the oldest congregations in the United States and originated with those 23 refugees from the Spanish Inquisition in Brazil in 1654. The present building still has religious items from the earliest days of the congregation and its small chapel is representative of the American colonial period; Temple Emanu-El (Reform) at Fifth Avenue and 65th Street is not only the city's largest, but the world's largest synagogue. The congregation was founded in 1848 and the building, built in 1929, can seat over 2,000 people; the Fifth Avenue synagogue at 5 East 62nd Street was, until early 1967, presided over by the then Rabbi Dr Immanuel Jakobovits, who later became the Chief Rabbi of Great Britain and the Commonwealth; the Park East synagogue at 163 East 67th Street on the very fashionable Upper East Side was founded in 1890 and is an historic landmark. Kehilath Jeshurun (Orthodox), 125 E. 85th Street, is a popular option if you are on the Upper East Side. On the Upper West Side, Lincoln Square Synagogue (Orthodox), 200 Amsterdam Avenue at 69th Street, and Ohab Zedek (Orthodox), 118 West 95th Street, are both very popular options.

Libraries, Museums, and Institutes of Learning

One of New York's living museums is the Eldridge Street Synagogue (14 Eldridge Street, 212-219-0888). At 108 years old, the Eldridge Street synagogue is a ghost of its former splendour. But, in its heyday at the turn of the century, it was among the busiest synagogues on the Lower East Side, and the first built for that purpose by New York's eastern European Jews. An official New York City landmark, and listed on the National Register of Historic Places, the synagogue is an ongoing restoration project. The synagogue functions as a museum and has a whole host of programmes.

In the same neighbourhood and sociologically related is the Lower East Side Tenement Museum (97 Orchard Street, 212-431-0233). Contrary to popular opinion, the word tenement does not mean slum housing, but a particular building design devised to house the masses of immigrants who came to New York in the latter part of the nineteenth century. Tenements are five- or six-storey walk up buildings distinguished by narrow entry halls and a central air shaft. Each floor contained four apartments. Toilet facilities, located in the hallway, were shared by all the residents. Baths were taken at numerous local public bath houses. The museum, located in a restored tenement built in 1863, shows visitors what tenement life was like via a model apartment. In addition, actors in period dress present 90-minute shows in a small theatre. This is how the vast majority of Jews lived when they first came to New York City.

Ellis Island National Monument (212-269-5755) was once the point of entry for Jews and other immigrants. Some five million Jews came to the United States between 1850 and 1948 and most were processed through immigration at Castle Garden (the present ferry ticket office) or, after 1890, Ellis Island.

The Jewish Museum (Fifth Avenue and 92nd Street, 212-423-3200) has been in existence since 1904. Under the auspices of the Conservative Jewish Theological Seminary, the museum has permanent and changing exhibits and programmes and an excellent collection of Jewish ritual and ceremonial objects.

The library at the Jewish Theological Seminary (3080 Broadway at 122nd Street, 212-678-8000), houses one of the greatest collections of Judaica and Hebraica in the world. Its holdings include a rare manuscript by Maimonides (the Rambam).

The YIVO Institute for Jewish Research (555 West 57th Street, 212-246-6080) houses a large collection of books, documents, photographs and recordings pertaining to Jewish life in Europe before the Holocaust.

Other libraries with large Judaica collections are at Yeshiva University (212-960-5400), the Judaica Collection at the New York Public Library (212-340-0849), New York University (212-998-1212), Columbia University (212-854-1754), the House of Living Judaism at Temple Emanu-El (212-744-1400) and the Leo Baeck Institute (212-744-6400). Inquire at each one individually as to availability of the collections.

The main Jewish universities and seminaries are Yeshiva University which offers undergraduate and graduate degrees in the arts, sciences and humanities, rabbinical study and professional degrees such as medicine and social work, including the renowned Albert Einstein College of Medicine in the Bronx; Hebrew Union College; Touro College and the Jewish Theological Seminary.

Neighbourhoods and areas of historical interest

Manhattan

The Lower East Side has physically changed very little in over a century. Cramped tenements and crowded, dirty streets have always characterised the area. But for the absence of vendors calling out 'I cash clothes' one can get a pretty good idea of what life looked like for Jews newly arrived in New York City from eastern European countries, although it is difficult to imagine the strangeness of a new language or being away from home for the first time.

Although the Lower East Side is not as Jewish as it once was and many Jewish shops have closed, it is appropriate that historical jaunts in New York begin in its tangle of streets and alleys. For the ancestors of some 80 per cent of American Jews, this was the first piece of America they saw. Now other immigrant groups call the Lower East Side home. Settlement houses such as the Henry Street Settlement and the Educational Alliance on East Broadway once served the Jewish immigrant population in their need to learn English and become Americanised. Still in existence, they provide services to current residents, Jewish and non-Jewish alike.

Many Jews still do business in the neighbourhood and the area is full of historic buildings, Jewish shops, foodstores and stores selling all manner of ritual items (kipot, taliltot, tefilin, siddurim, etc). Look along Essex, Orchard, Grand, Rivington, Hester and Canal streets.

One of the best guidebooks for this area (as well as the rest of New York City) is the *AIA* [American Institute of Architects] *Guide to New York City* by Elliot Willensky and Norval White. An organisation called Big Onion Walking Tours gives Lower East Side tours and they are worth a telephone call (212-439-1090).

You may notice that a number of churches on the Lower East Side used to be synagogues. They were re-consecrated as churches when the Jewish community dwindled. But in many cases you still can tell which were synagogues. Look for things like Stars of David on building cornerstones, darkened mezuzah shaped areas on doorposts, and shadows of Stars of David on building façades. They are quite evident if you look.

Synagogues of note in the area are the Bialystoker synagogue (7 Wilet Street); Beth Midrash HaGadol (60 Norfolk Street); First Roumanian American Congregation (89 Rivington Street); and the Eldridge Street Synagogue (14 Eldridge Street).

The only kosher winery in Manhattan is Schapiro's Kosher Winery (126 Rivington Street, 674-4404), founded in 1899. Call for tour information.

And no visit to the Lower East Side would be complete without a dairy meal at Ratner's (Delancy Street). It is the one remaining dairy restaurant in an area that used to support several. For Jewish New Yorkers it is a tie with the past, for visitors it is an experience not to be missed.

Along Second Avenue below 14th Street you can still see the remnants of the scores of Yiddish theatres that once lined the street. Note particularly the movie theatre on Second Avenue at 12th Street, currently the City Cinemas Village East. In the upper level auditorium you can get an idea of what the place looked like when stars like Molly Picon and Boris Tomeshevsky held forth on the stage.

Forty-seventh Street between Fifth Avenue and Avenue of the Americas is the diamond centre. Some 75 per cent of all the diamonds which enter the United States pass through here. As this is overwhelmingly a Jewish and Hasidic business, the street is bustling with diamond dealers concluding deals in the open market atmosphere that is pervasive. Most deals are made with a handshake. There are a number of small kosher restaurants up and down the block and on the mezzanines of office buildings.

Historical Cemeteries

Manhattan
Shearith Israel Cemeteries
Vestiges of early Jewish settlement in New York can be gleaned from the remnants of the community's first cemeteries. The following three are owned by New York's oldest congregation, Shearith Israel, the Spanish Portuguese Synagogue.

First Shearith Israel Graveyard: 55 St. James Place (between Oliver and James St), the first Jewish cemetery in New Amsterdam, was consecrated in 1656 and was located near the present Chatham Square. Its remains were moved to this location. It contains the remains of Sephardic Jews who emigrated from Brazil.

Second Cemetery of the Spanish and Portuguese Synagogue (1805–1829): 72-76 West 11th Street, just east of Sixth Avenue on the south side of the street.

Third Cemetery of the Spanish and Portuguese Synagogue (1829-1851): 98-110 west 21st Street, just west of Sixth Avenue on the south side of the street.

Brooklyn
Green-Wood Cemetery (Fifth Avenue and Fort Hamilton Parkway, Brooklyn) contains the graves of many prominent Jewish figures.

Queens
Fourth Cemetery of the Spanish and Portuguese Synagogue: Cypress Hills Street and Cypress Avenue, Queens. The beautiful chapel and gate were built in 1885.

Arts and Entertainment

As American entertainment is largely a secular Jewish enterprise, one need not look very far for Jewish references in plays and musicals. However, there are some dedicated Jewish theatrical companies and venues: the Jewish Repertory Company (212-831-2000); the American Jewish Theater (212-633-1588); the YM & YWHA (212-427-6000) has several outstanding lecture series, some with specific Jewish themes. For other events of Jewish interest consult one of the weekly listings magazines such as *Time Out New York* or *New York Magazine*, or the Sunday Arts & Leisure section of the *New York Times*. Jewish newspapers with events listings are *Jewish Week*, *Forward*, and *Jewish Press*, all available at most newsstands.

Jewish Neighbourhoods of Interest outside Manhattan

Brooklyn

Williamsburg was for many years the centre of Hasidic life in New York City. But in the last decade many rebbes and their followers have moved to the suburbs, particularly Rockland county. However, a trip to Williamsburg is still worthwhile.

Boro Park is almost completely orthodox and is almost a world apart from the rest of the city.

Crown Heights is populated by Hasidim of many sects, but particularly the Lubavitch, whose world headquarters is at 770 Eastern Parkway. The neighbourhood is not totally Jewish and there are often clashes (sometimes violent) between the Caribbean residents and Jewish residents.

New Jersey

Many towns in northern and central New Jersey are less than 40 minutes travel time by either car or public transport from Manhattan, and as such are part of metropolitan New York. They are: Bayonne, Clifton, Elizabeth, Englewood, Fairlawn, Hackensack, Hoboken, Jersey City, Newark, Passaic, Teaneck, Union and West New York.

Restaurants

By law in New York State, the selling of non-kosher food as kosher is a punishable fraud. Administered by the Kosher Law Enforcement Section of the New York State Department of Agriculture, heavy penalties are imposed on violators. An orthodox rabbi oversees the operation. Businesses selling kosher food must display proper signage, indicating under whose hashgacha they operate, and establishments which sell both kosher and non-kosher food must display that as well, with a sign in block letters no smaller than four inches high.

The Kosher Directory, issued by the Union of Orthodox Jewish Congregations, lists foods and services which bear the symbol. It is available for a charge by calling 212-563-4000. Other reliable kashruth insignias are Circle K and the Hebrew letter KOF-K.

Note that kosher packaged foods, including bread, meat, fish, cake, biscuits and virtually anything you can think of, are widely available in supermarkets throughout the New York metropolitan area. Many foodstores, especially on the Upper West Side of Manhattan and in Jewish neighbourhoods in Brooklyn and Queens, sell fresh kosher prepared meals as well.

Albany

Home Hospitality
Shabbos House
State University of New York, 316 Fuller Road
(518) 438-4227
Email: shabbos@albany.net

Mikvaot
Bnos Israel of the Capital District
190 Elm Street 12202

Synagogues

Conservative

Ohav Shalom
New Krumkill Rd 12208   (518) 489-4706
Temple Israel
600 New Scotland Av 12208   (518) 438-7858

Orthodox

Beth Abraham-Jacob
380 Whitehall Rd 12208
(518) 489-5819; 489-5179
Fax: (518) 489-5179
Email: mbomzer@aol.com
Chabad-Lubavitch Center of the Capital District
122 S. Main Av 12208   (518) 482-5781
Fax: (518) 482-3684
Email: chabad@albany.net
Shomray Torah
463 New Scotland Av 12208

Reform

B'nai Sholom
420 Whitehall Rd 12208   (518) 482-5283
Beth Emeth
100 Academy Rd 12208   (518) 436-9761
At this 160-year-old congregation, Rabbi Isaac Mayer Wise, founder of American Reform Judaism, served when he first arrived in the United States.
Daughters of Sarah Nursing Home
Washington Av. Extension 12208
(518) 456-7831
Traditional service, Sat. 9:15 am. Reform service, Fri. 3 pm.

Amsterdam

Synagogues

Conservative

Congregation of Sons of Israel
355 Guy Park Avenue 12010   (518) 842-8691

Beacon

Synagogues
Hebrew Alliance
55 Fishkill Avenue 12508   (914) 831-2012

Binghamton

Mikvaot
Beth David Synagogue
39 Riverside Drive 13905   (607) 722-1793
Fax: (607) 722-7121
Email: bethdavidsyn@juno.com

Synagogues
Community Center
500 Clubhouse Road 13903   (607) 724-2417
Fax: (607) 824-2311
Email: JCC13850@AOL.com

Conservative

Temple Israel
Deerfield Place, Vestal 13850   (607) 723-7461

Reform

Temple Concord
9 Riverside Drive 13905   (607) 723-7355

Buffalo

Media

Guides

Shalom Buffalo
787 Delaware Av,. 14209   (716) 886-7750
Fax: (716) 886-1367

Newspapers

Buffalo Jewish Review
15 Mohawk Street 14203   (716) 854-2192

Mikvaot
Mikva, 1248 Kenmore Avenue 14216
(716) 875-8451

Organisations
Jewish Federation of Greater Buffalo
787 Delaware Avenue 14209   (716) 886-7750
Fax: (716) 886-1367

Synagogues

Conservative

Beth El
2360 Eggert Road, Tonawanda 14223
(716) 836-3762
Hillel Foundation
40 Capen Blvd 14214   (716) 838-3232

Shaarey Zedek
621 Getzville Rd 14226   (716) 838-3232

Orthodox

B'nai Shalom
1675 N. Forest Rd 14221   (716) 689-8203
Beth Abraham
1073 Elmwood Av 14222   (716) 874-4786
Chabad House
3292 Main St., & N. Forest Rd
14214 &14068   (716) 688-1642

Saranac Synagogue
85 Saranac Avenue 14216   (716) 876-1284
                          Fax: (716) 833-7178
Daily Minyan.
Young Israel of Greater Buffalo
105 Maple Rd, Williamsville 14221
                               (716) 634-0212

Reconstructionist

Temple Sinai
50 Alberta Dr. 14226   (716) 834-0708

Reform

Beth Am
4660 Sheridan Dr 14221   (716) 633-8877
Beth Shalom
Union & Center Sts., Hamburg
Congregation Havurah
6320 Main St. 14221   (716) 874-3517
Judaic Museum of Temple Beth Zion
805 Delaware Avenue 14209-2095
                               (716) 886-7150
                          Fax: (716) 886-7152

Traditional

Kehilat Shalom
700 Sweet Home Rd 14226   (716) 885-6650

Catskills

The famous Catskills region, northwest of New York City, covers parts of Sullivan and Ulster counties. From the 1920s to the late 1960s, the large resort hotels formed the so-called Borscht Belt or Circuit of the entertainment industry. The term circuit, in this sense, comes from vaudeville wherein performers would go from theatre to theatre in various towns all over the United States within an ownership chain. Stars like Jerry Lewis, Milton Berle, Danny Kaye, Eddie Fisher, Sammy Davis Jr and others played to packed houses during the summer season and on holiday weekends during the rest of the year. Many of American show business's biggest names started by

singing, acting or telling jokes on stage on summer evenings in the Catskills. On Shabbat and holidays, the finest cantors could be heard. When a Jew said he or she was going to the mountains, it meant just one thing: the Catskills.

It was in the early part of the twentieth century that Jews from the slums of New York City's lower east side began to visit other Jews who lived and farmed in the Catskills in order to escape the scourge of tuberculosis and other diseases of poverty and crowded living conditions. The fresh air, space and fresh food was a restorative even if other living conditions were pretty rustic. Those Jewish farmers, seldom very successful at working the land, usually took in boarders to make ends meet and out of that grew boarding houses. Whole families would flee to the mountains to get a respite, however brief, from the city.

Boarding houses evolved into kuchaleins, a yiddish word which means to cook alone. To go to a kuchalein meant you shared living space with other families but did your own cooking. These evolved into bungalow colonies. Most bungalows were small and simple places, cheaply constructed and meant for very rudimentary living. It was an inexpensive vacation for what was becoming a burgeoning Jewish middle class barely a generation removed from their immigrant roots and the shtetls of Europe. Hundreds of colonies dotted the Catskills, and entire neighbourhoods would transplant themselves from city to country year after year. It bred another level of camaraderie and Jews who experienced it are wont to wax poetic when reminiscing.

But those boarding houses cum kuchaleins also evolved in another direction: the world renowned Catskills resort hotels. From their humble beginnings at the start of the twentieth century to their bittersweet nadir at its end, dozens of hotels became summer playgrounds for hundreds of thousands of Jews. There were vast opulent resorts like Grossingers, the Nevele, the Concord and Brown's as well as smaller, but no less ornate establishments like Stevensville, Brickman's, the Raleigh, and more haimische hotels like the Pioneer Country Club, Kutsher's, the Pines, the Pineview and several dozen others. Included in the price of a room were huge, multi-course meals, served three times a day. And to work that all off one merely had to avail oneself of every conceivable sport available on the premises.

A few hotels still remain though they are but shadows of their former selves. Maintenance tends to be lax and the facilities are frayed and worn. Some are no longer kosher and reflect the need to attract non-Jewish guests in order to remain viable.

The current generation, the baby-boomers, is more affluent and more cosmopolitan than the previous generation and so tends to go farther afield for holidays. The Catskills have for the most part become the vacation place for Hasidic Jews, who have larger families and lower incomes than their modern orthodox counterparts. They populate the bungalow colonies that generations ago represented the admixture of the Jewish community.

Note that the level of observance varies from hotel to hotel and travellers may want to inquire about this before booking.

Ellenville

Mikvaot
Congregation Ezrath Israel
Rabbi Herman Eisner Square 12428
(914) 647-4450/72
Fax: (914) 647-4472
Mikvah – call for hours.

Fallsburg / South Fallsburg

Hotels
The Pines Resort Hotel

Loch Sheldrake

Synagogues

Orthodox
Young Israel of Vacation Village
PO Box 650 12759   (914) 436-8359

Monticello

Hotels
Kutsher's Country Club
Daily services.

Mikvaot
Mikva, 16 North Street 12701
(914) 794-6757
Summer: Opens at sunset for two hours.
Winter: By appointment only.

Synagogues

Orthodox
Tifereth Israel
18 Landfield Avenue 12701   (914) 794-8470
Fax: (914) 794-8478
Daily services.

Reform
Temple Sholom
Port Jervis & Dillon Roads 12701
Daily services.

Woodbourne

Hotels
Chalet Vim
Glatt kosher.

Clifton Park

Synagogues

Conservative
Beth Shalom
Clifton Park, Center Road 12065
(716) 371-0608

Delmar

Synagogues

Orthodox
Delmar Chabad Center
109 Elsmere Avenue 12054   (716) 439-8280

Reconstructionist
Reconstructionist Havurah of the Capital District
98 Meadowland Street 12054 (716) 439-5870

Dewitt

Synagogues

Orthodox
Young Israel Shaarei Torah of Syracuse
4313 E Genesee Street 13214 (315) 446-6194
Fax: (315) 446-7936

Elmira

Synagogues
Shomray Hadath
Cobbles Park 14905

Reform

B'nai Israel
Water & Guinnip Streets 14905

Fleischmanns

Hotels

Kosher

Oppenheimer's Regis
(914) 254-5080
Fax: (914) 254-4399
Supervision: Rabbinate of K'hal Adas Jeshurun, NYC.
Ooen from Pesach to Succos. Off- season fax 1-732-367-5917

Geneva

Synagogues

Reform

Temple Beth El
755 South Main Street 14456   (315) 789-2945

Glens Falls

Synagogues

Conservative

Shaarey Tefila
68 Bay Street 12801   (518) 792-4945

Reform

Temple Beth El
3 Marion Avenue 12801   (518) 792-4364

Gloversville

Synagogues
Community Center
28 E. Fulton Street 12078

Conservative

Knesseth Israel
34 E. Fulton Street 12078   (518) 725-0649

Harrison

Synagogues

Orthodox

Young Israel of Harrison
207 Union Avenue 10528   (914) 777-1236

Haverstraw

Synagogues
Congregation Sons of Jacob
37 Clove Avenue 10927

Hudson

Synagogues

Conservative

Anshe Emeth
240 Jolsen Blvd. 12534   (518) 828-9040

Ithaca

Synagogues
Temple Beth El
402 N. Tioga Street 14850

Orthodox

Young Israel of Cornell
106 West Avenue 14850   (607) 272-5810

Lake Placid

Synagogues

Traditional

20 Saranac Avenue, PO Box 521 12946-0521
(518) 523-3876
Fax: (518) 891-3458

Long Island

By 1760 Jews had settled on Long Island, whose present-day Jewish population is around 500,000 with some 150 synagogues. Alhough two of New York City's five boroughs, Brooklyn and Queens, are geographically part of Long Island, when New Yorkers say Long Island they mean the counties of Nassau and Suffolk. Large concentrations of Jews are in the communities of West Hempstead, Plainview, Great Neck, Long Beach, Cedarhurst, Lawrence, Hewlett and Woodmere. The four latter are part of what is known as the Five Towns.

Booksellers
Zion Lion
444 West Jericho Turnpike, Huntington Station
11746 (516) 549-5155

Mikvaot
3397 Park Avenue, Oceanside 11572
(516) 766-3242

Restaurants
Te'Avone
64 Manetto Hall Road, Plainview 11803
(516) 822-4545

Baldwin

Restaurants
Ben's, 933 Atlantic Avenue (516) 868-2072

Commack

Community Organisations
Suffolk Jewish Communal Planning Council
74 Hauppage Road 11725 (516) 462-5826
Publishes "Suffolk Jewish Directory"

Restaurants

Meat

Pastrami 'N Friends
110a Commack Road 11725 (516) 499-9537

Dix Hills

Tourist Information
Jewish Geneaology Society of Long Island
37 Westcliff Drive 11746-5627
(516) 549-9532
Email: rsteinig@suffolk.lib.ny.us
Offers assistance to Jewish travellers about
their New York or US roots.

Elmont

Bakeries
Sapienza
1376 Hempstead Turnpike 11003
(516) 352-5232
Supervision: Kof-K.

Five Towns

Incorporates the towns of Cedarhurst, Hewlett,
Inwood, Lawrence and Woodmere.

Bakeries
Hungry Harbor Bakery
311 Central Avenue, Lawrence 11559
(516) 374-1131
Supervision: Vaad HaKashrus of the Five
Towns.
Moish's Bake Shop
536 Central Avenue, Cedarhurst
(516) 374-2525
Supervision: Vaad HaKashrus of the Five
Towns.
Zomick's Bake Shop
444 Central Avenue, Cedarhurst
(516) 569-5520
Supervision: Vaad HaKashrus of the Five
Towns.

Bagels
Gotta Getta Bagel
1033 Broadway, Woodmere 11598
(516) 374-5245
Supervision: Vaad HaKashrus of the Five
Towns.

Donuts
Donut Delite
125 Cedarhurst Avenue, Cedarhurst
(516) 295-5005
Supervision: Vaad HaKashrus of the Five
Towns.
Dunkin' Donuts
299 Burnside Avenue, Lawrence 11559
(516) 239-2052
Supervision: Vaad HaKashrus of the Five
Towns.

Delicatessens
Mauzone
341 Central Avenue, Lawrence 11559
(516) 569-6411
Supervision: Vaad HaKashrus of the Five
Towns.
Take-away.

Groceries
Gourmet Glatt Emporium
137 Spruce Street, Cedarhurst (516) 569-2662
Supervision: Vaad HaKashrus of the Five
Towns.
Supersol
330 Central Avenue, Lawrence 11559
(516) 295-3300
Supervision: Vaad HaKashrus of the Five
Towns.

Kashrut Information
Vaad HaKashrus of the Five Towns
859 Peninsula Blvd., Woodmere 11598
(516) 569-4536

Mikvaot
Peninsula Blvd., Hewlett 11557
(516) 569-5514

Restaurants
Chap-A-Nosh
410 Central Avenue, Cedarhurst
(516) 374-5100
Supervision: Vaad HaKashrus of the Five
Towns.
La-Pina, 600 Central Avenue, Cedarhurst
(516) 569-2922
Supervision: Vaad HaKashrus of the Five
Towns.
Oh Goodie, 540 Central Avenue, Cedarhurst
(516) 569-4663
Supervision: Vaad HaKashrus of the Five
Towns.

Dairy
Bagel Delight
598 Central Avenue, Cedarhurst
(516) 374-7644
Supervision: Vaad HaKashrus of the Five
Towns.
Delicious Kosher Dairy
698 Central Avenue, Cedarhurst
(516) 569-6725
Supervision: Vaad HaKashrus of the Five
Towns.
Jerusalem Pizza Plus
344 Central Avenue, Lawrence 11559
(516) 569-0074
Supervision: Vaad HaKashrus of the Five
Towns.
Pizza Pious
1063 Broadway, Woodmere 11598
(516) 295-2050
Supervision: Vaad HaKashrus of the Five
Towns.
Sabra Kosher Pizza
560 Central Avenue, Cedarhurst
(516) 569-1563
Supervision: Vaad HaKashrus of the Five
Towns.

Ultimate Yogurt Shop
602 Central Avenue, Cedarhurst
(516) 569-7821
Supervision: Vaad HaKashrus of the Five
Towns.

Meat
Cedar Club, 564 Central Avenue, Cedarhurst
(516) 374-1714
Supervision: Vaad HaKashrus of the Five
Towns.
Cho-Sen Island
367 Central Avenue, Lawrence 11559
(516) 374-1199
Supervision: Vaad HaKashrus of the Five
Towns.
Dave's Glatt Kosher Deli Restaurant
1508 Broadway, Hewlett   (516) 374-3296
Supervision: Vaad HaKashrus of the Five
Towns.
Jacob's Ladder
83 Spruce Street, Cedarhurst   (516) 569-3373
Glatt kosher.
King David, 550 Central Avenue, Cedarhurst
(516) 569-2920
Supervision: Vaad HaKashrus of the Five
Towns.
King David Delicatessen and Caterers
550 Central Avenue, Cedarhurst
(516) 569-2920
Supervision: Vaad HaKashrus of the Five
Towns.
Glatt kosher, shomer shabbat. 20 minutes
from JFK International Airport
Traditions
302 Central Avenue, Lawrence 11559
(516) 295-3630
Supervision: Vaad HaKashrus of the Five
Towns.
Wok Tov, 594 Central Avenue, Cedarhurst
(516) 295-3843
Supervision: Vaad HaKashrus of the Five
Towns.

Synagogues

Orthodox
Shaarey Tefila
25 Central Avenue, Lawrence 11559
Young Israel of North Woodmere
634 Hungry Harbor Road, North Woodmere
11581   (516) 791-5099
Email: info@yinw.org

Great Neck

Bakeries
Strauss Bake Shop
607 Middle Neck Road 11023   (516) 487-6853
Supervision: Vaad Harabonim of Queens.

Butchers
Great Neck Glatt
501 Middle Neck Road 11023   (516) 773-6328
                        Fax: (516) 773-4699
Supervision: Vaad Harabonim of Queens.

Media

Newspapers

Long Island Jewish Week
98 Cutter Mill Road 11020   (516) 773-3679
Long Island Jewish World
115 Middle Neck Road 11021   (516) 829-4000

Mikvaot
26 Old Mill Road 11023   (516) 487-2726

Restaurants

Meat

Colbeh
75 N. Station Plaza 11021   (516) 466-8181
Supervision: Kof-K.
Glatt kosher.
Hunan Restaurant
505/07 Middle Neck Road 11023
                           (516) 482-7912
Supervision: Vaad Harabonim of Queens.
Chinese food.
Shish Kabob Palace
90 Middle Neck Road 11021   (516) 487-2228
Supervision: Vaad Harabonim of Queens.

Pizzerias

Great Neck Kosher Pizza
770 Middle Neck Road 11024   (516) 829-2660
Supervision: Kof-K.
La Pizzeria
114 Middle Neck Road 11021   (718) 466-5114
Supervision: Vaad Harabonim of Queens.

Greenvale

Restaurants
Ben's, 140 Wheatley Plaza   (516) 621-3340

Lake Grove

Restaurants
Ben's, 135 Alexander Avenue   (516) 979-8770
                          Fax: (516) 979-8774
Supervision: Rabbi Buchler, Conservative.
Hours: 9 am to 10 pm.

Long Beach

Mikvaot
Sharf Manor, 274 W. Broadway 11561
                              (516) 431-7758

Nassau

Organisations
Jewish Federation of Greater Orange County
360 Powell Avenue 12550   (516) 562-7860

Synagogues
Route 20, Albany Street   (516) 477-6691

New Hyde Park

Kashrut Information
Long Island Commission of Rabbis
1300 Jericho Turnpike 11040   (718) 343-5993

Syosset

Representative Organisations
Conference of Jewish Organisations of Nassau County
North Shore Atrium, 6900 Jericho Turnpike
11791   (516) 364-4477
                          Fax: (516) 921-5092

UJA Federation
6900 Jericho Turnpike 11791   (516) 677-1800

Wantagh

Bakeries
B & B Bakery Bagels
2845 Jerusalem Avenue 11793
Supervision: Kof-K.
Pat Yisrael.

West Hempstead

Bakeries
The Bagel Gallery
540 Hempstead Turnpike 11552
                              (516) 483-7311
Supervision: Vaad Harabonim of Queens.

Butchers
J & M Glatt
177 Hempstead Avenue 11552
                              (516) 489-6926
Supervision: Vaad Harabonim of Queens.

Mikvaot
775 Hempstead Avenue 11552
(516) 489-9358

Restaurants

Pizzerias

Hunki's Kosher Pizza & Felafel
338 Hempstead Avenue 11552
(516) 538-6655
Supervision: Vaad Harabonim of Queens.

Monroe

Synagogues

Conservative

Congregation Eitz Chaim
County Route 105 10950 (914) 783-7424

Reform

Monroe Temple of Liberal Judaism
314 N. Main Street 10950

Monsey

Synagogues

Orthodox

Young Israel of Monsey and Wesley Hills Inc
58 Parker Blvd 10952 (914) 362-1838

Mount Vernon

Synagogues
Brothers of Israel
116 Crary Avenue 10550
Fleetwood
11 E. Broad Street 10552

Munsey

Delicatessens
Bubba's Bagels
Wesley Hills Plaza, Wesley Hills 10952
Sammy's Bagels
421 Route 59 10952

Restaurants
Al di La
455 Route 306, Wesley Hills 10952
Chai Pizza
94 Route 59 10952
Jerusalem Pizza & Restaurant
190 Route 59 10952
New York Café
Cot Route 59 & 306 10952

Meat

Fleigals Restaurant
43 Route 59 10952
Glatt kosher.
Pulkies
455 Route 306, Wesley Hills 10952
Glatt kosher.

New City

Delicatessens
Steve's Deli-Bake
179 South Main Street 10956 (914) 634-8749

Groceries
M&S Kosher Meats
191a South Main Street 10956
(914) 638-9494

Synagogues

Conservative

New City Jewish Center
47 Old Schoolhouse Road 10956
(914) 634-3619
Fax: (914) 634-3481
Email: ncjc@js1.com

Reform

Temple Beth Sholom
228 New Hampstead Road 10956

New Rochelle

Synagogues

Conservative

Bethel, Northfield Road

Orthodox

Anshe Shalom
50 North Avenue 10805 (914) 632-2426
Young Israel
1228 North Avenue 10804
Young Israel of New Rochelle
1228 North Avenue 10804 (914) 777-1236
Contact Rabbi on 835-5581

Reform

Temple Israel
1000 Pine Brook Blvd. 10804

New York City

Bronx

Bakeries
Gruenebaum Bakery
3530 Johnson Avenue 10463   (718) 884-5656
Supervision: Rabbi Jonathan Rosenblatt,
Riverdale Jewish Center.
Heisler's Pastry Shop
3601 Riverdale Avenue, at 236th Street,
Riverdale 10463   (718) 549-0770
Supervision: Westchester Vaad.
Mr Bagel of Broadway
5672 Broadway, Riverdale 10463
                             (718) 549-0408
Supervision: Rabbi Jonathan Rosenblatt,
Riverdale Jewish Center.

Booksellers
Judaica Book Store
3706 Riverdale Avenue 10463   (718) 601-7563

Butchers
Glatt Emporium
3711 Riverdale Avenue, Riverdale 10463
                             (718) 884-1200
Supervision: Rabbi Jonathan Rosenblatt,
Riverdale Jewish Center.
Glatt Shop
3540 Johnson Avenue 10463   (718) 548-4855
Supervision: Rabbi Jonathan Rosenblatt,
Riverdale Jewish Center.
Stock groceries as well.

Restaurants
Riverdelight
3534 Johnson Avenue, Riverdale 10463
                             (718) 543-4270
                        Fax: (718) 543-7545
Supervision: Vaad Harabonim of Riverdale.
Glatt Kosher. Grill, Deli and Middle-Eastern
Cuisine. Take-out and catering.
Second Helpings
3532 Johnson Avenue 10463   (718) 548-1818
Supervision: Rabbi Jonathan Rosenblatt,
Riverdale Jewish Center.
Yeshiva University: Bronx Center
Eastchester Rd. & Morris Park Avenue 10461
                             (718) 430-2131

Dairy
Corner Café and Bakery
3552 Johnson Avenue, Riverdale 10463
                             (718) 601-2861
Supervision: Rabbi Jonathan Rosenblatt,
Riverdale Jewish Center.

Main Event
3708 Riverdale Avenue, Riverdale 10463
                             (718) 601-6246
Supervision: Rabbi Jonathan Rosenblatt,
Riverdale Jewish Center.

Meat
Szechuan Garden Chinese Restaurant
3717 Riverdale Avenue, Riverdale 10463
                             (718) 884-4242
Supervision: Rabbi Jonathan Rosenblatt,
Riverdale Jewish Center.

Brooklyn

Bakeries

Donuts
Dunkin' Donuts
1410 Avenue J 11230
Supervision: Kof-K.
Pat Yisrael.
Dunkin' Donuts
2630 86th Street 11223   (718) 372-0650
Supervision: Kof-K.
Pat Yisrael.
Dunkin' Donuts
1611 Avenue M 11230   (718) 336-2641
Supervision: Kof-K.
Pat Yisrael.

Delicatessens
Eden Delicatessen and Steak House
5928 Glenwood Road 11236   (718) 209-4244
                        Fax: (718) 209-3268
Supervision: Kehilah (Flatbush).
Essex on Coney
1359 Coney Island Avenue 11230
                             (718) 253-1002
                        Fax: (718) 253-8322
Supervision: Kehilah (Flatbush).
Gourmet on J
1412 Avenue J 11230   (718) 338-9181
Supervision: Kehilah (Flatbush).
Meat. Take out only.
Kenereth
1920 Avenue U 11229   (718) 743-2473
Supervision: Kehilah (Flatbush).
Take out only.
Kings Glatt Deli
924 Kings Highway 11223   (718) 336-7500
Supervision: Kehilah (Flatbush).
Take out only.

Groceries

Mountain Fruit
1520 Avenue M 11230   (718) 998-3333
Fax: (718) 998-0726
Supervision: Kehilah (Flatbush).
Hashgacha is limited to bakery, store packaged
dry fruits and nuts, and candies.

Shop Smart
2640 Nostrand Avenue 11210 (718) 377-4166
Fax: (718) 252-2363
Supervision: Kehilah (Flatbush).

Hotels

Midwood Suites
1078 East 15 St. 11230   (718) 253-9535
Fax: (718) 253-3269
Email: shalom@midwoodsuites.com

The Crown Palace Hotel
570-600 Crown Street   (718) 604-1777
Glatt kosher.

The Park House Hotel
1206 48th Street 11219   (718) 871-8100

Libraries

Levi Yitzhak Library
305 Kingston Avenue 11213

Museums

The Chasidic Art Institute
375 Kingston Avenue

Organisations

Orthodox

Lubavitch Movement
770 Eastern Parkway 11213   (718) 221-0500
Fax: (718) 221-0985

Restaurants

La Casa Verde
811 Kings Highway 11223   (718) 339-9733

Lelot Tel Aviv
1910 Coney Island Avenue 11223
(718) 934-6786

Dairy

Garden of Eat-In
1416 Avenue J 11230   (718) 252-5289
Fax: (718) 252-1856
Supervision: Kehilah (Flatbush).

Ossie's Table
1314 50th Street   (718) 435-0635

Meat

Adelman's, 1906 Kings Highway
(718) 336-4915

Cachet Restaurant
815 Kings Highway, Midwood 11223
(718) 336-8600
Fax: (718) 615-2185
Supervision: OU.
Continental cuisine. Reservations only, parties
of 10 or more. Near D, Q, F trains, near buses.

Cafeteria
Crown Palace Hotel, 570-600 Crown Street
11213   (718) 604-1777

Chaap-a-Nosh
1426 Elm Avenue   (718) 627-0072
Supervision: ARK.
Glatt kosher.

Edna's Restaurant & Deli
125 Church Avenue 11202   (718) 438-8207

Gottlieb's Glatt Kosher
352 Roebling Street   (718) 384-9037

Jay & Lloyd's Kosher Deli
2718 Avenue U   (718) 891-5298

Jerusalem Steak House
533 Kings Highway 11223   (718) 336-5115

Kosher Delight Glatt Kosher
1223 Avenue J (E. 13th Street), Flatbush 11230
(718) 377-6873
Fax: (718) 253-6189
Supervision: Rav S.D. Beck and Vaad Rabonim
of Flatbush.
Hours: Sunday to Thursday, 11 am to 11 pm;
Friday, to 3 pm; Saturday, after Shabbat to 1
am. Near Q and D trains.
Major credit cards accepted.

Mama's Restaurant
906 Kings Highway 11223   (718) 382-7200
Supervision: Kehilah (Flatbush).

Shalom Hunan
1619 Avenue M   (718) 382-6000

Shang-Chai Glatt Kosher
2189 Flatbush Avenue 11234 (212) 377-6100

Sushi Kosher
1626 Coney Island Avenue 11230
(718) 338-6363
Fax: (718) 338-2922
Supervision: Kehilah (Flatbush).

Wok Mavin, 97-20A 64th Avenue, Rego Park
(718) 897-2888

Yun-Kee Glatt Kosher
1424 Elm Avenue,
cnr. E.15th Street & Avenue M
(718) 627-0072
Supervision: ARK.

Pizzerias

Chadash Pizza
1919 Avenue M 11230   (718) 253-4793
Supervision: Kehilah (Flatbush).

Kosher Hut
709 Kings Highway 11223   (718) 376-8996
Supervision: Kehilah (Flatbush).

Manhattan

Bakeries
H & H / The Excellent Bagel
2239 Broadway 10024   (212) 692-2435
Supervision: Kof-K.
Mom's Bagels of NY
15 West 45th Street 10036   (212) 764-1566
Supervision: Kof-K.
Pat Yisrael.

Delicatessens
Essen West
226 West 72nd Street 10023   (212) 362-1234
Supervision: OU.
Meat take out and caterers.
L'Chaim Caterers
4464 Broadway 10040   (212) 304-4852
Supervision: Kof-K.
Take out food store.
Lou G. Siegel
240 West 14th Street   (212) 921-4433
Supervision: OU.
Meat, take out only.
Second Avenue Delicatessan-Restaurant
156 2nd Avenue cnr. 10th Street
                              (212) 677-0606

Embassy
Consulate General
800 Second Avenue 10017
Permanent Mission of Israel to the United Nations
800 Second Avenue 10017

Kashrut Information
Agudath Israel World Organisation
84 William Street 10273   (212) 797-9600
The organisation will provide free of charge, a list of people in most major US cities who can provide kashrut information.

Libraries
Butler Library of Colombia University
Broadway at 116th Street 10027
Has some 6,000 Hebrew books and pamphlets, plus 1,000 manuscripts and a Hebrew psalter printed at Cambridge University in 1685 and used by Samuel Johnson at the graduation of the first candidates for bachelor's degrees.
New York University of Judaica and Hebraica
Housing a stunning collection of priceless items.

The Jewish Division of the New York Public Library
Fifth Avenue at 42nd Street 10017
Has 125,000 volumes of Judaica and Hebraica, along with extensive microfilm and bound files of Jewish publications, one of the finest collections in existence.

Museums
Jewish Museum
1109 Fifth Avenue 10028
Jewish Theological Seminary of America
3080 Broadway at 122nd Street 10027
Housing rare manuscripts, including a work in the hand of Maimonides, as well as Cairo Geniza fragments (on application to the librarian only). Has what is believed to be the greatest collection of Judaica and Hebraica in the world.
Leo Baeck Institute
129 E. 73rd Street 10021
Has a vast collection of books, manuscripts, letters and photographs of German Jewish authors, scientists, rabbis and communal leaders, as well as an art collection of the Jews of Germany.
The House of Living Judaism
5th Avenue and 65th Street
Frequently shows paintings and ritual objects. Twelve marble pillars symbolise the Twelve Tribes.
Theological Seminary of America
Fifth Avenue & 92nd Street 10028
An outstanding museum, with permanent displays of Jewish ritual and ceremonial art, along with notable paintings and sculptures.
Yeshiva University
Amsterdam Avenue, 185th Street 10033
The museum's salient feature is a permanent display of scale-model synagogues.
Yivo Institute for Jewish Research
555 West 57th Street 10019   (212) 246-6080
                              Fax: (212) 292-1892
The institute will be moving in early 1999 to: 15 West 16th Street, New York, NY 10011. The telephone and fax numbers listed may change. This Museum has a large collection of original documents on Jewish life, along with some 300,000 volumes, and thousands of photographs, music sheets, gramophone records, etc.

Organisations
UJA-Federation Resource Line
130 E. 59th Street 10022

Conservative

United Synagogue of America
155 Fifth Avenue 10010   (212) 533-7800

Orthodox

Agudat Israel World Organization
84 William Street 10273   (212) 797-9600
Union of Orthodox Jewish Congregations of America
333 Seventh Avenue 10001   (212) 563-4000
Fax: (212) 613-8333

Progressive

World Union for Progressive Judaism
838 Fifth Avenue 10021
(212) 249-0100 ext. 502
Fax: (212) 517-3940

Reform

Union of American Hebrew Congregations
633 Third Avenue 10017-6778
(212) 650-4000
Email: uahc@uahc.org

Sephardic

Union of Sephardic Congregations
8 West 70th Street 10023   (212) 873-0300

Religious Organisations

Young Israel National Office
3 West 16th Street 10011   (212) 929-1525
Fax: (212) 727-9526
Email: ncyi@youngisrael.org
Contact the Department of Synagogue Services at this number for information regarding the Young Israel shul nearest you.

Restaurants

Deniz, 400 East 57th 10022   (212) 486-2255
Pita Express
1470 2nd Avenue (77th Street)
(212) 249-1300
Glatt kosher.
Sammy's Restaurants
157 Chrystie Street   (212) 673-0330
Yeshiva University: Main Center
500 W. 185th Street 10033   (212) 960-5248
Yeshiva University: Mid-town Center
245 Lexington Avenue at 35th Street 10016
(212) 340-7712

Dairy

All-American Health Bar
24 E. 42nd Street   (212) 370-4525

American Cafe Health Bar and Pizza
160 Broadway 10038   (212) 732-1426
Supervision: Kof-K.
Chalav Yisrael.
Broadway's Jerusalem 2
1375 Broadway, at 38th Street 10018
(212) 398-1475
Fax: (212) 212-398-6797
Email: n.y.pies@.com
Supervision: OU.
Chalav Yisrael, Prs Yisruel. Home of the N.Y. Flying Pizza Pies. Visit the 'Jewish Wall of Fame'. 7.00am to 12.00pm. Saturday nights to 2.00am.
Cafe I II III
2 Park Avenue   (212) 685-7117
Cafe Roma, 175 W. 90th Street
(212) 875-8972
Diamond Dairy Kosher Lunchonette
2-4 W. 47th Street 10036   (212) 719-2694
On the gallery overlooking the diamond & jewelry exchange. Hours: Monday to Thursday, 7:30 am to 5 pm; Friday, to 2 pm.
Gourmet Garden
175 Madison Avenue 10016   (212) 545-7666
Fax: (212) 545-7445
Supervision: Kof-K.
Great American Health Bar
821 Third Avenue   (212) 758-0883
Great American Health Bar
35 W. 57th Street   (212) 355-5177
Joseph's Cafe
50 West 72 St   (212) 721-1943
La Bagel, 263 1st Avenue   (212) 388-9292
My Most Favorite Café
120 West 45th Street   (212) 997-5130
Supervision: OU.
Chalav Yisrael.
Ratner's Restaurant and Soup Carts
138 Delancey Street 10002   (212) 677-5588
Supervision: Kof-K.
Call for location of soup carts.
Va Bene
1589 Second Avenue 10028   (212) 517-4448
Fax: (212) 517-2258
Supervision: OU.
Chalav Yisrael Italian restaurant.
Vege-Vege II
544 3rd Avenue   (212) 679-4710
Vegetable Garden
15 East 40th Street 10016   (212) 545-7444
Supervision: Kof-K.
Vegetarian Heaven
364 W. 58th Street   (212) 956-4678

Village Crown Italian Dairy Cuisine
96 Third Avenue 10003
(212) 777-8816; 388-9639
Supervision: Kof-K.

Meat

Abigael's Grill and Caterers
9 East 37th Street 10016 (212) 725-0130
Fax: (212) 725-3577
Supervision: Kof-K.
Glatt kosher.
Alexi on 56
25 West 56th Street 10019 (212) 767-1234
Fax: (212) 767-8254
Supervision: OU.
Continental cuisine. Open for lunch and
dinner. Near public transportation.
Cafe Classico
35 West 57th Street (212) 355-5411
Glatt kosher.
Cafe Masada
1239 First Avenue (212) 988-0950
Chick Chack Chicken
121 University Place (212) 228-3100
Supervision: OU.
China Shalom II
686 Columbus Avenue 10025 (212) 662-9676
Supervision: Kof-K.
Glatt kosher.
Colbeh
43 West 39th Street 10018 (212) 354-8181
Supervision: Kof-K.
Glatt kosher.
Deli Glatt, 152 Fulton Street (212) 349-3622
Deli Kasbah
251 W. 85th Street (212) 496-1500
Supervision: Circle K.
Hours: Sunday to Thursday, 12 pm to 11 pm.
Deli Kasbah II
2553 Amsterdam Avenue (212) 568-4600
Dougie's BBQ
222 West 72nd Street 10023 (212) 724-2222
Supervision: OU.
Glatt kosher.
Galil, 1252 Lexington Avenue 10028
(212) 439-9886
Supervision: Kof-K.
Glatt Dynasty
1049 Second Avenue, East 55th & East 56th
Street 10022 (212) 888-9119
Fax: (212) 888-9163
Supervision: Kof-K.
Glatt kosher.
Grand Deli, 399-401 Grand Street
(212) 477-5200
Supervision: OU.

Haikara (First Class Restaurant)
1016 2nd Avenue (212) 355-7000
Supervision: OU.
Jasmine, 11 East 30 Street, between Madison
and 5th Avenues (212) 251-8884
Supervision: Vaad l'Kashrut Badatz Sepharadic.
Glatt kosher Persian and Middle Eastern
cuisine. Open Sunday to Friday, for lunch and
dinner.
Jerusalem Pita Glatt Kosher
212 E. 45th Street (212) 922-0009
Jewish Theological Seminary of America
cafeteria
3080 Broadway at 122nd Street 10027
(212) 678-8000
Kosher Delight Glatt Kosher
1359 Broadway (37th Street) (212) 563-3366
Kosher Tea Room
193 Second Avenue (212) 677-2947
Glatt kosher.
La Fontana
309 East 83rd Street 10028 (212) 734-6343
Supervision: Kof-K.
Glatt kosher.
Le Marais
150 W. 46th Street 10036 (212) 869-0900
Fax: (212) 869-1016
Supervision: Circle K.
Glatt kosher. Hours: Sunday to Thursday, 12
pm to 12 am; Friday, to 3 pm; Saturday,
October to May, one hour after sundown
to 1 am.
Levana
141 West 69th Street 10023 (212) 877-8457
Fax: (212) 595-7522
Email: levana@prodigy.net
Supervision: Kof-K.
Glatt kosher.
Mendy's Restaurant
61 East 34th Street 10016 (212) 576-1010
Supervision: OU.
Mendy's West
210 West 70th Street 10023 (212) 877-6787
Supervision: OU.
Mr. Broadway
1372 Broadway (212) 921-2152
Supervision: OU.
Pita Express
261 1st Avenue (15th Street) (212) 533-1956
Glatt kosher.
Siegel's Kosher Deli & Restaurant
1646 2nd Avenue (212) 288-3632

Tevere '84'
155 E. 84th Street 10028   (212) 744-0210
Supervision: OU.
Glatt kosher Italian restaurant. Private party
available. Open for lunch, brunch and dinner.

Village Crown
96 Third Avenue 10003   (212) 674-2061
Supervision: Kof-K.
Glatt kosher.

What's Cooking, Manhattan
18 E. 41st Street   (212) 725-6096
Breakfast and lunch are dairy. Dinner is meat.

Vegetarian

Madras Mahal
104 Lexington Avenue   (212) 684-4010

Synagogues

Conservative

Park Avenue Synagogue
50 East 87 Street 10128   (212) 369-2600
Fax: (212) 410-7879
United Synagogue of America
155 Fifth Avenue 10010   (212) 533-7800

Theatres

Dramatics

Jewish Repertory Theatre
c/o Midtown YMHA, 344 E. 14th Street
(212) 505-2667; 674-7200

Winery
Shapiro's Wine Company
124 Rivington Street   (212) 475-7383
In business since 1899. Providing free tours on
telephone call.

Queens

Bakeries
Aron's Bake Shop
71-71 Yellowstone Blvd, Forest Hills 11375
(718) 263-5045
Supervision: Vaad Harabonim of Queens.
Bagel King
116-26 Metropolitan Avenue, Kew Gardens
11418   (718) 847-3623
Supervision: Vaad Harabonim of Queens.
Beigel's Bakery
189-09 Union Turnpike, Flushing 11366
(718) 468-1243
Supervision: Vaad Harabonim of Queens.
G & I Bakeries
69-49 Main Street, Flushing 11367
(718) 261-1155
Supervision: Vaad Harabonim of Queens.
G & I Bakeries
72-22 Main Street, Flushing 11367
(718) 544-8736
Supervision: Vaad Harabonim of Queens.
Hot Bagels and Bialys
67-11 Main Street, Flushing 11367
(718) 575-1071
Supervision: Vaad Harabonim of Queens.
King David Bakery
77-51 Vleigh Place, Flushing 11367
(718) 969-6165
Supervision: Vaad Harabonim of Queens.
L & L Bakery
64-17 108th Street, Forest Hills 11375
(718) 997-1088
Supervision: Vaad Harabonim of Queens.
Queens Kosher Pita
68-36 Main Street, Flushing 11367
(718) 263-8000
Supervision: Vaad Harabonim of Queens.

PARK AVENUE SYNAGOGUE

Rabbi Emeritus **Judah Nadich**
Senior Rabbi **David H. Lincoln**
Rabbi **Kenneth A. Stern**
Asst. Rabbi **Miriam C. Berkowitz**
Senior Cantor **David Leftkowitz**
Cantor **Nancy Abramson**
Executive Director **Barrie Modlin**

50 East 87 Street, New York, NY 10128
Tel. (212) 369 2600 Fax (212) 410 7879

SERVICES
Mornings
Daily: 7.15am
Sundays & Holidays: 9.00am
Sabbath & Festivals: 9.15am

Evenings
Daily: 5.45pm
Fridays: 6.15pm

Donuts

Dunkin' Donuts
83-47 Parsons Blvd, Jamaica 11432
(718) 738-0465
Supervision: Vaad Harabonim of Queens.

Butchers

Abe's Glatt Kosher Meats
98-106 Queens Blvd, Forest Hills 11375
(718) 459-5820
Supervision: Vaad Harabonim of Queens.

Herman Glick's Sons
101-15 Queens Blvd, Forest Hills 11375
(718) 896-7736
Supervision: Vaad Harabonim of Queens.

Herskowitz Glatt Meat Market
164-08 69th Avenue, Hillcrest 11365
(718) 591-0750
Supervision: Vaad Harabonim of Queens.

S & L Glatt Kosher Meats
75-37 Main Street, Flushing 11367
(718) 459-4888
Supervision: Vaad Harabonim of Queens.

Super Glatt Meat
189-23 Union Turnpike, Flushing 11367
(718) 776-7727
Supervision: Vaad Harabonim of Queens.

Tov Hamativ
69-38 Main Street, Flushing 11367
(718) 263-7009
Supervision: Vaad Harabonim of Queens.

Delicatessens

Asian Glatt
67-21 Main Street, Flushing 11367
(718) 793-3061
Supervision: Vaad Harabonim of Queens.
Take out only.

Berso Foods
64-20 108th Street, Forest Hills 11375
(718) 275-9793
Supervision: Vaad Harabonim of Queens.
Take out only.

Mauzone Home Foods of Queens
69-60 Main Street, Flushing 11367
(718) 261-7723
Supervision: Vaad Harabonim of Queens.
Take out only.

Mauzone Take Home Foods
61-36 Springfield Blvd, Bayside 11364
(718) 225-1188
Supervision: Vaad Harabonim of Queens.
Take out only.

Maven Kosher Foods
188-09 Union Turnpike, Fresh Meadows 11366
(718) 479-5504
Supervision: Vaad Harabonim of Queens.
Take out only.

Meal Mart
72-10 Main Street, Flushing 11367
(718) 261-3300
Fax: (718) 261-3435
Supervision: Vaad Harabonim of Queens.
Catering and take out.

The Wok
100-19 Queens Blvd, Forest Hills 11375
(718) 896-0310
Supervision: Vaad Harabonim of Queens.
Chinese. Take out only.

Tov Caterers
97-22 63 Road, Rego Park 11374
(718) 896-7788
Supervision: Vaad Harabonim of Queens.
Take out only.

Groceries

Supersol
68-18 Main Street, Flushing 11367
(718) 268-6469
Supervision: Vaad Harabonim of Queens.

Wasserman Supermarket
72-68 Main Street, Flushing 11367
(718) 544-7413
Supervision: Vaad Harabonim of Queens.

Hotels

Washington Hotel
124-19 Rockaway Beach Blvd, Rockaway Park 11694
(718) 474-9671
Supervision: OU.

Ice Cream Parlors

Yogurt Planet
71-26 Main Street, Flushing 11367
(718) 793-8629
Supervision: Vaad Harabonim of Queens.

Restaurants

Ben's Best Deli Restaurant
96-40 Queens Blvd, Rego Park 11374
(718) 897-1700
Fax: (718) 997-6503
Email: bensbest@worldnet.att.net
Supervision: Vaad Harabonim.

Club Rafael
116-29 Queens Blvd, Forest Hills 11375
(718) 268-3308

Deli Master
184-02 Horace Harding Expressway, Fresh Meadows
(718) 353-3030

Jasa, 27-35 Crescent Street 11102
Jasa Senior Center
27-35 Crescent Street, Astoria (718) 728-9200
Seniors only.
Knish-Knosh
101-02 Queens Blvd, Forest Hills 11375
(718) 897-5554
On The Way, 69 54 Main Street, Flushing
(718) 544-6262

Dairy

Chef's Market
30-00 47th Avenue 11101   (718) 706-8070
Supervision: Vaad Harabonim of Queens.
Jerusalem Café
72-02 Main Street, Flushing 11367
(718) 520-8940
Supervision: Vaad Harabonim of Queens.
Main Street Kosher Corner
73-01 Main Street, Flushing 11367
(718) 263-1177
Supervision: Vaad Harabonim of Queens.

Meat

Annie's Kitchen
72-24 Main Street, Flushing 11367
(718) 268-0960
Supervision: Vaad Harabonim of Queens.
Chinese food.
Berso, 64-20 108th Street Forest Hills, Forest
Hills 11375   (718) 275-9793
Bombay Kitchen
113-25 Queens Blvd, Forest Hills 11375
(718) 263-4733
Burger Nosh
69-48 Main Street, Flushing 11367
(718) 520-1933
Supervision: Vaad Harabonim of Queens.
Chosen Garden
64-43 108th Street, Forest Hills 11375
(718) 275-1300
Supervision: Vaad Harabonim of Queens.
Chinese food.
Empire Kosher Roasters #1
100-19 Queens Blvd, Forest Hills 11375
(718) 997-7315
Supervision: Vaad Harabonim of Queens.
Empire Kosher Roasters #2
180-30 Union Turnpike, Flushing 11365
(718) 591-4220
Supervision: Vaad Harabonim of Queens.
Glatt Wok Express
190-11 Union Turnpike, Flushing 11366
(718) 740-1675
Supervision: Vaad Harabonim of Queens.
Chinese food. Take away service available.

Hapina
69-54 Main Street, Flushing 11367
(718) 544-6262
Supervision: Vaad Harabonim of Queens.
Hapisgah
147-25 Union Turnpike, Flushing 11367
(718) 380-4449
Supervision: Vaad Harabonim of Queens.
Kosher Haven
65-30 Kissena Blvd, Flushing 11367
(718) 261-0149
Supervision: Vaad Harabonim of Queens.
Located at Queens College.
Kosher International Restaurant
JFK Airport, Arrivals Bldg   (718) 656-1757
Kosher King
72-30 Main Street, Flushing 11367
(718) 793-5464
Supervision: Vaad Harabonim of Queens.
Pastrami King
124-24 Queens Blvd, Kew Gardens
(718) 263-1717
Pninat Hamizrach
178-07 Union Turnpike, Fresh Meadows 11365
(718) 591-3367
Supervision: Vaad Harabonim of Queens.
Stargate
73-27 Main Street, Flushing 11367
(718) 793-1199
Supervision: Vaad Harabonim of Queens.
Steakiat Mabat
68-36 Main Street, Flushing 11367
(718) 793-2926
Supervision: Vaad Harabonim of Queens.
Surf Deli
101-05 Queens Blvd, Forest Hills 11375
(718) 459-7875
Supervision: Vaad Harabonim of Queens.
Tashkent Glatt Kosher Restaurant
149-15 Union Turnpike, Flushing 11367
(718) 969-9810
Supervision: Vaad Harabonim of Queens.

Pizzerias

Benjy Kosher Pizza and Falafel
72-72 Main Street, Flushing 11367
(718) 268-0791
Supervision: Vaad Harabonim of Queens.
Dan Carmel Ice Cream and Pizza
98-98 Queens Blvd, Forest Hills 11375
(718) 544-8530
Supervision: Vaad Harabonim of Queens.
Hamakom Pizza
101-11 Queens Blvd, Forest Hills 11375
(718) 275-3992
Supervision: Vaad Harabonim of Queens.

King Solomon Pizza
75-43 Main Street, Flushing 11367
(718) 793-0710
Supervision: Vaad Harabonim of Queens.
Manna Kosher Pizza
68-28 Main Street, Flushing 11367
(718) 520-8754
Supervision: Vaad Harabonim of Queens.
Moshe's Kosher Pizza
181-30 Union Turnpike, Flushing 11366
(718) 969-1928
Supervision: Vaad Harabonim of Queens.
Shimon's Kosher Pizza
71-24 Main Street, Flushing 11367
(718) 793-1491
Supervision: Vaad Harabonim of Queens.
Spencer's Pizza
248-06 Union Turnpike, Bellerose 11426
(718) 347-5862
Supervision: Vaad Harabonim of Queens.

Staten Island

Kashrut Information

Directories

Organised Kashrus Laboratories
PO Box 218, Brooklyn   (718) 851-6428
Including the Circle K trademark.
The Dining Guide of the Jewish Press
(718) 330-1100
Providing information on where to get kosher
Won-Ton soup, couscous, hot pastrami and
corned (salt) beef sandwiches, gefilte fish,
hummus, tehina and much, much more.
UOJC, 333 7th Avenue 10001
(212) 563-4000

Newburgh

Kashrut Information
Agudas Israel
290 North Street 12550   (914) 562-5604

Museums
Gomez Mill House
Millhouse Road, Marlboro 12542
(914) 236-3126
Oldest Jewish residence maintained as a
museum.

Niagara Falls

Organisations
Jewish Federation of Niagara Falls
c/o of Beth Israel   (716) 284-4575

Synagogues

Conservative

Beth Israel
College & Madison Avenues 14305
(716) 285-9894

Reform

Beth El
720 Ashland Avenue 14301   (716) 282-2717

Orangeburg

Synagogues

Conservative

Orangetown Jewish Center
Independence Avenue 10962

Peekskill

Synagogues
First Hebrew Congregation
1821 E. Main Street 10566   (914) 739-0500

Port Chester

Synagogues

Conservative

Kneses Tifereth Israel
575 King Street 10573   (914) 939-1004

Poughkeepsie

Organisations
**Jewish Community Center of Dutchess
County**
110 Grand Avenue 12603   (914) 471-0430

Synagogues

Conservative

Temple Beth El
118 Grand Avenue 12603

Orthodox

Shomre Israel
18 Park Avenue 12603

Reform

Vassar Temple
140 Hooker Avenue 12601

Rochester

Bakeries
Brighton Donuts
Monroe Avenue   (716) 271-6940

Delicatessens

Brownstein's Deli and Bakery
1862 Monroe Avenue 14618
Fox's Kosher Restaurant and Deli
3450 Winton Place 14623

Media

Newspapers

Jewish Ledger
2525 Brighton-Henrietta Town Line R 14623

Organisations

Jewish Community Federation
441 E. Avenue 14607   (716) 461-0490

Restaurants

Meat

Jewish Home of Rochester Cafeteria
2021 S. Winton Road 14618

Saratoga Springs

Synagogues

Conservative

Shaare Tfille
260 Broadway 12866   (518) 584-2370

Orthodox

Congregation Mikveh Israel
26 Lafayette Street 12866   (518) 584-6338
Services in July & August. Kosher food
available.
Orthodox Minyan
510 1/2 Broadway 12866
                    (518) 437-1738; 584-3091

Reform

Temple Sinai
509 Broadway 12866   (518) 584-8730

Scarsdale

Synagogues

Magen David Sephardie Congregation
1225 Weaver Street 10583   (914) 633-3728

Orthodox

Young Israel of Scarsdale
1313 Weaver Street 10583   (914) 636-8686

Schenectady

Synagogues

Conservative

Agudat Achim
2117 Union Street 12309   (518) 393-9211

Orthodox

Beth Israel
2195 Eastern Parkway 12309   (518) 377-3700

Reform

Gates of Heaven
852 Ashmore Avenue 12309   (518) 374-8173

Sharon Springs

Hotels

Yarkony's Adler Spa Hotel
PO Box 328 13459
          (518) 284-2285 or 1 800 448-4314
                         Fax: (518) 284-2215
Supervision: OU.

Spring Valley

Delicatessens
GPG Deli
Main Street 10977

Dairy and Meat

Crest Hill Deli
279 Main Street 10977
Not under supervision.

Home Hospitality
Mendel & Margalit Zuber
32 Blauvelt Road, Monsey 10952
                         (914) 425-6213
The hospitable Zuber's write 'Anyone wishing
to spend a Shabbat or Yom Tov with us is
more than welcome. We are Lubavitch
Chasidim, glatt kosher.'

Hotels
Gartner's Inn
Hungry Hollow Road 10977   (914) 356-0875
Homowack Hotel
PO Box 369 12483
          (914) 647-6800; 800-243-4567
                         Fax: (914) 647-4908
Supervision: OU.
Glatt kosher.

Restaurants
Eli's Bagel Shop
58 N. Myrtle Avenue 10977
Mehadrin Restaurant
82 Route 59, Monsey 10952

Dairy

Sheli's Café and Pizza
126 Maple Avenue 10977   (914) 426-0105
Fax: (914) 362-5004
Email: shely@ucs.net
Supervision: Rabbi Breslaver.

Synagogues

Orthodox

Young Israel of Spring Valley
23 Union Road 10977   (914) 356-3363

Suffern

Synagogues
Bais Torah
89 West Carlton Road 10901   (914) 352-1343
Fax: (914) 352-0841
Email: yhaber@ou.org

Troy

Mikvaot
Troy Chabad Center
2306 15th Street 12180   (518) 274-5572

Synagogues

Conservative

Temple Beth El
411 Hoosick Street 12180   (518) 272-6113

Reform

Congregation Berith Shalom
167 3rd Street 12180   (518) 272-8872
Fax: (518) 272-8984

Utica

Organisations
Jewish Community Federation of the Mohawk Valley
2310 Oneida Street, Mohawk Valley 13501
(315) 733-2343
Fax: (315) 733-2346
The Federation supports the Jewish Community Center.

Synagogues

Conservative

Temple Beth El
1607 Genesee Street 13501

Orthodox

Congregation Zvi Jacob
112 Memorial Parkway 13501

Reform

Temple Emanu-El
2710 Genesee Street 13502

Vestal

Media

Newspapers
Reporter
500 Clubhouse Road 13850   (607) 724-2360
Fax: (607) 724-2311
Email: TReporter@AOL.com

Organisations
Jewish Federation of Broome County
500 Clubhouse Road 13850   (607) 724-2332
Fax: (607) 724-2311

White Plains

Restaurants

Meat

Lexington Glatt Kosher Restaurant
166 Mamaroneck Avenue 10601
(914) 682-7400
Glatt kosher.

Synagogues

Conservative

Temple Israel Center
280 Old Mamaroneck Road, at Miles Avenue
10605   (914) 948-2800
Fax: (914) 948-4755

Orthodox

Hebrew Institute of White Plains
20 Greenridge Avenue 10605   (914) 948-3095
Fax: (914) 949-4676
Email: hebinst@tdt.com
Young Israel
2 Gedney Way   (914) 683-YIWP
Young Israel of White Plains
2 Gedney Way 10605   (914) 683-YIWP

Reconstructionist

Bet Am Shalom
295 Soundview Avenue 10606

Reform

Jewish Community Center
252 Soundview Avenue 10606

Williamsville

Synagogues

Orthodox

Young Israel of Greater Buffalo
105 Maple Road 14221   (716) 634-0212

Woodridge

Hotels

The Lake House Hotel
12789   (914) 434-7800
Glatt kosher. Chalav Yisrael products only.
Open Pesach to Succot.

Yonkers

Synagogues

Conservative

Agudas Achim
21 Hudson Street 10701
Lincoln Park Center
323 Central Park Avenue 10704

Orthodox

Rosh Pinah
Riverdale Avenue 10705
Sons of Israel
105 Radford Avenue 10705

Reform

Temple Emanu-El
306 Rumsey Road 10705

North Carolina

Asheville

Synagogues

Conservative

Congregation Beth Israel
229 Murdoch Avenue 28804

Reform

Beth Ha-Tephila
43 N. Liberty Street 28801

Charlotte

Delicatessens

Shalom Park Sandwich Shoppe
5007 Providence Rd,   (704) 366-5007

The Kosher Mart & Delicatessen
Amity Gardens Shopping Center, 3840 E.
Independence Blvd 28205   (704) 563-8288
Fax: (704) 532-9111
Sandwiches and deli department are glatt
kosher. Groceries also sold here. Hours:
Monday to Wednesday, 10 am to 6 pm;
Thursday, to 7 pm; Friday to 3 pm; Sunday, to
3:30 pm; Shabbat, closed.

Libraries

Speizman Jewish Library
5007 Providence Road 28226

Media

Newspapers

Charlotte Jewish News
(704) 366-5007

Mikvaot

Chabad House
6619 Sardis Road 28270   (704) 366-3984
Fax: (704) 362-1423

Organisations

Jewish Community Center
5007 Providence Road 28226
Jewish Federation
5007 Providence Road 28226   (704) 366-5007
The Hebrew Academy & Social Services
5007 Providence Rd 28226

Synagogues

Conservative

Temple Israel
4901 Providence Road   (704) 362-2796

Orthodox

Chabad House
6619 Sardis Road 28270   (704) 366-3984
Fax: (704) 362-1423
Email: sardis@earthlink.net

Reform

Temple Beth El
5101 Providence Road 28207   (704) 366-1948

Durham

Kashrut Information

Leon Dworsky
1100 Leon Street, Apt. 28 27705

Organisations

Durham-Chapel Hill Jewish Federation and Community Council
205 Mt. Bolus Road, Chapel Hill 27514
(919) 967-6916

Synagogues

Conservative

Beth El
Watts Street 27701

Reform

Judea Reform Congregation
1955 Cornwallis Road 27705   (919) 489-7062
Fax: (919) 489-0611
Email: judeareform@mindspring.com

Fayetteville

Synagogues

Conservative

Beth Israel Congregation
2204 Morganton Road 28303   (919) 484-6462

Greensboro

Organisations

Greensboro Jewish Federation
5509 C West Friendly Avenue 27410-4211
(336) 852-5433
Fax: (336) 852-4346
Email: mfcgsonc@jon.cjfny.org

Synagogues

Conservative

Beth David
804 Winview Drive 27410   (336) 294-0006

Hendersonville

Synagogues

Agudas Israel Congregation
328 N. King Street, PO Box 668 28793

Raleigh

Groceries

Congregation of Sha'arei Israel
7400 Falls of the Neuse Road 27615
(919) 847-8986

Mikvaot

Congregation of Sha'arei Israel
7400 Falls of the Neuse Road 27615
(919) 847-8986

Organisations

Wake County Jewish Federation
3900 Merton Drive 27609   (919) 751-5459

Synagogue

Orthodox

Congregation of Sha'arei Israel
7400 Falls of the Neuse Road 27615
(919) 847-8986

Synagogues

Conservative

Beth Meyer
504 Newton Road 27615   (919) 848-1420

Orthodox

Congregation of Sha'arei Israel
7400 Falls of the Neuse Road 27615
(919) 847-8986

Reform

Temple Beth Or
5315 Creedmoor Road 27612
(919) 781-4895 Pre-school.

Wilmington

Synagogues

Conservative

Beth Jacob
1833 Academy Street 27101

Reform

Temple Emanuel
201 Oakwood Drive 27103   (919) 722-6640

North Dakota

Fargo

Synagogues

Orthodox

Fargo Hebrew Congregation
901 S. 9th Street 58103

Reform

Temple Beth El
809 11th Avenue S. 58103

Ohio

Akron

Organisations

Jewish Community Federation
750 White Pond Drive 44320   (216) 869-2424

Synagogues

Conservative

Beth El
464 S. Hawkins Avenue 44320

Orthodox

Anshe Sfard Synagogue
464 N.Revere Road 44333   (330) 867-7292
Fax: (330) 867-7719

Reform

Temple Israel
133 Merriman Road 44303

Beachwood

Synagogues

Orthodox

Young Israel of Beachwood
2463 South Green Road 44122
(216) 691-9007

Canton

Organisations

Jewish Community Federation
2631 Harvard Avenue 44709   (216) 452-6444

Synagogues

Conservative

Shaaray Torah
423 30th Street N.W. 44709

Orthodox

Agudas Achim
2508 Market Street N. 44704

Reform

Temple Israel
333 25th Street N.W. 44709

Cincinnati

Bakeries

Golf Manor, 2200 Losantiville Avenue
All pareve. Closed Shabbat.

Hot Bagels Factory
7617 Reading Road 45237
Supervision: Vaad Ho-ir of Cincinnati.
DBA Marx Hot Bagels also at 316 Northland
Blvd, 9701 Kenwood Road, 2327 Buttermilk
Crossings and I-75 Cres. Spgs, Kentucky. Open
daily, 6 am to 9 pm.

Hot Bagels Factory
477 E. Kemper Road 45246

Delicatessens

Bilkers
7648 Reading Road 45237

Groceries

Pilder's Kosher Foods
7601 Reading Road 45237

Toron's Meat
1436 Section Road 45237

Libraries

The Hebrew Union College-Jewish Institute of Religion
3101 Clifton Avenue 45220
One of the largest Jewish libraries in the world.
It is also has an art gallery of artefacts, houses
a collection Jewish 'objets d'art' and religious
and ceremonial appurtenances as well as rare
books and manuscripts.

Media

Newspapers

American Israelite
906 Main Street 45202
Oldest Anglo-Jewish weekly in the US.

Mikvaot

Kehelath B'nai Israel
1546 Beaverton Avenue 45237
(513) 761-5260

Organisations

Community Center
1580 Summit Road 45237   (513) 761-7500
Fax: (513) 761-0084

Jewish Federation
1811 Losantiville, Suite 320 45237
(513) 351-3800

Cleveland

Libraries
The Temple Museum of Religious Art Library.
University Circle, Silver Park 44106
Housing Abba Hillel Silver Archives (Jewish art objects, religious & ceremonial treasures, rare books and manuscripts.)

Media

Newspapers

Cleveland Jewish News
3645 Warrensville Center Road, Suite 230
44122

Mikvaot
1774 Lee Road 44118

Museums
Park Synagogue
3300 Mayfield Road 44118
Holding a collection of Jewish art and sculpture.

Organisations
Jewish Community Federation of Cleveland
1750 Euclid Avenue 44115   (216) 566-9200
With literally dozens of synagogues of each demonition, it is advisable to contact the local religious organisation for specific details.

Restaurants
Academy Party Center
Cellar, Hillel Building, CWRU, 11291 Euclid Av., 44106
Academy Party Center
4182 Mayfield Road 44121
Kinneret Kosher Restaurant
1869 S. Taylor Road 44118
Yacov's Restaurant
13969 Cedar Road 44118

Meat
Empire Kosher Kitchen
2234 Warrensville Center Road
                                    (216) 691-0006
Peking Kosher Chinese Restaurant
1841 S. Taylor Road 44118

Synagogues

Orthodox
Young Israel of Cleveland
14141 Cedar Road 44121   (216) 382-5740

Columbus

Bakeries
Block's Hot Bagels
6800 E. Broad Street 43068   (614) 575-9690
Supervision: Vaad Ho-ir of Columbus.
Baked goods only are kosher.
Block's Hot Bagels
2847 Festival Lane   (614) 798-1550
Supervision: Vaad Ho-ir of Columbus.
Baked goods only are kosher. Also, all 5 Block's Hot Bagels located inside the Kroger grocery stores at the Chambers, Gahanna, Pickerington, Reynoldsburg and Bethel Roads have supervised baked goods.
Block's Hot Bagels
3415 E. Broad Street   (614) 235-2551
Supervision: Vaad Ho-ir of Columbus.
Baked goods only are kosher.
Block's Hot Bagels
6115 McNaughten Center   (614) 863-0470
Supervision: Vaad Ho-ir of Columbus.
Baked goods only are kosher.

Delicatessens
Kosher Buckeye
2942 E. Broad Street 43209   (614) 235-8070
Supervision: Vaad Ho-ir of Columbus.

Groceries
Bexley Kosher Market
3012 E. Broad Street 43209   (614) 231-3653
Supervision: Vaad Ho-ir of Columbus.
Butcher as well.

Ice Cream Parlors
Graeters Ice Cream
1534 Lane Avenue   (614) 488-3222
Supervision: Vaad Ho-ir of Columbus.
Graeters Ice Cream
6255 Franz Road   (614) 799-2663
Supervision: Vaad Ho-ir of Columbus.
Graeters Ice Cream
2282 E. Main Street   (614) 236-2663
Supervision: Vaad Ho-ir of Columbus.

Mikvaot
Beth Jacob
1223 College Avenue 43209   (614) 237-8641

Representative Organisations
Jewish Federation
1175 College Avenue 43209   (614) 237-7686

Restaurants

Dairy

Sammy's New York Bagels
40 N. James Road 43213   (614) 237-2444
Fax: (614) 235-4177
Supervision: Vaad Ho-ir of Columbus.
Deli as well.

Meat

Yitzi's Kosher Dogs
207 E. 15th Avenue 43214   (614) 294-3296
Supervision: Vaad Ho-ir of Columbus.

Synagogues

Orthodox

Agudas Achim Synagogue
2767 E. Broad Street 43209   (614) 237-2747
Beth Jacob Congregation
1223 College Avenue 43209   (614) 237-8641
Nusach sefard; daily and Shabbat minyan.
Congregation Ahavas Sholom
2568 E. Broad Street 43209   (614) 252-4815
Fax: (614) 252-1316
Nusach sefard; daily and Shabbat minyan.

Dayton

Accommodation

Home Hospitality

Shomrei Emunah
1706 Salem Avenue 45406   (937) 274-6941
Please contact Mrs Maureen Barasch who will
arrange for accommodations.

Bakeries

Rinaldo's Bake Shoppe
910 W. Fairview Avenue   (513) 274-1311
Rinaldo's Bakery
910 West Fairview Avenue 45406
Supervision: Rabbi Hillel Fox, Beth Jacob
Congregation..
Certain products only, please ask for
certification certidicate.

Media

Newspapers

Dayton Jewish Advocate
4501 Denlinger Road 45426
The Dayton Jewish Advocate
(937) 854-4150 ext. 118
Published by the Jewish Federation of Greater
Dayton by Marshall Weiss, editor.

Mikvaot

556 Kenwood Avenue 45406

Organisations

Jewish Federation of Greater Dayton
4501 Denlinger Road 45426   (937) 854-4150
Jewish Federation of Greater Dayton
Jesse Phillips Building, 4501 Denlinger Rd.,
45426   (513) 854-4150
Fax: (513) 854-2850
Old Age Home
Covenant House, 4911 Covenant House Drive
45426   (937) 837-2651

Kollel

Dayton Community Kollel
1706 Salem Avenue 45406   (937) 274-6941
Email: KollelDayton@Juno.com
The Kollel offers classes in a variety of Judaic
topics in addition to schedule of Torah study.
Visitors are warmly welcomed. Please call for
details. There are no kosher restaurants, hotels
or butchers in Dayton or in the area. However,
the Kollel families will offer kosher hospitality.

Synagogues

Orthodox

Supervision: Rabbi Hillel Fox, Beth Jacob
Congregation..
7020 North Main Street 45415
(937) 274-2149
Supervision: Rabbi Hillel Fox, Beth Jacob
Congregation..
Shomrei Emunah/Young Israel of Dayton
1706 Salem Avenue 45406   (937) 274-6941
Fax: (937) 274-6941
Rabbi's study: (937)-277-4626. Shachris daily:
6:45am. Sundays and National holidays
8:30am. Shabbos and Yom Tov 9:15am.
Mincha and Maariv at sunset, call for details.
Young Israel of Dayton
1706 Salem Avenue 45406   (937) 274-6941

Traditional

Beth Jacob Synagogue

Supervision: Rabbi Hillel Fox, Beth Jacob
Congregation..
Runs a kosher restaurant approximately every
sixth Sunday.

Lorain

Synagogues

Conservative

Agudath B'nai Israel
1715 Meister Road 44053

Toledo

Synagogues
B'nai Israel
2727 Kenwood Blvd. 43606

Orthodox

Congregation Etz Chayim
3852 Woodley Road 43606

Reform

The Temple-Congregation Shomer Emunium
6453 Sylvania Avenue 43560

Westerville

Ice Cream Parlors
Graeters Ice Cream
1 State Street   (614) 895-0553
Supervision: Vaad Ho-ir of Columbus.

Worthington

Ice Cream Parlors
Graeters Ice Cream
654 Hight Street   (614) 848-5151
Supervision: Vaad Ho-ir of Columbus.

Youngstown

Mikvaot
Children of Israel
3970 1/3 Logan Way 44505

Organisations
Youngstown Area Jewish Federation
505 Gypsy Lane 44501   (216) 746-3251

Synagogues

Conservative

Beth Israel Temple Center
2138 E. Market Street, Warren 44483-6104
                                 (330) 395-3877
                            Fax: (330) 394-5918
             Email: bethisrael1@juno.com
Ohev Tzedek-Shaarei Torah
5245 Glenwood Avenue 44512
Temple El Emeth
3970 Logan Way 44505

Reform

Rodef Sholom
Elm Street & Woodbine Avenue 44505
Temple Beth Israel
840 Highland Road, Sharon 16146

Oklahoma

Oklahoma City

Bakeries
Ingrid's Kitchen
2309 N.W. 36th Street 73112

Organisations
Jewish Federation of Greater Oklahoma City
3022 N.W. Expressway, Suite 116 73112
                                 (405) 949-0111

Synagogues

Conservative

Emanuel Synagogue
900 N.W. 47th Street 73106

Reform

Temple B'nai Israel
4901 N. Pennsylvania Avenue 73112

Tulsa

Kashrut Information
Lubavitch of Oklahoma
6622 S. Utica Avenue
                     (918) 492-4499; 493-7006
Hospitality for travellers.

Media

Newspapers

Tulsa Jewish Review
2021 E. 71st Street 74136   (918) 495-1100

Museums
The Gershon & Rebecca Fenster Museum of
Jewish Art
1223 E. 17th Place 74120
Only Jewish Museum in the South-West. Well
worth a visit.

Organisations
Jewish Federation
2021 E. 71st Street 74136   (918) 495-1100

Synagogues

Conservative

B'nai Emunah
1719 S. Owasso Avenue 74120

Reform

Temple Israel
2004 E. 22nd Place 74114   (918) 747-1309
                            Fax: (918) 747-3564
              Email: templeis@ionet.net

Oregon

Ashland

Synagogues
Temple Emek Shalom-Rogue Valley Jewish
Community Center
PO Box 1092 97520　　(541) 488-2909

Eugene

Synagogues

Conservative

Beth Israel
42 W. 25th Avenue 97405　　(503) 485-7218

Portland

Groceries
Albertson's
5415 SW Beaverton Hillsdale Highway 97221
　　(503) 246-1713

Mikvaot
Ritualarium
1425 S.W. Harrison Street 97219
　　(503) 224-3409

Organisations
Jewish Federation of Portland
6651 S.W. Capitol Highway 97219
　　(503) 245-6219

Restaurants
Mittleman Jewish Community Center
(Kosher restaurant)
6651 S. W. Capitol Highway 97219
　　(503) 244-0111

Synagogues

Reform
Neveh Shalom Synagogue

Salem

Synagogues

Reconstructionist
Beth Shalom
1795 Broadway NE 97303　　(503) 362-5004

Pennsylvania

Allentown

Mikvaot
1834 Whitehall Street 18104　　(610) 776-7948

Organisations
Jewish Federation
702 22nd Street 18104　　(610) 821-5500

Restaurants

Meat

Abe's Place
1741 Allen Street 18104　　(610) 435-1735
Supervision: Lehigh Valley Kashrut
Commission.
Closed Shabbat. Call for hours. .
Glatt Kosher Community Center
702 N. 22nd Street 18104　　(610) 435-3571
Since opening hours vary according to season,
it is advisable to call before visiting.

Altoona

Synagogues

Conservative

Agudath Achim
1306 17th Street 16601

Reform

Temple Beth Israel
3004 Union Avenue 16602

Bala Cynwyd

Synagogues

Orthodox

Young Israel of the Main Line
PO Box 117 19004　　(215) 667-3255

Bethlehem

Synagogues

Conservative

Congregation Brith Sholom
Macada & Jacksonville Roads 18017

Orthodox

Agudath Achim
1555 Linwood Street 18017

Blue Bell

Synagogues

Conservative

Tiferet Bet Israel
1920 Skippack Pike 19422　　(610) 275-8797

Easton

Synagogues
B'nai Abraham
16th & Bushkill Streets 18042
Established 1888.

Reform
Temple Covenant of Peace
1451 Northampton Street 18042
(610) 253-2031
Fax: (610) 253 7973
Email: tcp@ fast.net
Established 1839.

Elkins Park

Synagogues

Orthodox
Young Israel of Elkins Park
7715 Montgomery Avenue 19027
(215) 635-3152
Web site:
www.philly-direct.com/frum/brisman.html

Erie

Organisations
Jewish Community Council
Suite 405, Professional Building
161 Peach St. 16501
(814) 455-4474
Fax: (814) 455-4475

Synagogues

Conservative
Brith Sholom Jewish Center
3207 State Street 16508

Reform
Anshe Hesed
10th & Liberty Streets 16502

Harrisburg

Caterers
Norman Gras
3000 Green Street 17110-1234
(717) 234-2196
Supervision: Rabbi Chaim Schertz.
Stocks kosher vending machines at the JCC,
3301 N. Front Street, Tel: 236-9555. Offers
catering for groups as well.
Norman Gras Catering
3000 Green Street 17110-1234
Glatt kosher.

Groceries
Bakeries Giant Food Store and Weis Market
Linglestown Road
Quality Kosher
7th Division Street 17110

Organisations
**United Jewish Community of Greater
Harrisburg**
100 Vaughn Street 17110
(717) 236-9555

Synagogues

Conservative
Beth El
2637 N. Front Street 17110
Chisuk Emuna
5th & Division Streets 17110

Orthodox
Kesher Israel
2945 N. Front Street 17110

Reform
Ohev Sholom
2345 N. Front Street 17110

Hazleton

Synagogues

Conservative
Agudas Israel
77 N. Pine Street 18201

Reform
Beth Israel
98 N. Church Street 18201

Johnstown

Organisations
United Jewish Federation
700 Indiana Street 15905
(814) 536-0647

Synagogues

Conservative
Beth Sholom Congregation
700 Indiana Street 15905

Lancaster

Organisations
Jewish Federation
2120 Oregon Pike 17601
(717) 597-7354

Synagogues
Jewish Community Center
2120 Oregon Pike 17601

Conservative
Beth El
25 N. Lime Street 17602

Orthodox
Degel Israel
1120 Columbia Avenue 17603

Reform
Temple Shaarei Shomayim
N. Duke & James Streets 17602

Levittown
Synagogues
Conservative
Congregation Beth El
21 Penn Valley Road, Fallsington 19054
(215) 945-9500

Reform
Temple Shalom
Edgley Road, off Mill Creek Pkwy. 19057
(215) 945-4154

McKeesport
Synagogues
Conservative
Tree of Life-Sfard
Cypress Avenue 15131

Orthodox
Gemilas Chesed
1400 Summit Street, White Oak 15131
(412) 678-9859

Reform
B'nai Israel
536 Shaw Avenue 15132

Melrose Park
Libraries
Tuttleman Library
Gratz College, Mandell Education Campus,
7601 Old York Road 19027   (215) 635-7304
Email: rhandau@gratz.edu
Specialised library of Judaic and Hebraic studies. Multilingual collection of approximately 100,000 books, periodicals, music and audio-visual materials. Special collections include a rare book room, a music library, and a Holocaust oral history archive. Open to the public.

Philadelphia
Bakeries
Arthur's Bakery
Academy Plaza, Red Lion and Academy Roads
19114   (215) 637-9146
Supervision: Rabbinical Assembly.
An additional location in the Northeast.
Bestcake Bakery
7594 Haverford Avenue 19151
(215) 878-1127
Email: rugalah@aol.com
Supervision: Orthodox Vaad of Philadelphia.
Closed Shabbat and holidays. Intersection Route 1 and Haverford Avenue (close to Route 3).
Buy the Dozen
219 Haverford Avenue
Narberth 19072   (610) 667-9440
Supervision: Orthodox Vaad of Philadelphia.
Wholesale bakery open to the public. Other products include: a variety of cookies and kamish bread (mandel), rugalach.
Dante's Bakery
Richboro Centre, Bustleton and Second Street Pikes, Richboro 18954   (215) 357-9599
Supervision: Rabbinical Assembly.
Hesh's Eclair Bake Shoppe
7721 Castor Avenue 19152   (215) 742-8575
Supervision: Vaad Hakashruth.
Closed on Shabbat.
Hutchinson's Classic Bakery
13023 Bustleton Pike 19116   (215) 676-8612
Supervision: Rabbinical Assembly.
Kaplan's New Model Bakery
901 Norht 3rd Street 19123   (215) 627-5288
Supervision: Rabbi Solomon Isaacson.
Lipkin and Sons Bakery
8013 Castor Avenue 19152   (215) 342-3005
Supervision: Rabbi Abraham Novitsky.
Masi-Schaber Wedding Cakes
1848 South 15th Street 19145
(215) 336-4557
Supervision: Rabbinical Council.
Michael's
6635 Castor Avenue 19149   (215) 745-1423
Supervision: Rabbi Dov Brisman.
Modern Kosher Meat Market
5948 Otgontz Avenue 19141   (215) 924-8259
Supervision: Vaad Hakashruth.
Moish's Addison Bakery
10865 Bustleton Avenue 19116
(215) 469-8054
Supervision: Rabbinical Assembly.

Rilling's Bakery
2990 Southampton Road 19154
(215) 698-6171
Supervision: Rabbinical Assembly.
The Village Baker
2801 South Eagle Road, Newton 18940
(215) 579-1235
Supervision: Rabbinical Assembly.
Viking Bakery
39 Cricket Avenue, Ardmore 19003
(215) 642-9227
Supervision: Rabbi Joshua Toledano.
Weiss Bakery
6635 Castor Avenue 19149   (215) 722-4506
Supervision: Rabbi Dov Brisman.
Closed on Shabbat.
Zach's Bakery
6419 Rising Sun Avenue 19111
(215) 722-1688
Supervision: Rabbinical Assembly.

Booksellers
Bala Judaica Center
222 Bala Avenue
Bala Cynwyd 19004   (610) 664-1303
Fax: (610) 664-4319

Because We Care
Mandell Education Campus
7603 Old York Raod, Melrose Park 19027
(215) 635-4774
Sends baskets of homemade cookies, candy
and food all over the Philadelphia area and out
of town. You can order by telephone. All
proceeds go to the Federation Allied Jewish
Appeal.

Gratz College
Old York Road and Melrose Avenue, Melrose
Park 19027   (215) 635-7300
Fax: (215) 635-7320
Email: gratzinfo@aol.com
Jerusalem Israeli Gift Shop
7818 Castor Avenue 19152   (215) 342-1452
Mazel Stuff
44 Antler Drive, Holland 18966
(610) 860-7744
**National Museum of American Jewish
History**
55 North 5th Street, Independence Mall East
19106-2197   (215) 923-3811
Fax: (215) 923-0763
Email: nmajh@nmajh.org
Web site: www.nmajh.org
Exhibition 'Creating American Jews' explores
the evolution of Jewish identity in America.

Neo Judiaca Gifts   (215) 922-1161
Provides mail-order and by-appointment sales
of Jewish giftware.
Raanan Enterprises
1096 Sparrow Road, Jenkintown 19046
(215) 886-1297
Provides mail-order and by appointment sales
of Jewish books, cassettes and giftware for
children. Provides merchandise for
organisation-sponsored Jewish bookfairs.
Rosen's Hebrew Books and Gifts
6743 Castor Avenue 19149   (215) 742-2397
Rosenberg Hebrew Book Store
6408 Castor Avenue 19149
Rosenberg Hebrew Book Store
409 Old York Road, Jenkintown 19046
(215) 884-1728; 800-301-8608
Fax: (215) 884-6648
Rosenberg Hebrew Book Store (Northeast)
6408 Castor Avenue 19149   (215) 744-5205
Fax: (215) 533-9248

Butchers
Aries Kosher Meats
6530 Castor Avenue 19149   (215) 533-3222
Supervision: Vaad Hakashruth.
Best Value Kosher Meat Center
8564 Bustleton Avenue 19152
(215) 342-1902
Supervision: Rabbi Dov Brisman.
Bustleton Kosher Meat Market
6834 Bustlton Avenue 19149   (215) 332-0100
Supervision: Rabbi Shalom Novoseller.
Glendale Meats
7730 Bustleton Avenue 19152
(215) 725-4100
Supervision: Vaad Hakashruth.
Main Line Kosher Meats
75621 Haverford Avenue 19151
(215) 877-3222
Supervision: Vaad Hakashruth.
Rhawnhurst Kosher Meat Market
8261 Bustleton Avenue 19152 (215) 742-5287
Supervision: Vaad Hakashruth.
Simons Kosher Meats and Poultry
6926 Bustleton Avenue 19149
(215) 624-5695
Supervision: Vaad Hakashruth.
Wallace's Krewstown Kosher Meat Market
8919 Krewstown Road 19115   (215) 464-7800
Supervision: Vaad Hakashruth.

Contact Information
Jewish Information and Referral Service
226 South 16th Street 19102   (215) 893-5821
Fax: (215) 545-1982
Email: 1youman@jon.cjfny.org
A free confidential service that provides
answers to questions about Jewish
organisations, institutions, community services
and various subjects of Jewish interest in the
five-county Greater Philadelphia area. JIRS is
the connection to the Jewish community. It is
open to callers during regular working hours.

Embassy
Consulate General
230 South 15th Street 19102

Groceries
Best Value Losher Meat Center
8564 Bustleton Avenue 19152
(215) 342-1902
Supervision: Rabbi Dov Brisman.
Kosher plus
7534 Haverford Avenue 19151
(215) 871-0774
Fax: (215) 871-0779
Supervision: Orthodox Vaad of Philadelphia.
Milk and Honey
7618 Castor Avenue 19152   (215) 342-3224
Supervision: Vaad Hakashruth.
R & R Produce and Fish
7551 Haverford Avenue 19151
(215) 878-6264
Supervision: Orthodox Vaad of Philadelphia.

Kashrut Information
Board of Rabbis of Greater Philadelphia
1616 Walnut Street 19103   (215) 985-1818
Ko Kosher Service
5871 Drexel Road 19131   (215) 879-1100
Supervision: (O).
Orthodox
Orthodox Vaad of Philadelphia
7505 Brookhaven Road 19151
Rabbi Shlomo Caplan (215) 473-0951 Rabbi
Aaron Felder (215) 745-2968 Rabbi Yehoshua
Kaganoff (215) 742-8421
Rabbinical Assembly
United Synagogue of Conservative, Judaism,
1510 Chestnut Street 19102   (215) 563-8814
Rabbinical Council of Greater Philadelphia
44 North 4th Street, Philadelphia 19106
(215) 922-5446
Fax: (215) 922-1550
Supervision: (O).

**Vaad Hakashruth and Beth Din of
Philadelphia**
1147 Gilham Street, Philadelphia 19111
(215) 725-5181
Fax: (215) 725-5182
Supervision: (O).

Landmarks
Beth Sholom Congregation
8231 Old York Road, Elkins Park 19027
(215) 887-1342
Conservative synagogue whose building is the
only synagogue ever designed by renowned
architect Frank Lloyd Wright.
**Congregation Beth T'fillah of Overbrook
Park**
7630 Woodbine Avenue 19151
(215) 477-2415
Conservative synagogue with a 10-foot high
replica of the Western Wall in its lobby.
Mikveh Israel Cemetery
8th and Spruce Streets 19107   (215) 922-5446
One of the oldest Jewish cemeteries in the
United States, with graves dating from 1740.
Interred here are Haym Solomon, Rebecca
Gratz and 21 veterans of the American
Revolution.
Monument to the Six Million Jewish Martyrs
16th Street and the Benjamin, Franklin
Parkway 19103
This memorial sculpture was the first public
Holocaust monument in the United States.
The Frank Synagogue
Albert Einstein Medical Center, Old York and
Tabor Roads 19141   (215) 456-7890
Modelled after first – and second – century
synagogues discovered in the Galilee region of
north central Israel, this small, historically
certified synagogue was originally dedicated
in 1901

Libraries
Philadelphia Jewish Archives Center
Balch Institute for Ethnic Studies, 18 South 7th
Street 19106   (215) 925-8090
Jewish community archives containing records
of agencies synagogues and community
organisations personal and family papers
autobiographies and memoirs and a
photograph collection Open to the public

Reconstructionist Rabbinical College Library
Church Road and Greenwood Avenue,
Wyncote 19095   (215) 576-0800
The Kaplan Library serves rabbinical students
and the general public 33,000 books and
periodicals in English Hebrew and other
languages The Kaplan Archives house
documents of the Reconstructionist
movement.

Talmudical Yeshivah Library
6063 Dexel Road 19131   (215) 477-1000
Library of Sefarim (Hebrew books on the Bible
the Talmud Responsa etc.) among the finest
of its kind in the city. Open for in-library work
to the general public by appointment.

Temple University
Paley Library, 13th Street and Berks Mall 19122
                                (215) 787-8231
Large collection of Judaica Hebraica and
Talmudic studies and literature in Hebrew and
in translation. Main stacks are open Borrowing
can be arranged through inter library loan

The Free Library of Philadelphia
Central Library, Logan Square 19103
                                (215) 686-5392
3,000-volume Moses Marx Collection of
Judaica central collection. Covers history liturgy
and bibliography with some books on
philosophy religion the Bible and the Talmud
Passover haggadahs. Open to the public.
Russian-language collection available at the
Northeast Regional Library.

University of Pennsylvania
Van Pelt Library, 3420 Walnut Street 19104
                                (215) 898-7556
Large collection of biblical studies rabbinics
Jewish history and medieval and modern
Hebrew language and literature. Stacks and
seminar rooms open to the public.

Media

Magazines

Inside Magazine
Jewish Publishing Group, 226 South 16th
Street 19102   (215) 893-5759
Quarterly magazine of Jewish lfe and style Sold
at news-stands and sent to all Jewish Exponent
and Jewish Times subscribers

Jewish Quarterly Review
420 Walnut Street 19106   (215) 238-1290
Scholarly Journal of the Annenberg Research
Institute published four times a year.

Shofar Magazine
P.O. Box 51591 19115   (215) 676-8304
Russian-language monthly magazine

Newspapers

Jewish Exponent
Jewish Publishing Group, 226 South 16th
Street, Philadelphia 19102   (215) 893-5700
Weekly newspaper covering world news of
Jewish interest and detailed information on
local activities including Jewish Federation of
Greater Philadelphia meetings and events.
Special sections include community and health
calendars singles and campus activities a
Russian-language column and synagogue
activities.

Jewish Post
P.O.Box 442, Yardley 19067   (215) 321-3443
Monthly newspaper serving Bucks County Pa
and Mercer County N.J.

Jewish Times
Jewish Publishing Group, 103A Tomlinson
Road, Huntingdon Valley 19006
                                (215) 938-1177
Weekly newspaper covering issues and
programs of interest to area Jewish residents
of the greater Northeast and Bucks County
including Jewish Federation of Greater
Philadelphia meetings and events. Special
sections include synagogue senior adult singles
and campus activities.

Mir, P.O. Box 6162, Philadelphia 19115
                                (215) 934-5512
Local weekly Russian-language newspaper

Radio & TV

Barry Reisman Show   (609) 365-5600
WSSJ (1310AM) Jewish music in Yiddish
Hebrew and English and Jewish news.
Mondays through Fridays 3.30 to 5.30pm
Sundays 9.30 am to 1 p.m..

Bucks County Jewish Life
                                (215) 949-1490
WBCB (1490AM) Rabbi Allan Tuffs hosts this
weekly Sunday morning radio program at 10
am

Comcast Cablevision of Philadelphia
4400 Wayne Avenue 19140   (215) 673-6600
Channel 66 (Cable Television) Half-hour
program on Jewish culture shown twice a
week in the evening usually midweek and
Sundays See local listings for exact time

Dialogue   (215) 878-9700
WPVI – TV (channel 6) Discussion Program on
religious issues sponsored by Delaware Valley
Media Ministry Sundays 6.30 to 7.30am

Keneseth Israel Sabbath Services
(215) 581-2100
Hour of Jewish worship for shut-ins the elderly and people unable to attend Sabbath services Saturdays 11am to noon
Pulse, WSSJ, Camden   (609) 365-5600
WSSJ (1310AM) Russian-language news and music program Sundays 9.30 to 10.30am

Raido & TV

Meridian   (609) 962-8000
Russian language program Saturdays 10 to 10.30 am

Mikvaot

Mikveh Association of Philadelphia (Ardmore)
Torah Academy, Wynnewood and Argyle Roads, Ardmore 19003   (610) 642-8679
Mikveh Association of Philadelphia (Northern)
7525 Loretto Avenue, Philadelphia 19111
(215) 745-3334

Museums

Balch Institute for Ethnic Studies
18 South 7th Street 19106   (215) 925-8090
Documents and interprets American multi-culturalism Research library has a Yiddish collection. Houses the Jewish Archives Center.
Borowsky Gallery
Jewish Community Centers of Greater, Philadelphia, 401 South Broad Street 19147
(215) 545-4400
Continuing exhibits of special interest to the Jewish community.
Fred Wolf Jr Gallery
Jewish Community Centers of Greater, Philadelphia, 10100 Jamison Avenue 19116
(215) 698-7300
Continuing exhibits of special interest to the Jewish community
Holocaust Awareness Museum
Gratz College, Mandell Education Campus, 7601 Old York Road, Melrose Park 19027
(215) 635-6480
Previously known as the Jewish Identity Center the Holocaust Awareness Museum contains donations form Holocaust survivors and concentration camp liberators. The collection documents and teaches the facts of genocide and dangers of ethnic hatred and bigotry.

National Museum of American Jewish History
55 North 5th Street, Independence Mall East 19106   (215) 923-3811
Fax: (215) 923-0763
Dedicated to documenting the American Jewish experience. With award-winning gift shop.
Philadelphia Congregation Rodeph Shalom
615 North Broad Street 19123 (215) 627-6747
Nationally recognised for exhibits of contemporary Jewish art and history. Permanent collection of 20th-century Jewish are and photographs.
Rosenbach Museum and Library
2010 Delancey Place 19103   (215) 732-1600
Fax: (215) 545-7529
Email: rosenb1@libertynet.org
The collection includes the first Haggadah printed in America and letters of the Gratz family of Philadelphia. Access to books is by appointment only.
Temple Judea Museum of Keneseth Israel
8339 Old York Road, Elkins Park 19027
(215) 887-8700
Fax: (215) 887-1070
This synagogue museum has four changing exhibits of Judaica and Jewish art each year.
U.S. Holocaust Memorial Museum
100 Raoul Wallenberg Place SW, Washington D.C. 20024   (202) 488-0400
Fax: (202) 488-2690
The permanent exhibition recommended for visitors 11 years and older presents a comprehensive history of the Holocaust through artefacts photographs films and eyewitness testimonies. There are other changing special exhibitions and an exhibition designed for children 8 years and older.

Organisations

Annenberg Research Institute
420 Walnut Street 19106   (215) 238-1290
Approximately 180,000 books and thousands of periodicals with emphasis on Judaic and Near Eastern studies. Rare book collection Archives of American Judaica particularly that of Philadelphia

Restaurants

Gratz College Cafeteria
Mandell Education Campus, Old York Road and Melrose Avenue, Melrose Park 19027
(215) 635-7300
Supervision: Rabbinical Council.

Hillel Dining Room
University of Pennsylvania, 202 South 36th
Street 19104 (215) 989-7391
Fax: (215) 898-8259
Supervision: Orthodox Vaad of Philadelphia.
Hours of operation are for lunch and dinner
during the school year.
Jonathan's
130 South 11th Street 19152 (215) 829-8101
Supervision: Rabbi Dov Brisman.

Dairy

Cherry Street Chinese vegeterian
1010 Cherry Street 19107 (215) 923-3663
Supervision: Rabbinical Assembly.
Oasis Falafel
17th Street Falafel, 17th and Market Streets
SW corner (vendor) 19103 (215) 879-6956
Fax: (215) 879-0925
Email: Falafel17@aol.com
Supervision: Orthodox, Mekor Baruch.
Hours: 11am to 3pm Monday to Friday.l
Shalom Pizza
7598A Haverford Avenue 19151
(215) 878-1500
Supervision: Orthodox Vaad of Philadelphia.
Chalav Yisrael pizza and Middle Eastern
cuisine. Around the corner from the Bestcake
Bakery. Take out or eat in. Hours: Sunday to
Thursday, 11 am to 9 pm; Friday, to 4 pm.
Tiberias Cafeteria
8010 Castor Avenue 19152 (215) 898-7391
Supervision: Orthodox Vaad of Philadelphia.

Meat

Dragon Inn
7628 Castor Avenue 19152 (215) 742-2575
Supervision: Rabbi Dov Brisman.
Maccabeam
128 South 12th Street 19107 (215) 922-5922
Supervision: Rabbinical Council.
Shalom Pizza
7598a Haverford Avenue (215) 878-1500
Supervision: Orthodox Vaad of Philadelphia.
Vegeterian, middle-eastern. Open 11.00 am to
9.00 pm daily. Friday closed at 4.00 pm
(winter at 2.00pm). Closed Shabbat.
Traditions Restaurant
9550 Bustleton Avenue 19115 (215) 677-2221
Supervision: Orthodox Vaad of Philadelphia.
Zenya Snack Bar
Jewish Community Centers of Greater,
Philadelphia, Red lion Road and Jamison
Avenue 19116 (215) 677-0280
Supervision: Ko Kosher Service.

Synagogue
Congregation Mikveh Israel
44 North 4th Street 19106 (215) 922-5446
Fax: (215) 922-1550
Web site: www.mikvehisrael.org
Spanish-Portuguese synagogue founded in
1740 Located on Independence Mall. Entrance
is shared with the National Museum of
American Jewish History. All Shabbat and
holiday services are conducted using historic
artifacts and tradition.

Synagogues

Orthodox
Young Israel of Oxford Circle
6427 Large Street 19149 (215) 725-7087
With dozens of synagogues of the various
demoninations in the area, travellers are
advised to contact a local religious
organisation for specific details.

Theatres
Theatre Ariel/Habima Ariel
P.O. Box 0334, Merion Station 19066
(215) 567-0670
Theatre productions, readings workshops mini-
performances and speakers all dedicated to
exploring the Jewish theatrical experience.

Tours of Jewish Interest
American Jewish Committee Historic Tour
117 South Seventeenth Street, Suite 1010
(215) 665-2300
Fax: (215) 665-8737
Tours, run by Simmi Hurwitz, may be arranged
to suit personal or group interests or needs.

Pittsburgh
Bakeries
Pastries Unlimited
2119 Murray Avenue 15217 (212) 521-6323
Pastries Unlimited
4743 Liberty Avenue (212) 681-0303

Booksellers
Pinskers Judaica Center
2028 Murray Avenue 15217
(412) 421-3033;1- 800-JUDAISM
(1-800-583-2476)
Fax: (412) 421-6103
Email: info@judaism.com

Groceries
Brauner's Emporium
2023 Murray Avenue 15217

Koshermart
2121 Murray Avenue 15217

Media

Newspapers

Pittsburgh Jewish Chronicle
5600 Baum Blvd   (412) 687-1000
                        Fax: (412) 687-5119
              Email: pittjewchr@aol.com

Mikvaot
2326 Shady Avenue 15217   (412) 422-8010

Museums
Holocaust Center of the United Jewish Federation
242 McKee Place 15213   (412) 682-7111
Serves as a living memorial by providing educational resources, sponsoring community activities, housing archives and cultural materials related to the Holocaust.

Organisations
Jewish Federation of Greater Wilkes-Barre and Community Center
60 S. River Street   (712) 822-4646
                        Fax: (712) 824-5966
United Jewish Federation of Greater Pittsburgh
234 McKee Place 15213   (412) 681-8000
                        Fax: (412) 681-8804
Houses all administrative office of the Federal and Community Relations Committee

Restaurants
Prime Kosher
1916 Murray Avenue 15217

Dairy

Yaacov's
2109 Murray Av, 15217   (412) 421-7208

Meat

Greenberg's Kosher Poultry
2223 Murray Avenue 15217
King David's
2020 Murray Avenue 15217   (412) 422-3370

Synagogues

Conservative

Ahavath Achim
Lydia & Chestnut Sts., Carnegie 15106
B'nai Israel
327 N. Negley Av. 15206
Beth El of South Hills
1900 Cochran Rd. 15220

Beth Shalom
Beacon & Shady Avs. 15217
New Light
1700 Beechwood Blvd. 15217
Parkway Jewish Center
300 Princeton Dr. 15235   (412) 823-4338
                        Fax: (412) 823-4338
Tree of Life
Wilkins & Shady Avs. 15217

Orthodox

Adath Israel
3257 Ward St. 15213
Adath Jeshurun
5643 E. Liberty Blvd. 15224
B'nai Emunoh
4315 Murray Av. 15217
B'nai Zion
6404 Forbes Av. 15217
Beth Hamedrash Hagodol
1230 Colwell St. 15219
Bohnei Yisroel
6401 Forbes Av. 15217
Kether Torah
5706 Bartlett St. 15217
Kneseth Israel
1112 N. Negley Av. 15206
Machsikei Hadas
814 N. Negley Av. 15206
Poale Zedeck
6318 Phillips Avenue 15217   (412) 421-9786
                 Web site: www.pzonline
Shaare Tefillah
5741 Bartlett St. 15217
Shaare Torah
2319 Murray Av. 15217
Shaare Zedeck
5751 Bartlett St. 15217
Torath Chaim
728 N. Negley Av. 15217
              (412) 362-7736; 362-0036
              Email: joeberger1@juno.com
Young Israel of Greater Pittsburgh
5831 Bartlett Street 15217-1636
                        (412) 421-7224

Reconstructionist

Dor Hadash
6401 Forbes Av. 15217

Reform

Rodef Shalom
4905 5th Av. 15213
Temple David
4415 Northern Pike, Monroeville 15146

Temple Emanuel
1250 Bower Hill Rd., South Hills 15243
Temple Sinai
5505 Forbes Av. 15217

Pottstown

Synagogues

Conservative

Congregation Mercy & Truth
575 N. Keim Street 19464

Reading

Organisations
Jewish Federation
1700 City Line St,. 19604   (610) 921-2766
Fax: (610) 921-2766
Email: sramati@epix.net

Synagogues

Conservative

Kesher Zion
Eckert & Perkiomen Streets 19602

Orthodox

Shomrei Habrith
2320 Hampden Blvd. 19604

Reform

Congregation Oheb Sholom
555 Warwick Drive, Wyomissing Hill 19610
(610) 375-6034
Fax: (610) 375-6036

Scranton

Butchers
Blatt's Butcher Block
420 Prescott Avenue 18510
(717) 342-3886; 800-221-4528
Fax: (717) 342-9711
Supervision: Rabbi Fine and Rabbi Herman of Scranton.
Glatt kosher meat, poultry, delicatessen and groceries. Also meat restaurant.

Organisations
Scranton-Lackawanna Jewish Federation
601 Jefferson Avenue 18510   (717) 961-2300
Fax: (717) 346-6147

Synagogues

Conservative

Temple Israel
Gibson Street & Monroe Avenue 18510

Orthodox

Beth Shalom
Clay Avenue at Vine Street 18510
Congregation Machzikeh Hadas
cnr. Monroe & Olive 18510
Ohev Zedek
1432 Mulberry Street 18510

Reform

Temple Hesed
Lake Scranton 18505

Sharon

Synagogues
Temple Beth Israel
840 Highland Avenue 16146

Wallingford

Synagogues

Conservative

Ohev Shalom
2 Chester Road 19086
The synagogue vestibule contains 12 stained glass panes (designed and executed by Rose Isaacson) each depicting a Jewish holiday.

Wilkes-Barre

Organisations
Jewish Federation of Greater Wilkes-Barre & Community Center
60 S. River Street   (712) 822-4146
Fax: (712) 824-5966

Synagogues

Conservative

Temple Israel
236 S. River Street 18702

Orthodox

Ohav Zedek
242 S. Franklin Street 18701   (717) 825-6619
Fax: (717) 825-6634
United Orthodox Synagogue
13 S. Welles Street 18702

Reform

B'nai B'rith
408 Wyoming Street, Kingston 18704

Williamsport

Synagogues

Conservative

Ohev Sholom
Cherry & Belmont Streets 17701

Reform

Beth Ha-Sholom
425 Center Street 17701

Yardley

Bakeries
Cramer Bakery
18 E. Afton Avenue 19067   (215) 493-2760

Contact Information
Rabbi Budow   (215) 493-1800

Rhode Island

Barrington

Synagogues

Reform

Temple Habonim
165 New Meadow Road 02806

Bristol

Synagogues

Conservative

United Brothers
215 High Street 02809

Cranston

Synagogues
Temple Torat Yisrael
330 Park Avenue 02905

Reform

Temple Sinai
30 Hagan Avenue 02920

Middletown

Synagogues

Conservative

Temple Shalom
223 Valley Road 02842   (401) 846-9002
                                Fax: (401) 682-2417

Narragansett

Synagogues
Congregation Beth David
Kingstown Road 02882   (401) 846-9002

Newport

Tours of Jewish Interest
Touro Synagogue
85 Touro Street 02840   (401) 847-4794
                                Fax: (401) 847-8121
The synagogue, designed by Peter Harrison and dedicated in 1763, is one of the finest examples of 18th-century Colonial architecture. It has been declared a national site by the US government. The Jewish cemetery, the second oldest in the US, dates back to 1677 and was immortalised in Longfellow's poem 'The Jewish Cemetery of Newport'. Judah Touro is buried here.

Pawtucket

Synagogues

Orthodox

Ohawe Shalom
East Avenue 02860
Young Israel of Pawtucket
671 East Avenue 02862   (401) 722-3146

Providence

Bakeries
Kaplan's Bakery   (401) 621-8107
Supervision: Rabbi Ephraim Berlinski, Vaad of Rhode Island.

Butchers
Marty Weissman's Butcher Shop
                                (401) 467-8903
Supervision: Rabbi Ephraim Berlinski, Vaad of Rhode Island.
Butcher shop only; 'Deli Counter' meat and hot dogs not under supervision.

Documentation Centres
Rhode Island Jewish Historical Association
                                (401) 863-2805
Has a vast amount of material regarding Colonial Jewry.

Kashrut Information
Brown University-RISD Hillel
80 Brown Street 02906   (401) 863-2805
                                Fax: (401) 863-1591
                                Email: spf@brown.edu
Vaad Hakashrut   (401) 331-9393

Media

Magazines
L'Chaim
130 Sessions Street 02906   (401) 421-4111

Mikvaot
401 Elmgrove Avenue 02906

Museums
Rhode Island Holocaust Memorial Museum
401 Elmgrove Avenue 02906
                                (401) 861-8800
The state memorial to the victims of the
Holocaust. Many survivors now living in Rhode
Island have donated memorabilia and personal
mementoes. There is also a garden of
remembrance.

Organisations
Jewish Federation of Rhode Island
130 Sessions Street 02906   (401) 421-4111

Synagogues

Conservative

Temple Emanu-El
99 Taft Avenue 02906

Orthodox

Beth Shalom
275 Camp Avenue 02906
Congregation Sons of Jacob
24 Douglas Avenue 02908
Mishkon Tfiloh
203 Summit Avenue 02906
Shaare Zedek
688 Broad Street 02907

Reform

Beth El
70 Orchard Avenue 02906

Warwick

Synagogues

Conservative

Temple Am David
40 Gardiner Street 02888

Westerly

Synagogues

Orthodox

Congregation Shaare Zedek
Union Street 02891

Woonsocket

Synagogues

Conservative

Congregation B'nai Israel
224 Prospect Street 02895   (401) 762-3651
                          Fax: (401) 762-3651

South Carolina

Charleston

Bakeries
Ashley Bakery
1662 Savannah Highway 29407
                                (803) 763-4125
Great Harvest Bread Company
975 Savannah Highway 29407 (803) 763-2055

Delicatessens
Nathan's Deli
1836 Ashley River Road 29407 (803) 556-3354
West Side Market and Deli
1300 Savannah Highway 29407
                                (803) 763-9988
                          Fax: (803) 763-4476
Kosher market, restaurant and catering. Open
Sunday to Friday.

Organisations
Jewish Federation and Community Center
1645 Raoul Wallenberg Blvd, PO Box 31298
29416   (803) 571-6565
                          Fax: (803) 556-6206

Synagogues

Reform

Beth Elohim
86 Hasell Street 29401   (803) 723-1090

Tours of Jewish Interest
Beth Elohim
86 Hasell Street 29401   (803) 723-1090
Dating from 1749, it is the birthplace of
Reform Judaism in the United States, the
Second oldest synagogue building in the
country, and the oldest surviving Reform
synagogue in the world. It has designated a
national historic landmark. A museum is
housed in the administration building next
door.

Columbia

Delicatessens
Groucho's
Five Points 29205

Organisations
Columbia Jewish Federation
4540 Trenholm Road, Cola 29206
(803) 787-2023

Synagogues

Conservative

Beth Shalom
5827 N. Trenholm Road 29206

Reform

Tree of Life
6719 Trenholm Road, Cola 29206
(803) 787-0580

Georgetown

Cemeteries

Although there are now very few Jews in Georgetown, and there is no synagogue, there is a very old Jewish cemetery, which is maintained by the city.

Myrtle Beach

Synagogues

Orthodox

Beth El
401 Highway 17 N., 56th Avenue 29577
(803) 449-3140
Chabad lubavitch
2803 N. Oak Street
(803) 626-6403

South Dakota

Aberdeen

Synagogues

Conservative

B'nai Isaac
202 N. Kline Street 57401
(605) 225-3404 or 7360

Rapid City

Synagogues

Reform

Synagogue of the Hills
PO Box 2320 57709
(605) 394-3310
Affiliated with UAHC. Services sporadic.

Tennessee
Chattanooga

Museums
Siskin Museum of Religious Artefacts
1 Siskin Plaza 37403
(423) 634-1700

Organisations
Jewish Community Federation
5326 Lynnland Terrace 47311
(423) 894-1317
Fax: (423) 894-1319

Synagogues

Conservative

B'nai Zion
114 McBrien Road 37411
(423) 894-8900

Orthodox

Beth Sholom
20 Pisgah Avenue 37411
(423) 894-0801

Reform

Mizpah Congregation
923 McCallie Avenue 37403
(423) 264-9771
Fax: (423) 267-9773
Email: admmizpahcong@juno.com

Memphis

Bakeries
Carl's Bakery
1688 Jackson Avenue 38107
(901) 276-2304
Supervision: Vaad Hakehilloth of Memphis.
Open daily except Shabbat and Monday.

Delicatessens
Rubenstein's
4965 Summer Avenue 38122
Closed Shabbat.

Kashrut Information
Vaad Hakehilloth of Memphis
Memphis Orthodox Jewish Community Council,
PO Box 41133 38104
(901) 767-2263
Fax: (901) 761-3788

Mikvaot
Baron Hirsch Congregation
369 Winter Oak Lane 38119

Organisations
Jewish Federation and Community Center
6560 Poplar Avenue 38138
(901) 767-7100

Restaurants

Dairy

Jon's Place
764 Mt. Moriah Road 38117   (901) 374-0600
Supervision: Vaad Hakehilloth of Memphis.
Open daily except Shabbat for dairy and fish
lunch and dinner.

Meat

M.I. Gottlieb's
5062 Park Avenue 38120   (901) 763-3663
Supervision: Vaad Hakehilloth of Memphis.
Hours: Sunday to Thursday, 9 am to 7 pm;
Friday, 7 am to 2:30 pm.

Synagogues

Conservative

Beth Sholom
482 S. Mendenhall Ave 38117

Orthodox

Anshei Sephard-Beth El Emeth
120 E.Yates Road N. 38117

Reform

Temple Israel
1376 E. Massey Road

Nashville

Mikvaot

Sherith Israel
3600 West End Avenue 37205 (615) 292-6614
                            Fax: (615) 463-8260

Organisations

**Jewish Federation of Nashville and Middle
Tennessee**
801 Percy Warner Blvd. 37205 (615) 356-3242
                            Fax: (615) 352-0056

Synagogues

Conservative

West End Synagogue
3814 West End Avenue 37205 (615) 269-4592
                            Fax: (615) 269-4695
           Email: office@westendsyn.org or
                      exec@westendsyn.org

Reform

The Temple
5015 Harding Road 37205   (615) 352-7620

Oak Ridge

Synagogues

Jewish Congregation of Oak Ridge
101 W. Madison Lane 37830   (615) 482-3581

Texas

Amarillo

Synagogues

Reform

Temple B'nai Israel
4316 Albert Street 79106   (806) 352-7191

Austin

Organisations

**Jewish Federation and Community Center of
Austin**
11713 Jollyville Road 78759   (512) 331-1144
                            Fax: (512) 331-7059

Synagogues

Conservative

Agudas Achim
4300 Bull Creek Road 78731
Congregation Beth El
8902 Mesa Drive 78759   (512) 346-1776

Orthodox

Chabad House
2101 Neuces Street 78705   (512) 499-8202
Mikvah on premises.

Reform

Temple Beth Israel
3901 Shoal Creek Blvd. 78756 (512) 454-6806

Beaumont

Synagogues

Temple Emanuel
1120 Broadway 7740   (409) 832-6131

Bellaire

Bakeries

Ashcraft
1301 N. First 77401

Corpus Christi

Synagogues

Conservative

B'nai Israel
3434 Fort Worth Street 78411 (512) 855-7308
Fax: (512) 855-7309

Reform

Temple Beth El
4402 Saratoga Street 78413

Dallas

Dallas stands at the western edge of the American South, both regionally and culturally. The Dallas Jewish community was founded in the decade following the Civil War by predominantly German Jews. The founders left their imprint in numerous institutions and a style of worship that reflects the German Reform Jewish culture of the mid-19th century. The social importance of German Jewish ancestry can still be seen in the Temple Emanu-El cemetery which is home to scores of 19th-century headstones bearing German regional names for eastern European birth-places.

The JCC sponsors a prestigious Jewish Arts Festival each August along with concerts and gallery exhibitions. Another highlight of the Jewish calendar is the Kosher Chile Cookoff, with participation from virtually all synagogues and other community organisations. A Holocaust Museum has served as a regional focal point for preserving the memory of the Shoah and teaching the lessons of hatred to a larger public. The present Jewish population in the Dallas area stands at approximately 35,000. For more information, see the Dallas Virtual Jewish Community website at www.dvjc.org.

Bakeries

Cakes of Elegance
9205 Skillman 75243 (214) 343-2253
Supervision: Vaad Hakashrus of Greater Dallas.
Minyards Kosher Bakery & Deli
714 Preston Forest Shopping Center 75230
Supervision: Vaad Hakashrus of Greater Dallas.
Neiman-Marcus Bakery
North Park (214) 363-8311
Supervision: Vaad Hakashrus of Greater Dallas.
Location only. Closed Sats.

Strictly Cheesecake
8139 Forest Lane, Suite 117, Forest Central Village 75243 (972) 783-6545
Supervision: Vaad Hakashrus of Greater Dallas.
Tom Thumb Bakery & Kosher Deli
11920 Preston Road 75230 (972) 392-2501
Supervision: Vaad Hakashrus of Greater Dallas.
Forest Lane only open 24 hours. Most Tom Thumb and Albertson grocery stores in North Dallas have a small kosher section for dried goods.

Caterers

Simcha Kosher Caterers
(972) 620-7293
Supervision: Vaad Hakashrus of Greater Dallas.
Prepares and delivers meals to order.

Community Organisations

Jewish Federation of Greater Dallas and Community Center
7800 Northaven Road, Suite A 75230
(214) 369-3313
Fax: (214) 369-8943
Email: dallasfed@jon.cjfny.org
The Center houses the Dallas Memorial Center for Holocaust studies and the Dallas Jewish Historical Society. There is a kosher kids café only on Sundays, under the supervision of the Vaad Hakashrus of Greater Dallas.

Delicatessens

Kosher Link
7517 Campbell Road 75230 (972) 248-3773
Fax: (972) 248-3931
Supervision: Vaad Hakashrus of Greater Dallas.
We prepare fresh meals to be sent to your hotel. Call if you need a menu faxed. Orders should be placed 24 hours ahead. Meals are glatt kosher. Hours: Sunday and Friday, 9 am to 3 pm; Monday to Thursday, to 6:30 pm.

Hotels

Grand Kempinski Hotel
15201 Dallas Parkway 75248 (972) 386-6000
Fax: (972) 404-1848
Sheraton Park Central
12720 Merit Drive 75240 (972) 385-3000
Westin Hotel
13340 Dallas Parkway (972) 934-9494
Supervision: Vaad Hakashrus of Dallas.
Lock-up kosher kitchens under the supervision of the Vaad Hakashrus of Dallas. There is some banquet service going on almost every weekend and it might be possible to arrange a kosher meal at the above three hotels.

Media

Newspapers

Texas Jewish Post
11333 N. Central Expressway 75230
Weekly publication. Includes weekly listing of synagogue services and times in the Greater Dallas area. Includes addresses and phone numbers.

Mikvaot

Congregation Tiferet Israel   (214) 397-3428
Call for appointment.

Religious Organisations

Dallas Area Torah Association (Kollel)
5840 Forest Lane 75230   (214) 987-3282
Fax: (214) 987-1764
Email: data@datanet.org
Web site: www.datanet.org
Mikvah Association
5640 McShann 75230   (972) 776-0037
Beeper: (972) 397-3428.
Rabbinic Association of Greater Dallas
6930 Alpha Road   (972) 661-1810
Vaad Hakashrus of Greater Dallas
7900 Northaven Road 75230
(214) 739-OKDK (6535)
Also known as 'Dallas Kosher', they can be contacted for all kashrut information.

Sites

Zaide Reuven's Esrog Farm   (972) 931-5596
Fax: (972) 931-5476
Email: ZRsEsrog@aol.com
Web site: members.aol.com/ARsEsrog
Dallas' only Esrog tree farm is open by appointment.

Synagogues

Conservative

Congregation Anshai Emet
5220 Village Creek Drive Plano
(972) 735-9818
Congregation Beth Emunah
75230   (972) 416-8016
Congregation Beth Torah
720 Lookout Richardson   (972) 234-1542
Congregation Shearith Israel
9401 Douglas 75230   (214) 361-6606

Orthodox

Chabad of Plano
(972) 596-8270
Congregation Ohev Shalom
6821 McCallum Blvd 75230   (972) 380-1292

Forest Lane Shul
7008 Forest Lane 75230   (214) 361-8600
Shaare Tefilla
6131 Churchill Way, off Preston Road 75230
(972) 661-0127
Fax: (972) 661-0150
Email: shaaretefilla@juno.com
Young Israel of Dallas
6504 Dykes Way 75230   (972) 386-7162

Reform

Congregation Beth-El Binah
Gay and Lesbian Center, 2701 Regan 75219
(214) 497-1591
Congregation Kol Ami
1887 Timbercreek
Flower Mound   (972) 539-1938
Congregation Ner Tamid
2312 Trinity Mills Road, Suites 160A and B,
Carrolton   (972) 416-9738
Temple Emanu-El
8500 Hillcrest Road 75230   (214) 706-0000
Fax: (214) 706-0025
Web site: www.tedallas.org
Temple Shalom
6930 Alpha Road 75230   (972) 661-1810

Traditional

Tiferet Israel Congregation
10909 Hillcrest Road 75230   (214) 691-3611

El Paso

Bakeries

Kahn's Bakery and Sweet Shop
918 N. Oregon Street 79901
Under rabbinical supervision.

Community Organisations

Chabad House
6515 Westwind 79912   (915) 584-8218
Have a mikva as well.
Jewish Federation
405 Wallenberg Drive 79912   (915) 584-4437

Museums

El Paso Holocaust Museum and Study Center
401 Wallenberg Drive 79912   (915) 833-5656

Synagogues

Conservative

B'nai Zion
805 Cherry Hill Lane 79912
Reform
Sinai, 4408 N. Stanton Street 79902

Fort Worth/Arlington

Synagogues

Conservative
Ahavath Shalom
4050 South Hulen 76109   (817) 731-4721
Beth Shalom
1211 Thannisch Drive   (817) 860-5448

Orthodox
Chabad-Lubavitch
6804 Del Prado   (817) 346-7700

Reform
Beth-El Congregation
207 W. Broadway 76104   (817) 332-7141
                       Fax: (817) 332-7157
Just south of downtown Fort Worth, offers a
full range of Shabbat and holiday worship
services and other programs for children and
adults. Call for service times and other
information.

Houston

Bakeries
Kroger Store 313
10306 S. Post Oak 77096
Supervision: Houston Kashruth Association.
LeMoulin
5645 Beechnut 77096
Supervision: Houston Kashruth Association.
New York Bagels
9724 Hillcroft 77096
Supervision: Houston Kashruth Association.
Randall's Bakery
Supervision: Houston Kashruth Association.
Can be found at seven locations: Clear Lake,
Sugar Land, Highway 6 & Memorial, Fondren &
Bissonnet, W. Bellfort & S. Post Oak, S. Gesner
& W. Bellfort, and Holcombe & Kirby.
Three Brothers
4036 S. Braeswood 77025
Supervision: Houston Kashruth Association.

Embassy
Consulate General
Suite 1500, 24 Greenway Plaza 77046

Kashrut Information
Houston Kashrut Association
9001 Greenwillow 77096   (713) 723-3850

Mikvaot
Chabad Lubavitch Center
10900 Fondren Road 77096

United Orthodox Synagogues
4221 S. Braeswood Blvd., 77096

Organisations
Jewish Federation of Greater Houston
5603 S. Braeswood Blvd. 77096
                       (713) 729-7000
                  Fax: (713) 721-6232
          Email: ujchouston@jon.cjfny.org

Restaurants
Nosher at the Jewish Community Center
5601 S. Braeswood 77096
Supervision: Houston Kashruth Association.

Meat
Drumsticks
10200 S. Main Street 77025
Supervision: Houston Kashruth Association.
Simon's Gourmet Kosher Foods
5411 Braeswood 77096
Supervision: Houston Kashruth Association.
Butcher shop as well.

Vegetarian
Madras Pavilion
3910 Kirby 77098
Supervision: Houston Kashruth Association.
Wonderful Vegetarian
7549 Westheimer 77063
Supervision: Houston Kashruth Association.

Synagogues

Conservative
B'rith Shalom
4610 Bellaire Blvd. 77401
Beth Am
1431 Brittmore Rd. 77043   (713) 461-7725
                       Fax: (713) 461-7773
One room and board is available to anyone
attending Services.
Beth Yeshurun
4525 Beechnut St. 77096
Congregation Shaar Hashalom
16020 El Camino Real 77062

Orthodox
Beth Rambam
11333 Braesridge Blvd. 77071
Young Israel of Houston
7823 Ludington Drive 77071   (713) 729-0719

Reform
Beth Israel
5600 N. Braeswood Blvd. 77096
Congregation for Reform Judaism
801 Bering Dr. 77057

Emanu-El
1500 Sunset Blvd. 77005
Jewish Community North
18519 Klein Church Rd., Spring 77039
Temple Sinai
783 Country Pl. 77079

Unaffiliated

K'nesseth Israel
cnr. Sterling & Commerce Sts., Baytown

Lubbock

Caterers

Vegetarian

Souper Salad
6703 Slide Road   (806) 794-0997

Groceries
Albertson's   (806) 794-6761
Good selection for Passover.
Lowe's Supermarket
82nd & Slide Rd
Good selection for Passover. Stocks matzot
and white fish.
United   (906) 791-0220
Good selection for Passover.

Synagogues
Congregation Shaareth Israel
6928 3rd Street 79424   (806) 794-7517
Mailing address: PO Box 93594, 79493-3594

San Antonio

Delicatessens
Delicious Food
7460 Callaghan Road 78229   (512) 366-1844

Museums
Holocaust Museum
8434 Ahern Drive 78216
Institute of Texan Cultures
Hemisphere Plaza, Downtown Riverfront

Organisations
Jewish Federation
8434 Ahern Drive 78216   (512) 341-8234

Synagogues

Conservative

Agudas Achim
1201 Donaldson Avenue 78228

Orthodox

Rodfei Sholom
3003 Sholom Drive 78230   (512) 492-4277
Mikvah on premises.

Reform
Beth El
211 Belknap Place 78212

Waco

Synagogues

Conservative

Agudath Jacob
4925 Hillcrest Drive 76710

Reform

Rodef Sholom
1717 N. New Road 76707   (254) 754-3703
                            Fax: (254) 754-5538

Utah

Salt Lake City

Organisations
United Jewish Federation of Utah
2416 East, 1700 South 84108 (801) 581-0102
                             Fax: (801) 581-1334

Synagogues

Reconstructionist

Chavurah B'yachad
P.O. Box 9115 84109   (801) 325-4539
                  Email: byachad@aol.com

Reform

Kol Ami
2425 E. Heritage Way 84109   (801) 484-1501

Vermont

Burlington

Synagogues

Conservative

Ohavi Zedek
188 N. Prospect Street 05401

Orthodox

Ahavath Gerim
cnr. Archibald & Hyde Streets 05401

Reform

Temple Sinai
500 Swift Street 05401

Virginia

Alexandria

Synagogues

Conservative

Agudas Achim
2908 Valley Drive 22302

Reform

Beth El Hebrew Congregation
3830 Seminary Road 22304

Arlington

Synagogues

Conservative

Arlington-Fairfax Jewish Congregation
2920 Arlington Blvd. 22204   (703) 979-4466
Daily Minyan and Shabbat services. Includes areas known as Crystal City, Rosslyn and Skyline.

Charlottesville

Synagogues
The Hillel Jewish Center
The University of Virginia, 1824 University Circle 22903   (804) 295-4963

Reform

Temple Beth Israel
301 E. Jefferson Street 22902   (804) 295-6382

Danville

Synagogues
Temple Beth Sholom
Sutherlin Avenue
This building is 95 years old, one of oldest synagogues in the South. Friday evening and holiday services.

Fairfax

Synagogues

Conservative

Congregation Olam Tikvah
3800 Glenbrook Road 22031   (703) 425-1880
                       Fax: (703) 425-0855
2 miles from Beltway Exit 6W.

Falls Church

Synagogues

Reform

Temple Rodef Shalom
2100 Westmoreland Street 22043
                       (703) 532-2217

Norfolk

Groceries

Meat

The Kosher Place
738 W. 22nd Street   (757) 623-1770
Supervision: Vaad Hakashrus of Tidewater.
Meats, deli, prepared foods. Hours: Monday to Thursday, 9 am to 6 pm; Friday, to 3 pm; Sunday, 10 am to 4 pm. Close to colonial Williamsburg and Virginia Beach.

Hotels
Sheraton Norfolk Waterside Hotel
777 Waterside Drive 23510   (757) 622-6664
Supervision: Va'ad.

Kashrut Information
Va'ad Hakashrut
c/o B'nai Israel   (804) 444-7361; 627-7358

Media

Magazines

Renewal Magazine
7300 Newport Avenue 23505
Quarterly publication

Newspapers

UJF Virginia News
7300 Newport Avenue 23505
Bi-weekly publication

Mikvaot
B'nai Israel Congregation
420 Spotswood Avenue 23517
                       (804) 627-7358

Va'ad Hakashrut

Organisations
United Jewish Federation of Tidewater
7300 Newport Avenue 23505   (804) 489-8040
                       Fax: (804) 489-8230

Synagogues

Conservative

Beth El
422 Shirley Av. 23517   (757) 625-7821
Fax: (757) 627-4905
Email: bethelc@erols.com
Temple Israel
7255 Granby St. 23505   (804) 489-4550

Reform

Ohef Sholom
Stockley Gdns. at Raleigh Av. 23507
(804) 625-4295
The Commodore Levy Chapel
Frazier Hall, Building C-7 (inside Gate 2),
Norfolk US Navy Station
Is the U.S. Navy's oldest synagogue. Services
are open to civilians. Inq. to the Jewish
Chaplain.

Richmond

Bakeries

Chesapeake Bagel Bakery
Willow Lawn Shopping Center, 5100
Monument Avenue 23226
Supervision: Vaad of Richmond.
Kosher bagels, challah and rolls.

Fishmongers

Andersons Fish
Willow Lawn Shopping Center, 5100
Monument Avenue 23226
Supervision: Vaad of Richmond.
Fresh fish.

Groceries

Hannafords
Willow Lawn Shopping Center, 5100
Monument Avenue 23226
Supervision: Vaad of Richmond.
Newly opened supermarket with a kosher deli.

Hotel

Kosher Retreat Center of Virginia
212 Gaskins Road 23233   (804) 740-2000
Fax: (804) 750-1341
Email: info@chabadofva.org
Kosher retreat center open year round.

Mikvaot

Young Israel
4811 Patterson Avenue 23226 (804) 353-3831
Fax: (804) 288-4381
Email: adere@juno.com

Museums

Beth Ahabah
1117 W. Franklin Street 23220
Also housing Jewish archives which are of
great historical interest.

Organisations

Jewish Community Federation
5403 Monument Avenue 23226
(804) 288-0045

Synagogues

Conservative

Or Atid
501 Parham Road 23229

Orthodox

Keneseth Beth Israel
6300 Patterson Avenue 23226
(804) 288-7953
Fax: (804) 673-9558
Email: kbi6300@erols.com
Young Israel of Richmond
4811 Patterson Avenue 23226
(804) 353-5831

Reform

Or Ami
9400 N. Huguenot Road 23235

Virginia Beach

Synagogues

Conservative

Kehillat Bet Hamidrash
952 Indian Lakes Blvd. 23464   (804) 495-8510
Temple Emanuel
25th Street 23451

Orthodox

Chabad Lubavitch
533 Gleneagle Drive 23462   (804) 499-0507

Reform

Beth Chaverim
3820 Stoneshore Road 23452-7965
(757) 463-3226
Fax: (757) 463-1134
Email: bethchaverim@ddaccess.com

Virginia Peninsula

Bakeries
Brenner's Warwick Bakery
240 31st Street, Newport News 23607
Supervision: Va'ad Hakashrut.

Mikvaot
Adath Jeshurun
12646 Nettles Drive, Newport News 23606

Organisations
**United Jewish Community of the Virginia
Peninsula**
2700 Spring Road, Newport News 23606
(804) 930-1422

Synagogues

Conservative

Rodef Shalom
318 Whealton Road, Hampton 23666

Reform

Temple Sinai
11620 Warwick Blvd., Newport News 23601

Traditional

B'nai Israel
3116 Kecoughtan Road, Hampton 23661

Washington

Aberdeen
Synagogues

Conservative

Temple Beth Israel
1219 Spur Street 98520   (360) 533-3784

Seattle

Bakeries
Bagel Deli, 340 15th Avenue E.
(206) 322-2471
Supervision: Va'ad HaRabanim of Greater
Seattle.
Bagel Oasis
2112 NE 65th Street   (206) 526-0525
Supervision: Va'ad HaRabanim of Greater
Seattle.
International Biscuit
5028 Wilson Avenue   (206) 722-5595
Supervision: Va'ad HaRabanim of Greater
Seattle.

Delicatessens
Bagel Deli, 1309 N.E. 43rd Street
(206) 634-3770
Betay Avone
113 Blanchard Avenue
Downtown Seattle 98121   (206) 448-5597
Supervision: Va'ad HaRabanim of Greater
Seattle.
Kosher Delight
47th Street and 6th Avenue
Park Deli
5011 South Dawson Street
Seward Park 98118   (206) 722-6674
Supervision: Va'ad HaRabanim of Greater
Seattle.
Park Deli
5011 S. Dawson Street, Seward Park 98118
(206) 722-NOSH
Fax: (206) 723-0364
Supervision: Va'ad HaRabanim of Greater
Seattle.
Hours: Sunday-Thursday 11.00am-8.00pm.
Friday 11.00am-3.00pm.

Kashrut Information
Va'ad HaRabanim
6500 52nd Avenue St 98118   (206) 760-0805
Fax: (206) 725-0347
Email: seavaad@aol.com

Libraries
**B'nai B'rith Hillel Foundation, University of
Washington**
4745 17th Av. N.E. 98105   (206) 527-1997
The University Library has a Jewish archives
section dealing with the Seattle community.

Media

Transcripts

The Jewish Transcript
2031 3rd Avenue 98121

Museums
Community Center
3801 E. Mercer Way, Mercer Island 98040
(206) 232-7115
A Holocaust memorial with a bronze sculpture
by Gizel Berman has been dedicated here.

Organisations
Jewish Federation of Greater Seattle
2031 3rd Avenue 98121   (206) 443-5400
**Stroum Jewish Community Center,
Northend Facility**
8606 35th Avenue NE 98115 (206) 526-8073
Fax: (206) 526-9958
Email: karenw@sjcc.org

Washington Association of Jewish Communities
2031 3rd Avenue 98121

Restaurants

Vegetarian

Bamboo Garden
364 Roy Street, near Seattle Center
(206) 282-6616
Supervision: Va'ad HaRabanim of Greater Seattle.

Spokane

Organisations

Jewish Community Council
North 221 Wall, Suite 500, Spokane 99201
(509) 838-4261

Synagogues

Conservative

Temple Beth Shalom
11322 E. 30th Street 99203   (509) 747-3304

West Virginia

Huntingdon

Synagogues

Conservative & Reform

B'nai Sholom
949 10th Avenue 25701   (304) 522-2980

Wisconsin

Madison

Organisations

Madison Jewish Community Council
6434 Enterprise Lane 53179   (608) 278-1808
Fax: (608) 278-7814
Email: morrison@jon.cjfny.org

Synagogues

Hillel Foundation
611 Langdon Street 53703

Conservative

Beth Israel Center
1406 Mound Street 53711

Orthodox

Chabad House
1722 Regent Street 53705   (608) 231-3450
Fax: (608) 231-3790

Reform

Beth El
2702 Arbor Drive 53711

Milwaukee

Community Organisations

Coalition for Jewish Learning
6401 North Santa Monica Boulevard 53217
(414) 962-8860
Fax: (414) 962-8852

Media

Directories

Milkwaukee Jewish Federation
1360 N. Prospect Avenue 53202
(414) 271-2992

Newspapers

Wisconsin Jewish Chronicle
1360 N. Prospect Avenue 53202
(414) 271-2992

Organisations

Milkwaukee Jewish Federation
1360 N. Prospect Avenue 53202
(414) 271-8338
Fax: (414) 271-7081
With more than a dozen synagogues in the area, travellers are advised to contact a local religious organisation for specific details.

Restaurants

Meat

Kosher Meat Klub
4731 West Burleigh 53210   (414) 449-5980
Fax: (414) 449-5985
Meat sandwiches, delicatessen and kosher groceries are available.
Shelley's Deliworks
4311 West Bradley Road 53223
(414) 365-8560
Fax: (414) 365-8526
Regular meals

Sheboygan

Synagogues

Traditional

Temple Beth El
1007 North Avenue 53083

Wyoming

Casper

Synagogues

Reform

Temple Beth El
4105 S. Poplar, PO Box 3534 82602
(307) 237-2330

Cheyenne

Synagogues

Conservative

Mount Sinai
2610 Pioneer Avenue 82001   (307) 634-3052
Gift shop and Mikvah by appointment.

Green River

Synagogues

Congregation of Beth Israel
PO Box 648 Green River Way 82935
(307) 875-4194

Laramie

Synagogues

Reform

Laramie JCC
PO Box 202 82070   (307) 745-8813

Uruguay

After the Conversos (Marranos) in the sixteenth century, there was no known Jewish community Uruguay until the late nineteenth century, when the country served as a stop-over on the way to Argentina. The Jewish population rose in the twentieth century, with immigration from the Middle East and eastern Europe. A synagogue had been opened by 1917. Despite restrictive immigration laws imposed against European Jews fleeing Nazism, 2,500 Jews managed to enter the country between 1939 and 1940. Further Jewish immigration followed, from Hungary and the Middle East, in the post-war period.

There are many Jewish organisations functioning in Urugauy, including Zionist and women's organisations. Kosher restaurants exist in Jewish institutions, and there are a number of synagogues.

GMT – 3 hours	Total Population 3,167,000
Country calling code (598)	Jewish Population 30,000

Montevideo

Embassy
Israel Embassy
Bulevar Artigas 1585-89   (442) 404-164/5/6
Fax: (442) 494-821

Groceries
Yavne, Cavia 2800   (2) 908-7869
Fax: (2) 707-0866

Media
Newspapers
Semanario Hebreo
Soriano 875/201   (442) 925-311
Spanish-language weekly. Editor also directs daily Yiddish radio programme.

Mikvaot
Adat Yiereim
Durazno 1183   (2) 711-1686
Fax: (2) 711-7736

Museums
Museo del Holocausto
Canelones 1084
Planta Baja

Restaurants
Kasherissimo
Camacua 623   (2) 915-0128
Supervision: Chief Rabbi Eliahu Birnbaum. The restaurant is situated in the Hebraica Macabi building.
Lubavich, Avda. Brasil 2704   (2) 708-5169

Dairy
Pizzeria Kasher
Sarmiento 2602   (2) 710-1420

Synagogues
Adat Israel
Democracia 2370
Anshei Jeshurun
Durazno 972
Bet Aharon, Harishona, Inca 2287
Comunidad Israelita Hungara
Durazno 972   (442) 908-456
Nueva Congregacion Israelita (Central European)
Wilson F Aldunete 1168   (442) 926-620
Social Isralite Adat Yeshurun
Alarcon 1396
Vaad Ha'ir, Canelones 828   (2) 900-6106
Fax: (2) 711-7736

Ashekenazi

Comunidad Israelita de Uruguay
Canelones 1084, Piso 1   (442) 925-750

Sephardi

Comunidad Israelita Sefardi
Buenos Aires 234, 21 de Setiembre 3111
    (442) 710-179
Templo Sefardi
de Pocitos L. Franzini 888

Tourist Sites
Memorial a Golda Meir
Reconquista y Ciudadela
Memorial al Holocausto del Pueblo Judio
Rambla Wilson, opposite campo de Golf

Uzbekistan

The ancient Jewish community in this central Asian republic is believed to have originated from Persian exiles in the fifth century. The Jews were subject to harsh treatment under the various rulers of the region, but still managed to become important traders in this area, which straddles the route between Europe and China and the east. In the late Middle Ages Jewish weavers and dyers were asked to help in the local cloth industry, and Bukhara became a key Jewish city after it became the capital of the country in the 1500s. Once the area had been incorporated into the Russian Empire in 1868, many Jews from the west of the Empire moved into Uzbekistan, and a further influx occurred when Uzbekistan was used to shelter Jews during the Nazi invasion of the Soviet Union – many subsequently set up home there.

The original Bukharan Jews are generally more religious than the Ashkenazim who entered the area in the nineteenth and twentieth centuries. There are Jewish schools in the area, and although there is no central Jewish organisation, there are many Jewish bodies operating on separate levels for the Ashkenazim and the Bukharans.

GMT + 5 to 6 hours
Country calling code (7)

Total Population 23,209,00
Jewish Population 20,000

Andizhan
Synagogues
7 Sovetskaya Street

Bukhara
Synagogues
20 Tsentralnaya Street

Katta-Kurgan
Synagogues
1 Karl Marx Alley

Kermine
Synagogues
36 Narimanov Street

Kokand
Synagogues
Dekabristov Street, Fergan Oblast

Margelan
Synagogues
Turtkilskaya Street, Fergan Oblast

Navoy
Synagogues
36 Narimanov Street

Samarkand
3,000 Jews live Samarkand. Many are Bukharan, and live in the special mahala, the quarter originally designated to Jews.
Although the single synagogue in use does not appear exciting from the outside, the inside is very interesting. There were other synagogues in the town, but they are not used any more. There is a Jewish school in the town.

Synagogues
5 Denauskaya Street
45 Respublikanskaya Street
34 Khudzumskaya Street

Tashkent
Embassy
Embassy of Israel
16A Lachuti Street, 5th floor

Synagogues
Gorbunova Street 62   (3712) 53-5447
9 Chkalov Street

Ashkenazi
77 Chempianov Street

Sephardi
3 Sagban Street   (3712) 40-0768

Venezuela

Settlement in Venezuela began in the early nineteenth century from the Caribbean. The Jews were granted freedom early (between 1819 and 1821), which encouraged more settlement. The community at that time was not religious. At the beginning of the twentieth century, some Middle Eastern Jewish immigrants organised a central committee for the first time. The powerful influence of the Catholic Church meant few Jews were accepted as immigrants in the pre-war rush to escape Nazi Europe.

After the war, however, the community began to expand, with arrivals from Hungary and the Middle East. The successful oil industry and the excellent Jewish education system attracted immigrants from other South American countries.

Today most Jews live in Caracas, the capital. Fifteen synagogues serve the country. The Lubavitch movement is present and maintains a yeshivah. Caracas has a Jewish bookshop and a weekly Jewish newspaper. Venezuela has an expanding Jewish community, in contrast to its South American neighbours. The oldest Jewish cemetery in South America, in Coro, with tombstones dating from 1832, is still in use today.

GMT – 4 hours
Country calling code (58)

Total Populatrion: 22,315,000
Jewish Population: 30,000

Caracas

Bakeries
Pasteleria Kasher
Avenida Los Proceres   (2) 515-086

Booksellers
Libreria Cultural Maimonides
Av Altamira Edif. Carlitos PB
San Bernardino   (2) 516-356
          Fax: (2) 524-242

Contact Information
Chabad-Lubavitch Centre
Apartado 5454 1010A   (2) 523-887

Delicatessens
La Belle Delicatesses
Av. Bogotá, Edif Santa María, Local 2
Los Caobos   (2) 781-7204
          Fax: (2) 781-7182
Kosher delicatessen and mini-market, restaurant and take-out.

Embassy
Embassy of Israel
Avenida Francisco de Miranda, Centro
Empresarial Miranda, 4 Piso Oficina 4-D,
Apartado Postal Los Ruices 70081
          (2) 239-4511; 239-4921
          Fax: (2) 239-4320

Groceries
Mini Market
Avenida Los Caobas   (2) 781-7204
Take away.

Hotels
Hotel Aventura

A short walk away from the Union Synagogue, convenient for Shabbat observers.
Hotel Avila

Next door to the Union Synagogue, convenient for Shabbat observers.

Media

Newspaper
Nuevo Mundo Israelita
Av Marques del Toro 9, Los Caobos

Mikvaot
Shomrei Shabbat Association Synagogue
Av Anauco
San Bernardino   (2) 517-197

Union Israelita de Caracas Synagogue & Community Centre
Av Marques del Toro 9
San Bernardino   (2) 552-8222
          Fax: (2) 552-7628
          Email: rabino@brener@eldish.net

Restaurants

Dairy

Caffé Pizzería La Finestra
Av. Principal de Las Palmas, Quinta Silvania
La Florida   (2) 793-6012
Supervision: Asociación Israelita de Venezuela.
Italian dairy

Papparazi
Calle Los Chaguaramos con Av. Mohedano
Centro Gerencial Mehedano
La Castellana 1070   (2) 266-4316
Supervision: Asociación Israelita de Venezuela.
Italian dairy.

Synagogues

Ashkenazi

Great Synagogue of Caracas
Av Francisco Javier Ustariz
San Bernardino   (2) 511-869

Shomrei Shabbat Assoc. Synagogue
Av Anauco, San Bernardino   (2) 517-197

**Union Israelita de Caracas Synagogue &
Community Centre**, Av Marques del Toro 9
San Bernardino   (2) 552-8222
                          Fax: (2) 552-7628
        Email: rabino@brener@eldish.net

Sepahrdi

Keter Tora
Av Lopez Mendez, San Bernardino

Sephardi

Bet El
Av Cajigal, San Bernardino   (2) 522-008

Shaare Shalom
Av Bogota, Quinta Julieta, Los Caobos
Tiferet Yisrael
Av MariperezLos Caobos   (2) 781-1942

Maracaibo

Community Organisations
Associación Israelita de Maracaibo
Calle 74 No 13-26   (61) 70333

Porlamar

Synagogues
Or Meir
Margarita Island
Mikva on premises.

Virgin Islands

Jews first began to settle on the island in 1655, taking advantage of liberal Danish rule. They were mainly traders in sugarcane, rum and molasses, and by 1796 a synagogue had been founded. The Jewish population of 400 in 1850 made up half of the islands' white community. There have been three Jewish governors.

    The community began to shrink after the Panama Canal was opened in 1914, and by 1942 only 50 Jews remained. Since 1945, the community has expanded again, with families arriving from the US mainland.

GMT – 4 hours   Total Population 106,000
Country calling code (1)   Jewish Population 300

St Thomas
Synagogues
St Thomas Synagogue
PO Box 266
Charlotte Amalie 00804   (809) 774-4312
This synagogue was built in 1833.

Services Friday at 8:00pm except holidays and first Friday monthly at 7:30pm. Visiting hours: Mon - Fri: 9:30am - 4:00pm.

Orthodox

Khal Hakodesh   (809) 779-2000
There is a conservative synagogue on the island of St Croix.

Yugoslavia

(Yugoslavia at present comprises Serbia and Montenegro.) The history of Serbian Jewry is both long and comparatively happy, with initial settlement in Roman times. After Turkish domination in 1389, the community continued to thrive and also prospered under Austrian rule in the eighteenth century. The nineteenth century saw some measures being taken against the Jews after Serbia became independent, but these were quickly redressed in 1889, following the Treaty of Berlin.

After 1918, Serbia was united with Croatia, Slovenia and the other south Slavic states into one country, known as Yugoslavia. The community suffered heavily under Nazi domination. The Jews were active in the Yugoslav partisans and, after liberation, many who had hidden or fought with the partisans began to return to their homes. Before the break-up of Yugoslavia, the Jews were allowed contact with other communities, including Israel. Since the civil war, some Jews still remain in the country, and there is a synagogue and a Talmud Torah school in Belgrade.

GMT + 1 hour
Country calling code (381)
Emergency Telephone (Police – 94) (Fire – 91)

Total Population 10,295,000
Jewish Population 2,500

Belgrade

Cemeteries
Jewish Cemetery

There are monuments to fallen fighters and martyrs of fascism, fallen Jewish soldiers in the Serbian army in the First World War here. In 1990 a new monument to Jews killed in Serbia was erected by the Danube, in the pre-war Jewish quarter Dorcol.

Community Organisations
Local Community
7 Kralja Petra Street 71a/11 11001
(11) 624-289

Museums
Jewish Museum
7 Kralja Petra Street 71a/1 11001
(11) 622-634
Fax: (11) 626-674
It is open daily from 10 am to 12 pm except Mondays.

Representative Organisations
Federation of Jewish Communities
7 Kralja Petra Street 71a/111, PO Box 841
11001
(11) 624-359/621-837
Fax: (11) 626-674

Synagogues
Birjuzova Street 19
Services are held Friday evenings and Jewish holidays.

Novi Sad

Cemeteries
Jewish Cemetery

There is a monument to the Jews who fell in the war and the victims of fascism. The synagogue here is no longer open but it's reported to be extremely beautiful, but is currently being converted to a concert hall.

Community Organisations
Community Offices
Jevrejska 11
(21) 613-882

Subotica

Community Organisations
Community Offices
Dimitrija Tucovica Street 13
28483

Zambia

The Jewish community began in the early twentieth century, with cattle ranching being the main attraction for Jewish immigrants. The community grew, and the copper industry was developed largely by Jewish entrepreneurs. With refugees from Nazism and a post-war economic boom, the Jewish community in the mid-1950s totalled 1,200. The community declined after independence in 1964.

Today, the Council for Zambian Jewry (founded in 1978) fulfils the role of the community's central body. Lusaka has a synagogue and the Zimbabwean community provides a connection to the small Zambian community but there are no education or similar services provided in the country.

GMT + 2 hours   Total Population 8,275,000
Country calling code (260)   Jewish Population Under 100
Emergency Telephone (Police, Fire and Ambulance – 999)

Lusaka
Synagogues
Lusaka Hebrew Congregation

Chachacha Road, POB 30020 (1) 229-190
Fax: (1) 221-428
Email: galaun@zamnet.zm

Zimbabwe

The first synagogue in Zimbabwe (formerly Rhodesia) was set up in 1894, in a tent in Bulawayo! The first Jews came from Europe (especially Lithuania), and they became involved in trade and managing hotels. They were joined in the 1920s and 1930s by Sephardis from Rhodes. Some senior politicians in the country were Jewish, including one prime minister.

The 1970s saw the turbulent transition to Zimbabwe and many Jews emigrated to escape the unrest. The community is now mainly Ashkenazi, with an important Sephardi component. Harare has both an Ashkenazi and a Sephardi synagogue; Bulawayo has a Sephardi synagogue. There are community centres in both the towns, and schools, although the latter have many local, non-Jewish pupils. There are also Zionist youth organisations.

GMT + 2 hours   Total Population 11,439,000
Country calling code (263)   Jewish Population 900

Bulawayo
Synagogues
Bulawayo Hebrew Congregation
Jason Moyo Street, PO Box 337 (9) 60829

Harare
Representative Organisations
Zimbabwe Jewish Board of Deputies
P.O. Box 1954   (4) 702506/7
Fax: (4) 702506

Hours of opening 8.30 a.m. to 12 noon
Synagogues
Harare Hebrew Congregation
Milton Park Jewish Centre, Lezard Avenue
POB 342   (4) 727-576
Sephardi Congregation
54 Josiah Chinamano Avenue, POB 1051
(4) 722-899

Availability of Kosher food in United Kingdom hotels

Hermolis meals (Supervised by Kedassia) can be delivered to a hotel or bed and breakfast in the country provided of couse the establishment has no objection.

Hotels chains known to accept such meals include Hilton, Sheraton and Marriott as well as such London hotels as The Ritz ,The Dorchester, The Grosvenor.

The catering department of the hotel should be informed that Hermolis food is required.

Hermolis may be contacted at 0181 810 4321 (Fax 0181 810 4331). There is a delivery charge.

Availability of Kosher food on cruise lines

Kosher food is obtainable on most cruise lines leaving the United Kingdom. The cruise line or travel agent should be informed at the time a booking is made.

The food comes in the form of pre-packed meals as on airplanes. It remains double wrapped until served as it is heated in the same ovens as other food.

Kosher Fish Around the World

Courtesy of Kashrut Division, London Beth Din,
and United Synagogue Publications Ltd

Common in Europe

UK	France	Holland	Italy	Spain
Anchovy	Anchois	Ansjovis	Acciuga	Anchoa, boqueron
Bass	Bar Commun	Zeebaars	Spigola	Lubina
Bream	Breme	Brasem	Brama	-
Brill	Barbue	Griet	Rombo, Liscio	Remol
Carp	Carpe	Karper	Carpa	Carpa
Cod	Cabillaud	Kabeljauw	Merluzzo, Bianco	Bacalao
Dab	Limande	Schar	Limande	Limanda
Flounder	Flet	Bot	Passera Pianuzza	Platija
Gurnard	Grondin	Poon	Pesce Capone	Rubios
Haddock	Aiglefin	Schelvis	Asinello	Eglefino
Hake	Merlu	Heek	Nasello	Merluza
Halibut	Fletan	Helibot	Halibut	Halilbut
Herring	Hareng	Hareng	Aringa	Arenque
Ling	Lingue	Leng	Molva	Maruca
Mackerel	Maquereau	Makreel	Maccerello	Caballa
Mullet	Mulet	Harder, aaldoe	Cefalo	Lisa
Perch	Perche	Baars	Pesce	Perca
Pike	Brochet	Snoek	Luccio	Lucio
Pilchard	Pilchard	Sardien	Sardina	Sardina
Plaice	Carrelet, Plie	Schol	Passera	Solla
Pollack	Lieu Jaune	Witte koolvis	Merluzzo Giallo	Abadejo
Roach	Gardon	Blankvoorn	Triotto	Bermejuela
Salmon	Saumon	Salm	Salmone	Salmon
Sardine	Sardine	Pelser, sardien	Sardina	Sardina
Sole	Sole	Tong	Sogliola	Lenguado
Sprat	Sprat	Sprot	Spratto	Espadin
Tench	Tanche	Zeelt	Tinca	Tenca
Trout	Truite	Forel	Trota	Trucha
Tuna	Thon	Tonijn	Tonno	Atun
Whiting	Merlan	Wijting	Merlano	Merlan

Kosher Fish Around the World

Courtesy of Kashrut Division, London Beth Din,
and United Synagogue Publications Ltd

Common in certain other countries

Australia

Baramundi
Barracouta
Barracuda
Blue Eye
Blue Grenadier
Butterfly fish
Flathead
Garfish
Groper
Harpuka
Jewfish
John Dory
Morwong
Northern Blue Fin
Orange Roughy
Red Emperor
Redfin
Skipjack (striped)
Snapper
Southern Blue Fin
Tailor
Terakiji
Trevally
Yellowfin

Hong Kong

Bigeye
Crevalle
Croaker
Grouper
Pampano
Scad
Whitefish

South Africa

Kabeljou
Kingklip
Maas banker
Red Roman
Seventy four
Steembrass
Stock Fish
Stump Nose

United State of America

Albacore
Barracuda
Bigeyes
Blackfish
Bluefish
Butterfish
Chub
Coalfish
Fluke
Grayling
Grouper
Kingfish
Mahimahi
Pickerel
Pompano
Porgy
Red Snapper
Sablefish
Snapper
Sunfish
Tilefish
Tilapia
Weakfish
Whitefish
Yellowtail

Index

A

Aachen	95
Aargau see Bremgarten	
Aberdeen (Scotland)	253
Aberdeen (NJ)	324
Aberdeen (SD)	380
Aberdeen (WA)	388
Acapulco	151
Acre see Akko	
Acton (MA)	306
Addis Ababa	63
Adelaide	9
Afula	119
Agadir	155
Agen	65
Ahmedabad	112
Aix-en-Provence	65
Aix-les-Bains	65
Ajaccio	93
Akko	119
Akron (OH)	364
Alabama	256
Alameda (CA)	260
Alaska	257
Albania	1
Albany (NY)	343
Alberta	35
Albuquerque (NM)	336
Alderney (C.I.)	253
Aldershot	224
Alexandria	61
Alexandria (LA)	300
Alexandria (VA)	386
Alfortville	83
Algarve	174
Algeria	1
Algiers	1
Alicante	193
Allentown (PA)	368
Alma-Ata	146
Alsenz	95
Altoona (PA)	368
Amarillo (TX)	381
Amazonas	29
Amberg	95
Amersfoort	160
Amherst (MA)	306
Amiens	66
Amstelveen see Amsterdam	

Amsterdam	160
Amsterdam (NY)	343
Anaheim (CA)	260
Anchorage (AK)	257
Ancona	138
Andernach	95
Andizhan	392
Andover (MA)	306
Angers	66
Ankara	211
Ann Arbor (MI)	317
Annapolis (MD)	302
Annecy	66
Annemasse	66
Annweiler	95
Antibes	66
Antony	83
Antwerp	22
Arad (Israel)	119
Arad (Romania)	176
Arcachon	66
Arcadia (CA)	260
Argentina	2
Arica	47
Arizona	257
Arkansas	259
Arleta (CA)	260
Arlington (MA)	306
Arlington (TX) see Fort Worth (TX)	
Arlington (VA)	386
Arlon	23
Arnhem	163
Arosa	203
Aruba	164
Ashdod	120
Asheville (NC)	362
Ashland (OR)	368
Asmara	63
Asnières	83
Asti	138
Astrakhan	179
Asunción	169
Athens (Greece)	106
Athens (GA)	290
Athis-Mons	83
Athol (MA)	306
Atlanta (GA)	290
Atlantic City (NJ)	324
Attleboro (MA)	306
Auburn (ME)	301

Index

Index

Index

Index

Index

Index

Index

Index

Index

Index

Index

Index

Index

Index

Index

T

Index

Index

Index to Advertisers

ADVERTISEMENT ORDER FORM 2000

Please complete and return Jewish Travel Guide form to us by 1 September 1999

Please reserve the following advertising space in
Jewish Travel Guide 2000:

☐ Full Page   £475   181 x 115 mm

☐ Half Page   £245   91 x 115 mm

☐ Quarter Page   £145   45.5 x 115 mm

(UK advertisers please note that the above rates are subject to VAT)
Special positions by arrangement

☐ Please insert the attached copy (If setting is required a 10% setting charge will be made.)

☐ Copy will be forwarded from our Advertising Agents (*see below*)

Contact Name: _____

Advertisers Name: _____

Address for invoicing: _____

_____

Tel: _____ Fax: _____

Signed: _____ Title: _____

VAT No: _____

Date: _____

Agency Name (if applicable): _____

Address: _____

_____

Tel: _____ Fax: _____

All advertisements set by the publisher will only be included if they have been signed and approved by the advertiser.

To the Advertising Department
Jewish Travel Guide
Vallentine Mitchell & Co. Ltd.
Newbury House, 890–900 Eastern Avenue, Newbury Park, Ilford, Essex IG2 7HH
Tel: +44(0)181-599 8866 Fax: + 44(0)181-599 0984. E-mail: jtg@vmbooks.com

Update for Jewish Travel Guide 2000

PUBLISHER'S REQUEST

Readers are asked kindly to draw attention to any errors or omissions. If errors are discovered, it would be appreciated if you could give up-to-date information, referring to page, place/institution, etc., and return this form to the Editor at the address given below.

With reference to the following entry:

Page:

Country:

Entry should read:

Kindly list on separate sheet if preferred.

Signed:_____ Date:_____

Name (BLOCK CAPITALS) _____

Address: _____

_____

Telephone: _____

SEND TO:

The Editor
Jewish Travel Guide
Vallentine Mitchell & Co. Ltd.
Newbury House, 890–900 Eastern Avenue,
Newbury Park, Ilford, Essex IG2 7HH
Fax: + 44(0)181-599 0984. E-mail: jtg@vmbooks.com

JEWISH TRAVEL GUIDE

New Entry Form

Name of Establishment: _____

_____

Category (circle one):

HOTEL	BUTCHER	MIKVAH
RESTAURANT	BOOKSELLER	KASHRUT INFORMATION
DELICATESSEN	MUSEUM	CONTACT INFORMATION
GROCERY	TOURIST SITE	JEWISH MEDIA
BAKERY	SYNAGOGUE	

Address of Establishment: _____

(Include Metropolitan area) _____

_____

_____

_____

City/ Town: _____

State: _____

Postcode: _____

Country: _____

Telephone, Fax, E-mail Numbers and Website: _____

_____

_____

_____

_____

(Please indicate country and city code) _____

_____

Supervision Details (who gives *Hashgacha*?): _____

_____

Contact Person: _____

Hours: _____

Your Name and Address (if different to above):_____

_____

_____

_____

Vallentine Mitchell & Co. Ltd

Newbury House,
900 Eastern Avenue,
Newbury Park, Ilford,
Essex IG2 7HH, UK
Tel: +44 (0)181 599 8866
Fax: +44 (0)181 599 0984
E-mail: jtg@vmbooks.com

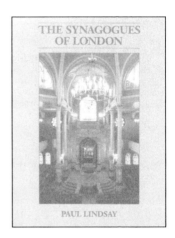

Double Jeopardy

Gender and the Holocaust

Judith Tydor Baumel

Double Jeopardy: Gender and the Holocaust is a collection of essays examining the Holocaust from the perspective of gender. The book is divided into seven sections, each focusing upon a different aspect of the discourse between gender and identity. Following an historical introduction deliniating the basic framework for understanding women's experiences during and shortly after the Holocaust, the volume explores the major research trends evincing themselves since the end of the Second World War. Topics examined include various aspects of women's experiences during the war years such as social interaction in crisis, leadership and martyrdom. Other essays illuminate Holocaust heroism through a gender sensitive approach, while yet an additional section - Postwar Life and Representation - focuses upon gender in a multicultural post-Holocaust society.

320 pages
0 85303 346 3
0 85303 345 5

January 1999
cloth £35.00/$49.50
paper £17.50/$25.00

The Exodus Affair

Holocaust Survivors and the Struggle for Palestine

Aviva Halamish

The Exodus 1947 affair was both a political and a human drama. On one level, it was composed of a series of political and operational decisions, and their subsequent implementation. On another level, it was a fascinating story, an absorbing and moving tale of heroism.

This book presents a number of new facts based on archival material never before exposed in research and new interpretations of some of the events that took place, all in a dramatic fashion. Filled with detail, the author is not scared of asking provocative questions.

352 pages   31 b/w photographs   June 1998
0 85303 342 0   cloth   £35.00
0 85303 347 1   paper   £18.00

The Journal of Holocaust Education

Editors: **Jo Reilly** (*Executive*), *Institute of Contemporary History and The Wiener Library;* **David Cesarani**, *University of Southampton;* **Colin Richmond**, *Keele University*

Devoted to all aspects of interdisciplinary Holocaust education and research, the journal aims to reach a wider audience including scholars in Britain and overseas, teachers inside and outside the University sector, students, and the general reader interested in both the Jewish and the non-Jewish experience. At a time when the subject is taught in more universities and schools than ever before, *The Journal of Holocaust Education* is well placed to act as an important resource and as a forum for debate for all those interested in Holocaust education.

ISSN 1359-1371 Volume 8 1999
Three issues per year: Summer, Autumn, Winter
Individuals £28/$45 Institutions £85/$130

VALLENTINE MITCHELL

Newbury House, 900 Eastern Avenue, Newbury Park, Ilford, Essex, IG2 7HH
Tel: +44 (0)181 599 8866   Fax: +44 (0)181 599 0984

North America
c/o ISBS, 5804 NE Hassalo Street, Portland, OR 97213 3644
Tel: 800 944 6190   Fax: 503 280 8832

website: www.vmbooks.com   email: sales@vmbooks.com

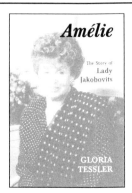